Divorce in the 70s: A Subject Bibliography

Compiled by Kenneth D. Sell

ORYX PRESS
1981

The rare Arabian Oryx is believed to have inspired the myth of the unicorn. This desert antelope became virtually extinct in the early 1960s. At that time several groups of international conservationists arranged to have 9 animals sent to the Phoenix Zoo to be the nucleus of a captive breeding herd. Today the Oryx population is nearing 300 and herds have been returned to reserves in Israel, Jordan, and Oman.

Copyright © 1981 by The Oryx Press
2214 North Central at Encanto
Phoenix, AZ 85004

Published simultaneously in Canada

Printed and Bound in the United States of America

Library of Congress Cataloging in Publication Data

Sell, Kenneth D.
  Divorce in the 70s.

  Includes indexes.
  1. Divorce—United States—Bibliography.
I. Title. II. Title: Divorce in the seventies.
Z7164.M2S396 [HQ834]   016.3068′9   81-38412
  ISBN 0-912700-81-5   AACR2

CONTENTS

Preface   v

Acknowledgements   v

Introduction   vii

I.   Social and Behavioral Science Literature   1

Alimony and Maintenance   3
Child Custody   3
Children of Divorced Parents   7
Desertion and Nonsupport   12
Divorce   12
Divorce (Economic Aspects)   17
Divorce (Historical Aspects)   18
Divorce (Medical Aspects)   19
Divorce (Statistics)   21
Divorce and Education   22
Divorce and Welfare   23
Divorce and Work   24
Divorce Counseling and Mediation   26
Divorced Persons   29
Father Absence   38
One-Parent Families   42
Remarriage   47
Separation   48
Stepparents and Stepchildren   49

II.   Legal Literature   51

Alimony and Maintenance   53
Annulment   57
Attorneys   58
Child Custody   59
Child Support   65
Conflict of Laws   70
Divorce   70
Divorced Persons   82
Domestic Relations   83
Domicile and Residence   85
Property Settlements   86
Separation   93
Taxes   93

III.   Judeo-Christian Literature   101

Doctrine, Theology, and Biblical Views   103
Practice and Ministry   106
Personal Aspects   108

IV.   Popular Literature   119

Alimony and Maintenance   121
Annulment   121
Child Custody   121
Child Support   123
Children of Divorced Parents   123
Desertion   125
Divorce   125
Divorce (Economic Aspects)   128
Divorce (Legal Aspects)   128
Divorce (in the Military Community)   131
Divorce and Work   132
Divorced Persons   132
Father Absence   136
One-Parent Families   136
Remarriage   138
Separation   139
Stepparents and Stepchildren   139

V.   Nonprint Materials on Divorce   141

Child Custody   143
Child Support   143
Children of Divorced Parents   143
Desertion   144
Divorce   144
Divorce Counseling   145
Divorced Persons   146
Father Absence   146
One-Parent Families   147
Religion and Divorce   147
Remarriage   147
Separation   148
Stepparents and Stepchildren   148

VI.   Addendum and Appendix   149

Addendum   151
Appendix   151

VII.   Indexes   153

Author Index   155
Geographic Index   174
Subject Index   179

PREFACE

The decade of the 1970s was extremely important for developments in the area of divorce in the United States. As the number of marital dissolutions increased, research on divorce increased manyfold over the previous decades. Social scientists probed many facets of the divorce process, attempting to discover the effect of divorce on the people involved. There was renewed interest during the decade in child custody, including father custody and joint custody, single-parent families, remarriage, and stepparenting. Divorce counseling and divorce mediation became recognized specializations in the human services field. New programs to help families during and after divorce were developed. As both sexes began to be considered as equals before the law, new issues were raised concerning alimony and maintenance, property settlements, and pensions. The fault system of divorce declined and was replaced by a variety of alternatives. Churches increasingly accepted divorce and divorced persons and explored new techniques for ministering to their divorced and single-parent constituencies. The mass media published hundreds of books and articles on divorce and divorce-related topics. This work documents these changes and innovations, as well as the responses of American social institutions to familial change in the decade of the 1970s.

The impetus for this bibliography originated in a pre-conference workshop on divorce sponsored by the Task Force on Divorce and Divorce Reform of the National Council on Family Relations in St. Louis, Missouri, October 1974. One of the purposes of the Task Force was to collect the increasing numbers of books, articles, and other materials on divorce. The Task Force report contained a 30-page bibliography of materials published between 1960 and 1974. When the Task Force was disbanded, this program of collection eventually ceased. From 1975 to 1978 my wife, a librarian and information scientist, and I, a family sociologist, collaborated on a book providing a systematic methodology for finding divorce information scattered throughout all areas of knowledge. In 1977, the Southeastern Council on Family Relations held its annual meeting in Lexington, Kentucky on the theme of "Divorce in the 1970s"; using the above methodology, I prepared a selected bibliography of books, research articles, dissertations, government documents, and films on divorce. The response on the part of divorce researchers, professors, and doctoral students was encouraging enough to continue this work with annual supplements. As the number of publications on divorce continued to increase throughout the decade, the need for a comprehensive bibliography was recognized.

It is hoped that this compilation will serve at least 2 important purposes: first, to avoid needless duplication of research already completed, and second, and perhaps more important, to identify areas where research is needed to expand our knowledge.

ACKNOWLEDGEMENTS

I am grateful to the indexers and abstractors of the journals that were used in compiling this bibliography, for without their careful work this volume would not have been possible, and to the librarians and technicians who have maintained their collections in an orderly and usable system, so that these materials could be easily located and examined. I am also extremely grateful to my wife Betty for her technical expertise, wisdom, and support during this project. Thanks to Jacquelyn Sims, reference librarian at Catawba College, for obtaining numerous difficult-to-locate articles through interlibrary loan, and Frances Wentz, documents librarian, for her continual referral of divorce information in government documents. I have appreciated the encouragement of this project by my colleagues Emily M. Brown and Helen J. Raschke. Thanks also to Susan Snider for typing the author index.

INTRODUCTION

Purpose. The purpose of this bibliography is to assemble the vast amount of information on divorce produced in the United States during the decade of the 1970s for the use of researchers, students, teachers, and practitioners in various fields. Since this information is scattered throughout thousands of sources, bringing this material together saves considerable time, makes it more accessible, and decreases the possibility of overlooking important information.

Scope. This bibliography is an attempt to list the majority of material (excluding fiction) written on divorce and divorce-related topics in the United States from 1970 through 1979, in all areas of knowledge, as a result of a systematic search of 73 index and abstract journals that were identified as sources of divorce information. The list of index and abstract journals searched is given in the Appendix. The key words and phrases developed in the work of Sell and Sell* were used in the systematic search. The indexes and abstracts were searched manually, since fewer than 20 had computer searching available. Almost all the items were examined by the compiler, with the exception of the nonprint materials and master's theses. Nearly 50 academic, legal, medical, theological, public, and other libraries, from Boston, Massachusetts to Tallahassee, Florida, were used in the course of this project.

Motion pictures for entertainment purposes, television programs, and newspaper articles are not included in this bibliography. Subject indexing is not presently available for the first 2 categories. Over 25 metropolitan newspapers were indexed during the 1970s, and a comprehensive list of all of the divorce articles in these newspapers would have produced more than 3,000 additional citations.

The goal of comprehensiveness cannot be fully attained because: (a) not all books are reported in the bibliographic system; (b) chapters in books are not usually indexed; (c) some periodicals are not indexed, some periodicals are only partially indexed, some periodicals are indexed for only part of the decade, and a few periodicals will not be indexed for another 2 or 3 years due to the time lag of a few of the index and abstract journals; and (d) only a small percentage of some materials, such as master's theses and law dissertations, are indexed. However, within these limitations, the aim of this work is comprehensiveness.

Arrangement. The items are arranged first by broad areas of knowledge. The items are then classified by topic within each chapter as indicated in the Table of Contents. Each topic is further subdivided as necessary. Each item is listed only once in the bibliography, even though many items could have been placed under more than one topic. Therefore, the Subject Index should be consulted to locate all of the items on a given topic. The general content of each major section is as follows:

I. Social and Behavioral Science. This includes the usual social science literature plus the social aspects of divorce found in the business, medical, and nursing literatures. The items in this section were written by professionals for other professionals.

II. Legal. This literature has been written generally by attorneys, judges, law professors, and students for the members of the legal profession. The tax aspects of divorce, alimony, and property settlements from the accountants' perspective are also included in this section.

III. Judeo-Christian. Most of this literature was written for laypersons. However, all the professional books and articles dealing with the religious aspects of divorce are also included in this chapter. The religious materials are classified by broad topic and then further divided by churches or denominations in most instances.

IV. Popular. This section includes secular books and magazine articles written for the general public in non-technical language. Popular treatments of legal subjects, such as do-it-yourself divorce books, and other nontechnical law books are included here.

V. Nonprint Materials. Here are listed 16mm motion pictures, filmstrips, slides, and videotapes produced primarily for nonprofessional audiences. Audio cassette tapes, produced primarily for professionals, are also included in this chapter.

VI. Addendum and Appendix. Two additional entries are included. Next, the appendix lists the titles and dates of the index and abstract journals that were checked, in order that the user may extend this search without omissions or duplications. Also, 12 unindexed periodicals that were searched are listed.

VII. Indexes. Three indexes are included. The Author Index lists the names of all authors and editors. The Geographic Index lists divorce information and statistics by city, state, and country. The Subject Index lists each item under one to 4 preassigned subject headings derived from the content of the item.

Entries. The entries for books and government documents in this bibliography generally conform to the Library of Congress entries in order to facilitate locating these materials in library card catalogs. Some entries contain special features. For example, an ''R'' at the end of an entry indicates a research article or book. The page and volume numbers of the abstracts of doctoral dissertations in *Dissertation Abstracts International* are given at the end of each doctoral dissertation citation, as well as

---

* Kenneth D. Sell and Betty H. Sell. *Divorce in the United States, Canada, and Great Britain: A Guide to Information Sources* (Detroit, MI: Gale Research, 1978.)

the number for ordering a copy of the dissertation from University Microfilms International. The superintendent of documents number, used for locating U.S. government documents, is indicated as appropriate for each document. When the document contains statistical information, the table numbers of the divorce information is given. Divorce data in the *1970 U.S. Census of Population, U.S. Vital Statistics,* the *Current Population Survey,* and the publications of the U.S. National Center for Health Sta-

tistics are extensively listed and indexed in order to make this divorce information more easily located.

Abbreviations. The following abbreviations are used in the citations: *DAI—Dissertation Abstracts International;* ed(s) —editor(s); ED—Education Document in the ERIC system (includes *Resources in Education*); and R—research article or book.

Kenneth D. Sell
Salisbury, North Carolina

I. Social and Behavioral Science Literature

ALIMONY AND MAINTENANCE

1. Cuse, Arthur. *Financial Guideline: Divorce*. Los Angeles: Guideline Publications, 1971.

2. Goodman, Ellen. "Who's Really Anti-male?" *Young Children,* vol. 34, no. 5 (1979): 12–13.

3. Kirkpatrick, Elizabeth K. "Alimony and Public Income Support: Fifteen Countries," *Social Security Bulletin,* vol. 40, no. 1 (1977): 36–39. R.

4. "Modern Compromise: Short Term Alimony," *Business Week,* 2553 (September 25, 1978): 171–72.

5. Seidenberg, Faith. "Alimony and the Older Woman," *Human Ecology Forum,* 7 (Fall 1976): 15–17.

6. Williams, Roger. "Alimony: The Short Goodbye," *Psychology Today,* vol. 11, no. 2 (1977): 71 + .

ALIMONY STATISTICS

7. U.S. Internal Revenue Service. *Statistics of Income: Individual Income Tax Returns: 1971*. Washington, DC: Government Printing Office, 1973 (T22.35/2:In 2/971) (Tables 1.5–1.9, 1.12, 2.3, 2.6, 4.1).

8. ———. *Statistics of Income: Individual Income Tax Returns: 1972*. Washington, DC: Government Printing Office, 1975 (T22.35/2:In 2/972) (Tables 1.3–1.5, 1.7, 2.2, 2.3, 2.21, 2.22).

9. ———. *Statistics of Income: Individual Income Tax Returns: 1973*. Washington, DC: Government Printing Office, 1976 (T22.35/2:In 2/973) (Tables 1.D, 1.3, 1.6, 2.1, 2.9).

10. ———. *Statistics of Income: Individual Income Tax Returns: 1974*. Washington, DC: Government Printing Office, 1977 (T22.35/2:In 2/974) (Tables 1.3, 2.1).

11. ———. *Statistics of Income: Individual Income Tax Returns: 1975*. Washington, DC: Government Printing Office, 1978 (T22.35/2:In 2/975) (Tables 1.3, 1.6, 2.2, 2.6, 5.2).

12. ———. *Statistics of Income: Individual Income Tax Returns: 1976*. Washington, DC: Government Printing Office 1979 (T22.35/2:In 2/976) (Tables 1.3, 1.6, 1.12, 2.3).

CHILD CUSTODY

13. Benedek, Richard S., and Benedek, Elissa P. "Child's Preference in Michigan Custody Disputes," *American Journal of Family Therapy,* vol. 7, no. 4 (1979): 37–43.

14. Benedek, Richard S.; Del Campo, Robert L.; and Benedek, Elissa P. "Michigan's Friends of the Court: Creative Programs for Children of Divorce," *Family Coordinator,* vol. 26, no. 4 (1977): 447–50.

15. "Beyond the Final Judgment: What Is in the Best Interest of the Child?" (editorial), *Conciliation Courts Review,* vol. 12, no. 1 (1974): iii.

16. Bleyer, Rosemary. "Responses to Children by Parents in Different Marital and Custodial Situations." Master's thesis, Georgia State University, 1979. R.

17. Buxton, Martin. "Applying the Guidelines of Beyond the Best Interests of the Child," *Child Psychiatry and Human Development,* vol. 7, no. 2 (1976): 94–102.

18. Charnas, Jane F. "Interdisciplinary Practice Use of the Concept of Psychological Parenthood in Contested Child Custody Cases Resulting from Divorce." D.S.W. diss., University of Utah, 1977 (*DAI* 38/5A, p. 3054, order # 7723098). R.

19. Coyne, Thomas A. "Who Will Speak for the Child?" In *The Rights of Children: Emergent Concepts in Law and Society,* compiled by Albert E. Wilkerson, pp. 193–211. Philadelphia, PA: Temple University Press, 1973.

20. Derdeyn, Andre P. "Child Custody Consultation," *American Journal of Orthopsychiatry,* vol. 45, no. 5 (1975): 791–801.

21. Desteian, John. "Interdisciplinary Approaches to Custody, Access and Conciliation," *Conciliation Courts Review,* vol. 16, no. 3 (1978): 13–16.

22. "Divorce, Children, Attorneys and Clinicians. Combined Use of Legal and Mental Health Resources to Solve Problems of Child Custody and Visitation," *Resources in Education 12 (1977). ERIC document ED 138 841.*

23. Duncan, Jane W. "Medical, Psychologic, and Legal Aspects of Child Custody," *Mayo Clinic Proceedings,* vol. 53, no. 7 (1978): 463–468.

24. Ferguson, Patricia L. "Kids Caught in Custody," *Conciliation Courts Review,* vol. 13, no. 1(1975): 10–11.

25. Floyd, Sally. "Child Custody: In Whose Best Interests?" *Union W.A.G.E.* 46 (March–April, 1978): 5.

26. Glasser, Claire L. "A Case for Counseling in Child Custody Cases," *Conciliation Courts Review*, vol. 13, no. 1 (1975): 12–13.

27. Goldstein, Joseph; Freud, Anna; and Solnit, Albert J. *Beyond the Best Interests of the Child*. New York: Free Press, 1973.

28. Gordon, Philip B.; Rapp, Don W.; and McKenry, Patrick C. "Judges' Knowledge of Key Child Development Concepts Related to Custody and Placement Decisions," *Conciliation Courts Review*, vol. 17, no. 3(1979): 41–46. R.

29. Gourley, Ruth L. "Trends in Custody Studies, Maricopa County, Arizona, 1972–1975," *Conciliation Courts Review*, vol. 13, no. 1 (1975): 14–17.

30. Hall, Douglas A., and Odencrantz, George D. "Involvement of Parents after Court Termination of Custody of Children—As Related to Support Order," *Public Welfare*, vol. 29, no. 2 (1971): 175–180. R.

31. Hansen, Robert W. "Guardians ad litem in Divorce and Custody Cases: Protection of the Child's Interests." In *The Rights of Children: Emergent Concepts in Law and Society*, compiled by Albert E. Wilkerson, pp. 239–43. Philadelphia, PA: Temple University Press, 1973.

32. Henning, James S. "Child Advocacy in Adoption and Divorce Cases," *Journal of Clinical Child Psychology*, vol. 5, no. 2 (1976): 50–53.

33. Jenkins, Richard L. "Maxims in Child Custody Cases," *Family Coordinator*, vol. 26, no. 4 (1977): 385–89.

34. Katz, Sanford N. "Who Looks after Laura?" In *Children's Rights Movement: Overcoming the Oppression of Young People*, edited by Beatrice Gross and Ronald Gross, pp. 48–54. Garden City, NY: Anchor Books, 1977.

35. Kubie, Lawrence S. "Provisions for the Care of Children of Divorced Parents: A New Legal Instrument." In *The Rights of Children: Emergent Concepts in Law and Society*, compiled by Albert W. Wilkerson, pp. 212–17. Philadelphia, PA: Temple University Press, 1973.

36. Rich, Adrienne C. "Husband-right and Father-right." In *On Lies, Secrets, and Silence*, pp. 215–22. New York: Norton, 1979.

37. Rosen, Rhona. "Some Crucial Issues concerning Children of Divorce," *Journal of Divorce*, vol. 3, no. 1 (1979): 19–25. R.

38. Rothschild, Carl J. "The Special Role for the Child and Family Psychiatrist in Divorce, Custody and Access Proceedings," *Conciliation Courts Review*, vol. 17, no. 2 (1979): 45–47.

39. Saxe, David B. "Some Reflections on the Interface of Law and Psychiatry in Child Custody Cases," *Journal of Psychiatry and Law*, vol. 3, no. 4 (1975): 501–14.

40. Seagull, Arthur A., and Seagull, Elizabeth A.W. "The Non-custodial Father's Relationship to his Child: Conflicts and Solutions," *Journal of Clinical Child Psychology*, vol. 6, no. 2 (1977): 11–15.

41. Solow, Robert A., and Adams, Paul L. "Custody by Agreement: Child Psychiatrist as a Child Advocate," *Journal of Psychiatry and Law*, vol. 5, no. 1 (1977): 77–100.

42. Stack, Carol B. "Who Owns the Child? Divorce and Child Custody Decisions in Middle-Class Families," *Social Problems*, vol. 23, no. 4 (1976): 505-15.

43. Taylor, Laura, and Werner, Emmy. "Child Custody and the Conciliation Courts," *Conciliation Courts Review*, vol. 16, no. 2 (1978): 25–32. R.

44. Woody, Robert H. "Family Counselors and Child Custody," *International Journal of Family Counseling*, vol. 6, no. 2 (1978): 81–88.

45. _____. "Sexism in Child Custody Decisions," *Personnel and Guidance Journal*, vol. 56, no. 3 (1977): 168–170.

46. Zuckerman, Jacob T. "Custody in Matrimonial Proceedings: Relations of Judge-Lawyer-Behavioral Expert," *Conciliation Courts Review*, vol. 8, no. 1 (1970): 27–29.

47. Zwink, William E. "Child Custody Principles in a Divorce Proceeding," *Conciliation Courts Review*, vol. 8, no. 2 (1970): 4–10.

BIBLIOGRAPHY

48. Weiss, Robert S. "Deciding the Custody of Children of Separating Parents: A Preliminary Literature Review," *Government Reports Announcements and Index* 26 (1976) 5K. PB-258 319/3GA.

CONTESTED CUSTODY

49. Alexander, Sharon J. "Protecting the Child's Rights in Custody Cases," *Family Coordinator*, vol. 26, no. 4 (1977): 377–82.

50. Burgoyne, Shirley J. "Child Custody and the Common Sense: Subjecting Your Custody Case to Realistic Analysis," *Family Law Reporter* 2 (August 3, 1976): 4051–59, monograph no. 20.

51. Chase, Gary A. "Criteria for Psychiatric Evaluations in Child Custody Contests," *Conciliation Courts Review*, vol. 15, no. 1 (1977): 19–27.

52. Derdeyn, Andre P. "A Consideration of Legal Issues in Child Custody Contests," *Archives of General Psychiatry*, vol. 33, no. 2 (1976): 165–71.

53. Holz, Marvin C. "Guidelines for Guardians ad litem—Custody Disputes," *Conciliation Courts Review*, vol. 15, no. 1 (1977): 13–18.

54. Kargman, Marie W. "A Court Appointed Child Advocate (Guardian ad litem) Reports on Her Role in Contested Child Custody Cases and Looks to the Future," *Journal of Divorce*, vol. 3, no. 1 (1979): 77–90.

55. Krell, Robert, "This Child Is Mine! The Battle Cry for Custody," *Canadian Psychiatric Association Journal*, vol. 23, no. 7 (1978): 433–39.

56. Lewis, Melvin. "The Latency Child in a Child Custody Conflict," *American Academy of Child Psychiatry Journal*, vol. 13, no. 4 (1974): 635–47.

57. Lindsley, Byron. "Custody Proceedings, Battlefield or Peace Conference?" *Conciliation Courts Review*, vol. 13, no. 1 (1975): 1–9.

58. Margolin, Frances M. "Counseling in Contested Custody and Visiting in a Court Setting," *Conciliation Courts Review*, vol. 8, no. 2 (1970): 11–13.

59. Miller, Emily. "Psychotherapy of a Child in a Custody Dispute," *American Academy of Child Psychiatry Journal*, vol. 15, no. 3 (1976): 441–52.

60. Nadeau, Judith S.; Fagan, Stephen H.; and Schuntermann, Peter. "Child Custody: The Adversarial Process as a Vehicle for Clinical Services," *Children Today*, vol. 7, no. 6 (1978): 14–17+.

61. Sanford, Jill L. "Contested Custody and the Judicial Decision-Making Process." Ph.D. diss., Florida State University, 1977 (*DAI* 38/9A, p. 5746, order # 7801513). R.

62. Weiss, Robert S. "Issues in the Adjudication of Custody When Parents Separate." In *Divorce and Separation: Context, Causes and Consequences*, edited by George Levinger and Oliver C. Moles, pp. 324–36. New York: Basic Books, 1979.

63. Weiss, Warren W., and Collada, Henry B. "Conciliation Counseling: The Court's Effective Mechanism for Resolving Visitation and Custody Disputes," *Family Coordinator,* vol. 26, no. 4 (1977): 444–46.

64. Westman, Jack C. "The Psychiatrist and Child Custody Cases," *American Journal of Psychiatry,* vol. 127, no. 12 (1971): 1687–88.

DETERMINATIONS AND EVALUATIONS

65. Awad, George A. "Basic Principles in Custody Assessments," *Canadian Psychiatric Association Journal,* vol. 23, no. 7 (1978): 441–47.

66. Cantor, Irwin, and Ferguson, Patricia L. "Family Counseling in the Conciliation Court: An Alternative to Custody Litigation," *Conciliation Courts Review,* vol. 14, no. 1 (1976): 1–16.

67. Cohen, Stanley N. "The Need to Assess the Custody Decision Process in Domestic Relations Courts—One Tentative Approach," *Conciliation Courts Review,* vol. 10, no. 2 (1972): 10–12.

68. Derdeyn, Andre P. "Child Custody Consultation." In *Annual Progress in Child Psychiatry and Child Development,* edited by Stella Chess and Alexander Thomas, pp. 538–51. New York: Brunner/Mazel, 1977.

69. Druckman, Joan M., and Rhodes, Clifton A. "Family Impact Analysis: Application to Child Custody Determination," *Family Coordinator,* vol. 26, no. 4 (1977): 451–58.

70. Duquette, Donald N. "Child Custody Decision-Making: The Lawyer-Behavioral Scientist Interface," *Journal of Clinical Child Psychiatry,* vol. 7, no. 3 (1978): 192–94.

71. ———. "Child Custody Decision-Making: The Lawyer–Behavioral Scientist Interface," *Resources in Education* 13 (1978). ERIC document ED 145 942.

72. Eder, Vera J. "The Use of Child Play as a Diagnostic Tool in Custody Evaluations," *Conciliation Courts Review,* vol. 14, no. 1 (1976): 17–20.

73. Isenhart, Mary-Alice. "Divorced Women: A Comparison of Two Groups Who Have Retained or Relinquished Custody of Their Children." Ph.D. diss., California School of Professional Psychology, San Diego, 1979 (*DAI* 40/10A, p. 5628, order # 8004344). R.

74. Kray, Dorothy J. "Influence of Sex of Judge, Child, and Parent, and Parent's Sexual Behavior on Child Custody Preference." Ph.D. diss., University of Southern California, 1977 (*DAI* 39/11B, p. 5562). R.

75. Lester, Eva P. "The Custody Assessment," *Canadian Psychiatric Association Journal,* vol. 23, no. 7 (1978): 429–30.

76. Littner, Ner. "The Doctor's Role in Contested Child Custody Matters," *Conciliation Courts Review,* vol. 9, no. 2 (1971): 34–36.

77. McDermott, John F., et al. "Child Custody Decision Making: The Search for Improvement," *American Academy of Child Psychiatry Journal,* vol. 17, no. 1 (1978): 104–16. R.

78. Milne, Ann. "Custody of Children in a Divorce Process: A Family Self-Determination Model," *Conciliation Courts Review,* vol. 16, no. 2 (1978): 1–10.

79. Musetto, Andrew P. "Child Custody and Visitation: The Role of the Clinician in Relation to Family," *Family Therapy,* vol. 5, no. 2 (1978): 143–50.

80. Nichols, Robert C., and Troester, James D. "Custody Evaluations: An Alternative?" *Family Coordinator,* vol. 28, no. 3 (1979): 399–407.

81. Robbins, Norman N. "Legal Standards for Determining 'Best Interests of Child,' " *Family Coordinator,* vol. 23, no. 1 (1974): 87–90.

82. Swerdlow, Edith L. "Mental Health Services Available to the Bench and Bar to Assist in Resolving Problems Relating to Custody and Visitation in Family Law Cases." *Journal of Clinical Child Psychology,* vol. 7, no. 3 (1978): 174–77.

83. Warner, Nancy S., and Elliott, Carla J. "Problems of the Interpretive Phase of Divorce-Custody Evaluations," *Journal of Divorce,* vol. 2, no. 4 (1979): 371–82.

84. Wolfington, Dave. "Child Custody Probe Questionnaire: A Structured Interview," *Conciliation Courts Review,* vol. 16, no. 2 (1978): 39–43.

85. Woody, Robert H. "Behavioral Science Criteria in Child Custody Determinations," *Journal of Marriage and Family Counseling,* vol. 3, no. 1 (1977): 11–18. R.

86. ———. "Child Custody Legal Proceedings: An Investigation of Criteria Maintained by Lawyers, Psychiatrists, Psychologists, and Social Workers." Sc.D.Hyg. diss., University of Pittsburgh, 1975 (*DAI* 36/6B, P. 2739, order # 7528717). R.

FATHER CUSTODY

87. Bartz, Karen W., and Witcher, Wayne C. "When Father Gets Custody," *Children Today,* vol. 7, no. 5 (1978): 2–6+.

88. Bernstein, Barton E. "Lawyer and Counselor as an Interdisciplinary Team: Preparing the Father for Custody," *Journal of Marriage and Family Counseling,* vol. 3, no. 3 (1977): 29–40.

89. Gersick, Kelin E. "Fathers by Choice: Characteristics of Men Who Do and Do Not Seek Custody of Their Children Following Divorce." Ph.D. diss., Harvard University, 1976. R.

90. ———. "Fathers by Choice: Divorced Men Who Receive Custody of Their Children." In *Divorce and Separation: Context, Causes and Consequences,* edited by George Levinger and Oliver C. Moles, pp. 307–23. New York: Basic Books, 1979. R.

91. Greene, Roberta S. "Custodial Single Fathers," *Conciliation Courts Review,* vol. 16, no. 2 (1978): 18–24. R.

92. Greif, Judith B. "Fathers, Children, and Joint Custody," *American Journal of Orthopsychiatry,* vol. 49, no. 2 (1979): 311–19. R.

93. Hanson, Shirley M. H. "Characteristics of Single Custodial Fathers and the Parent-Child Relationship." Ph.D. diss., University of Washington, 1979 (*DAI* 40/12A, p. 6438, order # 8013530). R.

94. Mendes, Helen A. "How Divorced Fathers Obtain Custody: A Review of Research," Conciliation Courts Review, vol. 17, no. 1 (1979): 27–30.

95. Salk, Lee. "On the Custody Rights of Fathers in Divorce," *Journal of Clinical Child Psychology,* vol. 6, no. 2 (1977): 49–50.

96. Santrock, John W., and Warshak, Richard A. "Father Custody and Social Development in Boys and Girls," *Journal of Social Issues,* vol. 35, no. 4 (1979): 112–25. R.

97. Warshak, Richard A. "The Effects of Father Custody and Mother Custody on Children's Personality Development." Ph.D. diss., University of Texas Health Science Center at Dallas, 1978 (*DAI* 40/2B, p. 940, order # 7918709). R.

98. Woody, Robert H. "Fathers with Child Custody," *Counseling Psychologist,* vol. 7, no. 4 (1978): 60–63.

HISTORY OF CUSTODY

99. Derdeyn, Andre P. "Child Custody: A Reflection of Cultural Change," *Journal of Clinical Child Psychology*, vol. 7, no. 3 (1978): 169–73.

100. ———. "Child Custody Contests in Historical Perspective," *American Journal of Psychiatry*, vol. 133, no. 12 (1976): 1369–76

HOMOSEXUAL PARENTS

101. Campbell, Ross W. "Child Custody When One Parent Is a Homosexual," *Conciliation Courts Review*, vol. 16, no. 3 (1978): 37–42.

102. Hitchens, Donna J.; Martin, Del; and Morgan, Mary. "An Alternative View to 'Child Custody—When One Parent is Homosexual,' " *Conciliation Courts Review*, vol. 17, no. 3 (1979): 27–30.

103. Nestor, Byron L. "Attitudes of Child Psychiatrists toward Homosexual Parenting and Child Custody," *Conciliation Courts Review*, vol. 17, no. 2 (1979): 21–23. R.

104. Riddle, Dorothy I. "Gay Parents and Child Custody Issues," *Resources in Education* 13 (1978). ERIC document ED 147 746.

JOINT CUSTODY

105. Abarbanel, Alice R. "Joint Custody Families: A Case Study Approach." Ph.D. diss., California School of Professional Psychology, San Francisco, 1977 (*DAI* 38/6B, P. 2840, order # 7727586). R.

106. ———. "Shared Parenting after Separation and Divorce: A Study of Joint Custody," *American Journal of Orthopsychiatry*, vol. 49, no. 2 (1979): 320–29. R.

107. Ahrons, Constance R. "The Binuclear Family: Two Households, One Family," *Alternative Lifestyles*, vol. 2, no. 4 (1979): 499–515. R.

108. Benedek, Elissa P., and Benedek, Richard S. "Joint Custody: Solution or Illusion?" *American Journal of Psychiatry*, vol. 136, no. 12 (1979): 1540–44.

109. Eder, Vicki. "Shared Custody: An Idea Whose Time Has Come," *Conciliation Courts Review*, vol. 16, no. 1 (1978): 23–25.

110. Elkin, Meyer. "Reflections on Joint Custody and Family Law" (editorial), *Conciliation Courts Review*, vol. 16, no. 3 (1978): iii–v.

111. Gaddis, Stephen M. "Joint Custody of Children: A Divorce Decision-Making Alternative," *Conciliation Courts Review*, vol. 16, no. 1 (1978): 17–22.

112. Grote, Douglas F., and Weinstein, Jeffrey P. "Joint Custody: A Viable and Ideal Alternative," *Journal of Divorce*, vol. 1, no. 1 (1977): 43–53.

113. Milne, Ann L., ed. *Joint Custody: A Handbook for Judges, Lawyers and Counselors*. Portland, OR: Association of Family Conciliation Courts, 1979.

114. Nehls, Nadine M. "Joint Custody of Children: A Descriptive Study." Master's thesis, University of Wisconsin—Madison, 1978.

115. O'Neil, Maureen. "Not Just a Visitor: Joint Custody as a Means of Extending the Parent Child Relationship beyond Divorce," *Perception*, vol. 1, no. 6 (1978): 36–37.

116. O'Neil, Maureen, and Leonoff, A. "Joint Custody: An Option Worth Examining," *Perception*, vol. 1, no. 2 (1977): 28–30.

117. Roman, Melvin. "The Disposable Parent," *Conciliation Courts Review*, vol. 15, no. 2 (1977): 1–11.

118. Roman, Mel, and Haddad, William. "The Case for Joint Custody," *Psychology Today*, vol. 12, no. 4 (1978): 96 + .

119. Sell, Kenneth D. "Joint Custody and Coparenting," *Resources in Education* 15 (1980). ERIC document ED 182 649.

120. Trombetta, Diane, and Lebbos, Betsey W. "Co-parenting: Everyone's Best Interest," *Conciliation Courts Review*, vol. 17, no. 3 (1979): 13–23.

VISITATION

121. Alexander, Sharon J. "Influencing Factors on Divorced Parents in Determining Vistation Arrangements." Ph.D. diss., Florida State University 1978 (*DAI* 40/2A, p. 1101, order # 7917013). R.

122. Benedek, Richard, and Benedek, Elissa P. "Postdivorce Visitation: A Child's Right," *American Academy of Child Psychiatry Journal*, vol. 16, no. 2 (1977): 256–71.

123. Bienenfeld, Florence. "Pay-Offs of Post-dissolution Visitation Counseling," *Conciliation Courts Review*, vol. 12, no. 2 (1974): 27–32.

124. Chase, Gary A. "Visitation Phobia," *Conciliation Courts Review*, vol. 16, no. 2 (1978): 33–38.

125. Elkin, Meyer. "Custody and Visitation: A Time for Change" (editorial), *Conciliation Courts Review*, iii–v.

126. ———. "Grandparents Are Also Forever" (editorial), *Conciliation Courts Review*, vol. 15, no. 2 (1977): iii–iv.

127. Kelly, Joan B., and Wallerstein, Judith S. "Part-time Parent, Part-time Child: Visiting after Divorce," *Journal of Clinical Child Psychology*, vol. 6, no. 2 (1977): 51–54.

128. Margolin, Frances M. "An Approach to Resolution of Visitation Disputes Postdivorce: Short-term Counseling." Ph.D. diss., United States International University, 1973 (*DAI* 34/4B, p. 1754, order # 7322680). R.

129. Markey, Christian E., Jr.; McIssac, Hugh; and Pike, Donald W. "Family Law Colloquim—Custody and Visitation—the Los Angeles Experience," *Conciliation Courts Review*, vol. 17, no. 1 (1979): 31–34.

130. Moore, Nancy V., and Davenport, Caroline V. "Custody and Visitation: An Explication of Prevalent Patterns," *Resources in Education* 14 (1979). ERIC document ED 168 702. R.

131. Musetto, Andrew P. "Evaluating Families with Custody or Visitation Problems," *Journal of Marriage and Family Counseling*, vol. 4, no. 4 (1978): 59–65.

132. Weiss, Warren W., and Collada, Henry B. "Role of the Conciliation Court in Visitation Disputes," *Conciliation Courts Review*, vol. 12, no. 2 (1974): 21–26.

CHILDREN OF DIVORCED PARENTS

133. Anderson, Hilary. "Children of Divorce," *Journal of Clinical Child Psychology,* vol. 6, no. 2 (1977): 41–44.

134. Bane, Mary J. "Children, Divorce and Welfare," *Wilson Quarterly,* vol. 1, no. 2 (1977): 89–94.

135. ———. "Marital Disruption and the Lives of Children," *Journal of Social Issues,* vol. 32, no. 1 (1976): 103–17. R.

136. ———. "Marital Disruption and the Lives of Children." In *Divorce and Separation: Context, Causes and Consequences,* edited by George Levinger and Oliver C. Moles, pp. 276–86. New York: Basic Books, 1979. R.

137. Bass, Howard L. "Children of Divorce," *Trial Lawyers Quarterly,* vol. 11, no. 1 (1975): 54–61.

138. Beal, Edward W. "Children of Divorce: A Family Systems Perspective," *Journal of Social Issues,* vol. 35, no. 4 (1976): 140–54.

139. Bernard, Janine M. "Divorce and Young Children: Relationships in Transition," *Elementary School Guidance and Counseling,* vol. 12, no. 3 (1978): 188–98.

140. Braun, Samuel J., and Sang, Dorothy M. "When Parents Split," *Day Care and Early Education,* vol. 4, no. 2 (1976): 26–29 +.

141. Buckley, Elizabeth Y. "Object Loss in Children of Divorce: Theoretical Considerations," *Smith College Studies in Social Work,* vol. 45, no. 1 (1974): 27–28.

142. Bumpass, Larry, and Rindfuss, Ronald R. "Children's Experience of Marital Disruption," *American Journal of Sociology,* vol. 85, no. 1 (1979): 49–65.

143. ———. "Children's Experience of Marital Disruption," *Resources in Education* 14 (1979). ERIC document ED 164 741. R.

144. Butler, Annie L. "Tender Topics: Children and Crises." *Resources in Education* 13 (1978). ERIC document ED 147 019.

145. Camara, Kathleen A. "Children's Construction of Social Knowledge: Concepts of Family and the Experience of Parental Divorce." Ph.D. diss., Stanford University, 1979 (*DAI* 40/7B, p. 3433, order # 8001844). R.

146. Cantor, Dorothy W. "Divorce: A View from the Children," *Journal of Divorce,* vol. 2, no. 4 (1979): 357–61.

147. "A Child of Divorce," *Journal of Emotional Education,* vol. 10, no. 3 (1970): 65–85.

148. Cline, Foster W. "Generalities concerning Children and Divorce," *Nurse Practitioner,* vol. 2, no. 4 (1977): 29–30.

149. Daniel, Ralph M. "Father-Child Intimacy in Divorced Families." Ph.D. diss., California School of Professional Psychology, San Francisco, 1977 (*DAI* 36/8B, p. 2854, order # 7727593). R.

150. Drinan, Robert F. "The Rights of Children in Modern America." In *The Rights of Children: Emergent Concepts in Law and Society,* compiled by Albert E. Wilkerson, pp. 37–46. Philadelphia, PA: Temple University Press, 1973.

151. Fenton, Norman S. "Tucson Child Petition Program," *Conciliation Courts Review,* vol. 13, no. 2 (1975): 6–8.

152. Fortinberry, Alicia. "Latent Stress of Divorce for Preschoolers," *Psychology Today,* vol. 13, no. 5 (1979): 26–27. R.

153. Freed, Rae. "The Emotional Attitudes Experienced by Children of Divorce in Relation to Their Parents." D.S.W. diss., University of Southern California, 1979 (*DAI* 39/12A, p. 7522). R.

154. Gardner, Richard A. "Parental Divorce and the Needs of Children," *Conciliation Courts Review,* vol. 13, no. 2 (1975): 1–5.

155. Glick, Paul C. "Children of Divorced Parents in Demographic Perspective," *Journal of Social Issues,* vol. 35, no. 4 (1979): 170–82. R.

156. Goldstein, Harris S. "Reconstituted Families: The Second Marriage and Its Children," *Psychiatric Quarterly,* vol. 48, no. 3 (1974): 433–40.

157. Greene, Karen L. "A Pilot Study: Differential Cultural Effects upon the Single Parent Child Demonstrated in Artwork," *Art Psychotherapy,* vol. 4, no. 3–4 (1977): 149–58. R.

158. Grey, Catherine. "Four Children," *Children Today,* vol. 1, no. 4 (1972): 7–12.

159. Grollman, Earl A., and Grollman, Sharon H. "How to Tell Children about Divorce," *Journal of Clinical Child Psychology,* vol. 6, no. 2 (1977): 35–37.

160. Hammond, Janice M. "A Comparison of Elementary Children from Divorced and Intact Families," *Phi Delta Kappan,* vol. 61, no. 3 (1979): 219. R.

161. Henning, James S., and Oldham, J. Thomas. "Children of Divorce: Legal and Psychological Crises," *Journal of Clinical Child Psychology,* vol. 6, no. 2 (1977): 55–59.

162. Hetherington, E. Mavis. "Divorce: A Child's Perspective," *American Psychologist,* vol. 34, no. 10 (1979): 851–58.

163. Hetherington, E. Mavis; Cox, Martha; and Cox, Roger. "Play and Social Interaction in Children Following Divorce," *Journal of Social Issues,* vol. 35, no. 4 (1979): 26–49. R.

164. Hodges, William F.; Wechsler, Ralph C.; and Ballantine, Constance. "Divorce and the Preschool Child: Cumulative Stress," *Journal of Divorce,* vol. 3, no. 1 (1979): 55–67. R.

165. Hozman, Thomas L., and Froiland, Donald J. "Children: Forgotten in Divorce," *Personnel and Guidance Journal,* vol. 55, no. 9 (1977): 530–33.

166. Jenkins, Shirley. "Children of Divorce," *Children Today,* vol. 7, no. 2 (1978): 16–20 +.

167. Johnson, Judy. "Help for the Handicapped Male Child of the Single Parent," *Pointer,* vol. 22, no. 1 (1977): 71–73.

168. Johnson, Lynell A. "Divorce, Father Absence, and Father-Child Relationship as Predictors of Preadolescent Children's Peer Relations and Perspective-Taking Performance." Ph.D. diss., Stanford University, 1979 (*DAI* 40/7B, p. 3483, order # 8001947). R.

169. Kelly, Joan B., and Wallerstein, Judith S. "Children of Divorce," *National Elementary Principal* 59 (October 1979): 51–64.

170. Kittleson, Mark J. "Divorce and Children," *Resources in Education* 14 (1979). ERIC document ED 169 026.

171. Kohn, Sherwood D. "Coping with Family Change," *National Elementary Principal,* vol. 59, no. 1 (1979): 40–50.

172. Lerner, Samuel. "Services to the Child in the Single Parent Family," *Journal of Jewish Communal Services*, vol. 55, no. 4 (1979): 369–74.

173. Levitin, Teresa E. "Children of Divorce: An Introduction," *Journal of Social Issues*, vol. 35, no. 4 (1979): 1–25.

174. McNeal Robert E. "A Study Comparing the Relationship of Broken Homes to the School Success of Junior High School Students." Ed.D. diss., George Washington University, 1973 (*DAI* 34/5A, p. 2173, order # 7325337). R.

175. Manfredi, Lynn A. "Divorce and the Preschool Child," *Day Care and Early Education*, vol. 4, no. 5 (1977): 18 + .

176. "More Than One-Third of U.S. Children Will Live in One-Parent Families as a Result of Broken Marriage," *Family Planning Perspectives*, vol. 11, no. 2 (1979): 115 + .

177. Muir, Martha F. "Children and Divorce: Opportunities for Continuing Research and Practical Applications" (editorial), *Journal of Clinical Child Psychology*, vol. 6, no. 2 (1977): 2.

178. Munger, Richard, and Morse, William C. "When Divorce Rocks a Child's World," *Educational Forum* 43 (May 1979): 428–33.

179. Pecot, Michael G. "When the Parents Are Divorced," *Childhood Education* vol. 46, no. 6 (1970): 294–95.

180. Phillips, E. Lakin. "Children's Reactions to Separation and Divorce," *Resources in Education* 12 1977. ERIC document ED 131 943.

181. Podell, Ralph J. "The Appointment of Guardians ad litem for Children in Divorce Proceedings—Why?" *Conciliation Courts Review*, vol. 11, no. 1 (1973): 19–22.

182. Rice, George P., Jr. "Children of Divorce," *Educational Forum*, vol. 34, no. 4 (1970): 457–61.

183. Richards, Arlene K., and Willis, Irene. "Effects on Adolescents of Living Arrangements Following Parental Separation or Divorce," *Journal of Pediatric Psychology*, vol. 2, no. 3 (1977): 135–37.

184. Roberts, Albert R., and Roberts, Beverly J. "Divorce and the Child: A Pyrrhic Victory?" In *Childhood Deprivation*, edited by Albert R. Roberts, pp. 84–97. Springfield, IL: Charles C Thomas, 1974.

185. Rogers, Rita R., et al. "Roundtable: Divorce," *Medical Aspects of Human Sexuality*, vol. 10, no. 1 (1976): 55–80.

186. Rubenstein, Carin. "The Children of Divorce as Adults," *Psychology Today*, vol. 13, no. 8 (1980): 74–75. R.

187. Santrock, John W. "Family Structure, Maternal Behavior and Moral Development in Boys." Ph.D. diss., University of Minnesota, 1973 (*DAI* 34/7B, p. 3474, order # 74744). R.

188. Schlesinger, Benjamin. "Children and Divorce: A Selected Review, *Conciliation Courts Review*, vol. 15, no. 1 (1977): 36–40.

189. ———. "Children of Divorce in Canada: The Law Reform Commission's Recommendations," *Journal of Divorce*, vol. 1, no. 2 (1977): 175–82.

190. Simpson, Jacqueline L. "The Effects of Parental Divorce on Individuals' Family Size Ideals, Desires, and Expectations." Ph.D. diss., Florida State University, 1978 (*DAI* 40/2A, p. 1096, order # 7917083). R.

191. "Small Boys Worst Victims of Divorce," *USA Today* 107 (June 1979): 2.

192. Stuart, Irving R., and Abt, Lawrence E., eds. *Children of Separation and Divorce*. New York: Grossman, 1972.

193. Sugar, Max. "Children of Divorce," *Pediatrics*, vol. 46, no. 4 (1970): 588–95.

194. ———. "Divorce and Children," *Southern Medical Journal*, vol. 63, no. 12 (1970): 1458–61.

195. Tessman, Lora H. *Children of Parting Parents*. New York: J. Aaronson, 1978.

196. Thomas, M. Donald. "Parent Education Cannot Be Neglected," *NASSP Bulletin* 61 (October 1977): 69–74.

197. Uslander, Arlene S. "Dick Lives with Dad, Jane Lives with Mom, So Who Gets Spot?" *Instructor*, vol. 89, no. 2 (1979): 78.

198. ———. "Divorce: You Too Must Pay Child Support," *Learning*, vol. 5, no. 6 (1977): 23 + .

199. Wald, Michael S. "Legal Policies Affecting Children: A Lawyer's Request for Aid," *Child Development*, vol. 47, no. 1 (1976): 1–5.

200. Wallerstein, Judith S., and Kelly, Joan B. "California's Children of Divorce," *Psychology Today*, vol. 13, no. 8 (1980): 67–68 + . R.

201. ———. "Children of Divorce: A Review," *Social Work*, vol. 24, no. 6 (1979): 468–75.

202. ———. "Divorce and Children." In *Basic Handbook of Child Psychiatry*, vol. 4 edited by Joseph D. Noshpitz, et al., pp. 339–47. New York: Basic Books, 1979.

203. Watson, Andrew S. "Contested Divorce and Children: A Challenge for the Forensic Psychiatrist." In *Legal Medicine Annual*, edited by Cyril H. Wecht, pp. 489–502. New York: Appleton-Century-Crofts, 1973.

204. Weisfeld, David, and Laser, Martin S. "Divorced Parents in Family Therapy in a Residential Treatment Setting," *Family Process*, vol. 16, no. 2 (1977): 229–36.

ADJUSTMENT TO DIVORCE

205. Desimone-Luis, Judith; O'Mahoney, Katherine; and Hunt, Dennis. "Children of Separation and Divorce: Factors Influencing Adjustment," *Journal of Divorce*, vol. 3, no. 1 (1979): 37–42. R.

206. Fulton, Julie A. "Parental Reports of Children's Post-Divorce Adjustment," *Journal of Social Issues*, vol. 35, no. 4 (1979): 126–39. R.

207. Gardner, Richard A. "Children of Divorce: Some Legal and Psychological Considerations," *Journal of Clinical Child Psychology*, vol. 6, no. 2 (1977): 3–6.

208. Hess, Robert D., and Camara, Kathleen A. "Post-Divorce Family Relationships as Mediating Factors in the Consequences of Divorce for Children," *Journal of Social Issues*, vol. 35, no. 4 (1979): 79–96. R.

209. Hetherington, E. Mavis; Cox, Martha; and Cox, Roger. "Beyond Father Absence: Conceptualization of the Effects of Divorce," *Resources in Education* 11 (1976). ERIC document ED 113 015. R.

210. Kurdek, Lawrence A., and Siesky, Albert E., Jr. "An Interview Study of Parents' Perceptions of Their Children's Reactions and Adjustments to Divorce," *Journal of Divorce*, vol. 3, no. 1 (1979): 5–17. R.

211. Raschke, Helen J. "Family Structure, Family Happiness, and Their Effect on College Students' Personal and Social Adjustment," *Conciliation Courts Review*, vol. 15, no. 2 (1977): 30–33. R.

212. Scheffner, David. "Psychiatric Consultation in the Post-Divorce Period," *Orange County Bar Journal*, vol. 1, no. 1 (1973): 45–50.

213. Toomin, Marjorie K. "The Child of Divorce." In *Therapeutic Needs of the Family: Problems, Descriptions, and Therapeutic Approaches,* edited by Richard E. Hardy and John G. Cull, pp 56–90. Springfield, IL: Charles C Thomas, 1974.

214. ———. "Understanding the Child of Divorce." In *Creative Divorce through Social and Psychological Approaches,* edited by Richard E. Hardy and John G. Cull, pp. 91–123. Springfield, IL: Charles C Thomas, 1974.

215. Ulfelder, Linda C. "The Adjustment of Children to Separation and Divorce." Master's thesis, University of Maryland, College Park, 1975. R.

216. Wallerstein, Judith S. "Children Who Cope in spite of Divorce," *Family Advocate,* vol. 1, no. 1 (1978): 2–5+.

217. ———. "Responses of Preschool Child to Divorce: Those Who Cope." In *Child Psychiatry: Treatment and Research,* edited by Mae F. McMillan and Sergio Henao, pp. 269–92. New York: Brunner/Mazel, 1977.

BEHAVIOR DISORDERS

218. Bendiksen, Robert A. "Death and the Child: An Anterospective Test of the Childhood Bereavement and Later Behavior Disorders Hypothesis." Ph.D. diss., University of Minnesota, 1974 (*DAI* 35/8A, p. 5549, order # 752086). R.

219. Bendiksen, Robert A., and Fulton, Robert. "Death and the Child: An Anterospective Test of the Childhood Bereavement and Later Behavior Disorders Hypothesis," *Omega,* vol. 6, no. 1 (1975): 45–59. R.

220. "Children of Divorce: How to Cope with Their Psychological Problems," *Business Week,* April 2, 1979: 102–04.

221. Grinnell, Richard M., Jr., and Chambers, Cheryl A. "Broken Homes and Middle-Class Delinquency: A Comparison," *Criminology,* vol. 17, no. 3 (1979): 395–400. R.

222. King, Richard. "The Effect of the Broken Home on the Number of Discipline Problems Encountered by High School Students." Master's thesis, State University College, Oswego (NY), 1973. R.

223. Kurdek, Lawrence A., and Siesky, Albert E. "Divorced Single Parents' Perceptions of Child-Related Problems," *Journal of Divorce,* vol. 1, no. 4 (1978): 361–70. R.

224. Perkowski, Stefan G. "Comment on Ackerman's 'Marital Instability and Juvenile Delinquency,' " *American Anthropologist,* vol. 74, no. 5 (1972): 1320–21.

225. Tooley, Kay. "Antisocial Behavior and Social Alienation Post Divorce: The Man of the House and His Mother," *American Journal of Orthopsychiatry,* vol. 46, no. 1 (1976): 33–42.

226. Woodbury, Roger, and Pate, Dove H. "The Relationship of Parental Marital Status to Measures of the Cognitive Vocational Maturity of Delinquents," *Educational and Psychological Measurement,* vol. 34, no. 4 (1974): 1013–15. R.

227. Woody, Jane D. "Children of Divorce: A Survey of Professional Services and Opinions in Omaha," *Review of Applied Urban Research,* vol. 5, no. 12 (1977): 1–3+. R.

COUNSELING

228. Eddy, John P., and Silverman, Manuel S. "Children of Divorce: Implications for Counseling," *Kappa Delta Pi Record,* vol. 11, no. 1 (1974): 7–8.

229. Felner, Robert D; Stolberg, Arnold; and Cowen Emory L. "Crisis Events and School Mental Health Referral Patterns of Young Children," *Journal of Consulting and Clinical Psychology,* vol. 43, no. 3 (1975): 305–10. R.

230. Gardner, Richard A. *Psychotherapy with Children of Divorce.* New York: J. Aaronson, 1976.

231. Hammond, Janice M. "Children of Divorce: Implications for Counselors," *School Counselor,* vol. 27, no. 1 (1979): 7–14. R.

232. Kalter, Neil. "Children of Divorce in an Outpatient Psychiatric Population," *American Journal of Orthopsychiatry,* vol. 47, no. 1 (1977): 40–51. R.

233. McConnell, Judith A. "A Proposed Model for Counseling Adolescent Children of Divorced Parents." Ph.D. diss., Texas A&M University, 1978 (*DAI* 39/11A, p. 6549, order # 7909219). R.

234. Martin, Gilbert I. "Helping the Child of Divorcing Parents," *Consultant,* vol. 13, no. 10 (1973): 44–45.

235. "Psychiatrists and Children," *Canadian Medical Association Journal,* vol. 115, no. 8 (1976): 793-96.

236. Rembar, James C. "Only Children of Divorce in an Outpatient Psychiatric Population." Ph.D. diss., University of Michigan, 1978 (*DAI* 39/10B, p. 5083, order # 7907153). R.

237. Ritchie, Agnes M., and Serrano, Alberto C. "Family Therapy in the Treatment of Adolescents with Divorced Parents." In *Therapeutic Needs of the Family: Problems, Descriptions and Therapeutic Approaches,* edited by Richard E. Hardy and John G. Cull, pp. 91–99. Springfield, IL: Charles C Thomas, 1974.

238. Rosenthal, Perihan A. "Sudden Disappearance of One Parent with Separation and Divorce: the Grief and Treatment of Preschool Children," *Journal of Divorce,* vol. 3, no. 1 (1979): 43–54.

239. Stewart, Robert J. "Effects of Traumatic and Nontraumatic Parental Separation in Clinically Evaluated Children." Ed.D. diss., Temple University, 1973 (*DAI* 34/4B, p. 1762, order # 7323365). R.

240. Toomin, Marjorie K. "Counseling Needs of the Child of Divorce." In *Techniques and Approaches in Marital and Family Counseling,* edited by Richard E. Hardy and John G. Cull, pp. 71–105. Springfield, IL: Charles C Thomas, 1974.

241. Westman, Jack C., et al. "Role of Child Psychiatry in Divorce," *Archives of General Psychiatry,* vol. 23, no. 5 (1970): 416–20.

EFFECTS OF DIVORCE ON CHILDREN

242. Anthony, E. James. "Children at Risk from Divorce: A Review." In *Children at Psychiatric Risk. The Child in His Family,* edited by E. James Anthony and Cyrille Koupernik, vol. 3, pp. 461–77. New York: John Wiley & Sons, 1974.

243. Benians, R. C. "Marital Breakdown and Its Consequences for Children," *Medico-Legal Journal,* vol. 45, no. 1 (1977): 19–28.

244. Brun, Gudrun. "Conflicted Parents: High and Low Vulnerability of Children to Divorce." In *Vulnerable Children. The Child in His Family,* edited by E. James Anthony, Cyrille Koupernick, and Colette Chiland, Vol. 4, pp. 253–59. New York: John Wiley & Sons, 1978. R.

245. Calvert, Sheryl E. "What Research Says about Children of Divorce." Master's thesis, Wisconsin State University, Platteville, 1971.

246. Cherlin, Andrew. "The Effects of Children on Marital Dissolution," *Demography,* vol. 14, no. 3 (1977): 265–72. R.

247. Cline, David W., and Westman, Jack C. "The Impact of Divorce on the Family," *Child Psychiatry and Human Development,* vol. 2, no. 2 (1971): 78-83. R.

248. Esman, Aaron H. "Unhappy Marriage and Its Effects on Children," *Medical Aspects of Human Sexuality,* vol. 5, no. 6 (1971): 37–47.

249. Felner, Robert D. "An Investigation of Crisis in Childhood: Effects and Outcomes in Children Experiencing Parental Death or Divorce." Ph.D. diss., University of Rochester, 1977 (*DAI* 39/3B, p. 1475, order # 7815274). R.

250. Gardner, Richard A. "Social, Legal, and Therapeutic Changes That Should Lessen the Traumatic Effects of Divorce on Children," *American Academy of Psychoanalysis Journal,* vol. 6, no. 2 (1978): 231–47.

251. Gonso, Jonni L. "The Effects of Parental Divorce on Children." Ph.D. diss., Indiana University, 1977 (*DAI* 38/11B, p. 5568, order # 7805598). R.

252. Jacobson, Doris S. "The Impact of Marital Separation/Divorce on Children: I. Parent-Child Separation and Child Adjustment," *Journal of Divorce,* vol. 1, no. 4 (1978): 341–60. R.

253. ———. "The Impact of Marital Separation/Divorce on Children: II. Interparent Hostility and Child Adjustment," *Journal of Divorce,* vol. 2, no. 1 (1978): 3–19. R.

254. ———. "The Impact of Marital Separation/Divorce on Children: III. Parent-Child Communication and Child Adjustment and Regression Analysis of Findings from Overall Study," *Journal of Divorce,* vol. 2, no. 2 (1978): 175–94. R.

255. Jones, F. Nolan. "The Impact of Divorce on Children," *Conciliation Courts Review,* vol. 15, no. 2 (1977): 25–29.

256. Kelly, Joan B., and Wallerstein, Judith S. "The Effects of Parental Divorce: Experiences of the Child in Early Latency," *American Journal of Orthopsychiatry,* vol. 46, no. 1 (1976): 20–32. R.

257. Kelly, Robert, and Berg, Berthold. "Measuring Children's Reactions to Divorce," *Journal of Clinical Psychology,* vol. 34, no. 1 (1978): 215–21. R.

258. Kirkland, Karyn K. "The Effect of Divorce on Adolescent Self-Esteem and Attitude toward School." Master's thesis, California State University, Long Beach, 1978. R.

259. Kulka, Richard A., and Weingarten, Helen. "The Long-term Effects of Parental Divorce in Childhood on Adult Adjustment," *Journal of Social Issues,* vol. 35, no. 4 (1979): 50–78. R.

260. Lewis, Doris. "Divorce and Its Effects on Children." Master's thesis, Bank Street College of Education, New York, 1979. R.

261. Littner, Ner. "The Effects on a Child of Family Disruption and Separation from One or Both Parents," *Conciliation Courts Review,* vol. 11, no. 1 (1973): 9–18.

262. Long, Sandra M. "Changes Experienced by the Young Child When There Has Been Parental Loss due to Divorce." Ph.D. diss., Indiana University, 1978 (*DAI* 39/12A, p. 7152, order # 7909697). R.

263. Longfellow, Cynthia. "Divorce in Context: Its Impact on Children." In *Divorce and Separation: Context, Causes and Consequences,* edited by George Levinger and Oliver C. Moles, pp. 287–306. New York: Basic Books, 1979.

264. Luepnitz, Deborah A. "Children of Divorce: A Review of the Psychological Literature," *Law and Human Behavior,* vol. 2, no. 2 (1978): 167–79.

265. ———. "Which Aspects of Divorce Affect Children?" *Family Coordinator,* vol. 28, no. 1 (1979): 79-85. R.

266. McDermott, John F., Jr. "Divorce and Its Psychiatric Sequelae in Children," *Archives of General Psychiatry,* vol. 23, no. 5 (1970): 421–27. R.

267. Magrab, Phyllis R. "For the Sake of the Children: A Review of the Psychological Effects of Divorce," *Journal of Divorce,* vol. 1, no. 3 (1978): 233–45.

268. Nosenzo, Maryann E. "The Effect of Divorce on the Self-Concept of Middle School Students." Master's thesis, State University College of New York, Oswego, 1978. R.

269. Reinhard, David W. "The Reaction of Adolescent Boys and Girls to the Divorce of Their Parents," *Journal of Clinical Child Psychology,* vol. 6, no. 2 (1977): 21–23. R.

270. ———. "The Reaction of Adolescent Boys and Girls to the Divorce of Their Parents." Ed.D. diss., University of Pennsylvania, 1971 (*DAI* 32/4B, p. 2408, order # 7125543). R.

271. Rohrlich, John A., et al. "The Effects of Divorce: A Research Review with a Developmental Perspective," *Journal of Clinical Child Psychology,* vol. 6, no. 2 (1977): 15–20.

272. Rosen, Rhona. "Children of Divorce: What They Feel about Access and Other Aspects of the Divorce Experience," *Journal of Clinical Child Psychology,* vol. 6, no. 2 (1977): 24–27. R.

273. Rubin, Lisa D., and Price, James H. "Divorce and Its Effects on Children," *Journal of School Health,* vol. 49, no. 10 (1979): 552–56.

274. Scherman, Avraham. "Divorce: Its Impact on the Family and Children," *Resources in Education* 14 (1979). ERIC document ED 172 133.

275. Scribner, John. "The Effects of Divorce on the Younger Adolescent." Master's thesis, Biola College, 1973. R.

276. Sorosky, Arthur D. "Psychological Effects of Divorce upon Adolescents," *Adolescence* 12 (Spring 1977): 123–36.

277. Theus, Robert. "Effects of Divorce upon School Children," *Clearing House,* vol. 50, no. 8 (1977): 364–65.

278. Wallerstein, Judith, and Kelly, Joan B. "The Effects of Parental Divorce: Experiences of the Child in Later Latency," *American Journal of Orthopsychiatry,* vol. 46, no. 2 (1976): 256–69. R.

279. ———. "The Effects of Parental Divorce: Experiences of the Preschool Child." In *Annual Progress in Child Psychiatry and Child Development,* edited by Stella Chess and Alexander Thomas, pp. 520–37. New York: Brunner/Mazel, 1977.

280. ———. "The Effects of Parental Divorce: Experiences of the Preschool Child," *American Academy of Child Psychiatry Journal,* vol. 14, no. 4 (1975): 600–16. R.

281. ———. "The Effects of Parental Divorce: The Adolescent Experience." In *Children at Psychiatric Risk.* The Child in His Family, edited by E. James Anthony and Cyrille Koupernik, Vol. 3, pp. 479–505. New York: John Wiley, 1974.

282. Wallerstein, Judith. "Effects of Divorce on Children, Research Findings, and Implications for Interviewing," *Conciliation Courts Review,* vol. 12, no. 1 (1974): 8–9.

283. Zimmerman, Beatrice S. "The Effect of Marital Dissolution on a Child." Master's thesis, Jersey City State College, 1974. R.

PERSONALITY DEVELOPMENT

284. Benedek, Richard S., and Benedek, Elissa P. "Children of Divorce: Can We Meet Their Needs?" *Journal of Social Issues,* vol. 35, no. 4 (1979): 155–69.

285. Berg, Berthold, and Kelly, Robert. "The Measured Self-Esteem of Children from Broken, Rejected and Accepted Families," *Journal of Divorce,* vol. 2, no. 4 (1979): 363–69. R.

286. Bessinger, Tina P. "The Relationship of Parental Divorce, during Adolescence, to Self-Concept." Ph.D. diss., University of Pittsburgh, 1976 (*DAI* 37/7A, p. 4220, order # 77682). R.

287. Cox, Martha J., and Cox, Roger D. "Socialization of Young Children in the Divorced Family," *Journal of Research and Developmental Education,* vol. 13, no. 1 (1979): 58–67.

288. Farson, Richard. "Parental Divorce: A Growth Experience for Children?" (letter to the editor), *American Journal of Orthopsychiatry,* vol. 48, no. 1 (1978): 183–85.

289. Hammond, Janice M. "Children of Divorce: A Study of Self-Concept, Academic Achievement, and Attitudes," *Elementary School Journal,* vol. 80, no. 2 (1979): 55–62. R.

290. ———. "Children of Divorce: A Study of Self-Concept, School Behaviors, Attitudes and Situational Variables." Ph.D. diss., University of Michigan, 1979 (*DAI* 40/2A, p. 672, order # 7916719). R.

291. Hetherington, E. Mavis. "Family Interaction and the Social, Emotional and Cognitive Development of Children Following Divorce." In *The Family: Setting Priorities,* edited by T. Berry Brazelton and Victor C. Vaughn, pp. 71–87. New York: Science and Medicine, 1979. R.

292. Hetherington, E. Mavis, et al. "Family Integration and Social, Emotional and Cognitive Development of Children Following Divorce," *Resources in Education* 13 (1978). ERIC document ED 156 328. R.

293. ———. "Development of Children in Mother-Headed Families." In *American Family: Dying or Developing,* edited by David Reiss and Howard A. Hoffman, pp. 117–45. New York: Plenum Press, 1979.

294. Isenberg, Roy M. "Personality Functioning in Latency Aged Children Prior to Parental Divorce." Ph.D. diss., University of Oklahoma, 1979 (*DAI* 40/10B, p. 5005, order # 8008649). R.

295. Kelly, Joan M. "Self-Concept Development in Parent Deprived Children: A Comparative Study," *Graduate Research Education and Related Disciplines,* vol. 6, no. 1 (1970): 30–48. R.

296. Lamb, Michael E. "The Effects of Divorce on Children's Personality Development," *Journal of Divorce,* vol. 1, no. 2 (1977): 163–74.

297. Lowenstein, Joyce S., and Koopman, Elizabeth J. "A Comparison of the Self-Esteem between Boys Living with Single-Parent Mothers and Single-Parent Fathers," *Journal of Divorce,* vol. 2, no. 2 (1978): 195–208. R.

298. Miller, Paul W. "The Effects of Father Contact on the Self-Concept of Children from Broken Homes." Master's thesis, California State University, Long Beach, 1976 (*Master's Abstracts* 15/1, p. 18, order # 1309085). R.

299. Moore, Nancy V., et al. "The Child's Development of the Concept of Family," *Resources in Education* 12 (1977). ERIC document ED 140 980. R.

300. Morrison, James R. "Parental Divorce as a Factor in Childhood Psychiatric Illness," *Comprehensive Psychiatry,* vol. 15, no. 2 (1974): 95–102. R.

301. Parish, Thomas S., and Taylor, James C. "Impact of Divorce and Subsequent Father Absence on Children's and Adolescents' Self-Concepts," *Journal of Youth and Adolescence,* vol. 8, no. 4 (1979): 427–32. R.

302. Raschke, Helen J., and Raschke, Vernon J. "Family Conflict and Children's Self-Concepts: A Comparison of Intact and Single-Parent Families," *Journal of Marriage and the Family,* vol. 41, no. 2 (1979): 367–74. R.

303. Stephens, Nancy, and Day, H. D. "Sex Role Identity, Parental Identification, and Self-Concept of Adolescent Daughters from Mother-Absent, Father-Absent, and Intact Families," *Journal of Psychology,* vol. 103, no. 2 (1979): 193–207. R.

304. Stolberg, Arnold L. "Cognitive and Behavioral Changes in Children Resulting from Parental Divorce and Consequent Environmental Changes." Ph.D. diss., University of South Florida, 1979 (*DAI* 40/7B, p. 3425, order # 8002204). R.

305. ———. "Parental Divorce, Death and Foster Home Placements as Related to Personality Profiles of Adolescents in Psychotherapy." Master's thesis, University of South Florida, 1977. R.

306. Stolberg, Arnold L., et al. "Parental Divorce, Death and Foster Home Placement as Related to Personality Profiles of Adolescents," *Resources in Education* 13 (1978). ERIC document ED 142 883. R.

307. Wallerstein, Judith S. "Some Observations Regarding the Effects of Divorce on the Psychoanalytic Development of the Pre-school Girl." In *Sexual and Gender Development of Young Children,* edited by Evelyn K. Oremland and Jerome D. Oremland, pp. 117–129. Cambridge, MA: Ballinger Pub., 1977.

308. Westman, Jack C. "Effect of Divorce on a Child's Personality Development," *Medical Aspects of Human Sexuality,* vol. 6, no. 1 (1972): 38–55.

309. ———. "Effect of Divorce on a Child's Personality Development," *Mental Health Digest,* vol. 4, no. 4 (1972): 24–28.

310. White, Sharon J. "Comparison of Self-Concept in Children from Broken and Non-broken Homes and Its Academic Relevance." Master's thesis, Tennessee Technological University, 1978. R.

STATISTICS

311. *Status of Children, 1977.* Washington DC: Department of Health, Education, and Welfare; Administration for Children, Youth and Families, 1977 (HE23.1009:977) (Tables 2.2, 2.3).

312. U.S. Bureau of the Census. *Characteristics of American Children and Youth: 1976.* Series P-23: Special Studies, No. 66. Washington, DC: Government Printing Office, 1978 (C3.186:P-23/66) (Tables 21, 23).

313. U.S. National Center for Health Statistics. *Children of Divorced Couples: United States Selected Years.* Series 21: Data on Natality, Marriage, and Divorce, No. 18. Washington, DC: Government Printing Office, 1970 (HE20.2210:21/18) (Fig. 1–8, Tables 1–26).

DESERTION AND NONSUPPORT

314. Johnson, Walter D. " 'Growing Pains' in Child Support: Non-compliance as an Ever-Increasing Problem," *Illinois Issues* April 1978: 7–9. R.

315. Pleck, Elizabeth H. "The Two-Parent Household: Black Family Structure in Late Nineteenth-Century Boston," *Journal of Social History,* vol. 6, no. 1 (1972): 3–31.

316. Snyder, Lillian M. "The Deserting, Nonsupporting Father: Scapegoat of Family Nonpolicy," *Family Coordinator,* vol. 28, no. 4 (1979): 594–98.

317. ———. "The Deserting Nonsupporting Father: Scapegoat of Family Nonpolicy," 1978. Washington, DC: *Resources in Education* 14 (1979). ERIC document ED 172 053.

318. ———. "The Impact of the Criminal Justice System in Baltimore on the Deserting Nonsupporting Father in Relation to the Fulfillment of His Role as Provider." D.S.W. diss., Columbia University, 1975 (*DAI* 36/12A, p. 8302, order # 7612786). R.

319. Todres, Rubiñ. "Runaway Wives: An Increasing North-American Phenomenon," *Family Coordinator,* vol. 27, no. 1 (1978): 17–21. R.

320. Winston, Marian P. *Nonsupport of Legitimate Children by Affluent Fathers as a Cause of Poverty and Welfare Dependence.* Rev. ed. Santa Monica, CA: Rand Corporation, 1974.

DIVORCE

321. Bentler, Peter M., and Newcomb, Michael D. "Longitudinal Study of Marital Success and Failure," *Journal of Consulting and Clinical Psychology,* vol. 46, no. 5 (1978): 1053–70. R.

322. Bertelsen, Judy. "Political Interest, Influence, and Efficacy: Differences between the Sexes and among Marital Status Groups," *American Politics Quarterly,* vol. 2, no. 4 (1974): 412–26. R.

323. Blanshard, Paul. "Voltaire on Adultery and Divorce," *Humanist,* vol. 34, no. 6 (1974): 42.

324. Blood, Robert O., Jr., and Blood, Margaret C. "Amicable Divorce: A New Lifestyle," *Alternative Lifestyles,* vol. 2, no. 4 (1979): 483–98.

325. Bohannan, Paul, ed. *Divorce and After.* Garden City, NY: Doubleday, 1970.

326. ———. "Divorce Chains, Households of Remarriage, and Multiple Divorcers." In *Divorce and After,* pp. 113–23. Garden City, NY: Doubleday, 1970.

327. Bohmer, Carol, and Lebow, Richard N. "Divorce Comparative Style: A Paradigm of Divorce Patterns. *Journal of Divorce,* vol. 2, no. 2 (1978): 157–73.

328. Brady, James B. "Divorce on Demand," *Humanist,* vol. 30, no. 3 (1970): 9–26.

329. Brockert, John E. "Marriage and Divorce in Utah and the United States," *Utah Economic and Business Review,* vol. 33, no. 2 (1973): 1+.

330. Brown, Prudence, and Fox, Hannah. "Sex Differences in Divorce." In *Gender and Disordered Behavior: Sex Differences in Psychopathology,* edited by Edith S. Gomberg and Violet Franks, pp. 101–23. New York: Brunner/Mazel, 1979.

331. Bumpass, Larry, and Sweet, James A. "Differentials in Marital Stability: 1970," *American Sociological Review,* vol. 37, no. 6 (1972): 754–66. R.

332. Burnstein, Jules. "The Psychosocial Consequences of Conjugal Visits in Prisons." Ph.D. diss., California School of Professional Psychology, San Francisco, 1976 (*DAI* 37/7B, p. 3599, order # 7630284). R.

333. Cashion, Barbara G. "Durkheim's Concept of Anomie and Its Relationship to Divorce," *Sociology and Social Research,* vol. 55, no. 1 (1970): 72–81.

334. Chester, Robert. *Divorce in Europe.* Leiden: Martinus Nijhoff Social Sciences Division, 1977.

335. ———. "Marital Stability and Social Mobility," *International Journal of Sociology of the Family,* vol. 8, no. 2 (1978): 159–70.

336. Christensen, Larry, and Wallace, Lee. "Perceptual Accuracy as a Variable in Marital Adjustment," *Journal of Sex and Marital Therapy,* vol. 2, no. 2 (1976): 130–36. R.

337. Cobe, Patricia. "Coping with Divorce," *Forecast for Home Economics,* vol. 22, no. 9 (1977): 68–69.

338. Cole, Charles L., and Powers, Edward A. "The Relationship between Divorce and Industrialization: Towards a Parsimonious Explanation," *International Journal of Sociology of the Family,* vol. 3, no. 1 (1973): 42–47. R.

339. Constantine, Larry L., and Constantine, Joan M. "Dissolution of Marriage in a Nonconventional Context," *Family Coordinator,* vol. 21, no. 4 (1972): 457–62.

340. Crawford, Don R. "A Yogi Looks at Divorce, Marriage, and Role of Marriage Counsellor," *Conciliation Courts Review,* vol. 12, no. 1 (1974): 25–26.

341. Cuff, E. C., and Francis, D. W. "Some Features of 'Invited Stories' about Marriage Breakdown," *International Journal of the Sociology of Language* 18 (1978): 111–33. R.

342. Dienstag, Eleanor. "Myth of Creative Divorce," *Psychology Today,* vol. 10, no. 11 (1977): 49+.

343. Dlugokinski, Eric. "A Developmental Approach to Coping with Divorce," *Journal of Clinical Child Psychology,* vol. 6, no. 2 (1977): 27–30.

344. Dranov, Paula. "What Every Agency Should Know about No-Fault Divorce," *Human Needs,* vol. 1, no. 10–11 (1973): 26–28.

345. Everly, Kathleen. "New Directions in Divorce Research," *Journal of Clinical Child Psychology,* vol. 6, no. 2 (1977): 7–10.

346. Fain, Harry M. "Family Law— 'Whither now'?" *Journal of Divorce,* vol. 1, no. 1 (1977): 31-42.

347. Farber, Bernard. *Family and Kinship in Modern Society.* Glenview, IL: Scott, Foresman, 1973.

348. Federico, Joseph. "The Marital Termination Period of the Divorce Adjustment Process," *Journal of Divorce,* vol. 3, no. 2 (1979): 93–106.

349. Fowler, Ray. "Alternatives to Divorce," *Conciliation Courts Review,* vol. 11, no. 1 (1973): 23–26.

350. Framo, James L. "The Friendly Divorce," *Psychology Today,* vol. 11, no. 9 (1978): 77+.

351. Fraydouni, Nasser. "An Intercultural Comparison of Marriage, Divorce and Marriage Role Expectations." Master's thesis, Emporia State University, 1978.

352. Glick, Paul C. "A Demographer Looks at American Families," *Journal of Marriage and the Family,* vol. 37, no. 1 (1975): 15–26. R.

353. Glick, Paul C., and Norton, Arthur J. "Marrying, Divorcing, and Living Together in the U.S. Today," *Population Bulletin,* vol. 32, no. 5 (1977): 3–39. R.

354. Gubrium, Jaber F. "Marital Desolation and the Evaluation of Everyday Life in Old Age," *Journal of Marriage and the Family,* vol. 36, no. 1 (1974): 107–13. R.

355. Hansen, Robert W. " 'Til Divorce Do Us Part,' " *Conciliation Courts Review,* vol. 8, no. 1 (1970): 30–32.

356. Hardy, Richard E., and Cull, John G., eds. *Creative Divorce through Social and Psychological Approaches.* Springfield, IL: Charles C Thomas, 1974.

357. Harshman, Gordon A. "Alternatives to Divorce and Their Implications." In *Therapeutic Needs of the Family: Problems, Descriptions and Therapeutic Approaches,* edited by Richard E. Hardy and John G. Cull, pp. 167–87. Springfield, IL: Charles C Thomas, 1974.

358. Hendrickson, Wendy E. "An Exploratory Study of Divorce as a Potential Differentiating Factor among Family Therapists." Ed.D. diss., Boston University, 1978 (*DAI* 39/5A, p. 2755, order # 7819744). R.

359. "High Costs of Divorce in Money and Emotions," *Business Week,* 2368 (February 10, 1975): 83–86+.

360. Hill, Charles T.; Rubin, Zick; and Peplaw, Letitia A. "Breakups before Marriage: The End of 103 Affairs," *Journal of Social Issues,* vol. 32, no. 1 (1976): 147–68. R.

361. ———. "Breakups before Marriage: The End of 103 Affairs." In *Divorce and Separation: Context, Causes and Consequences,* edited by George Levinger and Oliver C. Moles, pp. 64–82. New York: Basic Books, 1979. R.

362. Horn, Jack. "Personality and Divorce," *Psychology Today,* vol. 10, no. 5 (1976): 138+.

363. Houck, John H. "Marital Disruption and Divorce," *Psychiatric Annals,* vol. 5, no. 7 (1975): 294–99.

364. Howe, Ruth-Arlene W. "Divorce— Critical Issues for Legal and Mental Health Professionals," *Urban and Social Change Review,* vol. 10, no. 1 (1977): 15–21.

365. Johnson, Walter D. "In My Opinion: Establishing a National Center for the Study of Divorce," *Family Coordinator,* vol. 26, no. 3 (1977): 263–68.

366. Juhasz, Anne M. "A Concept of Divorce: Not Busted Bond but Severed Strand," *Alternative Lifestyles,* vol. 2, no. 4 (1979): 471–82.

367. Kenkel, William F., and Benson, Barbara. "Family Trends in Selected Nonsocialist Countries," *Resources in Education* 12 (1977). ERIC document ED 138 536. R.

368. Kohn, Sherwood D. "The Integrity of the Family," *National Elementary Principal,* vol. 55, no. 5 (1976): 48–58.

369. Kolodji, Joseph N. "Divorce in Shasta County, California." Master's thesis, California State University, Chico, 1976. R.

370. Kolodji, Joseph, and Carrico, Bill. "Divorce in Shasta County, California, 1975," *Conciliation Courts Review,* vol. 17, no. 1 (1979): 37–39. R.

371. Kraus, Sharon. "The Crisis of Divorce: Growth Promoting or Pathogenic?" *Journal of Divorce,* vol. 3, no. 2 (1976): 107–19.

372. Kunz, Phillip R., and Albrecht, Stan L. "Religion, Marital Happiness, and Divorce," *International Journal of Sociology of the Family,* vol. 7, no. 2 (1977): 227–32. R.

373. Leezenbaum, Ralph. "Divorce: A Penalty of the Ad Business?" *Marketing/ Communications,* vol. 298, no. 2 (1970): 24–27.

374. "Life in America: Who Gets Divorced?" *USA Today,* 107 (June 1979): 1.

375. Matthews, Stephen D. "Clinical Judgement in Parish Ministers, Pastoral Counselors, and Clinical Psychologists." Ph.D. diss., Adelphi University, 1976 (*DAI* 37/9B, p. 4693, order # 774330). R.

376. Mincer, Jacob. "Family Migration Decisions," *Journal of Political Economy,* vol. 86, no. 5 (1978): 749–73.

377. Moles, Oliver C., and Levinger, George. "Divorce and Separation" (Symposium), *Journal of Social Issues,* vol. 32, no. 1 (1976): 1–207. R.

378. Norton, Arthur J., and Glick, Paul C. "Marital Instability: Past, Present, and Future," *Journal of Social Issues,* vol. 32, no. 1 (1976): 5–20. R.

379. ———. "Marital Instability in America, Past, Present, and Future." In *Divorce and Separation: Context, Causes and Consequences,* edited by George Levinger and Oliver C. Moles, pp. 6–19. New York: Basic Books, 1979. R.

380. O'Brien, John E. "Violence in Divorce Prone Families," *Journal of Marriage and the Family,* vol. 33, no. 4 (1971): 692–98. R.

381. O'Connor, Nancy D. V. "An Exploration of the Effects of Anticipatory Grief versus Acute Grief on Recovery after Loss of Spouse among Divorced and Sepa-

rated Women." Ph.D. diss., University of Oregon, 1976 (*DAI* 37/9A, p. 5708, order # 774748). R.

382. Pearson, Willie, Jr., and Hendrix, Lewellyn. "Divorce and the Status of Women," *Journal of Marriage and the Family*, vol. 41, no. 2 (1979): 375–85. R.

383. Peskin, Tsipora R. "Divorce and the Adult Life Span: A Longitudinal Study." D.S.W. diss., University of California, Berkeley, 1976 (*DAI* 38/2A, p. 1026, order # 7715576). R.

384. Peters, John F. *Divorce*. Toronto: University of Toronto Press, 1979.

385. ———. "Divorce in Canada: A Demographic Profile," *Journal of Comparative Family Studies*, vol. 7, no. 2 (1976): 335–49. R.

386. ———. "Factors Associated with Divorce." In *Intimacy, Commitments, and Marriages: Development and Relationships*, edited by J. Ross Eshleman and Juanne N. Clarke, pp. 295–305. Boston, MA: Allyn and Bacon, 1978.

387. "Profile of Broken Families," *Metropolitan Life Statistical Bulletin* 51 (December 1970): 8–9. R.

388. Ravich, Robert A. "The Marriage/ Divorce Paradox." In *Progress in Group and Family Therapy*, edited by Clifford J. Sager and Helen S. Kaplan, pp. 531–36. New York: Brunner/Mazel, 1972. R.

389. Ricci, Isolina. "Divorce, Remarriage, and the Schools, *Phi Delta Kappan*, vol. 60, no. 7 (1979): 509–11.

390. Rice, David G. "Pseudo-divorce: A Factor in Marital Stability and Growth," *Psychotherapy: Theory, Research and Practice*, vol. 13, no. 1 (1976): 51–53.

391. ———. "Psychotherapeutic Treatment of Narcissistic Injury in Marital Separation and Divorce," *Journal of Divorce*, vol. 1, no. 2 (1977): 119–28.

392. Roberts, Wesley K., and Hart, Betty K. "Marriage, Divorce, and Society: A Report on a Symposium on Personal Adjustment to Transitions on Marital Status. Final Report," *Resources in Education* 12 (1977). ERIC document ED 141 728.

393. Rockwell, Richard C.; Elder, Glen H., Jr.; and Ross, David J. "Psychological Patterns in Marital Timing and Divorce," *Social Psychology*, vol. 42, no. 4 (1979): 399–404. R.

394. Rosen, Lawrence. "I Divorce Thee," *Transaction*, vol. 7, no. 8 (1970): 34–37.

395. Rosenblatt, Paul C., and Hillabrant, Walter J. "Divorce for Childlessness and the Regulation of Adultery," *Journal of Sex Research*, vol. 8, no. 2 (1972): 117–27. R.

396. Schoen, Robert. "California's Experience with Non-adversary Divorce," *Demography*, vol. 12, no. 2 (1975): 223–43. R.

397. Scudder, Townsend. "The Family— What Is Its Situation Today? Is It an Imperiled Institution?" Population Profiles: A Series of Units on Specific Topics for the Study of Demography, No. 17. *Resources in Education* 13 (1978). ERIC document ED 148 587.

398. Shorter, Edward. "Toward the Postmodern Family," *National Elementary Principal*, vol. 55, no. 5 (1976): 26–31.

399. Simons, Richard C., and Strauss, Dorothy. "Marital Dysfunction, Separation, and Divorce." In *Understanding Human Behavior in Health and Illness*, edited by Richard C. Simons and Herbert Pardes, pp. 344–55. Baltimore, MD: Williams and Wilkins, 1977.

400. Sobota, Walter L., and Cappas, A. Thomas. "Semantic Differential Changes Associated with Participation in a Public Lecture Series Describing the Emotional and Behavioral Consequences of Divorce," *Journal of Divorce*, vol. 3, no. 2 (1979): 137–51. R.

401. Sociological Resources for the Social Studies (Project). *Divorce in the United States*. Boston, MA: Allyn and Bacon, 1972.

402. Thompson, James G. "The Gillette Syndrome: A Myth Revisited?" *Wyoming Issues*, vol. 2, no. 2 (1979): 30–35. R.

403. Thornton, Arland. "Children and Marital Stability," *Journal of Marriage and the Family*, vol. 39, no. 3 (1977): 531–40. R.

404. ———. "Marital Instability Differentials and Interactions: Insights from Multivariate Contingency Table Analysis," *Sociology and Social Science Research*, vol. 62, no. 4 (1978): 572–595. R.

405. Vigderhous, Gideon, and Fishman, Gideon. "Social Indicators of Marital Instability, U.S.A., 1920–1969," *Social Indicators Research*, vol. 5, no. 3 (1978): 325–44. R.

406. Weed, James A. "Age at Marriage as a Factor in State Divorce Rate Differentials," *Demography*, vol. 11, no. 3 (1974): 361–75. R.

407. Weinstein, Arlene S., and Moskowitz, Joel A. " 'Let No Man Put Asunder,' " *New York State Journal of Medicine* 72 (September 15, 1972): 2347–49.

408. Weiss, Robert S. "New Marital Form: Marriage of Uncertain Duration." In *On the Making of America: Essays in Honor of David Riesman*, edited by Herbert J. Gans et al., pp. 221–33. Philadelphia, PA: University of Pennsylvania Press, 1979.

ATTITUDES

409. Alston, Jon P. "Review of the Polls," *Journal for the Scientific Study of Religion*, vol. 11, no. 3 (1972): 282–86. R.

410. Bernard, Jessie. "No News, but New Ideas." In *Divorce and After*, edited by Paul Bohannan, pp. 3–25. Garden City, NY: Doubleday, 1970.

411. "Californians Rank Presidential Candidate Qualities," *Public Opinion*, vol. 3, no. 6 (1975): 55.

412. Conley, John A., and O'Rourke, Thomas W. "Attitudes of College Students toward Selected Issues on Human Sexuality," *Journal of School Health*, vol. 43, no. 5 (1973): 286–92. R.

413. Hennigan, Joelyn L. "Attitudes toward the Survival of Marriage: A Survey of High School Seniors in Plaquemine, Louisiana." Master's thesis, Louisiana State University, Baton Rouge, 1978. R.

414. "Iowans See More Family Strife," *Public Opinion*, vol. 5, no. 2 (1977): 15.

415. Keller, Lillian M. "Marriage/Family/Child Counselors' Attitudes toward Divorce as Related to Selected Social Characteristics." Ph.D. diss., United States International University, 1976 (*DAI* 37/3A, p. 1806, order # 7620968). R.

416. "Minnesotans Concerned about Divorce Rate," *Public Opinion*, vol. 3, no. 1 (1975): 5.

417. "Most in Twin Cities Favor Automatic Divorce," *Public Opinion*, vol. 2, no. 3 (1974): 34.

BIBLIOGRAPHIES

418. Baker, Adrian J. "Divorce and One-Parent Family Counseling," *Resources in Education* 14 (1979). ERIC document ED 165 083.

419. Canada. Department of National Health and Welfare. Library. *Divorce: A Bibliographic Look at the World*. Ottawa: Health and Welfare Canada, 1977.

420. Israel, Stanley. *A Bibliography on Divorce*. New York: Bloch Publishing Co., 1974.

421. Kessler, Sheila. "Divorce Bibliography," *Resources in Education* 11 (1976). ERIC document ED 119 095.

422. McKenney, Mary. *Divorce: A Selected Annotated Bibliography*. Metuchen, NJ: Scarecrow Press, 1975.

423. Sell, Kenneth D. *Divorce in the 1970's: A Subject Guide to Books, Articles, Dissertations, Government Documents, and Film on Divorce in the United States, 1970–1976*. Preliminary ed. Salisbury, NC: Sell, 1977. Annual supplements.

424. Sell, Kenneth D., and Sell, Betty H. *Divorce in the United States, Canada, and Great Britain: A Guide to Information Sources*. Detroit, MI: Gale Research Co., 1978.

CAUSES OF DIVORCE

425. Birtchnell, John. "Some Possible Early Family Determinants of Marriage and Divorce," *British Journal of Medical Psychology* 47 (June 1974): 121–27. R.

426. Cherlin, Andrew J. "Social and Economic Determinants of Marital Separation." In *Government Reports Announcements Index*, Springfield, VA: 1978 (PB-274 296/3GA). R.

427. Deckert, Pamela, and Langelier, Regis. "The Late Divorce Phenomena: The Causes and Impact of Ending 20-Year-Old or Longer Marriages," *Journal of Divorce*, vol. 1, no. 4 (1978): 381–90. R.

428. Field, David L. "Primary Causes of Divorce in Teenage Marriages." Master's thesis, Drake University, 1976. R.

429. Karawia, Wafaa T. "Divorce in the United States." Master's thesis, California State University, Long Beach, 1979 (*Masters Abstract* 17/4, p. 292, order # 1313309). R.

430. Levinger, George, and Moles, Oliver C., eds. *Divorce and Separation: Context, Causes and Consequences*. New York: Basic Books, 1979. R.

431. Michael, Robert T. "Factors Affecting Divorce: A Study of the Terman Sample." Working Paper No. 147. Stanford, CA: National Bureau of Economic Research, 1976. R.

432. Mott, Frank L., and Moore, Sylvia F. "The Causes of Marital Disruption among Young American Women: An Interdisciplinary Perspective," *Journal of Marriage and the Family*, vol. 41, no. 2 (1979): 355–65. R.

433. ———. "The Causes of Marital Disruption among Young American Women: An Interdisciplinary Perspective," Columbus, OH: Center for Human Resources Research, Ohio State University, 1978. R.

434. ———. "The Causes of Marital Disruption among Young American Women: An Interdisciplinary Perspective," *Resources in Education* 13 (1978). ERIC document ED 156 923. R.

435. Mueller, Charles W., and Pope, Hallowell. "Marital Instability: A Study of Its Transmission between Generations," *Journal of Marriage and the Family*, vol. 39, no. 1 (1979): 83–93. R.

436. Pope, Hallowell, and Mueller, Charles W. "Intergenerational Transmission of Marital Instability: Comparisons by Race and Sex," *Journal of Social Issues*, vol. 32, no. 1 (1976): 49–66. R.

437. ———. "The Intergenerational Transmission of Marital Instability: Comparisons by Race and Sex." In *Divorce and Separation: Context, Causes and Consequences*, edited by George Levinger and Oliver C. Moles, pp. 99–113. New York: Basic Books, 1979. R.

438. Seglem, Betty S., and Hayes, Maggie P. "Reasons for Early Divorce," *Journal of Home Economics*, 69 (November 1977): 32–35. R.

ETHNIC GROUPS

439. Ackerman, Lillian A. "Marital Instability and Juvenile Delinquency among the Nez Perces," *American Anthropologist*, vol. 73, no. 3 (1971): 595–603. R.

440. Burch, Ernest S., Jr. "Marriage and Divorce among the North Alaskan Eskimos." In *Divorce and After*, edited by Paul Bohannan, pp. 152–81. Garden City, NY: Doubleday, 1970.

441. Chavis, William M., and Lyles, Gladys J. "Divorce among Educated Black Women." Tuskegee, AL: Division of Behavioral Science Research, Carver Research Foundation, Tuskegee Institute, 1974. R.

442. ———. "Divorce among Educated Black Women," *Journal of the National Medical Association*, vol. 67, no. 2 (1975): 128–34. R.

443. Eberstein, Isaac W., and Frisbie, W. Parker. "Differences in Marital Instability among Mexican Americans, Blacks and Anglos: 1960 and 1970," *Social Problems*, vol. 23, no. 5 (1976): 609–21. R.

444. Frisbie, W. Parker; Bean Frank D.; and Eberstein, Isaac W. "Patterns of Marital Instability among Mexican Americans, Blacks, and Anglos." In *The Demography of Racial and Ethnic Groups*, edited by Frank D. Bean and W. Parker Friesbie, pp. 143–63. New York: Academic Press, 1978.

445. Hampton, Robert L. "Husband's Characteristics and Marital Disruption in Black Families," *Sociological Quarterly*, vol. 20, no. 2 (1979): 255–66. R.

446. ———. "Marital Disruption among Blacks." Ph.D. diss., University of Michigan, 1976 (*DAI* 38/3A, p. 1685, order # 7718018). R.

447. Heinrich, Albert. "Divorce as an Integrative Social Factor," *Journal of Comparative Family Studies*, vol. 3, no. 2 (1972): 265–72. R.

448. Heiss, Jerold. "On the Transmission of Marital Instability in Black Families," *American Sociological Review*, vol. 37, no. 1 (1972): 82–92. R.

449. Sweet, James A., and Bumpass, Larry L. "Differentials in Marital Instability of the Black Population: 1970," *Phylon*, vol. 35, no. 3 (1974): 323–31. R.

450. Uhlenberg, Peter. "Marital Instability among Mexican Americans: Following the Patterns of Blacks?" *Social Problems*, vol. 20, no. 1 (1972): 49–56. R.

FEMINIST VIEWS

451. Hare-Mustin, Rachel T. "Biased Professional in Divorce Litigation," *Psychology of Women Quarterly*, vol. 1, no. 2 (1976): 216–22.

452. Pati, Prasanna K. "Costs of the New Feminism" (letter to the editor), *American Journal of Psychiatry*, vol. 134, no. 6 (1977): 704. [LTE]

453. Scott, Carol, and Oken, Jean. "Divorce as Survival: The Buck Stops Here," *Women—A Journal of Liberation*, vol. 2, no. 2 (1971): 14–15.

454. ———. "Divorce as Survival: The Buck Stops Here." In *Marriage and the Family: A Critical Analysis and Proposals for Change*, edited by Carolyn C. Perrucci and Dena B. Targ, pp. 308–12. New York: David McKay Co., 1974.

FERTILITY

455. Cohen, Sarah B., and Sweet, James A. "Impact of Marital Disruption and Remarriage on Fertility," *Journal of Marriage and the Family*, vol. 36, no. 1 (1974): 87–96. R.

456. Coombs, Lolagene C., and Zumeta, Zena. "Correlates of Marital Dissolution in a Prospective Fertility Study. A Research Note," *Social Problems,* vol. 18, no. 1 (1970): 92–102. R.

457. Freedman, Deborah S., and Thornton, Arland. "The Long-term Impact of Pregnancy at Marriage on the Family's Economic Circumstances," *Family Planning Perspectives,* vol. 11, no. 1 (1979): 6–13+. R.

458. Furstenberg, Frank F., Jr. "Premarital Pregnancy and Marital Instability," *Journal of Social Issues,* vol. 32, no. 1 (1976): 67–86. R.

459. ———. "Premarital Pregnancy and Marital Instability." In *Divorce and Separation: Context, Causes and Consequences,* edited by George Levinger and Oliver C. Moles, pp. 83–98. New York: Basic Books, 1979. R.

460. McCarthy, James, and Menken, Jane. "Marriage, Remarriage, Marital Disruption and Age at First Birth," *Family Planning Perspectives,* vol. 11, no. 1 (1979): 21–23+. R.

461. Rindfuss, Ronald R., and Bumpass, Larry L. "Fertility during Marital Disruption," *Journal of Marriage and the Family,* vol. 39, no. 3 (1977): 517–28. R.

462. ———. "Fertility during Marital Disruption," *Resources in Education* 12 (1977). ERIC document ED 129 674. R.

463. Sear, Alan M. "Pregnancy Timing, Marital Disruption and Associated Variables: A Record Linkage Analysis." Ph.D. diss., Purdue University, 1971 (*DAI* 32/2A, p. 1098, order # 7120541). R.

464. Thornton, Arland V. "Marital Disruption, Remarriage, and Childbearing," *Demography,* vol. 15, no. 3 (1978): 361–80. R.

INITIATION OF DIVORCE

465. Darsa, Stephanie D. "Initiation of Divorce as a Function of Locus of Control, Self-Actualization and Androgyny." Ph.D. diss., California School of Professional Psychology, Los Angeles, 1976 (*DAI* 37/9B, p. 4671, order # 776294). R.

466. Gunter, B. G. "Notes on Divorce Filing as Role Behavior," *Journal of Marriage and the Family,* vol. 39, no. 1 (1977): 95–98. R.

467. Levinger, George. "Marital Cohesiveness at the Brink: The Fate of Applications for Divorce." In *Divorce and Separation: Context, Causes and Consequences,* edited by George Levinger and Oliver C. Moles, pp. 137–50. New York: Basic Books, 1979. R.

468. Nevaldine, Anne. "Divorce: The Leaver and the Left." Ph.D. diss., University of Minnesota, 1978 (*DAI* 39/6A, p. 3867, order # 7823943). R.

INTERRACIAL DIVORCES

469. Miller, Michael H. "A Comparison of the Duration of Interracial with Intraracial Marriages in Hawaii," *International Journal of Sociology of the Family,* vol. 1, no. 1 (1971): 197–201. R.

470. Monahan, Thomas P. "Are Interracial Marriages Really Less Stable?" *Social Forces,* vol. 48, no. 4 (1970): 461–73. R.

471. ———. "Interracial Marriage and Divorce in Kansas and the Question of Instability of Mixed Marriages," *Journal of Comparative Family Studies,* vol. 2, no. 1 (1971): 107–20. R.

MIDDLE-AGE DIVORCES

472. Chambers, Marjorie B. "The Displaced Homemaker: Victim of Socioeconomic Change Affecting the American Family," *Journal of the Institute for Socioeconomic Studies,* vol. 3, no. 3 (1978): 68–76.

473. Cleveland, Martha. "Divorce in the Middle Years: The Sexual Dimension," *Journal of Divorce,* vol. 2, no. 3 (1979): 255–62.

474. Corcoran, Mary. "Economic Consequences of Marital Dissolution for Women in the Middle Years," *Sex Roles,* vol. 5, no. 3 (1979): 343–53. R.

475. Hayes, Maggie P. "Divorce in the Middle Years." Ed. D. diss., Oklahoma State University, 1976 (*DAI* 37/9A, p. 6093, order # 775092). R.

476. O'Brien, John E., Jr. "The Decision to Divorce: A Comparative Study of Family Instability in Early versus the Later Years of Marriage." Ph.D. diss., University of Wisconsin, 1971 (*DAI* 31/12A, p. 6748, order # 7112705). R.

477. Sommers, Tish, and Shields, Laurie. "The Economics of Aging Homemakers," *Journal of Home Economics,* vol. 71, no. 2 (1979): 16–19.

478. Turner, Nathan W. "Divorce in Midlife: Clinical Implications and Applications." In *Mid-life, Developmental and Clinical Issues,* edited by William H. Norman and Thomas J. Scaramella, pp. 149–77. New York: Brunner/Mazel, 1980.

479. Wright, Douglas. "Conference Focuses on Older Women," *Aging,* 275–276 (September–October 1977): 18–22.

KINSHIP AND DIVORCE

480. Anspach, Donald F. "Kinship and Divorce," *Journal of Marriage and the Family,* vol. 38, no. 2 (1976): 323–30. R.

481. Lager, Eric. "Parents-in-Law: Failure and Divorce in a Second Chance Family," *Journal of Marriage and Family Counseling,* vol. 3, no. 4 (1977): 19–23.

RECORDS

482. U.S. National Center for Health Statistics. *Vital Statistics Classification and Coding Instructions for Divorce Records. Data Preparation Instruction Manual, Part 7.* Washington, DC: Government Printing Office, 1975 (HE20.6208D26/pt. 7).

483. ———. *Handbook on Divorce Registration.* Washington, DC: Government Printing Office, 1978 (HE20.6208:D64).

484. U.S. Public Health Service. *Where to Write for Divorce Records: United States and Outlying Areas.* Washington, DC: Government Printing Office, 1978 (HE20.6202:D64/978).

485. "Where to Write for Divorce Records," *Army Lawyer* 27 (August 1978): 11–15.

RURAL-URBAN DIFFERENCES

486. Bacon, Lloyd. "Family Formation and Dissolution Patterns: Rural-Urban Differences," *Research in Education* 9 (1974). ERIC document ED 093 551. R.

487. Woodrow, Karen; Hastings, Donald W.; and Tu, Edward J. "Rural-Urban Patterns of Marriage, Divorce and Mortality: Tennessee 1970," *Rural Sociology,* vol. 43, no. 1 (1978): 70–84. R.

SOCIAL POLICY

488. Bronfenbrenner, Urie. "The Challenge of Social Change to Public Policy and Developmental Research," *Resources in Education* 11 (1976). ERIC document ED 113 056.

489. Dean, Gillian. "Impact and Feedback Effects: Divorce Policy and Divorce in the American States." Ph.D. diss., University of Wisconsin—Madison, 1974 (*DAI* 35/9A, p. 6205, order # 7426487). R.

490. Feldberg, Roslyn, and Kohen, Janet. "Family Life in an Anti-family Setting: A Critique of Marriage and Divorce," *Family Coordinator,* vol. 25, no. 2 (1976): 151–59.

491. National Council on Family Relations. *Task Force on Divorce and Divorce Reform, Report.* Edited by Emily M. Brown. Minneapolis, MN: The Council, 1973.

THEORIES OF DIVORCE

492. Johnson, Frank C. "A Test of a Social Exchange Model of Marital Stability." Ph.D. diss., Washington State University, 1978 (*DAI* 39/2A, p. 1137, order # 7811899). R.

493. Kuo, Eddie C. Y. *Field Theory as a Conceptual Framework for Divorce Study.* Singapore: Department of Sociology, University of Singapore, 1974.

494. Laner, Mary R. "Love's Labors Lost: A Theory of Marital Dissolution," *Journal of Divorce,* vol. 1, no. 3 (1978): 213–32. R.

495. ———. Love's Labors Lost: A Theory of Marital Dissolution." Ph.D. diss., Virginia Polytechnic Institute and State University, 1977 (*DAI* 37/11A, p. 7350, order # 7710838). R.

496. ———. "Saving Sinking Ships: Implications from a Theory of Marital Dissolution," *Journal of Marriage and Family Counseling,* vol. 4, no. 2 (1978): 51–57.

497. Levinger, George. "A Social Psychological Perspective on Marital Dissolution," *Journal of Social Issues,* vol. 32, no. 1 (1976): 21–47.

498. ———. "A Social Psychological Perspective on Marital Dissolution. In *Divorce and Separation: Context, Causes and Consequences,* edited by George Levinger and Oliver C. Moles, pp. 37–60. New York: Basic Books, 1979.

499. Lipman-Blumen, Jean. "Crisis Framework Applied to Macrosociological Family Changes: Marriage, Divorce, and Occupational Trends Associated with

World War II," *Journal of Marriage and the Family,* vol. 37, no. 4 (1975): 889–902. R.

500. Mohan, Raj P. "Cohesiveness and Dissolution of the Marital Relationship," *Indian Journal of Social Research,* vol. 11, no. 1 (1970): 51–57.

501. Nye, F. Ivan; White, Lynn; and Frideres, James S. "Role Competence, Profit, and Marital Dissolution," *International Journal of Contemporary Sociology,* vol. 14, no. 1–2, (1977): 74–86.

502. Toman, Walter. "The Duplication Theorem of Social Relationships as Tested in the General Population," *Psychological Review,* vol. 78, no. 5 (1971): 380–90. R.

503. Wallace, Arla S. "An Application of Attachment Theory to the Study of a Population of Court Referred Divorced People." Ph.D. diss., California School of Professional Psychology, 1977 (*DAI* 38/10B, p. 4994, order # 7802850). R.

DIVORCE (ECONOMIC ASPECTS)

504. Becker, Gary S.; Landes, Elizabeth M.; and Michael, Robert T. "An Economic Analysis of Marital Instability," *Journal of Political Economy,* vol. 85, no. 6 (1977): 1141–87. R.

505. Bianchi, Suzanne M., and Farley, Reynolds. "Racial Differences in Family Living Arrangements and Economic Well-Being: An Analysis of Recent Trends," *Journal of Marriage and the Family,* vol. 41, no. 3 (1979): 537–51. R.

506. Cherlin, Andrew. "Employment, Income, and Family Life: The Case of Marital Dissolution." In *Women's Changing Roles at Home and on the Job,* U.S. National Commission for Manpower Policy, pp. 157–78. Washington: DC: Government Printing Office, 1978 (Y3.M31:9/26). R.

507. Cohen, Alan L. "Economics, Marital Instability and Race." Ph.D. diss., University of Wisconsin, Madison, 1979 (*DAI* 40/5A, p. 2787, order # 7918148). R.

508. Combs, E. Raedene. "The Human Capital Concept as a Basis for Property Settlement at Divorce: Theory and Implementation," *Journal of Divorce,* vol. 2, no. 4 (1979): 329–56. R.

509. Cutright, Phillips. "Income and Family Events: Marital Instability," *Journal of Marriage and the Family,* vol. 33, no. 2 (1971): 291–306. R.

510. Day, Randal D. "The Effects of Marital Instability on Economic Well-Being." Ph.D. diss., Brigham Young University, 1979 (*DAI* 40/7A, p. 4258, order # 8000062). R.

511. Espenshade, Thomas J. "The Economic Consequences of Divorce," *Journal of Marriage and the Family,* vol. 41, no. 3 (1979): 615–25.

512. Hampton, Robert. "Marital Disruption: Some Social and Economic Consequences." In *Five Thousand American Families: Patterns of Economic*

Progress, Vol. 3, pp. 163–87. Ann Arbor, MI: University of Michigan, Survey Research Center, 1975. R.

513. Havens, Elizabeth. "Women, Work, and Wedlock: A Note on Female Marital Patterns in the United States," *American Journal of Sociology,* vol. 78, no. 4 (1973): 975–81. R.

514. Hoffman, Saul. "Marital Instability and the Economic Status of Women," *Demography,* vol. 14, no. 1 (1977): 67–76. R.

515. Hoffman, Saul, and Holmes, John. "Husbands, Wives and Divorce." In *Five Thousand American Families: Patterns of Economic Progress,* Vol. 4, pp. 23–75. Ann Arbor, MI: University of Michigan, Survey Research Center, 1976. R.

516. Johnson, Walter D. "The Economic Ramifications of Divorce Preparation through Counseling," *Conciliation Courts Review,* vol. 14, no. 1 (1976): 37–42.

517. Kerckhoff, Alan C. "Patterns of Marriage and Family Formation and Dissolution," *Journal of Consumer Research* 2 (March 1976): 261–75.

518. "Marketing Plans Will Change to Incorporate New Marriage-Divorce Patterns in Nation," *Commerce Today*, vol. 2, no. 17 (1972): 18.

519. Murray, Thomas J. "Business of Getting Divorced," *Duns*, vol. 99, no. 4 (1972): 85–86.

520. Sawhill, Isabel V. "Economic Perspectives on the Family," *Daedalus*, vol. 106, no. 2 (1977): 115–25.

521. Schutzer, A. I. "Look What's Happened to Those Divorce Laws," *Medical Economics* 54 (October 3, 1977): 178–79 + .

522. Seal, Karen L. "The Financial Implications of Divorce between Adversary and No-Fault Divorce Legislation." Ph.D. diss., United States International University, 1978 (*DAI* 40/2A, p. 1095, order # 7918194). R.

523. Shaw, Lois B. "Economic Consequences of Marital Disruption." In *Women's Changing Roles at Home and on the Job*, U.S. National Commission for Manpower Policy, pp. 180–203. Washington, DC: Government Printing Office, 1978 (Y3.M31:9/26). R.

524. ———. "Economic Consequences of Marital Disruption for Women in Their Middle Years." Columbus, OH: Center for Human Resource Research, Ohio State University, 1978.

525. Wiegner, Kathleen K. "High Cost Leaving," *Forbes* 123 (February 19, 1979): 44–49.

526. Wolf, Wendy C., and MacDonald, Maurice M. "The Earnings of Men and Remarriage," *Demography*, vol. 16, no. 3 (1979): 389–99. R.

LIFE INSURANCE

527. Guadagno, Mary Ann N. "Selected Factors Affecting Perceived Need for Life Insurance by Divorced Mothers." Ph.D. diss., The Ohio State University, 1978 (*DAI* 39/8B, p. 3784, order # 7902136).R.

RETIREMENT BENEFITS

528. "Pensions Land in Divorce Court," *Business Week* 2508 (November 7, 1977): 104 + .

SOCIAL SECURITY

529. Cockburn, Christine, and Hoskins, Dalmer. "Social Security and Divorced Persons," *International Social Security Review*, vol. 29, no. 2 (1976): 111–51. R.

530. "Men and Women: Changing Roles and Social Security," *Social Security Bulletin*, vol. 42, no. 5 (1979): 25–32.

531. "Task Force Report on Treatment of Women under Social Security," *Social Security Bulletin*, vol. 41, no. 5 (1978): 37–39.

WILLS

532. "Rewriting Your Will When Divorce Looms," *Business Week* 2442 (July 26, 1976): 126.

DIVORCE (HISTORICAL ASPECTS)

533. Bandel, Betty. " 'What the Good Laws of Man Hath Put Asunder,' " *Vermont History*, vol. 46, no. 4 (1978): 221–33.

534. Campbell, Eugene E., and Campbell, Bruce L. "Divorce among Mormon Polygamists: Extent and Explanations," *Utah Historical Quarterly*, vol. 46, no. 1 (1978): 4–23.

535. Candela, Joseph L. "Concern for Family Stability in American Opinion, 1880-1920." Ph.D. diss., University of Chicago, 1978 (*DAI* 39/1A, p. 425). R.

536. Cohn, Henry S. "Connecticut's Divorce Mechanism: 1636–1969," *American Journal of Legal History*, vol. 14, no. 1 (1970): 35–54.

537. Cott, Nancy F. "Divorce and the Changing Status of Women in Eighteenth-Century Massachusetts," *William and Mary Quarterly, Third Series*, vol. 33, no. 4 (1976): 586–614. R.

538. ———. "Eighteenth-Century Family and Social Life Revealed in Massachusetts Divorce Records," *Journal of Social History* 10 (Fall 1976): 20–43. R.

539. Edwards, Jerome E. "Mary Pickford's Divorce," *Nevada Historical Society Quarterly*, vol. 19, no. 3 (1976): 185–91.

540. Lasch, Christopher. "Divorce and the 'Decline of the Family.' " In *The World of Nations: Reflections on American History, Politics, and Culture*, pp. 35–43. New York: Vintage Books, 1972.

541. Littlefield, Daniel F., and Underhill, Lonnie E. "Divorce Seeker's Paradise, Oklahoma Territory, 1890–1897," *Arizona and the West*, vol. 17, no. 1 (1975): 21–34. R.

542. May, Elaine T. "The Pressure to Provide: Class, Consumerism, and Divorce in Urban America, 1880–1920," *Journal of Social History*, vol. 12, no. 2 (1978): 180–93. R.

543. ———. "The Pursuit of Domestic Perfection: Marriage and Divorce in Los Angeles, 1890–1920." Ph.D. diss., University of California, Los Angeles, 1975 (*DAI* 36/1A, p. 484, order # 7514060). R.

544. O'Neill, William L. "Divorce as a Moral Issue: A Hundred Years of Controversy." In *"Remember the Ladies": New Perspectives on Women in American History: Essays in Honor of Nelson Manfred Blake*, edited by Carol V. R. George. Syracuse, NY: Syracuse University Press, 1975.

545. Owsley, Harriet C. "The Marriages of Rachel Donaldson," *Tennessee Historical Quarterly*, vol. 36, no. 4 (1977): 479–92.

546. Scanzoni, John. "A Historical Perspective on Husband-Wife Bargaining Power and Marital Dissolution." In *Divorce and Separation: Context, Causes and Consequences*, edited by George Levinger and Oliver C. Moles, pp. 20–36. New York: Basic Books, 1979.

547. Stanton, Elizabeth C. "Need of Liberal Divorce Laws" (reprint of a September 1884 article), *North American Review* 261 (Summer 1976): 58–62.

548. Stern, Norton B. "Denouement in San Diego in 1888," *Western States Jewish History Quarterly*, vol. 11, no. 1 (1978): 49–55.

549. Weisberg, K. Kelly. " 'Under Greet Temptations Heer': Women and Divorce in Puritan Massachusetts," *Feminist Studies*, vol. 2, nos. 2–3 (1975): 183–93.

550. Weisberger, Bernard A. "Liberty and Disunion: Three Centuries of Divorce, American Style," *American Heritage*, vol. 22, no. 6 (1971): 22–25 + .

DIVORCE (MEDICAL ASPECTS)

551. Ladbrook, Dennis. "The Health and Survival of the Divorced," *Conciliation Courts Review*, vol. 14, no. 1 (1976): 21–33. R.

552. Ortmeyer, Carl E. "Variations in Mortality, Morbidity, and Health Care by Marital Status." In *Mortality and Morbidity in the United States*, edited by Carl L. Erhart and Joyce E. Berlin, pp. 159–88. Cambridge, MA: Harvard University Press, 1974.

553. Renne, Karen S. "Health and Marital Experience in an Urban Population," *Journal of Marriage and the Family*, vol. 33, no. 2 (1971): 338–50. R.

554. Seegel, V. F. "The Divorced Parent and the Hospitalized Child: Implications for the Hospital Staff," *Association for the Care of Children in Hospitals Journal* 7 (Fall 1978): 16–18.

555. Verbrugge, Lois M. "Marital Status and Health," *Journal of Marriage and the Family*, vol. 41, no. 2 (1979): 267–85. R.

MEDICAL CONDITIONS

556. Begleiter, Michael L.; Burry, V. F.; and Harris, David J. "Prevalence of Divorce among Parents of Children with Cystic Fibrosis and Other Chronic Diseases," *Social Biology*, vol. 23, no. 3 (1976): 260–64. R.

557. Belfer, Myron L.; Mulliken, John B.; and Cochran, Thomas C., Jr. "Cosmetic Surgery as a Antecedent of Life Change," *American Journal of Psychiatry*, vol. 136, no. 2 (1979): 199–201. R.

558. Chang, Frederic C., and Herzog, Briant. "Burn Morbidity: A Followup Study of Physical and Psychological Disability," *Annals of Surgery*, vol. 183, no. 1 (1976): 34–37. R.

559. Czajka-Narins, Dorice M.; Haddy, Theresa B.; and Kallen, David J. "Nutritional and Social Correlates in Iron Deficiency Anemia," *American Journal of Clinical Nutrition*, vol. 31, no. 6 (1978): 955-60. R.

560. "Diabetes via Divorce," *Human Behavior*, vol. 6, no. 5 (1977): 55. R.

561. El Ghatit, Ahmed Z., and Hanson, Richard W. "Marriage and Divorce after Spinal Cord Injury," *Archives of Physical Medicine and Rehabilitation*, vol. 57, no. 10 (1976): 470–72. R.

562. ———. "Outcome of Marriages Existing at the Time of a Male's Spinal Cord Injury," *Journal of Chronic Diseases*, vol. 28, nos. 7–8 (1975): 383–88. R.

563. Gath, Ann. "The Impact of an Abnormal Child Upon the Parents," *British Journal of Psychiatry* 130 (April 1977): 405–10. R.

564. Goodwin, Donald W., et al. "Alcohol Problems in Adoptees Raised Apart from Alcoholic Biological Parents," *Archives of General Psychiatry*, vol. 28, no. 2 (1973): 238–43. R.

565. Granat, Jay P. "Marital Disintegration among Parents of Mentally Retarded Adults and Adolescents: Implications for Psychological Counseling." Ph.D. diss., University of Michigan, 1978 (*DAI* 39/6A, p. 3469, order # 7822900). R.

566. Gruner, O. P. N., et al. "Mental Disorders in Ulcerative Colitis: Suicide, Divorce, Psychosis, Hospitalization for Mental Disease, Alcoholism and Consumption of Psychotropic Drugs in 178 Patients Subjected to Colectomy," *Diseases of the Colon and Rectum*, vol. 21, no. 1 (1978): 37–39. R.

567. Henoch, Monica J.; Batson, Jean W.; and Baum, John. "Psychosocial Factors in Juvenile Rheumatoid Arthritis," *Arthritis and Rheumatism* vol. 21, no. 2 (1978): 229–33. R.

568. Hoban, Christine, and Feinhandler, Sherwin. "Drinking Patterns among Single, Divorced and Separated Women— Meeting." *Alcoholism—Clinical and Experimental Research*, vol. 3, no. 2 (1979): 179.

569. Lansky, Shirley B., et al. "Childhood Cancer: Parental Discord and Divorce," *Pediatrics*, vol. 62, no. 2 (1978): 184–88. R.

570. Leck, Ian, et al. "Incidence of Cervical Cancer by Marital Status," *Journal of Epidemiology and Community Health*, vol. 32, no. 2 (1978): 108–10. R.

571. Martin, Patricia. "Marital Breakdown in Families of Patients with Spina Bifida Cystica," *Developmental Medicine and Child Neurology*, vol. 17, no. 6 (1975): 757–64. R.

572. Medsger, Anne R., and Robinson, H. "A Comparative Study of Divorce in Rheumatoid Arthritis and Other Rheumatic Diseases," *Journal of Chronic Diseases*, vol. 25, no. 5 (1972): 269–75. R.

573. "Rheumatoid Arthritis Linked to Broken Homes," *Medical World News* vol. 19, no. 8 (1978): 70.

574. Robinson, Mary J. "Sink or Swim: The Single-Parent Family with a Deaf Child," *Volta Review*, vol. 81, no. 5 (1979): 370–77.

575. Rosenblatt, S. M., et al. "Marital Status and Multiple Psychiatric Admissions for Alcoholism: A Cross Validation," *Quarterly Journal of Studies on Alcoholism*, vol. 32, no. 3 (1971): 1092–96. R.

576. Shufeit, Lawrence, and Wuster, Stanley. "Frequency of Divorce among Parents of Handicapped Children," *Resources in Education* 11 (1976). ERIC document ED 113 909. R.

577. Tew, B. J., and others. "Marital Stability Following the Birth of a Child with Spina Bifida," *British Journal of Psychiatry* 131 (July 1977): 79–82. R.

578. Wechsler, Henry, et al. "Social Characteristics and Blood Alcohol Level," *Quarterly Journal of Studies on Alcoholism,* vol. 33, no. 1 (1972): 132–47. R.

PHYSICIAN'S ROLE

579. Mott, Sylvester R., and Lira, Frank T. "Conceptual Approaches to Marital Discordance: An Overview for the Physician," *South Carolina Medical Association Journal,* vol. 71, no. 9 (1975): 287–89.

580. Schmidt, David D., and Messner, Edward. "The Role of the Family Physician in the Crisis of Impending Divorce," *Journal of Family Practice,* vol. 2, no. 2 (1975): 99–102.

STATISTICS

581. U.S. National Center for Health Statistics. *Characteristics, Social Contacts, and Activities of Nursing Home Residents, United States—1973–74.* Series 13: Data from the National Health Survey, No. 27. Washington, DC: Government Printing Office, 1977 (HE20.6209:13/27) (Tables 1,2,L).

582. ———. *Diabetes Mellitus Mortality in the United States—1950–67.* Series 20: Data on Mortality, No. 10. Washington, DC: Government Printing Office, 1971 (HE20.2210:20/10) (Tables A,5).

583. ———. *Differentials in Health Characteristics by Marital Status.* Series 10: Data from the Health Interview Survey, No. 104. Washington, DC: Government Printing Office, 1976 (HE20.6209:10/104) (Tables B,E,F,G,L, 1–29).

584. ———. *Expenses for Hospital and Institutional Care during the Last Year of Life for Adults Who Died in 1964 or 1965—United States.* Series 22: Data from the National Natality and Mortality Surveys, No. 11. Washington, DC: Government Printing Office, 1971 (HE20.2210:22/11) (Tables 9,17).

585. ———. *Hospital and Surgical Insurance Coverage United States—1968.* Series 10: Data from the Health Interview Survey, No. 66. Washington, DC: Government Printing Office, 1972 (HE20.2210:10/66) (Tables C,F,5).

586. ———. *Hospital and Surgical Insurance Coverage United States—1974.* Series 10: Data from the Health Interview Survey, No. 117. Washington, DC: Government Printing Office, 1977 (HE20.6209:10/117) (Tables D,5,68,70,72,74).

587. ———. *Hospital Discharges and Length of Stay: Short-stay Hospitals United States—1972.* Series 10: Data from the Health Interview Survey, no. 107. Washington, DC: Government Printing Office, 1976 (HE20.6209:10/107) (Tables 13, 19).

588. ———. *Measures of Chronic Illness among Residents of Nursing and Personal Care Homes, United States, June–August 1969.* Series 12: Data from the Institutional Population Survey, no. 24. Washington, DC: Government Printing Office, 1974 (HE20.6209:12/24) (Tables B,D,1,2).

589. ———. *Mortality from Selected Causes by Marital Status United States—Part A.* Series 20: Data on Mortality, no. 8a. Washington, DC: Government Printing Office, 1970 (HE20.2210:20/8a) (Tables 1–3,8–11,13, Figures 1,2).

590. ———. *Mortality from Selected Causes by Marital Status United States—Part B.* Series 20: Data on Mortality, no. 8b. Washington, DC: Government Printing Office, 1970 (HE20.2210:20/8b) (Tables 16,17,21,22, Figure 3).

591. ———. *National Nursing Home Survey: 1977, Summary for the United States.* Series 13: National Nursing Home Survey, no. 43. Washington, DC: Government Printing Office, 1979 (HE20.6209:13/43) (Tables 19,23,32,36,40).

592. ———. *Need for Dental Care among Adults, United States—1960–62.* Series 11: Data from the Health Examination Survey, no. 36. Washington, DC: Government Printing Office, 1970. (HE20.2210:11/36) (Tables E,F,5).

593. ———. *Persons Hospitalized by Number of Episodes and Days Hospitalized in a Year, United States—1972.* Series 10: Data from the National Health Survey, no. 116. Washington, DC: Government Printing Office, 1977 (HE20.6209:10/116) (Tables 6,13,27).

594. ———. *Persons Hospitalized by Number of Hospital Episodes and Days in a Year, United States—1968.* Series 10: Data from the Health Interview Survey, no. 64. Washington, DC: Government Printing Office, 1971 (HE20.2210:10/64) (Tables B,1, 19–21, 25).

595. ———. *Prevalence of Selected Digestive Conditions, United States—1975.* Series 10: Data from the Health Interview Survey, no. 123. Washington, DC: Government Printing Office, 1979 (HE20.6209:10/123) (Tables 2–14).

596. ———. *Tuberculin Skin Test Reaction among Adults 25–74 Years, United States—1971–72.* Series 11: Data from the National Health Survey, no. 204. Washington, DC: Government Printing Office, 1977 (HE20.6209:11/204) (Table 12).

597. U.S. National Institute of Mental Health. *Admission Rates by Age, Sex, and Marital Status: State and County Mental Hospitals, 1969.* Statistical Note, no. 32. Washington, DC: Government Printing Office, 1970 (HE20.2424:32) (Tables A–D).

598. ———. *Admission Rates by Marital Status: Outpatient Psychiatric Services, 1969.* Statistical Note, no. 35. Washington, DC: Government Printing Office, 1970 (HE20.2424:35) (Tables A,B).

599. ———. *Admission Rates to State and County Psychiatric Hospitals by Age, Sex and Marital Status—United States, 1975.* Statistical Note, no. 142. Washington, DC: Government Printing Office, 1977 (HE20.8116:142) (Tables 1a, 1b).

600. ———. *Admissions to Outpatient Psychiatric Services by Age, Sex, Color, and Marital Status, June 1970–May 1971.* Statistical Note, no. 79. Washington, DC: Government Printing Office, 1973. (HE20.2424:79) (Tables B,C,2,3).

601. ———. *Characteristics of Diagnosed and Missed Alcoholic Male Admissions to State and County Mental Hospitals, 1972.* Statistical Note, no. 124. Washington, DC: Government Printing Office, 1976. (HE20.8116:124) (Table 2).

602. ———. *Marital Status and Age of Male Admissions with Diagnosed Alcohol Disorders to State and County Mental Hospitals in 1972.* Statistical Note, no. 120. Washington, DC: Government Printing Office, 1975 (HE20.8116:120) (Figure 1, Tables B,1,2).

603. ———. *Marital Status, Living Arrangements, and Family Characteristics of Admissions to State and County Mental Hospitals and Outpatient Psychiatric Clinics: United States, 1970.* Statistical Note, no. 100. Washington, DC: Government Printing Office, 1974 (HE20.8116:100) (Tables 1-3).

604. ———. *Marital Status of Discharges from Psychiatric Inpatient Units of General Hospitals: United States, 1970–71. Part I: Analysis by Age, Color and Sex.* Statistical Note, no. 82. Washington, DC: Government Printing Office, 1973 (HE20.8116:82) (Figures 1,2, Tables A–D, 1–6).

605. ———. *Marital Status of Discharges from Psychiatric Inpatient Units of General Hospitals: United States, 1970–71. Part II: Analysis by Referral Source, Length of Stay and Primary Diagnosis.* Statistical Note, no. 83. Washington, DC: Govern-ment Printing Office, 1973 (HE20.8116:83) (Figures 1–3, Tables A,B,1–3).

606. ———. *Marital Status of Discharges from Psychiatric Inpatient Units of General Hospitals: United States, 1970–71. Part III: Analysis by Hospital Control.* Statistic-al Note, no. 84. Washington, DC: Govern-ment Printing Office, 1973 (HE20.8116:84) (Figure 1, Tables A,B,1,2).

607. ———. *Utilization of State and County Mental Hospitals by Spanish Amer-icans in 1972.* Statistical Note, no. 116. Washington, DC: Government Printing Office, 1975 (HE20.8116:116) (Tables 3a, 3b, 3c).

608. U.S. Veterans Administration. *Alco-holism and Problem Drinking, 1970–75: A Statistical Analysis of VA Hospital Pa-tients.* Washington, DC: Government Print-ing Office, 1977 (VA1.48/3.5) (Table 13).

609. ———. *Annual Report—Administra-tion of Veterans Affairs.* Washington, DC: Government Printing Office, 1978 (VA1.1:978) (Table 29).

DIVORCE (STATISTICS)

610. Carter, Hugh, and Glick, Paul C. *Marriage and Divorce: A Social and Eco-nomic Study.* Rev. ed. Cambridge, MA: Harvard University, Press, 1976.

611. "Growing Number Shows Preference for Own Home," *Commerce Today*, vol. 3, no. 4 (1972): 25.

612. Hetzel, Alice M. "Marriage and Di-vorce Statistics and the Health Depart-ment," *HSMHA Health Reports*, vol. 86, no. 7 (1971): 616–26.

613. Kop, P. P. A. M. "Fluctuations in Marriage and Divorce Frequencies in Rela-tion to the Month of Marriage," *Journal of Interdisciplinary Cycle Research*, vol. 5, nos. 3–4 (1974): 327–30. R.

614. "Marriage and Divorce," *Metropoli-tan Life Statistical Bulletin*, vol. 59, no. 4 (1978): 2–5.

615. Schoen, Robert, and Land, Kenneth C. "General Algorithm for Estimating a Markov-Generated Increment-Decrement Life Table with Applications to Marital-Status Patterns," *American Statistical Association Journal*, vol. 74, no. 368 (1979): 761–76.

616. U.S. Bureau of the Census. *Number, Timing, and Duration of Marriages and Divorces in the United States: June 1975.* Series P-20: Current Population Reports, no. 297. Washington, DC: Government Printing Office, 1976 (C3.186:P–20/297) (Tables B–H, K–T, 1–5).

617. ———. *Probabilities of Marriage, Divorce, and Remarriage.* Series, P-23: Special Studies, no. 32. Washington, DC: Government Printing Office, 1970 (C56.218:P-23/32) (Tables A,1,2).

618. ———. *Social Indicators, 1976.* Washington, DC: Government Printing Office, 1977 (C3.2:So1/2/976) (Tables 2/2b–2/4,2/8–2/12,2/16).

619. U.S. National Center for Health Sta-tistics. *Divorces by Marriage Cohort.* Series 21: Data on Natality, Marriage, and Divorce, no. 34. Washington, DC: Gov-ernment Printing Office, 1979 (HE20.6209:21/34) (Figures A–C, Tables 1–6).

620. ———. *Increases in Divorces, United States—1967.* Series 21: Data on Natality, Marriage and Divorce, no. 20. Washington, D.C.: Government Printing Office, 1970 (HE20.2210:21/20) (Figures 1–3, Tables A–J, 1–5).

621. ———. *Monthly Vital Statistics Re-port.* Washington, DC: Government Print-ing Office, monthly from 1963 (HE20.6009:vol. and no.).

622. ———. *Vital Statistics of the United States.* Washington, DC: Government Printing Office, annual from 1937 (HE20.6210:yr./vol.).

COHORT ANALYSIS

623. Ferris, Abbot L. "An Indicator of Marriage Dissolution by Marriage Cohort," *Social Forces*, vol. 48, no. 3 (1970): 356-65. R.

624. Land, Kenneth C. "Some Exhausti-ble Poisson Process Models of Divorce by Marriage Cohort," *Journal of Mathemati-cal Sociology*, vol. 1, no. 2 (1971): 213–32. R.

625. Preston, Samuel H., and McDonald, John. "The Incidence of Divorce within Cohorts of American Marriages Contracted since the Civil War," *Demography*, vol. 16, no. 1 (1979): 1–25.

PROBABILITIES OF DIVORCE

626. Caldwell, Steven B. "Models of First Marriage and Divorce in the United States: Combining Over-Time and Cross-Section Evidence." Ph.D. diss., Cornell University, 1975 (*DAI* 36/9A, p. 6328, order # 765904). R.

627. Glick, Paul C., and Norton, Authur J. "Frequency, Duration, and Probability of Marriage and Divorce," *Journal of Marriage and the Family*, Vol. 33, no. 2 (1971): 307–17. R.

628. Krishnan, P. "Divorce Tables for Females in the United States, 1960," *Jour-nal of Marriage and the Family*, vol. 33, no. 2 (1971): 318–20. R.

629. Krishnan, Parameswara, and Kayani, Ashraf K. "Model Divorce Tables," *Genus*, vol. 32, nos. 1–2 (1976): 109–27. R.

630. McCarthy, James. Comparison of the Probability of the Dissolution of the First and Second Marriages," *Demography*, vol. 15, no. 3 (1978): 345–59. R.

631. Preston, Samuel H. "Estimating the Proportion of American Marriages that End in Divorce," *Sociological Methods and Research*, vol. 3, no. 4 (1975): 435–60. R.

632. Schoen, Robert, and Nelson, Verne E. "Marriage, Divorce, and Mortality: A Life Table Analysis," *Demography*, vol. 11, no. 2 (1974): 267–90. R.

633. U.S. Bureau of the Census. *Social and Economic Variations in Marriage, Divorce and Remarriage: 1967*. Series, P-20: Current Population Reports, no. 223. Washington, DC: Government Printing Office, 1971 (C56.218:P–20/22). (Tables A,C,D,E,3,4,7,8,11–13).

RATES

634. Brown, George H. "Bulletin: Divorce Rate Jumps from 1 Percent to 2 Percent in 10 Years!" *Across the Board*, vol. 16, no. 7 (1979): 6–7.

635. Carlson, Elwood. Divorce Rate Fluctuations as a Cohort Phenomenon," *Population* (London), vol. 33, no. 3 (1979): 523–36. R.

636. Duchene, Josianne, and Wunsch, Guillame. "Measuring the Frequency of Divorce: A Comparative Analysis," *Population* 32 (September 1977): 53-68. R.

637. England, J. Lynn, and Kunz, Phillip R. "The Application of Age-Specific Rates to Divorce," *Journal of Marriage and the Family*, vol. 37, no. 1 (1975): 40–46. R.

638. Farley, Reynolds, and Hermalin, Albert I. "Family Stability. A Comparison of Trends between Blacks and Whites," *American Sociological Review*, vol. 36, no. 1 (1971): 1–17. R.

639. Fenelon, Bill. "State Variations in the United States Divorce Rates," *Journal of Marriage and the Family*, vol. 33, no. 2 (1971): 321–27. R.

640. Goetting, Ann. "Some Societal Explanations for the Rising Divorce Rate," *Family Therapy*, vol. 6, no. 2 (1979): 71–87.

641. Horiuchi, Shiro. "Decomposition of the Rise in Divorce Rates: A Note on Michael's Results," *Demography*, vol. 16, no. 4 (1979): 549–51. R.

642. Horn, Jack C. "Breakups—Is the Fever Dropping?" *Psychology Today*, vol. 13, no. 7 (1979): 27.

643. Krishnan, P., and Kayani, Ashraf K. "Estimates of Age Specific Divorce Rates for Females in the United States 1960–1969. *Journal of Marriage and the Family*, vol. 36, no. 1 (1974): 72–75. R.

644. Michael, Robert T. "The Rise in Divorce Rates, 1960–1974: Age-Specific Components," *Demography*, vol. 15, no. 2 (1978): 177–82. R.

645. ———. "Two Papers on the Recent Rise in U.S. Divorce Rates," Working paper no. 202. Stanford, CA: National Bureau of Economic Research, 1977. R.

646. Nichols, William. "Rising Divorce Rate," *Intellect*, vol. 103, no. 2366 (1974–75): 488.

647. Population Reference Bureau. "U.S. Trends in Marriage and Divorce, 1921–1974," *Social Education*, vol. 42, no. 1 (1978): 41–42.

648. Schoen, Robert. "California Divorce Rates by Age at First Marriage and Duration of First Marriage," *Journal of Marriage and the Family*, vol. 37, no. 3 (1975): 548–55. R.

649. Sharma, Prakash C., and Wan, Thomas. "Ecological Correlates of County Divorce Rates," *Indian Journal of Sociology*, vol. 2, no. 1 (1971): 51–58. R.

650. "Young Americans' Divorce Rate Triples," *Commerce America*, vol. 1, no. 2–3 (1976): 15.

DIVORCE AND EDUCATION

651. Bledsoe, Eugene. "Teaching about Divorce," *Today's Education*, vol. 66, no. 1 (1977): 31.

652. Damon, Parker. "When the Family Comes Apart: What Schools Can Do," *National Elementary Principal*, vol. 59, no. 1 (1979): 66–75.

653. Drake, Ellen A. "Helping the School Cope with Children of Divorce," *Journal of Divorce*, vol. 3, no. 1 (1979): 69–75.

654. Goldenberg, Ronald, and McNair, Bruce. "The Disruptive School," *Contemporary Education*, vol. 49, no. 3 (1978): 179–82.

655. Silvern, Steven B., and Yawkey, Thomas. "Divorce: Some Effects on and Teaching Strategies for Children," *Resources in Education* 10 (1975). ERIC document ED 103 114.

656. Wilson, Frank H. "Parental Involvement with Their Children's Education on the Junior High Level in Urban Schools." Ph.D. diss., Michigan State University, 1976 (*DAI* 37/6A, p. 3542, order # 7627164). R.

ACADEMIC ACHIEVEMENT

657. Conyers, Mary G. "Comparing School Success of Students from Conventional and Broken Homes," *Phi Delta Kappan*, vol. 58, no. 8 (1977): 647. R.

658. Pantell, Steven. "Children of Divorce and School Success." Master's thesis, California State University, Fresno, 1976–77. R.

659. Ryker, Millard J., et al. "Six Selected Factors Influencing Educational Achievement of Children from Broken Homes," *Education*, vol. 91, no. 3 (1971): 200–11. R.

660. Scott, Charles V. "The Effects of Family Structure on the Academic Status of Fifth Grade Students," Ed.D. diss., University of Oklahoma, 1974 (*DAI* 35/9A, p. 5695, order # 756554). R.

661. Thompson, Eugene W., and Smidchens, Uldis. "Single Parenting and Reading Comprehension Achievement," *Resources in Education* 15 (1980). ERIC document ED 179 952. R.

662. Webb, James B. "A Comparative Study of the Relation of Broken Homes to the School Success of High School Students." Ed.D. diss., George Washington University, 1970 (*DAI* 31/7A, p. 3187, order # 7027250). R.

CLASSROOM BEHAVIOR

663. Ellison, Edythe J. "Classroom Behavior and Psychosocial Adjustment of Children from Single– and Two–Parent Families. Ed.D. diss., University of California, Los Angeles, 1979 (*DAI* 40/4A, p. 1943, order # 7921391). R.

664. ———. "Classroom Behavior and Psychosocial Adjustment of Single– and Two–Parents Children," *Resources in Education* 14 (1979). ED 168 710. R.

665. Wallace, Richard J., Jr. "A Comparison of the Behavior of Stepchildren and Nonstepchildren in a School Setting." Master's thesis, California State University, Long Beach, 1978 (*Master's Abstracts* 17/3, p. 188, order # 1312779). R.

TEACHERS

666. Bentley, Eloise. "Children and Broken Homes: Sources for the Teacher," *Resources in Education* 12 (1977). ERIC document ED 128 735.

667. Black, Kathryn N. "What about the Child from a One-Parent Home?" *Teacher*, vol. 96, no. 5 (1979): 24–26.

668. Bledsoe, Eugene. "Divorce and Values Teaching, *Journal of Divorce*, vol. 1, no. 4 (1978): 371–79.

669. Chiodo, John J. "Teaching about the Family," *Curriculum Review*, vol. 16, no. 1 (1977): 73–74.

670. Cook, Jimmie, and Oaks, Mary Ann H. "Children in Crisis," *Early Years*, vol. 10, no. 4 (1979): 32±.

671. Halliwell, Anne S. "Working with Children of Divorced Parents," *Teachers and Writers*, vol. 8, no. 3 (1977): 18–25.

672. Main, Margaret H. "Most Terrible Moment," *Teacher*, vol. 96, no. 5 (1979): 66–67.

673. Santrock, John W., and Tracy, Russel L. "The Effects of Children's Family Structure Status on the Development of Stereotypes by Teachers," *Journal of Educational Psychology*, vol. 70, no. 5 (1978): 754–57. R.

674. ———. "The Effects of Children's Family Structure Status on the Development of Stereotypes by Teachers, *Resources in Education* 14 (1979). ERIC document ED 162 192. R.

675. Smith, Gloria S., and Scales, Alice M. "One-Parent Child and the Classroom Teacher," *Today's Teacher*, vol. 64, no. 4 (1975): 83–86.

DIVORCE AND WELFARE

676. Bahr, Stephen J. "Effects of Welfare on Marital Stability and Remarriage," *Journal of Marriage and the Family*, vol. 41, no. 3 (1979): 553–60. R.

677. Bernstein, Blanche, and Meezan, William, Jr. "The Impact of Welfare on Family Stability," *Government Reports Announcements and Index* 22 (1975) pp 5k. PB-244 179 8GA. R.

678. Bradbury, Katharine, et al. "The Effects of Welfare Reform Alternatives on the Family," *Resources in Education* 13 (1978). ERIC document ED 146 315.

679. ———. "Public Assistance, Female Headship, and Economic Well-Being," *Journal of Marriage and the Family*, vol. 41, no. 3 (1979): 519–35. R.

680. Cherlin, Andrew. "Divorcing Welfare from Marriage," *Psychology Today*, vol. 13, no. 2 (1979): 92.

681. *The Family, Poverty, and Welfare Programs: Factors Influencing Family Instability.* Prepared for the Subcommittee on Fiscal Policy of the Joint Economic Committee, Congress of the United States. Washington, DC: Government Printing Office, 1974 (Y4.Ec7:45/12pt.1).

682. Greenfield, Lawrence, and Falk, Mark. "Welfare Grant Reductions and Family Breakup among Working Poor," *Public Welfare*, vol. 31, no. 4 (1973): 26–31. R.

683. Hutchens, Robert M. "Welfare, Remarriage, and Marital Search," *American Economic Review* 69 (June 1975): 369–79. R.

684. Moles, Oliver C. "Marital Dissolution and Public Assistance Payments: Variations among American States," *Journal of Social Issues*, vol. 32, no. 1 (1976): 87–101. R.

685. ———. "Public Welfare Payments and Marital Dissolution: A Review of Recent Studies." In *Divorce and Separation: Context, Causes and Consequences*, edited by George Levinger and Oliver C. Moles, pp. 167–80.

686. Southwick, Lawrence, Jr. "Effect of Welfare Programs on Family Stability," *Review of Social Economy*, vol. 36, no. 1 (1978): 19–39. R.

687. Wolf, Wendy C., and MacDonald, Maurice M. "The Earnings of Males and Marital Disruption," *Resources in Education* 14 (1979). ERIC document ED 162 046. R.

AID TO FAMILIES WITH DEPENDENT CHILDREN (AFDC)

688. Burnside, Betty. "Changes in AFDC, 1969–1971," *Welfare in Review*, vol. 10, no. 2 (1972): 28–32.

689. Cutright, Phillips, and Madras, Patrik. "AFDC and the Marital and Family Status of Ever Married Women Aged 15–44: U.S., 1950–1970," *Sociology and Social Research*, 60 (April 1976): 314–27. R.

690. Goldsmith, Mary A. "AFDC Eligibility and the Federal Stepparent Regulation," *Texas Law Review*, vol. 57, no. 1 (1978): 79–100.

691. Honig, Marjorie. "AFDC Income, Recipient Rates, and Family Dissolution," *Journal of Human Resources*, vol. 9, no. 3 (1974): 303–22. R.

692. ———. "AFDC Income, Recipient Rates, and Family Dissolution—A Reply," *Journal of Human Resources*, vol. 11, no. 2 (1976): 250–60. R.

693. Minarik, Joseph J., and Goldfarb, Robert S. "AFDC Income, Recipient Rates, and Family Dissolution—a Comment," *Journal of Human Resources*, vol. 11, no. 2 (1976): 243–50. R.

694. Mudrick, Nancy R. "Use of AFDC by Previously High- and Low-income Households," *Social Service Review*, vol. 52, no. 1 (1978): 107–15. R.

695. North Carolina Division of Social Services, Comptroller Section, Reports and Program Analysis Branch. *Aid to Families with Dependent Children*. [Raleigh, NC]: Department of Human Resources, 1974.

696. U.S. Social Security Administration, Office of Research and Statistics. *Aid to Families with Dependent Children: A Chartbook*. [Washington]: Government Printing Office, [1978].

697. Wight, Jermy B. "Support Payments for AFDC Mothers: Getting Fathers to Pay," *Public Welfare* (US), vol. 30, no. 4 (1972): 59–62.

INCOME MAINTENANCE

698. Galligan, Richard J., and Bahr, Stephen J. "Economic Well-Being and Marital Stability: Implications for Income Maintenance Programs," *Journal of Marriage and the Family*, vol. 40, no. 2 (1978): 283–89. R.

699. Hannan, Michael, et al. "The Impact of Income Maintenance on the Making and Breaking of Marital Unions: Interim Report," *Resources in Education* 14 (1979). ERIC document ED 166 127. R.

700. Hannan, Michael T., and Tuma, Nancy B. "Income and Marital Events: Evidence from an Income-Maintenance Experiment," *American Journal of Sociology*, vol. 82, no. 6 (1977): 1186–1211. R.

701. Hannan, Michael T.; Tuma, Nancy B.; and Groenveld, Lyle P. "Income and Independent Effects on Marital Dissolution: Results from the Seattle and Denver Income-Maintenance Experiments," *American Journal of Sociology*, vol. 84, no. 3 (1978): 611–33. R.

702. Wolf, Douglas A. "Income Maintenance, Labor Supply, and Family Stability: An Empirical Analysis of Marital Dissolution." Ph.D. diss., University of Pennsylvania, 1977 (*DAI* 38/11A, p. 6839, order # 7806659). R.

DIVORCE AND WORK

703. Allan, Kathryn H. "First Findings of the 1972 Survey of the Disabled: General Characteristics," *Social Security Bulletin*, vol. 39, no. 10 (1976): 18–37. R.

704. Cherlin, Andrew. "Work Life and Marital Dissolution." In *Divorce and Separation: Context, Causes and Consequences*, edited by George Levinger and Oliver C. Moles, pp. 151–66. New York; Basic Books, 1979. R.

705. Hayghe, Howard. "Marital and Family Characteristics of the Labor Force in 1973," *Monthly Labor Review*, vol. 97, no. 4 (1974): 21–27. R.

706. ———. "Marital and Family Characteristics of Workers, March 1974," *Monthly Labor Review*, vol. 98, no. 1 (1975): 60–64. R.

707. ———. "Marital and Family Characteristics of the Labor Force," *Monthly Labor Review*, vol. 98, no. 11 (1975): 52–56. R.

708. ———. "Marital and Family Characteristics of Workers, March 1977," *Monthly Labor Review*, vol. 101, no. 2 (1978): 51–54. R.

709. Johnson, Beverly L. "Changes in Marital and Family Characteristics of Workers, 1970–78," *Monthly Labor Review*, vol. 102, no. 4 (1979): 49–52.

710. ———. "Women Who Head Families: Their Numbers Rise, Income Lags," *Monthly Labor Review*, vol. 101, no. 2 (1978): 32–37. R.

711. Johnson, Phyllis J. "Non-routine Management of Employment and Family Responsibilities by Divorced Mothers." Ph.D. diss., Ohio State University, 1978 (*DAI* 39/8B, p. 3785, order # 7902150). R.

712. Kriegsmann, John K., and Hardin, David R. "Does Divorce Hamper Job Performance?" *Personnel Administrator*, vol. 19, no. 2 (1974): 26–29. R.

713. Rosenthal, Kristine M., and Keshet, Harry F. "The Impact of Childcare Responsibilities on Part-time or Single Fathers," *Alternative Lifestyles*, vol. 1, no. 4 (1978): 465–91. R.

714. Santos, Fredericka P. "The Economics of Marital Status." In *Sex, Discrimination, and the Division of Labor*, edited by Cynthia B. Lloyd, pp. 244–68. New York: Columbia University Press, 1975.

715. *Selected Characteristics of Artists, 1970: Self-Employment, Migration, Household and Family*. Washington, DC: National Endowment for the Arts, 1978 (NF2.12:10).

716. Sherwood, Hugh C. "Is Business Prejudiced Against Single People?" *Industry Week*, 180 (February 25, 1974): 46 +

717. Waldman, Elizabeth. "Children of Working Mothers, March 1974," *Monthly Labor Review*, vol. 98, no. 1 (1975): 64–67. R.

718. Waldman, Elizabeth, and Whitmore, Robert. "Children of Working Mothers, March 1973," *Monthly Labor Review*, vol. 97, no. 5 (1974): 50–57. R.

719. Weinstein, Marc. "Women and Work," *Occupational Outlook Quarterly*, vol. 23, no. 2 (1979): 27–26.

BUSINESSPEOPLE

720. Murray, Thomas J. "High Cost of Executive Divorce," *Duns*, vol. 98, no. 4 (1971): 53–54 + .

DENTISTS

721. "Divorce, a Case Study—Her Side, Happy Ever After—Apart," *Texas Dental Journal*, vol. 94, no. 10 (1976): 6–9.

722. "Divorce—a Husband's Story, You've Heard Hers . . . Now Hear His," *Texas Dental Journal*, vol. 94, no. 12 (1976): 6–8.

723. "Divorce Dental Style," *Dental Management* 13 (March 1973): 34–38 + .

724. Walzer, Stuart B. "Dividing a Dental Practice in a California Marital Dissolution," *Southern California Dental Association Journal*, vol. 40, no. 4 (1972): 376–78.

DUAL-CAREER FAMILIES

725. Turner, Christopher. "Dual Work Household and Marital Dissolution," *Human Relations*, vol. 24, no. 6 (1971): 535–48.

LABOR FORCE PARTICIPATION

726. Grossman, Allyson S. "Divorced and Separated Women in the Labor Force—An Update," *Monthly Labor Review*, vol. 101, no. 10 (1978): 43–45. R.

727. ———. "The Labor Force Patterns of Divorced and Separated Women," *Monthly Labor Review*, vol. 100, no. 1 (1977): 48–53. R.

728. Hayghe, Howard. "Labor Force Activity of Married Women," *Monthly Labor Review*, vol. 96, no. 4 (1973): 31–36. R.

729. Johnson, Beverly L., and Hayghe, Howard. "Labor Force Participation of Married Women, March 1976," *Monthly Labor Review*, vol. 100, no. 6 (1977): 32–36. R.

730. Moore, Sylvia F. "The Short-term Effects of Marital Disruption on the Labor Supply Behavior of Young Women." Ph.d. diss., The Ohio State University, 1978 (*DAI* 39/8A, p. 5045, order # 7902192). R.

731. Rosenman, Linda S. "Marital Status Change and Labor Force Readjustments: An Analysis of Female Heads of Families." Ph.D. diss., Washington University, 1976 (*DAI* 37/12A, p. 7975, order # 7712480). R.

732. ———. "Marital Status Change and Labor Force Readjustments: An Analysis of Female Heads of Families," *Government Reports Announcements and Index* 3 (1978) 5I. PB-273 767/4GA. R.

733. Stokes, Kathleen D. "An Analysis of the Labor Force Behavior and Fertility of Remarried Women, Spouses Present, United States, 1970." Ph.D. diss., Columbia University, 1979 (*DAI* 40/6A, p. 3552, order # 7924991). R.

734. Taylor, Patricia A. "Women's Labor Force Participation and Marital Stability in the United States: A Panel Study." Ph.D. diss., University of Texas, Austin, 1976 (*DAI* 37/5A, p. 3217, order # 7626712). R.

735. U.S. Bureau of Labor Statistics. *U.S. Working Women: A Databook*. Washington, DC: Government Printing Office, 1977 (L2.3:1977).

736. Waldman, Elizabeth, and Young, Anne M. "Marital and Family Characteristics of Workers, March 1970," *Monthly Labor Review*, vol. 94, no. 3 (1971): 46–50. R.

737. Waldman, Elizabeth, and Gover, Kathryn R. "Marital and Family Characteristics of the Labor Force," *Monthly Labor Review*, vol. 95, no. 4 (1974): 4–8. R.

FAMILY LIFE SPECIALISTS

738. Glick, Paul C. "Marriage Experiences of Family Life Specialists," *Family Relations*, vol. 29, no. 1 (1980): 111–18. R.

MILITARY PERSONNEL

739. Gordon, Richard E., et al. "The Migratory Disabled Veteran," *Florida Medical Association Journal*, vol. 60, no. 9 (1973): 27–30. R.

740. Williams, John W. Jr. "Divorce and Dissolution in the Military Family." In *Families in the Military System*, edited by Hamilton I. McCubbin, Barbara B. Dahl, and Edna J. Hunter, pp. 209–36. Beverly Hills, CA: Sage Publishers, 1976.

741. Williams, John W., Jr. "Divorce in the Population of the United States and in a Homogeneous Subset of that Population (United States Air Force Officers) 1958–1970." Ph.D. diss., Mississippi State University, 1971 (*DAI* 32/4A, p. 2215, order # 7127030). R.

PHYSICIANS

742. Fuller, B. Latham. "One Couple's Approach to Malpractice Protection—Get a Divorce," *Medical Economics* 55 (October 16, 1978): 130–31 + .

743. Hittner, David. "What You'll Need to Know in Case of Divorce," *Medical Economics* 56 (February 19, 1979): 179–80 + .

744. Layne, Abner A. "Never Underestimate the High Cost of Divorce," *Medical Economics* 50 (November 26, 1973): 118–19 + .

745. Rosow, Irving, and Rose, K. Daniel. "Divorce among Doctors," *Journal of Marriage and the Family*, vol. 34, no. 4 (1972): 587–98. R.

746. ———. "Marital Stability among Physicians," *California Medicine*, vol. 116, no. 32 (1972): 95–99. R.

POLICE

747. Depue, Roger L. "Turning Inward: The Police Officer Counselor," *FBI Law Enforcement Bulletin*, vol. 48, no. 2 (1979): 8–12.

748. Durner, James A., et al. "Divorce: Another Occupational Hazard," *Police Chief*, vol. 42, no. 11 (1975): 48–53. R.

749. Fabricatore, Joseph M., and Dash, Jerry. "Suicide, Divorce, and Psycological Health among Police Officers," *Essence*, vol. 1, no. 4 (1977): 225–31. R.

750. Olmstead, Gerald T. "Divorce and the Police Profession: Marriage Dissolution among Deputy Sheriffs of Los Angeles Co." Master's thesis, California State University, Long Beach, 1973 (*Master's Abstracts* v. 11, p 347, order #M4330). R.

PROFESSIONAL WOMEN

751. Sparks, Zoe Ann D. "Socioeconomic Correlates of Divorced and Non-divorce among Professional Women in Arkansas." Ed.D. diss., University of Arkansas, 1977 (*DAI* 38/5A, p. 2471, order # 7723310). R.

SOCIOLOGISTS

752. Glenn, Norval D., and Keir, Margaret S. "Divorce among Sociologists Married to Sociologists," *Social Problems*, vol. 19, no. 1 (1971): 57–67. R.

UNEMPLOYMENT

753. Maio, Greta. Marital Instability and Unemployment among Whites and Non-Whites, the Moynihan Report Revisited—Again," *Journal of Marriage and the Family*, vol. 36, no. 1 (1974): 77–86. R.

DIVORCE COUNSELING AND MEDIATION

754. Auster, Simon L. "Divorce Counseling," *American Journal of Orthopsychiatry*, vol. 47, no. 3 (1977): 536–37. [LTE]

755. Bagby, Trudy K. "Divorce Groups," *The Group Leader's Workshop* 8 (January 1971): 25–28.

756. Baideme, Sally M.; Hill, Hank A.; and Serritella, Daniel A. "Conjoint Family Therapy Following Divorce: Alternative Strategy," *International Journal of Family Counseling*, vol. 6, no. 1 (1978): 55–59.

757. Beatrice, Dory K. "Divorce—Problems, Goals, and Growth Facilitation," *Social Casework*, vol. 60, no. 3 (1979): 157–65.

758. Bernstein, Barton E. "Lawyer and Counselor as an Interdisciplinary Team: Points for a Woman to Ponder in Considering the Basic Finances of Divorce," *Family Coordinator*, vol. 26, no. 4 (1977): 421–27.

759. ———. "Lawyer and Pastoral Counselor: A Team for Divorce Counseling," *Journal of Religion and Health*, vol. 16, no. 3 (1977): 223–32.

760. Black, Melvin, and Joffee, Wendy. "A Lawyer/Therapist Approach to Divorce," *Conciliation Courts Review*, vol. 16, no. 1 (1978): 1–5.

761. ———. "A Lawyer/Therapist Team Approach to Divorce," *Resources in Education*, (1978) 13 ERIC document ED 151 717.

762. Bonkowski, Sara E., and Wanner-Westly, Brenda. "The Divorce Group: A New Treatment Modality," *Social Casework*, vol. 60, no. 9 (1979): 552–57.

763. Bridges, Marybeth. "The Divorce Clinic," *Family Law Newsletter*, vol. 17, no. 2 (1977): 16–21. R.

764. Burchell, R. Clay. "Counseling the Formerly Married," *Clinical Obstetrics and Gynecology*, vol. 21, no. 1 (1978): 259–67.

765. Burdge, Walter A. "Divorce Adjustment Groups" (letter to the editor), *Personnel and Guidance Journal*, vol. 54, no. 10 (1976): 499.

766. Callahan, Betsy N. *"Separation and Divorce: Workshop Models for Family Life Education.* New York: Family Services Association of America, 1979.

767. Cassius, Joseph, and Koonce, Jay. "Divorce as a Final Option in Family Psychotherapy." In *Techniques and Approaches in Marital and Family Counseling*, edited by Richard E. Hardy and John G. Cull, pp. 11–26. Springfield, IL: Charles C Thomas, 1974.

768. Conway, Paul M. "To Insure Domestic Tranquility: Reconciliation Services as an Alternative to the Divorce Attorney," *Journal of Family Law*, vol. 9, no. 4 (1970): 408–24.

769. Crickmore, Jack. "Transition Institute," *The Group Leader's Workshop*, 15 (August 1972): 1–10.

770. Cull, John G., and Hardy, Richard E., eds. *Deciding on Divorce: Personal and Family Considerations*. Springfield, IL: Charles C Thomas, 1974.

771. DeFazio, V. J., and Klenbort, I. "A Note on the Dynamics of Psychotherapy During Marital Dissolution," *Psychotherapy: Theory, Research and Practice*, vol. 12, no. 1 (1975): 101–04.

772. Denton, David. "Social Workers' Views on and Experiences with Changing Family Life Styles, Marriage and Divorce Counseling, and the Need for New Treatment Techniques," Master's thesis, Boston University, 1977. R.

773. Donahoe, Mike. "Weekend Divorce Workshops," *The Group Leader's Workshop* 14 (July 1972): 1–10.

774. Dreyfus, Edward A. "Counseling the Divorced Father," *Journal of Marriage and Family Therapy*, vol. 5, no. 4 (1979): 79–85.

775. Elkin, Meyer. "Postdivorce Counseling in a Conciliation Court," *Journal of Divorce*, vol. 1, no. 1 (1974): 55–65.

776. Ferguson, Adelaide. "The Divorce Experience," *Conciliation Courts Review*, vol. 16, no. 1 (1978): 33–37.

777. Fisher, Bruce F. "Identifying and Meeting Needs of Formerly Married People through a Divorce Adjustment Seminar." Ed.D. diss., University of Northern Colorado, 1976 (*DAI* 37/11A, p. 7036, order # 7711057). R.

778. Fisher, Esther O. "Divorce Counseling and Values," *Journal of Religion and Health*, vol. 14, no. 4 (1975): 265–70.

779. ———. *Divorce: The New Freedom. A Guide to Divorcing and Divorce Counseling*. New York: Harper & Row, 1974.

780. ———. "A Guide to Divorce Counseling," *Family Coordinator*, vol. 22, no. 1 (1973): 55–61.

781. Freund, John. "Divorce and Grief," *Journal of Family Counseling*, vol. 2, no. 2 (1974): 40–43.

782. Frohlich, Newton. "Divorce Counseling: When a Physician Refers Only One Spouse for Psychotherapy," *Medical Annals of the District of Columbia*, vol. 41, no. 3 (1972): 176–78.

783. Froiland, Donald J., and Hozman, Thomas L. "Counseling for Constructive Divorce," *Personnel and Guidance Journal*, vol. 55, no. 9 (1977): 525–29.

784. Gillen, Frances C. "A Study of the Effects of Paraprofessionally Conducted Group Therapy on the Self Concept of Divorced or Separated Persons." Ed.D. diss., University of South Dakota, 1977 (*DAI* 37/8A, p. 4863, order # 773442). R.

785. Goldman, Janice, and Coane, James. "Family Therapy After the Divorce: Developing a Strategy," *Family Process*, vol. 16, no. 3 (1977): 357–62.

786. Graber, Richard F. "Therapeutic Counseling, When 'Divorce Crisis' Is the Diagnosis," Parts I & II, *Patient Care*, vol. 11, no. 6 (1977): 90+; vol. 11, no. 7 (1977): 106+.

787. Granvold, Donald K., and Welch, Gary J. "Intervention for Postdivorce Adjustment Problems: The Treatment Seminar," *Journal of Divorce*, vol. 1, no. 1 (1977): 81–92.

788. ———. "Structured, Short-term Group Treatment of Postdivorce Adjustment," *International Journal of Group Psychotherapy*, vol. 29, no. 3 (1979): 347–58.

789. Hardy, Richard E., and Cull, John G., eds. *Therapeutic Needs of the Family: Problems, Descriptions, and Therapeutic Approaches*. Springfield, IL: Charles C Thomas, 1974.

790. Hoffman, Richard C. "One Office's Success with Separation Counseling," *Family Law Newsletter*, vol. 15, no. 4 (1975): 1–2+.

791. Kane, Barbara. "Uncoupling Marriages," *Journal for Specialists in Group Work,* vol. 4, no. 2 (1979): 87–93.

792. Kessler, Sheila. *Beyond Divorce (Leader's Guide and Participant's Guide).* Atlanta, GA: National Institute for Professional Training in Divorce Counseling, 1977.

793. ———. "Building Skills in Divorce Adjustment Groups," *Journal of Divorce,* vol. 2, no. 2 (1978): 209–16. R.

794———. "Divorce Adjustment Groups," *Personnel and Guidance Journal,* vol. 54, no. 5 (1976): 251–55.

795. ———. "Divorce Adjustment Groups," *Resources in Education* 11 (1976). ERIC document ED 112 278.

796. ———. "Divorce Counseling," *Resources in Education* 12 (1977). ERIC document ED 131 371.

797. ———. "Divorce Counseling," *Resources in Education* 13 (1978). ERIC document ED 150 534.

798. Kressel, Kenneth, and Deutsch, Morton. "Divorce Therapy—In-Depth Survey of Therapists' Views," *Family Process,* vol. 16, no. 4 (1977): 413–43. R.

799. Kressel, Kenneth, et al. "Professional Intervention in Divorce: A Summary of the Views of Lawyers, Psychotherapists, and Clergy," *Journal of Divorce,* vol. 2, no. 2 (1978): 119–55. R.

800. Leader, Arthur L. "Family Therapy for Divorced Fathers and Others Out of Home," *Social Casework,* vol. 54, no. 1 (1973): 13–19.

801. Levine, Marcia W. "New Family Structures; Challenges to Family Casework," *Journal of Jewish Communal Service,* vo. 50, no. 3 (1974): 238–44.

802. McCulloch, Sandy. "Three Self-Assertive Exercises for Divorced or Singles Groups," *The Group Leader's Workshop* 15 (August 1972): 1–5.

803. Metcalfe, Barbara L. "An Internship Experience at the Family Divorce Counseling Service." Master's thesis, Western Michigan University, 1976 (*Master's Abstracts* 14/4, p. 228, order # 1308875). R.

804. Moerlin, Elinor B. "Competencies for the Divorced." Ed.D diss., University of Northern Colorado, 1977 (*DAI* 38/8B, p. 3960, order # 7730849). R.

805. Morris, James D., and Prescott, Mary R. "Adjustment to Divorce through Transactional Analysis," *Journal of Family Counseling,* vol. 4, no. 1 (1976): 66–69.

806. ———. "Facilitating Transition Groups on the College Campus," *Resources in Education* 9 (1974). ERIC document ED 092 832.

807. ———. "Transitional Groups: An Approach to Dealing with Post-Partnership Anguish," *Family Coordinator,* vol. 24, no. 3 (1975): 325–30.

808. Nichols, William C. "Divorce and Remarriage Education," *Journal of Divorce,* vol. 1, no. 2 (1977): 153–61.

809. Ostien, J. Keith. "Facilitating Adjustment to Divorce through Time-Limited, Individual, Self-Concept Based Psychotherapy." Ph.D. diss., Michigan State University, 1979 (*DAI* 40/9B, p. 4498, order # 8006174). R.

810. Prescott, Mary, and Morris, James D. "Transition Groups for Divorced and Separated Clients," *Journal for Specialists in Group Work,* vol. 4, no. 1 (1979): 34–39.

811. ———. "Transition Groups: Dealing with Postpartnership Adjustment on the College Campus," *Journal of College Student Personnel,* vol. 16, no. 3 (1975): 249.

812. Reid, Verna L. "The Influence of Group Counseling on the Recently Divorced." Ed.D. diss., Oklahoma State University, 1978 (*DAI* 39/8A, p. 4737, order # 7903731). R.

813. Salts, Connie J. "Effects of Post-separation/Postdivorce Counseling Groups on Adjustment and Self Concept." Ph.D. diss., Florida State University, 1979 (*DAI* 40/7A, p. 4262, order # 8001114). R.

814. Savage, Judith A. "The Impact of Changes on Service," *Conciliation Courts Review,* vol. 15, no. 2 (1977): 12–15.

815. Scarr, Daphne. "The Divorce Experience," *Probation Journal,* vol. 25, no. 1 (1978): 26–29.

816. Sheffner, David J., and Suarez, John M. "The Postdivorce Clinic," *American Journal of Psychiatry,* vol. 132, no. 4 (1975): 442–44.

817. Shelton, Sharon C., and Nix, Christine. "Development of a Divorce Adjustment Group Program in a Social Service Agency," *Social Casework,* vol. 60, no. 5 (1979): 309–12.

818. Suarez, John M.; Weston, Nancy L.; and Hartstein, Norman B. "Mental Health Interventions in Divorce Proceedings," *American Journal of Orthopsychiatry,* vol. 48, no. 2 (1978): 273–83.

819. Tubbs, Ace L. *Divorce Counseling: A Workbook for the Couple and Their Counselor.* Danville, IL: Interstate Printers & Publishers, 1973.

820. Vitousek, Betty M. "Divorce Experience Program," *Conciliation Courts Review,* vol. 15, no. 2 (1977): 37–38.

821. Wallerstein, Judith S., and Kelly, Joan B. "Divorce Counseling: A Community Service for Families in the Midst of Divorce," *American Journal of Orthopsychiatry,* vol. 47, no. 1 (1977): 4–22. R.

822. Welch, Gary J., and Granvold, Donald K. "Seminars for Separated/Divorced: An Educational Approach to Post-divorce Adjustment," *Journal of Sex and Marital Therapy,* vo. 3, no. 1 (1977): 31–39.

823. Whitaker, Carl A., and Miller, Milton H. "A Re-evaluation of 'Psychiatric Help' When Divorce Impedes." In *Progress in Group and Family Therapy,* edited by Clifford J. Sager and Helen S. Kaplan, pp. 521–30. New York: Brunner/Mazel, 1972.

824. White, Henry E., Jr. *Divorce—Attempting to Cope.* [Birmingham, AL]: White, 1978.

CHILDREN'S DIVORCE GROUPS

825. Bebensee, Barbara A. "Adjustment Counseling with Children of Divorced Parents," Ed.D. diss., College of William & Mary, 1979 (*DAI* 40/12A, p. 6148, order # 8014021). R.

826. Bernstein, Joanne E. "Helping Young Children Cope with Separation: A Bibliotherapeutic Approach," *Resources in Education* 14 (1979). ERIC document ED 170 695.

827. Cantor, Dorothy W. "School-Based Groups for Children of Divorce," *Journal of Divorce,* vol. 1, no. 2 (1977): 183–87.

828. Derdeyn, Andre P. "Children in Divorce: Intervention in the Phase of Separation," *Pediatrics,* vol. 60, no. 1 (1977): 20–27.

829. Gurney, Louise, and Jordon, Lucy. "Children of Divorce—A Community Support Group," *Journal of Divorce,* vol. 2, no. 3 (1979): 283–94.

830. Hozman, Thomas L., and Froiland, Donald J. "Families in Divorce: A Proposed Model for Counseling Children," *Family Coordinator,* vol. 25, no. 3 (1976): 271–76.

831. Kaplan, Stuart L. "Structural Family Therapy for Children of Divorce: Case Reports," *Family Process*, vol. 16, no. 1 (1977): 75–83.

832. Kelly, Joan B., and Wallerstein, Judith S. "Brief Interventions with Children in Divorcing Families," *American Journal of Orthopsychiatry*, vol. 47, no. 1 (1977): 23–39. R.

833. Kessler, Sheila, and Bostwick, Sylvia H. *Beyond Divorce: Coping Skills for Minors.* Atlanta, GA: National Institute for Professional Training in Divorce Counseling, 1977.

834. ———. "Beyond Divorce: Coping Skills for Children," *Journal of Clinical Child Psychology*, vol. 6, no. 2 (1977): 38–41.

835. Magid, Kenneth M. "Children Facing Divorce: A Treatment Program," *Personnel and Guidance Journal*, vol. 55, no. 9 (1977): 534–36.

836. Parker, Denise. "Impact of Divorce on the Lives of Children: Alleviating the Trauma of the Divorce Experience through Adult Strategies," *Resources in Education* 15 (1980). ERIC document ED 180 615.

837. Parks, Ann. "Children and Youth of Divorce in Parents without Partners, Inc.," *Journal of Clinical Child Psychology*, vol. 6, no. 2 (1977): 44–48.

838. Rogers, Clayton W. "Life Style Assessment of Children Experiencing Parental Separation or Divorce." Ed.D. diss., Oklahoma State University, 1978 (*DAI* 39/8A, p. 4738, order # 7903738). R.

839. Santella, Chris; Casperson, Paul; and Holdahl, Shirley. "Understanding and Coping with Family Change—The Children's Groups," *Conciliation Courts Review*, vol. 13, no. 1 (1975): 18–20.

840. Schulhofer, Edith. "Short Term Preparation of Children for Separation, Divorce, and Remarriage," *American Journal of Orthopsychiatry*, vol. 43, no. 2 (1973): 248–49.

841. Snyder, Peggy D. "A Model of a Child-Centered Intervention for Use with Families in the Process of Divorce," Ph.D. diss., United States International University, 1977 (*DAI* 39/10B, p. 5089, order # 7908427). R.

842. Wilkinson, Gary S., and Beck, Robert T. "Children's Divorce Groups," *Elementary School Guidance and Counseling*, vol. 11, no. 3 (1977): 205–14.

843. Wilkinson, Gary S. "Small Group Counseling with Elementary School Children of Divorce." Ph.D. diss., University of Florida, 1976 (*DAI* 37/10A, p. 6287, order # 778241). R.

844. Woody, Jane D. "Preventative Intervention for Children of Divorce," *Social Casework*, vol. 59, no. 9 (1978): 537–44.

DIVORCE EDUCATION

845. Green, Barbara J. "Helping Children of Divorce: A Multimodal Approach," *Elementary School Guidance and Counseling*, vol. 13, no. 1 (1978): 30–45.

846. Hyde, Heather R. "The Development of a Group Program for Separated or Divorced Parents." Master's thesis, University of British Columbia, 1979. R.

847. Khanlian, John F., et al. "Law and the Family: A High School Curriculum Guide," *Resources in Education* 13 (1978). ERIC document ED 153 932.

848. Snow, Barbara W. "The Single Parents' Potentials Program." Master's thesis, University of Utah, Salt Lake City, 1976. R.

849. Walker, Sharon G. "Factors Associated with Change in Divorced and Separated Persons Attending a Didactic Seminar." Ph.D. diss., Texas A&M University, 1979 (*DAI* 40/8B, p. 3975, order # 8003191). R.

850. Wiseman, Dennis G. "A Survey on the Instruction of the Subject of Marriage and Family, Pre-marital Relationships, and Divorce in Illinois Public Secondary Schools." Master's thesis, University of Illinois, Urbana, 1971. R.

DIVORCE MEDIATION

851. Coogler, O. J. "Divorce Mediation for 'Low Income' Families: A Proposed Model," *Conciliation Courts Review*, vol. 17, no. 1 (1979): 21–26.

852. ———. *Structured Mediation in Divorce Settlements: A Handbook for Marital Mediators.* Atlanta, GA: Family Mediation Association, 1977.

853. Coogler, O. J.; Weber, Ruth E.; and McKenry, Patrick C. "Divorce Mediations: A Means of Facilitating Divorce Adjustment," *Family Coordinator*, vol. 28, no. 2 (1979): 255–59.

854. Gaddis, Stephen M. "Divorce Decision Making: Alternatives to Litigation," *Conciliation Courts Review*, vol. 16, no. 3 (1978): 43–45.

855. Greenstone, James L. "An Interdisciplinary Approach to Marital Disputes Arbitration: The Dallas Plan," *Conciliation Courts Review*, vol. 16, no. 1 (1978): 7–15.

856. Haynes, John M. "Divorce Mediation: Theory and Practice of New Social Work Role." Ph.D. diss., Union (Ohio) Graduate School, 1978 (*DAI* 39/8A, p. 5149, order # 7903509). R.

857. ———. "Divorce Mediator: A New Role," *Social Work*, vol. 23, no. 1 (1978): 5–9.

858. Herrman, Margaret S.; McKenry, Patrick C.; and Weber, Ruth E. "Mediation and Arbitration Applied to Family Conflict Resolution—Divorce Settlement," *Arbitration Journal*, vol. 34, no. 1 (1979): 17–21. R.

859. Kelsey, Linda J. "Mediating Factors in Response to Divorce." Master's thesis, University of Connecticut, 1979. R.

860. Kessler, Sheila. "Counselor as Mediator," *Personnel and Guidance Journal*, vol. 58, no. 3 (1979): 194–96.

861. Kressel, Kenneth, et al. "Mediated Negotiations in Divorce and Labor Disputes: A Comparison," *Conciliation Courts Review*, vol. 51, no. 1 (1977): 91–112.

862. Lightman, Ernie S., and Irving, Howard H. "Conciliation and Arbitration in Family Disputes," *Conciliation Courts Review*, vol. 14, no. 2 (1976): 12–21.

863. Meroney, Anne E. "Mediation and Arbitration of Separation and Divorce Agreements," *Wake Forest Law Review*, vol. 15, no. 4 (1979): 467–86.

864. Tuchman, Bruce M., et al. "Mediated Negotiations in Divorce and Labor Disputes," *Resources in Education* 13 (1978). ERIC document ED 151 654. R.

DIVORCE PROCESS

865. Baginski, Joseph C. "The Process of Marriage and Divorce as Outcomes Interpersonal Perception." Master's thesis, California State University, Sacramento, 1978. R.

866. Bohannan, Paul. "The Six Stations of Divorce." In *Divorce and After*, edited by Paul Bohannan, pp. 29–55. Garden City, NY: Doubleday, 1970.

867. Bondurant, Stephen B. "The Divorce Process and the Stress of Separation." Ed.D. diss., University of Cincinnati, 1977 (*DAI* 39/2A, p. 669, order # 7812944). R.

868. Brown, Emily M. "Divorce Counseling." In *Treating Relationships*, edited by David H. L. Olson, pp. 399–429. Lake Mills, IA: Graphic, 1976.

869. ———. "A Model of the Divorce Process," *Conciliation Courts Review*, vol. 14, no. 2 (1976): 1–11.

870. Fisher, Bruce. "Rebuilding Blocks in the Divorce Process," *Journal of Extension* 15 (May–June 1977): 43–46.

871. ———. *When Your Relationship Ends: The Divorce Process Rebuilding Blocks*. Boulder, CO: Family Relations Learning Center, 1978.

872. Hackney, Gary R. "The Divorce Process and Psychological Adjustment." Ph.D. diss., University of North Dakota, 1975 (*DAI* 37/3B, p. 1434, order # 7618144). R.

873. Hobart, James F. "The Presentation and Empirical Validation of a Conceptual Model of Divorce." Ph.D. diss., University of Wisconsin, Milwaukee, 1975 (*DAI* 37/4B, p. 1902, order # 7613763). R.

874. Rasmussen, Paul K., and Ferraro, Kathleen J. "The Divorce Process," *Alternative Lifestyles*, vol. 2, no. 4 (1979): 443–60. R.

875. Salts, Connie. Divorce Process: Integration of Theory," *Journal of Divorce*, vol. 2, no. 3 (1979): 233–40.

876. Shepardson, Anne L. "Divorce and Renewal: The Experience of Three Women." Ph.D. diss., California School of Professional Psychology, San Diego, 1978 (*DAI* 39/5B, p. 2521, order # 7821945). R.

877. Steinberg, Joseph L. "The Therapeutic Potential of the Divorce Process," *American Bar Association Journal* 62 (May 1976): 617–20.

878. Wiseman, Reva S. "Crisis Theory and the Process of Divorce," *Social Casework*, vol. 56, no. 4 (1975): 205–12.

EVALUATION

879. Brown, Prudence, and Manela, Roger. "Client Satisfaction with Marital and Divorce Counseling," *Family Coordinator*, vol. 26, no. 3 (1977): 294–303. R.

880. Eckard, Joyce D. "A Program Evaluation of a Divorce Education Seminar." Master's thesis, Oklahoma State University, 1979. R.

881. Ritter, Barbara. "The Effects of Divorce Counseling Groups on Post-divorce Adjustment and Sexual Attitude Change." Master's thesis, Texas Woman's College, 1978. R.

882. Young, David M. "Consumer Satisfaction with the Divorce Workshop: A Follow-Up Report," *Journal of Divorce*, vol. 2, no. 1 (1978): 49–56. R.

883. ———. "The Divorce Experience Workshop: A Consumer Evaluation," *Journal of Divorce*, vol. 2, no. 1 (1978): 37–47. R.

WOMEN

884. Anderson, Margaret. "Counseling the No-Longer Married Woman," *Resources in Education* 11 (1976). ERIC document ED 117 630).

885. Aslin, Alice L. "Counseling 'Single-Again' (Divorced and Widowed) Woman," *Counseling Psychologist*, vol. 6, no. 2 (1976): 37–41.

886. Carter, Dianne K. "Counseling Divorced Women," *Personnel and Guidance Journal*, vol. 55, no. 9 (1977): 537–41.

887. Coché, Judith, and Goldman, Janice. "Brief Group Psychotherapy for Women after Divorce: Planning a Focused Experience," *Journal of Divorce*, vol. 3, no. 2 (1979): 153–60.

888. Lyman, Howard B. "Changes in Self-Image of Divorced Women Taking Single Again Course," *Resources in Education* 12 (1977):. ED 136 158. R.

889. McIvor, Daniel L., and Rosario, Anny. "Group Therapy for Women Going through Divorce," *Canadian Journal of Psychiatric Nursing*, vol. 20, no. 3 (1979): 11–13.

890. Phillips, Carol A. "Interaction of Divorced and Single Females in a Group Setting." Ed.D. diss., University of Tennessee, 1976 (*DAI* 37/11A, p. 7048, order # 7710795). R.

891. Rawlings, Edna I., and Carter, Dianne K. "Divorced Women," *Counseling Psychologist*, vol. 8, no. 1 (1979): 27–28.

DIVORCED PERSONS

892. Andress, Elizabeth L. "Marriage Role Expectations of Divorced Men and Women." Master's thesis, Virginia Polytechnic and State University, 1979. R.

893. Ard, Ben N., Jr. "Beyond Divorce: What Then?" *Rational Living*, vol. 12, no. 2 (1977): 31–34.

894. Bach, George R. "Creative Exits: Fight-Therapy for Divorcees." In *Women in Therapy: New Psychotherapies for a Changing Society*, edited by Violet Franks and Vasanti Burtle, pp. 307–25. New York: Brunner/Mazel, 1974.

895. Barnhill, Diane. "Divorce . . . Must One Be a Lonely Number," *Menninger Perspective*, vol. 6, no. 1 (1975): 5–9.

896. Bolhouse, Lana G. "Changes in Life Styles of Persons in the Post-Divorce Period." Master's thesis, Texas Woman's University, 1978. R.

897. Borenzweig, Herman. "The Punishment of Divorced Mothers," *Journal of Sociology and Social Welfare*, vol. 3, no. 3 (1976): 291–310.

898. Bradford, Lawrence J. "A Study to Identify Communicative Patterns in Marital Dyads Terminated by Divorce: A Grounded Theory Approach." Ph.D. diss., University of Colorado, Boulder, 1979 (*DAI* 40/4A, p. 1745, order # 7923209). R.

899. Brandwein, Ruth A., et al. "Women and Children Last: Divorced Mothers and Their Families," *Nursing Digest* 4 (January–February 1976): 39–43.

900. Brown, Carol A., et al. "Divorce: Chance of a New Lifetime," *Journal of Social Issues*, vol. 32, no. 1 (1976): 119–33. R.

901. Brown, Prudence, and Manela, Roger. "Changing Family Roles: Women in Divorce," *Journal of Divorce*, vol. 1, no. 4 (1978): 315–28. R.

902. Bryant, Barbara E. *American Women Today and Tomorrow*. [Washington, DC]: National Commission on the Observance of International Women's Year, Government Printing Office, 1977. R.

903. Chiriboga, David A., et al. "Divorce, Stress and Social Supports: A Study in Helpseeking Behavior," *Journal of Divorce*, vol. 3, no. 2 (1979): 121–35. R.

904. Colletta, Nancy D. "Support Systems after Divorce: Incidence and Impact," *Journal of Marriage and the Family*, vol. 41, no. 4 (1979): 837–46. R.

905. Culpepper, Emily E.; Meyners, Hazel S.; and Miller, Diane. *Coming Out of Marriage*. Somerville, MA: New England Free Press, 1973.

906. Cusick, Kathleen M. "A Comparison of the Constructs and Resource Choices of Divorced and Married Mothers." Ph.D. diss., California School of Professional Psychology, San Diego, 1978 (*DAI* 39/6B, p. 2977, order # 7822118). R.

907. Dries, Robert M. "The Divorced Woman: Measurement of Self-Actualization Change and Self-Concept." Ph.D. diss., United States International University, 1975 (*DAI* 36/2B, p. 884, order # 7518046). R.

908. Edwards, Marie. "Coupling and Recoupling vs The Challenge of Being Single," *Personnel and Guidance Journal*, vol. 55, no. 9 (1977): 542–45.

909. Everly, Kathleen G. "Leisure Networks and Role Strain: A Study of Divorced Women with Custody." Ph.D. diss., Syracuse University, 1978 (*DAI* 39/6A, p. 3865, order # 7823558). R.

910. Getz, Sandra, and Herman, Jeanne. "Sex Differences in Judgments of Male and Female Role Stereotypes," *Resources in Education* 10 (1975). ERIC document ED 099 711. R.

911. Glass, Shirley P., and Wright, Thomas L. "The Relationship of Extramarital Sex, Length of Marriage, and Sex Differences on Marital Satisfaction and Romanticism: Athanasiou's Data Reanalyzed," *Journal of Marriage and the Family*, vol. 39, no. 4 (1977): 691–703. R.

912. Goetting, Ann. "The Normative Integration of the Former Spouse Relationship," *Journal of Divorce*, vol. 2, no. 4 (1979): 395–414. R.

913. Gove, Walter R. "Sex, Marital Status, and Mortality," *American Journal of Sociology*, vol. 79, no. 1 (1973): 45–67. R.

914. Gray, Gloria M. "The Nature of the Psychological Impact of Divorce upon the Individual," *Journal of Divorce*, vol. 1, no. 4 (1978): 289–301. R.

915. ———. "Relationships among Feminist Values, Dependency, and Religiousness in a Group of Divorced Individuals." Ph.D. diss., United States International University, 1977 (*DAI* 39/11B, p. 5554, order # 7909553). R.

916. Greif, Judith B. "Child Absence: Fathers' Perceptions of Their Relationship to Their Children Subsequent to Divorce." D.S.W. diss., Adelphi University, 1977 (*DAI* 38/9A, p. 5714, order # 7800328). R.

917. Gruba, Glen H. "Homogeneous versus Heterogeneous Groups for Clients with Different Presenting Problems." Ph.D. diss., University of North Dakota, 1976 (*DAI* 38/1B, p. 358, order # 7714568). R.

918. Herrick, Jeannette E. "An In-Depth Study of Four Divorced Working-Class Women." Ed.D. diss., University of Massachusetts, 1977 (*DAI* 38/3A, p. 1835, order # 7722017). R.

919. Hetherington, E. Mavis; Cox, Martha; Cox, Roger. "The Aftermath of Divorce." In *Mother/Child, Father/Child Relations*, edited by Joseph H. Stevens, Jr., and Marilyn Mathews, pp. 149–76. Washington, DC: National Association for the Education of Young Children, 1978. R.

920. ———. "Divorced Fathers," *Family Coordinator*, vol. 25, no. 4 (1976): 417–27. R.

921. ———. "Divorced Fathers," *Psychology Today*, vol. 10, no. 11 (1977): 42–46.

922. Kelly, Janice M. "A Phenomenological Study of a Woman's Experience Separating from Marriage and Developing a Single Lifestyle." Ph.D. diss., University of Pittsburg, 1979 (*DAI* 40/9B, p. 4523, order #8004816). R.

923. Kitabchi, Gloria; Murrell, Patricia H.; and Crawford, Robert L. "Career/Life Planning for Divorced Women: An Overview," *Vocational Guidance Quarterly*, vol. 28, no. 2 (1979): 137–45.

924. Kitson, Gay C., and Sussman, Marvin B. "The Impact of Divorce on Adults," *Conciliation Courts Review*, vol. 15, no. 2 (1977): 20–24. R.

925. Kohen, Janet A.; Brown, Carol A.; and Feldberg, Roslyn. "Divorced Mothers: The Costs and Benefits of Female Family Control." in *Divorce and Separation: Context, Causes and Consequences*, edited by George Levinger and Oliver C. Moles. pp. 228–45. New York: Basic Books, 1979. R.

926. Leonard, Elizabeth D. "Rorschach Protocols of Fifty Individuals Who Represented Twenty-five Disrupted Marriages." Ph.D. diss., United States International University, 1976 (*DAI* 39/11B, p. 5565, order # 7909576). R.

927. McKenry, Patrick C.; White, Priscilla N.; and Price-Bonham, Sharon. "The Fractured Conjugal Family: A Comparison of Married and Divorced Dyads," *Journal of Divorce*, vol. 1, no. 4 (1978): 329–39. R.

928. Miller, Arthur A. "Reactions of Friends to Divorce." In *Divorce and After*, edited by Paul Bohannan, pp. 56–77. Garden City, NY: Doubleday, 1970.

929. Montgomery, Luetilla. "A Comparative Study of Post-Marital Attitudes of Blacks and Whites." Master's thesis, Alabama A&M University, 1979. R.

930. Moore, Kristin A., et al. "The Consequences of Age at First Childbirth: Marriage, Separation and Divorce," *Resources in Education* 14 (1979). ERIC document ED 164 698. Also in Springfield, VA: *Government Reports Announcements Index, 1979 (PB-289 053/1GA). R.*

931. Napier, Augustus Y. "The Rejection-Intrusion Pattern: A Central Family Dynamic," *Journal of Marriage and Family Counseling*, vol. 4, no. 1 (1978): 5–12.

932. Newsome, Oliver D. "Postdivorce Interaction: An Explanation Using Exchange Theory," Ph.D. diss., University of Iowa, 1976 (*DAI* 37/12A, 8001, order # 7713117). R.

933. Polizoti, Leo F. "The Efficacy of Direct Decision Therapy for Decreasing Indecision and Irrational Ideas and Increasing Self-Acceptance in Divorced Women." Ph.D. diss., United States International University, 1976 (*DAI* 36/10B, p. 5236, order # 768624). R.

934. Portuges, Stephen H. "The Crisis of Uncoupling." Ph.D. diss., University of Massachusetts, 1977 (*DAI* 38/4B, p. 1899, order # 7721491). R.

935. Rice, Joy K. "Divorce and a Return to School," *Journal of Divorce,* vol. 1, no. 3 (1978): 247–57.

936. Smart, Laura S. "An Application of Erikson's Theory to the Recovery-from-Divorce Process," *Journal of Divorce,* vol. 1, no. 1 (1977): 67–79.

937. Staal, Debra L. "Some Factors Affecting the Frequency of Dating among Formerly Married Persons." Master's thesis, University of Iowa, 1976. R.

938. Sullivan, Wallace E. "Some Personality Correlates of Marital Status." Ed.D. diss., Columbia Teachers College, 1976 (*DAI* 37/9B, p. 4764, order # 775760). R.

939. Sweet, James A. "The Living Arrangements of Separated, Widowed and Divorced Mothers," *Demography,* vol. 9, no. 1 (1972): 143–57. R.

940. Tcheng-Laroche, Francoise C. "Yesterday Wife and Mother, Today Head of Household: The Experience of a Group of Separated or Divorced Women," *Canada's Mental Health,* vol. 26, no. 3 (1978): 6–9. R.

941. Trypsiani, Marina. "The Relationship between Marital Status and Opposite Sex Friendships." Master's thesis, Roosevelt University, 1978. R.

942. Turner, Marcia C.; Tynan, Susan A.; and Gross, Steven J. "Staying—Or Splitting: What's Best for the Kids?" *International Journal of Family Counseling,* vol. 6, no. 1 (1978): 52–54.

943. Vaughn, Diane. "Uncoupling: The Process of Moving from One Lifestyle to Another," *Alternative Lifestyles,* vol. 2, no. 4 (1979): 415–42. R.

944. Wisconsin, Governor's Commission on the Status of Women. *Real Women, Real Lives: Marriage, Divorce, Widowhood.* Madison, WI: Governor's Commission on the Status of Women, 1978. Also in *Resources in Education* 13 (1978). ERIC document ED 161 778.

EMOTIONAL REACTIONS

945. Barrett, Roger K. "The Relationship of Emotional Disorder to Marital Maladjustment and Disruption." Ph.D. diss., Kent State University, 1973 (*DAI* 34/9B, p. 4651, order # 747299). R.

946. Bedell, Susanna E. "The Role of the Psychiatrist in Treating Divorce Cases" (letter to the editor), *American Journal of Psychiatry,* vol. 126, no. 9 (1970): 328.

947. Briscoe, C. William, and Smith, James B. "Depression and Marital Turmoil," *Archives of General Psychiatry,* vol. 29, no. 6 (1973): 811–17. R.

948. ———. "Depression in Bereavement and Divorce: Relationship to Primary Depressive Illness: A Study of 128 Subjects," *Archives of General Psychiatry,* vol. 32, no. 4 (1975): 439–43. R.

949. ———. "Psychiatric Illness: Marital Units and Divorce," *Journal of Nervous and Mental Disease,* vol. 158, no. 6 (1974): 440–45.

950. Briscoe, C. William, et al. "Divorce and Psychiatric Disease," *Archives of General Psychiatry,* vol. 29, no. 1 (1973): 119–25. R.

951. Brocki, Severine J. "Marital Status, Sex Status, and Mental Well Being." Ph.D. diss., Vanderbilt University, 1979 (*DAI* 40/10A, p. 5616, order # 8008288). R.

952. Brown, Evelyn C. "An Investigation of Risk Taking and Fear of Failure in Married and Divorced Women." Ph.D. diss., Texas Women's University, 1978 (*DAI* 39/3B, p. 1453, order # 7815588). R.

953. Gove, Walter R. "The Relationship between Sex, Sex Roles, Marital Status, and Mental Illness," *Social Forces,* vol. 51, no. 1 (1972): 34–44. R.

954. ———. "Sex, Marital Status, and Psychiatric Treatment," *Social Forces,* vol. 58, no. 1 (1979): 89–93. R.

955. Henry, B. W., and Overall, J. E. "Epidemiology of Marital Problems in a Psychiatric Population," *Social Psychiatry,* vol. 10, no. 3 (1975): 139–44. R.

956. Herman, Sonya J. "Divorce: A Grief Process," *Perspectives in Psychiatric Care,* vol. 12, no. 3 (1974): 108–12.

957. Lambert, Clinton E. Jr., and Lambert, Vickie A. "Divorce, a Psychodynamic Development Involving Grief," *Journal of Psychiatric Nursing,* vol. 15, no. 1 (1977): 37–42.

958. Offord, David R.; Allen, Nany; and Abrams, Nola. "Parental Psychiatric Illness, Broken Homes, and Delinquency," *American Academy of Child Psychiatry Journal,* vol. 17, no. 2 (1978): 224–38. R.

959. Overall, John E. "Associations between Marital History and the Nature of Manifest Psychopathology," *Journal of Abnormal Psychology,* vol. 78, no. 2 (1971): 213–21. R.

960. Peterson, Linda C. "Guilt, Attribution of Responsibility, and Resolution of the Divorce Crisis," *Image, Sigma Theta Tau National Honor Society of Nursing,* vol. 10, no. 2 (1978): 57. R.

961. ———. "Guilt, Attribution of Responsibility, and Resolution of the Divorce Crisis." Ed.D. diss., University of Massachusetts, 1978 (*DAI* 39/4B, p. 1703, order # 7818037). R.

962. Pokorny, Alex D., and Overall, John E. "Relationships of Psychopathology to Age, Sex, Ethnicity, Education, and Marital Status in State Hospital Patients," *Journal of Psychiatric Research* 7 (1970): 143–52. R.

963. Radloff, Lenore. "Sex Differences in Depression—Effects of Occupational and Marital Status," *Sex Roles,* vol. 1, no. 3 (1975): 249–65. R.

964. Rushing, William A. "Marital Status and Marital Disorder," *Social Forces,* vol. 58, no. 2 (1979): 540–56. R.

965. Schuckit, Marc A., et al. "Unrecognized Psychiatric Illness in Elderly Medical Surgical Patients," *Journal of Gerontology,* vol. 30, no. 6 (1975): 655–60. R.

966. Scoliard, Nancy B. "Divorce/Separation: An Examination of Self-Esteem and Support Systems in Female Headed, Single-Parent Families." Master's thesis, University of Rhode Island, 1979. R.

967. Scott, John A. "Dealing with Initial Isolation and Loneliness at the End of Marriage." In *Creative Divorce through Social and Psychological Approaches,* edited by Richard E. Hardy and John G. Cull, pp. 10–29. Springfield, IL: Charles C Thomas, 1974.

968. *Separation and Depression: Clinical and Research Aspects.* Edited by John P. Scott and Edward C. Senay. Washington, DC: American Association for the Advancement of Science, 1973. R.

969. Shapiro, Terry H. "A Comparison of Counseling MMPI Profiles of Couples Who Remain Married with Those Who Divorce." Ph.D. diss., University of Iowa, 1977 (*DAI* 38/7A, p. 3965, order # 7728514). R.

970. Spinks, William B., Jr. "A Comparison of MMPI Profile Characteristics of Divorcees with those of Marriage Counselees." Ph.D. diss., University of Southern Mississippi, 1974 (*DAI* 35/10B, p. 5139, order # 759610). R.

971. Vaughn, Thomas J., Jr. "Personality and Relationship Characteristics of Divorcing Parents." Ph.D. diss., University of Oklahoma, 1979 (*DAI* 40/12B, p. 5835, order # 8012298). R.

972. Vogel-Moline, Mary E. "The Effects of a Structured Group Treatment: On Self-Esteem and Depression of Divorced/Separated Persons." Ph.D. diss., Brigham Young University, 1979 (*DAI* 40/4A, p. 2294, order # 7922989). R.

973. Warheit, George J., et al. "Sex, Marital Status, and Mental Health: A Reappraisal," *Social Forces,* vol. 55, no. 2 (1976): 459–70. R.

974. Wood, Linda A. "Loneliness and Social Structure." Ph.D. diss., York University, 1976 (*DAI* 37/12B, p. 6414). R.

975. Woodruff, Robert A.; Guze, Samuel B.; and Clayton, Paula J. "Divorce among Psychiatric Out Patients," *British Journal of Psychiatry* 121 (1972): 289–92. R.

KINSHIP

976. Booth, Gerald V. "Kinship and the Crisis of Divorce." Ph.D. diss., Southern Illinois University, 1979 (*DAI* 40/6A, p. 3559, order # 7926296). R.

977. Mindel, Charles H. "Kinship Affiliation: Structure and Process in Divorce," *Journal of Comparative Family Studies,* vol. 3, no. 2 (1972): 254–64. R.

978. O'Brien, David J., and Garland, T. Neal. "Bridging the Gap between Theory, Research, Practice, and Policy Making: The Case of Interaction with Kin after Divorce," *Resources in Education* 13 (1978). ERIC document ED 153 101.

979. Spicer, Jerry W., and Hampe, Gary D. "Kinship Interaction after Divorce," *Journal of Marriage and the Family,* vol. 37, no. 1 (1975): 113–19. R.

PERSONAL GROWTH

980. Brown, Prudence. "Psychological Distress and Personal Growth among Women Coping with Marital Dissolution." Ph.D. diss., University of Michigan, 1976 (*DAI* 37/2B, p. 947, order # 7619092). R.

981. Singer, Laura J. "Divorce and the Single Life: Divorce as Development," *Journal of Sex and Marital Therapy,* vol. 1, no. 3 (1975): 254–62.

POSTDIVORCE ADJUSTMENT

982. Ansell, Charles. "Special Problems of Men." In *Creative Divorce through So-*
cial and Psychological Approaches, edited by Richard E. Hardy and John G. Cull, pp. 51–70. Springfield, IL: Charles C Thomas, 1974.

983. Boudreaux, Adrienne E. "Adjustment to the Divorce and Post-divorce Situation." Master's thesis, University of Utah, 1977. R.

984. Brown, Prudence. "A Study of Women Coping with Divorce." In *New Research on Women and Sex Roles,* edited by Dorothy McGuigan, pp. 252–61. Ann Arbor, MI: University of Michigan Center for Continuing Education, 1976.

985. Brown, Prudence; Perry, Lorraine; and Harburg, Ernest. "Sex Role Attitudes and Psychological Outcomes for Black and White Women Experiencing Marital Dissolution," *Journal of Marriage and the Family,* vol. 39, no. 3 (1977): 549–61. R.

986. Cull, John G., and Hardy, Richard E. "The Role of the Psychologist in Achieving Adjustment to Divorce." In *Creative Divorce through Social and Psychological Approaches,* edited by Richard E. Hardy and John G. Cull, pp. 3–9. Springfield, IL: Charles C Thomas, 1974.

987. Dawson, Dickson R. "Selected Factors in Divorce and Separation Adjustment: An Examination of Problem Areas, Reported Self Disclosure, Interaction with Significant Others and Attitudinal and Demographic Factors," Ph.D. diss., University of Missouri, Kansas City, 1978 (*DAI* 39/7A, p. 4056, order # 7900002). R.

988. Dixon, Beth. "Adjustment to Divorce," *Free Inquiry,* vol. 4, no. 1 (1976): 26–39. R.

989. Elvart, Ann C. "The Structure of the Lives of Middle-Aged Men during the Process of Separation and Divorce." Ph.D. diss., Northwestern University, 1979 (*DAI* 40/6B, p. 2834, order # 7927334). R.

990. Erskine, Rita K. "The Emotional Well-Being of Divorced Men in Comparison with Divorced Women." Master's thesis, Western Washington University, 1979. R.

991. Goethal, Kurt G. "A Follow-Up Study of a Skills Training Approach to Postdivorce Adjustment." Ph.D. diss., Texas Tech University, 1979 (*DAI* 40/8A, p. 4763). R.

992. Granvold, Donald K.; Pedler, Leigh M.; and Schellie, Susan G. "A Study of Sex Role Expectancy and Female Postdivorce Adjustment," *Journal of Divorce,* vol. 2, no. 4 (1979): 383–93. R.

993. Heritage, Jeanette G., and Daniels, Jack L. "Postdivorce Adjustment," *Journal of Family Counseling,* vol. 2, no. 2 (1974): 44–49. R.

994. Heritage, Lena J. G. "A Study of Selected Factors and Their Effect on Postdivorce Adjustment." Ph.D. diss., University of Southern Mississippi, 1971 (*DAI* 32/9A, p. 4950, order # 729076). R.

995. Jackson, Erwin D. "Descriptive Analysis of the Divorce Adjustment Process." Ph.D. diss., Florida State University, 1979 (*DAI* 40/10A, p. 5322, order # 8008606). R.

996. Johnson, Jill M. "Fathers and Mothers after Divorce: Contrasts in the Financial/Career and Domestic/Childrearing Aspects of Being a Single Parent." Master's thesis, University of Texas, Austin, 1979. R.

997. Kizer, Elizabeth J. "An Exploratory Analysis of Women's Communicative Behavior, Adjustment, and Role Redefinition Following Divorce." Ph.D. diss., Purdue University, 1978 (*DAI* 40/1A, p. 26, order # 7914916). R.

998. Laeger, Karen V. "Post-divorce Adjustment among Women." Master's thesis, Oklahoma State University, 1978. R.

999. Lenihan, Genie O. "Patterns of Response to the First Year of Divorce: Illustrative Case Studies of Persons Married Ten Years or Longer." Ph.D. diss., University of Illinois, Urbana-Champaign, 1979 (*DAI* 40/1B, p. 495, order # 7915382). R.

1000. McGinness, Susan K. "Relationship between Parent Adjustment and Preadolescent Adjustment to Divorce within a Specific Time Sequence." Ed.D. diss., North Texas State University, 1978 (*DAI* 39/7A, p. 4061, order # 7824656). R.

1001. MacKinnon, Dolores. "The Effects of Sex Differences, Divorce-Initiation and Time of Divorce Adjustment." Master's thesis, California State University, Hayward, 1974–75. R.

1002. Marcantonio, Clement. "A Profile Analysis of Selected Demographic and Personality Characteristics of Divorced Parties." Ed.D. diss., University of Northern Colorado, 1977 (*DAI* 38/11B, p. 5544, order # 7805509). R.

1003. Mayfield, Peter N. "Successful Adjustment to New Life Patterns and Interpersonal Relationships." In *Creative Divorce through Social and Psychological Approaches,* edited by Richard E. Hardy and John G. Cull, 30–50. Springfield, IL: Charles C Thomas, 1974.

1004. Mead, Margaret. "Anomalies in American Postdivorce Relations." In *Divorce and After*, edited by Paul Bohannan, pp. 97–112. Garden City, NY: Doubleday, 1970.

1005. Nelson, Geoffrey B. "Families Coping with the Loss of Father by Death or Divorce." Ph.D. diss., University of Manitoba, 1979 (*DAI* 40/8B, p. 3956). R.

1006. Pais, Jeanne S. "Social-Psychological Predictors of Adjustment for Divorced Mothers." Ph.D. diss., University of Tennessee, 1978 (*DAI* 39/8A, p. 5165, order # 7803460). R.

1007. Pais, Jeanne, and White, Priscilla. "Family Redefinition: A Review of the Literature Toward a Model of Divorce Adjustment," *Journal of Divorce*, vol. 2, no. 3 (1979): 271–81.

1008. Pett, Marjorie G. "Predictors of Post-divorce Adjustment of Single Parent Families." D.S.W. diss., University of Utah, 1979 (*DAI* 40/11A, p. 6009, order # 8009819). R.

1009. Raschke, Helen J. "The Role of Social Participation in Postseparation and Postdivorce Adjustment," *Journal of Divorce*, vol. 1, no. 2 (1977): 129–40. R.

1010. ———. "Social and Psychological Factors in Voluntary Postmarital Dissolution Adjustment." Ph.D. diss., University of Minnesota, 1974 (*DAI* 35/8A, p. 5549, order # 7502143). R.

1011. ———. "Sex Differences in Voluntary Post Marital Dissolution Adjustment," *Resources in Education* 12 (1977). ERIC document ED 140 183. R.

1012. Rose, Vicki L. and Price-Bonham, Sharon. "Divorce Adjustment: A Woman's Problem?" *Family Coordinator*, vol. 22, no. 3 (1973): 291–97.

1013. Saul, Suzanne C. "Relationship of Divorce Grief and Personal Adjustment in Divorced Persons Who Remarry or Remain Single." Ph.D. diss., University of Oklahoma, 1979 (*DAI* 40/12B, p. 5797, order # 8012293). R.

1014. Sherman, Linda K.G. "The Correlates of Happiness in Post-separation Adjustment." Ph.D. diss., University of Oregon, 1979 (*DAI* 40/10B, p. 5022, order # 8005800). R.

1015. Spanier, Graham B., and Casto, Robert F. "Adjustment to Separation and Divorce: An Analysis of 50 Case Studies," *Journal of Divorce*, vol. 2, no. 3 (1979): 241–53. R.

1016. ———. "Adjustment to Separation and Divorce: A Qualitative Analysis." In *Divorce and Separation: Context, Causes and Consequences*, edited by George Levinger and Oliver C. Moles, pp. 221–27. New York: Basic Books, 1979. R.

1017. Spanier, Graham B., and Fleer, Bryson. "Factors Sustaining Marriage: Factors in Adjusting to Divorce." In *Families Today—A Research Sampler on Families and Children*, edited by Eunice Corfman, pp. 205–31. Washington, DC: National Institute on Mental Health, Government Printing Office, 1979 (HE20.8131/2:1).

1018. Stoloff, Carolyn R. "The Impact of Changing Social, Sexual, and Occupational Contexts on Recently Divorced Women." Ph.D. diss., University of Michigan, 1979 (*DAI* 40/2B, p. 938, order # 7816820). R.

1019. Taibbi, Robert. "Transitional Relationships after Divorce," *Journal of Divorce*, vol. 2, no. 3 (1979): 263–69.

1020. Tatsuguchi, Rosalie K. "Post-divorce Adjustment by Women," Master's thesis, University of Hawaii, 1975. R.

1021. Thiessen, Jake D. "Facilitating Postdivorce Adjustment through Communication Skills Training." Ph.D. diss., Texas Tech University, 1979 (*DAI* 40/8B, p. 3974). R.

1022. Thompson, Bettye D. "An Analysis of the Social Characteristics, Social Adjustment, and Social Participation of Divorced Persons as Compared with Married Persons." Ph.D. diss., Texas Woman's University, 1978 (*DAI* 40/1A, p. 489, order # 7915888). R.

1023. Vernick, Sheila K. "Selected Correlates of Divorce and Postmarital Attachment." Ph.D. diss., University of Florida, 1979 (*DAI* 40/4B, p. 1873, order # 7921946). R.

1024. Zeiss, Antonette M., and Zeiss, Robert A. "Sex Differences in Initiation of Adjustment to Divorce," *Resources in Education* 14 (1979). ERIC document ED 165 017. R.

1025. Zusne, Helen. "Special Problems of Women." In *Creative Divorce through Social and Psychological Approaches*, edited by Richard E. Hardy and John G. Cull, pp. 71–90. Springfield, IL: Charles C Thomas, 1974.

SEXUAL BEHAVIOR

1026. Gebhard, Paul. "Postmarital Coitus among Widows and Divorcees." In *Divorce and After*, edited by Paul Bohannan, pp. 81–96. Garden City, NY: Doubleday, 1970.

1027. Patton, Robert D. "Sexual Attitudes and Behaviors of Single Parents." Ed.D. diss., University of Tennessee, 1976 (*DAI* 37/2A, p. 820, order # 7617736). R.

1028. Smith, Harold I. "Sex and Singleness the Second Time Around," *Christianity Today* 23 (May 25, 1979): 16–22. R.

SOCIAL CHARACTERISTICS

1029. Birdwell, Rawson P., Jr. "Androgeny, Femininity and Masculinity in Relation to Marital Status and Other Factors in a Population of Divorced and Married Middle Class Women, with Implications for Continuing Education." Ph.D. diss., Michigan State University, 1979. (*DAI* 10/12A, p. 6107, order # 8010674). R.

1030. Fonte, Verona H. "Demographic Variables and Self-Actualization for Divorced and Married Women." Ph.D. diss., California School of Professional Psychology, San Diego, 1976 (*DAI* 38/9B, p. 4452, order # 7732473). R.

1031. McCarthy, James F. "Patterns of Marriage Dissolution in the United States." Ph.D. diss., Princeton University, 1977 (*DAI* 38/7A, p. 4392, order # 7728128). R.

1032. McKenry, Patrick C. "A Comparison of Divorced and Married Dyads." Ph.D. diss., University of Tennessee, 1976 (*DAI* 37/11A, p. 7350, order # 7710786). R.

1033. Melton, Willie III. "Self-Satisfaction and Marital Stability among Black Males: Socioeconomic and Demographic Antecedents." Ph.D. diss., 1976 (*DAI* 37/8A, p. 5387, order # 772872). R.

1034. Thompson, Kendrick S. *The Divorce Profile, Differential Social Correlates in 1952 and 1972*. San Francisco, CA: R and E Research Associates, 1978. R.

1035. ———. "The Divorce Profile: Differential Social Correlates in 1952 and 1972." Ph.D. diss., Ohio State University, 1974 (*DAI* 35/8A, p. 5550, order # 753209). R.

1036. ———. "The Divorce Profile: Differential Social Correlates in 1952 and 1972," *International Journal of Sociology of the Family*, vol. 6, no. 2 (1976): 253–63. R.

STATISTICS

1037. U.S. Bureau of Labor Statistics. *Marital and Family Status of Workers by State and Area.* Washington, DC: Government Printing Office, 1978 (L2.71:545) (Tables 1–11).

1038. U.S. Bureau of the Census. *Characteristics of American Youth: 1974.* In its series, P–23: Special Studies, no. 51. Washington, DC: Government Printing Office, 1975. (C56.218:p-23/51) (Table 17).

1039. ———. *Characteristics of the Low-Income Population: 1973.* In its series, P–60: Consumer Income, no. 98. Washington, DC: Government Printing Office, 1975 (C56.218:P-60/98) (Table 17).

1040. ———. *Characteristics of the Population below the Poverty Level: 1972.* In its series, P–60: Consumer Income, no. 91. Washington, DC: Government Printing Office, 1973 (C56.218:P-60/91) (Table 16).

1041. ———. *Characteristics of the Population below the Poverty Level: 1974.* In its series, P-60: Consumer Income, no. 102. Washington, DC: Government Printing Office, 1976 (C3.186:P-60/102) (Table 16).

1042. ———. *Characteristics of the Population below the Poverty Level: 1975.* In its series, P-60: Consumer Income, no. 106. Washington, DC: Government Printing Office, 1977 (C3.186:P-60/106) (Tables 15,21).

1043. ———. *Characteristics of the Population below the Poverty Level: 1976.* In its series, P-60: Consumer Income, no. 115. Washington, DC: Government Printing Office, 1976 (C3.186:P-60/115) (Tables 15,21).

1044. ———. *Characteristics of the Population below the Poverty Level: 1977.* In its series, P-60: Consumer Income, no. 119. Washington, DC: Government Printing Office, 1979 (C3.186:P-60/119) (Tables 15,21).

1045. ———. *Demographic, Social, and Economic Profile of States: Spring 1976.* In its series, P-20: Current Population Reports, no. 334. Washington, DC: Government Printing Office, 1979 (C3.186:P-20/334) (Tables 2,11,12).

1046. ———. *Educational Attainment in the United States: March 1977 and 1976.* In its series, P-20: Current Population Reports, No. 314. Washington, DC: Government Printing Office, 1977 (C3.186:P-20/314) (Table 4).

1047. ———. *Household and Family Characteristics: March 1969.* In its series, P-20: Current Population Reports, No. 200. Washington, DC: Government Printing Office, 1970 (C56.218:P-20/200) (Tables 4,11,13,17).

1048. ———. *Household and Family Characteristics: March, 1970.* In its series, P-20: Current Population Reports, no. 218. Washington, DC: Government Printing Office, 1971 (C56.218:P-20/218) (Tables 4,13,17).

1049. ———. *Household and Family Characteristics: March 1972.* In its series, P-20: Current Population Reports, no. 246. Washington, DC: Government Printing Office, 1972 (C55.218:P-20/246) (Tables 1,4,5,7).

1050. ———. *Household and Family Characteristics: March 1973.* In its series, P-20: Current Population Reports, no. 258. Washington, DC: Government Printing Office, 1973 (C56.218:P-20/258) (Tables 4,17).

1051. ———. *Household and Family Characteristics: March 1974.* In its series, P-20: Current Population Reports, no. 276. Washington, DC: Government Printing Office, 1975 (C56.218:P-20-/276) (Tables 4,17).

1052. ———. *Household and Family Characteristics: March 1975.* In its series, P-20: Current Population Reports, no. 291. Washington, DC: Government Printing Office, 1976 (C3.186:P-20/291) (Tables 4,17).

1053. ———. *Household and Family Characteristics: March 1976.* In its series, P-20: Current Population Reports, no. 311. Washington, DC: Government Printing Office, 1977 (C3.186:P-20/311) (Tables 4,12,16).

1054. ———. *Household and Family Characteristics: March 1977.* In its series, P-20: Current Population Reports, no. 326. Washington, DC: Government Printing Office, 1978 (C3.186:P-20/326) (Tables 4,16).

1055. ———. *Household and Family Characteristics: March 1978.* In its series, P-20: Current Population Reports, no. 340. Washington, DC: Government Printing Office, 1979 (C3.186:P-20/340) (Tables 13,14,20,23).

1056. ———. *Household Money Income in 1973 and Selected Social and Economic Characteristics of Households.* In its series, P-60: Consumer Income, no. 96. Washington, DC: Government Printing Office, 1974 (C56.218:P-60/96) (Table 8).

1057. ———. *Household Money Income in 1974 and Selected Social and Economic Characteristics of Households.* In its series, P-60: Consumer Income, no. 100. Washington, DC: Government Printing Office, 1975 (C56.218:P-60/100) (Tables 3,4).

1058. ———. *Household Money Income in 1975 and Selected Social and Economic Characteristics of Households.* In its series, P-60: Consumer Income, no. 104. Washington, DC: Government Printing Office, 1977 (C3.186:P-60/104) (Tables 3,4,16).

1059. ———. *Marital Status and Family Status: March 1969.* In its series, P-20: Current Population Reports, no. 198. Washington, DC: Government Printing Office, 1970 (C56.218:P-20/198) (Tables F,1,6,9).

1060. ———. *Marital Status and Family Status: March 1970.* In its series, P-20: Current Population Reports, no. 212. Washington, DC: Government Printing Office, 1971 (C56.218:P-20/212) (Tables D,E,1,5,7).

1061. ———. *Marital Status and Living Arrangements: March 1971.* In its series, P-20: Current Population Reports, no. 225. Washington, DC: Government Printing Office, 1971 (C56.218:P-20/225) (Tables 1,5,6,7).

1062. ———. *Marital Status and Living Arrangements: March 1972.* In its series, P-20: Current Population Reports, no. 242. Washington, DC: Government Printing Office, 1972 (C56.218:P-20/242) (Tables F,1,5,7).

1063. ———. *Marital Status and Living Arrangements: March 1973.* In its series, P-20: Current Population Reports, no. 255. Washington, DC: Government Printing Office, 1973 (C56.218:P-20/255) (Tables A,B,1,5,7).

1064. ———. *Marital Status and Living Arrangements: March 1974.* In its series, P-20: Current Population Reports, no. 271. Washington, DC: Government Printing Office, 1974 (C56.218:P-20/271) (Tables E,F,G,1,5,6,7).

1065. ———. *Marital Status and Living Arrangements: March 1975.* In its series, P-20: Current Population Reports, no. 287. Washington, DC: Government Printing Office, 1975 (C56.218:P-20/287) (Tables E,F,G,1,5,6,7).

1066. ———. *Marital Status and Living Arrangements: March 1976.* In its series, P-20: Current Population Reports, no. 306. Washington, DC: Government Printing Office, 1977 (C3.186:P-20/306) (Tables E,G,H,1,5,6,8).

1067. ———. *Marital Status and Living Arrangements: March 1977.* In its series, P-20: Current Population Reports, no. 323. Washington, DC: Government Printing Office, 1978 (C3.186:P-20/323) (Tables F,G,1,5,6,8).

1068. ———. *Marital Status and Living Arrangements: March 1978.* In its series, P-20: Current Population Reports, no. 338. Washington, DC: Government Printing Office, 1979 (C3.186:P-20/338) (Tables C,F,1,5,6,8).

1069. ———. *Marital Status and Living Arrangements: March 1979.* In its series, P-20: Current Population Reports, no. 349. Washington, DC: Government Printing Office, 1980 (C3.186:P-20/349) (Tables C,D,F,G,H,1,5,6,8).

1070. ———. *Marriage, Divorce, and Remarriage by Year of Birth: June 1971.* In its series, P-20: Current Population Reports, no. 239. Washington, DC: Government Printing Office, 1972 (C56.218:P-20/239) (Tables AB,D–H,1–5,7–16).

1071. ———. *Marriage, Divorce, Widowhood, and Remarriage by Family Characteristics: June 1975.* In its series, P-20: Current Population Reports, no. 312. Washington, DC: Government Printing Office, 1977 (C3.186:P-20/312) (Tables A–N,R,S,1–10).

1072. ———. *Money Income in 1975 of Families and Persons in the United States.* In its series, P-60: Consumer Income, no. 105. Washington, DC: Government Printing Office, 1977 (C3.186,P-60/105) (Tables 2,45).

1073. ———. *Money Income in 1976 of Families and Persons in the United States.* In its series, P-60: Consumer Income, no. 114. Washington, DC: Government Printing Office, 1978 (C3.186:P-60/114) (Tables 2,45).

1074. ———. *Money Income in 1977 of Families and Persons in the United States.* In its series, P-60: Consumer Income, no. 118. Washington, DC: Government Printing Office, 1979 (C3.186:P-60/118) (Tables 2,45).

1075. ———. *Money Income in 1976 of Households in the United States.* In its series, P-60: Consumer Income, no. 109. Washington, DC: Government Printing Office, 1978 (C3.186:P-60/109) (Tables 6,18).

1076. ———. *Money Income in 1977 of Households in the United States.* In its series, P-60: Consumer Income, no. 117. Washington, DC: Government Printing Office, 1978 (C3.186:P-60/117) (Table 6).

1077. ———. *1976 Survey of Institutionalized Persons: a Study of Persons Receiving Long Term Care.* In its series, P-23: Special Studies, no. 69. Washington, DC: Government Printing Office, 1978 (C3.186.P-23/69) (Tables II. 11–II.15).

1078. ———. *Persons of Spanish Origin in the United States: March 1972 and 1971.* In its series, P-20: Current Population Reports, no. 250. Washington, DC: Government Printing Office, 1973 (C56.218:P-20/250) (Table 6).

1079. ———. *Persons of Spanish Origin in the United States, March 1973.* In its series, P-20: Current Population Reports, no. 264. Washington, DC: Government Printing Office, 1974 (C56.218:P20/264) (Tables E,5,6).

1080. ———. *Persons of Spanish Origin in the United States: March 1974.* In its series, P-20: Current Population Reports, no. 280. Washington, DC: Government Printing Office, 1975 (C56.218:P-20/280) (Tables 5,6).

1081. ———. *Persons of Spanish Origin in the United States: March 1975.* In its series, P-20: Current Population Reports, no. 290. Washington, DC: Government Printing Office, 1976 (C3.186.P-20/290) (Tables D,5,6).

1082. ———. *Persons of Spanish Origin in the United States: March 1976.* In its series, P-20: Current Population Reports, no. 310. Washington, DC: Government Printing Office, 1977 (C3.186:P-20/310) (Tables D,5,6).

1083. ———. *Persons of Spanish Origin in the United States: March 1977.* In its series, P-20: Current Population Reports, no. 329. Washington, DC: Government Printing Office, 1978 (C3.186:P-20/329) (Tables D,5,6).

1084. ———. *Persons of Spanish Origin in the United States: March 1978.* In its series, P-20: Current Population Reports, no. 339. Washington, DC: Government Printing Office, 1979 (C3.186:P-20/339) (Tables D,4,5,6).

1085. ———. *Perspectives on American Husbands and Wives.* In its series, P-23: Special Studies, no. 77. Washington, DC: Government Printing Office, 1978 (C3.186:P23/77) (Table 5).

1086. ———. *Population Profile of the United States: 1974.* In its series, P-20: Current Population Reports, no. 279. Washington, DC: Government Printing Office, 1975 (C56.218:P-20/279) (Tables 8,9).

1087. ———. *Population Profile of the United States: 1979.* In its series, P-20: Current Population Reports, no. 350. Washington, DC: Government Printing Office, 1980 (C3.186:P-20/350) (Fig. 3).

1088. ———. *Reasons for Interstate Migration: Jobs, Retirement, Climate, and Other Influences.* In its series, P-23: Special Studies, no. 81. Washington, DC: Government Printing Office, 1979 (C3.186:P-23/81) (Table 1).

1089. ———. *Social and Economic Characteristics of the Metropolitan and Nonmetropolitan Population: 1974 and 1970.* In its series, P-23, Special Studies, no. 55. Washington, DC: Government Printing Office, 1975 (C56.218:P-23/55) (Table 4).

1090. ———. *Social and Economic Characteristics of the Metropolitan and Nonmetropolitan Population: 1977 and 1970.* In its series, P-23, Special Studies, no. 75. Washington, DC: Government Printing Office, 1978 (C3.186:P-23/75) (Table 4).

1091. ———. *Social and Economic Characteristics of the Older Population: 1974.* In its series, P-23: Special Studies, no. 57. Washington, DC: Government Printing Office, 1975 (C56.218:P-23/57) (Tables 7,8,9).

1092. ———. *Social and Economic Characteristics of the Older Population: 1978.* In its series, P-23: Special Studies, no. 85. Washington, DC: Government Printing Office, 1979 (C3.186:P-23/85) (Tables 6,24).

1093. ———. *Social and Economic Status of the Black Population in the United States: An Historical View, 1790–1978.* In its series, P-23: Special Studies, no. 80. Washington, DC: Government Printing Office, 1979 (C3.186:P-23/80) (Tables 77,81,82,126).

1094. ———. *Social and Economic Status of the Black Population in the United States: 1973.* In its series, P-23: Special Studies, no. 48. Washington, DC: Government Printing Office, 1974 (C56.218:P-23/48) (Tables 52,67).

1095. ———. *1970 Census of Population. V.1, Characteristics of the Population,* part 1, *U.S. Summary,* sections 1 and 2. Washington, DC: Government Printing Office, 1972–73 (C3.223/9:970/v.1/pt.1,secs.1&2) (Tables 64,111,203,206,211,216,279,282,288,331,351).

1096. ———. *1970 Census of Population. V.1, Characteristics of the Population,* parts 2–52, *States.* Washington, DC: Government Printing Office, 1972–73 (C3.223/ 9:970/v.1/pts.2–52) (Tables 22,26,30,37,52,63,74,152,155,160,162,165).

1097. ———. *1970 Census of Population. V.1, Characteristics of the Population,* part 53, *Puerto Rico.* Washington, DC: Government Printing Office, 1972–73 (C3.223/ 9:970/v.1/pt.53) (Tables 21,24,30,121,129,132).

1098. ———. *1970 Census of Population. V.1, Characteristics of the Population,* part 55, *Virgin Islands.* Washington, DC: Government Printing Office, 1972–73 (C3.223/ 9:970/v.1/pt.55) (Table 6).

1099. ———. *1970 Census of Population. Vol.*2, Subject Report: PC(2)4D—*Age at First Marriage.* Washington, DC: Government Printing Office, 1972–73 (C3.223/ 10:970/v.2/pt.4D) (Table 4).

1100. ———. *1970 Census of Population.* Vol. 2, Subject Report: PC(2)1F—*American Indians.* Washington, DC: Government Printing Office, 1972–73 (C3.223/ 10:970/v.2/pt.1F) (Tables 5,8,12).

1101. ———. *1970 Census of Population.* Vol. 2, Subject Report: PC(2)10A—*Americans Living Abroad.* Washington, DC: Government Printing Office, 1972–73 (C3.223/10:970/v.2/pt.10A) (Tables 4,7,9,12,23,24,26,27,30).

1102. ———. *1970 Census of Population.* Vol. 2, Subject Report: PC(2)6A—*Employment Status and Work Experience.* Washington, DC: Government Printing Office, 1972–73 (C3.223/10:970/v.2/ pt.6A) (Tables 3,15,19–21).

1103. ———. *1970 Census of Population.* Vol. 2, Subject Report: PC(2)4A—*Family Composition.* Washington, DC: Government Printing Office, 1972–73 (C3.223/ 10:970/v.2/pt.4A) (Tables 4,8,18,19,22).

1104. ———. *1970 Census of Population.* Vol. 2, Subject Report: PC(2)7B—*Industrial Characteristics.* Washington, DC: Government Printing Office, 1972–73 (C3.223/10:970/v.2/pt.7B) (Table 46).

1105. ———. *1970 Census of Population.* Vol. 2, Subject Report: PC(2)1G—*Japanese, Chinese, and Filipinos in the United States.* Washington, DC: Government Printing Office, 1972–73 (C3.223/ 10:970/v.2/pt.1G) (Tables 5,8,12,20,23,27,35,38,42).

1106. ———. *1970 Census of Population.* Vol. 2, Subject Report: PC(2)9A—*Low Income Population.* Washington, DC: Gov-

ernment Printing Office, 1972–73 (C3.223/ 10:970/v.2/pt.9A) (Tables 12,21).

1107. ———. *1970 Census of Population. Vo. 2, Subject Report: PC(2)4C—Marital Status.* Washington, DC: Government Printing Office, 1972–73 (C3.223/10:970/ v.2/pt.4C) (Tables 1–9).

1108. ———. *1970 Census of Population.* Vol. 2, Subject Report: PC(2)2B—*Mobility for the State and the Nation.* Washington, DC: Government Printing Office, 1972–73 (C3.223/10:970/v.2/pt.2B) (Tables 3,32–34).

1109. ———. *1970 Census of Population.* Vol. 2, Subject Report: PC(2)1A—*National Origin and Language.* Washington, DC: Government Printing Office, 1972–73 (C3.223/10:970/v.2/pt.1A) (Tables 2,3,11,17).

1110. ———. *1970 Census of Population.* Vol. 2, Subject Report: PC(2)1B—*Negro Population.* Washington, DC: Government Printing Office, C3.223/10:970/v.2/pt.1B) (Tables 5,8,12).

1111. ———. *1970 Census of Population.* Vol. 2, Subject Report: PC(2)7A—*Occupational Characteristics.* Washington, DC: Government Printing Office, 1972–73 (C3.223/10:970/v.2/pt.7A) (Tables 31,32).

1112. ———. *1970 Census of Population.* Vol. 2, Subject Report: PC(2)7E—*Occupational and Residence in 1965.* Washington, DC: Government Printing Office, 1972–73 (C3.223/10:970/v.2/pt.7E) (Tables 13,14).

1113. ———. *1970 Census of Population.* Vol. 2, Subject Report: PC(2)4B—*Persons by Family Characteristics.* Washington, DC: Government Printing Office, 1972–73 (C3.223/10:970/v.2/pt.4B) (Tables 1,2,7–9).

1114. ———. *1970 Census of Population.* Vol. 2, Subject Report: PC(2)4E—*Persons in Institutions and Other Group Quarters.* Washington, DC: Government Printing Office, 1972–73 (C3.223/10:970/v.2/pt.4E) (Tables 16,24–27,54).

1115. ———. *1970 Census of Population.* Vol. 2, Subject Report: PC(2)6B—*Persons not Employed.* Washington, DC: Government Printing Office, 1972–73 (C3.223/ 10:970/v.2/pt.6B) (Tables 3,4).

1116. ———. *1970 Census of Population.* Vol. 2, Subject Report: PC(2)1C—*Persons of Spanish Origin.* Washington, DC: Government Printing Office, 1972–73 (C3.223/ 10:970/v.2/pt.1C) (Tables 6,11,14).

1117. ———. *1970 Census of Population.* Vol. 2, Subject Report: PC(2)1D—*Persons of Spanish Surname.* Washington, DC:

Government Printing Office, 1972–73 (C3.223/10:970/v.2/pt.1D) (Tables 8,11,15).

1118. ———. *1970 Census of Population.* Vol. 2, Subject Report: PC(2)6C—*Persons with Work Disability.* Washington, DC: Government Printing Office, 1972–73 (C3.223/10:970/v.2/pt.6C) (Table 2).

1119. ———. *1970 Census of Population.* Vol. 2, Subject Report: PC(2)1E—*Puerto Ricans in the United States.* Washington, DC: Government Printing Office, 1972–73 (C3.223/10:970/v.2/pt.1E) (Tables 5,8,15–18).

1120. ———. *1970 Census of Population.* Vol. 2, Subject Report: PC(2)6E—*Veterans.* Washington, DC: Government Printing Office, 1972–73 (C3.223/10:970/v.2/ pt.6E) (Tables 2,11).

1121. ———. *1970 Census of Population.* Vol. 2, Subject Report: PC(2)3A—*Women by Number of Children Ever Born.* Washington, DC: Government Printing Office, 1972–73 (C3.223/10:970/v.2/ pt.3A) (Tables 22,23,42,43).

1122. ———. *1970 Census of Population and Housing. Census Tract Reports.* 241 parts. Washington, DC: Government Printing Office, 1972 (C3.223/11:970/pts.1–241) (Table P-1).

1123. U.S. Dept. of Health, Education and Welfare. Division of Asian American Affairs. *Asian American Field Survey: Summary of the Data.* Washington, DC: Government Printing Office, 1977 (HE1.2:As4/2) (Tables 2.09–2.13, 3.09–3.13).

1124. U.S. Law Enforcement Assistance Administration. National Crime Survey. *Criminal Victimization in the United States, 1976.* Washington, DC: Government Printing Office, 1979 (J26.10:SD-NCS-N-9) (Table 10).

1125. U.S. National Center for Health Statistics. *Divorces: Analysis of Changes, United States, 1969.* In its series 21: Data on Natality, Marriage, and Divorce, no. 22. Washington, DC: Government Printing Office, (HE20:2210:21/22) (Figures 1–10, Tables A–Q, 1–22).

1126. ———. *Divorce and Divorce Rates United States.* In its series 21: Data on Natality, Marriage, and Divorce, no. 29. Washington, DC: Government Printing Office, 1978 (HE20.6209:21/29) (Figures 1–6, Tables A–M, 1–26).

1127. ———. *Contraceptive Utilization—United States.* In its series 23: Data from the National Survey of Family Growth, no. 2. Washington, DC: Government Printing Office, 1979 (HE20.6209:23/2) (Tables 19,20).

1128. ———. *Health Characteristics of Low-Income Persons*. In its series 10: Data from the Health Interview Survey, no. 74. Washington, DC: Government Printing Office, 1972 (HE20.2210:10/74) (Tables A,1).

1129. ———. *Marriages, Trends and Characteristics, United States*. In its series 21: Data on Natality, Marriage, and Divorce, no. 21. Washington, DC: Government Printing Office, 1971 (HE20.2210:21/21) (Figure 8, Tables E,5,6).

1130. ———. *Motor Vehicle Accident Deaths in the United States, 1950–67*. In its series 20: Data on Mortality, no. 9. Washington, DC: Government Printing Office, 1970 (HE20.2210:20/9) (Figures 10,11, Tables J,K,9).

1131. ———. *100 Years of Marriage and Divorce Statistics, United States 1867–1967*. In its series 21: Data on Natality, Marriage, and Divorce, no. 24. Washington, DC: Government Printing Office, (HE20.6209:21/24) (Figures 2–6, Tables B,C,E,F,1,2,4,6,9–22,24).

1132. ———. *Selected Symptoms of Psychological Stress, United States*. In its series 11: Data from the Health Examination Survey, no. 37. Washington, DC: Government Printing Office, 1970 (HE20.2210:11/37) (Table 17).

1133. ———. *Teenagers: Marriages, Divorces, Parenthood and Mortality*. In its series 21: Data on Natality, Marriages, and Divorce, no. 23. Washington, DC: Government Printing Office, 1973 (HE20.2210:21/23) (Figure 5, Tables Q,R,S).

1134. ———. *Use Habits among Adults of Cigarettes, Coffee, Aspirin and Sleeping Pills*. In its series 10: Data from the Health Interview Survey, no. 131. Washington, DC: Government Printing Office, 1979 (HE20.6209:10/131) (Tables 3,5,7,9).

1135. U.S. National Criminal Justice and Information Statistics Service. *Capital Punishment, 1977*. Washington, DC: Government Printing Office, 1978 (J26:10:SD–NPS–CP–6) (Tables 14,23,31).

1136. ———. *Capital Punishment, 1978*. Washington, DC: Government Printing Office, 1979 (J26.10:SD–NPS–CP–7) (Table 14).

STRESS

1137. Bloom, Bernard L.; Asher, Shirley J.; and White, Stephen W. "Marital Disruption as a Stressor: A Review and Analysis," *Psychological Bulletin*, vol. 85, no. 4 (1978): 867–94. R.

1138. ———. "Marital Disruption as a Stressful Life Event." In *Divorce and Separation: Context, Causes and Consequences*, edited by George Levinger and Oliver C. Moles, New York: Basic Books, 1979.

1139. Burlage, Dorothy D. "Divorced and Separated Mothers: Combining the Responsibilities of Bread-Winning and Childrearing." Ph.D. diss., Harvard University, 1978 (*DAI* 39/7B, p. 3483, order # 7901705). R.

1140. Chiriboga, David A., and Culer, Loraine. "Stress Responses among Divorcing Men and Women," *Journal of Divorce*, vol. 1, no. 2 (1977): 95–106. R.

1141. Hetherington, E. Mavis; Cox, Martha; and Cox, Roger. "Stress and Coping in Divorce: A Focus on Women." In *Psychology and Women: In Transition*, edited by Jeanne E. Gullahorn, pp. 95–128. Washington, DC: V. H. Winston & Sons, 1979. R.

1142. McMurray, Lucille. "Emotional Stress and Driving Performance: The Effect of Divorce," *Behavioral Research in Highway Safety*, vol. 1, no. 2 (1970): 100–14. R.

1143. Myers, Jerome K.; Lindenthal, Jacob J.; and Pepper, Max P. "Social Class, Life Events, and Psychiatric Symptoms." In *Stressful Life Events: Their Nature and Effects*, edited by Barbara S. Dohrenwend and Bruce P. Dohrenwend, pp. 191–205. New York: John Wiley, 1974.

1144. Pearlin, Leonard I., and Johnson, Joyce S. "Marital Status, Life-Strains and Depression," *American Sociological Review*, vol. 42, no. 5 (1977): 704–15. R.

1145. Raschke, Helen J. "The Development of a Post Separation/Post Divorce Problems and Stress Scale," *Resources in Education* 14 (1979): ERIC document ED 170 619.

1146. Tcheng-Laroche, Françoise, and Prince, Raymond H. "Middle Income, Divorced Female Heads of Families—Their Lifestyles, Health and Stress Levels," *Canadian Journal of Psychiatry*, vol. 24, no. 1 (1979): 35–42. R.

SUICIDE

1147. Bagley, Christopher, and Greer, Steven. "Clinical and Social Predictions of Repeated Attempted Suicide: A Multivariate Analysis," *British Journal of Psychiatry* 119 (1971): 515–21. R.

1148. Gove, Walter R. "Sex, Marital Status and Suicide," *Journal of Health and Social Behavior*, vol. 13, no. 2 (1972): 204–13. R.

1149. Heer, David, and MacKinnon, Douglas. "Suicide and Marital Status—Rejoinder to Rico-Velasco and Mynko," *Journal of Marriage and the Family*, vol. 36, no. 1 (1974): 6–11. R.

1150. Herman, Sonya J. "Women, Divorce and Suicide," *Journal of Divorce*, vol. 1, no. 2 (1977): 107–17. R.

1151. Jacobson, Gerald F., and Portuges, Stephen H. "Relation of Marital Separation and Divorce to Suicide: A Report," *Suicide and Life-Threatening Behavior*, vol. 8, no. 4 (1978): 217–24. R.

1152. Kraft, David P., and Babigian, Haroutun M. "Suicide by Persons with and without Psychiatric Contacts, *Archives of General Psychiatry*, vol. 33, no. 2 (1976): 209–15. R.

1153. Krauss, Herbert H., and Tesser, A. "Social Context of Suicide," *Journal of Abnormal Psychology*, vol. 78, no. 2 (1971): 222–28. R.

1154. Lester, David, and Beck, Aaron T. "Early Loss as a Possible 'Sensitizer' to Later Loss in Attempted Suicides," *Psychological Reports*, vol. 39, no. 1 (1976): 121–22. R.

1155. Morris, Jeffrey B., et al. "Notes toward an Epidemiology of Urban Suicide," *Comprehensive Psychiatry*, vol. 15, no. 6 (1974): 537–47. R.

1156. Rico-Velasco, Jesus, and Mynko, Lizabeth. "Suicide and Marital Status: A Changing Relationship?" *Journal of Marriage and the Family*, vol. 5, no. 2 (1973): 239–44. R.

1157. Schrut, Albert H., and Michels, Toni. "Suicidal Divorced and Discarded Women," *American Academy of Psychoanalysis Journal*, vol. 2, no. 4 (1974): 329–47. R.

1158. Schrut, Albert H. "Suicide Wish among Divorcees," *Intellect*, vol. 104, no. 2373 (1975–76): 418–19. R.

1159. Simon, Werner, and Lumry, Gayle K. "Suicide of the Spouse as a Divorce Substitute," *Diseases of the Nervous System*, vol. 31, no. 9 (1970): 608–12. R.

1160. Vigderhous, Gideon, and Fishman, Gideon. "The Impact of Unemployment and Family Integration on Changing Suicide Rates in the U.S.A., 1920–1969," *Social Psychiatry*, vol. 13, no. 4 (1978): 239–48. R.

FATHER ABSENCE

1161. Aldous, Joan. "Children's Perception of Adult Role Assignment: Father-Absence, Class, Race, and Sex Influences," *Journal of Marriage and the Family*, vol. 34, no. 1 (1972): 55–65. R.

1162. Atkinson, Brian R., and Ogston, Donald G. "Effect of Father Absence on Male Children in the Home and School," *Journal of School Psychology*, vol. 12, no. 3 (1974): 213–21. R.

1163. Bernhardt, Jeanne R. "The Young Child's Perception of the Father's Role Using a Comparison of Age, Sex, and Father-Absent, Father-Present Family Composition." Ph.D. diss., Brigham Young University, 1975 (*DAI* 35/10B, p. 4955, order # 758018). R.

1164. Biller, Henry B. *Paternal Deprivation: Family, School, Sexuality, and Society*. Lexington, MA: Lexington Books, 1974.

1165. Biller, Henry B., and Meredith, Dennis L. "The Invisible American Father." In *Sexual Issues in Marriage: A Contemporary Perspective*, edited by Leonard Gross, pp. 277–89. New York: Halsted Press, 1975.

1166. Colletta, Nancy D. "The Impact of Divorce: Father Absence or Poverty?" *Journal of Divorce*, vol. 3, no. 1 (1979): 27–35. R.

1167. Cook, Helen. "Big Brother for the Fatherless," *Elementary School Guidance and Counseling*, vol. 6, no. 2 (1971): 142–43.

1168. Davidson, Charles W.; Bell, Michael L.; and Gore, Delores. "The Prediction of Drug Use through Discriminate Analysis from Variables Common to Potential Secondary School Dropouts," *Journal of Educational Research*, vol. 72, no. 6 (1979): 313–16. R.

1169. Duke, Marshall P., and Lancaster, William, Jr. "A Note on Locus of Control as a Function of Father Absence," *Journal of Genetic Psychology*, vol. 129, no. 2 (1976): 335–36. R.

1170. Fakouri, M. Ebrahim. "Relationship among Differences in Fantasy Pattern, IQ, and Sex-Role Adaptation," *Psychological Reports* 44 (June 1979): 775–81. R.

1171. Gooblar, Howard M. "Double Bind: Aspects of the Communicational Style of the Father–Absent Family." Ph.D. diss., California School of Professional Psychology, Fresno, 1978 (*DAI* 39/8B, p. 4030, order # 7901804). R.

1172. Grossberg, Sidney H., and Crandall, Louise. "Father Loss and Father Absence in Pre-school Children," *Clinical Social Work Journal*, vol. 6, no. 2 (1978): 123–34.

1173. Hainline, Louise, and Feig, Ellen. "The Correlates of Childhood Father Absence in College-Aged Women," *Child Development*, vol. 49, no. 1 (1978): 37–42. R.

1174. Hamilton, Marshall L. *Father's Influence on Children*. Chicago: Nelson-Hall, 1977.

1175. Herzog, Elizabeth, and Sudia, Cecelia E. *Boys in Fatherless Families*. Washington, DC: U.S. Department of Health, Education, and Welfare, Office of Child Development, Children's Bureau, 1971.

1176. ———. "Children in Fatherless Families." In *Review of Child Development Research*, edited by Bettye M. Caldwell and Henry Ricciuti, pp. 141–232. Chicago: University of Chicago Press, 1973.

1177. ———. "Families without Fathers," *Childhood Education*, vol. 48, no. 4 (1972): 175–81.

1178. ———. "Fatherless Homes: A Review of Research." In *Readings in Child Development*, edited by I.R. Weiner, pp. 230–39. New York: John Wiley & Sons, 1972.

1179. Hunt, L. L., and Hunt, J. G. "Race and the Father-Son Connection: The Conditional Relevance of Father Absence for the Orientation and Identities of Adolescent Boys," *Social Problems*, vol. 23, no. 1 (1975–76): 35–52. R.

1180. Kestenbaum, Clarice J., and Stone, Michael H. "Effects of Fatherless Homes upon Daughters: Clinical Impressions Regarding Paternal Deprivation," *American Academy of Psychoanalysis Journal*, vol. 4, no. 2 (1976): 171–90. R.

1181. Kriesberg, Louis. *Mothers in Poverty: A Study of Fatherless Families*. Chicago: Aldine Publishing Co., 1970. R.

1182. Newman, Gustav, and Denman, Sidney B. "Felony and Paternal Deprivation: A Socio-Psychiatric Review," *International Journal of Social Psychiatry*, vol. 17, no. 1 (1970–71): 65–71. R.

1183. Pedersen, Frank A. "Does Research on Children Reared in Father-Absent Families Yield Information on Father Influences?" *Family Coordinator*, vol. 25, no. 4 (1976): 459–64.

1184. Polansky, Norman, et al. "Absent Father in Child Neglect," *Social Service Review* 53 (June 1979): 163–74. R.

1185. Santrock, John W., and Wohlford, Paul. "The Effects of Father Absence: Influence of the Reason for and the Onset of the Absence," *Proceedings of the 78th Annual Convention of the American Psychological Association* 5 (1970): 265–66. R.

1186. Seegmiller, Bonni R. "Effects of Maternal Employment on Sex-Role Differentials in Preschoolers," *Resources in Education* 15 (1980). ERIC document ED 175 579. R.

1187. Shinn, Marybeth. "Father Absence and Children's Cognitive Development," *Psychological Bulletin*, vol. 85, no. 2 (1978): 295–324.

1188. Vargon, Melanie M. "Effects of Father Absence on Women's Perception of 'Ideal' Mate and Father," Master's thesis, University of California, Davis. 1975. R.

1189. Vargon, Melanie M., et al. "Effects of Father Absence on Women's Perception of 'Ideal' Mate and Father," *Multivariate Experimental Clinical Research*, vol. 2, no. 1 (1976): 33–42. R.

BIBLIOGRAPHY

1190. Honig, Alice S. "Fathering: A Bibliography," *Resources in Education* 12 (1977). ERIC document ED 142 293.

BLACK FAMILIES

1191. Badaines, Joel S. "Identification, Imitation, and Sex-Role Preference in Father-Present and Father-Absent Black and Chicano Boys," *Journal of Psychology,* vol. 92, no. 1 (1976): 15–24. R.

1192. ———. "Identification, Imitation and Sex-Role Preference as a Function of Father-Absence and Father-Presence in Black and Chicano Boys." Ph.D. diss., University of South Carolina, 1972 (*DAI* 34/1B, p. 403, order # 7316294). R.

1193. Dean, Katherine I. "Father Absence, Feminine Identification, and Assertive-Aggressiveness: A Test of Compulsive Masculinity among Institutionalized Negro Juvenile Delinquents." Ph.D. diss., Florida State University, 1970 (*DAI* 31/9A, p. 4912, order # 716994). R.

1194. Earl, Loveline, and Lohmann, Nancy. "Absent Fathers and Black Male Children," *Social Work,* vol. 23, no. 5 (1978): 413–15. R.

1195. Glautz, Oscar. "Family Structure, Fate Control, and Counter-Normative Political Beliefs among Lower-Class Black Students," *College Student Journal,* vol. 10, no. 2 (1976): 121–25. R.

1196. Hartnagle, Timothy F. "Father Absence and Self Conception among Lower Class White and Negro Boys," *Social Problems,* vol. 18, no. 2 (1970): 152–63. R.

1197. Hunt, Janet G., and Hunt, Larry L. "Race, Daughters and Father-Loss: Does Absence Make the Girl Grow Stronger?" *Social Problems,* vol. 25, no. 1 (1977): 90–102. R.

1198. Keller, Peter A., and Murray, Edward J. "Imitative Aggression with Adult Male and Female Models in Father Absent and Father Present Negro Boys," *Journal of Genetic Psychology,* vol. 122, no. 2 (1973): 217–21. R.

1199. Masingale, Eula M. "Father-Absence as Related to Parental Role-Play Behavior." Ph.D. diss., Michigan State University, 1971 (*DAI* 32/12B, p. 7294, order # 7216475). R.

1200. Matthews, Graham P. "Father-Absence and the Development of Masculine Identification in Black Preschool Males." Ph.D. diss., University of Michigan, 1976 (*DAI* 37/03A, p. 1458, order # 7619189). R.

1201. Mumbauer, Corinne C., and Gray, Susan W. "Resistance to Temptation in Young Negro Children," *Child Development,* vol. 41, no. 4 (1970): 1203–07. R.

1202. Patterson, Sandra K. "Gender Identity as Seen in Drawings of Father Absent 5 to 7 Year Old Black Children," *Resources in Education* 12 (1977). ERIC document ED 141 463. R.

1203. Rubin, Roger H. "Adult Male Absence and the Self-Attitudes of Black Children," *Child Study Journal,* vol. 4, no. 1 (1974): 33–46. R.

1204. ———. *Matricentric Family Structure and the Self-Attitudes of Negro Children.* San Francisco, CA: R and E Research Associates, 1976. R.

1205. ———. "Matricentric Family Structure and the Self-Attitudes of Negro Children," *Resources in Education* 12 (1977). ERIC document ED 137 428. R.

1206. Sciara, Frank J. "Effects of Father Absence on the Educational Achievement of Urban Black Children," *Child Study Journal,* vol. 5, no. 1 (1975): 45–55. R.

1207. ———. "Father Absence, an Overlooked Factor in the Lack of Achievement of Black Children in Title I Schools," *Resources in Education* 12 (1977). ERIC document ED 137 493. R.

1208. Wasserman, Herbert L. "A Comparative Study of School Performance among Boys from Broken and Intact Black Families," *Journal of Negro Education,* vol. 41, no. 2 (1972): 137–41. R.

CHILDREN'S ACADEMIC ACHIEVEMENT

1209. Bernstein, Barbara E. "How Father Absence in the Home Affects the Mathematics Skills of Fifth-Graders," *Family Therapy,* vol. 3, no. 1 (1976): 47–59. R.

1210. Blanchard, Robert W., and Biller, Henry B. "Father Availability and Academic Performance among Third Grade Boys," *Developmental Psychology,* vol. 4, no. 3 (1971): 301–05. R.

1211. Brightman, Lloyd A. "The Differential Use of Interpersonal Resources by Father-Absent Adolescents as a Correlate of Their School Achievement." Ph.D. diss., Cornell University, 1971 (*DAI* 31/1A, p. 562, order # 7117093). R.

1212. Chapman, Michael. "Father Absence, Stepfathers, and the Cognitive Performance of College Students," *Child Development,* vol. 48, no. 3 (1977): 1155–58. R.

1213. Courtney, Dan E. "The Effect of Male Teachers on the Academic Achievement of Sixth Grade Father-Absent Boys." Ph.D. diss., Kansas State University, 1977 (*DAI* 38/9A, p. 5232, order # 7800807). R.

1214. Courtney, Dan, and Schell, Leo M. "The Effects of Male Teachers on the Reading Achievement of Father-Absent Sixth Grade Boys," *Reading Improvement,* vol. 15, no. 4 (1978): 253–56. R.

1215. Dawson, Paul. "Fatherless Boys, Teacher Perceptions, and Male Teacher Influence: A Pilot Study, Final Report," *Resources in Education* 6 (1971). ERIC document ED 048 616. R.

1216. Fowler, Patrick C. "Multivariate Assessments of the Effects of Early Father-Absence on the Educational Preparedness and Academic Achievement of Black Children." Ph.D. diss., University of Virginia, 1977 (*DAI* 38/7A, p. 4043, order # 7728616). R.

1217. Fowler, Patrick C., and Richards, Herbert C. "Father Absence, Educational Preparedness, and Academic Achievement: A Test of the Confluence Model," *Journal of Educational Psychology,* vol. 70, no. 4 (1978): 595–601. R.

1218. Lessing, Elsie E.; Zagorin, Susan W.; and Nelson, Dorothy. "WISC Subtest and IQ Score Correlates of Father Absence," *Journal of Genetic Psychology,* vol. 117, no. 2 (1970): 181–95. R.

1219. Longabaugh, Richard. "Mother Behavior as a Variable Moderating the Effects of Father Absence," *Ethos,* vol. 1, no. 4 (1973): 456–65. R.

1220. Mueller, E. Jane. "The Effects of Father Absence on Word Analysis Skills among Head Start Children," *Resources in Education,* 12 (1977). ERIC document ED 104 570. R.

1221. Parrow, Alan A. "Race, Father Absence and Educational Ambition of Adolescent Males," *Resources in Education* 13 (1978). ERIC document ED 148 984. R.

1222. Schell, Leo M., and Courtney, Dan. "Effect of Male Teachers on the Academic Achievement of Father-Absent Sixth Grade Boys," *Journal of Educational Research,* vol. 72, no. 4 (1979): 194–96. R.

1223. Sciara, Frank J. "Father Absence: An Overlooked Factor in the Academic Achievement of Urban Disadvantaged Children," *Resources in Education* 13 (1978). ERIC document ED 150–233. R.

1224. Sciara, Frank J., and Jantz, Richard K. "Father Absence and Its Apparent Effect on the Reading Achievement of Black Children from Low Income Families," *Journal of Negro Education*, vol. 43, no. 2 (1974): 221–27. R.

1225. Solomon, Daniel, et al. "Family Characteristics and Elementary School Achievement in an Urban Ghetto," *Journal of Consulting and Clinical Psychology*, vol. 39, no. 3 (1972): 462–66. R.

1226. Vroegh, Karen S. "The Relationship of Sex of Teacher and Father Presence-Absence to Academic Achievement." Ph.D. diss., Northwestern University, 1972 (*DAI* 33/10A, p. 5569, order # 7310310). R.

1227. ———. "The Relationship of Sex of Teacher and Father Presence-Absence to Academic Achievement," *Resources in Education* 8 (1973). ERIC document ED 070 026. R.

CHILDREN'S ADJUSTMENT

1228. Drayton, Ethel L. "The Effect of Father Absence upon Social Adjustment of Male and Female Institutionalized Delinquents." Ph.D. diss., Fordham University, 1978 (*DAI* 38/12A, p. 7223, order # 7808992). R.

1229. Kopf, Kathryn E. "Family Variables and School Adjustment of Eighth Grade Father-Absent Boys," *Family Coordinator*, vol. 19, no. 2 (1970): 145–50.

1230. Moerk, Ernst L. "Like Father like Son: Imprisonment of Fathers and the Psychological Adjustment of Sons," *Journal of Youth and Adolescence*, vol. 2, no. 4 (1973): 303–12. R.

1231. Steinberg, Marvin A. "Child's Coping Behaviors Related to Father Absence." Ph.D. diss., University of Texas, Austin, 1974 (*DAI* 35/1B, p. 490, order # 7414770). R.

1232. Summers, George M. "Paternal Deprivation and Adaptation: A Study of Differential Loss Management in Latency Age Father-Absent Boys." D.S.W. diss., Smith College of Social Work, 1970 (*DAI* 31/10, p. 5524, order # 719616). R.

1233. Young, Earl R., and Parish, Thomas S. "Impact of Father Absence during Childhood on the Psychological Adjustment of College Females," *Sex Roles*, vol. 3, no. 3 (1977): 217–27. R.

1234. ———. "Impact of Father Absence during Childhood on College Age Females' Psychological Adjustment," *Resources in Education* 13 (1978). ERIC document ED 149 216. R.

1235. Zold, Anthony C. "The Effects of Father Absence during Childhood on Later Adjustment: A Long Term Follow-Up." Ph.D. diss., University of Minnesota, 1975 (*DAI* 36/4B, p. 1648, order # 7521108). R.

CHILDREN'S BEHAVIOR

1236. Austin, Roy L. "Race, Father-Absence, and Female Delinquency," *Criminology*, vol. 15, no. 4 (1978): 487–504. R.

1237. Boone, Sherle L. "Effects of Fathers' Absence and Birth Order on Aggressive Behavior of Young Male Children," *Psychological Reports*, 44 (June 1979): 1223–29. R.

1238. Castellano, Vianne M. "The Effects of Early Father Absence and the Level of Antisocial Behavior on the Development of Social Egocentrism in Adolescent Mexican American Girls." Ph.D. diss., University of Southern California, 1978 (*DAI* 39/5A, p. 2825). R.

1239. Marcelous, Elinor W. "Investigation of the Father-Absent Family as a Causitive Factor in Juvenile Delinquency." Master's thesis, California State University, Hayward, 1979. R.

1240. Moran, Patricia A. "The Effects of Father Absence on Delinquent Males: Dependency and Hypermasculinity." Ph.D. diss., Saint Louis University, 1972 (*DAI* 33/3B, p. 1292, order # 7223978). R.

1241. Reyes, Tito F. "Father Absence and the Social Behavior of Preschool Children." Ph.D. diss., Michigan State University, 1977 (*DAI* 39/1A, p. 185, order # 7810100). R.

1242. Santrock, John W. "Effects of Father Absence on Sex-Types Behaviors in Male Children: Reason for Absence and Age of Onset of the Absence," *Journal of Genetic Psychology*, vol. 130, no. 1 (1977): 3–10. R.

1243. Schaengold, Marilyn. "The Relationship between Father-Absence and Encopresis," *Child Welfare*, vol. 56, no. 6 (1977): 386–94.

CHILDREN'S MORAL DEVELOPMENT

1244. Cox, Martha J. "The Effects of Father Absence and Working Mothers on Children." Ph.D. diss., University of Virginia, 1975 (*DAI* 36/7B, p. 3640, order # 7522139). R.

1245. Goldstein, Harris S. "Internal Controls in Aggressive Children from Father-Present and Father-Absent Families," *Journal of Consulting and Clinical Psychology*, vol. 39, no. 3 (1972): 512. R.

1246. Hoffman, Martin L. "Father Absence and Conscience Development," *Developmental Psychology*, vol. 4, no. 3 (1971): 400–06. R.

1247. Santrock, John W. "Father Absence, Perceived Maternal Behavior and Moral Development in Boys," *Child Development*, vol. 46, no. 3 (1975): 753–57. R.

CHILDREN'S PSYCHOLOGICAL DEVELOPMENT

1248. Baptiste, David A. "A Comparative Study of Mothers' Personality Characteristics and Childrearing Attitudes in Husband-Present and Husband-Absent Families." Ph.D. diss., Purdue University, 1976 (*DAI* 37/10A, p. 6263, order # 777414). R.

1249. Becker, Stephen. "Father Absence and Its Relationship to Creativity," *Graduate Research in Education and Related Disciplines*, vol. 7, no. 2 (1974): 32–52. R.

1250. Biller, Henry B. "Father Absence and Personality Development of Male Child," *Developmental Psychology*, vol. 2, no. 2 (1970): 181–201. R.

1251. ———. "The Father and Personality Development: Paternal Deprivation and Sex Role Development." In *The Role of the Father in Child Development*, edited by Michael E. Lamb, pp. 89–156. New York, John Wiley & Sons, 1976.

1252. ———. "The Mother-Child Relationship and Father-Absent Boy's Personality Development," *Merrill-Palmer Quarterly*, vol. 17, no. 3 (1971): 227–41. R.

1253. Biller, Henry B., and Bahm, Robert M. "Father Absence, Perceived Maternal Behavior, and Masculinity of Self-Concept among Junior High-School Boys," *Developmental Psychology*, vol. 4, no. 2 (1971): 178–81. R.

1254. Cantey, Richard E. "The Relationship of Father-Absence, Socioeconomic Status, and other Variables to Creative Abilities in Fifth-Grade Boys." Ph.D. diss., University of Southern California, 1973 (*DAI* 34/7A, p. 3981, order # 7331635). R.

1255. Gershansky, Ira S.; Hainline, Louise; and Goldstein, Harris S. "Maternal Differentiation, Onset and Type of Father's Absence and Psychological Differentiation in Children," *Perceptual and Motor Skills*, vol. 3, no. 2, pt. 2 (1978): 1147–52. R.

1256. Gourley, Ruth L. "Premarital Pregnancy as Related to Father-Absent Homes." *Conciliation Courts Review*, vol. 10, no. 2 (1972): 23–26.

1257. Hetherington, E. Mavis. "Effects of Father-Absence on Personality Development in Adolescent Daughters," *Developmental Psychology*, vol. 7, no. 3 (1972): 313–26. R.

1258. Hetherington, E. Mavis, and Deur, Jan L. "The Effects of Father Absence on Child Development," *Young Children*, vol. 26, no. 4 (1971): 233–48.

1259. Holman, Adele M. "The Impact of Father Absence on Achievement Motivation in Women." D.S.W. diss., Adelphi University, 1977 (*DAI* 39/1A, p. 468, order # 7810244). R.

1260. Hooker, Lizzie B. "The Race of Father-Absent Children as Related to Selected Aspects of Personality." Master's thesis, Fisk University, 1977–78. R.

1261. Imperio, Anne-Marie. "Ego Development, Father Status, and Perception of Parents in Psychopathic, Neurotic, and Subcultural Delinquents." Ph.D. diss., Fordham University, 1975 (*DAI* 36/8B, p. 4133, order # 764166). R.

1262. Kagel, Stephen A.; White, Raymond M.; and Coyne, James C. "Father-Absent and Father-Present Families of Disturbed and Nondisturbed Adolescents," *American Journal of Orthopsychiatry*, vol. 48, no. 2 (1978): 342–52. R.

1263. Kagel, Steven A. "Father-Absent Males, Sexual Identification, and Gender Identity." Ph.D. diss., Miami University, 1978 (*DAI* 39/4B, p. 1960, order # 7818678). R.

1264. McGuire, William J.; McGuire, Claire V.; and Winton, Ward. "Effects of Household Sex Composition on the Salience of One's Gender in the Spontaneous Self-Concept," *Journal of Experimental Social Psychology* 15 (January 1979): 77–90. R.

1265. Marino, Cena D., and McCowan, Richard J. "The Effects of Parent Absence on Children," *Child Study Journal*, vol. 6, no. 3 (1976): 165–82.

1266. Montare, Alberto, and Boone, Sherle. "Aggression and Paternal Absence: Racial Differences among Inner-City Males," *Resources in Education* 13 (1978). ERIC document ED 152 936. R.

1267. Oshman, Harvey P. "Some Effects of Father-Absence upon the Psychosocial Development of Male and Female Late Adolescents: Theoretical and Empirical Considerations." Ph.D. diss., University of Texas, Austin, 1975 (*DAI* 36/2B, p. 919, order # 7516719). R.

1268. Oshman, Harvey P., and Manosevitz, Martin. "Death Fantasies of Father-Absent and Father-Present Late Adolescents," *Journal of Youth and Adolescence*, vol. 7, no. 1 (1978): 41–48. R.

1269. Pedersen, Frank, et al. "Father Absence in Infancy," *Research in Education* 9 (1974). ED 085 088. R.

1270. Pedersen, Frank A.; Rubenstein, Judith L.; and Yarrow, Leon J. "Infant Development in Father-Absent Families," *Journal of Genetic Psychology*, vol. 135, no. 1 (1979): 51–61. R.

1271. Santrock, John W. "Influence of Onset of and Type of Paternal Absence on the First Four Eriksonian Developmental Crises," *Developmental Psychology*, vol. 3, no. 2 (1970): 273–74. R.

1272. ———. "Paternal Absence, Sex Typing, and Identification," *Developmental Psychology*, vol. 2, no. 2 (1970): 264–72. R.

1273. ———. "Relation of Type and Onset of Father Absence to Cognitive Development," *Child Development*, vol. 43, no. 2 (1972): 455–69. R.

1274. Shill, Merton A. "TAT Measures of Core Gender Identity (Castration Anxiety), Parental Introjects and Assertiveness in Father Absent Males," Ph.D. diss., University of Michigan, 1978 (*DAI* 39/10B, p. 5087, order # 7907168). R.

1275. Thompson, Beatrice R. "The Effects of Father Absence on the Arithmetic Achievement, Self-Concept and School Adjustment of Elementary School Children." Ph.D. diss., University of Georgia, 1978 (*DAI* 39/12A, p. 7254, order # 7914062). R.

1276. Trachtman, Richard S. "Father Absence during the Oedipal Phase of Development." D.S.W. diss., Smith College for Social Work, 1978 (*DAI* 39/6A, p. 3846, order # 7823719). R.

1277. van Bergen, Adriane. "Relationship of Early Father Absence on Sexual Attitudes and Self-Concept of Adult Women." Ph.D. diss., United States International University, 1976 (*DAI* 39/11B, p. 5528, order # 7909639). R.

CHILDREN'S SEX ROLE DEVELOPMENT

1278. Brody, Stephen A. "Men in the Nursery: The Effects of a Predominately Male Staffed Preschool on the Development of Gender Identity, Social Sex Role, and Attitudes toward Men of Father-Absent-Children." Ph.D. diss., California School of Professional Psychology, Los Angeles, 1978 (*DAI* 40/2B, p. 980, order # 7915770). R.

1279. Burns, Robert A. "The Effect of Father's Absence on the Development of the Masculine Identification of Boys in Residential Treatment." Ph.D. diss., Saint John's University, 1971 (*DAI* 32/7B, p. 4179, order # 722973). R.

1280. Drake, Charles T., and McDougall, Daniel. "Effects of the Absence of a Father and Other Male Models on the Development of Boys' Sex Roles," *Developmental Psychology*, vol. 13, no. 5 (1977): 537–38. R.

1281. Horowitz, June A. "An Exploratory Investigation of the Effects of Father Loss on the Adolescent Girls' Sex-Role Identity, Self-Esteem and Locus of Control," *Perspectives* 1 (March 1976): 10–12. R.

1282. Hull, Darrell M. "Examination of Three Maternal Characteristics in Relationship to Sex-Role Development in Father-Present and Father-Absent Children." Ph.D. diss., University of Washington, 1975 (*DAI* 37/2A, p. 807, order # 76–17507). R.

1283. Jones, Hugh E. "Father Absence During Childhood, Maternal Attitudes toward Men, and Sex-Role Development of Male College Students." Ph.D. diss., Michigan State University, 1975 (*DAI* 36/6B, p. 3047, order # 7527281). R.

1284. Muir, Martha F. "Differential Effects of Father Absence on Sex-Role Identity as a Function of Sex, Age at Time of Divorce, and Step-Parent Availability." Ph.D. diss., University of Oklahoma, 1977 (*DAI* 38/9A, p. 5744, order # 7732874). R.

1285. Pipher, Mary B. "The Effects of Father Absence on the Sexual Development and Adjustment of Adolescent Daughters and Their Mothers." Ph.D. diss., University of Nebraska, 1977 (*DAI* 38/2B, p. 913, order # 7716665). R.

CHILDREN'S SOCIAL DEVELOPMENT

1286. Atkins, Shirley M. "Opacity and Clarity in the Play Styles of Four-Year-Old Father-Absent and Father-Present Children." Ph.D. diss., University of Pittsburgh, 1975 (*DAI* 36/4A, p. 2043, order # 7522428). R.

1287. Brody, Steve. "Daddy's Gone to Colorado: Male-Staffed Child Care for Father-Absent Boys," *Counseling Psychologist*, vol. 7, no. 4 (1978): 33–36.

1288. Fox, Billy R. "Effect of Public Welfare, Affiliation, Absence of a Father Figure and Other Selected Variable Factors on the Development of Socialization, Maturity, Responsibility and Intrapersonal Structures of Values among Male High School Adolescents." Ph.D. diss., University of Southern Mississippi, 1972 (*DAI* 33/4A, p. 1864, order # 7226544). R.

1289. French-Wixson, Judith. "Differences between Father-Absent and Father-Present Fifth Grade Boys in Political Socialization." Ph.D. diss., Florida State University, 1976 (*DAI* 37/10A, p. 6337, order # 778582). R.

1290. LeCorgne, Lyle L., and Laosa, Luis M. "Father Absence in Low-Income Mexican-American Families: Children's Social Adjustment and Conceptual Differentiation of Sex Role Attributes," *Developmental Psychology*, vol. 12, no. 5 (1976): 470–71. R.

1291. Lowery, Donald W. "Classroom Dependency and Modeling Behavior of Father-Absent and Father-Present Preschool Boys with a Male Teacher." Ed.D. diss., Temple University, 1977 (*DAI* 39/2A, p. 759, order # 7812278). R.

1292. Nelsen, Edward, and Vangen, Patricia. "Impact of Father Absence on Heterosexual Behaviors and Social Development of Preadolescent Girls in a Ghetto Environment," *Resources in Education* 7 (1972). ERIC document ED 055 126. R.

ONE-PARENT FAMILIES

1293. Abraham, Willard. "The Single Parent Family," *Day Care and Early Education*, vol. 6, no. 4 (1979): 54.

1294. Baden-Marotz, Ramona, et al. "Family Form or Family Process? Reconsidering the Deficit Family Model Approach," *Family Coordinator*, vol. 28, no. 1 (1979): 5-14.

1295. Barringer, Kenneth D. "Self Perception of the Quality of Adjustment of Single Parents in Divorce Participating in Parents Without Partners Organizations." Ph.D. diss., University of Iowa, 1973 (*DAI* 34/7A, p. 4446, order # 7330895). R.

1296. Barry, Ann. "Research Project on Successful Single-Parent Families," *American Journal of Family Therapy*, vol. 7, no. 3 (1979): 65–73. R.

1297. Bernard, Jessie S., et al. *Self Portrait of a Family*. Boston: Beacon Press, 1978.

1298. Bond, Catherine. "The Challenge of Single Parenting," *Conciliation Courts Review*, vol. 14, no. 2 (1976): 26–28.

1299. Brandwein, Ruth A. "After Divorce: Focus on Single Parent Families," *Urban and Social Change Review*, vol. 10, no. 1 (1977): 21–25.

1300. Brandwein, Ruth A.; Brown, Carol A.; Fox, Elizabeth M. "Women and Children Last: The Social Situation of Divorced Mothers and Their Families," *Journal of Marriage and the Family*, vol. 36, no. 3 (1974): 498–514.

1301. Bronfenbrenner, Urie. "The Family Circle: A Study in Fragmentation," *National Elementary Principal*, vol. 55, no. 6 (1976): 11–25. R.

1302. Burgess, Jane K. "Single Parent Family: Social and Sociological Problem," *Family Coordinator*, vol. 19, no. 2 (1970): 137–44.

1303. Changing Family Conference (5th) University of Iowa. *The Single Parent Family*. Edited by Susan Burden. Iowa City, IA: University of Iowa, 1976.

1304. Cline, Brenda J. "A Construct Validity Study of Disengagement-Enmeshment: Some Individual, Family, and Sociocultural Correlates." Ph.D. diss., George Peabody College for Teachers, 1977 (*DAI* 38/5B, p. 2356, order # 7725090). R.

1305. Cobe, Patricia. "Parenting Alone," *Forecast for Home Economics* 24 (April 1979): 27.

1306. DeFronzo, James, and Warkov, Seymour. "Are Female-Headed Households Energy Efficient: A Test of Klausner's Hypothesis among Anglo, Spanish-Speaking, and Black Texas Households," *Human Ecology*, vol. 7, no. 2 (1979): 191–97. R.

1307. Dell, Paul F., and Appelbaum, Alan S. "Trigenerational Enmeshment: Unresolved Ties of Single-Parents to Family of Origin," *American Journal of Orthopsychiatry*, vol. 47, no. 1 (1977): 52–59.

1308. Dinerman, Miriam. "Catch 23: Women, Work, and Welfare," *Social Work*, vol. 22, no. 6 (1977): 472–77.

1309. Dresen, Sheila. "Adjusting to Single Parenting," *American Journal of Nursing*, vol. 76, no. 8 (1976): 1286–89.

1310. Duncan, Greg J. "Unmarried Heads of Households and Marriage." In *Five Thousand American Families: Patterns of Economic Progress*, pp. 77–115, vol. 4. Ann Arbor, MI: University of Michigan, Survey Research Center, 1974. R.

1311. Epstein, Marsha F. "Children Living in One-Parent Families," *Family Economics Review* 21 (Winter 1979): 21–23.

1312. Falk, Phyllis L. C. "One out of Five and Largely Ignored," *National Elementary Principal,* vol. 59, no. 1 (1979): 76–80.

1313. Farley, Florence S. "Scholastic Ability and Birth Order, Family Size, Sibling Age Spacing, and Parental Absence in Eighth and Ninth Graders: An Empirical Study of the Confluence Model." Ph.D. diss., Kent State University, 1977 (*DAI* 38/10A, p. 6008, order # 7802767). R.

1314. Horowitz, June A., and Perdue, Bobbie J. "Single-Parent Families," *Nursing Clinics of North America,* vol. 12, no. 3 (1977): 503–11.

1315. Hynes, Winifred J. "Single Parent Mothers and Distress: Relationships between Selected Social and Psychological Factors and Distress in Low-Income Single Parent Mothers." D.S.W. diss., Catholic University of America, 1979 (*DAI* 40/3A, p. 1686, order # 7920551). R.

1316. Jacobs, Laura J. "Problems of the Single Parent." Master's thesis, Bank Street College of Education, 1978.

1317. Jauch, Carol. "The One-Parent Family," *Journal of Clinical Child Psychology,* vol. 6, no. 2 (1977): 30–32.

1318. Kaplan, Howard B., and Pokorny, Alex D. "Self-Derogation and Childhood Broken Home," *Journal of Marriage and the Family,* vol. 33, no. 2 (1971): 328–37. R.

1319. Kaseman, Charlotte M. "The Single-Parent Family," *Perspectives in Psychiatric Care,* vol. 12, no. 3 (1974): 113–18.

1320. Kellam, Sheppard G., et al. "Family Structure and the Mental Health of Children," *Archives of General Psychiatry,* vol. 34, no. 9 (1977): 1012–22. R.

1321. Klausner, Samuel Z. "Social Order and Energy Consumption in Matrifocal Households," *Human Ecology,* vol. 7, no. 1 (1979): 21–39. R.

1322. Kruse, Janet K. "Self Esteem in Single-Parent Families." Master's thesis, University of Missouri, Columbia, 1979. R.

1323. Lipten, Claire R. "The Single Parent Family as an Alternative Lifestyle." Ph.D. diss., Wayne State University, 1979 (*DAI* 40/4A, p. 2292, order # 7921688). R.

1324. Loge, Betty J. "Role Adjustments to Single Parenthood: A Study of Divorced and Widowed Men and Women." Ph.D. diss., University of Washington, 1976 (*DAI* 37/7A, p. 4647, order # 77602). R.

1325. Long, Ann P. H. "Children's Perceptions of Peers from One-Parent Families." Ph.D. diss., Duke University, 1979 (*DAI* 40/12A, p. 6206, order # 8012041). R.

1326. McCarthy, Colman. "Mothers Struggling on Their Own," *National Elementary Principal,* vol. 55, no. 6 (1976): 52–53.

1327. Malouf, Roberta E. "Social Bases of Power in Single-Mother and Two-Parent Families." Ph.D. diss., University of Utah, 1979 (*DAI* 40/3B, p. 1374, order # 7920339). R.

1328. ———. "Social Bases of Power in Single and Two-Parent Families," *Resources in Education* 15 (1980). ERIC document ED 177 439. R.

1329. Moore, Kristin A., and Hofferth, Sandra L. "The Consequences of Age at First Childbirth: Female Headed Families and Welfare Recipiency," 1978. Springfield, VA: *Government Reports Announcements and Index* 4 (1979) 5K. PB-289 055/6GA. R.

1330. Morris, Lydia. "Women without Men: Domestic Organization and the Welfare State as Seen in a Coastal Community of Puerto Rico," *British Journal of Sociology* 30 (September 1979): 322–40. R.

1331. Myers, Martha M. "A Group Case Study of Divorced Single Parents." Master's thesis, John Carroll University, Cleveland, 1971. R.

1332. Nelson, Hal, et al. "Alternative Education and the Single-Parent Family," *Resources in Education* 12 (1977). ERIC document ED 141 928.

1333. Ohlson, E. LaMonte. "The Effects of the Female-Based Family and Birth Order on the Ability to Self-Disclose," *Journal of Psychology,* vol. 87, no. 1 (1974): 59–69. R.

1334. Patterson, Joya. "If You're a Woman and Head a Family," *Journal of Home Economics,* vol. 65, no. 1 (1973): 20–22.

1335. Porter, Blaine R. "Single-Parent Families." In *Building Family Strengths: Blueprints for Action,* edited by Nick Stinnett, Barbara Chesser, and John DeFrain, pp. 313–25. Lincoln, NE: University of Nebraska Press, 1979.

1336. Ricci, Isolina. "Dispelling the Stereotype of the 'Broken Home,' " *Conciliation Courts Review,* vol. 12, no. 2 (1974): 7–15.

1337. Ross, Heather L., and Sawhill, Isabel V. *Time of Transition: The Growth of Families Headed by Women.* Washington, DC: Urban Institute, 1975. R.

1338. Sawhill, Isabel V. "Women and Children on Their Own," *Challenge: The Magazine of Economic Affairs,* vol. 19, no. 4 (1976): 32–34.

1339. Schlesinger, Benjamin. "One Parent Families: Knowns and Unknowns," *Conciliation Courts Review,* vol. 17, no. 2 (1972): 41–44.

1340. Shackelford, James N. "A Comparison of the School Adjustment of Ninth Grade Students from Conventional Parent Families and from Single Parent Families in the Parkway School District." Ed.D. diss., Saint Louis University, 1978 (*DAI* 39/9A, p. 6053, order # 7908303). R.

1341. Smidchens, Uldis, and Thompson, Eugene. "Effects of Family Orientation within Socioeconomic Strata upon Basic Skill Achievement," *Resources in Education* 13 (1978). ED 156 931. R.

1342. Stone, Judith P. "Problems of the Single Parent of the Preschool Child," *Day Care and Early Education,* vol. 5, no. 3 (1978): 16–17.

1343. Talkington, Larry, and Simon, Barbara. "Comparison of Broken Home and Stable Home Retardates on Selected Variables," *Training School Bulletin,* vol. 67, no. 2 (1970): 131–36. R.

1344. Thompson, Cheryl L. "Perceptions of Intrafamilial Relationships in Single Parent Lower-Class Families and Male Adolescent Anti-social Behavior." Ph.D. diss., Adlephi University, 1978 (*DAI* 39/4B, p. 1972, order # 7817482). R.

1345. Vonderweidt, Joyce. "The Single Female Headed Family," *North Carolina Psychological Association Bulletin* (Spring 1976): 10–12.

1346. Weininger, Otto. "Effects of Parental Deprivation: An Overview of the Literature and Report on Some Current Research," *Psychological Reports,* vol. 30, no. 2 (1972): 591–612.

1347. Weiss, Robert S. "Going It Alone," *National Elementary Principal,* vol. 59, no. 1 (1979): 14–26+.

1348. ———. *Going It Alone: The Family Life and Social Situation of the Single Parent.* New York: Basic Books, 1979.

1349. ———. "A Preliminary Examination of Potential Contributions of Quality of Life Data to an Understanding of Single Parenting," *Government Reports Announcements and Index* 26 (1976) 5K. PB-258 318/5GA. R.

1350. Welsh, Jane A. "Women as Heads of Household," *National Association of Women Deans and Counselors, vol. 36, no. 3 (1973): 166–69.*

BIBLIOGRAPHY

1351. Burlage, Dorothy D. "A Preliminary Review of Research and Selected Bibliography Related to Separated and Divorced Mothers," *Government Reports Announcements and Index* 26 (1976) 5K. PB-258 317/7GA.

1352. Horner, Catherine T. *The Single Parent Family in Children's Books: An Analysis and Annotated Bibliography, with an Appendix on Audiovisual Material.* Metuchen, NJ: Scarecrow Press, 1978.

1353. National Council for One Parent Families. "One Parent Families—Selected Bibliography: Books, Pamphlets and Articles about Lone Parents and Their Children," *Readers Advisory Service,* vol. 4, no. 1 (1977).

1354. Schlesinger, Benjamin. *The One-Parent Family: Perspectives and Annotated Bibliography.* 3d rev. ed. Toronto: University of Toronto Press, 1975.

1355. ————. *The One-Parent Family: Perspectives and Annotated Bibliography.* 4th ed. Toronto: University of Toronto Press, 1978.

1356. *Varieties of Family Lifestyles: A Selected Annotated Bibliography.* Ottawa: Vanier Institute of the Family, 1977.

BLACK FAMILIES

1357. Farley, Reynolds, and Bianchi, Suzanne. "What Happened in the Decade after the Moynihan Report? A Look at Recent Trends in Family Structure among Blacks and Whites," *Resources in Education* 13 (1978). ERIC document ED 155 571. R.

1358. Hirsch, Seth L. "Home Climate in the Black Single-Parent, Mother-Led Family: A Social-Ecological, Interactional Approach." Ph.D. diss., United States International University, 1979 (*DAI* 40/9B, p. 4485, order # 8007637). R.

1359. LaPoint, Velma D. "A Descriptive Survey of Some Perceptions and Concerns of Black Female Single Parent Families in Lansing, Michigan." Ph.D. diss., Michigan State University, 1977 (*DAI* 38/3A, p. 1231, order # 7718504). R.

1360. Morris, Roger B. "Strengths of the Black Community: An Investigation of the Black Community and 'Broken Homes.' "

Ed.D. diss., Columbia University Teachers College, 1977 (*DAI* 38/3A, p. 1960, order # 7722276). R.

1361. Nelson, Kristine. "Children in Female-Headed Families: A Comparison of Blacks and Whites in California," *Journal of Social Science Research,* vol. 1, no. 4 (1978): 373–89. R.

1362. Osborne, Gwendolyn E. "Motherhood in the Black Community," *Crisis,* vol. 84, no. 10 (1977): 479 + .

1363. Savage, James E., Jr.; Adair, Alvis, V.; and Friedman, Philip. "Community-Social Variables Related to Black Parent-Absent Families," *Journal of Marriage and the Family,* vol. 40, no. 4 (1978): 779–86. R.

1364. Sawhill, Isabel V. "Black Women Who Head Families: Economic Needs and Economic Resources," *Resources in Education* 13 (1978). ERIC document ED 157 980.

1365. Snow, Jacquelyn E. "A Heuristic Study of Black Female Heads of Households and Black Females Who Are Not Heads of Households and Their Involvement with Their Children's Educational Development—Camden, New Jersey." Ed.D. diss., Rutgers University, 1976 (*DAI* 37/12A, p. 8002, order # 7713291). R.

1366. Staples, Robert. "Dating Behavior among Single Parents: The Case of the Black Middle Class," *Resources in Education* 14 (1979). ERIC document ED 170 403.

1367. Wilkinson, Charles B., and O'Connor, William A. "Growing Up Male in a Black Single-Parent Family," *Psychiatric Annals,* vol. 7, no. 7 (1977): 356–62. R.

CHILD-REARING

1368. Colletta, Nancy D. "Child-Rearing and Maternal Satisfaction in One- and Two-Parent Families," *International Journal of Sociology of the Family,* vol. 9, no. 1 (1979): 27–33. R.

1369. ————. "Divorced Mothers at Two Income Levels: Stress, Support and Child-Rearing Practices." Ph.D. diss., Cornell University, 1978 (*DAI* 38/12B, p. 6114, order # 7809466). R.

1370. Flanzer, Jerry P. "Can the Single Parent Parent as Well?" *Resources in Education* 14 (1979). ERIC document ED 166 626. R.

1371. Herz, Fredda M. "The Effects of Maternal Powerlessness and Isolation on the Adjustment of Children in Single Parent Families." Ph.D. diss., Rutgers University, 1978 (*DAI* 39/11B, p. 5647, order # 7910391). R.

1372. Honig, Alice S. "Child Care Alternatives and Options for Parents," *Viewpoints in Teaching and Learning,* vol. 55, no. 3 (1979): 57–65.

1373. Kelly, F. Donald, and Main, Frank O. "Sibling Conflict in a Single-Parent Family—Empirical Case Study," *American Journal of Family Therapy,* vol. 7, no. 1 (1979): 39–47. R.

1374. Klebanow, Sheila. "Parenting in the Single Parent Family," *American Academy of Psychoanalysis Journal,* vol. 4, no. 1 (1976): 37–48.

1375. Maye, Patricia A. "Single-Parent Family Communication with Child." Master's thesis, Boston University, 1977–78. R.

1376. Noller, Patricia. "Sex Differences in the Socialization of Affectionate Expression," *Developmental Psychology,* vol. 14, no.3 (1978): 317–19. R.

1377. Reinhart, Gail E. "One-Parent Families: A Study of Divorced Mothers and Adolescents Using Social Climate and Relationship Styles." Ph.D. diss., California School of Professional Psychology, San Francisco, 1977 (*DAI* 38/6B, p. 2881, order # 7727609). R.

1378. Rosenthal, David M. "Working and Non-working Mothers in Intact and Non-intact Families and Effects on the Child's Perception of the Parent Child Relationship, Educational Achievement, Self Concept, Occupational Aspirations, and Vocational Maturity." Ph.D. diss., State University of New York at Buffalo, 1978 (*DAI* 39/3A, p. 1871, order # 7817075). R.

1379. Singer, Karla. "A Comparative Study of Self-Concepts: Children from One-Parent Home Environments, Children from Two-Parent Home Environments." Ed.D. diss., Florida Atlantic University, 1978 (*DAI* 39/3A, p. 1409, order # 7814985). R.

1380. Sparer, Ellen A. "Gender Identity of Three Year Old Girls in Two Diverse Groups: Children of Single Mothers and Children of Couples." Ph.D. diss., California Professional School of Psychology, Berkeley, 1978 (*DAI* 39/7B, p. 3541, order # 7901757). R.

1381. Weisel, Joye E. "Single Mother Attitudes and Characteristics Related to the Self-Esteem of Her Son." Ph.D. diss., California School of Professional Psychology, Los Angeles, 1976 (*DAI* 37/9B, p. 4714, order # 776316). R.

COUNSELING AND TRAINING

1382. Bizer, Linda S. "Generality of Treatment Effects in Single Parent-Child Problem Solving." Ed.D. diss., University of Massachusetts, 1978 (*DAI* 39/3A, p. 1428, order # 7816234). R.

1383. Blechman, Elaine. "A Problem Solving Training Package for the Single Family," *Resources in Education* 11 (1976). ERIC document ED 122 174.

1384. Hajal, Fady, and Rosenberg, Elinor B. "Working with the One-Parent Family in Family Therapy," *Journal of Divorce,* vol. 1, no. 3 (1978): 259–69.

1385. Leavitt, Shelly, et al. "Parenting Alone Successfully: The Development of a Single-Parent Training Program." In *Building Family Strengths: Blueprints for Action,* edited by Nick Stinnett, Barbara Chesser, and John DeFrain, pp. 327–37. Lincoln, NB: University of Nebraska Press, 1979.

1386. Peck, Bruce B. "Psychotherapy with Fragmented (Father-Absent) Families," *Family Therapy,* vol. 1, no. 1 (1974): 27–42.

1387. Wolf, Abraham. "A Self-Help Program for One Parent Households," *Resources in Education* 10 (1975). ERIC document ED 106 473.

ECONOMIC ASPECTS

1388. Brightman, Carol. "Single Parenting: Money Helps," *Interracial Books for Children Bulletin,* vol. 9, nos. 4–5 (1978): 26–27.

1389. Nichols, Sharon Y. "Resource Management for Single Parents," *Journal of Home Economics,* vol. 71, no. 2 (1979): 40–41.

1390. Smith, Michael J. "The Correlates and Consequences of Family Status: A Longitudinal Perspective on the Single Parent Family." D.S.W. diss., Columbia University 1978 (*DAI* 39/4A, p. 2553, order # 7819441). R.

1391. Stein, Robert L. "The Economic Status of Families Headed by Women," *Monthly Labor Review,* vol. 93, no. 12 (1970): 3–10.

1392. "Welfare Reform: For Whom and By Whom? An Analysis of the Current Federal Strategy for the Low-Income Female-Headed Family with Children and Principles for Change," *Resources in Education* 14 (1978). ERIC document ED 156 763.

FATHERS

1393. Fast, Anita H. "The Father-Only Family: An Alternative Family Style." Ph.D. diss., Brandeis University, 1979 (*DAI* 40/7A, p. 4259, order # 7922700). R.

1394. Gasser, Rita D., and Taylor, Claribel M. "Role Adjustments of Single Parent Fathers with Dependent Children," *Family Coordinator,* vol. 25, no. 4 (1976): 397–401. R.

1395. Greenberg, Judith B. "Single-Parenting and Intimacy: A Comparison of Mothers and Fathers," *Alternative Lifestyles,* vol. 2, no. 3 (1979): 308–30. R.

1396. Greene, Roberta S. "Atypical Parenting: Custodial Single Fathers." Ph.D. diss., University of Maryland, 1977 (*DAI* 39/2A, p. 1136, order # 7811939). R.

1397. Keshet, Harry F. "Part-Time Fathers: A Study of Separated and Divorced Men." Ph.D. diss., University of Michigan, 1977 (*DAI* 38/3A, p. 1687, order # 7718043). R.

1398. Keshet, Harry F., and Rosenthal, Kristine M. "Fathering after Marital Separation," *Social Work,* vol. 23, no. 1 (1978): 11–18. R.

1399. ———. "Single-Parent Fathers: A New Study," *Children Today* vol. 7, no. 3 (1978): 13–19. R.

1400. Lewis, Ken. "Single Father Families: Who They Are and How They Fare," *Child Welfare,* vol. 57 (December 1978): 643–51.

1401. Lowenstein, Joyce S. "A Comparison of Self-Esteem between Boys Living with Single Parent Mothers and Boys Living with Single Parent Fathers." Ph.D. diss., University of Maryland, 1977 (*DAI* 39/2A, p. 1137, order # 7811943). R.

1402. Lutzke, Jim. "Single Fathers—Adjusting to a New Lifestyle," *U.S. Federal Extension Service Review,* vol. 46, no. 6 (1975): 18–19.

1403. Mendes, Helen A. "Single Fatherhood," *Social Work,* vol. 21, no. 4 (1976): 308–12. R.

1404. ———. "Single Fathers," *Family Coordinator,* vol. 25, no. 14 (1976): 439–44. R.

1405. Orthner, Dennis K.; Brown, Terry; and Ferguson, Dennis. "Single-Parent Fatherhood: An Emerging Family Life Style," *Family Coordinator,* vol. 25, no. 4 (1976): 429–37. R.

1406. "Reactions to 'Fathering After Divorce,' " *Social Work,* vol. 23, no. 4 (1978): 331–32 +.

1407. Schlesinger, Benjamin. "Single Parent Fathers: A Research Review," *Children Today,* vol. 7, no. 3 (1978): 12 +.

1408. Schlesinger, Benjamin, and Todres, Rubin. "Motherless Families: An Increasing Societal Pattern," *Child Welfare* 55 (October 1976): 553–58. R.

1409. Smith, Richard M. "Single-Parent Fathers: An Application of Role Transition Theory," *Resources in Education* 13 (1978). ERIC document ED 151 719.

1410. White, S. K. "Single Parent Fathers: Providing for the Child Care Tasks." Master's thesis, University of Alberta, 1977–78. R.

HOUSING

1411. Limmer, Ruth. "How Well Are We Housed? Female-Headed Households," *Resources in Education* 15 (1980). ERIC document ED 179 667.

1412. Plata, Maximo. "Housing Discrimination Toward One Parent Families with a Handicapped Son," *Exceptional Children,* vol. 46, no. 2 (1979): 132–33. R.

JUVENILE DELINQUENCY

1413. Andrew, June M. "Violence among Delinquents by Family Intactness and Size," *Social Biology* 25 (Fall 1978): 243–50. R.

1414. Chilton, Roland J., and Markle, Gerald E. "Family Disruption, Delinquent Conduct and the Effect of Subclassification," *American Sociological Review,* vol. 37, no. 1 (1972): 93–99. R.

1415. Datesman, Susan K., and Scarpitti, Frank R. "Female Delinquency and Broken Homes: A Reassessment," *Criminology,* vol. 13, no. 1 (1975): 33–55. R.

1416. Hennessy, Michael; Richards, Pamela J.; and Berk, Richard A. "Broken Homes and Middle Class Delinquency—A Reassessment," *Criminology,* vol. 15, no. 4 (1978): 505–28. R.

1417. Maskin, Michael B., and Brookins, Elwood. "The Effects of Parental Composition on Recidivism Rates in Delinquent Girls," *Journal of Clinical Psychology*, vol. 30, no. 3 (1974): 341–42. R.

1418. Offord, David R., et al. "Broken Homes, Parental Psychiatric Illness, and Female Delinquency," *American Journal of Orthopsychiatry*, vol. 49, no. 2 (1979): 252–64. R.

1419. Wilkinson, Karen. "Broken Family and Juvenile Delinquency: Scientific Explanation or Ideology?" *Social Problems*, vol. 21, no. 5 (1973–74): 726–39.

NEEDS OF ONE-PARENT FAMILIES

1420. Clayton, Patricia N. "Meeting the Needs of the Single Parent Family," *Family Coordinator*, vol. 20, no. 4 (1971): 327–36.

1421. Davis, Hermione G., and Finkel, Esther. "The Single Parent: A Growing Challenge to Communal Service," *Journal of Jewish Communal Service*, vol. 50, no. 3 (1974): 251–56.

1422. Javaras, Lee S. "One Parent Family: A Needs Assessment." Master's thesis, California State University, Hayward, 1974–75. R.

1423. Prewitt, Maryon P. W. "Divorced Mothers and Their Children: Basic Concerns." Ph.D. diss., University of Texas, Austin, 1974 (*DAI* 35/8A, p. 5178, order # 754441). R.

SEX ROLES

1424. Bunton, Peter L. "Mothers' and Children's Perception of the Maternal Role: Single, Dual Career, and Traditional Families." Ph.D. diss., University of Michigan, 1979 (*DAI* 40/5B, p. 2430, order # 7925119). R.

1425. Confusione, Michael J. "Single Mothers' Parental Attitudes, Behaviors, and Sex-Role Orientations." Ph.D. diss., California School of Professional Psychology, Fresno, 1979 (*DAI* 40/6B, p. 2818, order # 7927604). R.

1426. MacKay, Ann; Wilding, Paul; and George, Vic. "Stereotypes of Male and Female Roles and their Influence on People Attitudes to One Parent Families," *Sociological Review*, vol. 20, no. 1 (1972): 79–92. R.

1427. Rasmussen, Dennis D. "Sex Role Differentiation in One-Parent Families." Ph.D. diss., University of Wisconsin,

Madison, 1974 (*DAI* 35/11B, p. 5624, order # 757604). R.

SOCIAL CHARACTERISTICS

1428. Boyle, William. "The Single Parent Family: Some Social and Psychological Characteristics and Their Implications for Social Policy Decisions," *Resources in Education* 10 (1975). ERIC document ED 108 068.

1429. McEaddy, Beverly J. "Women Who Head Families, A Socioeconomic Analysis," *Monthly Labor Review*, vol. 99, no. 6 (1976): 3–9.

1430. Norton, Arthur J. "A Portrait of the One-Parent Family," *National Elementary Principal*, vol. 59, no. 1 (1979): 32–35; 36–39.

1431. Wattenberg, Esther, and Reinhardt, Hazel. "Female-Headed Families: Trends and Implication," *Social Work*, vol. 24, no. 6 (1979): 460–67.

SOCIAL POLICY

1432. Schorr, Alvin L., and Moen, Phyllis. "The Single Parent and Public Policy," *Social Policy*, vol. 9, no. 5 (1979): 15–21.

STRESS

1433. Burke, Sharon O. "Familial Strain and Development of Normal and Handicapped Children in Single and Two Parent Families." Ph.D. diss., University of Toronto, 1978 (*DAI* 39/7A, p. 4177). R.

1434. Culbreth, Marcene C. "A Comparison of the Male and Female Single-Parent Stress." Master's thesis, University of Louisville, 1975. R.

STATISTICS

1435. U.S. Bureau of the Census. *Female Family Heads*. In its series, P-23: Special Studies, no. 50. Washington, DC: Government Printing Office, 1974 (C56.218:P-23/50) (Tables 3,20,21).

1436. ———. *Households and Family Characteristics: March 1971*. In its series, P-20: Current Population Reports, no. 233. Washington, DC: Government Printing Office, 1972 (C56.218:P-20/233) (Tables C,4,13,17).

1437. ———. *Population Profile of the United States: 1975*. In its series, P-20: Current Population Reports, no. 292. Washington, DC: Government Printing Office, 1976 (C56.218:P-20/292) (Table 10).

1438. ———. *Population Profile of the United States: 1976*. In its series, P-20: Current Population Reports, no. 307. Washington, DC: Government Printing Office, 1977 (C3.186:P-20/307) (Tables 8,9,12).

1439. ———. *Population Profile of the United States: 1977*. Series P-20: Current Population Reports, no. 324. Washington, DC: Government Printing Office, 1978 (C3.186:P-20/324) (Tables 8,9,12).

1440. ———. *Population Profile of the United States: 1978*. Series, P-20: Current Population Reports, no. 336. Washington, DC: Government Printing Office, 1979 (C3.186:P-20/336) (Figure 3, Tables 8,11).

SUPPORT SYSTEMS

1441. Christensen, Larry, and McDonald Debbie. "Effect of a Support System on Single-Parent Families," *Psychology*, vol. 13, no. 3 (1976): 68–70. R.

1442. Heger, Donna T. "Supportive Service to Single Mothers and Their Children," *Children Today*, vol. 6, no. 5 (1977): 2–4 + .

1443. Jackson, Magnolia. "An Empirical Study of Single-Parent Families and Their Support Systems." Ph.D. diss., Case Western Reserve University, 1979 (*DAI* 39/11A, p. 6997, order # 7909357). R.

1444. Lewis, Ken. "Single Parent Families in Rural Communities," *Human Services in the Rural Environment*, vol. 3, no. 1 (1978): 7–18.

1445. Nuttall, Ena V. "The Support Systems and Coping Patterns of the Female Puerto Rican Single Parent," *Journal of Non-White Concerns in Personnel and Guidance*, vol. 7, no. 3 (1979): 128–37. R.

1446. "Report on the Activities of the Single Parent Resource Center, 1975–76," *Resources in Education* 13 (1978). ERIC document ED 153 140.

THEORY

1447. Mendes, Helen A. "Single-Parent Families—Typology of Life-Styles," *Social Work*, vol. 24, no. 3 (1979): 193–200.

1448. Rosenfeld, Jona M., and Rosenstein, Eliezer. "Towards a Conceptual Framework for the Study of Parent Absence Families," *Journal of Marriage and the Family*, vol. 35, no. 1 (1973): 131–35.

1449. Weiss, Robert S. "Growing Up a Little Faster, the Experience of Growing Up in a Single-Parent Household," *Journal of Social Issues*, vol. 35, no. 4 (1979): 97–111. R.

WORK

1450. Boyer, Sherry. "Tips for Working with Single Parents," *Instructor*, vol. 89, no. 2 (1979): 79.

1451. Hungerford, Nancy, and Paolucci, Beatrice. "Employed Female Single Parent," *Journal of Home Economics*, 69 (November 1979): 10–13.

1452. Waldman, Elizabeth, and Whitmore, Robert. "Children of Working Mothers," *Resources in Education*, 10 (1975). ERIC document ED 099 559.

1453. Waldman, Elizabeth, et al. "Working Mothers in the 1970's: A Look at the Statistics," *Monthly Labor Review*, vol. 102, no. 10 (1979): 39–49.

REMARRIAGE

1454. Cherlin, Andrew. "Remarriage as an Incomplete Institution," *American Journal of Sociology*, vol. 84, no. 3 (1978): 634–650.

1455. Dean, Gillian, and Gurak, Douglas T. "Marital Homogamy the Second Time Around," *Journal of Marriage and the Family*, vol. 40, no. 3 (1978): 559–70. R.

1456. Duberman, Lucile. "Becoming a Family: A Study of Reconstituted Families." Ph.D. diss., Case Western Reserve University, 1973 (*DAI* 38/8A, p. 5353, order # 742508). R.

1457. ———. *The Reconstituted Family: A Study of Remarried Couples and Their Children*. Chicago: Nelson-Hall, 1975. R.

1458. Glick, Paul C., and Norton, Arthur J. "Perspectives on the Recent Upturn in Divorce and Remarriage," *Demography*, vol. 10, no. 3 (1973): 301–14. R.

1459. Goetting, Ann. "The Normative Integration of the American Divorce Chain." Ph.D. diss., Western Michigan University, 1978 (*DAI* 39/2A, p. 1131, order # 7812841). R.

1460. Grigg, Susan. "Toward a Theory of Remarriage: A Case Study of Newburyport at the Beginning of the 19th Century," *Journal of Interdisciplinary History*, vol. 8, no. 2 (1977): 183–220. R.

1461. Jones, Shirley M. "Divorce and Remarriage: A New Beginning, a New Set of Problems," *Journal of Divorce*, vol. 2, no. 2 (1978): 217–27.

1462. Keith, Pat M.; Goudy, Willis J.; and Powers, Edward. "Marital Status, Family, Activity, and Attitudes toward Life," *International Journal of Sociology of the Family*, vol. 9, no. 1 (1979): 95–109. R.

1463. Kleinman, Judith; Rosenberg, Elinor; and Whiteside, Mary. "Common Developmental Tasks in Forming Reconstituted Families," *Journal of Marriage and Family Therapy*, vol. 5, no. 2 (1979): 79 86.

1464. Pritchard, James W. "Divorce-Remarriage: An Investigation of the Effects of Divorce and Related Variables on the Communication Style of Reconstituted Marriages." Ph.D. diss., California School of Professional Psychology, Fresno, 1976 (*DAI* 38/1B, p. 375, order # 7714267). R.

1465. Pullen, Robert L., Jr. "A Comparison of Family Role Structure in Remarriages and Original Marriages." Ph.D. diss., Florida State University, 1979 (*DAI* 40/7A, p. 4262, order # 8001111). R.

1466. Scarano, Thomas P. "Multivariate Informational Analysis: A Diagnostic Instrument for Measuring Social Interaction in Couples." Ph.D. diss., California School of Professional Psychology, Fresno, 1977 (*DAI* 37/8B, p. 4164, order # 772787). R.

1467. Schlesinger, Benjamin. "The Single Woman in Second Marriages," *Social Science*, vol. 49, no. 2 (1974): 104–09. R.

1468. Walker, Kenneth N.; Rogers, Joy; and Messinger, Lillian. "Remarriage after Divorce: A Review," *Social Casework*, vol. 58, no. 5 (1977): 276–85.

1469. Walker, Kenneth N., and Messinger, Lillian. "Remarriage after Divorce: Dissolution and the Reconstruction of Family Boundaries," *Family Process*, vol. 18, no. 2 (1979): 185–92.

BIBLIOGRAPHY

1470. Walker, Libby. "Annotated Bibliography of the Remarried, the Living Together, and Their Children," *Family Process*, vol. 18, no. 2 (1979): 193–212.

COUNSELING AND EDUCATION FOR REMARRIAGE

1471. Cameron, Catherine. "Remarriage Counseling: A Current Challenge," *Resources in Education* 13 (1978). ERIC document ED 154 261.

1472. Messinger, Lillian. "Remarriage between Divorced People with Children from Previous Marriages: A Proposal for Preparation for Remarriage," *Journal of Marriage and Family Counseling*, vol. 2, no. 2 (1976): 193–200.

1473. Messinger, Lillian; Walker, Kenneth N.; and Freeman, Stanley J. J. "Preparation for Remarriage Following Divorce: The Use of Group Techniques," *American Journal of Orthopsychiatry*, vol. 48, no. 2 (1978): 263–72.

1474. Whiteside, Mary F., and Auerbach, Lynn S. "Can the Daughter of My Father's New Wife Be My Sister? Families of Remarriage in Family Therapy," *Journal of Divorce*, vol. 1, no. 3 (1978): 271–83. R.

ECONOMIC ASPECTS

1475. Gregg, Gary. "Remarriage: Children and Money Are the Big Problems," *Psychology Today*, vol. 10, no. 6 (1976): 26+.

1476. Wolf, Wendy C., and MacDonald Maurice M. "The Earnings of Men and Remarriage" (Discussion Paper No. 537–39), *Resources in Education* 14 (1979). ERIC document ED 173 473. R.

EFFECTS ON CHILDREN

1477. Thies, Jill M. "Beyond Divorce: The Impact of Remarriage on Children," *Journal of Clinical Child Psychology*, vol. 6, no. 2 (1977): 59–61.

FERTILITY

1478. Levin, Martin L., and O'Hara, C. Joseph. "The Impact of Marital History of Current Husband on the Fertility of Remarried White Women in the United States," *Journal of Marriage and the Family*, vol. 40, no. 1 (1978): 95–102. R.

1479. O'Hara, Clinton J. "The Impact of Serial Marriage on the Fertility of White Serially Married American Women: 1955–1970." Ph.D. diss., Emory University, 1978 (*DAI* 39/7A, p. 4516, order # 7901469). R.

HUSBAND-WIFE RELATIONS

1480. Albrecht, Stan L. "Correlates of Marital Happiness among the Remarried," *Journal of Marriage and the Family*, vol. 41, no. 4 (1979): 857–67. R.

1481. Gilbert, Craig C. "A Comparison of Marital and Parent-Child Adjustment of Persons in Original Marriages and Remarriages." Ph.D. diss., United States International University, 1979 (*DAI* 40/7B, p. 3481, order # 7928690). R.

1482. Glenn, Norval D., and Weaver, Charles N. "The Marital Happiness of Remarried Divorced Persons," *Journal of Marriage and the Family*, vol. 39, no. 2 (1977): 331–37. R.

1483. Kizirian, Lucy B. "Remarriage: A Study of the Factors Leading to Success or Failure in Remarriage." Ph.D. diss., Florida State University, 1977 (*DAI* 38/12A, p. 7596, order # 7808960). R.

1484. Pascal, Harold J. "Need Interaction as a Factor in Marital Adjustment." Ph.D. diss., University of Miami, 1974 (*DAI* 35/4A, p. 2056, order # 23412). R.

1485. Schlesinger, Benjamin. "Husband-Wife Relationships in Reconstituted Families," *Social Science*, vol. 52, no. 3 (1977): 152–57.

1486. Stinnett, Charlotte A. "Life Satisfaction Following Re-Marriage in the Middle Years." Master's thesis, University of Oklahoma, 1979. R.

1487. White, Lynn K. "Sex Differences in the Effects of Remarriage on Global Happiness," *Journal of Marriage and the Family*, vol. 41, no. 4 (1979): 869–76. R.

MATE SELECTION

1488. Gurak, Douglas T., and Dean, Gillian. "The Remarriage Market: Factors Influencing the Selections of Second Husbands," *Journal of Divorce*, vol. 3, no. 2 (1979): 161–73. R.

1489. Nici, Janice. "Wives of Alcoholics as 'Repeaters,' " *Journal of Studies on Alcohol*, vol. 40, no. 7 (1979): 677–82. R.

1490. Peters, John F. "A Comparison of Mate Selection and Marriage in the First and Second Marriages in a Selected Sample of the Remarried Divorced," *Journal of Comparative Family Studies*, vol. 7, no. 3 (1976): 483–90. R.

STATISTICS

1491. Thornton, Arland. "Decomposing the Re-marriage Process," *Population Studies*, vol. 31, no. 2 (1977): 383–92. R.

1492. U.S. National Center for Health Statistics. *First Marriages: United States, 1968–1976*. In its series 21, Data on Natality, Marriage, and Divorce, no. 35. Washington, DC: Government Printing Office, 1979 (HE20.6209:21/35) (Figures 1,3,11,13,14, Tables A,M,N,Q).

1493. ———. *Remarriages United States*. In its series 21, Data on Natality, Marriage and Divorce, no. 25. Washington, DC: Government Printing Office, 1973 (HE20.6209:21/25) (Figures 1–5, Tables A–J, 1–7).

SEPARATION

1494. Bloom, Bernard L., et al. "Marital Separation: A Community Survey," *Journal of Divorce*, vol. 1, no. 1 (1977): 7–19. R.

1495. Cherlin, Andrew J. "Social and Economic Determinants of Marital Separation." Ph.D. diss., University of California, Los Angeles, 1976 (*DAI* 37/3A, p. 1827, order # 7621344). R.

1496. Chiancola, Samuel P. "The Process of Separation and Divorce: A New Approach," *Social Casework*, vol. 59, no. 8 (1978): 494–99.

1497. Chiriboga, David A. "Marital Separation and Stress," *Alternative Lifestyles*, vol. 2, no. 4 (1979): 461–70. R.

1498. Chiriboga, David A.; Roberts, John; and Stein, Judith A. "Psychological Well-Being during Marital Separation," *Journal of Divorce*, vol. 2, no. 1 (1978): 21–36. R.

1499. "Coming to Terms on a Separation," *Business Week* 2607 (October 15, 1979): 168–69+.

1500. Gongla, Patricia A. "Social Relationships after Marital Separation: A Study of Women with Children." Ph.D. diss., Case Western Reserve University, 1977 (*DAI* 38/9A, p. 5742, order # 7730987). R.

1501. Herman, Sonya J. "The Use of Time Limited Therapy and Its Effect on the Self-Concept of Separated Single Parents." D.N.Sc. diss., Catholic University of America, 1975 (*DAI* 36/3B, p. 1147, order # 7519529). R.

1502. Jaffe, Dennis T., and Kanter, Rosabeth M. "Couple Strains in Communal Households: A Four-Factor Model of the Separation Process." In *Divorce and Separation: Context, Causes and Consequences,* edited by George Levinger and Oliver C. Moles, pp. 114–33. New York: Basic Books, 1979. R.

1503. Lantz, Herman R. *Marital Incompatibility and Social Change in Early America.* Beverly Hills, CA: Sage Publishers, 1976.

1504. Levinger, George, and Moles, Oliver C. "In Conclusion: Threads in the Fabric," *Journal of Social Issues,* vol. 32, no. 1 (1976): 193–207.

1505. O'Farrell, Timothy J. "Marital Stability among Wives of Alcoholics: Reported Antecedents of a Wife's Decision to Separate from or Endure Her Alcoholic Husband." Ph.D. diss., Boston University, 1975 (*DAI* 36/4B, p. 1927, order # 7521006). R.

1506. Weiss, Robert S. "The Emotional Impact of Marital Separation," *Journal of Social Issues,* vol. 32, no. 1 (1976): 135–45.

1507. ———. "The Emotional Impact of Marital Separation." In *Divorce and Separation: Context, Causes and Consequences,* edited by George Levinger and Oliver C. Moles, pp. 201–10. New York, Basic Books, 1979.

1508. ———. *Marital Separation.* New York: Basic Books, 1975. R.

1509. Welker, Patricia Z. "Children's Perceptions of Parental Separation." Master's thesis, University of Nebraska, 1979. R.

ADJUSTMENT TO SEPARATION

1510. Forrest, Deborah A. "The Relationship between Adjustment to Marital Separation and Psychosomatic Complaints." Master's thesis, Pennsylvania State University, 1979. R.

1511. Meyers, Judith C. "The Adjustment of Women to Marital Separation: The Effects of Sex-Role Identification and of Stage in Family Life, as Determined by Age and Presence or Absence of Dependent Children." Ph.D. diss., University of Colorado, 1976 (*DAI* 37/5B, p. 2516, order # 7623656). R.

1512. Spanier, Graham B., and Anderson, Elaine A. "The Impact of the Legal System on Adjustment to Marital Separation," *Journal of Marriage and the Family,* vol. 41, no. 3 (1979): 605–13. R.

1513. White, Stephen W. "The Adjustment of Men to the Process of Marital Separation," Ph.D. diss., University of Colorado, 1979 (*DAI* 40/4B, p. 1921, order # 7923301). R.

COUNSELING

1514. Einbinder, Sandra S. "School Is One Step in Letting Go: A Pamphlet to Prepare Parents on How to Separate." Master's thesis, Bank Street College of Education, N4, 1977. R.

1515. Hight, Evelyn S. "A Contractual, Working Separation: A Step between Resumption and/or Divorce," *Journal of Divorce,* vol. 1, no. 1 (1977): 21–30.

1516. Jacobson, Gerald F., and Portuges, Stephen H. "Marital Separation and Divorce: Assessment of and Preventative Considerations for Crisis Intervention." In *Emergency and Disaster Management: A Mental Health Sourcebook,* edited by Howard J. Pared, H. L. P. Resniki, and Libbie G. Pared, pp. 433–41. Bowie, MD: Charles Press, 1976.

1517. Levy, Terry M., and Joffe, Wendy. "Counseling Couples through Separation: A Developmental Approach," *Family Therapy,* vol. 5, no. 3 (1978): 267–76.

1518. ———. "Counseling Couples through Separation: A Developmental Approach," *Resources in Education* 13 (1978). ERIC document ED 151 669.

1519. Toomin, Marjorie K. "Separation Counseling: A Structured Approach to Marital Crisis." In *Creative Divorce through Social and Psychological Approaches,* edited by Richard E. Hardy and John G. Cull, pp. 124–41. Springfield, IL: Charles C Thomas, 1974.

1520. ———. "Separation Counseling: A Structured Approach to Marital Crisis." In *Therapeutic Needs of the Family: Problems, Descriptions and Therapeutic Approaches,* edited by Richard E. Hardy and John G. Cull, pp. 148–66. Springfield, IL: Charles C Thomas, 1974.

SEXUAL BEHAVIOR

1521. Margolis, Randie. "Marital Separation and Extramarital Sex." Master's thesis, Pennsylvania State University, 1979. R.

SUPPORT SYSTEMS

1522. Putney, Richard S. "Support Systems of the Separated/Divorced." Ed.D. diss., University of Massachusetts, 1976 (*DAI* 37/1B, p. 529, order # 7614715). R.

STEPPARENTS AND STEPCHIDREN

1523. Gardner, Richard A. "Intergenerational Sexual Tensions in Second Marriages," *Medical Aspects of Human Sexuality,* vol. 13, no. 8 (1979): 77+.

1524. Visher, Emily B., and Visher, John S. *Stepfamilies: A Guide to Working with Stepparents and Stepchildren.* New York: Brunner/Mazel, 1979.

1525. Visher, John S., and Visher, Emily B. "Stepfamilies and Stepchildren." In *Basic Handbook of Child Psychiatry,* edited by Joseph D. Noshpitz et al., Vol. 4, pp. 347–53. New York: Basic Books, 1979.

1526. Wildemann, Ann P. "Perceptions and Attitudes toward Stepparenting." Ph.D. diss., Texas Woman's University, 1979 (*DAI* 40/12A, p. 6124, order # 8012188). R.

1527. Wilson, Kenneth L., et al. "Stepfathers and Stepchildren: An Exploratory Analysis from Two National Surveys," *Journal of Marriage and the Family,* vol. 37, no. 3 (1975): 526–36. R.

BIBLIOGRAPHY

1528. Espinoza, Renato, and Newman, Yvonne. *Stepparenting: With Annotated Bibliography*. National Institute of Mental Health, Center for Studies of Child and Family Mental Health. Washington, DC: Government Printing Office, 1979 (HE20.8102:St4).

1529. McCormick, Mona. *Stepfathers: What the Literature Reveals: A Literature Review and Annotated Bibliography*. La Jolla, CA: Western Behavioral Sciences Institute, 1974.

PROBLEMS OF STEPPARENTS

1530. Visher, Emily B., and Visher, John S. "Common Problems of Stepparents and their Spouses," *American Journal of Orthopsychiatry*, vol. 48, no. 2 (1978): 252–62.

1531. ———. "Major Areas of Difficulties for Stepparent Couples," *International Journal of Family Counseling*, vol. 6, no. 2 (1978): 70–80.

STEPFATHERS

1532. Biller, Henry, and Meredith, Dennis. *Father Power*. New York: David McKay Co., 1974.

1533. Buhr, Kenneth S. "Stress, Marital Interaction, and Personal Competence in Natural-Parent and Stepfather Families." Ph.D. diss., University of Southern California, 1975 (*DAI* 36/1A, p. 564, order # 7515519). R.

1534. Hodge, Harvey G. "Interpersonal Adjustment and the Utilization of Social Power by Stepfathers." Ph.D. diss., California School of Professional Psychology, Los Angeles, 1978 (*DAI* 40/8B, p. 3935, order # 8003264). R.

1535. LaRoche, Shirley S. "The Role of the Stepfather in the Family." Ph.D. diss., University of New Mexico, 1973 (*DAI* 34/5A, p. 2792, order # 7327800). R.

1536. Middleton, Glen S. "The Male Stepparent: His Role in the Stepchild Rearing Process." Ph.D. diss., Ohio State University, 1979 (*DAI* 40/10B, p. 5078, order # 8009315). R.

1537. Perkins, Terry F., and Kahan, James P. "Empirical Comparison of Natural-Father and Stepfather Family Systems," *Family Process*, vol. 18, no. 2 (1979): 175–83. R.

1538. Ragland, Francine L. "Stepfathers: An Analysis of the Role." Master's thesis, California State University, Long Beach, 1978 (*Master's Abstracts* 17/1, p. 92, order # 1312287). R.

1539. Rallings, E. M. "The Special Role of Stepfather," *Family Coordinator*, vol. 25, no. 4 (1976): 445–49.

1540. Stern, Phyllis N. "Integrative Discipline in Stepfather Families." D.N.S. diss., University of California, San Francisco, 1976 (*DAI* 37/10B, p. 4991, order # 775276). R.

1541. ———. Stepfather Families: Integration around Child Discipline," *Issues in Mental Health Nursing* 1 (Summer 1978): 49–56. R.

1542. Yahraes, Herbert, and Bohannan, Paul. "Stepfathers as Parents." In *Families Today—A Research Sampler on Families and Children*, edited by Eunice Corfman, pp. 347–62. NIMH Science Monograph no. 1. Washington, DC: Goverment Printing Office, 1979 (HE20.8131/2:1).

STEPMOTHERS

1543. Draughon, Margaret. "Stepmothers Model of Identification in Relation to Mourning in the Child," *Psychological Reports*, vol. 36, no. 1 (1975) 183–89.

1544. Nadler, Janice H. "The Psychological Stress of the Stepmother." Ph.D. diss., California School of Professional Psychology, Los Angeles, 1976 (*DAI* 37/10B, p. 5367, order # 776308). R.

1545. Rosenthal, Kristine M. and Keshet, Harry F. "The Not-Quite Stepmother," *Psychology Today*, vol. 12, no. 2 (1978): 82+.

1546. Sardanis-Zimmerman, Irene. "The Stepmother: Mythology and Self-Perception," Ph.D. diss., California School of Professional Psychology, San Francisco, 1977 (*DAI* 37/6B, p. 2884, order # 7727618). R.

STEPPARENTS

1547. Capaldi, Frederick, and McRae, Barbara. *Stepfamilies: A Cooperative Responsibility: A Positive Approach for Stepparents and Single Parents Considering Remarriage*. New York: New Viewpoints/Vision Books, 1979.

1548. Duberman, Lucile. "Step-Kin Relationships." *Journal of Marriage and the Family*, vol. 35, no. 2 (1973): 283–92. R.

1549. Duffin, Sharyn R. *Yours, Mine and Ours: Tips for Stepparents*. Rockville, MD: Dept. of HEW, National Institute of Mental Health, 1978 (HE20.8102:Y8/2).

1550. Jacobson, Doris S. "Stepfamilies: Myths and Realities," *Social Work*, vol. 24, no. 3 (1979): 202–07.

1551. Kavanaugh, Kathryn A. "A Preliminary Investigation of Family Relationships in Biological and Step Families." Master's thesis, University of Oregon, 1979. R.

1552. Keith, Judith A. Child Rearing Attitudes and Behavior Patterns of Natural Parents and Stepparents." Ph.d. diss., North Texas State University, 1977 (*DAI* 38/7A, p. 4396, order # 7729553). R.

1553. Medeiros, Julie P. "Relationship Styles and Family Environment of Stepfamilies." Ph.D. diss., California School of Professional Psychology, San Francisco, 1977 (*DAI* 38/9B, p. 4472, order # 7801688). R.

1554. Miller, Rosalie D. "The Stepfamily: A Guide to Single Parenting and Stepparenting." Master's thesis, California State University, Long Beach, 1979 (*Master's Abstracts* June 1980, order # 1313776). R.

1555. Mowatt, Marian H. "Group Psychotherapy for Stepfathers and Their Wives," *Psychotherapy: Theory, Research and Practice*, vol. 9, no. 4 (1972): 328–31.

1556. Oshman, Harvey, and Manosevitz, Martin. "Father Absence: Effects of Stepfathers upon Psychosocial Development in Males," *Developmental Psychology*, vol. 12, no. 5 (1976): 479–80. R.

1557. Parish, Thomas S., and Copeland, Terry F. "The Relationship between Self-Concepts and Evaluations of Parents and Stepparents," *Journal of Psychology*, vol. 101, no. 1 (1979): 135–38. R.

1558. Perkins, Terry F. "Natural-Parent Family Systems versus Step-Parent Family Systems." Ph.D. diss., University of Southern California, 1977 (*DAI* 38/10B, p. 5038). R.

1559. Ransom, Jane W.; Schlesinger, Stephen; and Derdeyn, Andre P. "A Stepfamily in Formation," *American Journal of Orthopsychiatry*, vol. 49, no. 1 (1979):: 36–43.

1560. Schulman, Gerda L. "Myths That Intrude on the Adaptation of the Stepfamily," *Social Casework*, vol. 53, no. 3 (1972): 131–39.

1561. Watson, Raymond. "A Forward Look: Creative Breakdown," *Conciliation Courts Review*, vol. 16, no. 2 (1978): 44–47.

II. Legal Literature

ALIMONY AND MAINTENANCE

1562. "Antenuptial Agreement Fixing Alimony Not Void ab initio," *Rutgers Camden Law Journal*, vol. 3, no. 1 (1971): 175–82.

1563. DuCanto, Joseph N. "The Case for More Frequent Use of Installment Payment of Lump Sum Alimony in Divorce Settlement Agreements and Judgments." *Law Notes*, 6 (January 1970): 35–42.

1564. *"Economics of Divorce: A Collection of Papers*. Chicago: American Bar Association, Section on Family Law, 1978.

1565. Ehrlich, Stanton L. "The New Deal on Alimony," *Trial*, vol. 8, no. 5 (1972): 22+.

1566. Freed, Doris J., and Foster, Henry H., Jr. "Economic Effects of Divorce," *Family Law Quarterly*, vol. 7, no. 4 (1973): 453–54.

1567. Freeman, Marvin A. "Should Spousal Support Be Abolished?" *Los Angeles Bar Bulletin*, vol. 48, no. 7 (1973): 236–41.

1568. Houle, Philip P., and Dubose, Eugene Z. "Nonsupport Contempt Hearing: Constitutional and Statutory Requirements," *New Hampshire Bar Journal*, vol. 14, no. 3 (1973): 165–85.

1569. "How Tax Court Distinguishes Alimony from Child Support Payments," *Taxation for Lawyers*, vol. 2, no. 5 (1974): 283–84.

1570. "How to Tell Alimony from Property Settlements," *Taxation for Accountants*, vol. 12, no. 1 (1974): 28–29.

1571. "Informality in Alimony Arrangements Is a Trap," *CPA Journal*, vol. 45, no. 2 (1975): 39.

1572. Inker, Monroe L.; Walsh, Joseph H.; and Perocchi, Paul P. "Alimony Orders Following Short-term Marriages," *Family Law Quarterly*, vol. 12, no. 2 (1978): 91–111.

1573. Krauskopf, Joan M., and Thomas, Rhona C. "Partnership Marriage: The Solution to an Ineffective and Inequitable Law of Support," *Ohio State Law Journal*, vol. 35 (1974): 558–600.

1574. Labovitz, Irving D. "Alimony . . . A Rose by Any Other Name May Not Provide the Same Cent," *Commercial Law Journal*, vol. 80, no. 8 (1975): 359–61.

1575. Landes, Elizabeth M. "Economics of Alimony," *Journal of Legal Studies*, vol. 7, no. 1 (1978): 35–63.

1576. Oelbaum, Harold. "Later Agreement Fails to Make Alimony Periodic," *Journal of Taxation*, vol. 37, no. 6 (1972): 355.

1577. ———. "Lump-Sum Payment Tied to Remarriage Can Be Alimony," *Journal of Taxation*, vol. 38, no. 3 (1973): 188–89.

1578. Oldham, J. Thomas. "Effect of Unmarried Cohabitation by a Former Spouse upon His or Her Right to Continue to Receive Alimony," *Journal of Family Law*, vol. 17, no. 2 (1979): 249–73.

1579. "Pension Fund Benefits Governed by the Federal Employee Retirement Income Security Act Are Subject to Court-Ordered Alimony and Child Support Payments," *Fordham Urban Law Journal*, vol. 7, no. 3 (1979): 693–703.

1580. Rollins, Elaine G. "Alimony Considerations under No-Fault Divorce Laws," *Nebraska Law Review*, vol. 57, no. 3 (1978): 792–816.

1581. Siller, Sidney. "For a Federal Divorce and Alimony Law," *Humanist*, vol. 31, no. 6 (1971): 27.

1582. Votolato, Arthur N., Jr. "Review of Recent Equal Protection Challenges to the Dischargeability-of-Alimony Provision of Section 17a(7) of the Bankruptcy Act," *Suffolk University Law Review*, vol. 13, no. 3 (1979): 506–23.

1583. White, Kenneth R., and Stone, R. Thomas, Jr. "Consumer Unit Scaling as an Aid in Equitably Determining Need under Maintenance and Child Support Decrees," *Family Law Quarterly*, vol. 13, no. 2 (1979): 231–49.

1584. Woody, Wayne S. "New Alimony Remedy?" *Louisiana Bar Journal*, vol. 19, no. 2 (1971): 151–56.

1585. Young, Carl D. "Dissolution of Marriage and the Bankruptcy Act of 1973: 'Fresh Start' Forgotten," *Indiana Law Journal*, vol. 52, no. 2 (1977): 469–85.

ENFORCEMENT OF ALIMONY

1586. Blank, Diane S., and Rone, Jemera. "Enforcement of Interspousal Support Obligations: A Proposal," *Women's Rights Law Reporter*, vol. 2, no. 4 (1975): 13–25.

1587. Foster, Henry H., Jr., and Freed, Doris J. "Modification, Recognition and Enforcement of Foreign Alimony Orders," *California Western Law Review*, vol. 11, no. 2 (1975): 280–96.

1588. Garrett, W. Walton. "Alimony and Child Support Enforcement," *Family Advocate*, vol. 1, no. 4 (1979): 18–21+.

1589. "Long-Arm Jurisdiction in Alimony and Custody Cases," *Columbia Law Review*, vol. 73, no. 2 (1973): 289–317.

FOREIGN DECREES

1590. Robertson, R. J., Jr. "Full Faith and Credit—Recognition of Retroactively Modifiable Foreign Alimony Decrees Denied," *Missouri Law Review*, vol. 40, no. 2 (1975): 335–41.

1591. Warder, Francis L., Jr. "Recognition of Modifiable Alimony Decrees," *West Virginia Law Review*, vol. 72, no. 3 (1970): 291–96.

MALE ALIMONY

1592. Detec, David A., and Thomas-More, Jane L. "Equal Protection Clause, State Alimony Statutes, Sex Discrimination," *Akron Law Review*, vol. 13, no. 1 (1979): 175–90.

1593. "Effect of Antenuptial Agreement in Awarding Husband Support," *Journal of Family Law*, vol. 13, no. 4 (1973–74): 622–25.

1594. Foster, Henry H., Jr., and Freed, Doris J. "Orr v. Orr—The Decision That Takes Gender out of Alimony," *Family Advocate*, vol. 1, no. 4 (1979): 6–9+.

1595. Henry, Ronald T. "Orr v. Orr: Predictable Result, Unpredictable Repercussions?" *Cumberland Law Review*, vol. 10, no. 2 (1979): 531–48.

1596. Hull, E. A. "Sex Discrimination and the Equal Protection Clause: An Analysis of Kahn v. Shevin and Orr v. Orr," *Syracuse Law Review,* vol. 30, no. 2 (1979): 639–74.

1597. Knight, Linda W. "Male Alimony in Light of the Sex Discrimination Decisions of the Supreme Court," *Cumberland Law Review,* vol. 6, no. 3 (1976): 589–610.

1598. Smith, Pamela J. "Alimony for Men—The Changing Law," *Florida State University Law Review,* vol. 7, no. 4 (1979): 687–700.

1599. "A Statutory Scheme Which Provides That Husbands, but Not Wives, May Be Required to Pay Alimony upon Divorce Violates the Equal Protection Clause of the Fourteenth Amendment," *Journal of Family Law,* vol. 18, no. 1 (1979): 192–97.

MODIFICATIONS

1600. Carey, J. Matthew. "Reduction in Alimony as a Result of Changes in Financial Condition: A Guide for the Practitioner," *Journal of Family Law,* vol. 15, no. 2 (1977): 300–13.

1601. Giacalone, David A. "The Drop Out Ex-Husband's Right to Reduce Alimony and Support Payments," *Family Law Reporter,* vol. 1 (September 9, 1975): 4065–71, monograph no. 10.

1602. Higgins, James R., Jr. "Modification of Spousal Support: A Survey of a Confusing Area of the Law," *Journal of Family Law,* vol. 17, no. 4 (1979): 711–40.

STATES AND TERRITORIES

Alimony: Alabama

1603. McRae, Ferrill D. "Alimony and Division of Property in Divorce Cases," *Alabama Lawyer,* vol. 33, no. 4 (1972): 426–41.

Alimony: Arkansas

1604. Beebe, Mike D. "Divorce—Effect of Independent Agreement on Modification of Decree," *Arkansas Law Review,* vol. 24, no. 4 (1971): 557–60.

Alimony: California

1605. "Enforceability of Second Wife's Guarantee of Husband's Support Obligation to First Wife," *Journal of Family Law,* vol. 14, no. 3 (1975–76): 484–88.

1606. Larson, Bianca G. "Equity and Economics: A Case for Spousal Support," *Golden Gate University Law Review,* vol. 8 (Spring 1979): 843–77.

1607. Miller, Ovvie. "Where Are We Now on Spousal Support? *California State Bar Journal,* vol. 53, no. 5 (1978): 302–06 + .

1608. Veith, Nancy A. "Rehabilitative Spousal Support: In Need of a More Comprehensive Approach to Mitigating Dissolution Trauma," *University of San Francisco Law Review,* vol. 12, no. 3 (1978): 493–524.

1609. Wasser, Dennis M. "Spousal Support and the Wife's Desire and Ability to Work," *Beverly Hills Bar Association Journal,* vol. 8, no. 2 (1974): 23–31.

Alimony: Colorado

1610. "Husband's Ability to Pay Support," *Journal of Family Law,* vol. 14, no. 3 (1975–76): 480–84.

Alimony: Connecticut

1611. "Enforceability of an Antenuptial Agreement Made in Contemplation of Divorce," *Journal of Family Law,* vol. 15, no. 4 (1976–77): 830–34.

Alimony: Florida

1612. Bowen, Henry C. "Antenuptial Agreements in Contemplation of Divorce," *West Virginia Law Review,* vol. 73, nos. 3–4 (1971): 339–43.

1613. "Continuance of Alimony into Deceased Ex-Husband's Estate," *Journal of Family Law,* vol. 13, no. 3 (1973–74): 620–22.

1614. Cypen, Irving, and Cypen, Stephen H. "Alimony for Husbands: Is There True Equality?" *Florida Bar Journal,* vol. 52, no. 3 (1978): 201–04.

1615. DeWeese, Allen. "Modifications of Alimony in Florida," *Florida Bar Journal,* vol. 32, no. 3 (1978): 192–98.

1616. Hernandez, Irma V. "Special Equities in Dissolution Proceedings," *University of Miami Law Review,* vol. 27, no. 1–2 (1972): 177–90.

1617. Jenkins, Elizabeth A. "Alimony in Florida: No-Fault Stops at the Courthouse Door," *University of Florida Law Review,* vol. 28, no. 2 (1976): 521–34.

1618. Power, Dierdre. "Validity of Prenuptial Agreement Fixing Alimony Recognized by Florida Supreme Court," *Creighton Law Review,* vol. 4, no. 1 (1970): 180–98.

1619. Sasser, Donald J. "Trends in Family Law," *Florida Bar Journal,* vol. 52, no. 3 (1978): 183–85.

1620. Scott, Sandra R. "Survey of Florida Alimony since Passage of the 1971 Dissolution of Marriage Act," *University of Florida Law Review,* vol. 28, no. 3 (1976): 763–86.

1621. White, Kenneth R., and Stone, R. Thomas, Jr. "Study of Alimony and Child Support Rulings with Some Recommendations," *Family Law Quarterly,* vol. 10, no. 1 (1976): 75–91.

1622. Zimmer, C. Thomas. "Public Policy, the Courts, and Antenuptial Agreements Specifying Alimony," *University of Florida Law Review,* vol. 23, no. 1 (1970): 113–33.

Alimony: Georgia

1623. Davies, Robert O. "Validity of Prenuptial Contracts Which Fix Alimony," *Georgia State Bar Journal,* vol. 14, no. 1 (1977): 18–20.

1624. "Economics of Divorce in Georgia: Toward a Partnership Model of Marriage," *Georgia Law Review* 12 (Spring 1978): 640–68.

1625. Ozburn, Samuel D. "Alimony Judgments Subject to Dormancy and Revival Statutes," *Mercer Law Review,* vol. 26, no. 1 (1974): 357–60.

Alimony: Illinois

1626. Emmons, Keith E. "Volid vs. Volid, Reconsideration of the Role of the Antenuptial Agreement in Illinois," *Loyola University (Chicago) Law Journal,* vol. 4, no. 2 (1973): 497–512.

1627. "Ex-wife's Entry into Religious Life Held Insufficient Grounds for Termination of Alimony Payments," *Journal of Family Law,* vol. 15, no. 2 (1976–77): 321–27.

1628. Kalcheim, Michael W. "Marital Property, Tax Ramifications, and Maintenance: Practice under the Illinois Marriage and Dissolution of Marriage Act—A Comparative Study," *Illinois Bar Journal,* vol. 66, no. 7 (1978): 388–400.

Alimony: Indiana

1629. Pennell, Stephen R. "Alimony in Indiana No-Fault Divorce," *Indiana Law Journal*, vol. 50, no. 3 (1975): 541–66.

1630. Rosen, Martin A. "Indiana's Alimony Confusion," *Indiana Law Journal*, vol. 45, no. 4 (1970): 595–605.

Alimony: Iowa

1631. Archbell, Roy A. "Iowa's Elimination of the Fault Concept in Alimony Awards," *Wake Forest Law Review*, vol. 9, no. 1 (1972): 152–58.

1632. Hogue, Jon. "Does No-Fault Divorce Portend No-Fault Alimony?" *University of Pittsburg Law Review*, vol. 34, no. 3 (1973): 486–99.

1633. "Regeneration of Alimony After a Second Marriage Has Been Annulled," *Journal of Family Law*, vol. 13, no. 4 (1973–74): 875–79.

Alimony: Kansas

1634. Hausheer, Myron. "Alimony Termination after a Voidable Remarriage," *Washburn Law Journal*, vol. 12, no. 3 (1973): 391–95.

1635. Lane, Gary L. "Survival of Obligor's Duties under Maintenance Decrees," *Washburn Law Journal*, vol. 12, no. 1 (1972): 92.

Alimony: Kentucky

1636. Smith, George A. "Alimony and Property Restoration—A Restatement," *Kentucky Law Journal*, vol. 60, no. 1 (1971): 236–45.

Alimony: Louisiana

1637. Bilbe, Kathleen. "Permanent Alimony: Wife's Earning Capacity Not Considered," *Southern University Law Review* 3 (Spring 1977): 266–77.

1638. "Deliberto v. Deliberto," *Journal of Family Law*, vol. 15, no. 4 (1977): 834–38.

1639. Gremillion, Glenn B. "Determination of Fault for Purposes of Permanent Alimony," *Loyola Law Review*, vol. 21, no. 4 (1975): 1012–19.

1640. Griffis, Charles B. "Pre-separation Fault Bars All Alimony Claims of the Spouse at Fault Regardless of Post-separation Fault of the Other Spouse," *Tulane Law Review*, vol. 53, no. 4 (1979): 1532–42.

1641. Guidry, Hervin A. "Louisiana's Forbidden Antenuptial Waiver of Alimony pendente lite," *Louisiana Law Review*, vol. 39, no. 4 (1979): 1161–72.

1642. Lewis, William E. "Alimony after Divorce: Tradition versus Reality," *Southern University Law Review* 3 (Spring 1977): 278–87.

1643. Longman, Douglas C., Jr. "Husband's Burden of Providing Alimony and Child Support," *Louisiana Law Review*, vol. 37, no. 3 (1977): 957–65.

1644. McIntosh, Phillip. "Nature of Alimony—Separate or Community Obligation?" *Louisiana Law Review*, vol. 37, no. 3 (1977): 965–73.

1645. Mouledoux, Andre J. "Alimony pendente lite: One-Way Street under Louisiana Civil Code Article 148," *Loyola Law Review*, vol. 22, no. 4 (1976): 1086–95.

1646. Ried, Diane E. "Alimony and Equal Protection: A Search for Rational Relationships," *Loyola Law Review*, vol. 22, no. 4 (1976): 103–60.

1647. ———. "Wife's Earning Capacity—Irrelevant to a Determination of Alimony Rights," *Loyola Law Review*, vol. 23, no. 2 (1977): 595–604.

1648. Robinson, George H., Jr. "Life Insurance as Alimony—Income Tax Aspects," *Louisiana Law Review*, vol. 34, no. 1 (1973): 114–21.

1649. Sherman, David R. "Husband's Right to Seek Permanent Alimony under Louisiana Law," *Loyola Law Review*, vol. 22, no. 1 (1976): 397–403.

1650. Tomeny, Ann E. "Alimony Recognition as a Civil Effect in Putative Marriages," *Loyola Law Review*, vol. 20, no. 2 (1973–74): 372–77.

1651. Zimmering, Paul L. "Relitigation of Fault for the Purpose of Alimony," *Tulane Law Review*, vol. 49, no. 4 (1975): 1161–67.

Alimony: Maine

1652. "Enforcement of Money Judgments and Divorce Decrees in Maine," *Maine Law Review*, vol. 24, no. 1 (1972): 99–122.

Alimony: Maryland

1653. "Alimony—Fault is to Be Considered in Awarding Alimony in an Absolute Divorce Based on Five Years of Uninterrupted Separation," *Maryland Law Review*, vol. 33, no. 4 (1973): 489–99.

1654. Baldwin, Rignal W., and Winner, Leslie. "Increase or Decrease of Permanent Alimony and Child Support Granted without the Necessity of Showing a Change in the Circumstances of Both Parties," *University of Baltimore Law Review*, vol. 3, no. 2 (1974): 328–34.

1655. "Divorce—Fault is Relevant in Determination of Alimony in Divorce Action Brought under No-Fault Prolonged Separation Statute," *Harvard Law Review*, vol. 87, no. 7 (1974): 1579–89.

1656. Strausberg, Gary I. "Abandoned Spouse: Alimony and Support Actions, and the Maryland Long Arm Statute," *Maryland Law Review*, vol. 37, no. 2 (1977): 227–66.

Alimony: Massachusetts

1657. Katz, Sanford N., and Inker, Monroe L. *Fathers, Husbands, and Lovers: Legal Rights and Responsibilities*. Chicago: American Bar Association, Section of Family Law, 1979.

Alimony: Missouri

1658. Beuche, Larry W. "No Revival of Alimony Following an Annulled 'Remarriage,' " *Missouri Law Review*, vol. 43, no. 4 (1978): 591–600.

1659. Breezeel, Gary L. "Spousal Maintenance in Missouri: The Old and the New," *Missouri Law Review*, vol. 41, no. 4 (1976): 570–81.

1660. Coleman, James P. "Missouri Experience with Garnishment under 42 U.S.C.,659," *Missouri Bar Journal*, vol. 33, no. 1 (1977): 40–45+.

1661. Constance, Richard. "Enforcement of Maintenance and Support under the Missouri Dissolution Act," *UMKC Law Review*, vol. 44 (Spring 1976): 416–37.

1662. Jones, Christopher. "Enforcement of Maintenance and Support Orders by Contempt Proceedings—Imprisonment for Debt," *Missouri Law Review*, vol. 42, no. 2 (1977): 325–31.

1663. Krauskopf, Joan M. "Applying the Maintenance Statute," *Missouri Bar Journal*, vol. 33, no. 2 (1977): 93–104.

1664. ———. "Maintenance: Theory and Negotiation," *Missouri Bar Journal*, vol. 33, no. 1 (1977): 24–32.

1665. Ruhland, Robert G. "Dissolution of Marriage under Missouri's New Divorce Law—Maintenance and Support," *Missouri Bar Journal*, vol. 29, no. 8 (1973): 516–19.

1666. Scott, Donald G. "Award of Nominal Maintenance to Preserve Jurisdiction to Modify," *Missouri Law Review*, vol. 43, no. 4 (1978): 754–62.

Alimony: Nebraska

1667. Berger, Penny. "Alimony Awards under No Fault Divorce Statutes," *Nebraska Law Review*, vol. 53, no. 1 (1974): 126–36.

1668. Hoffman, Judy. "First Decision by Nebraska Supreme Court under Nebraska's New No-Fault Marriage Dissolution Statutes Leaves Uncertain the Question of Whether Fault is to Be Excluded from the Post-dissolution Determination of Alimony and Property Settlement," *Creighton Law Review*, vol. 7, no. 2 (1974): 369–85.

Alimony: New Jersey

1669. *Matrimonial Decrees: Modification and Enforcement.* Newark, NJ; Institute for Continuing Legal Education, 1975.

1670. Richardson, J. Michael. "Husband Not Required to Reinstate Alimony upon Annulment of Wife's Second Marriage," *Drake Law Review*, vol. 21, no. 3 (1972): 645–48.

Alimony: New York

1671. Keleher, Thomas D. "Termination of Alimony under Section 248 of New York's Domestic Relations Law," *Albany Law Review*, vol. 43, no. 4 (1979): 967–78.

1672. Murphy, Richard H. "Impact of the Equal Rights Amendment on the New York State Alimony Statute," *Buffalo Law Review*, vol. 24 (Winter 1975): 395–418.

1673. Ullman, Lois. "Alimony Modification: Cohabitation of Ex-Wife with Another Man," *Hofstra Law Review*, vol. 7, no. 2 (1979): 471–98.

Alimony: Ohio

1674. "Collection of Temporary Alimony after Decree—Arrears Owed on Temporary Alimony Are Merged into the Final Decree and the Right to Enforce Does Not Extend Beyond the Decree—Colom v. Colom." *Capital University Law Review*, vol. 9, no. 2 (1979): 407–12.

1675. Kienzle, Susan L. "Proof of Former Wife's Unchastity as a Factor in a Proceeding to Modify an Alimony Award Based upon Agreement of the Parties," *University of Toledo Law Review*, vol. 8, no. 3 (1977): 783–95.

1676. Lavin, John J. "Divorce and Alimony, Separation Agreements, Jurisdiction of Court to Modify Impairment of Contract, Statutory Provisions," *Akron Law Review*, vol. 10, no. 2 (1976): 382–91.

1677. Lee, Joe. "In re Waller—Discharge of Debt: Alimony, Debt or Support," *American Bankruptcy Law Journal*, vol. 50, no. 2 (1976): 175–78.

1678. Reckling, William J. "The Court of Common Pleas Has Continuing Jurisdiction to Modify a Decree of Alimony for Sustenance Even Though the Decree Incorporates a Prior Separation Agreement," *University of Cincinnati Law Review*, vol. 45, no. 3 (1976): 717–23.

1679. Swift, David A. "Separation Agreements and the Modification of Alimony Awards in Ohio," *Ohio State Law Journal*, vol. 38, no. 3 (1977): 735–53.

1680. Tabac, William L. "Alimony and Child Support in Ohio: New Directions after Dissolution," *Cleveland State Law Review*, vol 26 (1977): 395–412.

Alimony: Oregon

1681. Aarnas, Laila E. "Determination of Spousal Support," *Oregon Law Review*, vol. 57, no. 4 (1978): 566–72.

1682. Sasaki, Joanne. "Unander v. Unander: Recognition of the Alimony Provision in Antenuptial Contracts," *Williamette Law Journal*, vol. 10, no. 1 (1973): 117–26.

Alimony: Pennsylvania

1683. Beck, Phyllis W. "Equal Rights Amendment: The Pennsylvania Experience," *Dickinson Law Review*, vol. 81, no. 3 (1977): 395–416.

1684. "Civil Contempt for Failure to Support—Limitation on Use of Pennsylvania Procedural Support Law in Incarceration of Indigent Defendants," *Dickinson Law Review*, vol. 81, no. 4 (1977): 851–57.

1685. Donley, Joseph M. "Alimony—Effect of Equal Rights Amendment," *Akron Law Review*, vol. 8, no. 2 (1974): 171–79.

1686. Donohue, William J. "Pennsylvania Declares the Wife's Right to Divorce from Bed and Board and Alimony pendente lite Unconstitutional in Light of the Equal Rights Amendment," *Dickinson Law Review*, vol. 78, no. 2 (1973): 402–12.

1687. "Effect of Pennsylvania's Equal Rights Amendment on Divorce a Mensa et Thoro," *Journal of Family Law*, vol. 13, no. 3 (1973–74): 629–31.

1688. Hunting, Margaret. "Support Law and the Equal Rights Amendment in Pennsylvania," *Dickinson Law Review*, vol. 77, no. 2 (1973): 254–76.

1689. Morrissey, Francis J., Jr. "Pennsylvania Primer for Alimony and Equitable Distribution," *Pennsylvania Bar Association Quarterly*, vol. 47, no. 4 (1976): 503–17.

Alimony: Puerto Rico

1690. Colón Rodríquez, Victor L. "La Institutión de Alimentos ante una Nueva Politica Publica del Estado," *Revista Juridica de la Universidad de Puerto Rico*, vol. 42, no. 2 (1973): 305–37.

1691. Vázquez Bote, Eduardo. "Los Alimentos al Ex-cónyuge, en el Divorcio Vincular: Notas Acerca de una Interpretación Armónica," *Revista de Derecho Puertorriqueño*, vol. 14 (abril-junio 1975): 677–85.

Alimony: South Dakota

1692. Bird, Thomas L. "Connolly v. Connolly: Antenuptial Agreements Settling Alimony," *South Dakota Law Review*, vol. 24, no. 2 (1979): 494–509.

Alimony: Tennessee

1693. Swann, Mary C. "Dischargeability of Domestic Obligations in Bankruptcy," *Tennessee Law Review*, vol. 43, no. 2 (1976): 231–73.

Alimony: Texas

1694. Gerken, Robert T., and Schultz, Phyllis. "Garnishment: 42 U.S.C. S. 659: The United States Cannot Be Made Party to a Texas Garnishment Proceeding to Enforce a Divorce Decree Which Divided Military Retired Pay as Community Property between Spouses," *Judge Advocate General's Journal*, vol. 30, no. 2 (1978): 221–28.

1695. Raup, Cal C. "State Court Jurisdiction: The Long-Arm Reaches Domestic Relations Cases," *Texas Tech Law Review*, 6 (Spring 1975): 1021–54.

Alimony: Virginia

1696. Holt, Joel H. "Support v. Alimony in Virginia: It's Time to Use the Revised Statutes," *University of Richmond Law Review*, vol. 12, no. 1 (1977): 139–56.

TRUSTS

1697. "Alimony Trust—Income Beneficiary of Section 71(a) Alimony Trust May Exclude Distributions Attributable to Tax-Exempt Interest When Computing Taxable Income," *Vanderbilt Law Review,* vol. 23, no. 2 (1970): 466–73.

1698. Boies, Judith. "Use of Trusts in Divorce Settlements," *New York University Institute of Federal Taxation,* vol. 30 (1972): 589.

1699. Del Cotto, Louis A. "Alimony Trust: Its Relationship with Subchapter J: The Right to Amortize Basis," *Tax Law Review,* vol. 33 (Summer 1978): 577–98.

1700. Gunn, Alan. "Douglas v. Willcuts Today: The Income Tax Problems of Using Alimony Trusts," *Cornell Law Review,* vol. 63, no. 5 (1978): 1022–52.

ANNULMENT

1701. "Annulment of a Marriage Rescinds Joint Returns," *Taxation for Lawyers,* vol. 5, no. 4 (1977): 216–17.

1702. Clinard, Keith A. "Reinstatement of Alimony under a Prior Divorce Decree after Annulment of Remarriage," *Wake Forest Law Review,* vol. 14, no. 2 (1978): 273–86.

1703. Grose, Madison. "Putative Spousal Support Rights and the Federal Bankruptcy Act," *UCLA Law Review,* vol. 25, no. 1 (1977): 96–124.

1704. Newman, Donald J. "Annulments—A Comparative Study of Jurisdiction and Recognition of Foreign Decrees," *Case Western Reserve Journal of International Law,* vol. 3, no. 2 (1971): 176–206.

STATES

Annulment: Arizona

1705. "Arizona Becomes the Second State to Adopt the Broad 'New York' Annulment Rule," *Washington University Law Quarterly* 3 (1971): 469–477.

1706. Hyman, Jeffrey A. "Religious Misrepresentation Held as a Ground for Annulment in Arizona," *Syracuse Law Review,* vol. 22, no. 4 (1971): 1180–86.

Annulment: California

1707. Osburn, Richard G. "Dissolution and Voidable Marriage under the California Family Law Act," *Loyola University of Los Angeles Law Review,* vol. 4, no. 2 (1971): 331–60.

Annulment: Georgia

1708. "Annulment in Georgia: A Product of Judicial Restraint and Legislative Confusion," *Georgia Law Review,* vol. 14, no. 1 (1979): 81–100.

Annulment: Louisiana

1709. Percy, Ryland. "Putative Marriages: What are 'Civil Effects'?" *Louisiana Law Review,* vol. 36, no. 2 (1976): 704–11.

1710. Wilkinson, Joseph C. "Civil Code Article 39 Unconstitutional as Applied to Venue Requirements in Actions for Annulment of Marriage, Separation, or Divorce," *Tulane Law Review,* vol. 53, no. 3 (1979): 973–83.

Annulment: Montana

1711. Molloy, Don. "Bad Laws Make Hard Cases: State ex rel Angvall v. District Court and the Law of Annulment in Montana," *Montana Law Review,* vol. 36, no. 2 (1975): 267–84.

Annulment: New Jersey

1712. Aliber, Stephen D. "Fraudulent Concealment of Narcotics Addiction as Grounds for Annulment," *Missouri Law Review,* vol. 38, no. 2 (1973): 287–91.

Annulment: New York

1713. Schultz, Thomas M. "Antenuptial Agreement—Void Marriage," *Duquesne Law Review,* vol. 9, no. 1 (1970): 135–41.

Annulment: Oklahoma

1714. Forst, Bradley P. "Annulment Controversy: Revival of Prior Alimony Payments," *Tulsa Law Journal,* vol. 13, no. 1 (1977): 127–45.

ATTORNEYS

1715. Berstein, Alan, and Zeisel, Elliot. "Cooperation between Legal and Psychotherapeutic Communities." *Family Law Newsletter*, vol. 17, no. 1 (1976): 5–6.

1716. Callner, Bruce W. "Boundaries of the Divorce Lawyer's Role," *Family Law Quarterly*, vol. 10, no. 4 (1977): 389–98.

1717. Church, Virginia A. "Counselor-at-Law: A Game of Chess," *Trial*, vol. 8, no. 5 (1972): 27+ .

1718. DuCanto, Joseph N. "The Age of Aquarius and the Matrimonial Lawyer," *Trial*, vol. 8, no. 5 (1972): 21.

1719. Hagy, James C. "Simultaneous Representation: Transaction Resolution in the Adversary System," *Case Western Reserve Law Review*, vol. 28, no. 1 (1977): 86–118.

1720. Huebner, Daniel L. "Scapegoating the Attorney, a Displacement of Marital Anguish," *Journal of Contemporary Psychotherapy*, vol. 9, no. 1 (1977): 112–15.

1721. Johnson, Flora. "What God Has Joined Together, These Men Put Asunder," *Student Lawyer*, vol. 6, no. 7 (1978): 18–24+ .

1722. Ray, Edward L. "If Your Client Is a Stepparent . . . ," *Family Advocate*, vol. 1, no. 3 (1979): 29–30.

1723. Sachs, Sidney S. "What a Family Lawyer Needs to Know about Psychiatry," *Family Law Reporter*, vol. 2 (December 7, 1976): 4013–18, monograph no. 22.

ADVERTISING

1724. Sell, Kenneth D. "Divorce Advertising—One Year after Bates," *Family Law Quarterly*, vol. 12, no. 4 (1979): 275–83. R.

ATTITUDES

1725. Herrman, Margaret S.; McKenry, Patrick C.; and Weber, Ruth E. "Attorneys' Perceptions of their Role in Divorce," *Journal of Divorce*, vol. 2, no. 3 (1979): 313–22. R.

1726. Johnson, Walter D. "Divorce, Alimony, Support, and Custody: a Survey of Judges' Attitudes in One State," *Family Law Reporter*, vol. 3 (November 9, 1976): 4001–12, monograph 22. R.

1727. Kressel, Kenneth, et al. "Professional Intervention in Divorce: Views of Lawyers, Psychotherapists, and Clergy." In *Divorce and Separation: Context, Causes and Consequences,* edited by George Levinger and Oliver C. Moles, pp. 246–72. New York: Basic Books, 1979. R.

1728. McKenry, Patrick C.; Herman, Margaret S.; and Weber, Ruth E. "Attitudes of Attorneys toward Divorce Issues," *Conciliation Courts Review*, vol. 16, no. 2 (1978): 11–17. R.

ATTORNEY-CLIENT RELATIONSHIP

1729. Bellison, Leonard E. "Changing Dynamics in Attorney-Client Relationship due to No-Fault Divorce Legislation," *Family Law Newsletter*, vol. 14, no. 1 (1973): 5–7.

1730. ———. "Changing Dynamics in Attorney-Client Relationship due to No-Fault Divorce Legislation," *Case and Comment*, vol. 79, no. 2 (1974): 30–31+ .

1731. Colton, Jerome G., and Austin, Jack F. "A Message to Our Client and His or Her Spouse Regarding Their Divorce," *Case and Comment*, vol. 77, no. 6 (1972): 14–15.

1732. Holder, Angela R. "Client Autonomy and Divorce Negotiations," *Family Law Newsletter*, vol. 17, no. 2 (1977): 11–14.

1733. Loucks, Richard R. "Explaining Divorce Proceedings to a Client," *Practical Lawyer*, vol. 20, no. 1 (1974): 83–87.

CLIENT INTERVIEWS

1734. Barrett, Leo J. "Initial Interview with a Divorce Client," *Practical Lawyer*, vol, 23, no. 4 (1977): 75–86.

1735. Carsola, Anthony T. "First Steps in Divorce—Initial Client Contract, Litigation Financing, Investigation, and Self Help," *Family Law Reporter* 3 (February 1, 1977): 4019–24, monograph no. 24.

1736. Groves, Patricia H. "Lawyer–Client Interviews and the Social Organization of Preparation for Court in Criminal and Di-

vorce Cases," Ph.D. diss., University of British Columbia, 1973 (*DAI* 34/7A, p. 4428). R.

1737. Moss, Milton O. "The Initial Interview in a Domestic Relations Case," *Practical Lawyer*, vol. 22, no. 1 (1976): 59–64.

1738. Sachs, Sidney S., and Goldman, Henry T. "The Crucial First Interview in a Divorce Case," *Family Law Reporter* 1 (January 17, 1975): 4013–20.

COUNSELING BY ATTORNEYS

1739. Elkins, James R. "Counseling Model for Lawyers in Divorce Cases," *Notre Dame Lawyer*, vol. 53, no. 2 (1977): 229–65.

1740. Freeman, Harrop A., and Weihofen, Henry. "Client Counseling in Negotiating the Terms of Divorce," *Practical Lawyer*, vol. 18, no. 4 (1972): 41–50.

1741. Merder, I. David. "Need for an Expanded Role for Attorney in Divorce Counseling," *Family Law Quarterly*, vol. 4, no. 3 (1970): 280–95.

1742. Mussehl, Robert C. "From Advocate to Counselor: The Emerging Role of the Family Law Practitioner," *Gonzaga Law Review*, vol. 12, no. 3 (1977): 443–54. R.

FEES

1743. Berlin, Gerald A. "Everything You Wanted to Know about Setting Matrimonial Case Fees But Have Been Afraid to Ask (Yourself)," *Case and Comment*, vol. 82, no. 1 (1977): 53–59.

1744. ———. "Everything You Wanted to Know about Setting Matrimonial Case Fees but Have Been Afraid to Ask (Yourself)," *Law Office Economics and Management*, vol. 18, no. 1 (1977): 47–56.

1745. Buchman, Arnold E. "Post Divorce Decree Awards of Counsel Fees," *Connecticut Bar Journal*, vol. 44, no. 3 (1970): 359–69.

1746. "Determining Fees in Divorce Cases," *Law Office Economics and Management*, vol. 18, no. 4 (1978): 506–13.

1747. Dienstag, Gary E. "Attorney Fees for Services Rendered in the Prosecution:

Or, Defense of Appeals from Post-decree Divorce Proceedings," *Illinois Bar Journal*, vol. 66, no. 10 (1978): 568-74 + .

1748. James, Frank S., III. "Contingent Fees in Domestic Relations Actions: The

Minority Rule(s)," *Journal of the Legal Profession*, vol. 3, no. 1 (1978): 209–16.

1749. Spellman, Howard H. "How Should the Adequacy of Compensation for the Wife's Attorney in Divorce Cases be Determined?" *Family Law Quarterly,* vol. 40, no. 1 (1970): 53–60.

1750. Stabile, Thomas P. "The Family Lawyers' Dilemma—'What Do You Mean You Have Been Reconciled, What About My Fees?' " *Orange County Bar Journal*, vol. 6, no. 1 (1979): 9–12.

CHILD CUSTODY

1751. Bank, Raymond L. "A Parent's Adultery Raises No Presumptions of Unfitness for Child Custody," *University of Baltimore Law Review*, vol. 7, no. 1 (1977): 141–50.

1752. Benedek, Elissa P. "Child Custody Laws: Their Psychiatric Implications," *American Journal of Psychiatry*, vol. 129, no. 3 (1972): 326–28.

1753. Benedek, Elissa P., and Benedek, Richard S. "New Child Custody Laws: Making Them Do What They Say," *Mental Health Digest*, vol. 4, no. 12 (1972): 52–55.

1754. ———. "New Child Custody Laws: Making Them Do What They Say," *American Journal of Orthopsychiatry*, vol. 42, no. 5 (1972): 825–34.

1755. Bishop, Thomas A. "Child Custody: An Overview," *Connecticut Bar Journal*, vol. 53, no. 4 (1979): 269–78.

1756. Bodenheimer, Brigitte M., and Neeley-Kvarme, Janet. "Jurisdiction over Child Custody and Adoption after Shaffer and Kulko," *University of California, Davis, Law Review*, vol. 12, no. 2 (1979): 229–53.

1757. Callow, William G. "Custody of the Child and the Uniform Marriage and Divorce Act," *South Dakota Law Review* 18 (Summer 1973): 550–58.

1758. "Child Custody: A Symposium," *Connecticut Bar Journal*, vol. 53, no. 4 (1979): 269–386.

1759. Fenton, Kennard L. "Minor's Rights in a Divorce Proceeding," *Missouri Bar Journal*, vol. 29, no. 7 (1973): 450–54 + .

1760. Fox, William. "Alimony, Property Settlement and Child Custody under the New Divorce Statutes: No-Fault Is Not Enough," *Catholic University Law Review*, vol. 22, no. 2 (1973): 365–84.

1761. Freed, Doris J., and Foster, Henry H., Jr. "Shuffled Child and Divorce Court," *Trial*, vol. 10, no. 3 (1974): 26 + .

1762. Hoffman, Blair W. "Restrictions on a Parent's Right to Travel in Child Custody Cases: Possible Consitutional Questions," *University of California, Davis, Law Review*, vol. 6 (1973): 181–94.

1763. Hudson, William E. "Family Law—Custody of Children," *Kentucky Law Journal*, vol. 71, no. 2 (1970): 529–36.

1764. Inker, Monroe L. "Expanding the Rights of Children in Custody and Adoption Cases," *Family Law Quarterly*, vol. 5, no. 4 (1971): 417–23. Also in *Journal of Family Law*, vol. 11, no. 2 (1971): 125–35.

1765. Jackson, Julie H. "Loss of Parental Rights as a Consequence of Conviction and Imprisonment: Unintended Punishment," *New England Journal of Prison Law* 6 (Fall 1979): 61–112.

1766. Kiefer, Louis. "Custody Meanings and Considerations," *Connecticut Bar Journal*, vol. 53, no. 4 (1979): 371–86.

1767. Lauerman, Nora. "Nonmarital Sexual Conduct and Child Custody," *University of Cincinnati Law Review*, vol. 46, no. 3 (1977): 647–724.

1768. Leonard, Martha F., and Provence, Sally. "The Development of Parent-Child Relationships and the Psychological Parent," *Connecticut Bar Journal*, vol. 53, no. 4 (1979): 320–29.

1769. Lightener, John. "An Attorneys Approach to Psychiatrists in Custody Cases," *American Academy of Psychiatry and the Law Bulletin*, vol. 4 (1976): 105–13.

1770. Lindsley, Byron F. "Custody Proceedings: Battlefield or Peace

Conference?" *American Academy of Psychiatry and the Law Bulletin*, vol. 4 (1976): 127–31.

1771. Marschall, Patricia H., and Gatz, Margaret J. "Custody Decision Process: Toward New Roles for Parents and the State," *North Carolina Central Law Journal*, vol. 7, no. 1 (1975): 50–72. R.

1772. Mnookin, Robert H. *Child, Family and State: Problems and Materials on Children and the Law*. Boston: Little, Brown & Co., 1978.

1773. Moody, Edward O. "The Proposed Arkansas Uniform Child Custody Jurisdiction Act," *University of Arkansas at Little Rock Law Journal*, vol. 1, no. 2 (1978): 332–54.

1774. Morris, Craig. "A Developmental Approach to Child Custody," *Connecticut Bar Journal*, vol. 53, no. 4 (1979): 330–42.

1775. Moskowitz, Lawrence A. "Divorce-Custody Dispositions: The Child's Wishes in Perspective," *Santa Clara Law Review*, vol. 18, no. 2 (1978): 427–52.

1776. National Conference of Commissioners on Uniform State Laws. *Matrimonial, Family, and Health Laws, with Annotations from State and Federal Courts*. Saint Paul, MN: West Publishing Co., 1973.

1777. Naturale, Cynthia. "Damages Awarded in Case of First Impression," *Trial*, vol. 14, no. 11 (1978): 30–31.

1778. Podell, Ralph J.; Peck, Harry F.; and First, Curry. "Custody—To Which Parent?" *Marquette Law Review*, vol. 56, no. 1 (1973): 51–68.

1779. ———. "Custody—To Which Parent?" *Family Law Newsletter*, vol. 13, no. 14 (1973): 5–6 + .

1780. Polaw, Bertram. "Child Custody—the Law and Changing Social Attitudes," *Family Law Newsletter,* vol. 13, no 3 (1972): 11–14.

1781. Rodgers, Thomas A. "The Crisis of Custody: How a Psychiatrist Can Be of Help," *American Academy of Psychiatry and the Law Bulletin* 4 (1976): 114–19.

1782. Sassower, Doris L. "Custody's Last Stand, *Trial,* vol. 15, no. 9 (1979): 14–17.

1783. Schiller, Donald C. "Child Custody: Evolution of Current Criteria," *De Paul Law Review,* vol. 26, no. 2 (1977): 241–58.

1784. Sheehan, John T., Jr. "Custody Awards of Minors," *New England Law Review,* vol. 6, no. 2 (1971): 201–11.

1785. Shepherd, Bobby E. "Death of the Custodial Parent and Jurisdiction to Modify the Decree," *Arkansas Law Review,* vol. 29, no. 1 (1975): 104–10.

1786. Slifkin, Morrie, and Mulligan, William G. "Custody and Visitation: The Judge's Viewpoint," *New York State Bar Journal,* vol. 48, no. 6 (1976): 450–60.

1787. Spencer, Janet M., and Zammit, Joseph P. "Mediation-Arbitration: A Proposal for Private Resolution of Disputes between Divorced or Separated Parents," *Duke Law Journal,* 5 (1976): 911–39.

1788. ———. "Reflections on Arbitration under the Family Dispute Services," *Arbitration Journal,* vol. 32, no. 2 (1977): 111–22.

1789. Trenker, Thomas R. "Modern Status of Maternal Preference Rule or Presumption in Child Custody Cases," *American Law Reports, Annotated, 3d. ser.* 70 (1976): 262–303.

1790. Trunnell, Thomas L. "Johnnie and Suzie, Don't Cry: Mommy and Daddy Aren't That Way," *American Academy of Psychiatry and the Law Bulletin* 4 (1976): 120–26.

1791. Uviller, Rena K. "Fathers' Rights and Feminism: The Maternal Presumption Revisited," *Harvard Women's Law Journal,* vol. 1, no. 1 (1978): 107–30.

1792. Weitzman, Lenore J., and Dixon, Ruth B. "Child Custody Awards: Legal Standards and Empirical Patterns for Child Custody, Support and Visitation after Divorce," *University of California, Davis, Law Review,* vol. 12, no. 2 (1979): 471–521. R.

1793. Yannacone, Victor J., Jr., and Grafton, Samuel. "Children or Chattels?" *Trial Lawyers Quarterly,* vol. 8, no. 3-4 (1972): 10–28.

1794. Young, Don J. "Evolving Judicial Concepts in Custody Cases," *Juvenile and Family Court Journal,* vol. 29, no. 2 (1978): 21–25.

1795. Young, Sheila. "Feminist Arguments for a Working Mother's Custody," *Women's Rights Law Reporter,* vol. 1, no. 6 (1974): 23–25.

BEST INTERESTS OF THE CHILD DOCTRINE

1796. Greenbaum, Martin, and Greenbaum, Richard. "In the Best Interest of the Child," *Florida Bar Journal,* vol. 50, no. 9 (1976): 532–36.

1797. Foster, Henry H., Jr. "Adoption and Child Custody: Best Interests of the Child?" *Buffalo Law Review,* vol. 22, no. 1 (1972): 1–16.

BEYOND THE BEST INTERESTS OF THE CHILD

1798. Crouch, Richard E. "Essay on the Critical and Judicial Reception of 'Beyond the Best Interests of the Child,' " *Family Law Quarterly,* vol. 13, no. 1 (1979): 49–103.

1799. Dembitz, Nanette. "Beyond the Best Interests of the Child': A Review and Critique," *The Record of the Association of the Bar of the City of New York,* vol. 29, no. 5-6 (1974): 456–63.

1800. Foster, Henry H., Jr. "Review of 'Beyond the Best Interests of the Child,' " *Willamette Law Journal,* 12 (Summer 1976): 545–56.

CHILD ADVOCATES

1801. Bersoff, Donald N. "Representation for Children in Custody Decisions: All That Glitters Is Not Gault," *Journal of Family Law,* vol. 15, no. 1 (1976-77): 27–49.

1802. Casasanto, Michael D. "Guardians ad litem: A Proposal to Better Protect the Interests of Children of Divorce," *New Hampshire Bar Journal,* vol. 20, no. 2 (1978): 35–60.

1803. Inker, Monroe L., and Perretta, Charlotte A. "A Child's Right to Counsel in Custody Cases," *Family Law Quarterly,* vol. 5, no. 1 (1971): 108–20.

1804. MacDonald, William E. "Case for Independent Counsel to Represent Children in Custody Proceedings," *New England Law Review,* vol. 7, no. 2 (1972): 351–60.

1805. Makaitis, Regina T. "Protecting the Interests of Children in Custody Proceedings: A Perspective on Twenty Years of Theory and Practice in the Appointment of Guardians ad litem," *Creighton Law Review,* vol. 12, no. 1 (1978): 234–55.

1806. Milmed, Paul K. "Due Process for Children: A Right to Counsel in Custody Proceedings," *New York University Review of Law and Social Change,* vol. 4, no. 2 (1974): 177–89.

1807. Mlyniec, Wallace J. "Child Advocate in Private Custody Disputes: A Role in Search of a Standard," *Journal of Family Law,* vol. 16, no. 1 (1977): 1–17.

1808. Wilcox, Maurice K.C. "Child's Due Process Right to Counsel in Divorce Custody Proceedings," *Hastings Law Journal,* vol. 27, no. 4 (1976): 917–50.

CHILD'S PREFERENCE

1809. Schowalter, John E. "View on the Role of the Child's Preference in Custody Litigation," *Connecticut Bar Journal,* vol. 53, no. 4 (1979): 298–300.

1810. Siegel, David M., and Hurley, Suzanne. "Role of the Child's Preference in Custody Proceedings," *Family Law Quarterly,* vol. 11, no. 1 (1977): 1–58.

1811. Speca, John M. "Role of the Child in Selecting His or Her Custodian in Divorce Cases," *Drake Law Review,* vol. 27, no. 3 (1977-78): 437–57.

CONTESTED CUSTODY

1812. Batt, John. "Child Custody Disputes: A Developmental-Psychological Approach to Proof and Decisionmaking," *Willamette Law Journal* 12 (Summer 1976): 491–510.

1813. Bellington, Janice E. "Best Interest of Child in Custodial Proceedings and Waiver of Jurisdictional Objection— Sommer v. Borovic," *De Paul Law Review,* vol. 27, no. 3 (1978): 853–69.

1814. Berdon, Robert I. "Child Custody Litigation: Some Relevant Considerations," *Connecticut Bar Journal,* vol. 53, no. 4 (1979): 279–97.

1815. Bodenheimer, Brigitte M. "Rights of Children and the Crisis in Custody Litigation: Modification of Custody in and out of State," *University of Colorado Law Review* 46 (Summer 1975): 495–508.

1816. Bradbrook, Adrian. "Relevance of Psychological and Psychiatric Studies to the Future Development of the Laws Governing the Settlement of Interparental Child Custody Disputes," *Journal of Family Law,* vol. 11, no. 4 (1972): 557–87.

1817. Cotroneo, Margaret. "At the Intersection of Family Systems and Legal Systems: Child Custody Decisions in Context," *Connecticut Bar Journal,* vol. 53, no. 4 (1979): 349–55.

1818. Katz, Lucy. "The Maternal Preferance and the Psychological Parent: Suggestions for Allocating the Burden of Proof in Custody Litigation," *Connecticut Bar Journal,* vol. 53, no. 4 (1979): 343–48.

1819. Landsman, Kim J., and Minow, Martha L. "Lawyering for the Child: Principles of Representation in Custody and Visitation Disputes Arising from Divorce," *Yale Law Journal,* vol. 87, no. 6 (1978): 1126–90.

1820. Mnookin, Robert H. "Child-Custody Adjudication: Judicial Functions in the Face of Indeterminacy," *Law and Contemporary Problems,* vol. 39, no. 3 (1975): 226–93.

1821. Smith, Elizabeth J. "Non-judicial Resolution of Custody Disputes and Visitation Disputes," *University of California, Davis, Law Review,* vol. 12, no. 2 (1979): 582–603.

1822. Winter, Edward J., Jr. "The Purpose, Planning, and Use of Depositions in Contested Child Custody Litigation," *American Journal of Trial Advocacy,* vol. 1, no. 1 (1977): 75–97.

1823. Woody, Robert H. "Psychologists in Child Custody." In *Psychology in the Legal Process,* edited by Bruce D. Sales, pp. 249–67. New York: Spectrum, 1977.

DETERMINATIONS

1824. Gozansky, Nathaniel. "Court-Ordered Investigations in Child Custody Cases," *Willamette Law Journal,* vol. 12 (Summer 1976): 511–26.

1825. Kirshner, Sheldon G. "Child Custody Determination—A Better Way!" *Journal of Family Law,* vol. 17, no. 2 (1979): 275–96.

1826. Levy, Alan M. "Child Custody Determination—Proposed Psychiatric Methodology and Its Resultant Case Typology," *Journal of Psychiatry and Law,* vol. 6, no. 2 (1978): 189–214.

1827. Okpaku, Sheila R. "Psychology: Impediment or Aid in Child Custody Cases?" *Rutgers Law Review,* vol. 29, no. 4 (1976): 1117–53.

1828. Shepherd, Robert E., Jr. "Solomon's Sword: Adjudication of Child Custody Questions," *University of Richmond Law Review,* vol. 8, no. 2 (1974): 151–200.

1829. Smith, Stephanie H. "Psychological Parents vs. Biological Parents: The Courts' Response to New Directions in Child Custody Dispute Resolution," *Journal of Family Law,* vol. 17, no. 3 (1979): 545–76.

FATHER CUSTODY

1830. Foster, Henry H. Jr., and Freed, Doris J. "Life with Father: 1978," *Family Law Quarterly,* vol. 11, no. 4 (1977): 321–63.

1831. Orthner, Dennis K., and Lewis, Ken. "Evidence of Single-Father Competence in Childrearing," *Family Law Quarterly,* vol. 13, no. 1 (1979): 27–47.

1832. Pick, Grant. "Father Knows Best: The New Trend in Child Custody," *Student Lawyer,* vol. 6, no. 9 (1978): 38–43.

1833. Solomon, Philip F. "The Fathers' Revolution in Custody Cases," *Trial,* vol. 13, no. 10 (1977): 33–37.

1834. ———. "The Fathers' Revolution in Custody Cases," *Case and Comment,* vol. 83, no. 3 (1978): 3–4 + .

1835. Title, Peter S. "Father's Rights to Child Custody in Interparental Disputes," *Tulane Law Review,* vol. 49, no. 1 (1974): 189–207.

FOREIGN DECREES

1836. Nyswonger, J. Stephen. "Child Custody and Foreign Judgments," *Washburn Law Journal,* vol. 11, no. 2 (1972): 305–09.

HISTORY

1837. Zainaldin, Jamil S. "Emergence of a Modern American Family Law: Child Custody, Adoption, and the Courts, 1796–1851," *Northwestern University Law Review,* vol. 73, no. 6 (1979): 1038–89.

HOMOSEXUAL PARENTS

1838. Davies, Rosalie C. "Representing the Lesbian Mother," *Family Advocate,* vol. 1, no. 3 (1979): 21–23 + .

1839. Hitchens, Donna, and Price, Barbara. "Trial Strategy in Lesbian Mother Custody Cases: The Use of Expert Testimony," *Golden Gate University Law Review,* vol. 9, no. 2 (1978–79): 451–79.

1840. Hunter, Nan D., and Polikoff, Nancy D. "Custody Rights of Lesbian Mothers: Legal Theory and Litigation Strategy," *Buffalo Law Review,* vol. 25, no. 3 (1976): 691–733.

1841. Payne, Anne T. "Law and the Problem Parent: Custody and Parental Rights of Homosexual, Mentally Retarded, Mentally Ill and Incarcerated Parents," *Journal of Family Law,* vol. 16, no. 4 (1978): 797–818.

INTERSTATE CUSTODY

1842. Fain, Harry M. "The Interstate Child Custody Problem Revisited," *Family Law Newsletter,* vol. 16, no. 1 (1975): 1 + .

1843. Hudak, Leona M. "Plight of the Interstate Child in American Courts," *Akron Law Review,* vol. 9, no. 4 (1975): 257–300.

1844. ———. "Seize, Run, and Sue: the Ignominy of Interstate Child Custody Litigation in American Courts," *Missouri Law Review,* vol. 39, no. 4 (1974): 521–49.

1845. Jarrett, John L. "Jurisdiction in Interstate Child Custody Disputes," *Gonzaga Law Review,* vol. 12, no. 3 (1977): 423–42.

JEWISH VIEWS ON CUSTODY

1846. Warburg, Ronald. "Child Custody: A Comparative Analysis," *Israel Law Review,* vol. 14, no. 4 (1979): 480–503.

JOINT CUSTODY

1847. "Award of 'Joint Custody,' " *Journal of Family Law,* vol. 14, no. 1 (1975): 154–56.

1848. Bodenheimer, Brigitte M. "Progress under the Uniform Child Custody Jurisdiction Act and Remaining Problems: Punitive Decrees, Joint Custody, and Excessive Modifications," *California Law Review,* vol. 65, no. 5 (1977): 978–1014.

1849. Bratt, Carolyn S. "Joint Custody," *Kentucky Law Review,* vol. 67, no. 2 (1979): 271–308.

1850. Cox, Mary J., and Cease, Lory. "Joint Custody: What Does It Mean? How Does It Work?" *Family Advocate*, vol. 1, no. 1 (1978): 10–13.

1851. Daniels, Deborah. "Reasonable Visitation or Divided Custody?" *Missouri Law Review*, vol. 42 (1977): 136–43.

1852. Evans, William H. "Custody and Visitation—Practical Problems at the Temporary Hearing before the Family Court Commissioner," *Wisconsin Bar Bulletin*, vol. 52 (June 1979): 16–21.

1853. Folberg, H. Jay, and Graham, Marva. "Joint Custody of Children Following Divorce," *University of California, Davis, Law Review*, vol. 12, no. 2 (1979): 523–81.

1854. Foster, Henry H., Jr., and Freed, Doris. "Joint Custody: A Viable Alternative?" *Trial*, vol. 15, no. 5 (1979): 26–31. Also in *New York Law Journal* 180 (November 9, 1978): 1–2; (November 24, 1978): 1+; (December 22, 1978): 1–3.

1855. Greif, Judith B. "Joint Custody: A Sociological Study," *Trial*, vol. 15, no. 5 (1979): 32–33.

1856. Haddad, William F., and Roman, Mel. "No-Fault Custody," *Family Law Review*, vol. 2, no. 2 (1979): 95–102.

1857. Jarobe, J. Michael. "A Case for Joint Custody after the Parents' Divorce," *Journal of Family Law*, vol. 17, no. 4 (1979): 741–62.

1858. Kehoe, Michael E., and Salituro, Patricia. "Making Joint Custody Work," *Wisconsin Bar Journal*, vol. 52 (November 1979): 28–30.

1859. Miller, David J. "Joint Custody," *Family Law Quarterly*, vol. 13, no. 3 (1979): 345–412.

1860. Nielson, Priscilla H. "Joint Custody: An Alternative for Divorced Parents," *UCLA Law Review*, vol. 26, no. 5 (1979): 1084–125.

1861. Parley, Louis. "Joint Custody: A Lawyer's Perspective," *Connecticut Bar Journal*, vol. 53, no. 4 (1979): 310–19.

1862. Rabbino, Anne A. "Joint Custody Awards: Towards the Development of Judicial Standards," *Fordham Law Review*, vol. 48, no. 1 (1979): 105–27.

1863. Ramey, Martha L.; Stender, Fay; and Smaller, Deborah. "Joint Custody: Are Two Homes Better Than One?" *Golden Gate University Law Review*, vol. 8 (1979): 559–81.

1864. Woolley, Persia. "Shared Custody: Demands by Parents, Discouraged by the Courts," *Family Advocate*, vol. 1, no. 1 (1978): 6–9+.

KIDNAPPING

1865. Bodenheimer, Brigitte M. "International Kidnapping of Children: The United States Approach," *Family Law Quarterly*, vol. 11, no. 1 (1977): 83–100.

1866. Cole, Tom. "Child Stealing," *Family Advocate*, vol. 1, no. 2 (1978): 33–34+.

1867. Coombs, Russell M. " 'Snatched' Child is Halfway Home in Congress," *Family Law Quarterly*, vol. 11, no. 4 (1977): 407–26.

1868. Fisk, Mary. "Child-Snatching," *Trial*, vol. 13, no. 10 (1977): 18+.

1869. Fleck, Charles J. "Child Snatching by Parents: What Legal Remedies for 'Flee and Plea'?" *Chicago—Kent Law Review*, vol. 55, no. 2 (1979): 303–17.

1870. Foster, Henry H., and Freed, Doris J. "Child Snatching and Custodial Fights: The Case for the Uniform Child Custody Jurisdiction Act," *Hastings Law Journal*, vol. 28, no. 4 (1977): 1011–26.

1871. ———. "Proposed Legislation on Child Abduction," *Family Law Journal*, vol. 17, no. 2 (1977): 1–3.

1872. Lewis, Jane A. "Legalized Kidnapping of Children by Their Parents," *Dickinson Law Review*, vol. 80, no. 2 (1976): 305–27.

1873. Lewis, Ken. "On Reducing the Child Snatching Syndrome," *Children Today*, vol. 7, no. 6 (1978): 19–21+.

1874. Martin, Allan L. "Child Abduction by a Relative: Maryland Enacts a Misdemeanor Offense to Deter Parental Child-Stealing," *University of Baltimore Law Review*, vol. 8, no. 2 (1979): 609–23.

1875. Sanders, Judith A. "Prevention of Child Stealing: The Need for a National Policy," *Loyola of Los Angeles Law Review*, vol. 11, no. 4 (1978): 829–66.

1876. Spillane, Dennis. "Child Snatching," *Human Rights*, vol. 7, no. 2 (1978): 46–50.

1877. Stern, Richard. "Stemming the Proliferation of Parental Kidnapping: New York's Adoption of the Uniform Child Custody Jurisdiction Act," *Brooklyn Law Review*, vol. 45, no. 1 (1978): 89–129.

1878. Timko, Andrea A. "Criminal Sanctions against 'Child-Snatching' in North Carolina," *North Carolina Law Review*, vol. 55, no. 6 (1977): 1275–89.

1879. Wallop, Malcolm. "Children of Divorce and Separation: Pawns in the Child-Snatching game," *Trial*, vol. 15, no. 5 (1979): 34–37.

MEDIATION

1880. King, Donald B. "Child Custody—A Legal Problem?" *California State Bar Journal*, vol. 54, no. 3 (1979): 156–58+.

1881. Pearson, Jessica. "The Denver Custody Mediation Project," *Colorado Lawyer*, vol. 8, no. 7 (1979): 1210–20.

POLICY

1882. Felner, Robert D.; Farber, Stephanie S.; and Kent, Judith S. "Toward the Development of a Social Policy for Child Custody: A Multidisciplinary Framework," *Connecticut Bar Journal*, vol. 53, no. 4 (1979): 301–09.

STATES AND TERRITORIES

Custody: Alaska

1883. Gruenberg, Max F., and Mackey, Robert D. "A New Direction for Child Custody in Alaska," *UCLA-Alaska Law Review*, vol. 6, no. 1 (1976): 34–49.

1884. "Johnson v. Johnson," *Journal of Family Law*, vol. 16, no. 3 (1978): 622–27.

Custody: California

1885. Bodenheimer, Brigitte M. "Multiplicity of Child Custody Proceedings—Problems of California Custody Law," *Stanford Law Review*, 23 (April 1971): 703–34.

1886. Hatherly, John E. "Role of the Child's Wishes in California Custody Proceedings," *University of California, Davis, Law Review* 6 (1973): 332–53.

1887. Lysaght, Brian C. "Children in Transit: Child Custody and the Conflict of Laws," *University of California, Davis, Law Review* 6 (1973): 160–80.

1888. Porter, Everette M., and Walsh, Joseph F. "Evolution of California's Child Custody Laws: A Question of Statutory Interpretation," *Southwestern University Law Review*, vol. 7, no. 3 (1975): 1–35.

Custody: Connecticut

1889. Balbirer, Arthur E. "Rights and Obligations of Custodial and Non-Custodial Parents in Connecticut," *Connecticut Bar Journal*, vol. 53, no. 4 (1979): 356–70.

1890. Berdon, Robert I. "Child's Right to Counsel in a Contested Custody Proceeding Resulting from a Termination of the Marriage," *Connecticut Bar Journal*, vol. 50, no. 2 (1976): 150–67.

Custody: Florida

1891. Cleveland, C. Anthony. "Child Custody—Interracial Marriage May Be Considered in Framing Custody Modification Orders," *Florida State University Law Review*, vol. 3, no. 2 (1975): 290–301.

1892. Frumkes, Melvyn B., and Elser, Marsha B. "Uniform Child Custody Jurisdiction Act—the Florida Experience," *Florida Bar Journal*, vol. 53, no. 11 (1979): 684–94.

1893. Kapner, Lewis, and Frumkes, Melvin B. "Trial of a Custody Conflict," *Florida Bar Journal*, vol. 52, no. 3 (1978): 174–78.

1894. Kutun, Barry, and Fox, Roberta. "Closing the Custody Floodgate: Florida Adopts the Uniform Child Custody Jurisdiction Act." *Florida State University Law Review*, vol. 6, no. 2 (1978): 409–22.

Custody: Georgia

1895. Lefco, Stanley M. "Child as a Party in Interest in Custody Proceedings," *Georgia State Bar Journal*, vol. 10, no. 4 (1974): 577–87.

1896. McGough, Lucy S., and Shindell, Lawrence M. "Coming of Age: The Best Interests of the Child Standard in Parent–Third Party Custody Disputes," *Emory Law Journal*, vol. 27, no. 2 (1978): 209–45.

Custody: Idaho

1897. Boyle, Larry M. "Paternal Custody of Minor Children in Idaho," *Idaho Law Review*, vol. 8, no. 2 (1972): 345–54.

1898. Graham, William T. "Uniform Child Custody Jurisdiction Act in Idaho: Purposes, Application, and Problems," *Idaho Law Review*, vol. 15, no. 2 (1979): 305–22.

Custody: Illinois

1899. Sproger, Charles E. "How to Win a Child Custody Action," *Illinois Bar Journal*, vol. 60, no. 2 (1971): 122–28.

1900. Taylor, Leigh H. "Child Custody Problems in Illinois," *De Paul Law Review*, vol. 24, no. 2 (1975): 521–31.

1901. Veverka, Donald T. "Right of Natural Parents to Their Children as against Strangers: Is the Right Absolute?" *Illinois Bar Journal*, vol. 61, no. 5 (1973): 234–40.

Custody: Indiana

1902. Bullard, Edward T. "Modification of Child Custody Awards in Indiana: The Need for Statutory Guidelines," *Indiana Law Journal* 47 (Fall 1971): 129–41.

Custody: Iowa

1903. Belson, Robert J. "Modification of Custody," *Drake Law Review*, vol. 24, no. 2 (1975): 396–408.

1904. "Mother Employed as a Masseuse Held Not Entitled to Custody of Child," *Journal of Family Law*, vol. 15, no. 1 (1976–77): 130-34.

1905. Payton, Patrick H. "Factors in Determining Child Custody in Iowa," *Drake Law Review*, vol. 20, no. 2 (1971): 383–95.

Custody: Kansas

1906. Barker, Edward L., and Hamman, Cathryn L. "Best Interests of the Child in Custody Controversies between Natural Parents; Interpretations and Trends," *Washburn Law Journal*, vol. 18, no. 3 (1979): 482–98.

1907. Green, Robert W. "Child Custody—Parent v. Third Party in Kansas," *Washburn Law Journal*, vol. 13, no. 2 (1974): 228–31.

1908. Metzger, Emily B. "Jurisdictional Guidelines in Matters of Child Custody: Kansas Adopts the Uniform Child Custody Jurisdiction Act," *University of Kansas Law Review*, vol. 27, no. 3 (1979): 469–81.

Custody: Kentucky

1909. Bratt, David A. "Paternal Custody of the Young Child under the Kentucky No-Fault Divorce Act," *Kentucky Law Journal*, vol. 66, no. 1 (1977–78): 165–83.

Custody: Louisiana

1910. Forrtenot, Gerald J. "Custody of Children by Writ of Habeas Corpus," *Loyola Law Review*, vol. 24, no. 2 (1978): 308–14.

1911. Gremillion, Jed G. "Louisiana Child Custody Disputes Between Parents and Non-parents," *Loyola Law Review*, vol. 25, no. 1 (1979): 71–92.

1912. Grimsal, A. Gregory. "The Bar to Interspousal Suit and the Paternal Preference Rule," *Tulane Law Review*, vol. 52, no. 2 (1978): 422–27.

1913. Hayden, Jan M. "Continuing Jurisdiction for Child Custody," *Louisiana Law Review*, vol. 38, no. 2 (1978): 613–19.

1914. Poole, Samuel N., Jr. "Maternal Preference and the Double Burden: Best Interest of Whom?" *Louisiana Law Review*, vol. 38, no. 4 (1978): 1096–108.

1915. Tritico, Lila. "Child Custody: Preference to the Mother," *Louisiana Law Review*, vol. 34, no. 4 (1974): 881–89.

1916. Truxillo, Douglas W. "Child Custody: Paternal Authority v. Welfare of the Child," *Louisiana Law Review*, vol. 35, no. 4 (1975): 904–13.

Custody: Maryland

1917. "Best Interests of the Child: Maryland Child Custody Disputes," *Maryland Law Review*, vol. 37, no. 3 (1978): 641–67.

1918. Levin, Marshall A. "Guardian ad litem in a Family Court," *Maryland Law Review*, vol. 34, no. 3 (1974): 341–81.

Custody: Michigan

1919. Ames, Loretta. "McDonald v. McDonald: Michigan Applies the Uniform Child Custody Jurisdiction Act," *Detroit College of Law Review* no. 1 (1978): 123–33.

1920. Mitchell, Marilyn H. "Mother's Career May Determine Custody Award to Father," *Wayne Law Review*, vol. 24, no. 3 (1978): 1159–71.

Custody: Minnesota

1921. "Court's Adoption of Uniform Child Custody Jurisdiction Act Offers Little Hope of Resolving Child Custody Conflicts," *Minnesota Law Review* 60 (April 1976): 820–38.

Custody: Mississippi

1922. Hunter, John L. "Child Custody—Rebutting the Presumption of Parental Preference," *Mississippi Law Journal* 43 (1972): 247–54.

Custody: Missouri

1923. Daniels, Deborah. "Reasonable Visitation or Divided Custody?" *Missouri Law Review*, vol. 42, no. 1 (1977): 136–43.

1924. Hutson, Brett A. "Tender Years Presumption in Missouri: A Judicial Anachronism," *St. Louis University Law Journal*, vol. 23, no. 4 (1979): 697–714.

1925. Krauskopf, Joan M. "Child Custody Jurisdiction under the UCCJA," *Missouri Bar Journal*, vol. 34, no. 6 (1978): 383–93.

1926. Smith, Gerald M. "Habeas Corpus in Child Custody Cases—What Hath the Writ Wrought?" *Missouri Bar Journal*, vol. 30, no. 3 (1974): 146–51+.

1927. Speca, John M. "Dissolution of Marriage under Missouri's New Divorce Law—Child Custody," *Missouri Bar Journal*, vol. 29, no. 8 (1973): 519–28

Custody: Montana

1928. Kilbourne, James C. "Gilmore v. Gilmore: Modifying Child Custody Awards," *Montana Law Review*, vol. 37, no. 2 (1976): 411–19.

Custody: New Hampshire

1929. Jones, Carroll F., and Huff, Glenn. "Child Custody Redetermination in New Hampshire," *New Hampshire Bar Journal*, vol. 17, no. 4 (1976): 238–46.

Custody: New Jersey

1930. Devine, James R. "Child's Right to Independent Counsel in Custody Proceedings: Providing the Effective 'Best Interests' Determination through the Use of a Legal Advocate," *Seton Hall Law Review*, vol. 6, no. 2 303–35

Custody: New York

1931. "Judge's Use of Extra Record Inquiry in Child Custody Cases—No Deprivation of Rights of Parties for Trial Court to Have Confidential Interview with Children without Parties' Consent and in Absence of Parents and Counsel. Lincoln v. Lincoln," *Albany Law Review*, vol. 34, no. 2 (1970): 473–81.

1932. Lynch, Dennis E. A. "New York's New Custody Act," *New York State Bar Journal*, vol. 51, no. 12 (1979): 624–27+.

Custody: Ohio

1933. Colburn, Virginia C. "Uniform Child Custody Jurisdiction Act: Its Provisions and Effects in Ohio," *Capital University Law Review*, vol. 7, no. 3 (1978): 453–68.

1934. "Family Law: Construing Ohio Revised Code 3109.05," *Capital University Law Review*, vol. 4, no. 2 (1975): 283–90.

1935. Kosicki, Evelyn L. "Child Custody Jurisdiction in Ohio—Implementing the Uniform Child Custody Jurisdiction Act," *Akron Law Review*, vol. 12, no. 1 (1978): 121–45.

1936. Rosenstock, George K. "Divorce Investigation Reports in Ohio Child Custody Determinations," *Case Western Reserve Law Review*, vol. 25, no. 2 (1975): 347–70.

Custody: Oklahoma

1937. Nay, William D. "Child Custody; Statutory Preference in Favor of the Mother Is Not Applicable in Proceedings to Modify a Prior Custody Order," *Tulsa Law Journal*, vol. 6, no. 2 (1970): 176–82.

1938. Trotter, Marcia. "Examining Oklahoma's Maternal Preference Doctrine: Gordon v. Gordon," *Tulsa Law Journal*, vol. 13, no. 4 (1978): 802–19.

Custody: Oregon

1939. "Child Custody—Adequate Showing of Change of Circumstances Was Not Demonstrated to Justify Order of Modification of Custody Provision in Divorce Decree," *Journal of Family Law*, vol. 16, no. 2 (1978): 301–08.

1940. Hatch, Jonathan C. "Legislative Opportunity for Oregon: The Uniform Child Custody Jurisdiction Act," *Willamette Law Journal* 7 (December 1971): 498–510.

Custody: Pennsylvania

1941. Badal, Cathy M. "Child Custody: Best Interests of Children vs. Constitutional Rights of Parents," *Dickinson Law Review*, vol. 81, no. 4 (1977): 733–54.

1942. Brosky, John G., and Alford, John G. "Sharpening Solomon's Sword: Current Considerations in Child Custody Cases," *Dickinson Law Review*, vol. 81, no. 4 (1977): 683–98.

1943. Gurevitz, Mark S. "Uniform Child Custody Jurisdiction Act—1977 Pa. Laws No. 20, 1–27," *Temple Law Quarterly*, vol. 51, no. 1 (1978): 139–52.

1944. Radcliff, David H. "Pennsylvania Child Custody: The Tender Years Doctrine—Reason or Excuse?" *Dickinson Law Review*, vol. 81, no. 4 (1977): 775–92.

1945. "Schall v. Schall," *Journal of Family Law*, vol. 17, no. 3 (1979): 587–91.

1946. Turner, Eric D. "Pennsylvania's New Child Custody Venue and Jurisdiction Legislation," *Pennsylvania Bar Association Quarterly*, vol. 49, no. 4 (1978): 471–91.

Custody: Puerto Rico

1947. Rivera Quintero, Márcia. "Las Adjudicaciones de Custodia y Patria Potestad en los Tribunales de Familia de Puerto Rico," *Revista del Colegio Abogados de Puerto Rico*, vol. 39, no. 2 (1978): 177–200.

Custody: South Dakota

1948. Chester, Stephanie A. "Tender Years Presumption: Do the Children Bear the Burden?" *South Dakota Law Review*, vol. 21, no. 2 (1976): 332–50.

Custody: Tennessee

1949. Cardwell, Ronald E. "Parental Custody of Minor Children," *Memphis State University Law Review*, vol. 5, no. 2 (1975): 223–34.

Custody: Texas

1950. Bernard, W. David and Johnson, Gary C. "Jurisdiction of Texas Courts in Interstate Child Custody Disputes: A Functional Approach," *Texas Law Review*, vol. 54, no. 5 (1976): 1008–046.

1951. Cage, Lowell T. "Article 4639a—Custody, Support, and Visitation re: Suits to Have these Rights Changed, Modified or Enforced," *Baylor Law Review*, *vol. 22, no. 4 (1970): 497–515.*

1952. Dibrell, Cooper G. "In a Child Custody Suit the Best Interests of the Child Serve to Lower the Traditional Requirements for Granting a New Trial Motion on the Basis of Newly Discovered Evidence,'' *Texas Tech Law Review*, vol. 8, no. 2 (1976): 568–75.

1953. Gault, Duncan. ''Grandparent—Grandchild Visitation,'' *Texas Bar Journal*, vol. 37, no. 5 (1974): 433–37.

1954. Hamilton, George. ''Some Domestic Relations Problems Connected with Children,'' *Texas Bar Journal*, vol. 33, no. 4 (1970): 283–90.

155. Jones, Marvin W. ''Child Custody Modification and the Family Code,'' *Baylor Law Review*, vol. 27, no. 4 (1975): 725–42.

Custody: Virginia

1956. Russell, Deborah M. '' 'Tender Years' Doctrine in Virginia,'' *University of Richmond Law Review*, vol. 12, no. 3 (1978): 593–605.

1957. Trapnell, Emily M. ''Uniform Child Custody Jurisdiction Act,'' *University of Richmond Law Review*, vol. 12, no. 4 (1978: 745–48.

Custody: West Virginia

1958. Tucker, Vicki O. ''Tender Years Presumption in Child Custody Determinations,'' *West Virginia Law Review*, vol. 81, no. 1 (1978): 149–57.

Custody: Wisconsin

1959. Berman, Robert S. ''Wisconsin and the Uniform Child Custody Jurisdiction Act: In Whose Hand Solomon's Sword.'' *Marquette Law Review*, vol. 61, no. 1 (1977): 79–121.

1960. Holz, Marvin C. ''The Child Advocate in Private Custody Disputes: The Wisconsin Experience,'' *Journal of Family Law*, vol. 16, no. 4 (1978): 739–49.

1961. Podell, Ralph J. ''The 'Why' behind Appointing Guardians ad litem for Children in Divorce Proceedings,'' *Marquette Law Review*, vol. 57, no. 1(1973): 103–10.

1962. Walther, David L. ''Uniform Child Custody Jurisdiction Act,'' *Marquette Law Review*, vol. 54, no. 2 (1971): 161–72.

STEPPARENTS

1963. Aulik, Elizabeth J. ''Stepparent Custody: An Alternative to Stepparent Adoption,'' *University of California, Davis, Law Review*, vol. 12, no. 2 (1974): 604–31.

TENDER YEARS DOCTRINE

1964. Jones, Cathy J. ''Tender Years Doctrine: Survey and Analysis,'' *Journal of Family Law*, vol. 16, no. 4 (1978): 695–738.

1965. Kram, Shirley W., and Frank, Neil. ''The Future of 'Tender Years,' '' *Trial*, vol. 12, no. 4 (1976): 14–15.

1966. Roth, Alan. ''Tender Years Presumption in Child Custody Disputes,'' *Journal of Family Law*, vol. 15, no. 3 (1976-77): 423–62

UNIFORM CHILD CUSTODY JURISDICTION ACT

1967. Hult, James M. ''Temporary Custody under the Uniform Child Custody Jurisdiction Act: Influence Without Modification,'' *University of Colorado Law Review*, vol. 48, no. 4 (1977): 603–20.

1968. Lozoff, Michael D. ''Due Process Dilemma of the Uniform Child Custody Jurisdiction Act,'' *Ohio Northern University Law Review*, vol. 6, no. 3 (1979): 586–96.

1969. Morris, Michael J. ''Uniform Child Custody Jurisdiction Act: An Attempt to Stop Child Rustling,'' *Willamette Law Journal*, vol. 12 (Summer 1976): 623–41.

VISITATION

1970. Allen, Michael L. ''Visitation Rights of a Grandparent over the Objection of a Parent: The Best Interests of the Child,'' *Journal of Family Law*, vol. 15, no. 1 (1976–77): 51–76.

1971. Bodenheimer, Bridgitte M. ''Equal Rights, Visitation, and the Right to Move,'' *Family Advocate*, vol. 1, no. 1 (1978): 19–21.

1972. Bruch, Carol S. ''Making Visitation Work: Dual Parenting Orders,'' *Family Advocate*, vol. 1, no. 1 (1978): 22–26+.

1973. Foster, Henry H., Jr., and Freed, Doris J. ''Grandparent Visitation: Vagaries and Vicissitudes,'' *Saint Louis University Law Journal*, vol. 23, no. 4 (1979): 643–75.

1974. Fournie, Judith A. ''Post-divorce Visitation: A Study in the Deprivation of Rights,'' *DePaul Law Review*, vol. 27, no. 1 (1977): 113–35.

1975. Henszcy, Benjamin N. ''Visitation by a Non-custodial Parent: What Is the 'Best Interest' Doctrine?'' *Journal of Family Law*, vol. 15, no. 2 (1976-77): 213–33.

1976. Johnson, Richard. ''Visitation: When Access Becomes Excess,'' *Family Advocate*, vol. 1, no. 1 (1979): 14–17+.

CHILD SUPPORT

1977. Berkowitz, Bernard J. ''Legal Incidents of Today's 'Step' Relationship: Cinderella Revisited,'' *Family Law Quarterly*, vol. 4, no. 3 (1970): 209–29.

1978. Bernet, Mary F. ''Child Support Provisions: Comments on the New Federal Law,'' *Family Law Quarterly*, vol. 9, no. 3 (1975): 491–526.

1979. Bosley, Wade R. ''Child Support—Protecting the Child's Interests,'' *Family Law Quarterly*, vol. 4, no. 3 (1970): 230–79.

1980. Eden, Philip. ''How Inflation Flaunts Court's Orders,'' *Family Advocate*, vol. 1, no. 4 (1979): 2–5.

1981. Fine, Amy R., and Dickson, Jane J. ''Family Law—Child Support,'' *Annual Survey of American Law*, (1977): 261–74.

1982. Howard, Margaret. "Relative Responsibility of AFDC: Problems Raised by to NOLEO Approach—'If at First You Don't Succeed. . . .'," *Urban Law Annual* (1975): 203–34.

1983. Hurowitz, Neil. "Some Basic Techniques for the Support Case," *Practical Lawyer,* vol. 22, no. 5 (1976): 13–22.

1984. Infausto, Felix. "New Federal Legislation Affecting Child Support," *Family Law Newsletter,* vol. 15, no. 4 (1975): 1+.

1985. Iseman, James M., Jr. "The Decline of Male Chauvinism?" *North Carolina Law Review,* vol. 54, no. 1 (1975): 97–107.

1986. Johnson, Walter D. "Child Support: Preventing Default," *Conciliation Courts Review,* vol. 16, no. 1 (1978): 27–32.

1987. Palmer, Helaine B. "Rising Divorce Rate: Familiarity Breeds Contempt," *Suffolk University Law Review,* vol. 11, no. 4 (1977): 1059–88.

1988. "Right of Federal Officers to Remove Garnishment Proceedings Instituted to Support Child Support Decreases," *Maryland Law Review,* vol. 37, no. 4 (1978): 779–808.

1989. Serratelli, Lori K., and Varin–Hommen, Alvora. "1974 Child Support Provisions: Constitutional Ramifications," *Capital University Law Review,* vol. 6, no. 2 (1976): 275–97.

1990. Walker, Charles M. "Domestic Relations: The Expanding Role of the Mother in Child Support," *Arkansas Law Review,* vol. 27, no. 1 (1973): 157–61.

1991. Weiner, Karen C. "Child Support: The Double Standard," *Florida State University Law Review,* vol. 6, no. 4 (1978): 1317–46.

AGE OF MAJORITY

1992. Di Piazza, Nicholas C. "Effects of the New Age of Majority on Preexisting Child Support Settlements," *Fordham Urban Law Journal* no. 2 (1977): 365–78.

1993. "State Statute Authorizing a Trial Court, in Its Discretion and under the Proper Circumstances, to Order Child Support, Including College Expenses, to Continue beyond a Child's Majority Held Constitutional," *Journal of Family Law,* vol. 17, no. 3 (1979): 604–11.

1994. Vanderlinde, Susan K. "Separation Agreement Provision for Child's College Education Held Binding in an Action for Child Support," *Buffalo Law Review* 27 (Spring 1978): 411–18.

1995. Veron, Enid L. "Parental Support of Post-majority Children in College: Changes and Challenges," *Journal of Family Law,* vol. 17, no. 4 (1979): 645–84.

1996. Washburn, Robert M. "Post-majority Support: Oh Dad, Poor Dad," *Temple Law Quarterly,* vol. 44, no. 3 (1971): 319–55.

ENFORCEMENT

1997. Anderson, Carol E. "Using Long-Arm Jurisdiction to Enforce Marital Obligations," *Journal of Family Law,* vol. 11 (1971): 67–80.

1998. Brockelbank, William, and Infausto, Felix. *Interstate Enforcement of Family Support (the Runaway Pappy Act).* 2d ed. Indianapolis, IN: Bobbs-Merrill Co., 1971.

1999. Cassetty, Judith. *Child Support and Public Policy: Securing Support from Absent Fathers.* Lexington, MA: D. C. Heath & Co., 1978.

2000. ———. "Child Support and Public Policy." Ph.D. diss., University of Wisconsin, Madison, 1977 (*DAI* 38/9A, p. 5714, order # 7723699). R.

2001. Council of State Governments. *Reciprocal State Legislation to Enforce the Support of Dependents.* Lexington, KY: The Council, 1971.

2002. Diaz, Robert E. "Pursuing the Elusive Nonsupporting Serviceman," *Air Force JAG Law Review,* vol. 14, no. 3 (1973): 123–45.

2003. Disanto, Edmund, and Podolski, Lawrence A. "Right to Privacy and Trilateral Balancing—Implications for the Family," *Family Law Quarterly,* vol. 13, no. 2 (1979): 183–229.

2004. "Domestic Relations Exception to Diversity Jurisdiction Bars Suit in Federal Court to Enforce Child Support Provision of Separation Agreement," *Rutgers Camden Law Journal,* vol. 7, no. 3 (1976): 603–08.

2005. Ehrlich, Stanton L. "New National Family Law—Garnish the Feds—Use the U.S. Courts," *Illinois Bar Journal,* vol. 65, no. 2 (1976): 70–75+.

2006. Foster, Henry H., Jr., and Freed, Doris J. "Enforcing Family Support Obligations," *Family Law Newsletter,* vol. 16, no. 2 (1975): 14–32.

2007. ———. "The Long Arm to Catch Pappy," *Trial,* vol. 8, no. 5 (1972): 23–26.

2008. Galvin, William R. "The Runaway Parents," *Trial,* vol. 12, no. 4 (1976): 20–21+.

2009. Locker, Barbara B. "Enforcement of Child Support Obligations of Absent Parents—Social Services Amendment of 1974," *Southwestern Law Journal,* vol. 30, no. 3 (1976): 625–46.

2010. "Making a Federal Case—Garnishment List Published," *Family Advocate,* vol. 2, no. 1 (1979): 38+.

2011. Miller, Steven R. "Federal Law and the Enforcement of Child Support Orders: A Critical Look at Subchapter 4 Part D of the Social Services Amendments of 1974." *New York University Review of Law and Social Change,* vol. 6, no. 1 (1976): 23–42.

2012. Phillips, B. Ellis, and Dworak, Richard F. "Federal Garnishment Statute: Its Impact in the Air Force," *Air Force Law Review,* vol. 18, no. 4 (1976): 70–80.

2013. Romero, Ernest J. "Garnishment of Military Wages," *Air Force Law Review,* vol. 17, no. 3 (1975): 1–16.

2014. Sellman, John R. "When Your Client Has Crossed the Line," *Family Advocate,* vol. 1, no. 4 (1979): 32–35.

2015. Stouder, Judith B. "Child Support Enforcement and Establishment of Paternity as Tools of Welfare Reform—Social Services Amendments of 1974, Pt. B, 42 U.S.C. p. 651–60 (supp. V, 1975)," *Washington Law Review,* vol. 52, no. 1 (1976): 169–92.

2016. U.S. Congress, House Committee on the Judiciary, Subcommittee on Claims and Governmental Relations. *Enforcement of Support Orders in State and Federal Courts: Hearing before the Subcommittee on Claims and Governmental Relations of the Committee on the Judiciary, House of Representatives, Ninety–third Congress, First Session, on H.R. 5405 and Related Bills . . . October 25, 1973.* Washington DC: Government Printing Office, 1974.

2017. U.S. Congress, Senate Committee on Finance. *Child Support and the Work Bonus. Hearing, Ninety-third Congress,*

First Session, on S. 1842, S. 2081 . . . September 25, 1973. Washington, DC: Government Printing Office, 1973.

2018. ———. *Child Support: Data and Materials: Background Information.* Washington, DC: Government Printing Office, 1975 (Y4.F49.C43/8).

2019. ———. *Staff Data and Materials on Child Support.* Washington, DC: Government Printing Office, 1979 (Y4.F49:C43/11).

2020. U.S. General Accounting Office. *New Child Support Legislation: Its Potential Impact and How to Improve It.* Washington, DC: Government Printing Office, 1976.

2021. U.S. Office of Child Support Enforcement. *Child Support Enforcement: Supplemental Report to the Congress for the Period Ending September 30, 1976.* Washington, DC: Government Printing Office, 1977 (HE1.53:976/supp.).

2022. ———. *Annual Report to the Congress on the Child Support Enforcement Program.* Washington, DC: Government Printing Office, 1976.

2023. Yearout, Megan. "Federal Wage Garnishment: Inadequate Protection for Wage Earners' Dependents," *Iowa Law Review,* vol. 64, no. 4 (1979): 1000–18.

ENFORCEMENT (STATES)

Enforcement: California

2024. California Legislature Joint Committee on Legal Equality. *Equal Rights for Homemakers, Community Property Laws, What Still Needs to Be Done, Enforcement of Child Support Laws: Transcript of Hearing of the Joint Committee on Legal Equality, Santa Barbara, California, February 27, 1976.* [Sacramento, CA]: The Committee, [1976].

Enforcement: Illinois

2025. Pacific Legal Foundation. *Child Support Enforcement Manual and Guide for the Bureau of Support Enforcement.* Illinois Department of Public Aid. Sacramento, CA, 1974.

Enforcement: Massachusetts

2026. Eltzroth, Marjorie. *P.L. 93–647, a Federal Dragnet in Violation of Human Rights?* [Boston ?]: Eltzroth, 1975.

2027. Massachusetts Advisory Council on Home and Family. *Support Laws, an Inquiry into Enforcement of Non-support.* Edited by Margaret K. Bisbee. Boston: The Council, 1972.

Enforcement: Michigan

2028. Chambers, David L. "Men Who Know They Are Watched: Some Benefits and Costs of Jailing for Nonpayment of Support," *Michigan Law Review,* vol. 75, no. 5 (1977): 900–40. R.

2029. Chambers, David L., and Adams, Terry K. *Making Fathers Pay, the Enforcement of Child Support.* Chicago: University of Chicago Press, 1979.

2030. Nelson, Robert L. "Family Support from Fugitive Fathers: A Proposed Amendment to Michigan's Long Arm Statute," *Prospectus,* vol. 3, no. 2 (1970): 399–423.

Enforcement: Texas

2031. Edmiston, Jane L. "Extradition and the Runaway Pappy," *Texas Tech Law Review,* vol. 2, no. 1 (1970): 81–87.

Enforcement: Wisconsin

2032. Wisconsin. Legislative Reference Bureau. *In Pursuit of Absent Fathers.* Prepared by Patricia V. Robbins. Madison, WI: Legislative Reference Bureau, 1974.

ESTIMATIONS

2033. Eden, Philip. "Economic Guidelines for Child Support," *Practical Lawyer,* vol. 24, no. 1 (1978): 25–44.

2034. ———. *Estimating Child and Spousal Support: Economic Guidelines for Judges and Attorneys.* San Mateo, CA: Western Book Journal Press, 1977.

MODIFICATIONS

2035. Giacalone, David A. "Guidelines for Child Support after Voluntary Reductions in Income," *Family Law Reporter* 2 (September 14, 1976): 4061–67, monograph no. 21.

STATES

Support: Alabama

2036. "Davenport v. Davenport," *Journal of Family Law,* vol. 17, no. 1 (1978): 158–62.

Support: Alaska

2037. Waxman, Robert M. "Child Support in Alaska: Time to Rethink Old Doctrine?" *UCLA–Alaska Law Review,* vol. 7, no. 2 (1978): 265–81.

Support: Arizona

2038. "Effect of Age of Majority on Prior Support Agreements," *Journal of Family Law,* vol. 13 (1973–74): 672–29.

2039. Wright, Robert L. "Community Assets and Separate Debts: Increased Community Vulnerability in Arizona," *Arizona State Law Journal,* (1975): 797–811.

Support: California

2040. Busch, Joseph P. "Role of the District Attorney in Civil and Criminal Child Support Enforcement," *Los Angeles Bar Bulletin,* vol. 47, no. 2 (1971): 56–61.

2041. "Effect of Parental Duty of Support on Eligibility for AFDC Benefits," *Journal of Family Law,* vol. 14, no. 3 (1975–76): 497–500.

2042. Gabler, Ronald G. "Impact of the ERA on Domestic Relations Law: Specific Focus on California," *Family Law Quarterly,* vol. 8, no. 1 (1974): 51–90.

2043. Goodman, Max A.; Oberman, I. Allan; and Wheat, Penny L. "Rights and Obligations of Child Support," *Southwestern University Law Review,* vol. 7, no. 1 (1975): 36–67.

2044. Hails, Judy. "In Loco Parentis and the Relevant Child," *Orange County Bar Journal,* vol. 2, no. 6 (1975): 712–32.

2045. Humphreys, Sarah A. L. "Kulko v. California Superior Court: Has the Long Arm Extended Too Far?" *Detroit College Law Review,* no. 1 (1979): 159–72.

2046. Nagata, Robert Y. "Mother Must Give Support Payments to Father Who Is in Custody of Children When Not Doing So Would Result in an Inequitable Situation," *San Diego Law Review,* vol. 7, no. 1 (1970): 134-40.

2047. Nakagawa, Mike K. "Termination of Parental Rights and Child Support Obligation—In re Marriage of O'Connell," *University of California, Davis, Law Review,* vol. 12, no. 2 (1979): 632–45.

2048. "Statute Which Imposed Criminal Penalty Upon Fathers Who Willfully Neglected to Support Their Minor Children Held Unconstitutional," *Journal of Family Law,* vol. 15, no. 3 (1976–77): 623–29.

2049. Zumbrun, Ronald A., and Parslow, Richard N. "Absent Parent Child Support: The California Experience," *Family Law Quarterly,* vol. 8, no. 3 (1974): 329–42.

Support: Colorado

2050. Yee, Lucy M. "What Really Happens in Child Support Cases: An Empirical Study of Establishment and Enforcement of Child Support Orders in the Denver District Court," *Denver Law Journal,* vol. 57, no. 1 (1979): 21–68. R.

Support: Connecticut

2051. Dusyn, Kenneth F. "Family Law: A Proposal for Marital Decree Support Fund for Minor Children," *Connecticut Law Review,* vol. 2, no. 3 (1970): 673–86.

2052. Lazorick, Paul S. "Obligations for Family Debts," *Connecticut Bar Journal,* vol. 44, no. 2 (1970): 236–44.

2053. Rosenberg, Herbert F. "Connecticut Family Expense Statute: Conn. Gen. Stat. par. 46–10," *Connecticut Bar Journal,* vol. 44, no. 2 (1970): 259–76.

Support: Florida

2054. Cristy, Carl W. "Child Support Enforcement in Broward County," *Florida Bar Journal,* vol. 52, no. 3 (1978): 214–15.

2055. Eldred, Quentin T. "The Use of Writs of Bodily Attachment in Child Support Enforcement," *Florida Bar Journal,* vol. 52, no. 3 (1978): 217.

2056. Fennessey, Robert E. "Child Support Payment Delinquency," *Florida Bar Journal,* vol. 52, no. 3 (1978): 216–17.

2057. Kelly, Clifton M. "Collecting Support for Children in Divorce Cases," *Florida Bar Journal,* vol. 44, no. 3 (1970): 142–43.

2058. Lupo, Mary E. "Domestic Relations: Three Special Defenses to Contempt," *Florida Bar Journal,* vol. 52, no. 3 (1978): 186–90.

2059. *Support, Custody, and Marital Property in Florida.* [Tallahassee, FL]: Florida Bar, Continuing Legal Education, 1978.

2060. Walsh, Michael R. "Enforcement—Some Practical Suggestions for an Age-Old Problem," *Florida Bar Journal,* vol. 52, no. 3 (1978): 210–13.

2061. White, Kenneth R., and Haulman, Clyde A. "Models for Court Use in Divorce Cases," *Florida Bar Journal,* vol. 52, no. 3 (1978): 179–82.

Support: Georgia

2062. Blau, Cecile A. "Law of Child Support in Georgia: A Morass," *Journal of Family Law,* vol. 14, no. 3 (1975–76): 464–75.

2063. "Georgia's Child Support Laws," *Georgia Law Review,* vol. 11, no. 2 (1977): 387–405.

2064. Goodman, Emmett L., Jr. "The Enforcement of a Foreign Modification of a Georgia Child Support Decree," *Mercer Law Review,* vol. 21, no. 3 (1970): 675–87.

2065. "Simonds v. Simonds," *Journal of Family Law,* vol. 17, no. 2 (1979): 375–78.

Support: Illinois

2066. Conti, Lee A. "Child Support: His, Hers, or Their Responsibility?" *De Paul Law Review,* vol. 25, no. 3 (1976): 707–24.

Support: Kansas

2067. McNeive, Peggy A. "Domestic Relations: Kansas Adopts Automatic Reduction of Child Support," *Washburn Law Journal,* vol. 19, no. 1 (1979): 175–81.

2068. Peggs, Jack. "Procedure and Defenses under the Kansas Uniform Reciprocal Enforcement of Support Act of 1970," *Kansas Bar Association Journal,* vol. 46, no. 4 (1977): 233–38.

2069. Russell, James R. "42 U.S.C. p. 659 and the Kansas Order of Garnishment," *Kansas Bar Association Journal* 48 (Spring 1979): 37–53.

2070. Schulman, R. E., and Rinn, Peter E. "Child Support and the New Federal Legislation," *Kansas Bar Association Journal,* vol. 46, no. 2 (1977): 105–14.

Support: Kentucky

2071. Bratt, David A. "Child Support, Life Insurance, and the Uniform Marriage and Divorce Act," *Kentucky Law Journal,* vol. 67, no. 1 (1978–79): 239–52.

2072. Fannin, David C. "Enforcement of Support Obligations: A Solution and Continuing Problems," *Kentucky Law Journal* vol. 61, no. 2 (1972–73): 322–33.

Support: Louisiana

2073. Cohan, Michael C. "Recovery of Attorneys Fees in an Action for Overdue Child Support Payments—A 'New' Exception to the General Rule?" *Loyola Law Review,* vol. 22, no. 1 (1976): 366–73.

2074. "Grandparents Ordered to Support Grandchildren under Family Responsibility Law in Divorce Proceeding," *Journal of Family Law* vol. 14 (1975): 324–28.

2075. Johnson, Thomas J., III. "Louisiana Adopts Uniform Laws: The Revised Uniform Reciprocal Enforcement of Support Act of 1968," *Loyola Law Review,* vol. 24, no. 1 (1978): 53–84.

Support: Maryland

2076. Ryan, William F., Jr. "Decriminalization of Non-support in Maryland—a Re-examination of a Uniform Act Whose Time has Arrived," *University of Baltimore Law Review,* vol. 7, no. 1 (1977): 97–106.

Support: Michigan

2077. Gebhart, Barton L. "Child Support Modification—Voluntary Reduction in Income Held Inadequate Reason to Deny Child Support Modification Absent Bad Faith," *Wayne Law Review,* vol. 25, no. 3 (1979): 951–60.

Support: Mississippi

2078. Milner, John E. "Parental Duty to Support a Subnormal Adult Child," *Mississippi Law Journal,* vol. 48, no. 2 (1977): 361–69.

Support: Missouri

2079. Hoyne, Stephen D. "Child Support in Missouri: The Father's Duty, the Child's Right, and the Mother's Ability to Enforce," *Missouri Law Review,* vol. 36, no. 3 (1971): 325–42.

2080. "Use of Uniform Reciprocal Enforcement of Support Act to Increase Support in Excess of That Ordered by a Foreign Divorce Decree," *Journal of Family Law,* vol. 15, no. 2 (1976–77): 327–31.

2081. Woods, Hammond C. "Fathers Have Eaten Sour Grapes and the Children's Teeth Are Set on Edge—Ezekiel 18:2," *Missouri Bar Journal*, vol. 26, no. 11 (1970): 560–65 + .

Support: New Mexico

2082. Hoffman, Mary F. "Guidelines for Modification of Child Support Awards: Spingola v. Spingola," *New Mexico Law Review*, vol. 9, no. 1 (1978–79): 201–10.

2083. McClelland, Muriel, and Eby, Lynn C. "Child Support Enforcement: The New Mexico Experience," *New Mexico Law Review*, vol. 9, no. 1 (1978–79): 25–43.

Support: New York

2084. Fisher, Mitchell S., and Saxe, David B. "Family Support Obligations: The Equal Protection Problem," *New York State Bar Journal*, vol. 46, no. 6 (1974): 441–46.

2085. Foster, Henry H., Jr.; Freed, Doris J.; and Midonick, Millard L. "Child Support: The Quick and the Dead," *Syracuse Law Review*, vol. 26, no. 4 (1975): 1159–94.

2086. "Marital Property: A New Look at Old Inequities," *Albany Law Review*, vol. 39, no. 1 (1974): 52–86.

2087. Pauley, Raymond J. "Mandatory Arbitration of Support Matters in the Family Courts," *New York State Bar Journal*, vol. 47, no. 1 (1975): 27 + .

2088. Podurgiel, William C. "Roe v. Doe: Child's Right to a College Education v. Parent's Right to Control," *Catholic Lawyer*, vol. 18, no. 2 (1972): 160 + .

2089. Sauber, Mignon, and Taittonen, Edith. *Guide for Determining the Ability of an Absent Parent to Pay Child Support.* New York: Research Planning Information Department, Community Council of Greater New York, [1977].

2090. Schwabe, Clara. "Separation Agreements and Stipulations of Settlement in Matrimonial Actions," *Trial Lawyers Quarterly*, vol. 12, no. 4 (1978): 94–98.

Support: North Carolina

2091. Heedy, Michael A. "Remedies—Domestic Relations: Garnishment for Child Support," *North Carolina Law Review*, vol. 56, no. 1 (1978): 169–79.

Support: Ohio

2092. Ahern, Stephen F. "The Effect of the Change in Age of Majority on Prior Divorce Decrees Providing for Child Support," *Akron Law Review*, vol. 8, no. 2 (1975): 338–51.

Support: Oklahoma

2093. Benson, Roger L. "Substantial Compliance with Child Support Orders," *Oklahoma Law Review*, vol. 25, no. 2 (1972): 269–77.

2094. Williams, Theodore J., Jr. "Increasing Support Award under Foreign Decree," *Tulsa Law Journal*, vol. 10, no. 1 (1974): 147–50.

Support: Oregon

2095. Higgins, Malcolm B. "Oregon's New Age of Majority Law and Existing Child Support Decrees," *Williamette Law Journal*, vol. 11, no. 1 (1974): 70–86.

Support: Pennsylvania

2096. Beckert, Paul R., Jr. "Duty of a Father under Pennsylvania Law to Support His Child in College," *Villanova Law Review*, vol. 18, no. 2 (1972): 243–68.

2097. Evans, Larry E. "Pennsylvania Equal Rights Amendment Reverses the Common Law Presumption That the Husband Because of His Sex, Should Bear the Primary Duty of Child Support," *Tulsa Law Journal*, vol. 10, no. 3 (1975): 485–92.

2098. "Limitation on Use of Pennsylvania Procedural Support Law in Incarceration of Indigent Defendants," *Dickinson Law Review*, vol. 81, no. 4 (1977): 851–57.

2099. Schmehl, John W. "Calculation of Child Support in Pennsylvania," *Dickinson Law Review*, vol. 81, no. 4 (1977): 793–814.

Support: South Carolina

2100. Arndt, Joseph M., III. "Domestic Relations: Child Support: Alimony," *South Carolina Law Review*, vol. 31, no. 1 (1979): 61–64 + .

Support: Texas

2101. Corrigan, Brian T. "Garnishment of Federal Income for Child Support and Alimony Obligations in Texas," *Texas Bar Journal*, vol. 41, no. 3 (1978): 245–47 + .

2102. Fullenweider, Donn C., and Feldman, David M. "Domestic Relations Judgments in Texas: Draftsmanship and Enforceability," *South Texas Law Journal*, vol. 18, no. 1 (1977): 1–30.

2103. Johnson, David W. "The Stepfather's Liability for and Right of Reimbursement against the Natural Father for Necessaries Furnished the Child," *Baylor Law Review*, vol. 22, no. 4 (1970): 580–87.

2104. Richmond-Hawkins, James. "Delinquent Child Support: Remedies, Limitations, and Laches," *Baylor Law Review*, vol. 28, no. 1 (1976): 197–204.

2105. Rudberg, Morton A. "Enforcing Divorce Judgments and Property Settlement Agreements in Texas," *Texas Tech Law Review*, vol. 5, no. 3 (1974): 645–58.

2106. Smith, Eugene L. "Texas Family Code and Commentary, Title 2: Commentary," *Texas Tech Law Review*, vol. 5, no. 2 (1974): 389–508.

2107. Stanton, L. Vance. "Development and Present Status of the Establishment, Modification and Enforcement of Child Support in Texas," *Texas Bar Journal*, vol. 34, no. 4 (1971): 325 + .

Support: Utah

2108. "A Review of Recent Utah Supreme Court Decisions. Part 10,B. Sex as a 'Suspect Criterion,' " *Utah Law Review*, no. 1 (1974): 164–66.

Support: Virginia

2109. *Report of the Department of Welfare and Institutions to the Governor and the General Assembly of Virginia.* Richmond, VA: Department of Welfare and Institutions, 1974.

Support: Washington

2110. Marshall, Patrick C. "Post-minority Child Support in Dissolution Proceedings," *Washington Law Review*, vol. 54, no. 2 (1979): 459–73.

2111. Mull, Richard L. "Administrative Adjudication of Child Support in Washington," *Gonzaga Law Review*, vol. 12, no. 3 (1977): 518–36.

Support: West Virginia

2112. Liotta, James A. "Child Support—Equal Obligations of Parents," *West Virginia Law Review*, vol. 77, no. 4 (1975): 808–15.

Support: Wisconsin

2113. "Voluntary Payment of Increased Child Support Does Not Raise Estoppel against Father to Deny Consent to an Increase in Obligatory Payments under Previous Judgment of Divorce," *Journal of Family Law*, vol. 15, no. 3 (1976–77): 629–35.

STATISTICS

2114. U.S. Bureau of the Census. *Divorce, Child Custody, and Child Support*. In its series, P-23: Special Studies, no. 84. Washington, DC: Government Printing Office, 1979 (C3.186:p-23/84) (Tables 1–10).

TEMPORARY

2115. Bair, Emily S. "How Much Temporary Support Is Enough?" *Family Advocate*, vol. 1, no. 4 (1979): 36–41 + .

UNIFORM RECIPROCAL ENFORCEMENT OF SUPPORT ACT

2116. [Arkansas Social Services]. *Register of Lists of Essential Information Concerning Uniform Reciprocal State Support Laws*. 4th ed. [Little Rock, AR: Arkansas Social Services], 1972.

2117. Doyle, Richard H., IV. "Uniform Reciprocal Legislation to Enforce Familial Duties of Support," *Drake Law Review*, vol. 25, no. 1 (1975): 206–27.

2118. Fox, William F. "The Uniform Reciprocal Enforcement of Support Act," *Family Law Reporter* 4 (May 2, 1978): 4017–26, monograph no. 4.

2119. ———. "Uniform Reciprocal Enforcement of Support Act," *Family Law Quarterly*, vol. 12, no. 2 (1978): 113–45.

CONFLICT OF LAWS

2120. Bierman, Jacquin D. "Ninth Circuit Reaffirms State Law as the Final Arbiter of Marital Status," *Journal of Taxation*, vol. 47, no. 1 (1977): 57.

2121. "Cocron v. Cocron," *American Journal of International Law*, vol. 70, no. 3 (1976): 571–73.

2122. Crouch, Richard E. "Interstate Aspects of Divorce Law," *Practical Lawyer*, vol. 24, no. 6 (1978): 27–34.

2123. "A Default Divorce Judgment Affecting Personal Rights of Defendant Is Entitled to Full Faith and Credit Where the Divorce Forum Acquired Personal Jurisdiction over Defendant under a Domestic Relations Long-Arm Statute," *Georgia Law Review*, vol. 11, no. 3 (1977): 683–93.

2124. "Divorce—Compulsory Compliance with an Anti-suit Injunction Issued by a Sister State Court Is not Required by Full Faith and Credit of Comity Principles," *Journal of Family Law*, vol. 17, no. 2 (1979): 387–92.

2125. Johnson, Joel. "State Assumption of Jurisdiction over a Divorce Action between Enrolled Reservation Indians," *North Dakota Law Review*, vol. 51, no. 1 (1974): 217–23.

2126. de Kemper, Magaly Bello. "Reconocimento en el Extranjero de las Sentencias Pronunciadas en Virtud de la Ley Numero 142 de 1971 Sobre Divorcio," *Revista de Derecho Puertorriqueño* 12 (Abril-Junio 1973): 439–46.

2127. Palsson, Lennart. *Marriage and Divorce in Comparative Conflict of Laws*. Leiden: Sijthoff, 1974.

2128. Shugrue, Noreen A. "The 'Rule of Validation' as a Solution to Matrimonial Tax Difficulties," *Connecticut Law Review*, vo. 9, no. 2 (1977): 282–93.

2129. Wilkerson, Pinkie C. "Foreign Divorces: A Question of Jurisdiction," *Southern University Law Review*, vol. 5, no. 1 (1978): 139–45.

DIVORCE

2130. Albers, Daniel T. "Judicial Discretion and the Doctrine of Recrimination," *Journal of Family Law* 11 (1972): 737–44.

2131. Berg, Pearl. "Are Fault Requirements in Divorce Actions Unconstitutional?" *Journal of Family Law*, vol. 16, no. 2 (1978): 265–79.

2132. Brodie, D.W. "Marriage and the New Biology," *Law and the Social Order* (1975): 177–90.

2133. *Cases and Materials on Family Law.* Compiled by Judith Areen. Mineola, NY: Foundation Press, 1978.

2134. Citron, Rebecca. "Spouse's Right to Marital Dissolution Predicated on the Partner's Contraceptive Surgery," *New York Law School Law Review* vol. 23, no. 1 (1977): 99–177.

2135. Clayton, Dorothy H. *Divorce Laws, 1929–1966.* Berkeley, CA: Institute of Governmental Studies, State Data Program, University of California, 1973.

2136. Collyer, Keith E. "The Marriage Is Irretrievably Broken," *Florida Bar Journal,* vol. 45, no. 9 (1971): 558–61.

2137. "Constitutional Law: Cause of Action Dismissed if Plaintiff Fails to Waive Privilege against Self–Incrimination," *Minnesota Law Review* 55 (1970): 348–53.

2138. Cowan, Thomas A. "Divorce in Utopia," *Indiana Law Journal* 46 (Winter 1971): 186–92.

2139. Danilov, Dan P. "Marriage and Divorce and the U.S. Immigration Laws," *Family Law Reporter* 4 (February 21, 1978): 4015–16, monograph 3.

2140. Davis, Helen G. "Let's Get Divorce out of the Courts," *Florida Bar Journal,* vol. 51, no. 8 (1977): 500–04.

2141. Fairbanks, James D. "Politics, Economics and the Public Morality: State Regulation of Gambling, Liquor, Divorce and Birth Control." Ph.D. diss., Ohio State University, 1975 (*DAI* 36/8A, p. 5509, order # 763423). R.

2142. Fisch, Edith L. "Legislation Revoking Testamentary Provisions for Former Spouse," *Trusts and Estates,* vol. 114, no. 10 (1975): 710–11.

2143. Foster, Henry H., Jr. "Marriage and Divorce in the Twilight Zone," *Arizona Law Review,* vol. 17, no. 2 (1975): 452–73.

2144. Halem, Lynne C. "Divorce and the Law: Pathology, Policy, and Practice." Ed.D. diss., Harvard University, 1977 (*DAI* 38/12A, p. 7595, order # 7808613). R.

2145. Hill, Thomas H., and Stogel, Elaine T. "Family Law—Innovative Approaches to Divorce Law and Its Incidents," *Annual Survey of American Law,* (1976): 359–81.

2146. Johnson, Walter D. "Special Code of Professional Responsibility in Domestic Relations Statutes?" *Family Law Quarterly* 9, no. 4 (1975): 595–614.

2147. Kahn, Robert W., and Kahn, Lawrence E. *The Divorce Lawyers' Casebook.* New York: St. Martin's Press, 1972.

2148. Keeffe, Arthur J. "Divorce Joins Death and Taxes as Good Business for Lawyers," *American Bar Association Journal* 64 (June 1978): 921.

2149. Lipton, Roslyn A. "Second Circuit Finds Marital Dispute Implicitly Exempted from the Federal Wiretapping Act," *Buffalo Law Review* 27 (Winter 1977): 139–56.

2150. Maxwell, Ralph B. "Divorce without Trauma," *Trial,* vol. 12, no. 4 (1976): 13 + .

2151. Mnookin, Robert H., and Kornhauser, Lewis. "Bargaining in the Shadow of the Law: The Case of Divorce," *Yale Law Journal,* vol. 88, no. 5 (1979): 950–97.

2152. Mnookin, Robert H. "Bargaining in the Shadow of the Law: The Case of Divorce," *Current Legal Problems* 32 (1979): 64–105.

2153. Myricks, Noel. "The Equal Rights Amendment: Its Potential Impact on Family Life," *Family Coordinator,* vol. 26, no. 4 (1977): 321–24.

2154. "Ninth Circuit Reaffirms State Law as the Final Arbiter of Marital Status," *Journal of Taxation* 47 (July 1977): 57.

2155. O'Flarity, James P. "Divorce Modern Style," *Trial,* vol. 8, no. 5 (1972): 15–16.

2156. Phelps, Joseph D. "Full Faith and Credit in Divorce Proceedings," *Alabama Lawyer,* vol. 36, no. 4 (1975): 556–65.

2157. "Privity, Preclusion, and the Parent-Child Relationship," *Brigham Young University Law Review* no. 3 (1977): 612–43.

2158. Problems and Solutions in Divorce or Dissolution of Marriage. Chicago: National Institute, American Bar Association, 1979.

2159. Records, T. Herbert. "Presumptions Respecting Marriage and Divorce," *Missouri Bar Journal,* vol. 28, no. 7 (1972): 329–34 + .

2160. Rheinstein, Max. *Marriage Stability, Divorce and the Law.* Chicago: University of Chicago Press, 1972.

2161. Robbins, Norman N. "End of Divorce—Beginning of Legal Problems," *Family Coordinator,* vol. 23, no. 2 (1974): 185–88.

2162. Rombauer, Marjorie D. "Marital Status and Eligibility for Federal Statutory Income Benefits: A Historical Survey," *Washington Law Review,* vol. 52, no. 3 (1977): 227–88.

2163. Sabalis, Robert F., and Ayers, George W. "Emotional Aspects of Divorce and Their Effects on the Legal Process," *Family Coordinator,* vol. 26, no. 4 (1977): 391–94.

2164. Sacco, Lynn A. "Wife Abuse: The Failure of Legal Remedies," *John Marshall Journal of Practice and Procedure,* vol. 11, no. 3 (1978): 549–77.

2165. Schwartz, Victor E. "Serious Marital Offender: Tort Law as a Solution," *Family Law Quarterly,* vol. 6, no. 3 (1972): 219–32.

2166. Seidelson, David E. "Interest Analysis and Divorce Actions," *Buffalo Law Review* 21 (Winter 1972): 315–37.

2167. Swink, Jack W. "How to Lose a Default Dissolution," *Los Angeles Bar Journal,* vol. 51, no. 9 (1976): 406–11.

2168. TenBrook, Tammany D. "Exclusion of Public from a Proceeding Merely Upon Request Is in Excess of Court's Power," *Miami Law Review,* vol. 30, no. 4 (1976): 1075–83.

2169. "Trend Analysis: The 'Changed Landscape' of Divorce Practice as an Ethical Minefield," *Family Law Reporter* 3 (July 19, 1977): 4031 39. Monograph no. 26.

2170. U.S. National Commission on the Observance of International Women's Year. Homemakers Committee. *The Legal Status of Homemakers.* Washington, DC: Government Printing Office, 1976–77 (Y3.W84:9/nos.).

2171. Van Zile, Philip T., III. "Reaching Equal Protection Under Law: Alternative Forms of Family and the Changing Face of Monogamous Marriage," *Detroit College of Law Review,* no. 1 (1975): 95–124.

2172. Wadlington, Walter. "Sexual Relations after Separation or Divorce: The New Morality and the Old and New Divorce Laws," *Virginia Law Review,* vol. 63, no. 2 (1977): 249–79.

2173. Walzer, Stuart B. "Divorce and the Professional Man," *Journal of the Beverly Hills Bar Association,* vol. 4, no. 6 (1970): 20–22 + . Also in *Family Law Quarterly,* vol. 4, no. 4 (1970): 363–72.

2174. Westman, Jack C., and Cline, David W. "Divorce Is a Family Affair," *Family Law Quarterly*, vol. 5, no. 1 (1971): 1–10.

2175. "Will Divorce Move out of the Courtroom?" *American Bar Association Journal* 64 (June 1978): 815.

BANKRUPTCY

2176. Arnold, David. "The Finality Doctrine Reviewed," *Washburn Law Journal*, vol. 12, no. 1 (1972): 77–81.

2177. Hammer, Bernard. "Matrimonial Litigation and Bankruptcy," *Family Law Newsletter*, vol. 17, no. 1 (1976): 2–3.

DEFENSES

2178. Hardisty, James H. "Insanity as a Divorce Defense," *Journal of Family Law*, vol. 12, no. 1 (1972–73): 1–61.

2179. Robbins, Norman N. "There Ought to Be a Law! To Condone or Condemn Condonation," *Family Coordinator*, vol. 20, no. 1 (1971): 74–76.

DIVORCE LAW REFORM

2180. Bodenheimer, Birgitte M. "New Approaches of Psychiatry: Implications for Divorce Reform," *Utah Law Review* 2 (1970): 191–220.

2181. Bohannan, Paul. "Some Thoughts on Divorce Reform." In *Divorce and After*, edited by Paul Bohannan. pp. 249–63. Garden City, NY: Doubleday, 1970.

2182. Clark, Homer H., Jr. "Divorce Policy and Divorce Reform," *University of Colorado Law Review* 42 (March 1971): 403–18.

2183. ———. "Divorce Reform in the Seventies?" *Colorado Quarterly*, vol. 19, no. 1 (1970): 77–95.

2184. "The Course of Change in Family Law," *Family Law Reporter* 5 (August 7, 1979): 4013–25, monograph no. 2.

2185. Feldman, Stephen R. "Statutory Proposal to Remove Divorce from the Courtroom," *Maine Law Review*, vol. 29, no. 1 (1977): 25–46.

2186. Foster, Henry H., Jr. "Divorce Reform and the Uniform Act," *Family Law Quarterly*, vol. 7, no. 2 (1973): 179–210.

2187. ———. "Divorce Reform and the Uniform Act," *South Dakota Law Review*, 18 (Summer 1973): 572–600.

2188. Foster, Henry H., Jr., and Freed, Doris J. "Divorce Reform: Brakes on Breakdown?" *Journal of Family Law*, vol. 13, no. 3 (1973-74): 443–93.

2189. ———. "Economic Effects of Divorce (as of June 1, 1973)," *Family Law Quarterly*, vol. 7, no. 3 (1973): 275–343.

2190. Gaylord, C.L. "Something Is Loose in the Marital Woods," *American Bar Association Journal* 59 (November 1973): 1306–09.

2191. Hussain, Syed Jaffer. "Divorce Laws and Reforms in America and in India: A Study in Comparative Law," Thesis, Harvard Law School, 1975.

2192. Kargman, Marie W. "The Revolution in Divorce Law," *Family Coordinator*, vol. 22, no. 2 (1973): 245–48.

2193. Monahan, Thomas P. "The National Divorce Legislation: Problems and Some Suggestions," *Family Coordinator*, vol. 22, no. 3 (1973): 353–57.

2194. Morrissey, Francis J., Jr. "Significant Developments in Divorce Legislation," *Pennsylvania Bar Association Quarterly*, vol. 44, no. 4 (1973): 567–73.

2195. Stetson, Dorothy M. "The Two Faces of Policy: Divorce Reform in Western Democracies," *Journal of Comparative Family Studies*, vol. 6, no. 1 (1975): 15–30.

2196. Zenor, Donna J. "Untying the Knot: The Course and Patterns of Divorce Reform," *Cornell Law Review*, vol. 59, no. 4 (1972): 649–67.

2197. Zuckman, Harvey L. "ABA Family Law Section v. the NCCUSL: Alienation, Separation and Forced Reconciliation over the Uniform Marriage and Divorce Act," *Catholic University Law Review*, vol. 24, no. 1 (1974): 61–74.

2198. ———. "Recent Developments in American Divorce Legislation," *Jurist*, vol. 35 (Winter 1975): 6–16.

2199. Zuckman, Harvey L., and Fox, William F. "Ferment in Divorce Legislation," *Journal of Family Law*, vol. 12, no. 4 (1973): 515–605.

2200. Zuckman, Jacob T. "New Divorce Laws—Will they Work?" *Conciliation Courts Review*, vol. 8, no. 2 (1970): 20–21.

DIVORCE LAW REFORM (STATES)

Reform: Arizona

2201. "Arizona Divorce Law: Time for a Better System," *Law and the Social Order* (1970): 621–40.

Reform: Arkansas

2202. Newbern, David, and Johnson, Phyllis H. "Uniform Marriage and Divorce Act: Analysis for Arkansas," *Arkansas Law Review*, vol. 28, no. 2 (1974): 175–98.

Reform: California

2203. Brody, Stuart A. "California's Divorce Reform: Its Sociological Implications," *Pacific Law Review*, vol. 1, no. 1 (1970): 223–32.

2204. Elkin, Meyer. "Family Law Reform: California's Constructive Break with Legal Tradition," *Conciliation Courts Review*, vol. 9, no. 1 (1971): 9–8.

2205. Krom, Howard A. "California's Divorce Law Reform: An Historical Analysis," *Pacific Law Review*, vol. 1, no. 1 (1970): 156–81.

Reform: Connecticut

2206. Cohen, Herbert L. "Divorce Reform—Another Point of View," *Connecticut Bar Journal*, vol. 47, no. 1 (1973): 88–98.

2207. "Proposal for Revision of the Connecticut Statutes Relative to Divorce: Statute and Commentary. Divorce Reform—Another Point of View," *Connecticut Bar Journal*, vol. 44, no. 3 (1970): 411–37.

Reform: Idaho

2208. Forgeron, Hy T. "What the Legislature Has Put Asunder: Section 36–603(8) and Divorce Reform," *Idaho Law Review*, vol. 8, no. 2 (1972): 331–36.

Reform: Illinois

2209. Auerbach, Marshall J. "Introduction to the New Illinois Marriage and Dissolution of Marriage Act," *Illinois Bar Journal*, vol. 66, no. 3 (1977): 132–37.

2210. Heyman, Michael G. "Illinois Marriage and Dissolution of Marriage Act: New Solutions to Old Problems," *John Marshall Journal of Practice and Procedure*, vol. 12, no. 1 (1978): 1–26.

Reform: Kentucky

2211. Humphrey, Stepehn L. "Kentucky Divorce Reform," *Journal of Family Law* 12 (1972–73): 109–50.

2212. Miller, Thomas W. "Kentucky's New Dissolution of Marriage Law," *Kentucky Law Journal* 61 (1972–73): 980–1002.

2213. Simms, Richard D. "Kentucky Divorce Venue Statute: A Call for Reform," *Kentucky Law Journal* 66 (1978): 724–40.

Reform: Michigan

2214. Lee, B. H. "Divorce Law Reform in Michigan," *University of Michigan Journal of Law Reform*, vol. 5, no. 3 (1972): 409–25.

Reform: Missouri

2215. Agatstein, Sylvan. "The Dissolution of Marriage Law—Lurking Quirks," *Missouri Bar Journal*, vol. 32, no. 3 (1976): 146–50.

2216. Ferriss, Franklin. "Dissolution of Marriage under Missouri's New Divorce Law—Temporary Orders," *Missouri Bar Journal*, vol. 29, no. 8 (1973): 504–07.

Reform: New Hampshire

2217. Anderson, G. Wells. "New Hampshire's Divorce Reform Act of 1971," *New Hampshire Bar Journal*, vol. 13, no. 4 (1972): 158–80.

Reform: New Jersey

2218. "1971 New Jersey Divorce Law," *Rutgers Law Review*, vol. 25, no. 3 (1971): 476–506.

Reform: New York

2219. Atkins, Michael B. "Developing Divorce Reform Law," *New York State Bar Journal*, vol. 45, no. 8 (1973): 545–51.

2220. Foster, Henry H., Jr., and Freed, Doris J. *The Divorce Reform Law: An Analysis.* Rochester, NY: Lawyers Co-Operative Publishing Co., 1970.

2221. Sassower, Doris L. "Matrimonial Law Reform: Equal Property Rights for Women," *New York State Bar Journal*, vol. 44, no. 6 (1972): 406–09.

2222. ———. "No-Fault Divorce and Women's Property Rights: A Rebuttal," *New York State Bar Journal*, vol. 45, no. 7 (1973): 485–89.

2223. Teitelbaum, Lee L. "Cruelty Divorce under New York's Reform Act: On Repeating Ancient Error," *Buffalo Law Review* 23 (Fall 1973): 1–42.

2224. Wolf, Edwin H. "Divorce Reform Law—A Lesson in Legislative Oversight," *Buffalo Law Review* 22 (Fall 1972): 173–80.

Reform: North Carolina

2225. Marschall, Patricia H. "Proposed Reforms in North Carolina Divorce Law," *North Carolina Central Law Journal*, vol. 8, no. 1 (1976): 35–52.

Reform: Ohio

2226. Cannell, John D. "Abolish Fault-Oriented Divorce in Ohio—As a Service to Society and to Restore Dignity to the Domestic Relations Courts," *Akron Law Review*, vol. 4, no. 1 (1971): 92–113.

2227. Jones, Robert B. "Ohio Divorce Reforms of 1974," *Case Western Reserve Law Review*, vol. 25, no. 4 (1975): 844–75.

2228. Norris, Allen E. "Divorce Reform: Ohio's Alternative to No–Fault," *State Government*, vol. 48, no. 1 (1975): 52–57.

Reform: South Dakota

2229. King, Rory P. "Marriage, Divorce and Custody Reform in South Dakota," *South Dakota Law Review*, vol. 18 (Summer 1973): 654–76.

Reform: West Virginia

2230. Parmer, David L. "Divorce Law Changes," *West Virginia Law Review*, vol. 72, nos. 1–2 (1969–70): 104–09.

Reform: Wisconsin

2231. Barnard, Charles P., and Sharenow, Eric. "Process Designed to Respond to Recent Divorce Law Reforms," *Wisconsin Bar Bulletin*, vol. 51, no. 11 (1979): 27–29.

DO-IT-YOURSELF DIVORCE

2232. Buesser, Frederick G., Jr. "The Kit Age and Unauthorized Practice (Divorce, Will and Corporation Kits)," *Unauthorized Practice News*, vol. 39, no. 1 (1974): 12–16.

2233. Resh, Warren H. " 'Do-It-Yourself' Divorce Kits and Services," *Wisconsin Bar Bulletin*, vol. 47, no. 1 (1974): 23–28 + .

2234. ———. "More on Do-It-Yourself Divorce Kits and Services," *Unauthorized Practice News*, vol. 37, no. 2 (1973): 59–73.

2235. Ryburn, Jack T. "The Dangers of Do-It-Yourself Dissolution," *Conciliation Courts Review*, vol. 11, no. 2 (1973): 1–2.

2236. Sell, Kenneth D. "Pro se Divorce: A Low Cost Alternative to the High Cost of Leaving," *New Directions in Legal Services*, vol. 3, no. 6 (1978): 163–68 + . R.

2237. "State Bar of Michigan v. Cramer, 1975," *Unauthorized Practice News*, vol. 40, no. 3 (1977): 290–91.

DO-IT-YOURSELF DIVORCE (STATES)

Do-It-Yourself: Alaska

2238. "Alaska Bar Association v. Foster, et al. (Divorce Kit)," *Unauthorized Practice News*, vol. 38, no. 1 (1974): 75–80.

Do-It-Yourself: California

2239. "California Restrains 'No-Fault Divorce Consultation Service,' " *Unauthorized Practice News*, vol. 38, no. 1 (1974): 44–54.

Do-It-Yourself: Colorado

2240. "Colorado Bar Association Starts Suit against Lay Divorce Specialists," *Unauthorized Practice News*, vol. 39, no. 2 (1975): 87–99.

Do-It-Yourself: Connecticut

2241. Cavenaugh, Ralph C., and Rhode, Deborah L. "The Unauthorized Practice of Law and pro se Divorce: An Empirical Analysis," *Yale Law Journal*, vol. 86, no. 1 (1976): 104–84. R.

2242. McLachlan, C. Ian. "Pro se Marriage Dissolution in Connecticut—Some Considerations," *Connecticut Bar Journal*, vol. 51, no. 1 (1977): 15–20.

Do-It-Yourself: Florida

2243. "More on Divorce Kits—Florida Bar v. Stupica," *Unauthorized Practice News*, vol. 39, no. 2 (1975): 116–22.

Do-It-Yourself: Minnesota

2244. "Minnesota Bar Wins Sweeping Victory against a Lay Practitioner of Divorce Law," *Unauthorized Practice News*, vol. 39, no. 3 (1975): 187–93.

Do-It-Yourself: Nevada

2245. "Nevada Divorce," *Unauthorized Practice News*, vol. 37, no. 1 (1973): 32–42.

Do-It-Yourself: New York

2246. Burke, George B. "New York 'Divorce Yourself' Enjoined," *Unauthorized Practice News*, vol. 37, no. 1 (1973): 22–31.

Do-It-Yourself: Oregon

2247. "Oregon Court Restrains Sale of Divorce Kits," *Unauthorized Practice News*, vol. 39, no. 1 (1974): 61–66.

2248. "Oregon Divorce Kit Case on Appeal," *Unauthorized Practice News*, vol. 39, no. 3 (1975): 194–95.

2249. "Oregon Supreme Court Modifies Trial Court Divorce Kit Decrees So as to Permit Sales of Kits but Affirms Injunction on Individual Services," *Unauthorized Practice News*, vol. 40, no. 1 (1976): 39–46. *Do-It-Yourselfer, Wiscon.*

2250. "More on 'Do-It-Yourself Divorce Kits,' " *Unauthorized Practice News*, vol. 38, no. 2 (1974): 131–32.

FILING FOR DIVORCE

2251. Friedman, Lawrence M., and Percival, Robert V. "Who Sues for Divorce? From Fault through Fiction to Freedom," *Journal of Legal Studies*, vol. 5, no. 1 (1976): 61–82. R.

2252. Gunter, B. G., and Johnson, Doyle P. "Divorce Filing as Role Behavior: Effect of No-Fault Law on Divorce Filing Patterns," *Journal of Marriage and the Family*, vol. 40, no. 3 (1978): 571–74. R.

FOREIGN DIVORCES

2253. Freed, Doris J. "Recognition and Enforcement Abroad of American Decrees and Judgments of Divorce, Alimony, Child Support and Custody," *Family Law Newsletter*, vol. 13, no. 3 (1972): 1–3.

2254. Fulton, James A. "Caribbean Divorce for Americans: Useful Alternative or Obsolescent Institution?" *Cornell International Law Journal*, vol. 10, no. 1 (1976): 116–33.

2255. Juenger, Frederich. "Recognition of Foreign Divorces—British and American Perspectives," *American Journal of Comparative Law*, vol. 20, no. 1 (1972): 1–37.

2256. Morris, J. H. C. "Recognition of American Divorces in England," *International and Comparative Law Quarterly*, vol. 24, no. 4 (1975): 635–42.

2257. "New York Court Enjoins Laymen from Foreign Divorce and Deportation Proceeding Practice," *Unauthorized Practice News* 38 (Spring 1974): 64–65.

2258. von Mehren, Arthur T., and Nadelmann, Kurt H. "The Hague Conference Convention of June 1, 1970 on Recognition of Foreign Divorce Decrees," *Family Law Quarterly*, vol. 5, no. 3 (1971): 303–68.

2259. White, Thomas C., and Cusick, David M. "Suggested Legislation Concerning Recognition of Certain Past and Future Foreign Divorce Decrees," *Connecticut Bar Journal*, vol. 49, no. 1 (1973): 75–87.

Foreign Divorces: Dominican Republic

2260. "Lay Operator of 24-Hour Dominican Divorce Service Enjoined, Held in Contempt, and Fined by Florida Supreme Court," *Unauthorized Practice news*, vol. 39, no. 1 (1974): 57–60.

2261. Streuk, Robert. "Isla of Hispaniola: American Divorce Haven?" *Case Western Reserve Journal of International Law*, vol. 5, no. 2 (1973): 198–209.

Foreign Divorces: Haiti

2262. Freed, Doris J. "Haitian Divorce Law Recognized as Valid by New York Supreme Court," *Family Law Newsletter*, vol. 14, no. 1 (1973): 13.

2263. "Haitian Divorce Solicitation in New Jersey Enjoined as Consumer Fraud," *Unauthorized Practice News* 37 (May 1973): 43–51.

2264. "Haitian Vacation: The Applicability of Sham Doctrine to Year-End Divorces," *Michigan Law Review*, vol. 77, no. 5 (1979): 1332–54.

2265. Perlstein, Robert S. "Recognition of Haitian–Dominican Divorce in New York," *Columbia Journal of Transnational Law*, vol. 11, no. 1 (1972): 158–75.

Foreign Divorces: Mexico

2266. Caballero, Romualdo C. "Reexamination of Mexican 'Quickie' Divorces," *International Lawyer*, vol. 4, no. 5 (1970): 871–81.

2267. Miller, Robert L. "Mexican Divorces Revisted," *Case and Comment*, vol. 84, no. 4 (1979): 43–47.

2268. Rosenbaum, Warren B. "Defective Mexican Divorce Decree Accorded New York Recognition due to Subsequent Appearance, through an Attorney of Party Absent from the Mexican Action," *Buffalo Law Review* 20 (Fall 1970): 296–304.

GROUNDS FOR DIVORCE

2269. Freed, Doris J. "Grounds for Divorce in the American Jurisdictions," *Family Law Quarterly*, vol. 6, no. 2 (1972): 179–212.

2270. ———. "Grounds for Divorce in the American Jurisdictions (as of June 1, 1974)," *Family Law Quarterly*, vol. 8, no. 4 (1974): 401–23.

2271. Freed, Doris J., and Foster, Henry, H., Jr. "Divorce in the Fifty States: An Outline," *Family Law Quarterly*, vol. 11, no. 3 (1977): 297–313.

2272. ———. "Divorce in the Fifty States: An Overview as of 1978," *Family Law Quarterly*, vol. 13, no. 1 (1979): 105–28.

2273. ———. "Divorce in the Fifty States: An Overview as of August 1, 1978," *Army Lawyer* (February 1979): 25–35.

2274. ———. "Divorce in the Fifty States: An Overview as of August 1, 1978," *Family Law Reporter* 4 (August 22, 1978): 4033–41, monograph no. 6.

2275. ———. "Divorce in the Fifty States: An Overview as of August 1, 1979," *Family Law Reporter* 5 (September 11, 1979): 4027–42.

2276. ———. "Family Law in the Fifty States: An Overview," *Family Law Reporter* 3 (September 6, 1977): 4047–52, monograph no. 28.

2277. ———. "Family Law in the Fifty States: An Overview," *Army Lawyer* (February 1978): 11–20.

2278. Weinstein, Meyer H. "Cruelty as a Ground for Divorce," *Decalogue Journal*, vol. 22, no. 1 (1972): 13–18.

INTERSTATE DIVORCE

2279. Schlender, E. Lee. "Handling a Divorce Case against an Out-of-State Defendant," *Practical Lawyer*, vol. 16, no. 6 (1970): 65–72.

INVALID DIVORCES

2280. Rosenberg, Edward D. "How Void Is a Void Decree, or the Estoppel Effect of Invalid Divorce Decrees," *Family Law Quarterly*, vol. 8, no. 4 (1974): 207–24.

NO-FAULT DIVORCE

2281. Case, Karen A. "No-Fault Divorce: Tax Consequences of Support, Maintenance and Property Settlement," *Wisconsin Bar Bulletin*, vol. 50, no. 11 (1977): 11–12+.

2282. Farrell, Michael F. "No Fault Divorce: A Time for Change?" *Suffolk University Law Review*, vol. 7, no. 1 (1972): 86–107.

2283. Freed, Doris J., and Foster, Henry, H. Jr. "Taking out the Fault but Not the Sting," *Trial*, vol. 12, no. 4 (1976): 10–12+.

2284. Ganley, Paul M.; Henry, Gaylord L.; and Porteus, Barbara D. "Divorce, Law and Psychology," *Hawaii Bar Journal*, vol. 7, no. 3 (1970): 73–108.

2285. Johnson, Walter D. *Marital Dissolution and the Adoption of No-Fault Legislation.* Springfield, IL: Illinois Legislative Studies Center, Sangamon State University, 1975.

2286. Kolb, Charles E. M. "Vestigial Fault in No-Fault," *New Hampshire Bar Journal*, vol. 18, no. 4 (1977): 238–49.

2287. Lavercombe, Robert R. "No-Fault Divorce?" *Educational Leadership*, vol. 31, no. 2 (1973): 134–36.

2288. McHugh, James T. "No-Fault Divorce," *Jurist* 35 (1975): 17–31.

2289. ———. "No-Fault Divorce Laws: An Overview and Criticism," *Catholic Lawyer*, vol. 18, no. 3 (1972): 237–42.

2290. Rheinstein, Max. "From Divorce as Punishment to No-Fault Divorce," *Revista del Colegio de Abogados de Puerto Rico*, vol. 33, no. 4 (1972): 523–39.

2291. Robbins, Norman N. "Have We Found Fault in No-Fault Divorce?" *Family Coordinator*, vol. 22, no. 3 (1973): 359–62.

2292. Schoenlaub, Fred E. "No-Fault Divorce, a Practical Approach to the Problems of Marital Failure," *Missouri Bar Journal*, vol. 27, no. 11 (1971): 579–83+.

2293. Steinberg, Joseph L. "Too Much Fault in No Fault Divorce," *Connecticut Law Tribune*, January 30, 1978.

2294. Steinbock, Delmar D., Jr. "Case for No-Fault Divorce," *Tulsa Law Journal*, vol. 10, no. 3 (1975): 427–35.

2295. Walker, Timothy B. "Beyond Fault: An Examination of Patterns of Behavior in Response to Present Divorce Laws," *Journal of Family Law*, vol. 10, no. 3 (1971): 267–99.

2296. Whaling, Michael J. "No Fault Concept: Is this the Final Stage in the Evolution of Divorce?" *Notre Dame Lawyer*, vol. 47, no. 4 (1972): 959–75.

NO-FAULT DIVORCE AND DIVORCE RATES

2297. Jones, Mary S. "An Historical Geography of Changing Divorce Law in the United States." Ph.D. diss., University of North Carolina, Chapel Hill, 1978 (*DAI* 40/1A, p. 461, order # 7914370). R.

2298. Mazur-Hart, Stanley F. "Effects of No-Fault Divorce: An Interrupted Time Series Quasi-Experiment." Ph.d. diss., University of Nebraska, 1976 (*DAI* 37/5B, p. 2573, order # 7625882). R.

2299. Mazur-Hart, Stanley F., and Berman, John J. "Changing from Fault to No-Fault Divorce: An Interrupted Time Series Analysis," *Journal of Applied Psychology*, vol. 7, no. 4 (1977): 300–12. R.

2300. Sell, Kenneth D. "Divorce Law Reform and Increasing Divorce Rates in the United States," *Current Issues in Marriage and the Family*, edited by J. Gipson Wells., pp. 290–308. 2d ed. New York: Macmillan Publishing Co., 1979. R.

2301. Stetson, Dorothy M., and Wright, Gerald C., Jr. "Effects of Laws on Divorce in American States," *Journal of Marriage and the Family*, vol. 37, no. 3 (1975): 537–47. R.

2302. Wright, Gerald C., Jr., and Stetson, Dorothy M. "The Impact of No-Fault Divorce Law Reform on Divorce in American States," *Journal of Marriage and the Family*, vol. 40, no. 3 (1978): 575–80. R.

NO-FAULT DIVORCE (STATES)

No-Fault: Alabama

2303. Ferguson, Harld L., Jr. "Incompatibility of Temperament and Irretrievable Breakdown—What Will They Mean in Alabama?" *Cumberland Samford Law Review*, vol. 3, no. 3 (1972): 434–49.

2304. Furner, Joanne F., and Ohle, B. Robert. "Fault or No-Fault Divorce for Alabama?" *Alabama Lawyer*, vol. 33, no. 1 (1972): 46–57.

No-Fault: California

2305. Berg, Elayne C. "Irreconcilable Differences: California Courts Respond to No-Fault Dissolutions," *Loyola University of Los Angeles Law Review*, vol. 7, no. 3 (1974): 453–88.

2306. Bolas, Donald M. "No-Fault Divorce: Born in the Soviet Union?" *Journal of Family Law*, vol. 14 (1975): 31–65.

2307. Goddard, Wendell H. "Report of California's New Divorce Law: Progress and Problems," *Family Law Quarterly*, vol. 6, no. 4 (1972): 405–21.

2308. Hayes, James A. "California Divorce Reform: Parting Is Sweet Sorrow," *American Bar Association Journal* 56 (July 1970): 660–63.

2309. Hogoboom, William P. "California Family Law Act of 1970: 18 Months Experience," *Missouri Bar Journal*, vol. 27, no. 11 (1971): 584–89.

2310. ———. "The California Family Law Act of 1970: 21 Months Experience," *Conciliation Courts Review*, vol. 9, no. 1 (1971): 5–8.

2311. Mass, Earl H., Jr.; Cantwell, Robert E., III; and Hervey, James E. "Divorce without Fault: Good, Bad or What?" *Conciliation Courts Review*, vol. 10, no. 2 (1972): 1–9.

2312. Olson, Lester, "California Divorce Laws—Will they Work?" *Conciliation Courts Review*, vol. 8, no. 1 (1970): 25–26.

2313. Saul, Edwin S. "Proof of a No-Fault Divorce Case," *Los Angeles Bar Bulletin*, vol. 45, no. 3 (1970): 99–102+.

2314. Walker, Timothy B. "Disarming the Litigious Man: A Glance at Fault and California's New Divorce Legislation," *Pacific Law Review*, vol. 1, no. 1 (1970): 182–222.

No-Fault: Connecticut

2315. Heffernan, John. "Finding Fault with No-Fault Divorce: The Proposed Connecticut Divorce Statute," *Connecticut Bar Journal,* vol. 47, no. 1 (1973): 99–106.

2316. McAnerney, Robert M., and Schoonmaker, Samuel V., III. "Connecticut's New Approach to Marriage Dissolution," *Connecticut Bar Journal,* vol. 47, no. 4 (1973): 375–415.

No-Fault: Delaware

2317. Ferrell, Ruth M. "No-Fault Divorce," *Women Layers Journal,* vol. 62, no. 1 (1976): 27–29.

2318. Gallagher, John T. "No-Fault Divorce in Delaware," *American Bar Association Journal* 59 (August 1973): 873–75.

No-Fault: Florida

2319. Church, Virginia A. "Faults in Florida No-Fault Divorce," *Florida Bar Journal,* vol. 45, no. 9 (1971): 568–74.

2320. Clark, Mary F. "Florida's No-Fault Divorce: Is It Really No-Fault?" *Florida State University Law Review,* vol. 4, no. 4 (1976): 504–22.

No-Fault: Georgia

2321. Gozansky, Nathaniel E. "No-Fault Divorce Comes to Georgia," *Georgia State Bar Journal,* vol. 10, no. 1 (1973): 9–15.

No-Fault: Illinois

2322. Auerbach, Marshall J. "No-Fault Divorce: Truth in Ending," *Chicago Bar Record,* vol. 56, no. 4 (1975): 210–14.

2323. Baer, Joseph W., and Davis, Muller. " 'Merit' in No-Fault Divorce," *Illinois Bar Journal,* vol. 60, no. 10 (1972): 766–75.

2324. Friedman, James T. "No-Fault Divorce Legislation—A Comparison of the CBA and ISBA Proposals," *Chicago Bar Record,* vol. 56, no. 4 (1975): 198–208.

2325. Johnson, Walter D. *Policy Implications of Divorce Reform: The Illinois Example.* Springfield, IL: Illinois Legislative Studies Center, Sangamon State University, 1979.

No-Fault: Iowa

2326. Farrell, Margaret D. "Under Iowa's No-Fault Dissolution of Marriage Procedure Evidence of the Conduct of the Parties Which Tends to Place Fault for the Marriage Breakdown Must Be Disregarded as a Factor in Awarding Property Settlement or Allowance of Alimony or Support Money," *University of Cincinnati Law Review,* vol. 42, no. 1 (1973): 127–36.

2327. German, Judith M. "Dissolution of Marriage in Iowa: Collateral Determinations under the No-Fault Concept," *Drake Law Review,* vol. 22, no. 3 (1973): 584–99.

2328. Peters, Jack W. "Iowa Reform of Marriage Termination," *Drake Law Review,* vol. 20, no. 2 (1971): 211–26.

2329. Sass, Stephen L. "The Iowa No-Fault Dissolution of Marriage Law in Action," *South Dakota Law Review* 18 (Summer 1973): 629–53.

No-Fault: Kansas

2330. Kennalley, John M. "Incompatibility Divorce in Kansas—A Movement Toward No-Fault Divorce," *Washburn Law Journal,* vol. 14, no. 2 (1975): 349–54.

2331. Schulman, R. E. "Fault or No Fault: The Divorce Lawyers Dilemma," *Kansas Bar Association Journal,* vol. 41, no. 2 (1972): 129–34 + .

2332. ———. "Incompatibility: A 'New' Approach to the Dissolution of Marriage," *University of Kansas Law Review,* vol. 20, no. 2 (1972): 227–37.

No-Fault: Kentucky

2333. Bilby, John W. "Kentucky No Fault Divorce: Theory and the Practical Experience," *Journal of Family Law,* vol. 13, no. 3 (1973–74): 567–85.

No-Fault: Maryland

2334. Tennery, Elizabeth. "No Fault Divorce: Craze or Cure?" *Women Lawyers Journal,* vol. 62, no. 1 (1976): 30–31.

No-Fault: Massachusetts

2335. Hoffman, Richard G.; Inker, Monroe L.; and Volterra, Max. "No-Fault Divorce in Massachusetts: An Explanation of Chapter 698," *Massachusetts Law Quarterly,* vol. 61, no. 2 (1976): 78–80 + .

No-Fault: Michigan

2336. Honigman, Jason L. "What 'No-Fault' Means to Divorce," *Michigan State Bar Journal,* vol. 51, no. 1 (1972): 16–24.

2337. Institute for Continuing Legal Education. University of Michigan—Wayne State University. *Michigan's New No-Fault Divorce Law.* Ann Arbor, MI: The Institute, 1971.

2338. Snyder, George E. "Divorce Michigan Style—1972 and Beyond," *Michigan State Bar Journal,* vol. 50, no. 12 (1971): 740–45.

No-Fault: Mississippi

2339. Adkinson, Clayton J.M. "No-Fault Divorce: A Proposal for Mississippi," *Mississippi Law Journal,* vol. 45, no. 1 (1974): 179–207.

No-Fault: Missouri

2340. McEvoy, Lawrence T. "Impact of No-Fault Divorce: The Missouri Experience," *State Government,* vol. 51, no. 2 (1978): 95–105. R.

2341. Shapiro, Lee S. "Dissolution of Marriage under Missouri's New Divorce Law—Grounds," *Missouri Bar Journal,* vol. 29, no. 8 (1973): 501–04.

2342. Thayer, Charlotte P. "Dissolution of Marriage under Missouri's New Divorce Law—Introduction," *Missouri Bar Journal,* vol. 29, no. 8 (1973): 496–500.

No-Fault: Nebraska

2343. Frank, Alan H.; Berman, John J.; and Mazur-Hart, Stanley F. "No-Fault Divorce and the Divorce Rate: The Nebraska Experience—An Interrupted Time Series Analysis and Commentary," *Nebraska Law Review,* vol. 58, no. 1 (1979): 1–99. R.

2344. Van Pelt, Samuel. "No Fault Divorce: A Re-examination of Nebraska Law," *Nebraska Law Review,* vol. 54, no. 1 (1975): 27–45.

No-Fault: New York

2345. Bronstein, Eli H. "No-Fault Divorce, Alimony, and Property Settlement," *New York State Bar Journal,* vol. 45, no. 4 (1973): 241–45.

2346. "Divorce Reform Law—'Nonfault Ground' Based on Separation Decree Held Retroactive," *New York Law Forum,* vol. 16, no. 2 (1970): 508–15.

No-Fault: Ohio

2347. Rose, Clayton W., Jr. "Non-Fault Divorce in Ohio," *Ohio State Law Journal,* vol. 31, no. 1 (1970): 52–65.

No-Fault: Oregon

2348. Leo, Roger J. "Oregon's No-Fault Marriage Dissolution Act," *Oregon Law Review,* vol. 51, no. 4 (1972): 715–26.

2349. Stevenson, Victoria. "Oregon's No-Fault Divorce Law: Effect on Custody, Property Division, and Support," *Oregon Law Review,* vol. 55, no. 2 (1976): 267–77.

No-Fault: Washington

2350. Holman, Nancy A. "A Law in the Spirit of Conciliation and Understanding: Washington's Marriage Dissolution Act," *Gonzaga Law Review,* vol. 9, no. 1 (1973): 39–56.

No-Fault: Wisconsin

2351. Wisconsin. Legislative Reference Bureau. *An Emerging Trend: The Nonfault Concept of Divorce.* [Madison, WI]: The Bureau, 1971.

2352. ———. *The Legislative Response to Divorce: A Survey of No-Fault Divorce.* Madison, WI: The Bureau, 1976.

STATES AND TERRITORIES

Divorce: Alabama

2353. Thornton, J. Edward. "Marriage Vows: Who Cares about Them?" *Alabama Lawyer,* vol. 35, no. 2 (1974): 158–81.

Divorce: Arizona

2354. Smith, Charles M. *Arizona Divorce Manual.* Tucson, AZ: Arizona Law Institute, 1972.

Divorce: Arkansas

2355. "An Antenuptial Agreement Obtained by the Husband through Design, Cognitive Planning, and Concealment, Which Constitutes Fraud and Overreaching, is Void," *Journal of Family Law,* vol. 16, no. 4 (1978): 823–30.

2356. Cathey, Maurice. "Ante-nuptial Agreements in Arkansas—Divorce Provisions," *Arkansas Law Review,* vol. 29, no. 2 (1976): 480–85.

2357. Mobley, Richard. "Arkansas Divorce—Do We Have Problems?" *Arkansas Law Review,* vol. 23, no. 4 (1970): 601–18.

2358. Vasser, Albert G. "Doctrine of Recrimination—Denial of Decree on the Grounds of Equal Fault," *Arkansas Law Review,* vol. 24, no. 4 (1971): 550–56.

Divorce: California

2359. Baron, Robert E. C. "In re Marriage of McKim—Playacting and the New Family Law Act," *Southwestern University Law Review,* vol. 4, no. 2 (1972): 325–29.

2360. Johnson, Charles W. "The Family Law Act: A Guide to the Practitioner," *Pacific Law Journal,* vol. 1, no. 1 (1970): 147–55.

2361. Langum, David J. "Expatriate Domestic Relations Law in Mexican California," *Pepperdine Law Review,* vol. 7, no. 1 (1979): 41–66.

2362. Machtinger, Steven N. "Domestic Relations Problems of California Prisoners," *University of California, Davis, Law Review,* 6 (1973): 313–31.

2363. Nelson, Meredith A. "California Family Law Act," *Prospectus,* vol. 3, no. 2 (1970): 425.

2364. "Nonresident Father Subjected to Personal Jurisdiction of State of Child's Residence," *Journal of Family Law,* vol. 16, no. 2 (1978): 316–21.

2365. Pitcairn, Robert A., Jr. "No Fault Dissolution of Marriage—Petitioner Must Personally Appear at the Dissolution Hearing and Testify to Irreconcilable Differences unless Exceptional Circumstances Are Shown," *University of Cincinnati Law Review,* vol. 41, no. 4 (1972): 996–1001.

2366. Porter, Everette M. "Practice and Procedure under the California Family Law Act of 1969," *Conciliation Courts Review,* vol. 8, no. 2 (1970): 14–19.

2367. Reppy, Susan W. "End of Innocence: Elimination of Fault in California Divorce Law," *UCLA Law Review* 17 (June 1970): 1306–32.

2368. Wenke, Robert A. *Marital Settlement Agreement and Form Book.* Los Angeles: Richter Law Book Co., 1971.

2369. Widmann, Randall M. "Divorce Without Marriage: The Subject Matter Jurisdiction Anomaly in California," *Santa Clara Law Review,* vol. 16, no. 1 (1975): 129–46.

Divorce: Colorado

2370. "Divorce: A Discussion," *Denver Law Journal,* Special Issue (1971): 55–64.

Divorce: Connecticut

2371. Gordon, Victor M. "Uncontested Divorce Evidence," *Connecticut Bar Journal,* vol. 46, no. 2 (1972): 338–64. R.

2372. Schoonmaker, Samuel V., III, and Balbirer, Arthur E. "Survey of 1974 Developments in Connecticut Family Law," *Connecticut Bar Journal,* vol. 49, no. 1 (1975): 1–23.

2373. ———. "Survey of 1974–1975 Developments in Connecticut Family Law," *Connecticut Bar Journal,* vol. 50, no. 1 (1976): 67–80.

2374. ———. "Survey of 1976 Developments in Connecticut Family Law," *Connecticut Bar Journal,* vol. 51, no. 1 (1977): 2–14.

Divorce: District of Columbia

2375. "Authority of Court to Order Mother to Submit Her Child to Blood-Grouping Tests to Determine Issue of Adultery," *Journal of Family Law,* vol. 15, no. 3 (1976–77): 592–97.

2376. Green, Samuel, and Long, John V. "Real and Illusory Changes of the 1977 Marriage and Divorce Act," *Catholic University Law Review* 27 (Spring 1978): 469–513.

Divorce: Florida

2377. Florida Bar. Continuing Legal Education. *Florida Dissolution of Marriage,* [Tallahassee, FL]: Florida Bar, 1976.

2378. Murray, Daniel E. "Family Law," *University of Miami Law Review* vol. 30, no. 1 (1976): 108–67.

2379. Orthwein, Stephen A. "The Privilege against Self-Incrimination," *St. Louis University Law Journal* 15 (Summer 1971): 662–68.

2380. Reynolds, Jason G. "Avoiding Self-Incrimination in Marriage Dissolution Proceedings," *Florida Bar Journal,* vol. 50, no. 9 (1976): 528–31.

2381. Shankweiler, Richard T. "Statutory Marriage Counseling," *Florida Bar Journal*, vol. 45, no. 9 (1971): 566–67.

2382. Waybright, Roger J. "Silver of Hatred: Financial Aspects of Divorce," *Florida Bar Journal*, vol. 44, no. 3 (1970): 134–40.

Divorce: Georgia

2383. Carswell, Kenneth R. "Summary Judgment for Divorce Required When One Spouse Swears to Irretrievable Breakdown," *Mercer Law Review*, vol. 28, no. 1 (1976): 409–12.

2384. "A Default Divorce Judgment Affecting Personal Rights of Defendant Is Entitled to Full Faith and Credit Where the Divorce Forum Acquired Personal Jurisdiction over Defendant under a Domestic Relations Long-Arm Statute," *Georgia Law Review*, vol. 11, no. 3 (1977): 683–93.

2385. "In Determining Whether a Marriage Is Irretrievably Broken, the Court May Consider All Relevant Evidence Including That Previously Admitted in Another Action," *Journal of Family Law*, vol. 14, no. 4 (1975–76): 629–33.

2386. Little, Jeannette. " 'Minimum Contacts' Concept of in Personam Jurisdiction Extended to Domestic Relations Litigation," *Mercer Law Review*, vol. 29, no. 1 (1977): 341–46.

2387. McConaughey, Dan E., and Hinchey, John W. *Georgia Divorce, Alimony, and Child Custody*. Atlanta, GA: Harrison Co., 1973.

2388. Steinbeck, Mark A. "Bold New Procedure in Divorce Actions," *Mercer Law Review*, vol. 27, no. 1 (1975): 331–34.

Divorce: Hawaii

2389. *The Hawaii Divorce Manual: An Innovative Systems Approach for Hawaii Attorneys and Their Staff: A Cooperative Effort*. Edited by Robert J. LeClair. [Honolulu, HI]: Hawaii State Bar Association, 1975.

2390. "The Problem of the 'Newcomer's Divorce,' " *Maryland Law Review*, vol. 30, no. 4 (1970): 367–82.

Divorce: Idaho

2391. Younger, Judith T. "Not Equal Yet," *Idaho Law Review*, vol. 13, no. 2 (1977): 227–45.

Divorce: Illinois

2392. Baker, David A. "Divorce Jurisdiction after the 1977 Amendment to the Illinois Long Arm Statute: Extending a Legal Doctrine or Creating a Legal Hallucination?" *Loyola University of Chicago Law Journal*, vol. 9, no. 4 (1978): 893–909.

2393. Beigler, Jerome S. "The 1971 Amendment of the Illinois Statute on Confidentiality: A New Development in Privilege Law," *American Journal of Psychiatry*, vol. 129, no. 3 (1972): 311–15.

2394. Bundesen, Russell. "Mental Cruelty in Illinois—After Five years," *Illinois Bar Journal*, vol. 61, no. 12 (1973): 628–35.

2395. Dickinson, Robert J. "Elimination of Recrimination in Illinois," *Chicago Bar Record*, vol. 52, no. 5 (1971): 238–49.

2396. "Divorce Action—Recrimination a Valid Defense," *University of Illinois Law Forum* no. 1 (1974): 169–76.

2397. Hunter, Robert L. "Divorce in Cook County," *Illinois Bar Journal*, vol. 60, no. 10 (1972): 776–83.

2398. Schiller, Donald C. "Injunctive Relief without Notice—Preliminary Injunction or Temporary Restraining Order," *Chicago Bar Record*, vol. 52, no. 6 (1971): 304–09.

2399. Valiulis, Anthony. "Kech v. Kech, Routine or Novel Approach to the Applicability of Full Faith and Credit to Foreign Divorce and Custody Decrees?" *Loyola University of Chicago Law Journal*, vol. 4, no. 2 (1973): 594–602.

Divorce: Indiana

2400. Ancel, Sorell J. "Effect of the Indiana Divorce Law upon the Application of Section 17a(7) of the Bankruptcy Act," *Indiana Law Review*, vol. 12, no. 2 (1979): 379–95.

2401. Hopson, Dan. *Summary of the New Indiana Dissolution of Marriage Law*. Indianapolis, IN: Indiana Continuing Legal Education Forum, 1973.

2402. Storer, Janet K. "O'Connor v. O'Connor: Recrimination in Retreat," *Indiana Legal Forum*, vol. 3, no. 2 (1970): 538–46.

Divorce: Iowa

2403. *The Dissolution of Marriage Law. Selected Problems in Administering Iowa Trusts and Estates. Placement Interviews with Seniors*. [Iowa City, IA]: University of Iowa College of Law, [1970].

Divorce: Kansas

2404. Glenn, Grant M. "Effect of Change in Age of Majority upon Parents' Duty of Support," *University of Kansas Law Review*, vol. 23, no. 1 (1974): 181–88.

Divorce: Kentucky

2405. Coleman, Susan L. "Tax Implications of the Uniform Marriage and Divorce Act: Does the Davis Rule Still Apply in Kentucky?" *Kentucky Law Journal* 66 (1978): 889–909.

2406. Humphrey, Stephen L. "Kentucky Divorce Reform," *Journal of Family Law*, vol. 12, no. 1 (1972–73): 109–50.

2407. Massey, Raymond. "Effect of the Equal Rights Amendment on Kentucky's Domestic Relations Laws," *Journal of Family Law* 12 (1972–73): 151–59.

Divorce: Louisiana

2408. Berman, Diana D. "Divorce: Demise of the Doctrine of Recrimination in Louisiana," *Loyola Law Review*, vol. 24, no. 4 (1978): 776–81.

2409. Pascal, Robert A. "Louisiana's 1978 Matrimonial Regimes Legislation," *Tulane Law Review*, vol. 53, no. 1 1978): 105–34.

2410. Toney, Felicia G. "Abrogation of the Doctrine of Recrimination: A Step toward Reality," *Southern University Law Review*, vol. 4, no. 1 (1978): 263–71.

Divorce: Maryland

2411. "Divisible Divorce in Maryland—Does it Exist? Dachman v. Dachman," *Maryland Law Review*, vol. 30, no. 1 (1970): 63.

2412. *Maryland Divorce and Separation Law*. Edited by John W. Ester. Baltimore, MD: Maryland Institute for Continuing Professional Education of Lawyers, 1979.

Divorce: Massachusetts

2413. Freeman, Haskell C. "ABC's of Massachusetts Divorce Practice and Procedure." *Boston Bar Association Journal*, vol. 24, no. 1 (1980): 5–26.

2414. ————. *Massachusetts Divorce Practice and Procedure*. Boston: Massachusetts Continuing Legal Education—New England Law Institute, 1979.

2415. Harvard Legal Bureau. "Divorce Procedures Guide." Rev. August 1977. Typewritten. [Cambridge, MA: Harvard Legal Bureau, 1977.]

2416. Harvey, John V., and McGovern, Sheila E. *Massachusetts Divorce System.* Melrose, MA: Massachusetts Divorce System, 1971.

2417. Massachusetts Continuing Legal Education. New England Law Institute, Inc. *Massachusetts Divorce Practice and Procedure.* Boston: MCLE-NELI, 1977.

2418. ———. *Compendium of Massachusetts Divorce Law, Rules, and Practices.* Boston: MCLE-NELI, 1979.

Divorce: Michigan

2419. Chardavoyne, David G. "Wills—Implied Revocation—Effect of Divorce," *Wayne Law Review,* vol. 21, no. 4 (1975): 1265–77.

2420. Klarman, Barbara. "Marital Agreements in Contemplation of Divorce," *University of Michigan Journal of Law Reform,* vol. 10, no. 3 (1977): 397–412.

2421. *Michigan Family Law: The Contested Divorce Case: Course Handbook.* Ann Arbor, MI: Institute of Continuing Legal Education, 1976.

Divorce: Minnesota

2422. Haugh, William E., and Helland, Mark D. *Dissolution of Marriage.* Eau Claire, WI: Legal Systems, Inc., 1978.

Divorce: Mississippi

2423. Furby, Tommy E. "Effect of Divorce on Tenancy by the Entirety in Mississippi," *Mississippi Law Journal,* vol. 48, no. 2 (1977): 352–60.

2424. Griffith, Benjamin E. "Habitual Cruel and Inhuman Treatment—Absence of Proof that Defendant's Conduct was Proximate Cause of Separation Precludes Granting Divorce Absolute on Ground of Habitual Cruel and Inhuman Treatment," *Mississippi Law Journal,* vol. 45, no. 4 (1974–75): 1073–81.

Divorce: Missouri

2425. "Dissolution of Marriage Under Missouri's New Divorce Law—Forms," *Missouri Bar Journal,* vol. 29, no. 8 (1973): 529–41.

2426. Riederer, Henry A. "Marriage Dissolution Trends: An Analysis of a Missouri Bar Survey," *Family Law Quarterly,* vol. 4, no. 2 (1970): 184–207. R.

2427. Shapiro, Lee S. "Topical Index of New Missouri Law of Dissolution—R.s. Mo. Chapter 452," *Missouri Bar Journal,* vol. 31, no. 5 (1975): 365–69.

2428. Triplett, Timothy W. "Confidential Communications Privilege of Husband and Wife: Application under the Missouri Dissolution Statute," *Missouri Law Review,* vol. 43, no. 2 (1979): 235–49.

Divorce: Montana

2429. Townsend, Karen. "Uniform Marriage and Divorce Act: New Statutory Solutions to Old Problems," *Montana Law Review,* vol. 37, no. 1 (1976): 119–30.

Divorce: Nebraska

2430. Curry, Douglas L. "Personal Jurisdiction in Divorce Proceedings," *Nebraska Law Review,* vol. 51, no. 1 (1971): 159–71.

2431. Henderson, Roger C. "Practice and Problems under Nebraska's New Divorce Laws," *Nebraska Law Review,* vol. 52, no. 1 (1972): 1–23.

2432. Nebraska Continuing Legal Education, Inc. and Committee on Family Law of the Nebraska State Bar Association. *"Domestic Relations Practice": Current Issues and Tax Implications* (seminar report). Lincoln, NB: Nebraska Continuing Legal Education, 1977.

Divorce: New Hampshire

2433. *Family Law—Anatomy of a Divorce Case from Initial Conference to Final Hearing and Beyond, with Special Emphasis on Tax Consequences of Property Settlements.* Manchester, NH: New Hampshire Bar Association, 1977.

Divorce: New Jersey

2434. "C. v. C.: Judicial Erosion of the Beleaguered Doctrine of Recrimination," *Rutgers Law Review,* vol. 24, no. 4 (1970): 770–83.

2435. *Matrimonial Practice Course.* Newark, NJ: Institute for Continuing Legal Education, 1974.

2436. New Jersey. Divorce Law Study Commission. *Final Report to the Governor and the Legislature (Pursuant to P.L. 1967 c. 57 as Amended by P.L. 1968, c. 170 and P.L. 1969, c. 25), May 11, 1970.* Trenton, NJ: The Commission, 1970.

2437. New Jersey. Legislature. General Assembly. Judiciary Committee. *Public Hearing . . . on Assembly Bill no. 1100 (Revises Statutes Concerning Divorce) Held October 30, 1970.* Trenton, NJ: Legislature, [1970].

2438. Silverman, Paul N. *Marriage, Divorce, and Separation: With Forms.* 4th ed. Saint Paul, MN: West Publishing Co., 1978.

Divorce: New Mexico

2439. Behles, Jennie D., and Behles, Daniel J. "Equal Rights in Divorce and Separation," *New Mexico Law Review,* vol. 3, no. 1 (1973): 118–35.

Divorce: New York

2440. Cohen, Richard B. "Justice for the Poor? A Look at the Right to Counsel for Indigents in Divorce Litigation," *New York Law School Law Review,* vol. 22, no. 1 (1976): 87–102.

2441. "Declaratory Judgment to Determine the Validity of an ex parte Divorce Can be Brought upon the Procuring Thereof, but the Statute of Limitations Does Not Commence to Run until the Right to Bring a Coercive Action Accrues," *Brooklyn Law Review,* vol. 36, no. 3 (1970): 493–98.

2442. "Divorce—Cruel and Inhuman Treatment," *New York Law Forum,* vol. 21, no. 1 (1975): 131–49.

2443. Foster, Henry H., Jr., and Freed, Doris J. *Divorce, Separation and Annulment.* Law and the Family: New York: Dissolution of the Family Unit, vol. 1, 1972. *Economic Aspects, Custody, Taxes.* vol. 2, 1978. Rochester, NY: Lawyers Co-Operative Pub. Co.

2444. "From the Legislature to the Court of Appeals: New York's Conversion Divorce under Domestic Relations Law Section 170," *Fordham Law Review,* vol. 38, no. 4 (1970): 767–85.

2445. Gershenson, Milton G. *New York Matrimonial Practice.* New York: Practising Law Institute, 1978.

2446. Haberle, Therese M. "Sex-Based Discrimination in New York Statutory Law: A Roadmap for Legislative Reform," *St. John's Law Review,* vol. 50, no. 1 (1975): 152–78.

2447. "Marital Fault v. Irremediable Breakdown: The New York Problem and the California Solution," *New York Law Forum,* vol. 16, no. 1 (1970): 119–64.

2448. *Matrimonial Matters: Latest Developments under New York Divorce Law.* New York: Practising Law Institute, 1973.

2449. *Matrimonial Matters: What the General Practitoner Should Know about the Latest Developments under New York Divorce Law.* New York: Practising Law Institute, 1974.

2450. *Matrimonial Matters: What the General Practitioner Should Know about the Latest Developments under New York Divorce Law.* New York: Practising Law Institute, 1975.

2451. *Matrimonial Matters: What the General Practitioner Should Know about Developments and Probable New Direction under New York Matrimonial Law, 1976.* New York: Practising Law Institute, 1976.

2452. "Subdivision (5) Section 170 of Domestic Relations Act Which Provides for Non-Fault Divorce after Decree of Separation Has Retroactive Effect. Gleason v. Gleason," *Albany Law Review,* vol. 34, no. 3 (1970): 715–20.

2453. *Tactics and Strategy under the New Divorce Law.* New York: Practising Law Institute, 1970.

2454. Weiler, Robert K. "Right to Assigned Counsel in Divorce Actions and the Effect of Matter of Smiley: Setting the Boundaries in a New Frontier," *Albany Law Review,* vol. 40, no. 3 (1976): 513–42.

2455. Zett, James, Edmonds, Michael E.; and Schwartz, Stanley A. *Matrimonial Actions.* New York: Matthew Bender & Co., 1971.

Divorce: North Carolina

2456. Napier, Douglas W. "Amendment of Pleadings to Conform to Evidence," *Wake Forest Law Review,* vol. 12, no. 2 (1976): 405–22.

2457. Sugar, Harriet S. "New Rules for an Old Game: North Carolina Compulsory Counterclaim Provision Applies in Divorce Suits," *North Carolina Law Review,* vol. 57, no. 3 (1979): 439–48.

Divorce: North Dakota

2458. Opland, David V. "Marriage and Divorce for the Devil's Lake Indian Reservation," *North Dakota Law Review,* vol. 47, no. 2 (1971): 317–34.

Divorce: Ohio

2459. Haine, William R. "The Doctrine of Recrimination in Divorce Cases," *St. Louis University Law Journal* 15, (Winter 1970): 326–36.

2460. Haldy, Ronald L. "Ohio Divorce Reform Act: Half-Stepping to the Modern Drummer," *Ohio Northern Law Review,* vol. 2, no. 3 (1975): 508–23.

2461. Milligan, J.R. "Dissolution of Marriage—'Fresh Air in the Family Court,' " *Akron Law Review,* vol. 8, no. 3 (1975): 338–97.

2462. Oppenheimer, Randolph C. "Antenuptial Contract in Ohio," *Case Western Reserve Law Review,* vol. 28, no. 4 (1978): 1040–73.

Divorce: Oklahoma

2463. "Availability of Forum non conveniens in Divorce Actions," *Oklahoma Law Review,* vol. 27, n o. 3 (1979): 567–70.

2464. Rogers, Lynn C. "Post-marital Squabbles and the Harassing Ex-spouse," *Oklahoma Law Review,* vol. 28, no. 2 (1975): 404–12.

Divorce: Pennsylvania

2465. "Anti-Suit Injunction: Vehicle for Change in Divorce Jurisdiction?" *University of Pittsburg Law Review,* vol. 32, no. 1 (1970): 92–103.

2466. "Grounds as Affecting Subsequent Rights," *Journal of Family Law,* vol. 13, no. 4 (1973–74): 871–72.

2467. Hoch, Jered L. "Arrival of Divisible Divorce in Pennsylvania," *Dickinson Law Review,* vol. 77, no. 2 (1973): 401–14.

2468. Morrissey, Francis J., Jr. "Living Apart as a Ground for Divorce," *Pennsylvania Bar Association Quarterly,* vol. 41, no. 4 (1970): 439–48.

2469. Perlberger, Norman. "Marital Residence—A Strategic Battleground," *Dickinson Law Review,* vol. 81, no. 3 (1977): 699–707.

2470. Raphael, Robert; Frank, Frederick N.; and Wilder, Joanne R. "Divorce in America: The Erosion of Fault," *Dickinson Law Review,* vol. 81, no. 4 (1977): 719–31.

2471. Willoughby, Barry M. "Incompetency and Divorce Laws: Protective or Defective?" *Dickinson Law Review,* vol. 83, no. 2 (1979): 339–65.

Divorce: Puerto Rico

2472. Belén, Frías, Ana. "Reconocimiento y Validez de una Sentencia Final," *Revista Jurídica de la Univ. de Puerto Rico,* vol. 40 (1971): 645–53.

2473. Fiol Matta, Liana. "Las Medidas Temporeras en la Acción de Divorcio," *Revista del Colegio de Abogados de Puerto Rico,* vol. 33, no. 2 (1972): 197–242.

2474. Menéndez Menéndez, Emilio. *Lecciones de Derecho de Familia.* [Río Piedras]: Editorial Universitaria, University de Puerto Rico, 1976.

2475. Silva-Ruiz, Pedro F. "El Divorcio: Reconocimiento de las Sentendias Dominicanas in Puerto Rico," *Revista de Derecho Puertorriqueño,* vol. 12, no. 48 (1973): 447–72.

2476. Vázquez Bote, Eduardo, "Reforma del Derecho de Familia en Derecho Puertorriqueño, vol. 16, no. 1 (1976): 91–105.

Divorce: South Carolina

2477. Crystal, Nathan M. "Ethical Problems in Marital Practice," *South Carolina Law Review,* vol. 30, no. 2 (1979): 321–62.

Divorce: South Dakota

2478. Wheeler, Ronald J. "Recrimination—A Doctrine for the Past," *South Dakota Law Review,* vol. 15, no. 2 (1970): 366–75.

Divorce: Tennessee

2479. Cohen, Neil P. "Critical Survey of Developments in Tennessee Family Law in 1976–77," *Tennessee Law Review,* vol. 45, no. 3 (1978): 432–55.

2480. Creswell, Richard W. "Proposed Tennessee Family Law Act in Context," *Tennessee Law Review,* vol. 41, no. 3 (1974): 463–501.

2481. Garrett, W. Walton, *Tennessee Divorce, Alimony, and Child Custody.* Norcross, GA: Harrison Co., 1978.

2482. Gillen, Rebecca O. "Domestic Relations—Jurisdiction—Extension of Comity to Foreign-Nation Divorce," *Tennessee Law Review*, vol. 46, no. 1 (1978): 238–51.

2483. Parker, James O. "Defenses to Divorce Confined to those Prescribed by Statute," *Memphis State University Law Review*, vol. 9, no. 2 (1979): 346–55.

2484. Shepperd, Sarah Y. "Divorce—Restrictions on Recrimination," *Tennessee Law Review*, vol. 46, no. 2 (1979): 461–71.

2485. Tennessee General Assembly Legislative Council Committee. *Study on Domestic Relations Laws and Procedures*. Nashville, TN: The Committee, 1970.

2486. West, William K., Jr. "New Office of Divorce Referee in Shelby County, *Memphis State University Law Review*, vol. 4, no. 1 (1973): 33–38.

Divorce: Texas

2487. Bonesio, W.M. "Marriage and Divorce under the Texas Family Code," *Houston Law Review*, vol. 8, no. 1 (1970): 101–36.

2488. "Full Faith and Credit versus State Interest: The Last-in-Time Rule in Texas," *Texas Law Review*, vol. 55, no. 1 (1976): 127–45.

2489. Hatten, William M., and Brown, Robert T. " 'Impressions of a Domestic Relations Judge,' " *South Texas Law Journal* 13 (1972): 250–68.

2490. Johannes, Jack. *Forms for Divorce and Annulment under the Family Code*. Austin, TX: State Bar of Texas, 1970.

2491. McKnight, Joseph W. "Texas Family Code and Commentary, Title 1: Commentary," *Texas Tech Law Review*, vol. 5, no. 2 (1974): 281–388.

2492. *Marriage Dissolution in Texas*. [Austin, TX]: State Bar of Texas, Professional Development Program, 1978.

2493. Moseley, Jim. "Court Awarded Attorney's Fees in Divorce—'Necessities' or 'Factors in Property Division'?" *Baylor Law Review*, vol. 29, no 1 (1977): 172–79.

2494. Sampson, John J. "Jurisdiction in Divorce and Conservatorship Suits," *Texas Tech Law Review*, vol. 8, no. 1 (1976): 159–254.

2495. ———. "Long-Arm Jurisdiction Marries the Texas Family Code," *Texas Bar Journal*, vol. 33, no. 10 (1975): 1023+.

2496. Turley, Edward W., Jr. "Wife's Right to Support Payments in Texas," *South Texas Law Journal*, vol. 16 (1974): 1–56.

2497. Volk, Michael D. "Award of Attorney's Fees in Divorce Litigation in Texas," *Houston Law Review*, vol. 13, no. 5 (1976): 1016–40.

2498. Weintraub, Russell J. "Texas Long-Arm Jurisdiction in Family Law Cases," *Southwestern Law Journal*, vol. 32, no. 3 (1978): 965–84.

Divorce: Virginia

2499. *Dissolving a Marriage*. Roanoke, VA: Joint Committee on Continuing Legal Education of the Virginia Bar Association, 1978.

2500. Phelps, Arthur W. *Divorce and Alimony in Virginia and West Virginia*. 2d ed. Charlottesville, VA: Michie Co., 1970.

2501. *Separation and Divorce*. [Richmond, VA]: Joint Committee on Continuing Legal Education of the Virginia Bar and the Virginia Bar Association, 1976.

2502. *Separation and Divorce*. Richmond, VA: Joint Committee on Continuing Legal Education of the Virginia Bar Association and Virginia State Bar, with the Bar Association of the City of Richmond, 1971.

2503. Virginia Advisory Legislative Council. *Separation and Divorce: Report of the Virginia Advisory Legislative Council to the Governor and the General Assembly of Virginia*. Richmond, VA: Commonwealth of Virginia, Department of Purchases and Supply, 1975.

2504. Wadlington, Walter. "A Case of Insanity and Divorce," *Virginia Law Review*, vol. 56, no. 1 (1970): 12–36.

Divorce: Washington

2505. Holman, Nancy A., and Noland, Jane. "Agreement and Arbitration: Relief to Over-litigation in Domestic Relations Disputes in Washington," *Willamette Law Journal*, vol. 12 (Summer 1976): 527–44.

2506. Rieke, Luvern V. "Dissolution Act of 1973: From Status to Contract?" *Washington Law Review*, vol. 49, no. 2 (1974): 375–421.

Divorce: Wisconsin

2507. Di Pronio, Blaise. "Abolition of Guilt in Marriage Dissolution: Wisconsin's Adoption of No-Fault Divorce," *Marquette Law Review*, vol. 61, no. 4 (1978): 672–90.

2508. Gaylord, C. L. "McMurtrie Affair," *Wisconsin Bar Bulletin*, vol. 45, no. 2 (1972): 20–26.

2509. Gibson, Helen E. "Voluntary Separation as Grounds for Divorce in Wisconsin," *Wisconsin Law Review*, (1972): 1215–28.

2510. Perkins, Sandra L. "1977 Amendments to the Wisconsin Family Code," *Wisconsin Law Review*, no. 3 (1978): 882–903.

2511. *Wisconsin Legal Systems: Divorce*. Edited by K. Richard Olson and Jerold E. Aubry. Eau Claire, WI: Legal Systems, 1978.

TRIALS

2512. Foster, Henry H., Jr. "Trial Marriages and Divorce Trials," *Conciliation Courts Review*, vol. 11, no. 1 (1973): 1–8.

2513. Glieberman, Herbert A. "Discovery Tactics in a Divorce Case," *Trial*, vol. 11, no. 2 (1975): 56–58.

2514. Glosband, Benjamin A., and Di Mento, Carol A. G. "Trial Preparation in Divorce Litigation," *Trial*, vol. 15, no. 5 (1979): 38–40.

UNIFORM MARRIAGE AND DIVORCE ACT

2515. American Bar Association. "Uniform Family Code, 1970," Springfield, VA: *Government Reports Announcements Index*, 1974 (PB-235 810/9GA).

2516. Family Law Reporter. *Desk Guide to Uniform Marriage and Divorce Act*. Washington, DC: Bureau of National Affairs, 1974.

2517. Levy, Robert J. "Comments on the Legislative History of the Uniform Marriage and Divorce Act," *Family Law Quarterly*, vol. 7, no. 4 (1973): 405–12.

2518. ———. "A Symposium on the Uniform Marriage and Divorce Act—Introduction," *South Dakota Law Review* 18 (Summer 1973): 531–37.

2519. Merrill, Maurice H. "Section 305: Genesis and Effect," *South Dakota Law Review* 18 (Summer 1973): 538–50.

2520. National Conference of Commissioners on Uniform State Laws Special Committee on Divorce. Robert J. Levy. "Uniform Marriage and Divorce Legislation: A Preliminary Analysis," *Government Reports Announcements and Index* 1 (1971) 5K. PB-236 781/1GA. R.

2521. O'Connell, Frederick P. "Marriage, Divorce, and the Uniform Marriage and Divorce Act," *New York Law Forum*, vol. 17, no. 4 (1972): 983–1049.

2522. Podell, Ralph J. "The Case for Revision of the Uniform Marriage and Divorce Act," *Family Law Quarterly*, vol. 7, no. 2 (1973): 169–78.

2523. ———. "The Case for Revision of the Uniform Marriage and Divorce Act," *South Dakota Law Review*, vol 18 (Summer 1973): 601–10.

2524. "Proposed Revised Uniform Marriage and Divorce Act," *Family Law Quarterly*, vol. 7, no. 2 (1975): 135–67.

2525. "Reconciliation and the Uniform Marriage and Divorce Act," *South Dakota Law Review* 18 (Summer 1973): 611–28.

2526. "Uniform Marriage and Divorce Act," *Family Law Quarterly*, vol. 5, no. 2 (1971): 123–251.

DIVORCED PERSONS

2527. Franks, Maurice R. "Federal Relief for Male Divorce Litigants," *Case and Comment*, vol. 80, no. 3 (1975): 14 + .

2528. ———. "Federal Remedies for Sexual Discrimination against Male Divorce Litigants," *Colorado Lawyer*, vol. 4, no. 2 (1975): 231–38.

2529. "Rights of Stepparents," *Journal of Family Law*, vol. 17, no. 4 (1979): 830–41.

2530. Schlissel, Stephen W. " 'Holding out' or 'Holding up'—An Ex-Wife's Right to Live with Her Boyfriend, Etc." *Nassau Lawyer* 23 (April 1976): 293–305.

2531. Wolf, Judi, and Wolf, Marshall J. "Books can Help—Bibliotherapy for Families Facing Divorce," *Family Advocate*, vol. 1, no. 2 (1978): 18–23.

INDIGENTS

2532. Boerner, Laurel L. "Boddie v. Connecticut: Eroding Civil Court Barriers to Indigents," *South Dakota Law Review* 17 (Winter 1972): 269–73.

2533. Brooks, Charles. "Boddie v. Connecticut: The Rights of Indigents in a Divorce Action," *Journal of Family Law* 11 (1971): 121–27.

2534. Bruce, Jackson M. "Does Virginia Deny Indigents the Right to Divorce?" *University of Richmond Law Review*, vol. 12, no. 4 (1978): 735–38.

2535. Burnett, Dennis J. "In Forma Pauperis: Boddie v. Connecticut and the Nebraska Statute," *Nebraska Law Review*, vol. 51, no. 3 (1972): 475–85.

2536. Burstein, Carole. "Application of Curator Statutes to Absent, Indigent Defendants in Divorce Proceedings," *Loyola Law Review*, vol. 19, no. 3 (1973): 771–79.

2537. Cohen, Warren H. "Divorce Filing Fees in Indian Tribal Courts: A First Look after Boddie v. Connecticut," *Law and the Social Order*, (1975): 540–57.

2538. Dart, John M., Jr. "Constitutional Law: Free Divorce for the Indigent," *University of Florida Law Review*, vol. 24, no. 1 (1971): 180–84.

2539. Du Val, Kathleen. " 'Thou Shalt Not Ration Justice,' " *Journal of Family Law* 11 (1972): 589–601.

2540. Goff, Thomas J. "Legal Aid Divorce Representation and Conflict of Interests," *University of California, Davis, Law Review* 6 (1973) 294–312.

2541. Goldberger, Gustav. "Legal Aid Divorces—a Practical Approach," *American University Law Review*, vol. 20, no. 1 (1970): 30–38.

2542. Gromek, Carl L. "Right of Access to the Courts for Indigents Seeking Judicial Dissolution of Their Marriage," *Journal of Urban Law*, vol. 43, no. 2 (1971): 438.

2543. Hollstein, Richard W., and Stiles, Michael R. "Indigent's Right to an in forma pauperis Proceeding in Pennsylvania Divorce Litigation—Analysis and a Proposal," *Villanova Law Review*, vol. 16, no. 2 (1970): 283–322.

2544. Kaplan, Alan S. "Validity of Requiring Indigent to Pay Court Costs in Divorce Proceeding," *Suffolk University Law Review*, vol. 8, no. 1 (1973): 165–82.

2545. Laser, Alvin. "Divorce—Indigent's Right to Avoid Payment of Filing Fees," *Arkansas Law Review*, vol. 26, no. 1 (1972): 87–93.

2546. Lee, James R. "Access to Divorce Courts for Indigents," *Tulane Law Review*, vol. 46, no. 4 (1972): 799–806.

2547. McAninch, William S. "Constitutional Right to Counsel for Divorce Litigants," *Journal of Family Law*, vol. 14, no. 4 (1975–76): 509–33.

2548. Matano, Gary R. "Towards a Constitutional Right to Counsel in Matrimonial Litigation," *Fordham Urban Law Journal*, vol. 4, no. 3 (1976): 515–30.

2549. Nelson, N. Royce. "A State's Denial to Indigents of Access to Its Courts in a Divorce Proceeding Due to Financial Barriers is a Violation of Due Process," *University of Kansas Law Review*, vol. 20, no. 3 (1972): 554–66.

2550. Noelker, Timothy. "Uniform Child Custody Jurisdiction Act: The Difficulties It Presents for Poor People," *Clearinghouse Review*, vol. 11, no. 3 (1977): 222–23.

2551. Saul, Elward L. "Divorce—Indigent Plaintiff—Fees of Curator for Non-Resident Defendant," *Loyola Law Review*, vol. 21, no. 1 (1975): 256–63.

2552. Wall, John E. "Access to Courts—Seeking Divorce Decree," *Duquesne Law Review*, vol. 10, no. 1 (1971): 123–27.

DOMESTIC RELATIONS

2553. Abrahams, Samuel. *Law in Family Conflict*. New York: Law-Arts Publishers, 1970.

2554. Dakin, Carol F. *Family Law—For Law School and Bar Examinations*. Saint Paul, MN: West Publishing Co., 1975.

2555. Fain, Harry M. "Family Law—'Whither Now?' " *Journal of Divorce*, vol. 1, no. 1 (1977): 31–42.

2556. Foley, Leander J., and McMillian, Theodore. *Family Law*. Reno, NV: National College of the State Judiciary, 1976.

2557. Glendon, Mary A. *State, Law, and Family: Family Law in Transition in the United States and Western Europe*. Amsterdam and New York: North Holland Pub. Co., 1977.

2558. Henry, Linda. "The Role of Long Arm Statutes," *Washburn Law Journal*, vol. 10, no. 3 (1971): 487–92.

2559. Katz, Sanford N. *When Parents Fail: The Law's Response to Family Breakdown*. Boston: Beacon Press, 1971.

2560. Knowles, Laurence W. "Expanding Jurisdiction Over Domestic Relations Cases," *Journal of Family Law*, vol. 11, no. 1 (1971): 49–66.

2561. Krause, Harry D. *Family Law in a Nutshell*. Saint Paul, MN: West Publishing Co., 1977.

2562. Legalines, Inc. *Family Law*. Los Angeles: College Bookstore, 1973.

2563. McMillian, Theodore. *Family Law*. Reno, NV: National College of the State Judiciary, 1972.

2564. Talley-Morris, Neva B. *Family Law Practice and Procedure Handbook*. Englewood Cliffs, NJ: Prentice-Hall, 1973.

2565. Webb, Garn H, and Bianco, Thomas C. *Domestic Relations: Analysis and Explanation*. New York: Holt, Rinehart & Winston, 1970.

ANTENUPTIAL AGREEMENTS

2566. Bowen, Henry C. "Domestic Relations—Antenuptial Agreements in Contemplation of Divorce," *West Virginia Law Review*, vol. 73, nos. 3–4 (1971): 339–43.

2567. Clark, Homer H., Jr. "Antenuptial Contracts," *University of Colorado Law Review* 50 (Winter 1979): 141–164.

2568. Evans, Gayle S. "Antenuptial Contracts Determining Property Rights upon Death or Divorce," *UMKC Law Review*, vol. 47, no. 1 (1978): 31–54.

2569. Rac, Frank. "Modern Theory and Practice of Antenuptial Agreements," *John Marshall Journal of Practice and Procedure*, vol. 5, no. 1 (1971): 179–204.

2570. Swisher, Peter N. "Divorce Planning in Antenuptial Agreements: Toward a New Objectivity," *University of Richmond Law Review*, vol. 13, no. 2 (1979): 175–95.

2571. Wenke, William F., and O'Hare, William S. "Antenuptial Agreements: Litigating Their Validity upon Dissolution of Marriage," *Orange County Bar Journal*, vol. 6, no. 2 (1979): 216–30.

CASES

2572. Clark, Homer H. *Cases and Problems on Domestic Relations*. 2d ed. Saint Paul, MN: West Publishing Co., 1974.

2573. ———. "*1977 Supplement to Cases and Problems on Domestic Relations, Second Edition*. Saint Paul, MN: West Publishing Co., 1977.

2574. Enochs, Elizabeth. *Problems and Solutions on Domestic Relations: Based on Standard Case and Text Books*. Irving-on-Hudson, NY: American Legal Publications, 1975.

2575. Foote, Calib; Levy, Robert J.; and Sander, Frank A. E. *Cases and Materials on Family Law*. Boston; Little, Brown & Co., 1976.

2576. Foster, Henry H., Jr. *Ploscowe, Foster, and Freed's Family Law: Cases and Materials: 1977 Supplement*. Boston: Little, Brown & Co., 1977.

2577. Krause, Harry D. *Family Law: Cases and Materials*. Saint Paul, MN: West Publishing Co., 1976.

2578. Paulsen, Monrad; Wadlington, Walter; and Goebel, Julius, Jr. *Cases and Other Materials on Domestic Relations*. 2d ed. Mineola, NY: Foundation Press, 1974.

2579. Paulsen, Monrad and, Wadlington, Walter. *Statutory Materials on Family Law*. 2d ed. Mineola, NY: Foundation Press, 1974.

2580. Phillips, Earl. *Cases and Materials on Domestic Relations*. Mimeographed. New York: Fordham Law School, 1978.

2581. Ploscowe, Morris; Foster, Henry H., Jr.; and Freed, Doris J. *Family Law: Cases and Materials*. 2d ed. Boston: Little, Brown & Co., 1972.

COURTS

2582. Elkin, Meyer. "Conciliation Courts: The Reintegration of Disintegrating Families," *Family Coordinator*, vol. 22, no. 1 (1973): 63–71.

2583. ———. "More Than a Divorce Court," *Trial*, vol. 8, no. 5 (1972): 19–20+.

2584. *Family Court Proceedings* by James Zett and others. New York: Matthew Bender & Co., 1972.

2585. Foster, Henry H., Jr. "Devil's Advocate. [Private Practice of Jurisprudence in Family Court]." *American Academy of Psychiatry and Law Bulletin*, vol. 6, no. 1 (1978): 118–21.

2586. Kay, Herma H. "A Family Court: The California Proposal." In *Divorce and After*, edited by Paul Bohannan. pp. 215–48. Garden City, NY: Doubleday, 1970.

2587. Maddi, Dorothy L. "Effect of Conciliation Court Proceedings on Petitions for Dissolution of Marriage," *Journal of Family Law* 13 (1973–74): 495–566. R.

2588. Nelson, James E. "New York Conciliation and Divorce," *Albany Law Review*, vol. 37, no. 4 (1973): 751–75.

2589. Nisnewitz, Freda S. "Matrimonial Conciliation: Theory and Practice," *Brooklyn Law Review*, vol. 37, no. 2 (1971): 366–86.

2590. Orlando, Frank A. "Conciliation Programs: Their Effect on Marriage and Family Life," *Florida Bar Journal*, vol. 52, no. 3 (1978): 218–21.

2591. Robbins, Norman N. "There Ought to Be a Law! Will Arbitration Ease the Crowded Divorce Docket?" *Family Coordinator*, vol. 19, no. 4 (1970): 374–76.

2592. Shipman, Gordon. "In My Opinion: The Role of Counseling in the Reform of Marriage and Divorce Proceedings," *Family Coordinator,* vol. 26, no. 4 (1977): 395–407.

2593. Woodard, Francis M., and Bahr, Stephen J. "The Pros and Cons of a Family Court: An Empirical Evaluation," *Conciliation Courts Review,* vol. 17, no. 2 (1979): 1–11. R.

2594. ———. "The Pros and Cons of a Family Court: An Empirical Evaluation," *Resources in Education* 15 (1980). ERIC document ED 179 892. R.

COURT COUNSELING

2595. McLaughlin, Jon M. A. "Court-Connected Marriage Counseling and Divorce—The New York Experience," *Journal of Family Law* 11 (1971–72): 517–56.

2596. MacLean, John V. "Marriage Counseling through the Divorce Courts—Another Look," *South Carolina Law Review* 28 (March 1977): 687–701.

2597. "Mandatory Counseling—The Lecture Series of the Salt Lake City Family Court," *Conciliation Courts Review,* vol. 9, no. 2 (1971): 11–33.

2598. Sonne, John C. "On the Question of Compulsory Marriage Counseling as Part of Divorce Proceedings," *Family Coordinator,* vol. 23, no. 3 (1974): 303–05.

STATES AND TERRITORIES

Domestic Relations: California

2599. *Attorney's Guide to Family Law Act Practice,* by Marvin Freeman, et al. 2d ed. Berkeley, CA: Continuing Education of the Bar, [1972].

2600. Faber, Stuart J. *Handbook of Family Law.* 2d ed. Los Angeles: Lega-Books, 1978.

2601. Freeman, Marvin A., et al. *Attorney's Guide to Family Law Practice.* Berkeley, CA: California Continuing Education of the Bar, 1970, 1972.

2602. Goddard, John L. *Family Law Practice.* Saint Paul, MN: West Publishing Co., 1972.

Domestic Relations: Connecticut

2603. Balbier, Arthur E., and McLachlin, C. Ian. "Survey of Developments in Connecticut Family Law," *Connecticut Bar Journal,* vol. 53, no. 5 (1979): 391–422.

Domestic Relations: Florida

2604. Florida Family Law. [Tallahassee, FL]: Florida Bar, Continuing Legal Education, 1972.

Domestic Relations: Georgia

2605. *Program Materials: Seminars on Georgia Family Law.* Athens, GA: The Institute of Continuing Legal Education in Georgia, 1973.

2606. *Seminar on Legal and Practical Problems in Family Law.* Athens, GA.: Institute of Continuing Legal Education in Georgia, 1978.

2607. Stubbs, Robert S., II. *Marriage and Divorce in Georgia.* Atlanta, GA: Emory University School of Law, [n.d.].

Domestic Relations: Illinois

2608. Illinois Family Law. I. *Handling Matrimonial Cases.* Springfield, IL: Illinois Institute on Continuing Legal Education, 1972.

2609. Illinois Family Law. II. *Legal Problems of the Illinois Family.* Springfield, IL.: Illinois Institute for Continuing Legal Education, 1973.

2610. Illinois Family Law. I. *Matrimonial Law.* Springfield, IL: Illinois Institute for Continuing Education, 1975.

Domestic Relations: Louisiana

2611. Pascal, Robert A. *Louisiana Family Law Course.* Baton Rouge, LA: Claitor's Pub. Division, 1973.

Domestic Relations: Michigan

2612. Rowse, Ruth A., and Brevitz, Ruth A., eds. *Michigan Family Law.* Ann Arbor, MI: Institute of Continuing Legal Education, 1978.

Domestic Relations: Minnesota

2613. Minnesota State Bar Association, Family Law Committee. *Minnesota Family Law.* [Minneapolis, MN]: University of Minnesota, 1971.

Domestic Relations: Missouri

2614. Missouri Bar Committee on Legal Education. *Missouri Family Law.* 2d ed. Jefferson City, MO: Missouri Bar, 1976.

Domestic Relations: New Jersey

2615. Institute for Continuing Legal Education. *Family Law.* Newark, NJ: Institute for Continuing Legal Education, 1976.

2616. New Jersey. *Family Court Study Commission. Report.* Trenton, NJ: 1972.

2617. New Jersey Institute for Continuing Legal Education. *Family Law Workbook.* Newark, NJ: The Institute, 1973.

2618. Skoloff, Gary N. *New Jersey Family Law Practice.* 3d ed. Newark, NJ: Institute for Continuing Legal Education, 1976.

2619. ———. *Survey of New Jersey Law, Part II, Family Law.* Newark, NJ: Institute for Continuing Legal Education, 1976.

Domestic Relations: New York

2620. Biskind, Elliott L. *Boardman's New York Family Law.* New York: Clark Boardman Co., 1979.

2621. Foster, Henry H., Jr., and Freed, Doris J. *New York Matrimonial Law: A Brief Commentary.* Rochester, NY: Lawyer's Cooperative Pub. Co., 1973.

2622. New York (State). Legislative Commission on Expenditure Review. *Marital Conciliation in New York State Supreme Court; Program Audit 4.1.171, August 16, 1971.* Albany, 1971.

2623. *New York Matrimonial Practice, 1977.* New York: Practising Law Institute, 1977.

2624. Rothenberg, Charles. *Matrimonial Litigation: Strategy and Techniques.* New York: Practising Law Institute, 1972.

2625. ———. *Matrimonial Litigation: Strtegy and Techniques.* New York: Practising Law Institute, 1974.

Domestic Relations: Ohio

2626. *Anderson's Ohio Family Law, Containing Text, Statutes, Forms, Rules, and Checklists: A Revision of Meier's Ohio Family Law.* Cincinnati, OH: W. H. Anderson Co., 1975.

2627. Milligan, John R. *Family Law.* Saint Paul, MN: West Publishing Co., 1975.

Domestic Relations: Pennsylvania

2628. Momijan, Albert and Perlberger, Norman. *Pennsylvania Family Law*. Philadelphia: George T. Bissel Co., 1978.

Domestic Relations: Puerto Rico

2629. Portuondo y de Castro, José. *Derecho Matrimonial Canonico Puertorriqueño*. Mimeographed. Ponce, PR: Catholic University Law School, 1974.

Domestic Relations: Texas

2630. Ledbetter, Jack W. *Texas Family Law*. 5th ed. [Austin, TX]: University of Texas, Austin, 1978.

2631. Rasor, Reba G., and Smith, Donald R. *Texas Family Practice Manual*. Austin, TX: Professional Development Program, State Bar of Texas, 1976.

2632. Simkins, Loy M. *Texas Family Law: With Forms*. Speer's 5th ed. San Francisco, CA: Bancroft-Whitney Co., 1975.

2633. State of Texas. *Family Code*. Saint Paul, MN: West Publishing Co., 1975.

Domestic Relations: Virginia

2634. Phelps, Arthur W. *Domestic Relations in Virginia, with Forms*. 3d ed. Charlottesville, VA: Michie Co., 1977.

Domestic Relations: West Virginia

2635. Morris, William O. *Cases and Statutes Relating to Domestic Relations in West Virginia*. Morgantown, WV: [Morris], 1973.

DOMICILE AND RESIDENCE

2636. Cromley, Brent R. "Home Is Where I Hang My Divorce Decree: A Critical Appraisal of Sosna v. Iowa," *California Western Law Review*, vol. 12, no. 3 (1976): 452–74.

2637. Freeman, Patricia. "Constitutional Law: New Distaste for Equal Protection Analysis," *University of Florida Law Review*, vol. 27, no. 3 (1975): 839–48.

2638. Hall, Clifford. "Cruse v. Chittum: Habitual Residence Judicially Explored," *International and Comparative Law Quarterly*, vol. 24, no. 1 (1975): 1–30.

2639. Robertson, Bruce A. "Jurisdiction over Non-domiciliary Service Members: Time to Adopt a New Jurisdictional Analysis," *Washington Law Review*, vol. 52, no. 3 (1977): 369–94.

2640. "Unified Jurisdictional Test Applied to in Personam Jurisdiction," *Washington University Law Quarterly* no. 4 (1978): 797–807.

2641. Veléz Torres, Berenith A. "El Domicilio de los Cónyuges in la Legislación de 1976," *Revista de Derecho Puertorriqueño*, vol. 16, no. 2 (1977): 261–84.

MILITARY

2642. Borgen, Mack. "Determination of Domicile," *Military Law Review*, vol. 65 (Summer 1974): 133–49.

2643. Walton, Abbott B., Jr. "Absence of Domicile in Military Divorces: Faith and Due Process Requirements," *Alabama Law Review*, vol. 22, no. 2 (1970): 304–18.

RESIDENCY REQUIREMENTS

2644. Akers, Monte E. "State's One Year Residence Requirement for Divorce Is Constitutionally Permissible," *Houston Law Review*, vol. 12, no. 5 (1975): 1153–66.

2645. Anderson, R. Dennis, and Lutes, Dennis L. "Demise of the Durational Residence Requirement," *Southwestern Law Journal* 26 (August 1972): 538–68.

2646. Bain, Jeffrey M. "One-Year Durational Residency Requirement for Dissolution of Marriage Is Not Violative of Equal Protection," *University of Miami Law Review*, vol. 29, no. 4 (1975): 817–26.

2647. Boone, Gregory K. "Durational Residency Requirements: The Alaskan Experience," *UCLA–Alaska Law Review*, vol. 6, no. 1 (1976): 50–66.

2648. "The Constitutionality of State Durational Residence Requirements for Divorce," *Texas Law Review*, vol. 51, no. 3 (1973): 585–95.

2649. Cybulski, Donald. "Constitutionality of Divorce Durational Residency Statute," *Case Western Reserve Law Review*, vol. 26, no. 2 (1976): 527–54.

2650. "Divorce Residency Requirements," *New York Law School Law Review*, vol. 22, no. 1 (1976): 121–31.

2651. "Divorce Residency Requirement Does Not Infringe Right to Travel, Deny Access to Divorce Courts, or Create Irrebuttable Presumption," *University of Illinois Law Forum* no. 2 (1975): 254–63.

2652. "Durational Residency Requirements for Divorce," *Journal of Family Law* 13 (1973–74): 872–75.

2653. "Durational Residency Requirements for Divorce," *University of Pennsylvania Law Review*, vol. 123, no. 1 (1974): 187–205.

2654. "Durational Residency Requirement for Divorce Held Not to Violate Fourteenth Amendment," *University of Richmond Law Review*, vol. 10, no. 2 (1976): 418–26.

2655. "Durational Residence Requirements from Shapiro through Sosna: The Right to Travel Takes a New Turn," *New York University Law Review*, vol. 50, no. 3 (1975): 622–80.

2656. Fischer, James M. "Constitutionality of State Durational Residence Requirements for Divorce," *University of Kansas Law Review*, vol. 24, no. 1 (1975): 173–93.

2657. Freed, Doris J., and Foster, Henry H., Jr. "Durational Residency Requirements as Prerequisites for Divorce Jurisdiction," *Family Law Quarterly,* vol. 9, no. 3 (1975): 555–71.

2658. Getto, Charles A. "Sosna v. Iowa: A New Equal Protection Approach to Durational Residency Requirements?" *UCLA Law Review,* vol. 22 (August 1975): 1313–41.

2659. Heard, Drew R. "Sosna v. Iowa: Mootness and Class Actions; Durational Residency Requirement for Divorce," *Baylor Law Review,* vol. 28, no. 1 (1976): 138–50.

2660. Johnson, Sandra R. "Residency Requirements for Divorce," *North Carolina Law Review,* vol. 52, no. 6 (1974): 1279–88.

2661. Keeffe, Arthur J. "Sticking It Out for a Year: Iowa's Residency Require-ment," *American Bar Association Journal* 62 (July 1976): 922–23.

2662. Kolyer, Peter R. "State Durational Residence Requirements for Divorce: How Long Is Too Long?" *Washington and Lee Law Review,* vol. 31, no. 2 (1974): 359–83.

2663. Luker, William H. "Durational Residency Requirements for Divorce," *Arkansas Law Review,* vol. 29, no. 3 (1975): 415–26.

2664. McKeown, H. Mary. "One Year Durational Residence Requirement for Divorce Held Unconstitutional by Alaska Supreme Court," *Cumberland–Samford Law Review,* vol. 5, no. 2 (1974): 331–38.

2665. Mills, Carol S. "Durational Residency in Divorce," *Capital University Law Review,* vol. 3, no. 1 (1974): 182–96.

2666. Pauline, G. David. "Constitutionality of a Residency Requirement in State Divorce Law," *Dickinson Law Review,* vol. 76, no. 1 (1971): 183–96.

2667. Pierce, David E. "Durational Residency Requirements for Divorce," *Washburn Law Journal,* vol. 15, no. 1 (1976): 149–54.

2668. Sachs, Sidney S., and Goldman, Henry T. "Constitutionality of Durational Residency Requirements for Divorce," *Family Law Reporter* 1 (November 12, 1974): 4001–04. monograph no. 71.

2669. Salinger, Robert M. "One Year Residency Requirement for Divorce is Constitutional," *Wisconsin Law Review* (1975): 875–900.

2670. Sheridan, Thomas I., III. "Class Action Suit to Invalidate Divorce Residency Requirement Not Moot, but Statute is Upheld," *Fordham Law Review,* vol. 43, no. 5 (1975): 857–70.

PROPERTY SETTLEMENTS

2671. Aresty, Joel M. "How to Avoid Creating Some Common Title Problems in Real Estate Litigation," *Florida Bar Journal,* vol. 52, no. 1 (1978): 29–32.

2672. Barrett, John D. "Community Property States—Property Settlement Incident to Divorce," *Tax Adviser,* vol. 6, no. 2 (1975): 81–82.

2673. Berger, Vivian O. "Legal Status of the Family Home," *American Journal of Comparative Law,* vol. 27, supplement (1978): 55–65.

2674. Boies, Judith. "Use of Trusts in Divorce Settlements," in *Institute on Federal Taxation, New York University, Proceedings, 1971,* pp. 589–608. Albany, 1972.

2675. Branca John G. "Dischargeability of Financial Obligations in Divorce: The Support Obligation and the Division of Marital Property," *Family Law Quarterly,* vol. 9, no. 2 (1975): 405–34.

2676. Campbell, Regis W. "Interspousal Transfers," Part 1, *Community Property Journal,* vol. 6, no. 3 (1979): 286–360; Part 2, vol. 6, no. 4 (1979): 395–446.

2677. Case, Karen A. "Divorce, the Anti-Davis Trend—Property Settlement," *Wisconsin Bar Bulletin,* vol. 52 (October 1979): 7–10.

2678. DuCanto, Joseph N. "The Cunning Calculator: The Family Lawyer's Best Friend," *Family Advocate,* vol. 1, no. 4 (1979): 26–31.

2679. ———. "Determination of Property Settlement," *Family Law Newsletter,* vol. 17, no. 1 (1976): 1+.

2680. ———. "Determination of Issue of Property Settlement as Opposed to 'Periodic Payments' (A/K/A 'Alimony')," *Chicago Bar Record,* vol. 55, no. 3 (1973): 130–39.

2681. ———. "Property Settlements in the Reflected Light of the Davis and Lester Cases," *American Academy of Matrimonial Lawyers Journal,* vol. 1, no. 1 (1970): 28–39.

2682. Ethridge, Deborah. "Rice Acreage Allotments," *Baylor Law Review,* vol. 26, no. 3 (1974): 376–84.

2683. Foley, Daniel M. "Investigative Auditing in Marital Dissolutions," *Orange County Bar Association Journal,* vol. 6, no. 3 (1979): 273–78.

2684. Foster, Henry H., Jr. "Equitable Distribution and Equal Protection," *Family Law Newsletter,* vol. 17, no. 3 (1977): 16–20.

2685. Foster, Henry H., Jr., and Freed, Doris J. "From a Survey of Matrimonial Laws in the United States: Distribution of Property upon Dissolution," *Community Property Journal,* vol. 3, no. 4 (1976): 231–35.

2686. ———. "Marital Property and the Chancellor's Foot," *Family Law Quarterly,* vol. 10, no. 1 (1976): 55–73; vol. 10, no. 2 (1976): 137–59; and vol. 10, no. 3 (1976): 203–45.

2687. Glieberman, Herbert A. "How to Negotiate Divorce Settlements," *Trial,* vol. 10, no. 6 (1974): 50–51.

2688. Grigg, Linda L. "Economics of Divorce: Alimony and Property Awards," *University of Cincinnati Law Review,* vol. 43, no. 1 (1974): 133–63.

2689. Halpern, Gerard, and Seaton, Lloyd, Jr. "Property Settlements in Marriage Dissolutions," *Arkansas Business and Economic Review* 8 (Summer 1975): 4–7.

2690. Hauver, Constance L. "Divorce Situation: Trusts and Trust Provisions," *Real Property, Probate and Trust Journal,* vol. 10, no. 4 (1975): 633–39.

2691. Kulzer, Barbara A. "Law and the Housewife: Property, Divorce and Death," *University of Florida Law Review,* vol. 28, no. 1 (1975): 1–55.

2692. McClure, Jerry. "Restricted Community Property: Disposition in Divorce," *Tax Adviser,* vol. 5, no. 4 (1974): 217.

2693. Mortland, Jean A. "Courts Construe Provisions for Testamentary Trusts and Effect of Remarriage and Divorce of Spouse (New Fiduciary Decisions)," *Estate Planning,* vol. 6, no. 5 (1979): 315–16.

2694. ———. "Effect of Divorce on Will Leaving Property to Spouse (New Fiduciary Decisions)," *Estate Planning,* vol. 6, no. 5 (1979): 315.

2695. Nodgaard, John C., and Pickler, Harold T. "Community Property in a Common Law Jurisdiction: A Seriously Neglected Area of the Law," *Washburn Law Journal,* vol. 16, no. 1 (1976): 77–101.

2696. "Oral Agreement Recorded in Court Becomes Written," *Taxation for Lawyers,* vol. 5, no. 3 (1976): 167.

2697. "Property, Maintenance, and Child Support Decrees under the Uniform Marriage and Divorce Act," *South Dakota Law Review* 18 (Summer 1973): 559–71.

2698. Rheinstein, Max. "Division of Marital Property," *Willamette Law Journal* 12 (Summer 1976): 413–40.

2699. Skoloff, Gary N. "The Way We Were," *Family Advocate,* vol. 1, no. 4 (1979): 22–25.

2700. Stephenson, Don C. "Recognition of Gain in Property Settlements Pursuant to Divorce—Wiles v. Commissioner," *Southwestern Law Journal* 28 (Winter 1974): 1073–79.

2701. Sutherland, James E. "ABA Family Law Section Program: The Economics of Divorce (in a Community Property Division)," *Community Property Journal,* vol. 4, no. 1 (1977): 47–51.

2702. Wiley, Thomas W. "Community Property in a Common Law State," *Practical Lawyer,* vol. 21, no. 1 (1975): 81–83.

Community Property

2703. Bodenheimer, Brigitte M. "Community without Community Property: The Need for Legislative Attention to Separate–Property Marriages under Community Property Laws," *California Western Law Review,* vol. 8, no. 3 (1972): 381–423.

2704. Cross, Harry M. "Community Property: A Comparison of the Systems in Washington and Louisiana," *Louisiana Law Review,* vol. 39, no. 2 (1979): 479–89.

2705. Larkin, Mark D. "Keeping Your Community Property File Up to Date," *California CPA Quarterly,* vol. 42, no. 2 (1974): 40.

2706. "Social Security as Community Property: Will Supreme Court Get Another Chance?" *Community Property Journal,* vol. 6, no. 2 (1979): 145–52.

Education As Property

2707. "Divorcee Claims Property Rights in Ex-mate's Degrees," *Chronicle of Higher Education* 13 (September 20, 1976): 12.

2708. Dostart, Thomas J. "Professional Education as a Divisible Asset in Marriage Dissolutions," *Iowa Law Review,* vol. 64, no. 3 (1979): 705–21.

2709. "An Education Obtained by One Spouse during Marriage Held Not to Be Property Which Can Be Divided upon Dissolution—Graham v. Graham," *Journal of Family Law,* vol. 17, no. 1 (1978): 182–85.

2710. Flynn, Jon R. "In re Marriage of Graham: Education Acquired during the Marriage—For Richer or Poorer?" *John Marshall Journal of Practice and Procedure,* vol. 12, no. 3 (1979): 709–30.

2711. Howard, Jeffrey C. "Education Degree Does Not Constitute Marital Property Subject to Division between Spouses upon Divorce," *Tulsa Law Journal,* vol. 13, no. 3 (1978): 646–57.

2712. Jacobson, Robert L. "Court Rejects Divorcee's Claim of Rights in Husband's Degree," *Chronicle of Higher Education* 16 (April 3, 1978): 2.

2713. Pinnell, Robert E. "Divorce after Professional School: Education and Future Earning Capacity May Be Marital Property," *Missouri Law Review,* vol. 44, no. 2 (1979): 329–40.

2714. Stulting, Janet S. "Graduate Degree Rejected as Marital Property Subject to Division upon Divorce: In re Marriage of Graham," *Connecticut Law Review,* vol. 11, no. 1 (1978): 62–74.

2715. Sullivan, James J. "Interest of the Community in a Professional Degree," *Louisiana Law Review,* vol. 39, no. 4 (1979): 1106–31.

Evaluation of Property

2716. Biederman, Frana. "Putting a Value on: Art and Antiques," *Family Advocate,* vol. 2, no. 1 (1979): 18–21 +.

2717. Brown, Bertram R. "Putting a Value on: Real Estate," *Family Advocate,* vol. 2, no. 1 (1979): 28–31.

2718. Ford, Jon R. "Putting a Value on: Farm and Ranch Property," *Family Advocate,* vol. 2, no. 1 (1979): 22–25.

2719. Hauserman, Nancy R., and Fethke, Carol. "Valuation of a Homemaker's Services," *Trial Lawyer's Guide* 22 (Fall 1978): 249–66.

2720. Jersin, Nikki K. "Putting a Value on: Personal Property," *Family Advocate,* vol. 2, no. 1 (1979): 14–16.

2721. Kennedy, Fred, and Thomas, Bruce. "Putting a Value on: Education and Professional Goodwill," *Family Advocate,* vol. 2, no. 1 (1979): 3–5 +.

2722. Munson, Douglas A. "Putting a Value on: Insurance Policies," *Family Advocate,* vol. 2, no. 1 (1979): 10–13.

2723. Perocchi, Paul, and Walsh, Joe. "Putting a Value on: Closely Held Corporations," *Family Advocate,* vol. 2, no. 1 (1979): 32–34 +.

2724. Projector, Murray. "Putting a Value on: A Pension Plan," *Family Advocate,* vol. 2, no. 1 (1979): 37 +.

2725. ———. "Valuation of Retirement Benefits in Marriage Dissolutions," *Los Angeles Bar Bulletin,* vol. 50, no. 6 (1975): 229–38.

2726. Udinsky, Jerald H. "Economist's Views on Community Property," *Community Property Journal,* vol. 6, no. 1 (1979): 52–60.

2727. ———. "Inflation, Interest Rates, and Community Property Valuation," *Community Property Journal,* vol. 6, no. 3 (1979): 279–85.

2728. Walker, Barth P. "Putting a Value on: Oil and Gas," *Family Advocate,* vol. 2, no. 1 (1979): 7–9 +.

LIFE INSURANCE

2729. Abbin, Byrle M., and Carlson, David K. "Significant Recent Developments Concerning Estate Planning," part 2, *Tax Adviser,* vol. 10, no. 4 (1979): 206–19.

2730. Auerbach, Marshall J. "Pitfalls of Using National Service Life Insurance in Divorce Settlements," *Law Notes* (January 1971): 33–36.

2731. Broden, Barry C. "Life Insurance in Divorce Situations," *Taxes* 1976,54(8),512-516. Also available in *Insurance Law Journal* 11 (May 1976): 277–81.

2732. D'Amico, John, Jr. "How to Handle Some Common Life Insurance Problems," *Practical Lawyer*, vol. 24, no. 5 (1978): 13–23.

2733. Flamion, Allen. "Divorce Decrees and Policy Provisions," *American Society of Chartered Life Underwriters Journal*, vol. 27, no. 3 (1973): 24–27.

2734. Grande, Donald I. "Divorce Situation: The Proper use of Insurance," *Real Property, Probate and Trust Journal*, vol. 10, no. 4 (1975): 652–56.

2735. "Life Insurance Paid to Ex–wife Is Deductible by Estate," *Taxation for Accountants*, vol. 16, no. 6 (1976): 341.

2736. "Life Insurance Paid to Ex-wife Is Deductible by Estate," *Taxation for Lawyers*, vol. 5, no. 1 (1976): 39.

2737. "Life Insurance Proceeds Paid to Decedent's Divorced Wife Deductible," *Estates, Gifts and Trusts Journal* (July–August 1976): 33–34.

2738. Saks, Howard J. "Life Insurance Policies in Divorce Settlements," *Estate Planning*, vol. 4, no. 6 (1977): 366.

2739. Schmidt, Ted A. "Common Law Concepts of Life Insurance in Community Property Jurisdictions: Recommendations for a Practical Approach," *Arizona Law Review*, vol. 18, no. 1 (1976): 182–206.

2740. Smith, Richard P. "Effects of Divorce on Life Insurance Policies," *North Dakota Law Review*, vol. 46, no. 4 (1970): 417–23.

2741. ———. "The Effect of Divorce on Life Insurance Policies," *Law Notes* 6 (July 1970): 97–102.

2742. "Tax Effects of Life Insurance Premiums in Divorce Settlements," *New York Certified Public Accountant* vol. 41, no. 10 (1971): 777–78.

2743. "Transfer by Wife Was Indirect Gift of Ex-husband," *Insurance Law Journal* 662 (March 1978): 180.

PROFESSIONAL GOODWILL AS PROPERTY

2744. Adams, Fred M. "Is Professional Goodwill Divisible Community Property?" *Community Property Journal*, vol. 6, no. 1 (1979): 61–78.

2745. ———. "Professional Goodwill as a Community Property: How Should Idaho Rule?" *Idaho Law Review*, vol. 14, no. 2 (1978): 473–91.

2746. Billingsley, Nancy. "Exclusion of Professional Good Will from Partition on Divorce," *Houston Law Review* vol. 10, no. 4 (1973): 966–72.

2747. Durkin, John J. "Divorce and Dissolution: Goodwill," *Gonzaga Law Review*, vol. 15, no. 1 (1979): 243–52.

2748. Norton, George N. "Professional Goodwill—Its Value in California Marital Dissolution Cases," *Community Property Journal*, vol. 3, no. 1 (1976): 9–18.

2749. Overton, Philip R., and Stone, Sam V., Jr. "Medicine and the Law—Court Holds 'Good Will' Not a Community Asset," *Texas Medicine* 69 (December 1972): 106.

2750. Walzer, Stuart B. "Divorce and the Professional Man," *Family Law Quarterly*, vol. 4, no. 4 (1970): 363–72.

2751. ———. "Marital Dissolution: Valuation of Good Will in Business and Professional Practices," *Southern California Tax Institute* 27 (1975): 377–414.

PROFESSION AS PROPERTY

2752. "Inman v. Inman," *Journal of Family Law*, vol. 17, no. 4 (1979): 826–30.

2753. "Kentucky Includes License to Practice Dentistry in Marital Property Division," *Washington University Law Quarterly* 1979(4), 1175–81.

2754. Loper, Amy T. "Horstmann v. Horstmann: Present Right to Practice a Profession as Marital Property," *Denver Law Journal*, vol. 56, no. 4 (1979): 677–90.

2755. Walzer, Stuart B. "Dividing an Accounting Practice in a California Marital Dissolution," *California CPA Quarterly*, vol. 40, no. 1 (1972): 25–26.

RETIREMENT BENEFITS

2756. "Attachment of Pensions in Divorce Actions: Does ERISA or State Law Govern?" *Employee Benefit Plan Review*, vol. 32, no. 12 (1978): 20 + .

2757. Bass, Gill E. "ERISA and the Treatment of Pensions etc., as Property Divisible in Divorce," *Family Law Reporter* 4 (January 31, 1978): 4009–13. Monograph no. 2.

2758. Calof, Michael P. "Community Property Rights in Pensions—Some Legal and Procedural Considerations," *California State Bar Journal*, vol. 51, no. 3 (1976): 206–08 + .

2759. Dickinson, Lloyd J. "Divorce Situation: Role of Retirement Plans," *Real Property, Probate and Trust Journal*, vol. 10, no. 4 (1975): 644–51.

2760. Dutton, Diana. "Wife's Community Interest in Her Husband's Qualified Pension or Profit–sharing Plan," *Texas Law Review*, vol. 50, no. 2 (1972): 334–50.

2761. "ERISA Preemption Moves towards Supreme Court Test," *Community Property Journal*, vol. 6, no. 2 (1979): 131–44.

2762. Fink, Albert J., and Victor, Edward G. "Slicing the Pension Pie: Tax Problems Involved in Spousal Division of Unmatured Pension Benefits," *Los Angeles Bar Bulletin*, vol. 49, no. 5 (1974): 186–95.

2763. Foster, Henry H., Jr., and Freed, Doris J. "Spousal Rights in Retirement and Pension Benefits," *Journal of Family Law*, vol. 16, no. 2 (1978): 187–211.

2764. Gudebski, John J., and Jovonich, Susan. "Retirement Pay: A Divorce in Time Saved Mine," *Hastings Law Journal*, vol. 24, no. 2 (1973): 347–58.

2765. Hardie, L. Glenn. "How to Handle an Employee's Retirement Benefits in Negotiating a Divorce Settlement," *Taxation for Lawyers*, vol. 7, no. 2 (1978): 92–96.

2766. ———. "Pay Now or Later: Alternatives in the Disposition of Retirement Benefits on Divorce," *California State Bar Journal*, vol. 53, no. 2 (1978): 106–11.

2767. Hardie, L. Glenn, and Reisman, Louis A. "Employee Benefit Plans and Divorce: Type of Plan, Date of Retirement, and Income Tax Consequences as Factors in Dispositions," *Community Property Journal*, vol. 5, no. 3 (1978): 179–86.

2768. Hartstein, Gordon. "In re Marriage of Brown: Every Family Lawyer Knows What It's Done—Do You Know What It Can Do?" *Pepperdine Law Review*, vol. 4, no. 1 (1977): 147–55.

2769. Jennings, Kathryn A. "Attachment of Pension Benefits under ERISA," *Northwestern University Law Journal*, vol. 74, no. 2 (1979): 255–83.

2770. Johnson, Charles W., and Jones, Robert C. "How Community Property Laws Affect Employee Benefit Plans," *Community Property Journal*, vol. 3, no. 1 (1976): 3–8.

2771. ———. "How Community Property Laws Affect Employee Benefit Plans," *Pension and Profit-sharing Tax Journal*, vol. 3, no. 2 (1977): 155–63.

2772. Karch, Gary C. "ERISA Preemption of Divorce Decree Enforcement against Pension Plans," *Wisconsin Law Review* 1 (1979): 277–92.

2773. Kaufman, Michael. "Legal and Malpractice Consequences of Divorce on the Entitlement of the Wife and Dependents to Social Security Benefits," *Beverly Hills Bar Association Journal*, vol. 11, no. 3 (1977): 38–42.

2774. Kroll, Arthur H., and Tauber, Yale D. "Divorce under ERISA: The Controversy between Retirement Plans and Aggrieved Spouses Continues." In *Institute on Federal Taxation, New York University, Proceedings, 1978*, vol. 27, pp. 1–54. New York: Mathew Bender & Co., 1979.

2775. "Law Gives Divorcees Stake in Pensions," *Department of State Newsletter* 205 (October 1978): 27.

2776. Levin, Noel A. "Spousal Support Draws Conflicting Rulings," *Pension World*, vol. 14, no. 10 (1978): 64–67.

2777. "More on Hisquierdo: Amicus Briefs," *Community Property Journal*, vol. 6, no. 2 (1979): 153–89.

2778. Pearl, William. "Pensions and Divorce," *Pension World*, vol. 12, no. 7 (1976): 61.

2779. "Pensions and Marital Property," *Family Law Newsletter*, vol. 17, no. 4 (1977): 11 + .

2780. Schuppert, Ken, and Watson, Clark. "Pension Plans as Property in Divorce Proceedings," *American Journal of Trial Advocacy*, vol. 3, no. 1 (1979): 89–100.

2781. Stanley, Marjorie T. "Financial Theory and the Valuation of Defined Contribution Retirement Accounts in a Community Property Divorce," *Community Property Journal*, vol. 5, no. 1 (1978): 57–59.

2782. Trudgeon, Jon H. "Effects of Divorce upon Qualified Retirement Benefits," *Labor Law Journal*, vol. 29, no. 12 (1978): 786–95.

2783. Van der Veer, Hugh G. "ERISA: Does It Prohibit a State Court from Attaching Plan Benefits?" *University of Pittsburgh Law Review*, vol. 40, no. 1 (1978): 47–69.

Retirement Benefits (Military)

2784. Belt, Terry L., and McDonald, Scott K. "Cearly v. Cearly: Non-vested Military Retirement Benefits in Texas," *Texas Bar Journal*, vol. 40, no. 7 (1977): 571–73.

2785. Borgen, Mack, and Todd, Stephen. "Equitable Distribution of Property—Division of Military Retired Pay," *Army Lawyer* (June 1976): 9–10.

2786. Bowman, Gene. "Lump Sum Division of Military Retired Pay," *Idaho Law Review*, vol. 12, no. 2 (1976): 197–215.

2787. Bruce, Larry B. "Unsettled Question of the Military Pension: Separate or Community Property," *California Western Law Review*, vol. 8, no. 3 (1972): 522–535.

2788. Goldberg, B. Abbott. "Is Armed Services Retired Pay Really Community Property?" *State Bar of California Journal*, vol. 48, no. 1 (1973): 13–17 + .

2789. Lynch, Nancy N. "Military Retirement Benefits: Community Property as Earned during Marriage," *Houston Law Review*, vol. 14, no. 4 (1977): 925–35.

2790. MacMillan, Dalphine. "Treatment of Retired Military Pay in a Divorce Action," *Judge Advocate General's Journal*, vol. 27, no. 3 (1973): 392–401.

2791. Sandbote, Louis J. "Military Retirement Benefits as Community Property: New Rules from the Supreme Court?" *Baylor Law Review*, vol. 24, no. 2 (1972): 235–50.

2792. Strackbein, Howard E. "Ex-wife may Bring Garnishment Proceedings to Secure her Share of Ex-husband's Military Retirement Pay under the Federal Consent Statute," *St. Mary's Law Journal*, vol. 9, no. 3 (1978): 581–89.

2793. Sumner, David W. "Division of Military Retirement Pay upon Dissolution of Marriage," *Arkansas Law Review*, vol. 31, no. 3 (1977): 522–28.

2794. Young, D. Michael. "Disposition of Military Retirement Pay upon Dissolution of a Marriage," *Community Property Journal*, vol. 2, no. 4 (1975): 239–56 + .

2795. ———. "Disposition of Military Retired Pay upon Dissolution of a Marriage," *Washington Law Review*, vol. 50, no. 2 (1975): 505–39.

Retirement Benefits (Railroad)

2796. Drummond, Paul A. "Benefits Awarded under the Railroad Retirement Act Are Not Community Property Subject to Division upon Divorce," *St. Mary's Law Journal*, vol. 11, no. 2 (1979): 535–49.

2797. Young, Rowland L. "Railroad Act Benefits Not Community Property," *American Bar Association Journal* 65 (March 1979): 452 + .

Retirement Benefits (States)

Retirement Benefits: California

2798. Berger, Michael J. "In re Marriage of Brown: An Equal Division of Pension Rights?" *Southwestern University Law Review*, vol. 9, no. 3 (1977): 671–86.

2799. Gamblin, Joanne. "ERISA Creates Problems in Divorce, Council Told [California]," *Business Insurance* 12 (April 17, 1978): 33.

2800. Hoover, John K. "The Characterization of State Disability Retirement Benefits after Dissolution," *Pepperdine Law Review*, vol. 3, no. 1 (1975): 205–11.

2801. McNamara, T. Neal. "California Community Property Aspects of Executive Compensation." In *Southern California Tax Institute, 1978*, pp. 151–91. New York: Matthew Bender & Co., 1978.

2802. Maher, Thomas E. "Pensions and Community Property—An Anomaly," *Orange County Bar Journal*, vol. 5, no. 3 (1978): 265–68 + .

2803. Maloney, Joseph E. "Preemption of California Community Property Law by ERISA: Congressional Intent and Judicial Interpretation," *Pacific Law Journal*, vol. 10, no. 2 (1979): 881–903

2804. Paoli, Sylvia. "Pension Right and Community Property: From French to Brown," *Western State University Law Review*, vol. 4, no. 1 (1976): 91–104.

2805. Pattiz, Henry A. "In a Divorce or Dissolution Who Gets the Pension Rights: Domestic Relations Law and Retirement Plans," *Pepperdine Law Review*, vol. 5, no. 2 (1978): 191–281.

2806. Reppy, William A., Jr. "Community and Separate Interests in Pensions and Social Security Benefits after Marriage of Brown and ERISA," *UCLA Law Review*, vol. 25, no. 3 (1978): 417–546.

2807. Rozsman, John S. "Distribution of Pension Benefits: Time Runs out on the Time Rule," *Pacific Law Journal*, vol. 10, no. 2 (1979): 847–60.

2808. Spector, Barbara. "Retirement Benefits Which Vest following Marital Dissolution Are Divisible as Community Property to the Extent That Such Benefits Derive from Employment During Marriage until the Date of Separation," *Santa Clara Law Review*, vol. 17, no. 3 (1977): 734–40.

Retirement Benefits: Louisiana

2809. Kupperman, Stephen H. "Relation of Community Property and Forced Heirship to Employee Retirement Plans," *Tulane Law Review*, vol. 51, no. 3 (1977): 645–68.

2810. Le Van, Gerald. "Allocating Deferred Compensation in Louisiana," *Louisiana Law Review*, vol. 38, no. 1 (1977): 35–48.

2811. Simon, Michael J. "Toward a More Equitable Distribution of Pension Benefits," *Southern University Law Review*, vol. 3, no. 1 (1976): 51–75.

Retirement Benefits: Missouri

2812. Shaw, John W. "Husband's 'Vested' Interest in Retirement Plan Is Divisible as Marital Property," *Missouri Law Review*, vol. 42, no. 1 (1977): 143–52.

Retirement Benefits: Oklahoma

2813. Smith, Dianne. "Pensions as Property Subject to Equitable Division upon Divorce in Oklahoma," *Tulsa Law Review*, vol. 14, no. 1 (1978): 168–89.

Retirement Benefits: Texas

2814. Anderson, R. Dennis. "Military Retirement Benefits as Community Property," *Southwestern Law Journal* 25 (May 1971): 340–50.

2815. Carmichael, H. Alan. "United States Has Not Consented to Be Sued in Garnishment Proceedings to Enforce Texas Court's Division of Community Military Retirement Benefits," *Texas Tech Law Review*, vol. 10, no. 2 (1978): 214–227.

2816. Carmody, Mary E. "Military Retirement Benefits—Prior to Accrual, Military Retirement Pension Earned during Coverture is Community Property Subject to Division at Time of Divorce," *St. Mary's Law Journal*, vol. 9, no. 1 (1977): 135–44.

2817. Corrigan, Brian T. "Federal Retirement Benefits in Texas," *Army Lawyer* 27 (April 1978): 4–13.

2818. Parsons, Lynne W. "Valdez v. Ramirez: A New Element to Consider in Determining Community Property Rights in Retirement Benefits," *South Texas Law Journal*, vol. 19, no. 3 (1978): 729–36.

2819. Rennick, Charles H. "Apportionment of Community Property Interests in Prospective Military Retirement Benefits upon Divorce," *St. Mary's Law Journal*, vol. 9, no. 1 (1977): 72–86.

2820. Sage, Joseph F. "Military Retired Pay in Texas: A New Outlook," *St. Mary's Law Journal*, vol. 7, no. 1 (1975): 28–37.

2821. Swann, Tommy J. "Direct Payment of Vested Firemen's Relief and Retirement Fund Benefits to Non-member Spouse on Division of Community Property Pursuant to Divorce Is Permissible," *Texas Tech Law Review*, vol. 9, no. 1 (1977): 173–83.

STATES

Property Settlements: Alaska

2822. Dumon, Denise M. "Property Division upon Divorce in Alaska: An Analysis of the 1968 Statutory Amendments," *UCLA-Alaska Law Review*, vol. 6, no. 2 (1977): 218–43.

Property Settlements: Arizona

2823. Adler, Jan M. "Arizona's All-or-Nothing Approach to the Classification of Gain from Separate Property: High Time for a Change," *Community Property Journal*, vol. 6, no. 2 (1978): 190–224.

2824. ———. "Arizona's All-or-Nothing Approach to the Classification of Gain from Separate Property: High Time for a Change," *Arizona Law Review* 20 (1978): 597–628.

2825. Torrez, Barbara J. "Arizona Property Division upon Marital Dissolution," *Arizona State Law Journal* 2 (1979): 411–37.

Property Settlements: California

2826. Cline, Stephen R. "California's Divorce Reform: Its Effect on Community Property Awards," *Pacific Law Journal*, vol. 1, no. 1 (1970): 310–20.

2827. Davis, Michael E. "Valuation of Professional Goodwill upon Marital Dissolution," *Southwestern University Law Review*, vol. 7, no. 1 (1975): 186–205.

2828. Evensen, Martha A. "Dissolution of Marriage after Discharge in Bankruptcy: the Not-So-Fresh Start Doctrine," *Pacific Law Journal*, vol. 10, no. 2 (1979): 861–79.

2829. Fain, Harry M. "Effect of Property Distribution on Spousal Support in California," *Community Property Journal*, vol. 5, no. 3 (1978): 187–96+.

2830. Gach, Linda. "Mix-Hicks Mix: Tracing Troubles under California's Community Property System," *UCLA Law Review*, vol. 26, no. 5 (1979): 1231–60.

2831. Grant, Isabella H. "How Much of a Partnership Is Marriage?" *Hastings Law Journal*, vol. 23, no. 1 (1971): 249–57.

2832. Jones, David L. "Drafting the Property settlement Agreement with Substituted Assets," *California State Bar Journal*, vol. 51, no. 2 (1976): 133–37.

2833. Lurvey, Ira H. "Professional Goodwill on Marital Dissolution: Is It Property or Another Name for Alimony?" *California State Bar Journal*, vol. 52, no. 1 (1977): 27–30+.

2834. McKisson, Michael P. "Postdissolution Suits to Divide Community Property: A Proposal for Legislative Action," *Pacific Law Journal*, vol. 10, no. 2 (1979): 825–45.

2835. Munson, Douglas A. "Forgotten Community Property Asset: An Overview of the Individual Whole Life Insurance Policy at the Time of Marital Dissolution," *California State Bar Journal*, vol. 53, no. 5 (1978): 310–17.

2836. Oliver, Stephen R. "For Apportionment of Community Business Where Appreciation is Attributable to the Husband's Efforts after Separation, the Corporate Entity May Be Disregarded If Justified by the Facts," *Santa Clara Law Review*, vol. 16, no. 3 (1976): 682–90.

2837. Propper, Grant E. "Judgment of Dissolution and the Agreement—Incorporation, Merger, Integration and Approval," *Los Angeles Bar Journal*, vol. 51, no. 4 (1975): 177–85.

2838. Rutter, J. E. T. "Promissory Note to Equalize Division—Solving the Tammen Problem," *Orange County Bar Association Journal*, vol. 5, no. 3 (1978): 207–12.

2839. Seal, Karen. "A Decade of No-Fault Divorce; What It Has Meant Financially for Women in California," *Family Advocate*, vol. 1, no. 4 (1979): 10+. R.

2840. State Bar of California Committee on Continuing Education of the Bar. *California Marital Termination Settlements.* Supplemented by Clifford R. Anderson, Jr., and Clarence E. Fleming, Jr., Berkeley, CA: California Continuing Education of the Bar, 1975.

2841. Walzer, Stuart B. *California Marital Termination Settlements.* Berkeley, CA: California Continuing Education of the Bar, 1971.

Property Settlements: Florida

2842. Murphy, Michael C. "Implied Partnership: Equitable Alternative to Contemporary Methods of Postmarital Property Distribution," *University of Florida Law Review*, vol. 26, no. 2 (1974): 221–35.

Property Settlements: Georgia

2843. "Impact of the Revolution in Georgia's Divorce Law on Antenuptial Agreements," *Georgia Law Review*, vol. 11, no.2 (1977): 406–25.

Property Settlements: Idaho

2844. FitzMaurice, Gregory. "Status in Idaho Community Property Law of the Living-Separate-and-Apart Doctrine," *Idaho Law Review*, vol. 13, no. 2 (1971): 295–307.

Property Settlements: Illinois

2845. Johnson, S. Greg. "Property Provisions of New Illinois Marriage and Dissolution of Marriage Act Are Constitutional—The Exact Nature of the Interest of the Non-titleholding Spouse during the Marriage Still Needs Clarification," *Southern Illinois University Law Journal* 4 (178): 598–610.

2846. Kalcheim, Michael W. "Marital Property, Tax Ramifications, and Maintenance: Practice under the Illinois Marriage and Dissolution of Marriage Act—A Comparative Study," *Illinois Bar Journal*, vol. 66, no. 6 (1979): 324–41+.

2847. Neumark, Victor. "Property Rights in Divorce," *Illinois Bar Journal*, vol. 62, no. 5 (1974): 242–52.

Property Settlements: Indiana

2848. Combs, Elizabeth R. "The Development of a Set of Propositional Guidelines and Their Implementation of Use in Decision Making at Dissolution of Marriage in Indiana." Ph.D. diss., Purdue University, 1977 (*DAI* 38/10A, p. 6278, order # 7803211). R.

Property Settlements: Kansas

2849. Cohen, Keith D. "Property Settlements in Divorce and Kansas Senate Bill #907," *Kansas Bar Association Journal*, vol. 47, no. 4 (1978): 275–85.

Property Settlements: Kentucky

2850. Coffman, Jennifer B. "Restoration of Property: Illusory Barrier to Interspousal Gifts," *Kentucky Law Journal*, vol. 67, no. 1 (1978–79): 173–211.

Property Settlements: Louisiana

2851. Gonzalez, Carmen C. "Husband's Recovery of Personal Injury Damages after Judicial Separation," *Louisiana Law Review*, vol. 36, no. 4 (1976): 1029–39.

2852. Lee, Wayne J. "Judicial Dissolution of the Marital Community in Louisiana," *Tulane Law Review*, vol. 49, no. 1 (1974): 167–88.

2853. Pascal, Robert A. "Matrimonial Regimes," *Louisiana Law Review*, vol. 39, no. 3 (1979): 697–703.

2854. Spaht, Katherine S., and Samuel, Cynthia. "Equal Management Revisited: 1979 Legislative Modifications of the 1978 Matrimonial Regimes Law," *Louisiana Law Review*, vol. 40, no. 1 (1979): 83–145.

2855. Wise, Sherry M. "Settlement of a Community Partnership Interest upon Separation or Divorce," *Tulane Law Review*, vol. 51, no. 3 (1977): 700–16.

Property Settlements: Maryland

2856. Peters, Paula. "Property Disposition upon Divorce in Maryland: An Analysis of the New Statute," *University of Baltimore Law Review*, vol. 8, no. 2 (1979): 377–410.

Property Settlements: Massachusetts

2857. Inker, Monroe L.; Walsh, Joseph H.; and Perocchi, Paul P. "Alimony and Assignment of Property: The New Statutory Scheme in Massachusetts," *Journal of Family Law*, vol. 11, no. 1 (1977): 59–82.

2858. ———. "Alimony and Assignment of Property: The New Statutory Scheme in Massachusetts," *Suffolk University Law Review*, vol. 10, no. 1 (1975): 1–24.

Property Settlements: Missouri

2859. Agatstein, Sylvan. "Dissolution of Marriage Act—Property Rights and Wrongs," *Missouri Bar Journal*, vol. 34, no. 7 (1978): 451–58.

2860. Bild, Brian. "Dissolution of Marriage and the Finality of Judgments, *Missouri Bar Journal*, vol. 35, no. 4 (1979): 241–44.

2861. Brown, J. Michael. "Personal Injury Damages as Marital Property in Missouri," *Missouri Law Review*, vol. 41, no. 4 (1976): 603–08.

2862. Fowler, Ray, and Krauskopf, Joan. "Dissolution of Marriage under Missouri's New Divorce Law—Property Provisions," *Missouri Bar Journal*, vol. 29, no. 8 (1973): 508–16.

2863. Haines, Marjorie W. "Division of Property Which Has Increased in Value," *Missouri Law Review*, vol. 42, no. 3 (1977): 479–85.

2864. ———. "Tax Consequences of Interspousal Property Transfers pursuant to a Missouri Dissolution," *Missouri Law Review*, vol. 44, no. 1 (1979): 92–113.

2865. Krauskopf, Joan M. "Missouri Property at Marriage Dissolution," *Missouri Law Review*, vol. 43, no. 2 (1978): 157–98.

2866. ———. "Theory for 'Just' Division of Marital Property in Missouri," *Missouri Law Review*, vol. 41, no. 2 (1976): 165–78.

2867. Power, Richard W. "Well Begun Is Half Done: Community Property for Missouri," *St. Louis University Law Journal*, vol. 21, no. 2 (1977): 308–16.

2868. Smith, Craig A. "Marital Property and Transmutation in a Non-community Property State—Conversion from Separate to Marital Property," *Missouri Law Review*, vol. 43, no. 4 (1978): 770–79.

Property Settlements: Nebraska

2869. Greene, Scott. "Comparison of the Property Aspects of the Community Property and Common-Law Marital Property Systems and Their Relative Compatibility with the Current View of the Marriage Relationship and the Rights of Women,'' *Creighton Law Review,* vol. 13, no. 1 (1979): 71–119.

Property Settlements: New Jersey

2870. Covino, John A. ''Divorce—New Jersey's Decision on the Eligibility of Assets for Equitable Distribution,'' *Dickinson Law Review,* vol. 79, no. 3 (1975): 526–38.

2871. ''Life Insurance—Divorce Property Settlements—Relative Rights of Beneficiaries—New Jersey's Inflexible Approach,'' *Rutgers Law Review,* vol. 25, no. 1 (1970): 189–98.

2872. Neustadt, Leslie B. ''Painter v. Painter: Equitable Distribution of Marital Assets upon Divorce,'' *Temple Law Quarterly,* vol. 48, no. 2 (1975): 397–413.

2873. Rhett, Teel O. ''New Jersey Courts Make First Equitable Distributions of Property under New Divorce Act,'' *Seton Hall Law Review,* vol. 4, no. 1 (1972): 311–28.

2874. Tischler, Saul. ''Distribution of Property upon Divorce,'' *New Jersey Law Journal* 94 (December 2, 1971): 1+.

Property Settlements: New Mexico

2875. Spring, Frank L. ''In-Migration of Couples from Common Law Jurisdictions: Protecting the Wife at the Dissolution of the Marriage,'' *New Mexico Law Review,* vol. 9, no. 1 (1978–79): 113–30.

Property Settlements: New York

2876. *Drafting Matrimonial Agreements and Property Settlements.* New York: Practising Law Institute, 1971.

2877. *Drafting the Matrimonial Settlement Agreement: Strategies and Techniques.* New York: Practising Law Institute, 1977.

2878. Foster, Henry H., Jr., and Freed, Doris J. ''Marital Property Reform in New York: Partnership of Co-equals?'' *Family Law Quarterly,* vol. 8, no. 2 (1974): 169–205.

2879. Kalman, Benjamin. *Property and the Marital Home: A Guide to the Property Aspects of Matrimonial Practice in New York.* Brooklyn, NY: Central Book Co., 1974.

Property Settlements: Ohio

2880. Marks, Ronald A. ''Community Property Primer for Ohio Lawyers,'' *Ohio Northern University Law Review,* vol. 5, no. 3 (1978): 631–41.

Property Settlements: Oklahoma

2881. Powell, Morgan K. ''Relevant Factors in the Division of Jointly Acquired Property,'' *Oklahoma Law Review,* vol. 23, no. 3 (1970): 288–93.

2882. Simpson, Lee K. ''The Role of Joint Industry in the Determination of What Is Jointly Acquired Property,'' *Oklahoma Law Review,* vol. 32, no. 1 (1979): 214–20.

2883. Stamets, Connie S. ''Husband and Wife: Drafting an Antenuptial Contract in Oklahoma,'' *Oklahoma Law Review,* vol. 32, no. 1 (1979): 220–34.

Property Settlements: Oregon

2884. Fetterly, Patricia C. ''Oregon Marital Property Laws: Can Both Separation and Equality Be Achieved?'' *Oregon Law Review,* vol. 57, no. 1 (1977): 152–70.

Property Settlements: Tennessee

2885. James, H. Wynne, III. ''Property Transfers in Tennessee pursuant to Divorce or Separation: Possible Tax-Free Consequences,'' *Tennessee Law Review,* vol. 41, no. 2 (1974): 339–56.

Property Settlements: Texas

2886. Castleberry, James N., Jr. ''Constitutional Limitations on the Division of Property upon Divorce,'' *St. Mary's Law Journal,* vol. 10, no. 11 (1978): 37–73.

2887. Dulick, H. L. ''Foreign Divorce and Texas Community Property,'' *Community Property Journal,* vol. 3, no. 4 (1976): 236–40.

2888. ———. ''Foreign Divorce and Texas Community Property,'' *Baylor Law Review,* vol. 28, no. 2 (1976): 425–31.

2889. ''Goodwill of a Professional Practice Acquired after Marriage Is Held to be Community Property in the State of Texas,'' *Texas Southern University Law Review,* vol. 2, no. 2–3 (1973): 383–89.

2890. Groves, Linda C. ''In Property Division upon Divorce, the Trial Court Cannot Divest Spouse of Separate Realty and Transfer Title to Other Spouse,'' *Texas Tech Law Review,* vol. 9, no. 1 (1977): 232–36.

2891. Locke, Carey P. ''Professional Corporation May Have Valuable Goodwill, apart from Person of Individual Member, That Must Be Considered in Property Set-

tlement on Divorce,'' *St. Mary's Law Journal,* vol. 11, no. 1 (1979): 222–37.

2892. McKnight, Joseph W. ''Division of Texas Marital Property on Divorce,'' *St. Mary's Law Journal,* vol. 8, no. 3 (1976): 413–85.

2893. McMullen, Richard. ''Pleading Separate Property in a Divorce Case,'' *Baylor Law Review,* vol. 27, no. 4 (1975): 784–92.

2894. Morell, Jerry. ''Division of Property on Divorce—Spouse Cannot Be Divested of Title to Separate Real Property under Texas Family Code Sec. 3.63,'' *St. Mary's Law Journal,* vol. 9, no. 2 (1977): 331–40.

2895. Muse, Diane. ''Division of Separate Real Property in Divorce Action: Eggemeyer v. Eggemeyer,'' *Southwestern Law Journal,* vol. 31, no. 4 (1977): 934–39.

2896. Price, Randall K. ''Determining the Liability of Community Property,'' *Baylor Law Review,* vol. 29, no. 3 (1977): 608–19.

2897. Sampson, John J. ''Common Law Property in a Texas Divorce: After Eggemeyer, the Deluge?'' *Texas Bar Journal,* vol. 42, no. 2 (1979): 131–38.

2898. Sokolik, J. Brian. ''Division of Marital Property on Divorce: A Proposal to Revise Section 3.63,'' *St. Mary's Law Journal,* vol. 7, no. 1 (1975): 209–27.

2899. Westbrook, Craig. ''Acceptance of Benefits and the Right to Appeal: Divorce,'' *Baylor Law Review,* vol. 31, no. 1 (1979): 81–94.

2900. Williams, Ronald G. ''Section 5.22 of the Texas Family Code: Control and Management of the Marital Estate,'' *Southwestern Law Journal* 27 (December 1973): 837–64.

Property Settlements: Utah

2901. Henderson, Robert H. ''Effect in Utah of a Divorce and Property Settlement on a Previously Executed Will—A Need for Legislation,'' *Utah Law Review* 2 (1972): 177–92.

Property Settlements: Washington

2902. Crandall, Patricia I. ''Property Dispositions in Dissolution Proceedings: The Criteria in Washington,'' *Gonzaga Law Review,* vol. 12, no. 3 (1977): 492–504.

2903. Phelps, Nancy C. ''Antenuptial and Postnuptial Contracts in Washington,'' *Washington Law Review,* vol. 54, no. 1 (1978): 135–58.

SEPARATION

2904. Anderson, Elaine A. "Satisfaction with the Legal System and Adjustment to Marital Separation," Ph.D. diss., Pennsylvania State University, 1979 (*DAI* 40/1A, p. 484, order # 7915696). R.

2905. ———. "Satisfaction with the Legal System and Adjustment to Marital Separation," *Resources in Education* 14 (1979): ERIC document ED 172–21. R.

2906. Lindey, Alexander. *Separation Agreements and Antenuptial Contracts.* Albany, NY: Matthew Bender & Co., 1973.

2907. Mortland, Jean A. "Spousal Election Allowed Where Couple Were Living Apart under Separation Decree," *Estate Planning,* vol. 4, no. 6 (1977): 338–39.

STATES AND TERRITORIES

Separation: California

2908. Brown, James M. "Living Separate and Apart under Section 5118 of the Family Law Act—Effects and Implications of the Baragry Decision," *Western State University Law Review,* vol. 6, no. 1 (1978): 183–98.

2909. Bruch, Carol S. "Legal Import of Informal Marital Separations: A Survey of California Law and a Call for Change," *California Law Review,* vol. 65, no. 5 (1977): 1015–85.

Separation: Florida

2910. Collyer, Keith E. "Separation as a Ground for Divorce," *Florida Bar Journal,* vol. 44, no. 8 (1970): 438–40.

Separation: Louisiana

2911. deBessonet, Cary. "Suggested Move in the Direction of No-Fault Separation," *Southern University Law Review,* vol. 3, no. 1 (1976): 31–39.

2912. Kelly, Dennis M. "Is a Louisiana Wife Liable for Federal Income Taxes on Income Earned by Her Husband Pending a Judgment of Separation?" *Loyola Law Review,* vol. 23, no. 1 (1977): 98–121.

Separation: Maryland

2913. Fairbanks, Joseph M. "Offers of Reconciliation in Maryland Divorce Law," *Maryland Law Review,* vol. 30, no. 1 (1970): 49–62.

Separation: Missouri

2914. Blond, Irwin E. "Separation Agreements in Missouri," *Missouri Law Review,* vol. 35, no. 3 (1970): 350–66.

Separation: New Jersey

2915. "Rebutting the Presumption against Reconcilability in the New Jersey Separation Statute: A Recommendation," *Rutgers Camden Law Journal,* vol. 6, no. 3 (1975): 592–609.

Separation: Florida

2916. Thompson, M. Karen. "New Jersey Equitable Distribution Statute Applied to Separation Agreements Executed Prior to Statute's Effective Date," *Rutgers Law Review,* vol. 38, no. 1 (1978): 376–90.

Separation: North Carolina

2917. Dean, Paula D. "The Enforceability of Arbitration Clauses in North Carolina Separation Agreements," *Wake Forest Law Review,* vol. 15, no. 4 (1979): 487–505.

2918. Narron, James W. "Separation Agreements—Implied Release of Intestate Share," *Wake Forest Law Review,* vol. 10, no. 2 (1974): 273–78.

Separation: Oklahoma

2919. Stack, Steve. "Enforcement of Separation Agreements," *Oklahoma Law Review,* vol. 24, no. 2 (1971): 252–56.

Separation: Puerto Rico

2920. Ortiz Alvarez, Pedro E. "La Causal de Separación en nuesto Estatuto de Divorcio," *Revista de Derecho Puertorriqueño* 13 (Julio–diciembre, 1973): 69–108.

2921. Trías Grimes, Peter. "La Tributación de Conyuges Separados," *Revista Juridica de la Universidad de Puerto Rico,* vol. 39, no. 3 (1970): 499–512.

TAXES

ALIMONY

2922. "Alimony v. Child Support: When May Deduction Be Taken?" *Taxation for Accountants,* vol. 8, vol. 1 (1972): 37.

2923. "Alimony Deduction Requires Living Apart from Spouse," *Journal of Taxation,* vol. 47, no. 2 (1977): 95.

2924. "Alimony Held Deductible Even Where Spouses Live Together," *Taxation for Accountants,* vol. 21, no. 2 (1978): 74.

2925. "Are Payments to Wife's Relatives Deductible Alimony?" *Taxation for Lawyers,* vol. 2, no. 3 (1973): 182–83.

2926. Benford, Gary A. "Federal Income Tax Consequences of Divorce and Separation," *Journal of Family Law,* vol. 16, no. 4 (1978): 779–76.

2927. Bierman, Jacquin D. "Periodic Payments of Community not Alimony," *Journal of Taxation,* vol. 50, no. 4 (1979): 240–41.

2928. Borghese, Phyllis. "Living in the Same House Does Not a Separation Make," *National Public Accountant*, vol. 23, no. 2 (1978): 31.

2929. ———. "Wife's Share of Legal Fees for Alimony Tax Deductible," *National Public Accountant*, vol. 20, no. 11 (1975): 30–31.

2930. "Can Tax Status of Alimony Change?" *Taxation for Accountants*, vol. 20, no. 5 (1978): 269.

2931. "Can Tax Status of Alimony Change?" *Taxation for Lawyers*, vol. 7, no. 1 (1978): 51.

2932. "Classifying Payments as Alimony or Support Difficult," *Taxation for Lawyers*, vol. 4, no. 4 (1976): 217–18.

2933. Davies, John H. "Taxation of Alimony: Policies, Problems and a Proposal," *University of Miamia Law Review*, vol. 31, no. 5 (1977): 1355–1408.

2934. "Deduction Lost as Court Fixes 'Alimony' as Child Support," *Taxation for Accountants*, vol. 20, no. 3 (1978): 162–63.

2935. "Deduction Lost as Court Fixes 'Alimony' as Child Support," *Taxation for Lawyers*, vol. 7, no. 1 (1978): 40–41.

2936. Diss, William T. "Periodic Payments to Former Spouse May Be Nondeductible," *Tax Adviser*, vol. 4, no. 1 (1973): 27–28.

2937. "Error in Calculation Nearly Bars Alimony Deduction," *Taxation for Lawyers*, vol. 6, no. 3 (1977): 162.

2938. Garian, Harry Z. "Alimony Claims vs. Estate Valued on Basis of Acturial Tables not Actual Events," *Tax Adviser*, vol. 3, no. 6 (1972): 374–75.

2939. ———. "Alimony 'Voluntarily' Paid after Remarriage Is not 'Alimony' for Tax Purposes," *Tax Adviser*, vol. 2, no. 2 (1971): 119–20.

2940. ———. "Contingent Payments Held Alimony despite Brevity of Installment Period," *Tax Adviser*, vol. 3, no. 7 (1972): 439.

2941. ———. "Nunc pro tunc Alimony Order 'May Be' Recognized Retroactively," *Tax Adviser*, vol. 2, no. 11 (1972): 692.

2942. ———. "Periodic Payments not Taxable 'Alimony' after Obligation to Pay Terminates under State Law," *Tax Adviser*, vol. 3, no. 5 (1972): 308–09.

2943. Garian, Harry Z., and Kalben, John F. "Cost of Term Life Insurance Held Alimony Where Ex-Wife's Beneficial Interest in Ordinary Policy Was Conditional," *Tax Adviser*, vol. 2, no. 8 (1971): 504–05.

2944. ———. "Voluntarily Assumed Obligations Treated as Taxable Alimony," *Tax Adviser*, vol. 2, no. 5 (1971): 315–16.

2945. Halpert, David H. "Planning for Shifting Taxable Income in Divorce and Separation." In *Institute on Federal Taxation, New York University Proceedings, 1978*, pp. 34–77. New York: Matthew Bender & Co., 1979.

2946. Harris, John W. "Federal Income Tax Treatment of Alimony Payments—The 'Support' Requirement of the Regulations," *Hastings Law Journal*, vol. 22, no. 1 (1970): 53–85.

2947. "Has CA-2 Ruled on Whether a Term Life Insurance Premium Is Alimony?" *Journal of Taxation*, vol. 47, no. 6 (1977): 341–42.

2948. Hobbet, Richard D. "Avoiding the Creation-of-Income Trap on a Return of Capital in Alimony Situations," *Journal of Taxation*, vol. 35, no. 6 (1971): 384–86.

2949. Hoffman, Arthur S. "Informality in Alimony Arrangements Is a Trap," *CPA Journal*, vol. 45, no. 2 (1974): 39.

2950. "How to Lose Tax Benefits for Alimony and Dependents," *Taxation for Accountants*, vol. 22, no. 6 (1979): 341.

2951. "Is Husband Married to his Ex-wife's Tax Return?" *Taxation for Lawyers*, vol. 5, no. 4 (1977): 207.

2952. "Is Lump-Sum Settlement of Alimony Obligation Taxable?" *Taxation for Lawyers*, vol. 4, no. 2 (1975): 108.

2953. Jensen, Herbert L. "High-Income Individuals and the Tax Reform Act of 1976," *Taxes—The Tax Magazine*, vol. 55, no. 6 (1977): 405–10.

2954. Joyner, Robert C. "Alimony: Income Taxation of Installment Payments," *University of Florida Law Review*, vol. 24, no. 3 (1972): 499–516.

2955. Levine, Aaron. "Proper Tax Treatment of Payments under a Divorce Decree Can Be Elusive," *Taxation for Accountants*, vol. 12, no. 4 (1974): 202–07.

2956. Linett, E. S. "Sec. 483 Inapplicable to Nondeductible Alimony," *Tax Adviser*, vol. 7, no. 7 (1976): 439–40.

2957. "Living in Same House Kills Deduction for Support Payments," *Practical Accountant*, vol. 10, no. 4 (1977): 8+.

2958. Practising Law Institute (New York City). *Impact of Taxes on Matrimonial Agreements: A Video Handbook*. New York: Practising Law Institute, 1976.

2959. "No Alimony Deduction Allowed for Term Insurance Premium," *Practical Accountant*, vol. 5, no. 3 (1972): 10+.

2960. Parker, Allan J. "Some 1977 Developments in Estate and Gift Taxation," *Practical Lawyer*, vol. 24, no. 8 (1978): 59+.

2961. "Paying 'Alimony' Does not Make One Single," *Taxation for Accountants*, vol. 19, no. 4 (1977): 200.

2962. "Paying 'Alimony' Does not Make One Single," *Taxation for Lawyers*, vol. 6, no. 3 (1977): 168.

2963. " 'Periodic' Payments of Community not Alimony," *Journal of Taxation*, vol. 50, no. 4 (1979): 240–41.

2964. "Periodic v. Lump-Sum: Crucial in Alimony Taxation," *Taxation for Accountants*, vol. 9, no. 2 (1972): 105–06.

2965. Peschel, John L. "Income Taxation of Alimony Payments Attributable to Transferred Property: Congressional Confusion," *Tulane Law Review*, vol. 44, no. 2 (1970): 223–50.

2966. Pitcher, Griffith F. "Planning Tax Treatment of Payments to Spouse Is Major Factor in Divorce Settlements," *Taxation for Accountants*, vol. 17, no. 1 (1976): 22–26.

2967. ———. "Planning Tax Treatment of Payments to Spouse Is Major Factor in Divorce Settlements," *Taxation for Lawyers*, vol. 5, no. 1 (1976): 4–8.

2968. "Remarriage Can Render Alimony Nontaxable," *Taxation for Accountants*, vol. 6, no. 2 (1971): 73.

2969. Sander, Frank A. E. *Tax Aspects of Divorce*. Minneapolis, MN: National Practice Institute for Continuing Legal Education, 1978.

2970. Sloane, L. "How Does IRS View Alimony and Child Support?" *American Journal of Nursing*, vol. 78, no. 2 (1978): 293.

2971. Tarantino, Dominic A. "Alimony: The '76 Act's Effect on Mini- and Maxi-tax," *Tax Adviser*, vol. 8, no. 7 (1977): 409–10.

2972. "Taxation: Alimony Taxation," *St. John's Law Review*, vol. 46, no. 3 (1972): 547–50.

2973. "Tax Pitfalls in Planning Alimony Arrangements," *Taxation for Accountants*, vol. 16, no. 3 (1976): 184–85.

2974. "Tax Pitfalls in Planning Alimony Arrangements," *Taxation for Lawyers*, vol. 5, no. 1 (1976): 43–44.

2975. "Tax Treatment of Alimony Should Be Settled in Divorce Negotiations," *Taxation for Accountants*, vol. 7, no. 5 (1971): 317.

2976. "Ten-Year Payments as Split of Community Property," *Taxation for Accountants*, vol. 22, no. 6 (1979): 353–54.

2977. "Ten-Year Payments as Split of Community Property," *Taxation for Lawyers*, vol. 8, no. 2 (1979): 128.

2978. Tomlinson, Allen. "Post-mortem Alimony Payments," *Tax Adviser*, vol. 2, no. 12 (1971): 738.

2979. "When Is Alimony Periodic?" *Taxation for Accountants*, vol. 11, no. 5 (1973): 268.

2980. Wolfstone, Gary L. "Alimony Taxation—The Contingency Doctrine Challenged," *Harvard Journal on Legislation*, vol. 9, no. 1 (1971): 156–70.

ALIMONY TRUSTS

2981. Del Cotto, Louis A. "Alimony Trust: Its Relationship with Subchapter J: The Right to Amortize Basis," *Tax Law Review* 33 (Summer 1978): 577–98.

2982. Gerhart, Frederick J. "Substantial Support Exists for Amoritizing Life Income Interest in an Alimony Trust," *Journal of Taxation*, vol. 44, no. 3 (1976): 167–70.

2983. Gilreath, James R. "How to Use a Trust to Satisfy Taxpayer's Obligations under a Divorce Decree," *Taxation for Lawyers*, vol. 8, no. 3 (1979): 132–35.

2984. Kessler, Stuart, and Safier, I. Jay. "Alimony Trust," *CPA Journal*, vol. 46, no. 11 (1976): 60–61.

2985. "No Gain on Transfer to Trust Created to Pay Alimony," *Journal of Taxation*, vol. 51, no. 6 (1979): 372–73.

2986. Teitell, Conrad. "Charitable Remainder Trusts—Alimony and Sprinkling Varieties," *Trusts & Estates*, vol. 115, no. 11 (1976): 757–60.

2987. Zaritsky, Howard M. "Special Trusts and Unique Problems: Grantor Trusts after the Grantor's Death, Alimony Trusts, and Foreign Trusts versus Domestic Trusts." In *Institute on Federal Taxation, New York University, 1978*, pp. 42–59. New York: Matthew Bender & Co., 1979.

AVOIDANCE OF TAXES BY DIVORCE

2988. Feld, Alan L. "Divorce, Tax–Style," *Taxes—The Tax Magazine*, vol. 54, no. 10 (1976): 608–12.

2989. "Off-Again, On-Again Marriages Treated as Sham by IRS," *Journal of Taxation*, vol. 45, no. 4 (1976): 246.

2990. "Some Divorce-Remarriages are Sham Transactions Says IRS," *Taxation for Lawyers*, vol. 5, no. 2 (1976): 114–15.

CHILD CUSTODY

2991. Klein, Michael F., Jr. "Some Divorced Parents Eligible for Refunds under New IRS Ruling," *CPA Journal*, vol. 43, no. 7 (1973): 594.

2992. Nichols, George D. "Dependency Exemptions for Children of Divorced or Separated Parents," *Missouri Law Review*, vol. 37, no. 4 (1972): 718–26.

2993. "Physical Custody is Key to Exemption," *Taxation for Accountants*, vol. 22, no. 2 (1979): 81.

2994. "Residence Title Affects Dependency Exemption," *Taxation for Lawyers*, vol. 7, no. 4 (1979): 244–45.

CHILD SUPPORT

2995. Borghese, Phyllis. "Divorced Wife Can Include New Spouse's Child Support Contributions," *National Public Accountant*, vol. 18, no. 12 (1973): 34.

2996. "Divorced Husband Wins Dependency Exemption a New Way," *Practical Accountant*, vol. 5, no. 3 (1972): 8 +.

2997. "Exemptions for Children of Divorced Parents," *Taxation for Accountants*, vol. 16, no. 1 (1976): 57.

2998. "Exemptions for Children of Divorced Parents," *Taxation for Lawyers*, vol. 4, no. 5 (1976): 313.

2999. Flater, Morris E. "Burden of Proof Required of a Parent Claiming Child Exemption," *Washington and Lee Law Review*, vol. 29, no. 1 (1972): 29–43.

3000. Garian, Harry Z. "Divorced Parents: 'Clear Preponderance of Evidence' Suffices for Special Exemption Rule," *Tax Adviser*, vol. 3, no. 2 (1972): 124–25.

3001. ———. "General, not Sec. 151(e), Rules Apply When Divorced Parents Don't Dispute Exemption for Children." *Tax Adviser*, vol. 3, no. 4 (1972): 250–51.

3002. "How Stepfather's Support Affects Exemption for Child," *Taxation for Accountants*, vol. 20, no. 5 (1978): 302–03.

3003. "How Stepfather's Support Affects Exemption for Child," *Taxation for Lawyers*, vol. 7, no. 1 (1978): 41.

3004. Linett, E. S. "Sec. 152(e): Support for Child Provided by Custodial Parent's Spouse Attributed to Parent," *Tax Adviser*, vol. 9, no. 6 (1978): 373–74.

3005. "No Exemption Where Agreement not Specific," *Taxation for Accountants*, vol. 22, no. 6 (1979): 373–74.

3006. "Residence Title Affects Dependency Exemptions," *Taxation for Accountants*, vol. 21, no. 6 (1978): 349.

3007. "Special Rule for Dependents after Divorce: IRS Revises and Clarifies Its Application," *Taxation for Accountants*, vol. 10, no. 6 (1973): 362–63.

3008. "Taxpayers Cannot Change Child Support to Alimony," *Taxation for Accountants*, vol. 21, no. 4 (1978): 241–42.

3009. Ward, Larry D. "Characterizing Payments Made pursuant to Divorce Decree: Support vs. Property Settlement," *Review of Taxation of Individuals*, vol. 1, no. 3 (1977): 264–66.

DIVORCE

3010. "Alimony Payments: The Periodic v. Installment Problems," *Taxation for Accountants*, vol. 9, no. 3 (1972): 178.

3011. Amerine, Janet. "Taxation: Taxability of Property Transferred pursuant to Divorce Decree," *Washburn Law Journal*, vol. 18, no. 2 (1979): 397–403.

3012. Anderson, John A. "Transfer of Appreciated Property pursuant to Divorce: Taxable Event in Oregon?" *Oregon Law Review*, vol. 53, no. 4 (1974): 544–56.

3013. Anglea, Berneice. "Tax Aspects of Divorce and Separation," *Tulane Tax Institute* 26 (1977): 1–27.

3014. Arvidson, R. Regner. "Federal Income Taxes and Marital Dissolutions—Selected Problems," *Connecticut Bar Journal*, vol. 52, no. 3 (1978): 220–34.

3015. "Avoiding Generation-Skipping Tax on Divorce," *Journal of Taxation*, vol. 48, no. 1 (1978): 63.

3016. Barnett, Bernard. "Danger! Don't Disregard Double Deductions," *Tax Adviser*, vol. 2, no. 1 (1971): 33–37.

3017. Bashinsky, Thomas M. "Income Taxation: The Tax Reform Act of 1976 Changes the Treatment of the Individual Taxpayer's Alimony and Child Care Payments," *Cumberland Law Review*, vol. 9, no. 1 (1978): 177–94.

3018. Bernstein, Lawson F. "Handling Problems of Divorce and Separation." In *New York University Institute on Federal Taxation, 1976*, vol. 34, pp. 139–61. New York: Matthew Bender & Co., 1977.

3019. Biblin, Allan E. "Transfer of Community Property in Divorce Has Tax Consequences in Common Law States," *Journal of Taxation*, vol. 49, no. 3 (1978): 168–72.

3020. ———. "Divorce, Taxes, and Community Property: Some Current Cases, Problems and Concerns." In *Southern California Tax Institute, 1978*, pp. 571–607. New York: Matthew Bender & Co., 1978.

3021. Bierman, Jacquin D. "Prepayment Proviso Is no Bar to Alimony Deduction," *Journal of Taxation*, vol. 42, no. 4 (1975): 216–17.

3022. ———. "Tax Court Equates Void Marriages with Voidable Ones for Tax Purposes," *Journal of Taxation*, vol. 40, no. 4 (1974): 250.

3023. ———. "Ten-Year Periodic Payment Can Precede Final Decree," *Journal of Taxation*, vol. 41, no. 4 (1974): 223.

3024. ———. "Transfer of over 50 Percent of Joint Property Creates Taxable Gain," *Journal of Taxation*, vol. 41, no. 4 (1974): 223–24.

3025. Borghese, Phyllis. "Marital Status for Tax Filing," *National Public Accountant*, vol. 21, no. 9 (1976): 38–39.

3026. ———. "Household Absence Because of Marital Discord Does Not Bar Use of Head of Household Rates," *National Public Accountant*, vol. 20, no. 7 (1975): 33.

3027. ———. "Second Time Around not Necessarily Better," *National Public Accountant*, vol. 20, no. 4 (1970): 35–36.

3028. Brockhouse, John D., and Brandzel, Jacob R. "Litigation Awards and Expenses: Tax Consequences to Defendants and Plaintiffs," *Tax Adviser*, vol. 3, no. 10 (1972): 624–32.

3029. Chapman, Benson J., and Strassler, Philip F. "Divorce and Separation: Recent Income Tax Developments," vol. 7, no. 10 (1976): 592–98.

3030. Coates, William H. "Tax Incidents of a Nebraska Divorce," *Nebraska CPA* 11 (Spring 1976): 14–17+.

3031. Cobb, Anita D. "Section 152(e) of the Internal Revenue Code of 1954: A Present Need for Congressional Review," *Connecticut Law Review*, vol. 6, no. 1 (1973): 125–41.

3032. Commerce Clearing House. *Tax Planning in Divorce and Separation*. Chicago: Commerce Clearing House, 1975.

3033. "Correction of Divorce Decree Has Tax Effect," *Taxation for Accountants*, vol. 19, no. 4 (1977): 242.

3034. "Correction of Divorce Decree Has Tax Effect," *Taxation for Lawyers*, vol. 6, no. 3 (1977): 191–92.

3035. Cronkhite, John A. "Pre-divorce Tax Planning Can Conserve After-tax Dollars and Control Hidden Tax Difficulties," *Taxation for Accountants*, vol. 6, no. 1 (1971): 46–50.

3036. Crouch, Garrett R., II. "Lodging Deemed Furnished by Divorced Parent Who Is Entitled to Exclusive Use and Occupancy," *Missouri Law Review*, vol. 41, no. 2 (1976): 305–09.

3037. Crown, Jeffrey L. "Divorce, Remarriage, and the Marital Deduction," *Estates, Gifts and Trusts Journal* (September–October, 1978): 18–19.

3038. Curtis, Orlie L. "Should Federal Income Tax Consequences of Divorce Depend on State Property Law?" *Southern California Law Review*, vol. 46, no. 6 (1976): 1401–40.

3039. Daniels, Eugene O. "Tax Problems of a Broken Marriage," *Practical Accountant*, vol. 3, no. 5 (1970): 40–48.

3040. Del Cotto, Louis A. "Sales and Other Dispositions of Property under Section 1001: The Taxable Event, Amount Realized and Related Problems of Basis," *Buffalo Law Review*, vol. 26, no. 2 (1977): 219–359.

3041. Delevett, J. Allen F., Jr. "Federal Income Tax Aspects of Divorce and Separation," *American Bar Association Journal* 61 (April 1975): 503–07.

3042. ———. "Federal Gift and Estate Tax Aspects of Divorce and Separation," *American Bar Association Journal* 64 (February 1978): 272–75.

3043. "Divorce and Remarriage Can Erase Marital Deduction," *Taxation for Lawyers*, vol. 5, no. 2 (1976): 97–98.

3044. DuCanto, Joseph N. "Divorce and the High Cost of Leaving: Three Modern Tax Tales," *Taxes*, vol. 51, no. 12 (1973): 860–80.

3045. ———. "Federal Tax Law: Where You Divorce Does Make a Difference," *Loyola University of Chicago Law Journal*, vol. 9, no. 2 (1978): 397–411.

3046. ———. "Federal Tax Treatment of Transfers of 'Marital Property' under the New Illinois Marriage and Dissolution of Marriage Act," *Chicago Bar Record*, vol. 59, no. 5 (1978): 286–90+.

3047. ———. "Tax Aspects of Separation and Divorce," *Family Law Newsletter*, vol. 16, no. 2 (1975): 15–21; and no. 3 (1975): 11–23.

3048. ———. "Tax Developments in Family Law," *Family Law Newsletter*, vol. 17, no. 2 (1977): 1+; no. 3 (1977): 1+; and no. 4 (1977): 1+.

3049. Elliott, Patricia C. "Women: Their Changing Status and Income Tax Law," *The Woman CPA*, vol. 34, no. 3 (1972): 5–8.

3050. Engler, Calvin. "How to Increase After-tax Income of Both Parties When Divorce or Separation Is Contemplated," *Taxation for Accountants*, vol. 23, no. 3 (1979): 170–74.

3051. "Father Gets Medical Deduction for Payments through Ex-wife," *Taxation for Lawyers*, vol. 5, no. 4 (1977): 230.

3052. Fetterly, Patricia C. "Taxation—Has the Doctrine of United States v. Davis Been Mitigated?" *Oregon Law Review*, vol. 57, no. 2 (1978): 365–70.

3053. Freeland, James J.; Lind, Stephen A.; and Stephens, Richard B. *Cases and Materials on Fundamentals of Federal Income Taxation*. 2d ed. Mineola, NY: Foundation Press, 1977.

3054. Frisch, Robert E. "How to Avoid Tax Complications When Arranging a Divorce Settlement," *Taxation for Accountants*, vol. 20, no. 1 (1978): 20–25.

3055. ———. "How to Avoid Tax Complications When Arranging a Divorce Settlement," *Taxation for Lawyers*, vol. 6, no. 4 (1978): 222–27.

3056. Godeke, Dan A. "Federal Income Tax Treatment of Gains and Losses in Divorce and Separation Property Settlements," *St. Louis University Law Journal* 20 (1975): 181–98.

3057. Graves, Edward S. "Federal Taxation in Separation and Divorce," *Washington and Lee Law Review*, vol. 29, no. 1 (1972): 1–25.

3058. ———. "How to Protect Your Client from Tax Disaster When Divorce Clouds Gather," *Taxation for Accountants*, vol. 8, no. 5 (1972): 308–14.

3059. Gunn, Alan. "Federal Income Tax Effects of the Missouri Version of the Uniform Divorce Act," *Washington University Law Quarterly* 2 (1974): 227–62.

3060. Harmelink, Philip J., and Shurtz, Nancy E. "How to Control the Tax Consequences of Payments in Divorces and Legal Separations," *Taxation for Accountants*, vol. 18, no. 2 (1977): 112–16.

3061. ———. "Tax Effects in Divorce Planning," *CPA Journal*, vol. 47, no. 10 (1977): 27–32.

3062. Harter, Richard M. "Divorce Situation: Tax Implications of Employee Benefit Arrangements," *Real Property, Probate and Trust Journal*, vol. 10, no. 4 (1975): 657–62.

3063. Henson, John P. "Federal Tax Aspects of Divorce and Separation," *Mississippi Law Journal*, vol. 4, no. 44 (1973): 740–65.

3064. Hollis, Robert A. "Financial and Tax Aspects of Divorce and Separation," *Kansas Bar Association Journal*, vol. 41, no. 4 (1972): 357–60 + .

3065. Holzman, Robert S. "Intrafamily Transactions Can Yield a Surprising Number of Deductible Items," *Taxation for Accountants*, vol. 13, no. 2 (1974): 92–95.

3066. "How Divorce can Create Generation-Skipping Problems," *Journal of Taxation*, vol. 47, no. 3 (1977): 191.

3067. Hjorth, Roland L. "Community Property Marital Settlements: The Problem and a Proposal," *Washington Law Review*, vol. 50, no. 2 (1975): 231–75.

3068. ———. "Tax Consequences of Post-dissolution Support Payment Arrangements," *Washington Law Review*, vol. 51, no. 1 (1976): 233–71.

3069. "Invalid Divorce Can Throw Tax Obligation into Turmoil," *Taxation for Accountants*, vol. 15, no. 4 (1975): 218.

3070. "Invalid Divorce Can Throw Tax Obligation into Turmoil," *Taxation for Lawyers*, vol. 4, no. 3 (1975): 172.

3071. Keating, Gerald. "Information Required by the Practitioner in Divorce Proceedings," *National Public Accountant*, vol. 23, no. 1 (1978): 8–9.

3072. Klein, Michael F., Jr. "Transfer of Residence in Connection with Divorce," *CPA Journal*, vol. 43, no. 7 (1973): 593–94.

3073. Kleinbard, Martin. "Matrimonial Law—Impact of Federal Taxes." In *Institute on Federal Taxation, New York University, 1973*, pp. 1679–98. New York: Matthew Bender & Co., 1974.

3074. Kuntz, Joel D. "Simplification of the Definition of Periodic Payments in Internal Revenue Code Section 71," *University of Cincinnati Law Review*, vol. 47, no. 1 (1978): 213–28.

3075. "Landmark Tax Cases: Gilmore and Patrick—Origin of Expense Determines Deductibility," *Taxation for Accountants*, vol. 6, no. 6 (1971): 349.

3076. Leonard, Robert H. "Divorce or Separation from a Tender Trap to a Tax Trap?" *UMKC Law Review*, vol. 42, no. 1 (1973): 133–54.

3077. Levine, Aaron. "Successful Divorce Negotiations Require Careful Attention to the Tax Implications," *Taxation for Lawyers*, vol. 2, no. 4 (1974): 232–38.

3078. Mahoney, Dennis C. "Divorce: Tax Free Swaps of Jointly Owned Business and Personal Assets," *Wisconsin CPA* 119 (June 1978): 8 + .

3079. "Marital Breakup Pointers," *New York Certified Public Accountant*, vol. 41, no. 12 (1971): 952–53.

3080. "Marital Property Transfers May Yield Loss Too," *Taxation for Accountants*, vol. 6, no. 6 (1971): 354.

3081. Meeker, Larry K. "Federal Income Tax Implications of Divorce," *Washburn Law Journal*, vol. 14, no. 2 (1975): 219–40.

3082. Meldman, Robert E., and Ryan, Karen C. "Federal Tax Consequences of Divorce," *Marquette Law Review*, vol. 57, no. 2 (1974): 229–48.

3083. Nathan, Max, Jr. "Tax Aspects of Separation and Divorce," *Tulane Tax Institute* 20 (1971): 258–75.

3084. New York State Bar Association. Personal Income Committee. "Report on the Davis Rule regarding Property Settlements in Divorce or Separation," *Review of Taxation of Individuals*, vol. 3, no. 1 (1979): 30–40.

3085. Olsen, Shirley. "Community Property: Planning for Division in Divorce," *Tax Adviser*, vol. 6, no. 5 (1975): 291–92.

3086. Payne, Raymond J. "Selected Tax Problems Related to Separation and Marital Dissolution," *Connecticut Bar Journal*, vol. 53, no. 1 (1979): 48–59.

3987. Perkins, Cheryl G. "Certain Tax Consequences of Divorce," *Oregon Certified Public Accountant* 30 (April 1978): 7.

3088. Pitcher, Griffith F. "Tax Implications of Divorce or Separation Do not End with Payments to Spouse," *Taxation for Accountants*, vol. 17, no. 2 (1976): 112–16.

3089. ———. "Tax Implications of Divorce or Separation Do Not End with Payments to Spouse," *Taxation for Lawyers*, vol. 5, no. 2 (1976): 68–72.

3090. Robertson, Edward H. "Fritz & Marilyn & Mike & Susanne," *Taxes—The Tax Magazine*, vol. 51, no. 5 (1973): 268–72.

3091. Rombro, Robert A. "Federal Income Tax Aspects of Conjugal Split-Ups: A General Survey," *Barrister*, vol. 6, no. 3 (1979): 21–28 + .

3092. "Rules for Exemption after Divorce Don't Always Apply," *Taxation for Accountants*, vol. 8, no. 4 (1972): 252.

3093. Samuels, Dorothy J. "New Benefits Available for Care of Dependent or Spouse under the Tax Reform Act of 1976," *Taxation for Lawyers*, vol. 5, no. 4 (1977): 240–42.

3094. Sander, Frank A. E., and Gutman, Harry L. *Tax Aspects of Divorce and Separation*. Washington, DC: Tax Management, Bureau of National Affairs, 1975.

3095. "Separate Estimated Payments Credited Only to Filer," *Journal of Taxation*, vol. 47, no. 2 (1977): 118.

3096. Sherwood, Hugh C. "Divorce and Taxes: When They Must Mix," *Dental Management* (February 15, 1975): 75–78.

3097. "Should State Courts Determine Federal Tax Policy?" *University of Colorado Law Review*, vol. 47, no. 3 (1976): 533–51.

3098. Solomon, Howard B. "Balance Sheet Liabilities: Divorce, Maritals and Their Agreements." In *Institute on Federal Taxation, New York University, 1976*. New York: Matthew Bender & Co., 1977.

3099. "Sources of Estimated Tax Payments Are Irrelevant," *Taxation for Lawyers*, vol. 6, no. 4 (1978): 219–20.

3100. Stratman, Steven F. "Significance of Divorce Invalidation Decrees for Purposes of Internal Revenue Code Sec. 2056(a)," *Notre Dame Lawyer*, vol. 52, no. 4 (1977): 702–32.

3101. Taggart, John Y. *Some Tax Aspects of Separation and Divorce*. 2d ed. Chicago: American Bar Association, 1975.

3102. "Tax Effect of Subsequent Change in Divorce Decree," *Taxation for Lawyers*, vol. 1, no. 2 (1972): 112–13.

3103. "Tax Effects of Invalid Divorce Still Unclear," *Taxation for Accountants*, vol. 19, no. 1 (1977): 47–48.

3104. "Tax Effects of Invalid Divorce Still Unclear," *Taxation for Lawyers*, vol. 6, no. 2 (1977): 98.

3105. "Tax Effects of Invalid Divorce Still Unclear," *Estate Planning*, vol. 4, no. 6 (1977): 326–27.

3106. Thomas, Lowell S., Jr. *Tax Consequences of Marriage, Separation, and Divorce*. 2d ed. Philadelphia, PA: American Law Institute—American Bar Association Committee on Continuing Professional Education, 1976.

3107. Turley, Edward W., Jr. "Divorce and Taxes—Texas Style," *Texas Law Review*, vol. 48, no. 4 (1970): 721–65.

3108. U.S. Internal Revenue Service. *Tax Information for Divorced and Separated Individuals*. Washington, DC: Government Printing Office, 1978 (T22.44/2.504/11).

3109. "Valuation of the Right to Support for Purposes of the Federal Tax System," *Columbia Law Review* 1 (1972): 132–61.

3110. Vaughn, Jack M. "Basic Tax Principles in Divorce Negotiations," *Community Property Journal*, vol. 4, no. 4 (1977): 194–212.

3111. ———. "Community Property Divorce: A Comprehensive Tax Planning Approach," *Community Property Journal*, vol. 2, no. 3 (1975): 148–54.

3112. ———. "Community Property Divorce: Preparing the Tax Returns," part 2, *Community Property Journal*, vol. 2, no. 4 (1975): 213–24.

3113. ———. "Community Property States—Preparing Tax Returns for the Year of Divorce," *Taxes*, vol. 52, no. 3 (1974): 141–58.

3114. ———. "Texas Divorce—Planning the Tax Results," *Texas Bar Journal*, vol. 38, no. 10 (1975): 1035 + .

3115. Vollman, Stanton H. "Allocation of Joint Income Tax Liability in Contemplation of Divorce," *Tax Adviser*, vol. 2, no. 2 (1971): 104–05.

3116. Walker, Mike. "Tax Consequences of Divorce in New Mexico," *New Mexico Law Review*, vol. 5, n o. 2 (1975): 233–78.

3117. Wegher, Arnold C. "Deductibility of Fees for Professional Services—Accountant or Attorney." In *Institute on Federal Taxation, New York University, 1975*, pp. 163–87. New York: Matthew Bender & Co., 1976.

3118. Weisbard, George L. "$750-Deduction Is Not the Only Tax Benefit That a Qualified Dependent Can Provide," *Taxation for Accountants*, vol. 10, no. 6 (1973): 338–42.

3119. Wenig, Mary M. "Use of Life Insurance in Divorce and Separation Agreements." In *Institute on Federal Taxation, New York University, 1970*, pp. 837–52. New York: Matthew Bender & Co., 1971.

3120. Wenke, William F., and Evans, John F. "Developments in the Taxation of Dissolution Actions," *Orange County Bar Journal*, vol. 4, no. 4 (1977): 385–400.

3121. Weston, David L. "Saving Taxes by Giving Dependency Exemptions to Divorced Spouse with Lower Income," *Tax Adviser*, vol. 4, no. 7 (1973): 426.

3122. *What You Should Know about Taxes and Marital Split-Ups*. Federal Taxes Report Bulletin, No. 27 (June 2, 1977). Englewood Cliffs, NJ: Prentice-Hall, 1977.

3123. "When Are Decedent's Marital Obligations Deductible?" *Taxation for Lawyers*, vol. 3, no. 6 (1975): 355.

3124. Whittenburg, Gerald E., and Bost, John C. "Special Problems on the Disposition of a Personal Residence pursuant to a Community Property Divorce," *Community Property Journal*, vol. 6, no. 4 (1979): 385–94.

3125. "Wife May Avoid Tax on Income from Divorce-Connected Trust," *Journal of Taxation*, vol. 40, no. 6 (1974): 333–34.

3126. "Wilkinson, Carl E. "Who Is the Surviving Spouse in Divorce and Remarriage Cases?" *Trusts and Estates*, vol. 116, no. 12 (1977): 784–88.

3127. "Will Section 121 Replacement Elections Foster Annulments?" *Journal of Taxation*, vol. 51, no. 1 (1979): 63.

3128. Zabel, William D. "Income, Estate, and Gift Tax Consequences of Marital Settlements," *Institute on Estate Planning*, vol. 13, no. 14 (1979): 1–58.

ESTATE PLANNING

3129. Abbin, Byrle M.; Daskal, Robert H.; and Carlson, David K. "Significant Recent Developments concerning Estate Planning," part 3, *Tax Adviser*, vol. 7, no. 5 (1976): 288–98.

3130. American Bar Association. Section of Real Property, Probate and Trust Law. Committee on Tax and Estate Planning. "Estate Planning through Family Bargaining," *Real Property, Probate and Trust Journal*, vol. 8, no. 2 (1973): 233–70.

3131. Schick, Roy J. "Divorce and Estate Planning," *Life Insurance Selling*, vol. 53, no. 6 (1978): 72 + .

ESTATE TAXES

3132. Ben-Horin, Giora. "Recent Cases Highlight the Estate and Gift Tax Implications of Divorce," *Journal of Taxation*, vol. 34, no. 2 (1971): 87–91.

3133. Carp, Gerald I. "Estate Tax Considerations in Using Life Insurance with Marital Settlements: Current Developments," *Insurance Law Journal* 647 (1976): 737–44.

3134. ———. "Estate Tax Considerations in Using Life Insurance with Marital Settlements: Current Developments," *Taxes*, vol. 55, no. 4 (1977): 282–87.

3135. "Claim v. Bequest: What Are the Distinguishing Factors?" *Estate Planning*, vol. 4, no. 5 (1977): 286.

3136. "Estate Tax Deduction for Payments Required under Separation Agreements or Divorce Decrees," *CPA Journal*, vol. 48, no. 12 (1978): 82–84.

3137. "Ex-wife's Support Rights Fully Deductible under 2053," *Estate Planning*, vol. 5, no. 6 (1978): 341.

3138. "Ex-wife's Support Rights Fully Deductible under 2053," *Journal of Taxation*, vol. 49, no. 2 (1978): 94.

3139. Huffaker, John B. "Divorce Invalidated after Death Erases Marital Deduction and Estate Plans," *Journal of Taxation*, vol. 45, no. 3 (1976): 154–55.

3140. ———. "Insurance Paid to Ex-wife Deductible by Estate Says TC," *Journal of Taxation*, vol. 43, no. 1 (1975): 48–49.

3141. Linett, E. S. "Estate Tax: Insurance Proceeds Paid to Ex-spouse per Divorce Decree Not Taxable to Insured's Estate," *Tax Adviser*, vol. 7, no. 6 (1976): 376–77.

3142. Mulligan, Michael D. "When Are Divorce-Related Payments Deductible as Claims against Estate?" *Estate Planning*, vol. 6, no. 4 (1979): 210–13.

3143. Peschel, John L., and Spurgeon, Edward D. "Trusts Incident to Separation and Divorce." In *Federal Taxation of Trusts, Grantors and Beneficiaries—Income, Estate, Gift Taxation*, pp. 1–30. Boston, MA: Warren, Gorham and Lamont, 1978.

3144. "Postponed Support Allowed as Deductible Estate Claim," *Estate Planning*, vol. 5, no. 5 (1978): 272–73.

3145. "Postponed Support Allowed as Deductible Estate Claim," *Taxation for Accountants*, vol. 21, no. 1 (1978): 32.

3146. "Postponed Support Allowed as Deductible Estate Claim," *Taxation for Lawyers*, vol. 7, no. 2 (1978): 106.

3147. Schlenger, Jacques T., and Dykes, William T. F. "Life Insurance Proceeds Paid to Decedent's Former Spouse Includable in Decedent's Gross Estate under Section 2042(2) and Deductible under Section 2053(a)(4) Where Decedent Was Required by Divorce Decree to Name Former Spouse as Beneficiary and to Pay Premium," *Estate Planning*, vol. 4, no. 1 (1976): 37–38.

3148. Schlenger, Jacques T., and Garrett, David J. "Deduction from Gross Estate Permitted for Excess Value of Surviving Spouse's Right to Receive Support Payments from inter vivos Trust," *Estate Planning*, vol. 1, no. 4 (1974): 235–36.

LEGAL FEES

3149. "Many Legal Expenses Incident to a Divorce Are Deductible," *Taxation for Lawyers*, vol. 6, no. 6 (1978): 330–31.

3150. "Many Legal Expenses Incident to a Divorce Are Deductible," *Taxation for Accountants*, vol. 20, no. 3 (1978): 183–84

PROPERTY SETTLEMENTS

3151. Aardal, Danny C. "Federal Taxation of Divorce Property Settlements and the Amiable Fictions of State Law," *Denver Law Journal*, vol. 52, no. 3 (1975): 799–826.

3152. Alcott, Mark H. "Selected Tax Problems in Matrimonial Disputes and Settlements." In *Institute on Federal Taxation, New York University, 1978*, pp. 33-1–33-18. New York: Matthew Bender & Co., 1979.

3153. Argue, Douglas W., and Cook, James J. "Tax Aspects of Property Divisions in Divorce," *Los Angeles Bar Bulletin*, vol. 45, no. 7 (1970): 288–92.

3154. Basi, Bart A., and Weinstein, Elliott W. "Internal Revenue Code and its Impact on Divorce Settlements," *Taxes*, vol. 53, no. 3 (1975): 132–53.

3155. Bonavich, Peter. "Allocation of Private Pension Benefits as Property in Illinois Divorce Proceedings," *De Paul Law Review*, vol. 29, no. 1 (1979): 1–46.

3156. Bost, T. G. "Divorces in Community Property States: Selected Tax Problems." In *Institute on Federal Taxation, New York University, 1978*, pp. 35-1–35-32. New York: Matthew Bender & Co., 1979.

3157. Ceravolo, Anthony J. "Federal Income Tax Consequences of Appreciated Property Transfers under the Illinois Marriage and Dissolution of Marriage Act," *DePaul Law Review*, vol. 27, no. 3 (1978): 815–36.

3158. Connally, John B., III. "Taxes on Community Income Are Debts of the Community, and the Wife Is Not Obligated to Pay the Tax on One-Half of that Income from Her Separate Property," *Texas Law Review*, vol. 49, no. 3 (1971): 562–68.

3159. Cronkhite, John A. "Analyze Divorce Settlement to Get Desired Tax Effect," *Taxation for Lawyers*, vol. 1, no. 1 (1972): 40–46.

3160. Deutsch, Ellen S. "New Approach to the Transfer of Appreciated Property pursuant to Divorce," *Catholic University Law Review*, vol. 25, no. 3 (1976): 616–33.

3161. Dickinson, Martin B., Jr. "Federal Income Tax Treatment of Divisions of Property: Marital Property Settlements, Estate and Trust Distributions, and Other Transactions," *University of Kansas Law Review* 18 (Winter 1970): 193–236.

3162. Dillingham, Charles, and Turner, Bruce E. "Incorrectly Computing the Basis of Property Can Prove Costly to Taxpayer," *Taxation for Lawyers*, vol. 4, no. 5 (1976): 278–86.

3163. "Divorce Settlement Sets Section 1239 Treatment," *Journal of Taxation*, vol. 46, no. 1 (1977): 46–47.

3164. DuCanto, Joseph N. "Federal Income Tax Effect of Novation of Marital Settlement Agreements," *Loyola University of Chicago Law Journal*, vol. 3, no. 2 (1972): 237–46.

3165. ———. "Negotiating and Drafting Property Settlement Agreements in the Reflected Light of the Davis and Lester Cases," *De Paul Law Review*, vol. 19, no. 4 (1970): 717–36.

3166. "Federal Income Tax Consequences of Property Settlements in Common Law States and under the Uniform Marriage and Divorce Act: A Proposal," *Maine Law Review*, vol. 29, no. 1 (1977): 73–111.

3167. Glickfeld, Bruce S.; Rabow, Jerome A.; and Schwartz, Herbert E. "Federal Income Tax Consequences of Marital Property Settlements." In *University of Southern California Tax Institute, 1974*, pp. 307–46. New York: Matther Bender & Co., 1974.

3168. Gokel, Ruth L. "Income Tax—Property Settlement in Divorce—An Unsettled Area of Settled Law," *Florida State University Law Review*, vol. 6, no. 1 (1978): 175–85.

3169. Grach, Brian. "Divorce Situation: Tax Implications of Settlements," *Real Property, Probate and Trust Journal*, vol. 10, no. 4 (1975): 640–43 + .

3170. Harris, Steven M., and Ravikoff, Ronald B. "Controlling the Tax Effects of Transfers of Life Insurance or Annuities in Divorces," *Journal of Taxation*, vol. 47, no. 2 (1977): 92–96.

3171. "How Not to Dispose of Property in a Marital Settlement," *Practical Accountant*, vol. 10, no. 4 (1977): 71.

3172. Hull, Addis E. "New Uniform Divorce Laws: The Davis Decision." In *Institute on Federal Taxation, New York University, 1978*, pp. 36-1–36-17. New York: Matthew Bender & Co., 1979.

3173. "Interest Cannot Be Imputed in a Property Settlement," *Taxation for Accountants*, vol. 17, no. 1 (1976): 54.

3174. "Interest Cannot Be Imputed in a Property Settlement," *Taxation for Lawyers*, vol. 5, no. 2 (1976): 99.

3175. Lawson, Gary B. "Tax Implications of Using Appreciated Property in a Property Settlement," *Journal of Taxation*, vol. 42, no. 1 (1975): 58–60.

3176. Levi, Jeffrey H. "Tax Consequences of the Maryland Marital Property Act," *University of Baltimore Law Review*, vol. 9, no. 1 (1979): 12–36.

3177. McKenney, Paul L. B. "Divorce Property Settlement Tax Pitfalls and Solutions," *Michigan State Bar Journal*, vol. 57, no. 12 (1978): 1006–08 + .

3178. ———. "Divorce Property Settlement Tax Pitfalls and Solutions," *Michigan CPA*, vol. 30, no. 6 (1979): 23–24 + .

3179. "Marital Settlements," *CPA Journal* 49 (September 1979): 48–50.

3180. Middlebrook, Janet S. "Eggemeyer v. Eggemeyer: An Exercise in Judicial Legislation?" *Houston Law Review*, vol. 14, no. 4 (1977): 1104–14.

3181. Mills, Robert A. "Community/Joint Tenancy—Avoiding a Tax Double-Play: Touch the Basis," *University of Southern California Tax Institute, 1979*, pp. 951-70. New York: Matthew Bender & Co., 1979.

3182. "Property Settlement Can Result in Loss of Capital Gains," *Taxation for Lawyers*, vol. 5, no. 3 (1976): 178.

3183. "Rent Held Alimony but Not Mortgage Payments," *Taxation for Accountants*, vol. 21, no. 2 (1978): 120.

3184. "Rent Held Alimony but Not Mortgage Payments," *Taxation for Lawyers*, vol. 7, no. 2 (1978): 125–26.

3185. Rosel, James. "Tax Consequences of Divisions of Jointly Owned and Community Property Incident to Divorce," *University of Florida Law Review*, vol. 27, no. 4 (1975): 1033–43.

3186. Rutter, Paul S. "Future Tax Consequences in Community Property Divisions: An Analysis of the California Approach," *UCLA Law Review*, vol. 24, no. 6 (1977): 1354–87.

3187. Spjut, Robert J. "Income Tax Consequences of Equal Divisions of Community Property in California: Collins and the New Divorce Law," *University of San Francisco Law Review*, vol. 4, no. 2 (1970): 397–419.

3188. Stechert, Robert B. "Property Settlement pursuant to Divorce as a Taxable Event," *Washburn Law Journal*, vol. 13, no. 1 (1974): 169–73.

3189. Stigamire, James C. "Internal Revenue Service Case Settlement Procedures." In *University of Southern California Tax Institute, 1979*, pp. 1073–84. New York: Matthew Bender & Co., 1979.

3190. Vaughn, Jack M. "What the Property Settlement Agreement Should Say about Income Taxes," *Community Property Journal*, vol. 4, no. 1 (1977): 29–36.

3191. Victor, Edward G. "Divorce and Deferred Compensation Arrangements." In *University of Southern California Tax Institute, 1971*, pp. 469–93. New York: Matthew Bender & Co., 1972.

3192. Ward, Larry D. "Divorce Property Settlement Generates Ordinary Income under Code Section 1239," *Review of Taxation of Individuals*, vol. 1, no. 2 (1977): 159–62.

REMARRIAGE

3193. "Remarriage Doesn't Convert Alimony to Child Support," *Taxation for Lawyers*, vol. 5, no. 3 (1976): 166.

SEPARATION

3194. Bruch, Carol S. "Effect of Informal Marital Separations on Personal Income Taxation," *Tax Adviser*, vol. 9, no. 8 (1978): 470–77.

3195. Higgins, Warren, and Horvitz, Jerome S. "Tax Considerations for Separated Married Couples," *Taxes*, vol. 53, no. 3 (1975): 154–60.

3196. "Redemption of Estranged Spouse's Stock not Taxable," *Taxation for Lawyers*, vol. 7, no. 6 (1979): 356.

3197. Sandor, Paul E. "Residence: Appeals Officer Recalls Tough Tax Issues," *Connecticut CPA*, vol. 42, no. 2 (1978): 16–17.

3198. "Spouses under One Roof Can Be Living 'Separately' Says CA-8," *Journal of Taxation*, vol. 49, no. 3 (1978): 172.

3199. "Taxpayers Living in Same House Are Not Separated," *Taxation for Accountants*, vol. 19, no. 5 (1977): 273.

3200. Wakeford, Herbert W. "Flaws in Separation Agreement Could Cause Loss of Tax Benefits," *Tax Adviser*, vol. 3, no. 12 (1972): 740–41.

III. Judeo-Christian Literature

DOCTRINE, THEOLOGY AND BIBLICAL VIEWS

ANNULMENT

Church of Jesus Christ of Latter-Day Saints

3201. "Seminar Spotlights Single Parents," *Church News* 46 (November 27, 1976): 4+.

Jewish

3202. Rakeffet-Rothkoff, Aaron. "Annulment of Marriage within the Context of Cancellation of the GET," *Tradition,* vol. 15, no. 1–2 (1975): 173–85.

Roman Catholic

3203. "Annulments to Be Handled Twice as Fast," *National Catholic Reporter* 6 (July 3, 1970): 15.

3204. "Canonist Norms Meet Dire Need," *National Catholic Reporter* 10 (June 21, 1974): 24.

3205. "Canonist Says Annulment Mentality among Catholics," *Our Sunday Visitor* 67 (May 14, 1978): 3.

3206. "Canonists Will Push to Keep Annulment Norms," *National Catholic Reporter* 10 (October 16, 1973): 6.

3207. Catoir, John T. *Catholics and Broken Marriage.* Notre Dame, IN: Ave Maria Press, 1979.

3208. Coulter, James A. "The Pastoral Problem of Annulments," *Furrow* 29 (November 1978): 680–88.

3209. Doherty, Dennis J. "Marriage Annulments: Some Theological Implications," *Jurist,* vol. 38, no. 1–2 (1978): 180–89.

3210. Donahue, Charles, Jr. "Comparative Reflections on the 'New Matrimonial Jurisprudence' of the Roman Catholic Church," *Michigan Law Review,* vol. 75, no. 5–6 (1977): 994–1020.

3211. Donnelly, Francis. "Helena Decision of 1924," *Jurist,* vol. 36, no. 2 (1976): 442–49.

3212. Filteau, Jerry. "Experimental Annulment Norms Continue," *National Catholic Reporter* 9 (July 6, 1973): 5.

3213. "Forum Major Remarries: Annulment Brings Flak," *National Catholic Reporter* 11 (February 7, 1975): 20.

3214. Gibeau, Dawn. "New Grounds Cause Rise in Annulments," *National Catholic Reporter* 10 (November 2, 1973: 1+.

3215. Green, Thomas J. "Homosexuality and the Validity of Marriage—The Developing Jurisprudence," *Linacre Quarterly,* vol. 43, no. 3 (1976): 196–207.

3216. ———. "Psychological Grounds for Church Annulments: Changing Canonical Practice," *Social Thought* 4 (Spring 1978): 47–59.

3217. Haring, Bernard. "Internal Forum Solutions to Insoluble Marriage Cases," *Jurist* 30 (January 1970): 21–30.

3218. Hettinger, Clarence J. "Marriage Consent in Post-conciliar Law," *Homiletic and Pastoral Review* 78 (January 1978): 30–32+.

3219. Kelleher, Stephen J. "Annulments and Dissolutions of Particular Marriages," *Catholic Mind,* vol. 70, no. 1267 (1972): 17–25.

3220. ———. "Catholic Annulments: A Dehumanizing Process: Lifting Excommunications for Divorce and Remarriage Is not Enough," *Commonweal,* vol. 104, no. 12 (1977): 363–68.

3221. Kenny, Walter F. "Homosexuality and Nullity—Developing Jurisprudence," *Catholic Lawyer,* vol. 17, no. 12 (1971): 110–22.

3222. Komora, Edward J. "Narcissism: Its Relation to Personality Disorders and Church Marriage Annulments," *Catholic Lawyer,* vol. 24, no. 4 (1979): 313–26.

3223. Lebel, Robert R. "Genetic Grounds for Annulments," *Jurist,* vol. 36, no. 2 (1976): 317–27.

3224. McFadden, Leo E. "Pope Speeds Up Marriage Cases," *National Catholic Reporter* 7 (June 18, 1971): 1+.

3225. Natale, Samuel M., and Wolff, Richard J. "Annulment in the Church Today," *Catholic Charismatic,* vol. 2, no. 1 (1977): 24–28.

3226. "New Norms for Marriage Annulment Cases," *Catholic Mind,* vol. 68, no. 1246 (1970): 53–64.

3227. "New Pontifical Document on Marriage Cases," *L'Osservatore Romano* (English Edition) 219 (June 8, 1972): 4.

3228. "Pope Gives Hopes on Marriage Norms," *National Catholic Reporter* 10 (March 8, 1974): 5.

3229. Reinhardt, Marion J. "Incidence of Mental Disorder," *Catholic Lawyer,* vol. 18, no. 3 (1972): 195–205.

3230. Reinhardt, Marion J., and Arella, Gerard J. "Essential Incompatibility as Grounds for Nullity of Marriage," *Catholic Lawyer,* vol. 16, no. 2 (1970): 173–87.

3231. Saltzman, Leon. "Catholic Annulment and Civil Divorce," *America* 140 (May 5, 1979): 367–69.

3232. Shanahan, Louise. "Ecclesiastical Annulment," *Marriage and Family Living* 58 (May 1976): 2–6.

3233. Tierney, Terence E. *Annulment: Do You Have a Case?* New York: Alba House, 1978.

3234. "Vatican Extends Marriage Norms," *National Catholic Reporter* 10 (June 21, 1974): 24.

3235. "Vatican Orders Ceiling on Annulment Case Fees," *National Catholic Reporter* 9 (November 10, 1972): 15.

3236. Wrenn, Lawrence G. "The American Procedural Norms," *American Ecclesiastical Review* 165 (November 1971): 175–86.

Canon Law

3237. "Can the Vatican Hear?" (editorial), *National Catholic Reporter* 14 (October 28, 1977): 10.

3238. Catoir, John T. "When the Courts Don't Work," *America* 125 (October 9, 1971): 254–57.

3239. Green, Thomas J. "Marriage Nullity Procedure in the Schema de Processibus," *Jurist,* vol. 38, no. 3–4 (1978): 311–414.

3240. "The Judge: A Case History," *New Catholic World* 217 (May 1974): 121–25.

3241. Kenkelen, Bill. "Canon Lawyers Fear for Annulment Process," *National Catholic Reporter* 13 (October 21, 1977): 1+.

3242. ———. "U.S. Annulments not in Danger: Vatican Criticizes," *National Catholic Reporter* 14 (March 24, 1978): 3.

3243. Maida, Adam J., ed. *The Tribunal Reporter; A Comprehensive Study of the Grounds for the Annulment of Marriage in the Catholic Church.* Huntington, IN: Our Sunday Visitor, 1970.

3244. Marshner, William H. *Annulment or Divorce? A Critique of Current Tribunal Practice and the Proposed Revision of Canon Law.* Triangle, VA: Crossroads Books, 1978.

3245. Noonan, John T. *Power to Dissolve; Lawyers and Marriages in the Courts of the Roman Curia.* Cambridge, MA: Belknap Press of Harvard University Press, 1972.

3246. Reinhardt, Marion J. "Error as the Quality of the Person in Canon Law," *Catholic Lawyer*, vol. 2, no. 1 (1974): 44–59.

3247. "Scholars Attempt to Affect Canon Law on Marriage," *National Catholic Reporter* 11 (May 30, 1975): 15.

3248. Towey, Damian. "Annulments," *Sign*, vol. 56, no. 6 (1977): 5–8.

Tribunals

3249. Arella, Gerard J. "Case for the Marriage Court," *America*, vol. 127, no. 12 (1972): 316–20.

3250. Cuenin, Walter J. " 'Tribunals Are Good, but . . .,' " *National Catholic Reporter* 15 (May 25, 1979): 11.

3251. Gibeau, Dawn. "Marriage Courts Need Revamping, Canon Lawyers Say," *National Catholic Reporter* 10 (October 26, 1973): 1+.

3252. James, Edward. "Marriage Tribunals: Another Viewpoint," *America* 140 (May 5, 1979): 370–71.

3253. Knox, L. Mason. "The Tribunal Explosion: A 21-Fold Increase in Canonical Marriage Cases in a Six-Year Period," *America* 135 (October 16, 1976): 226–28.

3254. MacEoin, Gary. "Tribunal Speeds Up Annulments," *National Catholic Reporter* 8 (March 3, 1972): 1+.

3255. Maher, John. "Marriage Tribunals Should Be Abolished," *National Catholic Reporter* 10 (November 9, 1973): 5.

3256. Mungavan, Mary. "Church Marriage Courts: It's Not Who You Know but Where You Go," *U.S. Catholic* 42 (June 1978): 13–18.

3257. Natale, Samuel M. "The Tribunal Vetitum: Limit Setting and Confrontation," *Studia Canonica*, vol. 12, no. 2 (1978): 365–75.

3258. Petosa, Jason. "Tribunals Substandard; Marriage." *National Catholic Reporter* 11 (September 5, 1975): 4.

3259. Pfnausch, Edward G. "The Question of Tribunals," *America* 139 (November 18, 1978): 352–54.

3260. Provost, James H. "A Candid Look at the Marriage Tribunal," *Marriage and Family Living* 61 (April 1979): 12–15.

3261. ———. "Remarks Concerning Proofs and Presumptions," *Jurist*, vol. 39, no. 3–4 (1979): 456–70.

3262. Sanson, Robert J. "A Preliminary Investigation for Marriage Annulment?" *Studia Canonica*, vol. 11, no. 1 (1977): 37–66.

3263. Stewart, Oliver (pseudonym). *Divorce—Vatican Style.* London: Oliphants, 1971.

3264. Vath, William R. "The Parish Priest and the Tribunal," *Homiletic and Pastoral Review* 78 (June 1978): 27–32+.

3265. West, Morris L., and Francis, Robert. *Scandal in the Assembly: A Bill of Complaints and a Proposal for Reform in the Matrimonial Laws and Tribunals of the Roman Catholic Church.* New York: William Morrow & Co., 1970.

3266. Wrenn, Lawrence G. "Marriage Tribunals and the Expert," *National Guild of Catholic Psychiatrists Bulletin* 25 (1979): 53–68.

DIVORCE

Jewish

3267. Geller, Markham J. "Elphantine Papyri and Hosea 2,3," *Journal for the Study of Judaism*, vol. 8, no. 20 (1977): 139–48.

Protestant

3268. Catchpole, David R. "The Synoptic Divorce Material as a Traditio-Historical Problem," *John Rylands Library Bulletin*, vol. 57, no. 1 (1974): 92–127.

3269. Fennel, Justus J. "Contributions to a Theology of Divorce in the Light of Process Theology and Crisis Intervention Theory and Practice." Ph.D. diss., Boston University, 1979 (*DAI* 39/12A, p. 7390, order # 7912140).

3270. Fischer, James A. "I. Cor. 7:8–24—Marriage and Divorce," *Biblical Research* 23 (1978): 26–36.

3271. Gangel, Kenneth O. "Toward Biblical Theology of Marriage and Family," *Journal of Psychology and Theology*, vol. 5, no. 1 (1977): 55–69; no. 2 (1977): 150–62; no. 3 (1977): 247–59; no. 4 (1977): 318–31.

3272. Geldard, Mark. "Jesus' Teaching on Divorce: Thoughts on the Meaning of Porneia in Matthew 5:32 and 19:9," *Churchman* (London), vol. 92, no. 2 (1978): 134–43.

3273. Hosier, Helen K. *The Other Side of Divorce.* New York: Hawthorne Press, 1975.

3274. Kysar, Myrna, and Kysar, Robert. *The Asundered: Biblical Teachings on Divorce and Remarriage.* Atlanta, GA: John Knox Press, 1978.

3275. Sinks, Robert F. "Theology of Divorce," *Christian Century* 94 (April 20, 1977): 376–79.

Christian and Missionary Alliance

3276. Woodcock, Eldon. "The Case for Staying Put: First Corinthians 7:17–28," *The Alliance Witness* 113 (April 5, 1978): 23–24.

3277. ———. "Divorce and Remarriage," *Alliance Witness*, vol. 113, no. 6 (1978): 25–26.

Christian Reformed Church

3278. Jewett, Paul K. "Divorce: A Theological Statement," *The Reformed Journal*, vol. 27, no. 1 (1977): 21–25.

3279. Verhey, Allen. "Divorce in the New Testament," *The Reformed Journal*, vol. 26, no. 5 (1976): 17–19; no. 6 (1976): 28–31.

Evangelical

3280. Allen, C. Ermal. "Divorce and Remarriage: Another Look," *Christian Standard* 113 (May 7, 1978): 7.

3281. Barron, Gene. "God Hates Divorce . . . But Loves the Divorced," *Christian Standard* 114 (January 14, 1979): 12–14.

3282. Barton, Freeman. "Jesus and Paul on Divorce," *Henceforth* 8 (Fall 1979): 15–31.

3283. Boice, James M. "The Biblical View of Divorce," *Eternity,* vol. 21, no. 12 (1970): 19–21.

3284. Bustanoby, Andre. "When Wedlock Becomes Deadlock, Biblical Teaching on Divorce," *Christianity Today* 19 (June 20, 1975): 4–6; 19 (July 18, 1975): 11–14.

3285. Coleman, William M. "Divorce Court in Jesus' Day," *Eternity,* vol. 28, no. 6 (1977): 54+.

3286. Conway, Jim. "Divorce . . . And You," *His* 39 (April 1979): 1–2+.

3287. Ensworth, George. " 'This Marriage Cannot Be Saved': What Christians Say the Bible Says about Divorce," *Eternity,* vol. 27, no. 6 (1976): 11–15.

3288. Hurley, Virg. "God Hates Divorce—But Loves His People," *Christian Standard* 110 (May 4, 1975): 9–10.

3289. Lundbom, Jack R. "What about Divorce?" *The Covenant Quarterly* 36 (November 1978): 21–27.

3290. Peters, George W. "The New Testament and Remarriage of the Divorced," *Moody Monthly,* vol. 70, no. 6 (1970): 26–31.

3291. ———. "Putting Asunder What God Has Joined Together," *Christian Medical Society Journal* 7 (Winter 1976): 9–19.

3292. ———. "What God Says about Divorce," *Moody Monthly* 78 (June 1978): 40–42.

3293. ———. "What the Bible Says about Divorce," *Moody Monthly* 70 (May 1970): 34–35+.

3294. Piper, Thomas S. "Joseph's Grounds for Divorce," *Good News Broadcaster* 34 (December 1976): 16.

3295. Powers, B. Ward. "Divorce and the Bible," *Interchange,* vol. 23, no. 1 (1978): 149–74.

3296. Ryrie, Charles C. *You Mean the Bible Teaches That . . .* Chicago: Moody Press, 1974.

3297. Sanders, James L. "Marriage outside of Paradise," *The New Pulpit Digest* 57 (July–August 1977): 14–18.

3298. Stein, Robert H. " 'Is It Lawful for a Man to Divorce His Wife?' " *Journal of the Evangelical Theological Society,* vol. 22, no. 2 (1979): 115–21.

3299. Stott, John R. W. *Divorce—The Biblical Teaching.* Downers Gove, IL: Inter-Varsity Press, 1971.

3300. Wilson, Wallace R. "An Examination of the Problem of Divorce and Remarriage," *voice,* vol. 55, no. 2 (1976): 4–5+. no. 3 (1976): 6–7; no. 4 (1976): 30–31.

3301. *Your Marriage Can Be Great: Including Forty Chapters Dealing Directly or Indirectly with the Crucial Problems of Divorce and Remarriage.* Edited by Thomas B. Warren. Jonesboro, AR: National Christian Press, 1978.

Methodist

3302. Crum, Robert A. "Divorce in the Human Perspective," *Engage/Social Action* 5 (December 1977): 57–58.

Reformed Church in America

3303. Jewett, Paul K. "Divorce: A Theological Statement," *Church Herald* 34 (August 19, 1977): 17.

Southern Baptist

3304. Hendricks, William L. "Divorce, Remarriage and the New Testament Concept of Forgiveness," *Search,* vol. 2, no. 1 (1971): 36–43.

3305. Lester, Andrew D. "Christ and Divorce," *Royal Service* 72 (July 1977): 29–30.

3306. Tolbert, Malcolm. "The Gospel and Failure in Marriage," *Theological Educator,* vol. 7, no. 2 (1977): 13–14.

Roman Catholic

3307. Byron, Brian. "I Cor. 7:10–15: A Basis for Future Catholic Discipline on Marriage and Divorce?" *Theological Studies,* vol. 34, no. 3 (1973): 429–45.

3308. Connery, John R. "Moral Education and Development," *Today's Catholic Teacher* 11 (November–December 1977): 16–17.

3309. Fitzmyer, Joseph A. "The Matthean Divorce Texts and Some New Palestine Evidence," *Theological Studies,* vol. 37, no. 2 (1976): 197–226.

3310. May, William E. "Moral Education and Development; Marriage and Divorce," *Today's Catholic Teacher* 11 (October 1977): 30–31+.

3311. Olsen, V. Norskov. *The New Testament Logia on Divorce. A Study of Their Interpretation from Erasmus to Milton.* Tübingen: Mohr (Siebeck), 1971.

3312. Stock, Augustine. "Matthean Divorce Texts," *Biblical Theology Bulletin* 8 (February 1978): 24–33.

3313. Vawter, Bruce. "Divorce and the New Testament," *Catholic Biblical Quarterly,* vol. 39, no. 4 (1977): 528–42.

3314. ———. "What the New Testament Says about Divorce," *National Catholic Reporter* 15 (May 25, 1979): 10.

INDISSOLUBILITY OF MARRIAGE

Church of Jesus Christ of Latter-Day Saints

3315. Cullimore, James A. "Marriage Is Intended to Be Forever," *Ensign of the Church of Jesus Christ of Latter Day Saints* 1 (June 1971): 93–94.

Eastern Orthodox

3316. Meyendorff, Jean. *Marriage: An Orthodox Perspective.* 2d ed. Crestwood, NY: St. Vladmir's Seminary Press, 1975.

Roman Catholic

3317. "Canonists Seek Annulment Alternatives: Nonsacramental Unions Suggested," *National Catholic Reporter* 15 (October 27, 1978): 28.

3318. Cunningham, Thomas G. "Indissolubility as Paradox," *Jurist,* vol. 38, no. 3–4 (1978): 434–44.

3319. Donovan, Michael L. *The Vicarious Power of the Church over the Marriage Bond* (An analysis of its nature and function in light of a new interpretation of Matthew 19:12). Rome: Catholic Book Agency, 1972.

3320. Felici, P. "Indissolubility of Marriage and Solution of the Marriage Bond," *L'Osservatore Romano* (English edition) 402 (December 11, 1975): 6–7.

3321. Grenier, Henri. "Can We Still Speak of the Petrine Privilege?" *Jurist* 38 (Winter–Spring 1978): 158–62.

3322. Hallett, Garth. "Whatever You Loose Shall Be Loosed: The Indissolubility of Marriage," *America,* vol. 133, no. 9 (1975): 188–90.

3323. Hire, Richard P. "Our Catholic Faith: Dissolution of the Marriage Bond," *Our Sunday Visitor* 64 (July 13, 1975): 4–5.

3324. International Theological Commission. "Propositions on the Doctrine of Christian Marriage," *Origins* 8 (September 28, 1978): 235–39.

3325. John Paul II. "Address to a General Audience about the Unity and Indissolubility of Marriage," *L'Osservatore Romano* (English edition) 598 (September 10, 1979): 1 + .

3326. "Judge Upholds Indissolubility," *National Catholic Reporter* 11 (November 22, 1974): 2.

3327. Kuntz, J. M. "Is Marriage Indissoluble?" *Journal of Ecumenical Studies*, vol. 7, no. 2 (1970): 333–37.

3328. Lehmann, Karl. "Indissolubility of Marriage and Pastoral Care of the Divorced Who Remarry," *International Catholic Review: Communio*, vol. 1, no. 3 (1974): 219–42.

3329. "Marriage: A Covenant of Indissoluble Love," *Our Sunday Visitor Magazine* 67 (October 15, 1978): 9.

3330. Nowell, Robert. "British Expert Says Church's Marriage Laws Still Insist on Indissolubility," *Our Sunday Visitor* 64 (October 5, 1975): 3.

3331. Orsy, Ladislas. "An Evaluation of 'New Applications of Canon 1127,' " *Jurist* 38 (Winter–Spring 1978): 163–70.

3332. ———. "More about Canon 1127: The Power of the Diocesan Tribunal," *Jurist*, vol. 39, no. 3–4 (1979): 447–55.

3333. Palmer, Paul F. "Indissolubility: A Kinship Bond," *Priest* 34 (Apirl 1978): 28–32.

PRACTICE AND MINISTRY

BIBLIOGRAPHY

Protestant

3334. Polson, Leonard. "Books on Divorce," *Moody Monthly* 78 (July–August 1978): 46–47.

3335. Tinder, Donald. "Recent Books on Divorce," *Christianity Today* 23 (May 1979): 38–42.

Roman Catholic

3336. Kennedy, Robert T., and Finnegan, John T. "Select Bibliography on Divorce and Remarriage in the Catholic Church Today." In *Ministering to the Divorced Catholic*, edited by James J. Young, pp. 260–73. New York: Paulist Press, 1979.

3337. Kircher, Kathleen. "Books for the Divorced," *National Catholic Reporter* 15 (May 25, 1979): 10.

COUNSELING

Protestant

3338. Barnhart, Joe E., and Barnhart, Mary A. "Saint Paul and Divorce: Divorce Counseling for Devout Christians," *Journal of Divorce*, vol. 1, no. 2 (1977): 141–51.

3339. Goot, Mary V. "Broken Marriages: And the Christian Counselor's Task," *The Reformed Journal* 26 (November 1976): 9–11.

3340. Martin, John R. *Divorce and Remarriage; A Perspective for Counseling.* Scottdale, PA: Herald Press, 1974.

3341. Paige, Roger. *Dealing with Divorce,* Independence, MO: Herald Publishing House, 1979.

3342. Small, Dwight H. "Prophet Hosea—God's Alternative to Divorce for the Reasons of Infidelity," *Journal of Psychology and Theology*, vol. 7, no. 2 (1979): 133–40.

Roman Catholic

3343. Christie, Lyle E. "Counseling the Client Who Is Mourning a Divorce," *Catholic Charities Review* 56 (October 1972): 1–11.

3344. "New Orleans Reaches out to Divorced with Seminars," *National Catholic Reporter* 13 (March 4, 1977): 5.

DIVORCE MINISTRY

Jewish

3345. Glustrom, Simon. "The Duty of the Synagogue to Its Widows and Divorcees," *United Synagogue Review Quarterly* 26 (Spring 1973): 14–15.

Protestant

American Baptist

3346. Eppinger, Paul. "Global Gospel: Local Action Possibilities," *Foundations*, vol. 20, no. 4 (1977): 362–65.

Evangelical

3347. Coleman, William L. "Ministering to the Divorced," *Christianity Today* 19 (June 20, 1975): 29–30.

3348. "The Divorced—One Church's Point of Contact," *Eternity* 27 (June 1976): 15.

3349. Wood, Britton. "The Formerly Married—The Church's New Frontier," *United Evangelical Action* 34 (Fall 1975): 24–26.

Methodist

3350. Hayashi, Janet W. "Seattle's Divorce Lifeline," *United Methodists Today*, vol. 2, no. 6 (1975): 36–37.

3351. "Ministry with Young Adults: The Single Parent," *Adult Leader* 11 (December–February 1978–1979): 10.

3352. Santon, Marshall. "Ministering to Divorced Church Members," *Circuit Rider*, vol. 1, no. 5 (1977): 6–7.

Reformed Church In America

3353. Atwood, Andrew. "A Grace-full Response to Divorce," *Church Herald* 32 (July 25, 1975): 18–19.

Southern Baptist

3354. Bailey, Robert W. "Beginning a Ministry to Single and Single-Again Adults," *Deacon* 8 (July–September 1978): 24–25.

3355. Brown, Autry. "Developing Attitudes toward Divorce," *Church Training* 2 (August 1972): 14–15.

3356. Calvert, Stuart. "Ministering in Crisis: Divorce," *Royal Service* 62 (December 1977): 54–56.

3357. Hullum, Everett. "The Family of God," *Home Missions* 48 (May 1977): 8–15.

3358. Lindahl, Alan. "An Evaluation of Divorced Single Parents' Views of Local Church Ministries." D.Min. diss., Eastern Baptist Theological Seminary, 1979 (*DAI* 40/3A, p. 1708, order # 7920267). R.

3359. Ryan, Robert S. "Ministering to the Divorced," *Deacon* 8 (October–December 1977): 4 + .

3360. Stubblefield, Jerry. "Adults without Partners, a Needed Emphasis," *Outreach* 6 (June 1976): 12–13.

3361. Whetstone, James D. "A Divorce Adjustment Seminar Taught from a Christian Perspective with a Goal of Ministry to and by Divorced." D.Min. diss., Southeastern Baptist Theological Seminary, 1978. R.

Roman Catholic

3362. Ament, Richard J. "People with Dignity: A Pastoral Program for the Divorced Catholic," *Living Light* 13 (Winter 1976): 577–81.

3363. Curtin, William B. "The Phantom Spouse: Communion to Divorced and Remarried," *Priest*, vol. 28, no. 9 (1972): 9–19.

3364. DeZutter, Albert. "Clergy Unit: Reconcile Ex-priests, Remarrieds," *National Catholic Reporter* 11 (March 21, 1975): 1–2.

3365. Dickey, Gordon. *Divorced Catholics: An Imperative for Social Ministries.* Washington, DC: National Conference of Catholic Charities, 1974.

3366. "Dissent '76: Victims of Broken Marriages Need Pastoral Ministry," *National Catholic Reporter* 12 (January 30, 1976): 16–17.

3367. Emswiler, James P., and Pfnausch, Edward G. *Divorced and Separated Catholics: A Guide to Ministry.* Winona, MN: Saint Mary's College Press, 1979.

3368. Gardiner, Anne M. "Reaching out to the Divorced," *Today's Parish* 11 (September 1979): 16–18.

3369. Green, Thomas J. "Canonical-Pastoral Reflections on Divorce and Remarriage," *Living Light* 13 (Winter 1976): 560–75.

3370. ———. "Ministering to Marital Failure," *Chicago Studies* 18 (Fall 1979): 327–44.

3371. Kosnik, Anthony. "The Pastoral Care of those Involved in Canonically Invalid Marriages," *Jurist* 30 (January 1970): 31–44.

3372. McAndrew, David T. "Pastoral Ministry to the Invalidly Married," *Homiletic and Pastoral Review*, vol. 73, no. 6 (1973): 26–30.

3373. *Ministering to the Divorced Catholic.* Edited by James J. Young. New York: Paulist Press, 1979.

3374. "Ministry to Separated, Divorced and Remarried Persons: Symposium," *Living Light* 13 (Winter 1976): 547–600.

3375. Nessel, William J. "The Catholic Divorcee: A Pastoral Approach," *Homiletic and Pastoral Review*, vol. 73, no. 6 (1973): 10–14 + .

3376. Nowak, Clara J. "Healing the Wounded: Evangelizing the Divorced and Separated," *Today's Parish* 10 (September 1978): 15–16.

3377. Onaitis, Susan. "The Pain of Divorce—What Is the Church Doing to Help?" *St. Anthony Messenger*, vol. 80, no. 12 (1973): 22–27.

3378. Papa, Mary. "No Fault Concept Changes Divorce in the U.S.," *National Catholic Reporter* 9 (March 2, 1973): 1 + .

3379. Sheehan, Frank X. "Ministering to Divorced Catholics," *Today's Parish* 10 (May–June 1978): 44–45.

RITUALS FOR DIVORCE

Protestant

3380. Feigenbaum, Dolly. "Divorce Ceremonies," *Transactional Analysis Journal*, vol. 7, no. 2 (1977): 160–62.

3381. Norman, Sam R. "Ceremony for the Divorced," *Journal of Pastoral Care* 33 (March 1979): 60–63.

3382. Shideler, Mary M. "An Amicable Divorce," *Christian Century*, vol. 88, no. 18 (1971): 553–55.

Methodist

3383. "Divorce Rituals Proposed in New Church Resource," *United Methodist Newscope*, vol. 4, no. 43 (1976): 4.

3384. Elliot, Ralph E. "A Divorce Service," *Quest* 2 (May–June 1978): 120.

3385. Johnson, Dick. "More on Divorce Rituals," *Engage/Social Action* 6 (June 1978): 45 + .

3386. ———. "Ritual for Divorce?" *Engage/Social Action* 5 (October 1977): 15–16.

Southern Baptist

3387. Johnson, Larry. "The Unwedding (Satirical Copy for a Divorce Ceremony)," *Theological Educator*, vol. 7, no. 2 (1977): 14–15.

Roman Catholic

3388. " 'Rite of Divorce' Enacted during Mass," *National Catholic Reporter* 9 (November 3, 1972): 17.

PERSONAL ASPECTS

CHILDREN OF DIVORCED PARENTS

Church of Jesus Christ of Latter-Day Saints

3389. Anderson, Geraldine P. "Explaining Divorce to Children," *Ensign of the Church of Jesus Christ of Latter Day Saints* 2 (November 1972): 56–58.

Protestants

3390. McDaniel, Charles-Gene. "Children in Divorce Cases; The Wisdom of Solomon Challenged," *Christian Century* 89 (February 16, 1972): 202–04.

Evangelical

3391. Belz, Joel. "The Question of Custody," *Presbyterian Journal* 37 (August 23, 1978): 13 + .

3392. Hendricks, Howard. "When Your Parents Split," *Moody Monthly* 79 (October 1978): 132–35.

3393. Jarrett, Rose. "When a Child Has to Choose," *Christian Herald* 100 (February 1977): 32–34 + .

3394. Lewis, Larry. "Picking Up the Pieces," *Campus Life* 37 (November 1978): 44–45.

3395. Spinnanger, Ruthe T. *Better Than Divorce*. Plainfield, NJ: Logos International, 1978.

3396. "When My Parents Split Up," *His* 39 (April 1979): 9–14.

Lutherans

3397. Bredehoft, David. "Divorce and the Child," *Lutheran Education*, vol. 114, no. 4 (1979): 224–30.

Methodists

3398. Brubaker, Ellen A. "When Family Life Changes," *Accent on Youth* 11 (May 1979): 3–5.

3399. Carr, Jo. "My Own Parents—Divorced?" *Accent on Youth* 9 (November 1976): 8 + .

3400. Jeffrey, Shirley H. "Focus: The Single Parent—How Do the Children Fare?" *Christian Home* 10 (October 1977): 25 + .

3401. ———. "Nothing but the Truth," *Christian Home* 12 (September 1979): 22.

3402. Oden, Marilyn B. "The Nullified Nest When Parents Part," *Christian Home* 10 (February 1978): 8–10.

Seventh Day Adventists

3403. Dobson, James C. "Attitudes toward Motherhood," *Life and Health* 92 (May 1977): 30–31.

3404. Holbrook, Betty. "Melissa Has Two—Again," *Advent Review and Sabbath Herald* 154 (November 24, 1977): 11.

Southern Baptists

3405. Kavanaugh, Karen. "Dear Diary: Maybe He's My Father," *Home Life* 28 (June 1974): 12.

3406. McCroskey, Doris. "If Your Child's Marriage Should Fail," *Home Life* 31 (July 1977): 34–36.

3407. Thompson, Dorothy K. "Youth and Today's Issues: Divorce—Alone in the Middle," *Youth Leadership* 8 (October 1977): 38–41.

3408. Williams, Nelda. "The Children of Divorce: Patterns for Ministry," *Children's Leadership* 9 (January–March 1979): 17–18.

3409. Wooldridge, Barbara. "Children Are Not Possessions," *Home Life* 33 (January 1979): 12–13.

Roman Catholics

3410. Cargill, Joan. "Understanding the One-Parent Child in the Classroom," *Living Light* 13 (Winter 1976): 599–600.

3411. Drinan, Robert F. "Children's Rights," *America* 122 (January 10, 1970): 4–5.

3412. Young, James J. "The Religious Educator and the Children of Divorce," *Living Light* 13 (Winter 1976): 588–98.

DIVORCE

3413. Bontrager, G. Edwin. *Divorce and the Faithful Church*. Scottdale, PA: Herald Press, 1978.

3414. Carroll, Anne K. *From the Brink of Divorce: How to Save Your Marriage*. Garden City, NY: Doubleday, 1978.

3415. "A Few Show Reservations on Divorce," *National Catholic Reporter* 10 (September 13, 1974): 5.

3416. "Loving Gesture; Religion," *Economist* 263 (May 14, 1977): 47–48.

3417. McCarthy James. "Religious Commitment, Affiliation, and Marriage Dissolution." In *The Religious Dimension: New Directions in Quantitative Research,* edited by Robert Wuthnow, pp. 179–97. New York: Academic Press, 1979. R.

3418. Meyer, D. Eugene. "Avoid Divorce and Have Stories with Happy Endings," *Religious Humanism,* vol. 7, no. 4 (1973): 177–78.

3419. Rosenthal, Erich. "Divorce and Religious Intermarriage: The Effect of Previous Marital Status upon Subsequent Marital Behavior," *Journal of Marriage and the Family,* vol. 32, no. 3 (1970): 435–40. R.

3420. Shivanandan, Mary. "Fidelity, the Forgotten Virtue," *Marriage and Family Living* 59 (November 1977): 1–4.

3421. Shrum, Wesley. "Religion and Marital Instability: A Change in the 1970s?" *Review of Religious Research,* vol. 21, no. 2 (1980): 135–47. R.

3422. Walker, Joyce W. *Divorce: How to Prevent or Survive It*. Bountiful, UT: Horizon Publishers, 1976.

3423. Weinglass, Janet; Kressel, Kenneth; and Deutsch, Morton. "The Role of the Clergy in Divorce: An Exploratory Survey," *Journal of Divorce,* vol. 2, no. 1 (1978): 57–82. R.

Church of Jesus Christ of Latter-Day Saints

3424. Cullimore, James A. "What Happens When a Couple Gets a Temple Divorce," *New Era* 5 (December 1975): 14–15.

3425. "Divorce Insurance," *Church News* 43 (February 3, 1973): 16.

3426. "A Family in Heaven," *Church News* 44 (June 8, 1974): 16.

3427. Faust, James E. "The Enriching of Marriage," *Ensign of the Church of Jesus Christ of Latter-Day Saints* 7 (November 1977): 9–11.

3428. Hoopes, Margaret H. "Alone through Divorce," *Ensign of the Church of Jesus Christ of Latter-Day Saints* 2 (November 1972): 52–55.

3429. Kimball, Spencer W. *Marriage.* Salt Lake City, UT: Deseret Book Co., 1978.

3430. ———. *Marriage and Divorce: An Address.* Salt Lake City, UT: Deseret Book Co., 1976.

3431. ———. "The Time to Labor Is Now," *Ensign of the Church of Jesus Christ of Latter-Day Saints* 5 (November 1975): 4–6.

3432. Lee, Harold B. "President Harold B. Lee's General Priesthood Address," *Ensign of the Church of Jesus Christ of Latter-Day Saints* 4 (January 1974): 96–101.

3433. Taylor, Henry D. "Divorce Clearances for those Married in the Temple and Divorced Civilly," *Ensign of the Church of Jesus Christ of Latter-Day Saints* 6 (February 1976): 34–35.

3434. "Those Broken Homes," *Church News* 43 (November 3, 1973): 16.

Eastern Orthodox

3435. Larentzakis, Gregor. "Marriage, Divorce and Remarriage in the Orthodox Church," *Theology Digest,* vol. 26, no. 3 (1978): 232–34.

3436. Maloney, George A. "Catholicism, Orthodoxy and Divorce," *Diakonia,* vol. 7, no. 4 (1972): 297–300.

3437. ———. "Oeconomia: A Corrective to Law," *Catholic Lawyer,* vol. 17, no. 2 (1971): 90–109.

3438. Melia, Elias. "Divorce in the Orthodox Church," *Diakonia,* vol. 10, no. 3 (1975): 280–82.

3439. Patsavos, Lewis J. "The Orthodox Position on Divorce," *Diakonia,* vol. 5, no. 1 (1970): 4–15.

3440. ———. "The Orthodox Position on Divorce." In *Ministering to the Divorced Catholic,* edited by James J. Young, pp. 51–61. New York: Paulist Press, 1979.

Jewish

3441. Bulka, Reuven P. "Divorce: The Problem and the Challenge," *Tradition,* vol. 16, no. 1 (1976): 127–33.

3442. Fields, Sidney. "The Beth Din in Action," *Jewish Digest* 23 (February 1978): 57–59.

3443. Fisher, Jerry. "Rap Session," *Keeping Posted—Union of Hebrew Congregations,* vol. 20, no. 7 (1975): 21–23.

3444. Greenberg, Blu. "Jewish Divorce Law: If We Must Part Let's Part as Equals," *Lilith,* vol. 1, no. 3 (1977): 26–29.

3445. Greenberg, Simon. "And He Writes Her a Bill of Divorcement," *Conservative Judaism,* vol. 24, no. 3 (1970): 75–141.

3446. Haut, Irwin H. "A Problem in Jewish Divorce Law: An Analysis and Some Suggestions," *Tradition,* vol. 16, no. 3 (1977): 29–49; no. 5 (1977): 191–94.

3447. Landes, Aaron. "The Open Forum: The Ante-nuptial Agreement," *Conservative Judaism,* vol. 26, no. 3 (1972): 61–63.

3448. Lang, Judith. "Divorce and the Jewish Woman: A Family Agency Approach," *Journal of Jewish Communal Service,* vol. 54, no. 3 (1978): 220–28.

3449. Lipman, Eugene F. "The Rabbi and Divorce," *Central Conference of American Rabbis,* vol. 24, no. 4 (1977): 29–34.

3450. Maller, Allen S. "Jewish-Gentile Divorce in California," *Jewish Social Studies,* vol. 37, no. 3–4 (1975): 279–90. R.

3451. ———. "A Religious Perspective on Divorce," *Journal of Jewish Communal Services,* vol. 55, no. 2 (1978): 192–94.

3452. Meislin, Bernard J. "Jewish Divorce in American Courts," *Journal of Family Law,* vol. 16, no. 1 (1978): 19–35.

3453. Rabinowitz, Stanley. "The Megillah and the Get," *Conservative Judaism,* vol. 26, no. 3 (1972): 64–69.

3454. Raphael, Marc L. "To Be Jewish and Divorced in Columbus, Ohio," *Jewish Spectator* 41 (Winter 1976): 58–60.

3455. Rayner, John D. "Divorce—Jewish Style," *Jewish Digest* vol. 15, no. 8 (1970): 29–32.

3456. Schecter, Martha J. "Civil Enforcement of the Jewish Marriage Contract," *Journal of Family Law,* vol. 9, no. 4 (1970): 425–32.

3457. Sorosky, Arthur D. "Family Disintegration and the Role of the Paraprofessional in the Synagogue," *Reconstructionist* 42 (December 1976): 18–28.

3458. Stickman, H. Norman. "A Note on the Text of Babylonian Talmud Git. 6a," *Jewish Quarterly Review,* vol. 66, no. 3 (1976): 173–75.

3459. Wenham, Gordon J. "The Restoration of Marriage Reconsidered," *Journal of Jewish Studies,* vol. 30, no. 1 (1979): 36–40.

Protestants

3460. Arnold, William V., et al. *Divorce: Prevention or Survival.* Philadelphia, PA: Westminster Press, 1977.

3461. Avakian, Spurgeon. "Divorce—California Style," *Presbyterian Life,* vol. 23, no. 11 (1970): 11–15.

3462. Barnwell, William. "Gays and the Divorced: Similar Scars," *Christian Century* 95 (January 4, 1978): 29–30.

3463. Becker, Russell J. *When Marriage Ends.* Philadelphia, PA: Fortress Press, 1971.

3464. Hudson, Robert L. *"Til Divorce Do Us Part"; A Christian Looks at Divorce.* Nashville, TN: Thomas Nelson, 1973.

3465. Oglesby, William B., Jr. "Divorce and Remarriage in Christian Perspective," *Pastoral Psychology,* vol. 25, no. 4 (1977): 282–93.

3466. Olshewsky, Thomas M. "A Christian Understanding of Divorce," *Journal of Religious Ethics,* vol. 7, no. 1 (1979): 117–38.

3467. Peppler, Alice S. *Divorced and Christian.* St. Louis, MO: Concordia Publishing House, 1974.

3468. Schaper, Donna. "Marriage: The Impossible Commitment?" *Christian Century* 96 (June 20, 1979): 669–72.

3469. Vayhinger, John M. *Before Divorce.* Philadelphia, PA: Fortress Press, 1971.

3470. Willimon, William H. "The Risk of Divorce," *Christian Century* 96 (June 20, 1979): 666–69.

Christian Reformed Church

3471. Smedes, Lewis B. "Divorce: An Ethical Response," *The Reformed Journal* 26 (October 1976): 10–13.

Church of God

3472. Sterner, R. Eugene. "On Marriage and Divorce," *Vital Christianity* 95 (August 24, 1975): 2–3.

3473. Withrow, Oral C. "Divorce Is a Sad Thing," *Vital Christianity* 93 (April 29, 1973): 5–6; and 93 (May 13, 1973): 9–11.

Church of the Brethern

3474. Berkebile, James M. "Here I Stand," *Brethern Life* 21 (Summer 1976): 160–64.

3475. Gibble, Kenneth L. "Divorce, Remarriage and the Good News," *Brethern Life* 21 (Summer 1976): 151–55.

3476. Roop, Eugene E., et al. "Symposium on Divorce and Remarriage," *Brethern Life* 21 (Summer 1976): 133–64.

3477. ———. "Two Become One Become Two," *Brethern Life* 21 (Summer 1970): 133–37.

3478. Wilson, Leland. "Living in Sin," *Brethern Life* 21 (Summer 1976): 147–51.

3479. Zunkel, C. Wayne. "Can a Divorce Be Forgiven?" *Brethern Life* 21 (Summer 1976): 155–59.

Episcopal

3480. Edwards, O. C., Jr., and Holmes, U. T., III. "Marriage and Mating: Creation, Society and Jesus," *Anglican Theological Review, Supplementary Series* 2 (September 1973): 4–27.

Evangelical

3481. Bustanoby, Andre. *But I Didn't Want a Divorce: Putting Your Life Back Together.* Grand Rapids, MI: Zondervan Publishing House, 1978.

3482. Cerling, C. E., Jr. "When Love Fails; Consultation on Divorce and Remarriage Meeting," *Christianity Today* 21 (November 19, 1976): 54–55.

3483. "Divorce and Christian Ethics," (editorial), *Presbyterian Journal* 35 (November 24, 1976): 12.

3484. "Divorce and Remarriage" (editorial), *Christianity Today* 33 (May 25, 1979): 8–9.

3485. "Divorces Unlimited," *Presbyterian Journal* vol. 34, no. 18 (1975): 10–11.

3486. Ellis, Paul N. "Divorce: The Dilemma of Discipline," *Wesleyan Advocate* (May 26, 1975): 11.

3487. Ellisen, Stanley A. *Divorce and Remarriage in the Church.* Grand Rapids, MI: Zondervan Publishing House, 1977.

3488. Franke, Carl W. "Must We Be Legalistic about Divorce? *Christian Herald,* vol. 95, no. 2 (1972): 37–38.

3489. Gay, Arthur. "Restoring the Divorced Christian," *United Evangelical Action,* vol. 37, no. 1 (1978): 15–17.

3490. "The Growing Divorce Blight" (editorial), *Presbyterian Journal* 35 (September 1, 1976): 12.

3491. Halverson, Richard. "No Spiritual Grounds for Divorce," *Good News Broadcaster* 32 (March 1974): 11.

3492. Leggett, Marshall J. "The Christian and Divorce," *Christian Standard* 111 (November 21, 1976): 4–6.

3493. Lloyd, Ann. *The Divorce Syndrome.* New York: Manor Books, 1977.

3494. McKenna, David L. "In the World," *United Evangelical Action,* vol. 31, no. 2 (1972): 4–5+.

3495. Martin, Norma, and Levitt, Zola. *Divorce: A Christian Dilemma.* Scottdale, PA: Herald Press, 1977.

3496. Meier, Paul D. "Divorce Is Never Necessary," *United Evangelical Action* 34 (Fall 1975): 15–17.

3497. ———. "Is Divorce Ever Necessary?" *Christian Medical Society Journal* 7 (Winter 1976): 2–8.

3498. Petri, Darlene. *The Hurt and Healing of Divorce.* Elgin, IL: David C. Cook Publishing Co., 1976.

3499. Ramm, Bernard L. "Survey of Church Views on Divorce," *Eternity,* vol. 27, no. 6 (1976): 51–52.

3500. Saucy, Robert L. "Husband of One Wife," *Bibliotheca Sacra* 131 (July–September 1974): 229–240.

3501. Shank, J. Ward. "Divorce—Don't Beg the Issue," *Presbyterian Journal* 34 (September 10, 1975): 9–10.

3502. Shaw, Jean. "Divorce in the Church: A Five Act Play," *Eternity* 27 (June 1976): 13.

3503. Smedes, Lewis B. "Infidelity, Marriage and Divorce," *Christian Heritage* 38 (March 1977): 4–7+.

3504. Smith, Bruce L. "Till Death Us Do Part?" *Christianity Today,* vol. 14, no. 8 (1970): 5–10.

3505. Smith, Chuck. "Advice on Divorce," *Christian Life* 39 (June 1977): 19+.

3506. [Smith, Helen.] *Divorce and Remarriage . . .* [Huger, SC: 1974?]

3507. Spooner, A Boyce. "Solomon's Sword," *Presbyterian Life,* vol. 34, no. 50 (1976): 10+.

3508. Woodson, Leslie H. *Divorce and the Gospel of Grace.* Waco, TX: Word Books, 1979.

Lutheran

3509. Brett, Wesley E. "A Survey of the Concept of Marriage, Divorce, and Remarriage in the Writings of Martin Luther." Master's thesis, Wake Forest University, 1978. R.

3510. Schmidt, Katherine. "Divorce—Where Do We Go from Here?" *Lutheran Witness,* vol. 95, no. 6 (1976): 8–9.

3511. Scott, Karen. "Is There Life After Divorce?" *Lutheran,* vol. 10, no. 14 (1972): 11–14.

Mennonite

3512. Dick, LaVernae J. "The Question of Divorce," *Mennonite* 92 (November 29, 1977): 702.

3513. "How Mennonite Churches Handle Divorce and Remarriage," *Christian Living* 25 (July 1978): 4–7.

Methodist

3514. Barringer, Kenneth D. "The Successful Divorce," *Christian Home* vol. 5, no. 5 (1974): 35+.

3515. Cannon, Melissa. "To Stand Alone," *Face to Face,* vol. 5, no. 11 (1973): 12–20.

3516. Crady, Luther, Jr. "Divorce as Treatment," *Christian Home* (April 1978): 24–25.

3517. Evans, David S. "Do Sex Issues Cause Divorce?" *Engage/Social Action,* vol. 3, no. 5 (1975): 23.

3518. ———. "Marriage or Divorce," *Christian Action,* vol. 3, no. 10 (1971): 33–36.

3519. Hickman, Hoyt L. "Worship and the Challenge of Change," *Circuit Rider,* vol. 1, no. 1 (1976–77): 3+.

3520. Mace, David R. "Divorce, New Style," *Christian Home* 9 (January 1977): 26.

3521. Peak, Lynda. "Married no More; What Now?" *Together,* vol. 15, no. 6 (1971): 18.

3522. Ramsey, James L. "Some Understandings about Divorce," *Cross/Talk,* vol. 5, no. 2, pt. 9 (1976):.

Nazarene

3523. Parrott, Leslie. "The Alternative to Divorce," *Herald of Holiness* 59 (November 11, 1970): 6–7.

3524. Reed, Gerald. "For Better, for Worse," *Herald of Holiness* 61 (February 16, 1972): 4–5.

Pentecostal

3525. Cox, W. O. "Is Divorce the Answer?" *Pentecostal Evangel* 3149 (September 15, 1974): 6–7.

3526. Ward, C. M. "Divorce Is not the Answer," *Pentecostal Evangel* 3193 (July 20, 1975): 6–7.

Reformed Church In America

3527. Boyd, Mary. "Whom God Has Joined Together," *Church Herald* 29 (December 29, 1972): 11.

3528. "I'm Glad I Didn't Get a Divorce," *Church Herald* 34 (April 29, 1977): 15–16.

Seventh Day Adventist

3529. "Annual Council Passes Action on Conciliation, Divorce, and Remarriage," *Advent Review and Sabbath Herald* 154 (February 17, 1977): 12–18.

3530. Barton, Kaye. "How to Save a Marriage," *Insight* 7 (November 16, 1976): 4–9.

3531. Bradley, W. P. "Honor between the Sexes," *Sabbath School Lesson Quarterly* 327 (January 1977): 64–71.

3532. Campbell, Alma L. "The 'I' in Divorce," *Advent Review and Sabbath Herald* 153 (August 12, 1976): 10–11.

3533. Earle, George R. "Marriage—Endless Happiness?" *Message Magazine* 42 (November 1976): 4–7.

3534. Fordham, W. W. "Sour Marriage," *Message Magazine,* vol. 38, no. 4 (1972): 17–19.

3535. Hoehn, G. H. "Fewer Divorces" (letter to the editor), *Advent Review and Sabbath Herald* 154 (November 17, 1977): 11.

3536. Jewett, Richard. "Is Divorce the Only Solution?" *These Times* 86 (March 1977): 23.

3537. Lamp, Herschel C. "Divorce and Remarriage" (letter to the editor), *Advent Review and Sabbath Herald* 154 (April 21, 1977): 12.

3538. Maxwell, Mervyn. "May a Bible Christian Get a Divorce?" *Signs of the Times* 99 (January 1972): 24.

3539. ———. "Should I Get a Divorce?" *Signs of the Times* 99 (February 1972): 29.

3540. Moore, Marvin. "Divorce, Remarriage and Church Discipline," *Spectrum* 10 (May 1979): 20–22.

3541. Neff, David, and Neff, LaVonne. "Marriage and Divorce as Jesus Saw Them," *These Times,* vol. 81, no. 7 (1972): 3–6.

3542. Ray, LaVon. "The 'Other Man' Every Wife Needs," *Advent Review and Sabbath Herald* 152 (July 3, 1975): 16–17.

3543. Reynolds, Louis B. "Divorce Is Never the Perfect Answer," *Life and Health,* vol. 87, no. 2 (1972): 18–19 +.

3544. Scragg, Walter R. L. "The Inside Outsiders," *Advent Review and Sabbath Herald* 154 (February 10, 1977): 10.

3545. Shryock, Harold. "Aftermath of Divorce," *Life and Health,* vol. 86, no. 8 (1971): 24–25.

3546. Wilson, Neal C. ["Comment on Annual Council Actions on Divorce, Remarriage and Church Membership."] *Advent Review and Sabbath Herald* 154 (February 17, 1977): 18–19.

3547. Winslow, Gerald. "Divorce, Remarriage and Adultery," *Spectrum* 7 (Summer 1975): 2–11.

Southern Baptist

3548. Barnard, Everett. "Factors Causing Divorce," *Adult Leadership* 2 (May 1972): 10–11.

3549. Bloskas, John D. "The High Cost of Divorce," *Home Life* 33 (March 1979): 20–22.

3550. Burns, Robert J. "Divorce and Remarriage: A Pastoral Perspective." Master of Theology thesis, Southeastern Baptist Theological Seminary, 1972.

3551. Drakeford, John W. "When Marriage Is Terminated," *Home Life* 29 (May 1975): 32–33.

3552. Hunter, Laura. "What Do You Do with the Pictures?" *Home Life* 32 (August 1978): 26–27.

3553. "Is There Still Time?" *Home Life* 24 (July 1970): 10–+.

3554. Knight, George W. "The Question of Divorce" (editorial), *Home Life* 31 (July 1977): 4.

3555. McAlister, Cecil M. "Why So Many Divorces?" *Home Life* 33 (September 1979): 44–46.

3556. Madden, Myron C. "Divorce or Not?" (letter to the editor), *Home Life* 28 (August 1974): 18.

3557. Petty Charles. "Current Attitudes and Practices of Southern Baptists regarding Divorce." Ph.D. diss., Southwestern Baptist Theological Seminary, 1970. R.

3558. Pinson, William M., Jr. "Divorce in Jesus' Day," *Sunday School Lesson Illustrator,* vol. 2, no. 1 (1976): 10–12.

3559. Rowatt, G. Wade. "Divorce: An Open Perspective for the Church," *Review and Expositor* 74 (January 1977): 51–61.

Worldwide Church of God

3560. Armstrong, Herbert. "Alarming Rise in Divorce Poses Major Threat to U.S. and Western World," *Plain Truth* 38 (November 1973): 1 +.

3561. Parnell, Patrick A. ". . . Till Divorce Do Us Part," *Plain Truth* 39 (May 1974): 8–11.

Roman Catholic

3562. Abad Salvador, Federico. *Problematica del Divorcio en Puerto Rico.* Guadalajara, Spain: Editorial OPE, 1971.

3563. Berry, Newton. "Portrait of a Family Conservationist," *Marriage and Family Living* 60 (October 1978): 10–13.

3564. Bevilacqua, Anthony J. "ERA in Debate—What Can It Mean for Church Law?" *Catholic Lawyer,* vol. 24, no. 2 (1979): 117–26.

3565. "Bishops Won't Oppose No-Fault Reform," *National Catholic Reporter* 10 (March 15, 1974): 13.

3566. Bosco, Antoinette. "Divorce and Remarriage," *Catholic Mind,* vol. 70, no. 1264 (1972): 41–47.

3567. ———. "Explosive New Interpretation of Divorce and Remarriage," *Marriage and Family Living,* vol. 54, no. 1 (1972): 2–11.

3568. Breen, Joseph. "Church Divorce Laws: They Don't Make Sense," *U.S. Catholic,* vol. 41, no. 1 (1976): 30–31.

3569. Breig, James. "Divorce: The Issue That Hits Home," *Our Sunday Visitor Magazine* 67 (October 15, 1978): 8–9; 67 (October 22, 1978): 16–17; 67 (October 29, 1978): 4–5; 67 (November 5, 1978): 3 + ; 67 (November 12, 1978): 6–7; 67 (November 19, 1978): 16–17 + .

3570. "Christians Divorced and Remarried," *IDOC International* 5 (June 13, 1970): 48–52.

3571. Coleman, Gerald D. "Pastoral Theology and Divorce," *American Ecclesiastical Review* 169 (April 1975): 256–69.

3572. Conroy, Donald B. "The Statistics and Crisis of Divorce," *Living Light* 13 (Winter 1976): 547–52.

3573. Curran, Charles E. "Divorce and Remarriage: Two Signs of the Times," *National Catholic Reporter* 10 (October 18, 1974): 7 + .

3574. ———. "Divorce: Catholic Theory and Practice in the U.S." *American Ecclesiastical Review*, vol. 168, no. 1 (1974): 3–34; no. 2 (1974): 75–95.

3575. ———. "The Gospel and Culture: Christian Marriage and Divorce Today," *Social Thought*, vol. 2, no. 1 (1976): 9–28.

3576. ———. *New Perspectives in Moral Theology.* Notre Dame, IN: University of Notre Dame Press, 1974.

3577. Davis, Charles. "When Two Persons Divorce, One Usually Gets Hurt," *National Catholic Reporter* 8 (March 24, 1972): 7.

3578. Delooz, Pierre. "The Western Family, a Prospective Evaluation," *Cross Currents* 23 (Winter 1974): 419–35.

3579. DeRanitz, Richard. "Should the Roman Church Recognize Divorce?" *Listening* 6 (Winter 1971): 60–70.

3580. "The Dissolution of Marriage in Favor of the Faith," *Jurist* 34 (Summer-Fall 1974): 418–23.

3581. "Divorced but Catholic," *National Catholic Reporter* 13 (October 22, 1976):12.

3582. "Divorce: Discipline and Compassion" (Editorial), *America* 139 (November 18, 1978): 345–46.

3583. "Divorce, Remarriage and the Catholic Bishop Tacey and Cardinal Krol," *Catholic Mind*, vol. 70, no. 1267 (1972): 5–9.

3584. Doherty, Dennis J. *Divorce and Remarriage: Resolving a Catholic Dilemma.* St. Meinrad, IN: Abbey Press, 1974.

3585. ———. "Divorced and Remarriage: Catholics and Credibility," *Catholic Theological Society of America Proceedings* 30 (1975): 121–28.

3586. Dunigan, Vincent. "Catholics Rethink the Unthinkable, the Divorced and Remarried," *Priest*, vol. 31, no. 7–8 (1975): 20–23.

3587. Durkin, Mary G., and Hitchcock, James. *Divorce.* Chicago: Thomas More Press, 1979.

3588. "Excommunication Tag Lifted from Divorced," *National Catholic Reporter* 13 (May 13, 1977): 3.

3589. Farley, Leo C., and Reich, Warren T. "Toward 'An Immediate Internal Forum Solution' for Deserving Couples in Canonically Insolvable Marriage Cases," *Jurist* 30 (January 30): 45–74.

3590. Farley, Margaret. "Society and Ethics: Divorce and Remarriage," *Catholic Theological Society of America Proceedings* 30 (1975): 111–19.

3591. Fehren, Henry. "Consider the Sparrow," *U.S. Catholic* 43 (August 1978): 41–43.

3592. Fogarty, Gerald P. "Historical Origin of the Excommunications of Divorce and Remarried Catholics Imposed by the Third Plenary Council of Baltimore," *Jurist*, vol. 38, no. 3–4 (1978): 426–33.

3593. Foley, Leonard. "What Divorced Catholics Are Saying," *St. Anthony Messinger* 83 (July 1975): 28–33.

3594. Gaffney, James. "Marriage and Divorce," *New Catholic World* 222 (January–February 1979): 20–23.

3595. Gallagher, Charles. "Divorce," *Our Sunday Visitor* 66 (July 10, 1977): 14.

3596. ———. "A Note of Recognition: To Those Who Are Divorced and Have Chosen not to Remarry," *Our Sunday Visitor* 65 (February 25, 1977): 11.

3597. ———. "The Tragedy of Divorce," *Our Sunday Visitor* 66 (August 21, 1977): 13.

3598. Gerhartz, Johannes G. "Can the Church Dissolve Sacramental Marriages?" *Theology Digest*, vol. 21, no. 1 (1973): 28–32.

3599. Gibeau, Dawn. "Curran Supports Change in Teaching on Divorce," *National Catholic Reporter* 10 (October 18, 1974): 1 + .

3600. Graham, George P. "Catholics, Divorce and Annulment," *USA Today* 107 (January 1979): 47–48.

3601. Greeley, Andrew M. "The Sexual Revolution among Catholic Clergy," *Review of Religious Research*, vol. 14, no. 2 (1973): 91–100. R.

3602. Guentert, Kenneth. "A Tough and Tender Solution for Divorced Catholics," *U.S. Catholic*, vol. 41, no. 12 (1976): 12–13.

3603. Haughey, John. "Can Anyone Say Forever?" *New Catholic World*, vol. 218, no. 1304 (1975): 65–68.

3604. Heffernan, Virginia A. "Divorce and Remarriage in the Contemporary United States," *International Catholic Review: Communio*, vol. 1, no. 3 (1974): 285–92.

3605. Hertel, James R. "Divorce and Remarriage," *St. Anthony Messenger*, vol. 80, no. 11 (1973): 8–12.

3606. Hitchcock, James. "Family Values and Moral Revisionism," *International Catholic Review: Communio*, vol. 1, no. 3 (1974): 309–16.

3607. Kaler, Patrick. "Has the Church Gone Soft on Divorce?" *Liguorian* 66 (June 1978): 53–58.

3608. Kelleher, Stephen J. *Divorce and Remarriage for Catholics?* Garden City, NY: Doubleday, 1973.

3609. ———. "Intolerable Marriage: Ten Years Later, Looking Back, Looking Ahead," *America* 139 (November 18, 1978): 355-57.

3610. ———. "The Laity, Divorce and Remarriage," *Commonweal* 102 (November 7, 1975): 521–24.

3611. Kelly, William. *Pope Gregory II on Divorce and Remarriage.* Rome: Universita Gregoriana, 1976.

3612. Knox, L. Mason. "Divorce in the Roman Catholic Church: An Ecumenical Evaluation," *American Ecclesiastical Review* 16 (May 1975): 342–58.

3613. McCarron, Gerald J. "Divorce and the Catholic Church," *Journal of Religion and Health*, vol. 14, no. 2 (1975): 113–19.

3614. McCormick, Richard A. "Divorce and Remarriage," *Catholic Mind* 73 (November 1975): 42–57.

3615. ———. "Divorce and Remarriage; Notes on Moral Theology," *Theological Studies*, vol. 36, no. 1 (1975): 100–17.

3616. ———. "Notes on Moral Theology: April–September, 1970," *Theological Studies,* vol. 32, no. 1 (1971): 107–22.

3617. McHale, John. "Divorce," *Marriage and Family Living,* vol. 56, no. 9 (1974): 32.

3618. McHugh, James T. "No-Fault Divorce," *Jurist* 5 (Winter 1975): 17–31.

3619. ———. "No-Fault Divorce Laws: An Overview and Critique," *Jurist* 32 (Spring 1972): 266–72.

3620. McMahon, Mary S. "Can you Afford a Divorce?" *Liguorian* 62 (March 1974): 23–25.

3621. Martelet, Gustave. "Christological Theses on the Sacrament of Marriage," *Origins* 8 (September 14, 1978): 200–04.

3622. May, William E. "Marriage, Divorce, and Remarriage," *Jurist* 37 (Summer–Fall 1977): 266–86.

3623. O'Brien, Patricia. "Divorce Is a Scream: Reprint from *Chicago Sun-Times,*" *U.S. Catholic,* vol. 40, no. 10 (1975): 37.

3624. O'Callaghan, Denis. "Annulment versus Divorce," *Furrow* 27 (September 1976): 525–30.

3625. O'Meara, Frank. "Why Moral Theologians Are Wishy-Washy," *U.S. Catholic,* vol. 40, no. 8 (1975): 37–39.

3626. Palmer, Paul F. "When a Marriage Dies," *America,* vol. 132, no. 7 (1975): 126–28.

3627. Pantoga, Fritzie. "Broken Marriages: Picking Up the Pieces," *U.S. Catholic,* vol. 42, no. 7 (1977): 6–10.

3628. Pellegrino, M. "Cardinal Pellegrino of Turin Makes Statements on Divorce," *L'Osservatore Romano* (English edition) 96 (January 29, 1970): 10.

3629. Perry, Joseph N. "Teenage Marriages: What the Church Is Doing," *Living Light* 13 (Winter 1976): 553–59.

3630. Peter, Val J. "Divorce and Remarriage," *International Catholic Review: Communio,* vol. 3, no. 1 (1974): 261–74.

3631. "The Pontifical Document on Marriage Cases," *L'Osservatore Romano* (English edition) 170 (July 1, 1971): 11.

3632. Provost, James. "Divorced and Remarried Catholics," *Chicago Studies,* vol. 14, no. 2 (1975): 218–224.

3633. Rashke, Richard. "Can the Church Cope with the 'New' Family?" *New Catholic World,* vol. 218, no. 1306 (1975): 148–52.

3634. Ratner, Helen. "Divorce and Remarriage," *America,* vol. 129, no. 10 (1973): 245.

3635. Riga, Peter J. "Divorce and Remarriage in the Catholic Church," *U.S. Catholic,* vol. 38, no. 3 (1973): 18–20.

3636. Rue, James J. "Divorce and Remarriage," *Liguorian* 64 (July 1976): 43–45.

3637. Rue, James J., and Shanahan, Louise. *A Catechism for Divorced Catholics.* Chicago: Franciscan Herald Press, 1978.

3638. ———. *The Limbo World of the Divorced.* Chicago: Franciscan Herald Press, 1979.

3639. Sattler, Henry V. "Divorce and Remarriage in the Church," *American Ecclesiastical Review,* vol. 167, no. 8 (1973): 553–73.

3640. Savitsky, Charles, Jr. " 'Catholic Family Can Survive' Is Priest's Message of Hope." *Our Sunday Visitor* 67 (March 4, 1979): 1.

3641. Shepherd, Herman (pseudonym). "Should There Be 'Amnesty' for Divorced Catholics?" *Our Sunday Visitor* 1975, 64 (June 22, 1975): 1 + .

3642. Toolan, David S. "Divorce and Remarriage," *Commonweal,* vol. 98, no. 2 (1973–74): 503–05.

3643. Tracy, Robert E., and Krol, John. "Divorce, Remarriage and the Catholic: Two Statements," *Catholic Mind,* vol. 70, no. 1267 (1972): 5–8.

3644. True, Michael, and Young, James. "Divorce and Remarriage," *Commonweal,* vol. 101, no. 7 (1974): 185–90.

3645. "What Did the Bishops Decide about Divorce and Remarriage?" *Origins* 7 (June 16, 1977): 56.

3646. Whelan, Charles M. "Divorced Catholics: A Proposal," *America* 131 (December 7, 1974): 363–65; (discussion) 131 (December 7, 1974): 362; (letter to the editor) 132 (January 11, 1975): 12–14; (letter to the editor) 132 (March 15, 1975): 182.

3647. Wieser, Francis. "Divorce, Remarriage and the Sacraments," *Catholic Mind,* vol. 69, no. 1251 (1971): 34–38.

3648. Winiarski, Mark. "Divorce, Remarriage Woes Vex U.S. Church," *National Catholic Reporter* 15 (December 29, 1978): 1 + .

3649. Wrenn, Lawrence G., ed. *Divorce and Remarriage in the Catholic Church.* New York: Newman Press, 1973.

3650. ———. "It's Unbelievable, yet I Believe it," *National Catholic Reporter* 7 (June 11, 1971): 5–A.

3651. Young, James J. "Divorce: A Window on Today's Family," *Origins* 7 (November 17, 1977): 344–49.

3652. ———. "Divorced Catholics Are Surviving," *New Catholic World* 218 (July-August 1975): 174–77.

3653. ———. "Divorce in Contemporary Church and Society," *Urban and Social Change Review,* vol. 10, no. 1 (1977): 26–27.

3654. ———. "Six Factors in a Climate of Change," *America* 139 (November 18, 1978): 347–51.

3655. ———. "Wanted: Amnesty for Divorced Catholics," *U.S. Catholic,* vol. 49, no. 6 (1975): 13–14.

DIVORCED CLERGY

Protestant

Christian Reformed Church

3656. Myers, Allen. "Divorce—A Personal Perspective," *The Reformed Journal,* vol. 26, no. 4 (1976): 17–19.

Evangelical

3657. Adams, Jay. "Divorced Clergy" (letter to the editor), *Presbyterian Journal* 37 (February 28, 1979): 18–19.

3658. Bouma, Mary L. *Divorce in the Parsonage.* Minneapolis, MN: Bethany Fellowship, 1979.

3659. Callen, Barry L. "Love—No Matter What," *Vital Christianity* 97 (June 12, 1977): 11.

3660. "The Divorce Dilemma: A Symposium," *Logos Journal,* vol. 8, no. 6 (1978): 17–29.

3661. Galloway, Dale E. *Dream a New Dream: How to Rebuild a Broken Life.* Wheaton, IL: Tyndale House Publishers, 1975.

Lutheran

3662. Braaten, Carl E. "Sex, Marriage, and the Clergy," *Dialog,* vol. 18, no. 3 (1979): 169–74.

3663. Jordahl, Leigh. "Another Word on Clerical Divorce and Remarriage," *Dialog,* vol. 15, no. 3 (1976): 222–23.

3664. ———. "On Clerical Divorces," *Dialog,* vol. 14, no. 3 (1975): 223–25.

3665. Stickley, William. "On Divorced Clergy, a Response," *Dialog,* vol. 15, no. 2 (1976): 148–49.

Methodists

3666. "Bishops Take Concerned Stance on Clergy Divorce," *United Methodist Newscope* 6 (April 7, 1978): 1.

3667. "Bishops Urged Not to Treat Divorce Lightly," *United Methodist Newscope* 6 (March 31, 1978): 3.

3668. Cauthen, William H. "Divorce in the Clergy of an Annual Conference of the United Methodist Church." D.Min. diss., Candler School of Theology, Emory University, 1979. R.

3669. "Committee Asks Bishops for Divorce Session," *United Methodist Newscope,* vol. 44, no. 5 (1977): 1.

3670. Gilbert, Douglass W. "A Broken Vessel and God's Grace," *Circuit Rider* 3 (February 1979): 6.

3671. Henzlik, William C. "Divorce and the Appointment System," *Today's Ministry,* vol. 2, no. 3 (1975): 72–75.

3672. "I'm a Divorced Minister," *Faith/at/Work* 91 (April 1978): 32–34.

3673. Lowder, Paul D. "Forgivable Sin: Clergy Divorce," *Circuit Rider* 3 (February 1979): 8 + .

3674. Minehart, Gordon. "Clergy Careers: Divorce and Appointments," *Circuit Rider* 2 (October 1977): 20–22.

3675. Snow, M. Lawrence. "Grace for Divorce," *Today's Ministry* 2 (March 1975): 76 + .

3676. White, C. Dale. "The Bishops Address Clergy Divorce," *Circuit Rider* 3 (June 1979): 19–20.

3677. ———. "If Your Pastor Gets a Divorce," *United Methodist Today,* vol. 2, no. 4 (1975): 21–25.

3678. Williams, Foster J. "Preventing Divorce in the Parsonage," *Today's Ministry,* vol. 2, no. 3 (1975): 68–71.

Presbyterian

3679. Hutchinson, Ira W., and Hutchison, Katherine R. "The Impact of Divorce upon Clergy Career Mobility," *Journal of Marriage and the Family,* vol. 41, no. 4 (1979): 847–55. R.

3680. Ruark, Katherine L. "Clergy Divorce and Subsequent Career Mobility," Ph.D. diss., Florida State University, 1977 (*DAI* 38/9A, p. 5746, order # 7801511). R.

Roman Catholic

3681. Winiarski, Mark. "Divorced Priests Can Be Rehabilitated," *National Catholic Reporter* 14 (September 1, 1978): 6.

DIVORCED PERSONS IN THE CHURCH

Church of Jesus Christ of Latter-Day Saints

3682. Anderson, Wayne J. *Alone, but Not Lonely: Thoughts for the Single, Widowed or Divorced Woman.* Salt Lake City, UT: Deseret Book Co., 1973.

3683. Christensen, John C. "A Descriptive Study of the Religious Differences between Divorced and Non-divorced Individuals." Ed.D. diss., Brigham Young University, 1978 (*DAI* 39/11A, p. 6996, order # 7911873). R.

Protestants

3684. Krebs, Richard. *Alone Again: A Christian Psychologist Offers Courage and Renewal to the Newly Widowed and Divorced.* Minneapolis, MN: Augsburg Publishing House, 1978.

Christian Reformed Church

3685. Claerbaut, David. "The Church and Divorced People," *The Reformed Journal,* vol. 27, no. 3 (1977): 13–15.

3686. Harmelink, Herman, III. "Divorce: A Pastor's View," *The Reformed Journal,* 27 (April 1977): 22–24.

Evangelicals

3687. Chase, Mary T. "A Plea for the Divorced," *Alliance Witness,* vol. 112, no. 14 (1977): 10.

3688. Crook, Roger H. *An Open Book to the Christian Divorcee.* Nashville, TN: Broadman Press, 1974.

3689. Davey, James. "Liberty for Some: Views on Divorced Persons by the Christian Missionary Alliance," *Christianity Today* 20 (June 4, 1976): 45.

3690. Hensley, John C. *Coping with Being Single Again.* Nashville, TN: Broadman Press, 1978.

3691. Larson, Philip M. "A Divorce Analysis: For Those Considering Divorce," *Church Management* 50 (November–December 1973): 15.

3692. Pentacost, Dorthy H. "The Divorcee," *Good News Broadcaster* 29 (April 1971): 18–19.

3693. Smoke, Jim. *Growing through Divorce.* Irvine, CA: Harvest House Publishers, 1976.

3694. Tompkins, Iverna, and Harrell, Irene B. *How to Be Happy in No Man's Land: A Book for Singles.* Plainfield, NJ: Logos International, 1975.

Methodists

3695. Holland, Ronald E. "Divorce as a Quest for Personal Power," *Circuit Rider* 1 (September 1977): 7–10.

3696. McClanahan, John H. "They're Getting a Divorce," *Contempo* 5 (November 1974): 12–14.

Southern Baptists

3697. Barnard, Everett. "Constructive Attitudes toward Divorced Persons," *Adult Leadership* 2 (June 1972) 14–15.

3698. Herring, Clyde L. "Dilemma: The Church and the Divorcee," *People* 2 (June 1972): 32–35.

3699. Pinder, Robert H. "Understanding the Divorced Person," *Adult Leadership* 5 (January 1975): 10–12.

3700. Potts, Nancy. "Helping Persons Going through Divorce," *Home Life* 31 (July 1977): 24–26.

3701. Ray, Rayburn W. "Marriage on the Rocks," *People* 1 (May 1971): 33–35 + .

3702. "What Is the Policy of Your Church concerning Ordaining as Deacons Men Who Are Divorced?" *Baptist Program* (March 1977): 27–28.

3703. Young, Amy R. *By Death or Divorce: It Hurts to Loose.* Denver, CO: Accent Books, 1976.

Roman Catholics

3704. Beifuss, Joan. "Sex and the Divorced Catholic," *National Catholic Reporter* 15 (May 25, 1979): 9 + .

3705. Casey, Rick. "Divorced Catholics out of the Closet," *National Catholic Reporter* 10 (November 2, 1973): 3–4.

3706. ———. "Divorced See Need to Rethink Marriage," *National Catholic Reporter* 9 (November 3, 1972): 1 + .

3707. Cosgrove, Thomas H. "What Divorced Catholics Need Most," *Liguorian* 61 (March 1973): 28–31.

3708. Edmonds, Patty. "Church Responding to Divorced Catholics," *National Catholic Reporter* 14 (October 28, 1977): 1 + .

3709. ———. "Divorced Catholics: Helping Those Who Help Themselves," *National Catholic Reporter* 13 (November 5, 1976): 1–2 + .

3710. Jackson, Lorraine D. "What My Divorce Did for Me," *Liguorian* 66 (September 1978): 48–51.

3711. Kelleher, Stephen J. "Divorced Catholics: Starting Fires in a Cold Church," *U.S. Catholic* 43 (June 1978): 6–12.

3712. Kern, Patricia. "The Divorced Catholic," *Our Sunday Visitor Magazine* 68 (May 6, 1979): 8–9; 68 (May 20, 1979): 8–10.

3713. McCarthy, Abigail. "The Displaced Homemaker," *Commonweal*, vol. 103, no. 2 (1976): 38 + .

3714. Marroni, E. "Factors Influencing the Adjustment of Separated or Divorced Catholics," Master's thesis, Norfolk State College, 1977. R.

3715. Mullaney, Tom. "Divorced Catholics Ask Amnesty for Remarried," *National Catholic Reporter* 11 (November 8, 1974): 3.

3716. ———. "The Divorced: Nary a Stereotype," *National Catholic Reporter* 11 (November 22, 1974): 4.

3717. Paolin, Jo. "Divorced Need No 'Joan of Arc,' " *National Catholic Reporter* 15 (May 25, 1979): 16.

3718. Ripple, Paula. *The Pain and the Possibility: Divorce and Separation among Catholics.* Notre Dame, IN: Ave Maria Press, 1978.

3719. Rue, James J., and Shanahan, Louise. "The Limbo World of the Divorced," *Family Digest*, vol. 28, no. 2 (1972): 48–52.

3720. ———. *The Divorced Catholic.* Paramus, NJ: Paulinist/Newman Press, 1972.

3721. "Says Divorced Catholics Support Church on Marriage," *Our Sunday Visitor* 67 (July 23, 1978): 3.

3722. Shanahan, Louise. "Divorced Catholics," *Family Digest*, vol. 25, no. 4 (1970): 10–15.

3723. ———. "How Catholic Divorcees Can Help Each Other," *Liguorian* 65 (March 1977): 38–42.

Groups

3724. Brown, Gerald L. "The Rhetoric of Divorced Catholics Groups and the Founding of a National Organization." Ph.D. diss., Temple University, 1979 (*DAI* 40/5A, p. 2351, order # 7923983). R.

3725. Casey, Rick. "Divorced Catholics Form National Group," *National Catholic Reporter* 12 (November 28, 1975): 1 + .

3726. Dickey, Gordon. "Divorced Catholics: Imperative for Pastoral Ministry." Master of social work thesis, Catholic University, 1974. R.

3727. "Divorced in Conflict over Church Study Says," *National Catholic Reporter* 10 (August 2, 1974): 16.

3728. Farrell, William P. "A Parish Plan for the Divorced Catholic," *Living Light* 13 (Winter 1976): 582–87.

3729. "Ministry to Divorced Spreads out of Boston," *National Catholic Reporter* 10 (May 3, 1974): 20.

3730. "Separated, Divorced Catholics' Conference Elects First Officers," *National Catholic Reporter* 12 (January 30, 1976): 17.

3731. Young, James J. "The Divorced Catholics Movement," *Journal of Divorce*, vol. 2, no. 1 (1978): 83–97.

FRIENDSHIP WITH DIVORCED PERSONS

3732. Cole, C. Donald. "What to Say to a Divorced Friend," *Moody Monthly* 76 (March 1976): 25–26.

3733. Ripple, Paula. "What to Do When Good Friends Divorce: Interview," *U.S. Catholic* 44 (October 1979): 6–11.

3734. Webb, Carla F. "How to Handle a Divorce When It's Not Your Own," *Marriage and Family Living* 61 (May 1979): 14–15.

ONE-PARENT FAMILIES

Jewish

3735. Bubis, Gerald B. "The Single Parent Family," *Reconstructionist*, vol. 42, no. 1 (1976): 7–10.

3736. Hofstein, Saul. "Perspectives on the Jewish Single-Parent Family," *Journal of Jewish Communal Service*, vol. 54, no. 3 (1978): 229–40.

Protestant

Evangelical

3737. Carter, Velma, and Leavenworth, J. Lynn. *Putting the Pieces Together.* Valley Forge, PA: Judson Press, 1977.

3738. Stewart, Suzanne. *Parent Alone.* Waco, TX: Word Books, 1978.

3739. Watts, Virginia. *The Single Parent.* Old Tappan, NJ: Fleming H. Revell Co., 1976.

Methodist

3740. Barringer, Kenneth D. "Focus: The Single Parent—Confronting the Relationships with the Larger Family," *Christian Home* 10 (November 1977): 24–25 + .

3741. ———. "Focus: The Single Parent—How to Deal with Depression," *Christian Home* 9 (September 1976): 26 + .

3742. Brower, Elizabeth. "Warren Village: Community for One-Parent Families," *Response* 11 (May 1979): 12–15.

3743. Cutshaw, Gina. "The Church and the Single Parent," *Church School*, vol. 7, no. 10 (1975): 1–3.

3744. Gilbert, John P. "Single Parent Families," *Adult Leader*, vol. 3, no. 3 (1971): 8–9.

3745. Haney, Daniel Q. "Hard on Single Dads," *Christian Home* 11 (August 1979): 15 + .

3746. Jeffrey, Shirley H. "Focus: The Single Parent—Anger, Honesty and Understanding," *Christian Home* 9 (August 1977): 22–23.

3747. ———. "Focus: The Single Parent—Can You Play Today?" *Christian Home* 10 (December 1974): 24.

3748. ———. "Hold Me," *Christian Home* 11 (June 1979): 24 + .

3749. ———. "Focus: The Single Parent—I Am Loveable and Capable," *Christian Home* 9 (October 1976): 26 + .

3750. ———. "Focus: The Single Parent—Loneliness," 9 (November 1976): 28 + ; 9 (December 1976): 28 + ; 9 (January 1977): 27–28.

3751. ———. "Money, Money, Money," *Christian Home* 11 (August 1979): 23.

3752. ———. "Focus: The Single Parent—On Thy People Pour Thy Power," *Christian Home* 10 (January 1978): 27.

3753. ———. "Focus: The Single Parent—Vulnerable Persons," *Christian Home* 10 (September 1977): 24–25.

3754. McClure, Cecilia A. "Christmas as a Single Parent," *Christian Home* 12 (November 1979): 17–18.

Reformed Church in America

3755. Grab, Nancy H. "Single Parents and the Church," *Church Herald* 34 (April 29, 1977): 13–15.

Southern Baptist

3756. Keeton, H. Dale. "What about Single Parents—Ostracize or Harmonize," *Outreach,* vol. 6, no. 4 (1976): 8–9.

3757. Peak, Paul. "Ministering to Single Parents," *Deacon* 8 (October–December 1977): 10–12.

Roman Catholic

3758. Bosco, Antoinette. "When Marriage Ends—And Parenthood Remains," *Marriage and Family Living,* vol. 56, no. 5 (1974): 12–15.

PERSONAL NARRATIVES

Church of Jesus Christ of Latter-Day Saints

3759. Arnold, Marilyn. "After Divorce, My Ward Went the Extra Several Miles," *Ensign of the Church of Jesus Christ of Latter Day Saints* 5 (June 1975): 48–51.

3760. Baxter, Lynn. "The Christmas I Learned to Love Again," *Ensign of the Church of Jesus Christ of Latter Day Saints* 5 (December 1975): 33–35.

3761. "Surviving Divorce," *Ensign of the Church of Jesus Christ of Latter Day Saints* 8 (February 1978): 13–15.

3762. Western, Joset F. "Continuing as a Whole Person," *Ensign of the Church of Jesus Christ of Latter Day Saints* 5 (June 1975): 53–54.

Protestant

Evangelicals

3763. "Christopher, I Hear You Have Left Your Wife," *Eternity* 29 (April 1978): 26–27.

3764. "Divorced but Not Forsaken," *Moody Monthly* 78 (June 1978): 43–45.

3765. "Divorce: Triumph over Tragedy," *Wesleyan Advocate* 137 (April 16, 1979): 13–14.

3766. Ellingson, Catherine. "At Wit's End—God," *Herald of Holiness* 61 (February 2, 1972): 3–4.

3767. Emrich, Ernestine H. "I Chose Honesty," *Brethern Life* 21 (Summer 1976): 138–47.

3768. Harris, Elizabeth C. "When Love Is Not Enough," *Christian Life* 32 (July 1970): 34–35.

3769. Hunter, Brenda. *Beyond Divorce: A Personal Journey,* Old Tappan, NJ: Fleming H. Revell Co., 1978.

3770. Hurst, Gloria. *No Valley Too Deep.* Chicago: Moody Press, 1978.

3771. "I'm Hurting—Please Help," *Christian Medical Society Journal* 7 (Winter 1976): 26–30.

3772. "Jesus Is Enough," *Good News Broadcaster* 36 (February 1978): 41–42.

3773. Landrum, Faye. "I Gave God the Pieces," *Christian Life* 36 (February 1975): 30+.

3774. Smith, Sue. "Divorce from Inside the Wall," *Eternity* 27 (June 1976): 14.

3775. Stewart, Suzanne. *Divorced! I Wouldn't Have Given a Nickel for Your Chances.* Grand Rapids, MI: Zondervan Publishing House, 1974.

3776. Tengbom, Mildred. "When a Marriage Falls Apart," *Christian Life* 37 (September 1975): 30–31+.

3777. "Tenth Anniversary," *Presbyterian Journal,* vol. 35, no. 18 (1976): 9–11.

3778. Tompkins, Iverna. "I Was Saved—But My Marriage Wasn't," *Eternity* 27 (June 1976): 12.

Methodists

3779. Lamb, Jane. "Alone/Responsible," *Christian Home,* vol. 4, no. 7 (1972): 8–11.

Pentecostals

3780. Harris, Thelma. "Divorce Is a Lonely Road," *Pentecostal Evangel* 3380 (February 18, 1979): 4–5.

3781. Miller, Pauline. "Sometimes We're Happy . . . ," *U.S. Catholic* 6 (June 1975): 25–30.

Seventh Day Adventists

3782. Hirschmann, Maria A. *Please Don't Shoot: I'm Already Wounded.* Wheaton, IL: Tyndale House Publishers, 1979.

Southern Baptists

3783. "Divorce, a Haunting Reality," *Home Life* 31 (July 1977): 6–7.

3784. Duncan, Lois. "Still God's Child," *Home Life* 28 (June 1974): 10.

3785. "I Said No to Divorce," *Home Life* 28 (February 1974): 34.

3786. "Lonely Graduation," *Home Life* 31 (July 1977): 33.

3787. McKay, Richard W. "She May Walk Again," *Home Life* 24 (July 1970): 11+.

3788. Morgan, Marilyn. "Discoveries from Divorce," *Home Life* 33 (October 1978): 31.

3789. "My Parents Divorced," *Home Life* 26 (September 1972): 6–7.

3790. Sanders, Marie. "Then Came the Loneliness," *Home Life* 32 (July 1978): 20–22.

3791. Taylor, Gail. "The Awakening," *Home Life* 33 (June 1979): 12.

3792. Wooldridge, Barbara. "Faith and Loneliness," *Home Life* 33 (June 1979): 38–39.

Roman Catholics

3793. Geaney, Dennis J. "Till Divorce Do Us Part," *U.S. Catholic,* vol. 40, no. 4 (1975): 6–13.

3794. Medeiros, Gladys. "Women Alone," *Our Sunday Visitor* 68 (May 20, 1979): 8.

3795. Quoist, Michel. "My Parents Are Divorced," *U.S. Catholic,* vol. 40, no. 4 (1975): 14–16.

3796. Stevens, Marie. "Church Courts: How They Made Her Suffer," *National Catholic Reporter* 7 (June 11, 1971): 1–A+.

REMARRIAGE

Protestant

3797. Burton, John D. "A Pastor Looks at Remarriage," *Christian Ministry* 7 (May 1976): 11–13.

3798. Perske, Robert. "That Second Marriage Service: A Pastoral Worksheet," *Journal of Pastoral Care,* vol. 28, no. 1 (1974): 17–22.

Evangelical

3799. Brown, Bob W. *Getting Married Again: A Christian Guide for Successful Remarriage.* Waco, TX: Word Books, 1979.

3800. Peters, George W. "What God Says about Remarriage," *Moody Monthly* 78 (July 1978): 42–45.

3801. Small, Dwight H. *The Right to Remarry.* Old Tappan, NJ: Fleming H. Revell Co., 1975.

Southern Baptist

3802. Cardwell, Albert L. "Can Remarriage to the Same Mate Succeed?" *Home Life* 33 (August 1979): 14.

3803. Forlines, Fay. "Daddy Married Again Today," *Home Life* 29 (February 1975): 10–11.

3804. Hudson, R. Lofton. "Marriage the Second Time Around," *Home Life* 31 (July 1977): 12–14.

3805. "If a Couple Asked You to Conduct Their Marriage Ceremony, and You Discovered One or Both Were Divorced, What Would You Do? Why?" *Baptist Program* (August 1974): 23.

3806. Platts, Barbara. "A Summer of Adjustment," *Home Life* 32 (July 1978): 8–10.

Seventh Day Adventists

3807. "Free to Marry Again?" (question and answer, *Message Magazine,* vol. 38, no. 7 (1972): 16.

Roman Catholic

3808. " 'America' Urges Acceptance of Second Marriage," *National Catholic Reporter* 11 (December 13, 1974): 3.

3809. Bassett, William W. "Divorce and Remarriage: The Catholic Search for a Pastoral Reconciliation," *American Ecclesiastical Review,* vol. 162, no. 1 (1970): 20–36; no. 2 (1970): 92–105.

3810. "Cardinal's Statement on 'Good Conscience' Procedures," *Social Justice Review,* vol. 65, no. 6 (1972): 200.

3811. "The Church, the Law and Marriage," *America,* vol. 127, no. 10 (1972): 251+.

3812. Clemente, Virginia. "The Remarriage Trap," *National Catholic Reporter* 15 (May 25, 1979): 13+.

3813. Curtin, William B. "The Dilemma of Second Marriage," *America,* vol. 129, no. 4 (1973): 88–99.

3814. "Debate . . . On Kelleher and Divorce," *National Catholic Reporter* 11 (May 9, 1975): 14.

3815. "Divorced Catholics: A Proposal," *America,* vol. 132, no. 1 (1975): 12–14.

3816. "Invalid Marriage Means no Communion, Delegates Say: The Eucharist, Bread of Life, Bread for Life, Meeting," *Our Sunday Visitor* 64 (March 28, 1976): 3.

3817. Kelleher, Stephen J. "Remarriage," *National Catholic Reporter* 11 (April 18, 1975): 5+.

3818. McDevitt, Anthony. "Excommunication and the Right of Catholics in Second Marriage to the Eucharist," *Catholic Mind* 75 (May 1977): 43–51.

3819. "Meet Vetoes Communion for Twice-Wed," *National Catholic Reporter* 12 (March 26, 1976): 20.

3820. O'Donnell, Cletus S. "A Statement on the Bishops' Vote to Lift the Penalty of Excommunication for Divorced Catholics Who Have Remarried," *Catholic Mind* 75 (November 1977): 6–8.

3821. ———. "Divorced Catholics Who Have Remarried; Bishops Vote to Repeal Excommunication," *Origins* (May 19, 1977): 765–66.

3822. Palmer, Paul F. "Can the Church Condone Second Marriages?" *Priest,* vol. 32, no. 1 (1976): 28–33.

3823. Provost, James. "Reconciliation of Catholics in Second Marriages," *Origins* 8 (September 14, 1978): 204–08.

3824. "Reforming Our Discipline: Second Marriages" (editorial), *America,* vol. 131, no. 18 (1974): 362.

3825. "Remarriage after Psychic Incapacity?" *Jurist* 34 (Winter-Spring 1974): 107–11.

3826. "Tells Remarried Catholics to Take Communion," *National Catholic Reporter* 7 (October 8, 1971): 3+.

3827. Wakin, Edward. "They Remarried in Good Conscience," *U.S. Catholic,* vol. 38, no. 6 (1973): 19–22.

3828. Young, James J. "Remarrieds Rejoice: I'm Back In," *National Catholic Reporter* 14 (February 10, 1978): 14.

SEPARATION

3829. Becker, Carmelita D. "When All Else Has Failed," *Marriage and Family Living* 61 (January 1979): 10–11.

3830. Brubaker, Ellen A. "If Your Parents Have Separated . . . ," *Face to Face,* vol. 8, no. 3 (1976): 47–49.

3831. Landgraf, John R. "The Impact of Therapeutic Marital Separation on Spouses in Pastoral Marriage Counseling." Th.D. diss., School of Theology at Claremont, 1973 (*DAI* 33/10B, p. 5021, order # 73-9118). R.

3832. Van Wade, David, and Van Wade, Sarah. *Second Chance: A Broken Marriage Restored.* Plainfield, NJ: Logos International, 1975.

STEPPARENTS

Protestant

Methodist

3833. Erhard, Tom. "I'm Never Going to Call Him Dad," *Accent on Youth* 11 (May 1979): 7–14.

3834. McClenaghan, Judy C., and Most, Bruce W. "Stepmothering: Make His Child Love You," *Christian Home* 12 (October 1979): 20–22.

Southern Baptist

3835. Capaldi, Frederick, and McRae, Barbara. "Can Stepfamilies Work?" *Solo,* vol. 3, no. 5 (1979): 28–29.

3836. Jameson, Mark. "Helpful Hints for Stepparents," *Home Life* 33 (April 1979): 46–47.

3837. Madden, Myron C. "Problems as a Stepmother" (letter to the editor), *Home Life* 28 (September 1974): 20.

3838. Wellborn, Jacquelyn. "Stepmother," *Home Life* 30 (May 1976): 32–33.

IV. Popular Literature

ALIMONY AND MAINTENANCE

3839. "Alimony: It Ain't What It Used to Be," *New Woman* 6 (September–October 1976): 36+.

3840. "A Ban on Alimony?" *Newsweek* 83 (January 7, 1974): 47.

3841. Brady, Kathleen. "How to Get a Good Settlement: Negotiating a Fair Divorce Settlement. Inverview with Louis Nizer," *Harper's Bazaar* 109 (July 1976): 45+.

3842. ———. "Should You Accept Alimony? Interview with Betty Friedan," *Harper's Bazaar* 109 (July 1976): 45+.

3843. Chan, Janet. " 'Maintenance': An Alternative to Alimony," *McCalls* 102 (September 1975): 36.

3844. Coburn, Judith. "Intelligent Woman's Guide to Sex," *Mademoiselle* 85 (May 1979): 58.

3845. Franks, Maurice R. *How to Avoid Alimony*. New York: Saturday Review Press, 1975.

3846. Larson, Alan. "EDP Keeps Tabs on Wife Supporters: Dane County, Wis.," *American City* 86 (May 1971): 82.

3847. MacDonald, Steve. "Alimony Blues," *New York Times Magazine* (March 16, 1975): 20+.

3848. "Who Should Pay Alimony? Divorce Lawyer Doris Sassower Offers a Surprising Answer," *People* 7 (March 28, 1977): 59–60+.

ALIMONY FOR MALES

3849. "It's Official: Alimony Is a Two-Way Street," *U.S. News and World Report* 86 (March 19, 1979): 9.

3850. Meade, Marion. "Alimony for Men," *New Woman* 2 (June–July 1972): 54–55+.

3851. Morganthau, Tom, and Camper, Diane. "Equalimony," *Newsweek* 93 (March 19, 1979): 40.

3852. "The Price of Equality," *Newsweek* 93 (May 14, 1979): 129.

ANNULMENT

3853. "Debate over Catholic Marriage," *Time* 96 (July 6, 1970): 64+.

3854. "Divorce for Catholics?" *Time* 102 (November 12, 1973): 100.

3855. "Love Impediment," *Newsweek* 82 (October 1, 1973): 71.

3856. Nobile, Philip. "Brooklyn, Reno of the Catholic Church," *New York* 11 (June 12, 1978): 47–50.

3857. "Rota Revolt," *Time* 100 (November 13, 1972): 100.

CHILD CUSTODY

3858. Ashby, Deborah H. "Revenge: The Endless War," *Single Parent* 19 (November 1976): 11–13.

3859. Baum, Charlotte. "What to Do When You Both Want Custody," *New Woman* 7 (September–October 1977): 32+.

3860. Bernard, Will. "Who Gets the Children?" *Women's Day* 42 (June 26, 1979): 144.

3861. Briles, Ingrid. "I Gave Up My Children," *Ladies Home Journal* 96 (June 1979): 48+.

3862. Buchanan, Margaret R. "Courts, Custody, and Confusion," *Delaware Today* 14 (February 1976): 27–28+.

3863. Carro, Geraldine, and Solnit, Albert. "Who Gets the Kids? An Expert Talks about Custody," *Ladies Home Journal* 93 (January 1976): 70.

3864. "The Custody Referees," *Human Behavior,* vol. 4, no. 9 (1975): 62+.

3865. Elliot, Elizabeth, and Susco, Wendy. "Legal Briefs, Custody," *Working Woman* 3 (October 1978): 8.

3866. Epstein, Alan. "Summer Father," *Redbook* 151 (June 1978): 67–68+.

3867. Hall, Sarah M. "A Sioux Mother Battles White In-Laws for her Child in the

Bitter Case of Brokenleg v. Butts," *People* 11 (June 25, 1979): 71–72.

3868. Koch, Joanne. "Healthy Criticism: Let's Be More Just in Child Custody Decisions," *Today's Health* 50 (November 1972): 68–70.

3869. Mayleas, Davidyne. "New Options in Child Custody," *Harper's Bazaar* 111 (September 1978): 231–32.

3870. Noble, June, and Noble, William. *The Custody Trap.* New York: Hawthorn Books, 1975.

3871. Ramos, Suzanne. *The Complete Book of Child Custody.* New York: G. P. Putnam's Sons, 1979.

3872. Silverman, Stephen M. "Life without Mother," *American Film* 4 (July–August 1979): 50–55.

3873. Thompson, Dorothy. "Children's Rights: On Custody and the Law," *Single Parent* 21 (May 1978): 14–16.

3874. "Two on the Seesaw," *Time* 99 (January 31, 1972): 13–14.

3875. "Who Gets the Children?" *Time* 99 (January 31, 1972): 61.

3876. Woody, Robert H. *Getting Custody: Winning the Last Battle of the Marital War.* New York: Macmillan, 1978.

3877. Woolley, Persia. *The Custody Handbook.* New York: Summit Books, 1979.

3878. Young, Gregory. "Law for Everyday Living: Child Custody," *Sepia* 27 (September 1978): 38.

CONTESTED CUSTODY

3879. "Children Chase," *Time* 101 (April 9, 1973): 82.

3880. Feder, Chris W. "Custody Battles: More Fathers are Winning," *McCalls* 101 (May 1974): 50–51.

3881. "Lollipop War," *Redbook* 141 (September 1973): 48 + .

3882. Smilgis, Martha. "A Mother's Battle for Custody of Her Sons Brings Cher into the Case—With Lawyers," *People* 11 (April 30, 1979): 41–41.

FATHER CUSTODY

3883. Davidson, Jessica. "A Woman Who Gave up Custody of Her Children," *New Woman* 1 (December 1971): 44 + .

3884. Dougherty, Ruth. "Fathers with Custody," *Parents' Magazine* 52 (October 1977): 56–57 + .

3885. ———. "When a Mother Gives Up Her Child," *Parents' Magazine* 53 (May 1978): 46–47 + .

3886. James, Adrienne. "What Happens to Mother When Father Takes Custody of the Child?" *Vogue* 168 (September 1978): 122 + .

3887. Molinoff, Daniel D. "Life with Father," *New York Times Magazine* (May 22, 1977): 12–17.

3888. Victor, Ira, and Winkler, Win A. *Fathers and Custody.* New York: Hawthorn Books, 1977.

3889. Winter, Edward J. *Father Winning Child Custody Cases: "How Children Can Come Out the Winner": A Guide for Lawyers and Laymen to Help Children Win Contested Child Custody Litigation.* Miami, FL: River Trails Pub., 1975.

HOMOSEXUAL PARENTS

3890. Gibson, Gifford G. *By Her Own Admission: A Lesbian Mother's Fight to Keep Her Own Son.* Garden City, NY: Doubleday, 1977.

JOINT CUSTODY

3891. Abrahams, Sally. "Joint Custody Controversy," *New York* 12 (June 18, 1979): 56–61.

3892. Bakos, Susan. "Joint Custody: The No-Lose Agreement," *St. Louis* 11 (May 1979): 115–17 + .

3893. Baum, Charlotte. "Best of Both Parents," *New York Times Magazine* (October 6, 1976): 44–46 + .

3894. "Coparenting: What the Experts Say," *San Francisco Bay Guardian* 11 (February 13, 1977): 8.

3895. Dancey, Elizabeth. "Who Gets the Kids? New Solutions for the Big Dilemma," *Ms* 5 (September 1976): 70–72 + .

3896. Deitz, Susan. "Joint Custody: A Growing Trend," *Single Parent* 19 (September 1976): 17.

3897. Fager, Chuck. "Coparenting: Sharing the Children of Divorce," *San Francisco Bay Guardian* 11 (February 13, 1977): 7.

3898. Galper, Miriam. *Co-parenting, Sharing your Child Equally: A Source Book for the Separated or Divorced Family.* Philadelphia, PA: Running Press, 1978.

3899. Goldscheider, Robert. "Not Only on Sunday," *Parents' Magazine* 49 (May 1974): 40 + .

3900. Goodman, Emily J. "Custody Sharing: The American Way of Divorce," *Viva* 3 (May 1976): 113–14.

3901. Goodman, Emily J. "Joint Custody," *McCalls* 102 (August 1975): 34.

3902. Haddad, William F., and Roman, Mel. *The Disposable Parent: The Case for Joint Custody.* New York: Holt, Rinehart, and Winston, 1978.

3903. "Happy Daddies: The Case for Half-time Fathers," *Human Behavior,* vol. 7, no. 11 (1978): 37.

3904. Holly, Marcia. "Joint Custody: The New Haven Plan," *Ms* 5 (September 1976): 70–71.

3905. Humphrey, Kyler. "Joint Custody and Missouri Law," *St. Louis* 11 (July 1979): 14 + .

3906. Kellogg, Mary A. "Joint Custody," *Newsweek* 89 (January 24, 1977): 56–57.

3907. Lichtenstein, Grace. "Living with Parents Who Live Apart," *Seventeen* 38 (March 1979): 170 + .

3908. Molinoff, Daniel. "Days Here, Days There," *Single Parent* 22 (April 1979): 9–12 + .

3909. Morgenstern, Debora. "Joint Custody: When Divorced Parents Share," *McCalls* 107 (December 1979): 55.

3910. "One Child, Two Homes," *Time* 113 (January 29, 1979): 61.

3911. Spock, Benjamin. "Joint Custody and the Father's Role," *Redbook* 153 (October 1979): 77 + .

3912. Ware, Ciji. "Joint Custody: One Way to End the War," *New West* 4 (February 26, 1979): 42 + .

3913. Woolley, Persia. "Who Keeps the Children? Mother, Father, or Both." *Vogue* 169 (May 1979): 300–02.

KIDNAPPING

3914. "Child Snatching Epidemic Stirs a Storm," *U.S. News and World Report* 87 (September 3, 1979): 57.

3915. Chu, Daniel, and Sciolino, Elaine. "Family Affair: Child-Snatching," *Newsweek* 88 (October 18, 1976): 24 + .

3916. Clifford, Garry. "Arnold Miller Grieves for His Stolen Son and Fights for Laws That Might Bring Him Back," *People* 11 (March 19, 1979): 22 + .

3917. ———. "For Five Years Arnold Miller Searched, Prayed, Crusaded—And Finally Found His Abducted Son," *People* 11 (May 7, 1979): 45–46.

3918. Demeter, Anna. *Legal Kidnapping: What Happens to a Family When the Father Kidnaps Two Children.* Boston, MA: Beacon Press, 1977.

3919. Gittelson, Natalie. "Parents as Kidnappers," *McCalls* 103 (August 1976): 39.

3920. "I Kidnapped My Own Son," *Good Housekeeping* 189 (October 1979): 26+.

3921. McGrady, Patrick Jr. "Have You Seen This Child?" *Ladies Home Journal* 91 (November 1974): 86+.

3922. "Moving to Stop Child Snatching," *Time* 111 (February 27, 1978): 85.

3923. Shapiro, Andrew O. "Child Snatching: A Cautionary Tale," *New York* 11 (October 9, 1978): 128–29+.

3924. Van Gelder, Lindsy. "Beyond Custody: When Parents Steal Their Children," *Ms* 6 (May 1978): 52–53+.

3925. Wallop, Malcolm. "Children of Divorce and Separation: Pawns in the Child-Snatching Game," *Single Parent* 22 (December 1979): 11–13+.

3926. Westgate, Bob. "The Seize and Run Game," *Single Parent* 19 (September 1976): 18–19.

3927. Williams, Dennis A. "The Mellon Feud," *Newsweek* 87 (March 29, 1976): 30.

CHILD SUPPORT

3928. Cannell, Lin. "Wanted: For Child Support," *Single Parent* 21 (June 1978): 7–9.

3929. "Child Support Delinquents. Does Jail Help the Problem?" *Human Behavior* 7 (September 1978): 67.

3930. Cowley, Susan C., et al. "Paying Their Dues," *Newsweek* 85 (February 24, 1975): 55–56.

3931. Luboff, Eileen B., and Posner, Constance L. *How to Collect Your Child Support and Alimony.* Occidental, CA: Nolo Press, 1977.

3932. Shaffer, Helen B. "Child Support," *Editorial Research Reports* (January 25, 1974): 63–80.

3933. "Society's Child," *Newsweek* 77 (January 11, 1971): 60–61.

3934. "Woman Pays Husband Back Alimony to Avoid Jail," *Jet* 53 (February 9, 1978): 34.

CHILD SUPPORT (ENFORCEMENT)

3935. Hayden, Trudy R. "The Rights of Parents and Children," *Current* (February 1977): 24–31.

3936. Steele, Richard, and Sciolino, Elaine. "Tracer of Lost Fathers," *Newsweek* 88 (December 20, 1976): 30.

3937. Stephen, Beverly. "Getting Child Support from Runaway Fathers," *McCalls* 104 (June 1977): 84–85.

3938. Ungar, Sanford J. "Reports and Comment: Washington: Bill to Collect Child-Support Payments from Delinquent Fathers," *Atlantic,* vol. 236, no. 6 (1975): 16+.

3939. Walsh, Lawrence. "Daddy's Day in Court," *Ms* 3 (January 1975): 19.

CHILDREN OF DIVORCED PARENTS

3940. Adams, Jane. "Divorce—The Positive Side," *Harper's Bazaar* 112 (February 1979): 134–35.

3941. "After Divorce Guide for You and Your Children—Symposium," *Harper's Bazaar* 109 (July 1976): 44–47+.

3942. Arlen, Michael J. "Saturday Father," *McCalls* 100 (February 1973): 36–40.

3943. Bettelheim, Bruno. "Bringing Up Children," *Ladies Home Journal* 90 (March 1973): 30+.

3944. Black, Kathryn N. "Children and Divorce," *Single Parent* 21 (January–February 1978): 16–17+.

3945. "Breaking Up Is Hard—On whom?" *Senior Scholastic* 101 (October 9, 1972): 17.

3946. Bridgers, Sue E. "Salvaging Something," *American Girl,* vol. 55, no. 9 (1972): 44–45.

3947. Buttenweiser, Helen R. "Children Are Not Chattels," *Single Parents* 16 (March 1973): 7+.

3948. "A Child's Guide to Divorce," *Time* 96 (October 26, 1970): 63.

3949. "Child's Point of View," *Time* 104 (September 30, 1974): 65.

3950. Constantine, Diane. "That Was My Father . . . ," *Single Parent* 21 (June 1978): 11–12+.

3951. LeDubovay, Diane. "You and Your Love and His Children," *Vogue* 164 (September 1974): 302.

3952. "The Divorced Child," *Human Behavior* 6 (September 1977): 60–61.

3953. "Divorce in the Family," *Current Health* 5 (March 1979): 18–20.

3954. Dreskin, Wendy. "Larry Gets a Divorce," *Single Parent* 20 (December 1977): 17–19.

3955. "A Father with Custody of Two, Dr. Lee Salk Tells How to Help Children Cope with Divorce," *People* 9 (June 1978): 55–56+.

3956. Friggens, Paul. "If You Spoil the Marriage, Spare the Child," *Reader's Digest* 106 (June 1975): 155–58.

3957. Garai, Josef E. "Children of Divorce: Healing Their Special Hurt," *Parents' Magazine* 48 (March 1973): 46+.

3958. Gardner, Richard A. *The Parents Book about Divorce.* Garden City, NY: Doubleday, 1977.

3959. Kessler, Sheila, and Bostwick, Sylvia H. "Daddy Honks the Horn Outside," *Single Parent* 20 (October 1977): 13–15+.

3960. King, Barbara. "Children of Split Homes: What's True and False," *New Woman* 7 (January–February 1977): 53–55+.

3961. Meredith, Nancy G. "When Parents Divorce," *Parents' Magazine* 46 (January 1971): 44+.

3962. "Middle Class Deviants: The Broken-Home Delinquency Connection," *Human Behavior* 8 (May 1979): 59–60.

3963. Pascoe, Elizabeth J. "Helping Children Survive Divorce," *Woman's Day* 39 (August 1976): 2+.

3964. Rubin, Estelle. "The Sunday Father," *Harper's Bazaar* 109 (July 1976): 47+.

3965. Rubin, Theodore I. "Psychiatrist's Notebook," *Ladies Home Journal* 93 (November 1976): 62.

3966. Salk, Lee. "Divorce: How to Protect Your Children," *Harper's Bazaar* 111 (September 1978): 228–29+.

3967. Schlesinger, Benjamin. "Kids Talk about Divorce," *Single Parent* 22 (July–August 1979): 19–20+.

3968. Smith, Gloria S., and Scales, Alice M. "One-Parent Child and the Classroom Teacher," *Today's Education* 64 (November 1975): 83–86.

3969. Steinzor, Bernard. *When Parents Divorce: A New Approach to Relationships.* New York: Pocket Books, 1970.

3970. Tener, Elizabeth. "Your Parents' Divorce: How to Survive It," *Co-ed* 22 (May 1977): 40+.

3971. Urbanski, Wanda. "Growing Up in a Broken Home," *Seventeen* 33 (September 1974): 118–19+.

3972. Velie, Lester. "Love, Marriage, and Crime," *Reader's Digest* 101 (August 1972): 79–83.

3973. Vigeveno, H. S., and Claire, Anne. *Divorce and the Children.* Glendale, CA: G. L. Regal Books, 1979.

3974. Weiss, Robert S. "Can Your Children Survive Divorce?" *Harper's Bazaar* 109 (July 1976): 46–47.

3975. Winter, Walter T. "What about the Children?" *San Francisco* 18 (September 1976): 14–15.

3976. Wood, Abigail. "When Your Parents Remarry: Questions and Answers," *Seventeen* 35 (November 1976): 98+.

3977. Wortman, Ruth. "Divorce: Its Problems Follow the Child to Camp," *Camping Magazine* 51 (June 1979): 10–11+.

3978. "Your Children: Growing up Divorced" (special section), *Harper's Bazaar* 111 (September 1978): 228–31+.

3979. "Your Opinion: Where Do You Stand When Your Parents Divorce?" *Young Miss* 24 (April 1977): 60–61.

ADJUSTMENT TO DIVORCE

3980. Demarest, Vicci. "How to Handle Your Parents' Divorce," *Young Miss* 20 (March 1973): 38–42.

3981. King, Barbara. "Children of Divorce: How to Help Them When the Split Comes," *Town and Country* 130 (October 1976): 135+.

3982. Little, Suzanne. "Helping Children Cope with Divorce," *McCalls* 103 (August 1976): 38.

3983. Matluck, Hannah. "Where Do You Stand When Your Parents Divorce?" *Young Miss* 24 (January 1977): 30–34.

3984. Robinson, Louie. "House Divided; Child of Broken Home Adjusts to Double Life," *Ebony* 29 (August 1974): 74–78.

3985. Robson, Bonnie E. *My Parents Are Divorced, Too: What Teenagers Experience and How They Cope.* Toronto: Dorset Press, 1979.

3986. Spock, Benjamin. "How Divorced Parents Can Help Their Children," *Redbook* 149 (July 1977): 22+.

3987. ———. "How Divorced Parents Can Help Their Children Adjust," *Redbook* 136 (March 1971): 33–34+.

COMMUNICATION ABOUT DIVORCE

3988. Bettelheim, Bruno. "Dialogue with Mothers: Helping Children Accept Divorce," *Ladies Home Journal* 89 (February 1972): 26+.

3989. Grollman, Earl A. *Talking about Divorce: A Dialogue between Parent and Child.* Boston, MA: Beacon Press, 1975.

3990. ———. "Talking about Divorce," *Ms* 5 (October 1976): 77–78.

DIVORCE EDUCATION AND COUNSELING

3991. "Divorce in Technicolor: Believable Films Help Youngsters Adjust," *Human Behavior* 7 (December 1978): 40.

3992. Francke, Linda B., and Smith, Sunde. "Split Screen," *Newsweek* 85 (April 21, 1975): 58–59.

3993. Gardner, Sandra. "Divorced Kids—Organizing to Help Each Other," *Senior Scholastic* 112 (November 15, 1979): 9–11.

3994. "Help for Kids of Divorced Parents," *Co-ed* 25 (January 1980): 58.

3995. Jennes, Gail. "Her Parents' Divorce Shocked Gabrielle Reem; Now She Helps Other Kids Pick Up the Pieces," *People* 11 (May 21, 1979): 104+.

3996. Olds, Sally W. "Separation Counseling," *McCalls* 102 (August 1975): 33–34.

3997. O'Reilly, J. "In Massachusetts: 'Divorced Kids,' " *Time* 113 (June 11, 1979): 6–7.

EFFECTS OF DIVORCE ON CHILDREN

3998. Cosneck, Bernard J. "The Effects of Divorce on Children," *Single Parent* 16 (March 1973): 6+. R.

3999. McCall, Robert, and Stocking, Holly. "What Divorce Will Do to Your Child," *Oklahoma Observer* 11 (July 25, 1979): 9.

4000. Marks, Jane. "Divorce in the Family—How it Affects the Children's Expectations of Marriage," *Glamour* 73 (May 1973): 164+.

4001. Reinhart, John B. "Divorce: Its Effect on Children," *PTA Magazine* 67 (October 1972): 11–14.

4002. Streshinsky, Shirley. "How Divorce Really Affects Children: A Major Report," *Redbook* 147 (September 1976): 70 + .

PERSONAL NARRATIVES

4003. "Dear Judge Fenton . . ." (letters from the Children of Divorcing Couples), *Newsweek* 86 (August 18, 1975): 59.

4004. "Gold, Tracy M. "What My Parents' Divorce Means to Me," *Seventeen* 32 (June 1973): 114 + .

DESERTION

4005. Brenton, Myron. "Looking at the Runaway: Who? What? Why? Where? When?" *New Woman*, vol 8, no. 4 (1978): 76–83.

4006. ———. *The Runaways: Children, Husbands, Wives and Parents*. Boston, MA: Little, Brown & Co., 1978.

4007. "Crackdown on Runaway Parents," *U.S. News and World Report* 86 (February 12, 1979): 50.

4008. "Gaining Ground: A Plan to Lasso Runaway Fathers," *U.S. News and World Report* 81 (November 15, 1976): 99–101.

4009. Gunther, Max. "Wives Who Run Away," *Ladies Home Journal* 88 (February 1971): 66 + .

4010. "My Husband Deserted Me," *Good Housekeeping* 175 (August 1972): 14 + .

4011. "Why So Many Wives are Running Away," *U.S. News and World Report* 80 (February 23, 1976): 24–25.

DIVORCE

4012. Abeel, Erica. "Divorce Fever: Is It an Epidemic?" *New York Magazine*, vol. 7, no. 4 (1974): 46–51.

4013. Adam, John H., and Adam, Nancy W. *Divorce: How and When to Let Go*. Englewood Cliffs, NJ: Prentice-Hall, 1979.

4014. Addeo, Edmond G., and Burger, Robert E. *Inside Divorce: Is It What You Really Want?* Radnor, PA: Chilton Book Co., 1975.

4015. Allman, T.D. "Why We Can't Stay Married," *American Home* 80 (February 1977): 66 + .

4016. Andrew, Jan. *Divorce and the American Family*. New York: Franklin Watts, 1978.

4017. Athearn, Forden. *How to Divorce Your Wife: The Man's Side of Divorce*. Garden City, NY: Doubleday, 1976.

4018. Bailey, Fred, Jr. "Divorce: Is It Destroying the American Family?" *Better Homes and Gardens* 51 (September 1973): 2 + .

4019. Baker, Russell. "Batting .667," *New York Times Magazine* (July 8, 1973): 6.

4020. Baskin, Henry, and Kiel-Friedman, Sonya. *I've Had It, You've Had It!* Los Angeles: Nash Publishing Corp., 1974.

4021. "Bazaar's After-divorce Survival Guide—Symposium," *Harper's Bazaar* 109 (July 1976): 26–31 + .

4022. Blackwell, Robert. *The Fighter's Guide to Divorce*. Chicago: Regnery, 1977.

4023. Block, Jean L. "What the Carters Are Doing to Wipe out Divorce in Washington," *Good Housekeeping* 184 (June 1977): 109 + .

4024. "Branded or Barefaced?" *Time, Supplement* 107 (May 17, 1976): 61.

4025. Bry, Adelaide. "Divorce Dilemma—Do You Really Want That Divorce? A Quiz," *New Woman* 1 (December 1971): 8.

4026. Carroll, Katherine. "Divorce Dilemma," *New Woman* 2 (June–July 1972): 30 + .

4027. Cassidy, Robert. *What Every Man Should Know about Divorce*. Washington, DC: New Republic Books, 1977.

4028. Costa, Simeon. "Grandparents: Sometimes They Come in Six-Packs," *Retirement Living* 18 (July 1978): 24–26.

4029. Dannenberg, Linda. "Getting through the Bad Times," *Ladies Home Journal* 95 (May 1978): 166–68.

4030. *David I. Levine Enterprises, Seminar Division, Presents All about Divorce, and Lots about Marriage* (Madison Square Garden Arena, October 23, 1976). Portsmouth, VA: The Division, [1976].

4031. David, Lester, "Case of Teenage Divorce," *Seventeen* 35 (August 1976): 256–57.

4032. Davis, Douglas. "Divorce-Go-Round," *Newsweek* 84 (July 1, 1974): 11.

4033. Davis, Flora. "Sad but Necessary Facts about Divorce," *Redbook* 149 (May 1977): 223 + .

4034. Dreifus, Claudia. "Decree for a Degree, an Equal Opportunity Divorce," *Ms* 4 (September 1975): 19.

4035. Duncan, T. Roger, and Duncan, Darlene. *You're Divorced, but Your Children Aren't*. Englewood Cliffs, NJ: Prentice-Hall, 1979.

4036. Durbin, Karen. "Premarital Divorce," *Harper's* 248 (May 1974): 8.

4037. Edmonds, Mim R. "Divorce Traps," *Cosmopolitan* 175 (December 1973): 96 + .

4038. Epstein, Joseph. *Divorced in America: Marriage in an Age of Possibility*. New York: E. P. Dutton, 1974.

4039. Felder, Raoul L. *Divorce: The Ways Things Are, Not the Ways Things Should Be*. New York: World Publishing Co., 1971.

4040. Ferguson, Larry. "Divorce: Winner Takes All," *Argosy* 382 (December–January 1975–76): 34–36.

4041. Flanagan, William. "Plain Talk about Divorce: Good Counsel? 'Tis Cheap," *New York* 9 (August 9, 1976): 59.

4042. ———. "Splitting at the 'Y,'" *New York* 9 (October 18, 1976): 91.

4043. Francke, Linda. "An American Divorce," *Newsweek* 83 (March 11, 1974): 58.

4044. Gabor, Zsa Zsa. *How to Catch a Man, How to Keep a Man, How to Get Rid of a Man.* New York: Doubleday, 1970.

4045. Gettleman, Susan, and Markowitz, Janet. *The Courage to Divorce.* New York: Simon & Schuster, 1974.

4046. ———. "No Corpse, No Death," *Single Parent* 18 (March 1975): 5–7 + .

4047. Gittelson, Natalie. "Divorce: Suburban Style," *Harper's Bazaar* 107 (June 1974): 24 + .

4048. Gordon, Bud. "How to Spot the Early Warning Signs of Divorce," *New Woman* 6 (September–October 1976): 36.

4049. Greene, Roberta. *Till Divorce Do You Part.* 2d ed. Pittsburgh: KNOW, 1972.

4050. Grollman, Earl A., and Sams, Marjorie L. *Living through Your Divorce.* Boston, MA: Beacon Press, 1978.

4051. Hallett, Kathryn. "Discover When/ How to Let Go," *New Woman* 4 (September–October 1974): 80–88.

4052. Haspel, Eleanor C. *Marriage in Trouble: A Time of Decision.* Chicago: Nelson-Hall, 1976.

4053. Hirsch, Barbara B. *Divorce, What Every Woman Needs to Know.* Chicago: H. Regnery, 1973.

4054. Hormann, Elizabeth. "Divorce Survival Kit," *Single Parent* 19 (December 1976): 11–13 + .

4055. Hunt, Morton M. "Maybe Divorce Was Good for You," *Single Parent* 13 (April 1970): 4–8 + .

4056. Hunt, Morton, and Hunt, Bernice. *The Divorce Experience.* New York: McGraw-Hill, 1977.

4057. ———. "The Divorce Experience," *Book Digest* 5 (January 1978): 154–74.

4058. ———. "For Women Who Wonder about Divorce: A Major Report," *Redbook* 149 (September 1979): 92 + .

4059. Johnson, Nora. "Journey of a Divorce," *Cosmpolitan* 178 (April 1975): 200–04.

4060. Kalish, Richard. "The Second Time Around," *Single Parent* 21 (November 1975): 8–10 + .

4061. Kessler, Sheila. *The American Way of Divorce: Prescriptions for Change.* Chicago: Nelson-Hall, 1975.

4062. Krantzler, Mel. *Creative Divorce: A New Opportunity for Personal Growth.* New York: M. Evans & Co., 1973.

4063. ———. "Focus on Mel Krantzler and Creative Divorce. Interview," *Harper's Bazaar* 107 (January 1974): 50 + .

4064. Lichtenstein, Grace. "Now the Poor Can Get Divorced, Too," *New York Times Magazine* (April 26, 1970): 30 + .

4065. Maynard, Fredelle. "How to Tell When It's Over," *Woman's Day* 41 (April 24, 1978): 84 + .

4066. Mead, Margaret. "Too Many Divorces, Too Soon," *Redbook* 142 (February 1974): 72 + .

4067. Melman, Carla. "Divorce: A Community Affair," *Single Parent* 17 (April 1974): 8–12.

4068. Moffett, Robert K., and Scherer, Jack F. *Dealing with Divorce.* Boston, MA: Little, Brown, 1976.

4069. "More and More Broken Marriages," *U.S. News and World Report* 73 (August 14, 1973): 30.

4070. Mulligan, Elizabeth. "Divorce Court: Scene of Decay," *Marriage,* vol. 52, no. 4 (1970): 38–43.

4071. Murray, Thomas J. "The Business of Getting Divorced," *Duns,* vol. 99, no. 4 (1972): 85–86.

4072. Ogg, Elizabeth. *Divorce.* New York: Public Affairs Committee, 1975 (Public Affairs Pamphlet #528).

4073. Olds, Sally W. "Is Divorce Contagious?" *Ladies Home Journal* 94 (February 1977): 81 + .

4074. Pearce, William W., and Hoffer William. *Caught in the Act: The True Adventures of a Divorce Detective.* New York: Stein & Day, 1976.

4075. Polatin, Phillip, and Philtine, Ellen C. "Divorce: From the Man's Point of View," *Single Parent* 17 (November 1974): 5–10 + .

4076. Popenoe, Paul. "Toward Fewer Divorces," *Marriage,* vol. 52, no. 6 (1970): 50–52.

4077. "Protestants Offer a Ritual to Mark the End of a Marriage," *People* 6 (December 13, 1976): 95.

4078. Raab, Robert A. *Coping with Divorce.* New York: Richards Rosen Press, 1979.

4079. Reice, Sylvie. "Surviving the Divorce Epidemic," *Family Circle* 88 (November 1975): 84 + .

4080. Rubin, Theodore I. "When Is Divorce the Answer?" *Ladies Home Journal* 95 (November 1978): 82.

4081. Salk, Lee. *What Every Child Would Like Parents to Know about Divorce.* New York: Harper & Row, 1978.

4082. "Separation and Divorce: A Reader Survey," *McCalls* 106 (November 1978): 125–26.

4083. Shaw, Leslie. "Divorce Dilemma," *New Woman* 1 (June 1971): 15 + .

4084. Sheresky, Norman, and Mannes, Marya. *Uncoupling: The Art of Coming Apart.* New York: Viking Press, 1972.

4085. Sheridan, Kathleen. *Living with Divorce.* Chicago: Thomas More Press, 1977.

4086. Silden, Isobel. "Problems of Divorce," *Dynamic Years* 14 (March–April 1979): 35–36.

4087. Singleton, Mary A. "Trouble Spots after the Marriage Is Over," *New Woman* 6 (May–June 1976): 23–26.

4088. Spikol, Art. "It's Not the End of the World," *Philadelphia* 69 (February 1979): 100–03 + ; *St. Louis* 19 (October 1978): 75 + .

4089. "Status of Divorcées: Moving Up After Splitting Up," *Human Behavior* 8 (April 1979): 50.

4090. Stoddard, Maynard G. "For Better or for Worse," *Saturday Evening Post* 251 (December 1979): 58–59 + .

4091. Sundbye, Ronald L. "Clergymen Speak Up on Marriage and Divorce: Divorce—Sensible Style," *Single Parent* 13 (March 1970): 4 + .

4092. Taylor, Geraldine. "Strength," *Essence* 5 (February 1975): 58 + .

4093. "Throwaway Marriages—Threat to the American Family," *U.S. News and World Report* 78 (January 13, 1975): 43–44.

4094. Trager, Olive. "Healthy Divorce," *Harper's Bazaar* 105 (June 1972): 42–43.

4095. Tucker, Carll. "On Splitting," *Saturday Review* 5 (January 21, 1978): 64.

4096. Vanton, Monte. *Marriage, Grounds for Divorce.* Burbank, CA: Victoria Press, 1977.

4097. Viorst, Judith. "It's Never a Nice Divorce," *Redbook* 142 (January 1974): 29 + .

4098. Walder, Eugene. *How to Get out of an Unhappy Marriage or Unhappy Relationship.* New York: G. P. Putnam's Sons, 1978.

4099. Walker, Greta. "The Facts of Divorce," *Galmour* 74 (February 1974): 162+.

4100. "Who Stays Married Longer," *U.S. News and World Report* 73 (October 30, 1972): 39.

4101. Williams, Mona. "Waiting out His Divorce . . . ," *Cosmopolitan* 173 (April 1972): 112+.

4102. Wright, H. Norman. *An Answer to Divorce.* Irvine, CA: Harvest House Publishers, 1977.

4103. Younger, Judith T. "Love Is Not Enough: Divorce and Feminism," *New Republic* 174 (June 19, 1976): 8–9.

CAUSES OF DIVORCE

4104. Cornish, Edward. "The Future of the Family: Intimacy in an Age of Loneliness," *Futurist* 13 (February 1979): 45–58.

4105. "The Real Reasons for Divorce," *Pageant* 32 (August 1976): 12–17.

4106. Taylor, Robert B. "Behind the Surge in Broken Marriages," *U.S. News and World Report* 86 (January 22, 1979): 52–53.

DIVORCE COUNSELING AND MEDIATION

4107. "Cleaning Up after Divorce," *Human Behavior* 6 (December 1977): 29.

4108. Hunt, Morton and Hunt, Bernice. "Surviving a Divorce," *Family Circle* 92 (August 28, 1979): 49–50.

4109. Kiester, Edwin, Jr. "How Divorce Counselors Sweeten the Sour Taste of Separation," *Today's Health* 53 (November 1975): 46–50.

4110. Lobsenz, Norman M. "Divorce Settlements without Legal Strife: Family Mediation Center of Atlanta," *McCalls* 103 (June 1976): 35.

4111. Maynard, Fredelle. "Must Divorce Be So Painful?" *Woman's Day* 37 (June 1974): 48+.

4112. ———. "Must Divorce Be So Painful?" *Reader's Digest* 105 (July 1974): 98–101.

4113. "Separation Pains," *Human Behavior,* vol. 5 no. 1 (1976): 30.

DIVORCE PROCESS

4114. Olds, Sally W. "Stages of Divorce: How Families Learn to Love Again," *Ladies Home Journal* 96 (September 1979): 118+.

4115. O'Phelan, Lou. "Take Five: Come Alive!" *Single Parent* 21 (September 1978): 17–19.

DIVORCE RATES

4116. Gordon, Michael. "Exploding the High Divorce Rate Myth," *Family Circle,* vol. 81, no. 6 (1972): 18–21.

4117. "Permissive Laws and Divorce Rates," *Human Behavior,* vol. 5, no. 3 (1976): 63.

4118. "Rising Divorce Rate," *Intellect* 103 (May 1975): 488.

4119. "Surge in Easy Divorces—And the Problems They Bring," *U.S. News and World Report* 76 (April 22, 1974): 43–45.

ETIQUETTE

4120. Rabwin, Marcella. "Divorce Etiquette," *Cornet* 14 (December 1976): 58–63.

4121. Sherberg, Ellen. "Divorce Etiquette," *St. Louis* 10 (January 1978): 39–42.

FOREIGN DIVORCES

4122. "Demise of the Quckie Divorce," *Time* 96 (November 16, 1970): 96.

4123. "Divorce, Caribbean Style," *Time* 98 (August 30, 1971): 43.

4124. "Divorce, Mexican Style," *Newsweek* 76 (August 24, 1970): 43.

4125. Wolfe, Linda. "The Urban Strategist/Divorce—Dominican Style," *New York,* vol. 5, no. 5 (1972): 58–60.

FRIENDLY DIVORCES

4126. Austin, Eugene. *The Practical Aspects of Amicable Divorce.* Foley, MO: Austin, 1979.

4127. Cadden, Vivian. "Myth of the Civilized Divorce," *Redbook* 140 (February 1973): 89+.

4128. Klemesrud, Judy. "Still Friends after Divorce, Ex Husband/Wife Teams," *New Woman* 6 (May–June 1976): 43–44.

HUMOR

4129. Cookson, Bernard. *Till Divorce Do Us Part.* London: Dobson, 1976.

4130. Erikson, Alden. "Divorce—Hollywood Style," *Playboy,* vol. 18, no. 2 (1971): 159–63.

4131. Gallin, Martin. "Divorce—American Style," *Law Office Economics and Management,* vol. 11, no. 2 (1970): 309–11.

JEWISH DIVORCE

4132. Wolynski, Mara. "I Do. I Don't: A Jewish Marriage and Divorce," *Village Voice* 24 (August 20, 1979): 38+.

ROMAN CATHOLIC DIVORCE

4133. "Catholic Divorce," *Newsweek* 80 (August 7, 1972): 60.

4134. Ryan, Michael. "Uncoupling Catholics," *Boston Magazine* 67 (April 1975): 46–49+.

STATES

4135. DePalma, Anthony. "Divorce, New Jersey Style," *New Jersey Monthly* 3 (November 1978): 61–65+.

4136. Ephron, Nora. "Divorce, Maryland Style," *New York* 7 (January 28, 1974): 52–53.

4137. Flanagan, William. "Divorce, New York Style," *New York* 9 (April 12, 1976): 71–72.

4138. ———. "Divorce, New York Style," *New York* 9 (June 21, 1976): 71.

4139. Koch, Lew. "Divorce, Chicago Style," *Chicago* 24 (July 1975), 131–137.

4140. Shartar, Martin. "Divorce Atlanta Style: The Male Trauma," *Atlanta* 16 (July 1976): 48–52.

4141. Shultz, Susan. "The Truama of Divorce," *Phoenix* 13 (April 1978): 50–53+.

4142. Van Gelder, Lawrence. "Divorce, California Style," *McCalls* 106 (January 1979): 41.

DIVORCE (ECONOMIC ASPECTS)

4143. Auerbach, Sylvia. "And So They Were—Divorced," *Cosmpolitan* 182 (May 1977): 154 + .

4144. "Divorce: Make Sense, Not War," *Money,* vol. 2, no. 2 (1973): 28–32.

4145. "Divorcees and Dollars," *Human Behavior,* vol. 4, no. 9 (1975): 61.

4146. Gross, Paul. "Finances of Divorce," *House and Garden* 148 (November 1976): 30 + .

4147. Lake, Alice. "Divorcées: The New Poor," *McCalls* 103 (September 1976): 18 + .

4148. Lavoie, Rachel. "Who Gets What in a Divorce," *Money,* vol. 7, no. 4 (1978): 66–69.

4149. Lemov, Penelope. "The High, High Costs of Breaking Up," *Washingtonian* 12 (April 1977): 205–09.

4150. "Money Side of Divorce," *Changing Times* 27 (September 1973): 29–32.

4151. Seixas, Suzanne. "Divorced Mother's Fears for Tomorrow," *Money,* vol. 7, no. 7 (1978): 85–86 + .

4152. Shapiro, Andrew O. "Bills and Divorcement," *New York* 12 (February 5, 1979): 58–59.

4153. Tarrant, Marguerite. "The Divorcee's Dilemma, or Making Do with Less," *Money,* vol. 3, no. 12 (1974): 85 + .

4154. Yates, Martha. "Finances: Getting Down to Basics," *Harper's Bazaar* 109 (July 1976): 29 + .

4155. "Your Rights as a Divorcee," *Family Circle* 92 (November 1, 1979): 52 + .

DIVORCE INSURANCE

4156. Mead, Margaret. "Divorce Insurance: A New Idea," *Redbook* 142 (March 1974): 38 + .

4157. Pascoe, Jean. "Divorce Insurance," *McCalls* 100 (April 1973): 49.

4158. "Wedding Present," *Newsweek* 81 (January 29, 1973): 64.

FARMS

4159. Farm Divorces: Splitting the Farm Business," *Successful Farmer* 76 (May 1978): 7.

4160. Gilles, Jean. "Divorce Can Split Up a Farm as Well as a Marriage," *Farm Journal* 102 (April 1978): 53–55.

4161. Lane, Laura. "His and Hers Estate Plans . . . How to Protect the Children of an Earlier Marriage," *Farm Journal* 102 (September 1978): 39–41.

PROPERTY SETTLEMENTS

4162. Ashley, Paul. *Oh Promise Me but Put It in Writing: Living Together Arrangements, without, during, and after Marriage.* New York: McGraw-Hill, 1978.

4163. Kosner, Alice. "Rich Divorcees/Impoverished Ex-Husbands," *Cosmpolitan* 180 (April 1976): 212 + .

4164. "Pensions Land in Divorce Court," *Business Week* 2508 (November 7, 1977): 104.

4165. Wiegner, Kathleen K. "The High Cost of Leaving," *Forbes* 123 (February 19, 1979): 44–49.

DIVORCE (LEGAL ASPECTS)

4166. Bass, Howard L., and Rein, M. L. *Divorce Law: The Complete Practical Guide.* Englewood Cliffs, NJ: Prentice-Hall, 1978.

4167. ———. *Divorce or Marriage: A Legal Guide.* Englewood Cliffs, NJ: Prentice-Hall, 1976.

4168. Callahan, Parnell J. T. *The Law of Separation and Divorce.* 3d ed., rev. Dobbs Ferry, NY: Oceana Publications, 1970.

4169. ———. *The Law of Separation and Divorce.* 4th ed., rev. Dobbs Ferry, NY: Oceana Publications, 1979.

4170. Cantor, Donald J. *Escape from Marriage: How to Solve the Problems of Divorce.* New York: William Morrow & Co., 1971.

4171. DeWolf, Rose. *The Bonds of Acrimony.* Philadelphia, PA: J. B. Lippincott Co., 1970.

4172. Doppler, George F. *America Needs Total Divorce Reform—Now!* New York: Vantage Press, 1973.

4173. Doyle, R. F. *Rape of the Male.* St. Paul, MIN: Poor Richard's Press, 1976.

4174. Dunn, George T. *How to Protect Yourself and Children in Divorce: An Authoritative Guide to Help Women toward Successful Proceedings before and after the Divorce.* Syracuse, NY: Limestone Pub. Co., 1978.

4175. Frolich, Newton. *Making the Best of It: A Common-Sense Guide to Negotiating Divorce.* New York: Harper & Row, 1971.

4176. Kohut, Nester C. *Divorce for the Unbroken Marriage.* Madison, WI: Family Law Publications, 1973.

4177. Kole, Janet. "New Grounds for Divorce," *Harper's Bazaar* 109 (July 1976): 44 + .

4178. Mayer, Michael F. *Divorce and Annulment in the 50 States.* 3d ed., rev. New York: Arco Books, 1975.

4179. " 'Men's Lib' Movement Trains Its Guns on Divorce Courts," *U.S. News and World Report* 83 (September 12, 1977): 42.

4180. Nordstrom, Ervin E. *God Knows I Tried: Divorce in America.* Port Washington, NY: Ashley Books, 1979.

4181. "Who Files for Divorce," *Human Behavior* 6 (August 1977): 45.

ATTORNEYS

4182. Bedell, Susan. "Divorce Dilemma," *New Woman* 1 (September 1971): 10 + .

4183. Goulden, Joseph. "Divorce Lawyers: A Glimpse under the Rocks," *Penthouse* 8 (February 1977): 62 + .

4184. Green, Tony. "Wickedest War of All," *Philadelphia Magazine* 69 (December 1978): 185–92 + .

4185. Sopkin, Charles. "The Roughest Divorce Lawyers in Town," *New York* 7 (November 4, 1974): 52–56.

DO-IT-YOURSELF DIVORCE

4186. "Barber Nicks Divorce Lawyers," *Business Week* 2239 (July 29, 1972): 44.

4187. Barkin, Robert. "Divorce Kits," *McCalls* 104 (March 1977): 45.

4188. Dean, George W. *How to Divorce without Lawyers.* Louisville, KY: Touchstone, 1972.

4189. "Do-It-Yourself Divorce," *Newsweek* 78 (November 8, 1971): 71.

4190. Downey, Charles E. "Do-It-Yourself Kits for Doctoring and Lawyering," *Money* 8 (August 1979): 71–72.

4191. Flanagan, William. "You Don't Need a Lawyer to Get a Divorce—But It Helps," *New York* 9 (December 6, 1976): 107–108.

4192. Goodman, Emily J. "Do-It-Yourself Divorce," *McCalls* 101 (April 1974): 35.

4193. Gordon, Kathie. "Do-It-Yourself Divorce," *Cosmpolitan* 183 (October 1977): 214 + .

4194. Levine, David I. *How to Get a Divorce without a Lawyer.* New York: Bantam Books, 1979.

Do-It-Yourself: Arizona

4195. Moore, Lynn S. *Splitting Up! A Guide to Divorce with or without a Lawyer in the State of Arizona, with the Forms You Will Need to Obtain your Divorce.* [s.l.]: D. W. Giboney, 1975.

4196. Wainwright, Sally. *Arizona Divorce without a Lawyer.* Tucson, AZ: Omen Press, 1973.

Do-It-Yourself: California

4197. Boyance, Rudolph E. *Manual for Divorce, Propia Persona.* Los Angeles: California Divorce Council, 1973.

4198. California Divorce Council. *Steps 1[–5] of our 5 Step Manual for Divorce: Propia Persona.* Los Angeles: The Council, 1976.

4199. Diamond, S. J. "The Trials of a California Do-It-Yourself Advocate," *People* 3 (May 26, 1975): 42–43.

4200. Greene, Freda. "Do-It-Yourself Divorce," *Coronet* 14 (June 1976): 35–38.

4201. Rogers, Harry E. *How to Do a California Divorce.* Carmel-by-the-Sea, CA: Self Help Publications, 1977.

4202. Sherman, Charles E. *How to Do Your Own Divorce in California; With the Forms You Will Need to Do It.* Berkeley, CA: Nolo Press, 1975.

Do-It-Yourself: Colorado

4203. Hamilton, Harper. *The No Fault Divorce Guide.* Boulder, CO: Hamilton Press, 1978.

4204. Johnson, James E. *The Divorce Book.* Boulder, CO: Pine Tree Books, 1979.

4205. Williams, David, and Black, Paul. *The $27 Divorce: A Practical Guide to the Do-It-Yourself Divorce.* Denver, CO: Asterisk Press, 1972.

Do-It-Yourself: Florida

4206. Brill, Steven. "Divorce Florida Style," *Esquire* 90 (July 4, 1978): 14 + .

4207. Hinson, Sandra. "Want a Divorce? Rosemary Furman Can Get It for You Wholesale—But Lawyers Are Trying to Stop Her," *People* 10 (August 21, 1978): 80.

Do-It-Yourself: Illinois

4208. Wysong, Robert J. *Divorce in Chicago without a Lawyer.* Chicago: Consumers Publishing Co., 1974.

Do-It-Yourself: Indiana

4209. Taylor, Vincent S. *How to Do Your Own Divorce in Indiana.* [Bloomington, IN]: Taylor, [1978].

Do-It-Yourself: Maine

4210. Divorce Reform, Inc. *Do Your Own Divorce in Maine.* Ashville, ME: Cobblesmith, 1974.

Do-It-Yourself: Massachusetts

4211. Jancourtz, Isabella. *The Massachusetts Woman's Divorce Handbook.* Weston, MA: Jancourtz, 1974.

Do-It-Yourself: New Jersey

4212. Carpenter, Teresa. "Law: Divorce Thyself," *New Jersey Monthly* 1 (June 1977): 13.

4213. Sommer, Leslie. *How to Get a Divorce with or without a Lawyer.* Cherry Hill, NJ: Evans-Taylor, 1978.

Do-It-Yourself: New York

4214. Allen, Charles M. *How to Get a New York Divorce for under $100.* New York: Allen Advertising Co., 1973.

4215. Green, Mark. "Divorce, Long Island Style," *New York* 12 (June 1979): 51–54.

4216. Weathers, Diane. "Cut-rate Divorce," *Newsweek* 93 (February 26, 1979): 93.

Do-It-Yourself: North Carolina

4217. Barrier, Joseph L., and Teague, Franklin L. *Divorce Kit.* Charlotte, NC: Barrier & Teague, 1978.

4218. McGee, Michael H. *Do Your Own Divorce in North Carolina.* Freeport: ME: Cobblesmith, 1978.

Do-It-Yourself: Oregon

4219. Feminist Divorce Collective. *Parting: A Handbook for Self-Help Divorce in Oregon, Legal Forms Included*. Portland, OR: Women's Place, 1976.

Do-It-Yourself: Pennsylvania

4220. Gates, Samuel K. *Divorce in Pennsylvania: A People's Guide: What You Should Know If You're Thinking of Divorce*. York, PA: Liberty Cap Books, 1975.

4221. Polis, Sheri. "Divorce on a Shoestring," *Philadelphia* 69 (February 1978): 158.

Do-It-Yourself: Texas

4222. Gilstrap, Frank. *How to Do Your Own Texas Divorce for under $35*. Arlington, TX: How-to Press, 1974.

Do-It-Yourself: Virginia

4223. Howell, John C. *The No Fault Divorce Guide*. [Leesburg, VA]: Citizens Law Library, 1979.

4224. Kalenik, Sandra, and Bernstein, Jay S. *How to Get a Divorce: A Practical Handbook for Residents of the District of Columbia, Maryland, Virginia Who Are Contemplating Separation and Divorce*. Washington, DC: Washingtonian Books, 1976.

Do-It-Yourself: Vermont

4225. McCarren, V. Louise, and Nicholson, Deirdre T. *Non-Lawyer's Guide to Getting a Divorce in Vermont*. Middlebury, VT: Addison, 1977.

Do-It-Yourself: Washington

4226. Giboney, Daniel W. *So You Want a Divorce: How to Do It Yourself for the State of Washington*. Opportunity, WA: Printed by Spokane Valley Herald for Giboney, 1973.

Do-It-Yourself: Wisconsin

4227. Milwaukee Legal Services. *Divorce in Milwaukee County: How to Do It Yourself: A Manual to Instruct People How to Represent Themselves in Divorce Actions in the Milwaukee County Legal System*. Milwaukee, WI: Milwaukee-Legal Services, 1976.

LEGISLATION

4228. Mitchelson, Marvin M. *Made in Heaven, Settled in Court*. Los Angeles: J. P. Tarcher, 1976.

4229. Shapiro, Andrew O. "New Divorce Bill," *New York* 12 (May 14, 1979): 66 + .

4230. "What Price Divorce?" *Editorial Research Reports* 2 (September 25, 1974): n.p.

4231. Wylie, Evan M. "The Disgrace of Our Divorce Laws," *Good Housekeeping* 170 (April 1970): 98 + .

NO-FAULT

4232. Brackley, Judith. Divorce, Massachusetts Style: Finding Fault with No-Fault," *Boston Phoenix* (September 28, 1976): 6–7.

4233. Calbreath, Dean. "Split Decisions," *San Francisco* 21 (February 1979): 60–63.

4234. "California Style," *Time* 95 (January 12, 1970): 8.

4235. DeWolf, Rose. "No Fault Divorce: Myths of American Marriage," *Nation* 216 (April 23, 1973): 527–29.

4236. Falconer, Barbara. "California: Is Divorce without Guilt Working?" *McCalls* 98 (April 1971): 41.

4237. Goldstone, Patricia. " 'Til Debt Do We Part," *New West* 3 (April 24, 1978): 80.

4238. Gough, Aidan R. "California Shows How: Divorce without Squalor," *Nation* 210 (January 12, 1970): 17–20.

4239. Lobsenz, Norman N. "No-Fault Divorce: Is It Working?" *Reader's Digest* 112 (March 1978): 113–16.

4240. Murray, Robert M. *Divorce in Virginia: All You Need to Know Simply Explained*. [s.l.]: Murray, 1976.

4241. Nebraska. Governor's Commission on the Status of Women. *"No-Fault" Divorce: a Resource Book and Discussion Guide for Nebraska Women's Organizations*. Lincoln NB: The Commission, 1977.

4242. "No-Fault Divorces," *Human Behavior*, vol. 2, no. 12 (1973): 61.

4243. "No-Fault Divorces—They're Catching On," *U.S. News and World Report* 74 (June 4, 1973): 41–42.

4244. "Now, the Era of Mail-Order Divorces," *U.S. News and World Report* 86 (January 8, 1979): 8.

4245. "Pennsylvania vs. No Fault," *Philadelphia* 69 (February 1978): 154.

4246. Shaffer, Helen B. "No-Fault Divorce," *Editorial Research Reports* (October 10, 1973): 779–96.

4247. "Surge in No-Fault Divorce and Its Spreading Impact," *U.S. News and World Report* 83 (July 25, 1977): 76.

4248. Swords, Betty. "No-Fault Divorce Has Some Faults," *McCalls* 101 (February 1974): 53

4249. Velie, Lester. "What's Killing Our Marriages?" *Reader's Digest* 102 (June 1973): 152–56.

4250. Wheeler, Michael. *No-Fault Divorce*. Boston: Beacon Press, 1974.

STATES

4251. Block, Winston J. *The Ins and Outs of Illinois Divorce Law in Plain English*. Joliet, IL: Bloch, 1976.

4252. Braun, Julius. *Surviving Divorce: A Primer of Marital Dissolution*. Hicksville, NY: Exposition Press, 1975.

4253. Canudo, Eugene R. *Marriage, Divorce and Adoption Laws of New York*. Jamacia, NY: Gould, 1971.

4254. Eddy, R. Lee, III. *What You Should Know about Marriage, Divorce, Annulment, Separation and Community Property in Louisiana*. New York: Exposition Press, 1974.

4255. Garrity, Robert W. *Minnesota Divorce Law*. Minneapolis, MN: Wellington Pub. Co., 1972.

4256. Harkey, Ira, III. "Divorce: Louisiana Takes a More Liberal Look at Some Outdated Laws," *New Orleans* 12 (May 1978): 38–42.

1257. Koch, Harry W. *California Marriage and Dissolution Law*. Rev. ed. San Francisco, CA: Ken-Books, 1976.

4258. McConaughey, Dan E., and Ross, Michele. *Georgia Handbook on Divorce, Alimony, and Child Custody*. Layman's ed. Norcross, GA: Harrison Co., 1977.

4259. Maloy, Richard H. W. *Your Questions Answered about Florida Divorce Law*. Miami, FL: Windward Publishing, 1977.

4260. ———. *Your Questions Answered about Florida Law and Family Relationships in Life and Death*. Miami, FL: Windward Publishing, 1978.

4261. ———. *Your Questions Answered about Florida Law and Your Continuing Obligations after Divorce.* Miami, FL: Windward Publishing, 1978.

4262. Olen, Stanley. *Screwed by Lawyers and Judges.* Chatham, NJ: Olen, 1977.

4263. Palley, Michael R., and Schwartz, Lawrence I. *Divorce, California Style.* Los Angeles: Raymond Pub. Co., 1970.

4264. Tittle, Diane. "Ohio's New Divorce—Easy as Flicking Your Bic!" *Cleveland* 5 (February 1976): 42–47.

4265. Voeckler, Pamela R. P. *Divorce: What You Should Know about No Fault*

Divorce in Georgia. [Union City, GA]: Voeckler, 1976].

SUITS

4266. Epstein, Edward Z. *Notorious Divorces.* Secaucus, NJ: Lyle Stuart, 1976.

4267. Hennen, Claudia M. "Frontlines: Egads, He's Out Loose," *Mother Jones* 4 (December 1979): 12.

4268. Smilgis, Martha. "Soraya Khashoggi Is Suing for $2 Billion," *People* 12 (August 1979): 34.

4269. Thistle, Frank. "The World's Weirdest Divorces," *Pageant* 32 (January 1977): 26–31.

TAXES

4270. Cherney, Walter. "Single Parents and Income Taxes," *Single Parent* 13 (January–February 1970): 3–5+.

4271. Dorfman, John R. "Dealing the Tax Man out of a Divorce," *Money* 6 (June 1977): 81–88.

4272. Hanks, George F.; Hensley, Dennis E.; and Summers, William J. "What Every Divorced Woman Should Know about Taxes," *Essence* 9 (March 1979): 66–67+.

4273. "Testing Those Tax Divorces," *Newsweek* 94 (September 24, 1979): 109.

DIVORCE (IN THE MILITARY COMMUNITY)

4274. Covill, Bruce. "Cutting Up Retiree's Paycheck: Spouses Disagree," *Air Force Times* 37 (April 18, 1977): 16.

4275. ———. "Military Retired Pay: 'Property' or 'Income'?" *Air Force Times* 37 (Apirl 11, 1977): 33.

4276. ———. "Paying till Death Do Us Part: Divorce Ruling," *Air Force Times* 37 (April 25, 1977): 14.

4277. Ewing, Lee. "State Order on Garnishment Backed," *Air Force Times* 36 (March 29, 1976): 4.

4278. ———. "U.S. to Help Trace Fathers Who Skip out," *Air Force Times* 36 (August 27, 1975): 4.

4279. "Ex-Spouses May Win Claim on Retired Pay—Bill Launched in House," *Air Force Times* 38 (March 20, 1978): 2.

4280. "400 Have Pay Garnisheed for Child Support, Alimony," *Air Force Times* 35 (August 6, 1975): 18.

4281. "Garnishment Policies Detailed," *Air Force Times* 36 (April 12, 1976): 12.

4282. "Garnishment Rules Clarified," *Air Force Times* 36 (November 5, 1975): 3.

4283. Gerow, Ann. "Interim Rules Issued on Garnishment," *Air Force Times* 35 (February 26, 1975): 3.

4284. "Limits Set on Garnishing," *Air Force Times* 37 (June 20, 1977): 1.

4285. "Navy Rights and Benefits: Medical and Health Care," *All Hands* 744 (January 1979): 34–41.

4286. "New Ruling on Divorce Hikes BAQ," *Air Force Times* 30 (July 15, 1970): 16.

4287. Plattner, Andy. "Panel Eyes Benefits for Ex-spouses," *Air Force Times* 38 (November 7, 1977): 1+.

4288. "P.O.W. Divorce Surge," *Time* 105 (June 9, 1975): 41.

4289. "Retired Money Eyed as Divorce Pay," *Air Force Times* 37 (October 18, 1976): 11.

4290. "Retirement Pay (Can't Be Attached) as Property," *Air Force Times* 38 (May 29, 1978): 3.

4291. Rogers, Jim. "Divorce, the Last Alternative," *Soldiers,* vol. 32, no. 11 (1977): 6–10.

4292. "Several Methods Finalize Divorce" (Law and You Series), *Air Force Times* 31 (January 20, 1971): 21.

4293. Thomas, Lucille, and Quinn, Garnet. "Divorce: Confessions of Two Service Wives," *Air Force Times, Times Magazine Supplement* 37 (April 18, 1977): 6–10+.

4294. "What Divorce Proceedings Entail" (Law and You Series), *Air Force Times* 31 (January 6, 1971): 30.

4295. Williams, John W., Jr. "Divorce and the Air Force Family," *Air Force Times* 57 (October 1974): 54–57.

DIVORCE AND WORK

4296. "Divorced Execs: It's Lonely at the Top," *Human Behavior* 7 (December 1978): 49–50.

4297. "Doctors and Divorce," *Human Behavior,* vol. 2, no. 4 (1973): 39 + .

4298. Flanagan, William. "No Divorce at the Top," *Esquire* 91 (June 19, 1979): 8–10.

4299. "Highly Paid Women, Divorce Prone: Study," *Jet* 22 (November 22, 1979): 25.

4300. "Interview Tips for Divorced Women," *Family Circle* 91 (August 7, 1978): 80 + .

4301. Miller, Ann M. "Do Working Wives Risk Divorce?" *McCalls* 103 (September 1976): 42.

4302. "Politicians and Divorce," *Editorial Research Service* 11 (July 27, 1978): n.p.

DIVORCED PERSONS

4303. Armstrong, Ann. *On Your Own.* London: Aldous Books, 1974.

4304. Armstrong, Ron, and Hover, Dorothea. "Starting Over after Divorce . . . What?" *Single Parent,* vol. 22, no. 8 (1979): 5–8 + .

4305 . Baroni, Diane. "The New Divorcées," *Comsopolitan* 176 (March 1974): 60 + .

4306. Bedell, Susanna. "Divorce Dilemma: Going to a Party Alone," *New Woman* 1 (November 1971): 20 + .

4307. Berman, Eleanor. "Overcoming Guilt," *Harper's Bazaar* 112 (February 1979): 133 + .

4308. Berson, Barbara, and Bova, Ben. *Survival Guide for the Suddenly Single.* New York: St. Martin's Press, 1974.

4309. Bliss, Elsie. "Single Bliss," *Single Parent* 22 (October 1979): 9–10 + .

4310. Butler, C. O. "Long Distance Father," *Single Parent* 19 (October 1976): 11–12 + .

4311. Carro, Geraldine. "How Parents Can Talk Back to the School System," *Ladies Home Journal* 96 (July 1979): 67.

4312. "Coming to Grips with Your Post-divorce Blues," *Business Week* 2317 (February 9, 1974): 77–78.

4313. Comisky, Myra. "With Eyes Wide Open," *Single Parent* 22 (May 1979): 13–14 + .

4314. Cooper, Arthur. "Is There Life after Divorce?" *Penthouse* 8 (February 1977): 35.

4315. Cowan, Ronnie. "Divorce without Marriage: The Curious Case of Lee Marvin's Common-Law Wife; Interview," *Ladies Home Journal* 90 (October 1973): 78 + .

4316. Curran, Jan G., and Wetton, Marcy B. *The Statue of Liberty Is Cracking Up: A Guide to Loving, Leaving, and Living Again.* New York: Harcourt Brace Jovanovich, 1979.

4317. Day, Ingeborg. "How I Stayed Friends with my Mother-in-Law," *Ms* 7 (November 1978): 12–18.

4318. Decter, Midge. *The Liberated Woman and Other Americans.* New York: Coward, McCann & Geoghegan, 1971.

4319. "Divorce in the Barrios," *Human Behavior,* vol. 2, no. 1 (1973): 51 + .

4320. "Divorce: Men Have Rights Too," *Harper's Weekly* 64 (May 9, 1975): 11.

4321. Fleming, Jennifer B., and Washburne, Carolyn K. "The First Six Months," *Harper's Bazaar* 109 (July 1976): 27 + .

4322. Flinn, Richard. *The Third Breed.* Phoenix: Ross Publications, 1976.

4323. Ford, Charlotte. "Modern Woman's Guide to the Etiquette of Divorce," *Ladies Home Journal* 95 (March 1978): 79 + .

4324. Furfine, Allen. "Outside Father," *Single Parent* 22 (May 1979): 15 + .

4325. Gertz, Kathryn R. "ERA and the Liberated Divorce," *Harper's Bazaar* 109 (July 1976): 45 + .

4326. Green, Leslie. "Why I Miss Being Married," *Woman's Day* vol. 38, no. 2 (1974): 51 + .

4327. Greene, A. C. "Heartbreak Hotel," *D Magazine—The Magazine of Dallas* 4 (November 1977): 104–07.

4328. Helmlinger, Trudy. "The Pain of Leaving," *New Woman* 6 (July–August 1977): 77 + .

4329. Hinson, Sandra. "A Divorced Doctor Is Adopting the Little Girl He Saved from Dying of Cystic Fibrosis," *People* 12 (October 15, 1979): 113 + .

4330. Hoffman, James W. "Is Divorce Fattening?" *Weight Watchers* 11 (June 1978): 10–13.

4331. Horn, Jack. "Personality and Divorce," *Psychology Today,* vol. 10, no. 5 (1976): 138 + .

4332. Hunt, Morton, and Hunt, Bernice. "What's New in the World of the Formerly Married," *Single Parent* 20 (October 1977): 10–12 + .

4333. Irwin, Lee J. "Can This Divorce Be Saved?" *Single Parent* 22 (September 1979): 15–16 + .

4334. Jason, Judy. "Single in the 70's," *Single Parent* 21 (March 1978): 15–18.

4335. Jensen, Marilyn. "For Better or Worse," *Single Parent* 21 (December 1978): 26 + .

4336. Johnson, Stephen M. *First Person Singular: Living the Good Life Alone*. Philadelphia, PA: J.B. Lippincott Co., 1977.

4337. ———. "How to Say Good-by," *Cosmopolitan* 183 (December 1977): 154 + .

4338. Jones, Judy. "When a Husband Walks out," *New Woman* 5 (March–April 1975): 30.

4339. Kalish, Richard A. "Dear Divorced Friend," *Single Parent* 21 (June 1978): 5–6.

4340. Kapit, Hanna. "It's the Parent Who 'Suffers the Most!'" *Single Parent* 13 (January–February 1970): 6–10.

4341. Kempton, Beverly. "Decision Training for Divorcees," *McCalls* 102 (March 1975): 52.

4342. Kosner, Alice. "Starting Over: What Divorced Women Discover," *McCalls* 106 (March 1979): 22 + . R.

4343. Krantzler, Mel. "Learning to Love Again," *Cosmopolitan* 185 (July 1978): 204 + .

4344. ———. "Learning to Love Again," *Cosmopolitan* 181 (August 1976): 90–98.

4345. Krantzler, Mel, and Schwenkmeyer, Barry. "Self-Renewal: Divorce's Surprising Dividend," *Cosmpolitan* 179 (July 1975): 176–79.

4346. LaBarre, Harriet. "To Be Happily Divorced, Avoid This Deadly Trap," *New Woman* 6 (September–October 1976): 37–40.

4347. Lehr, Claire J. "Fathers in Name Only," *Parents' Magazine* 52 (May 1977): 44 + .

4348. Lewis, Shawn D. "Divorce: How to Survive One of the Worst Times of Your Life," *Ebony* 34 (July 1979): 53–56 + .

4349. Lobsenz, Norman M. "How Divorced Young Mothers Learn to Stand Alone," *Redbook* 138 (November 1971): 83 + .

4350. McCall, Robert, and Stocking, Holly. "The Pain of Divorce," *Oklahoma Observer* 11 (July 10, 1979): 7.

4351. McConnell, Lynda L. "Jingle the Holiday Blues," *Single Parent* 19 (December 1976): 5–7.

4352. McCourtney, Lorena. "The Dangerous Age," *Coronet* 15 (April 1977): 46–49.

4353. McKinney, Sally. "How Can You Say Goodbye?" *Single Parent* 21 (June 1978): 13–15 + .

4354. ———. "Where Is Everybody Anyway?" *Single Parent* 20 (November 1977): 7–8 + .

4355. Markham, Margaret. "How Does Divorce Affect Your Health?" *Harper's Bazaar* 109 (July 1976): 28 + .

4356. Mayleas, Davidyne. "The Stress of Divorce," *Harper's Bazaar* 112 (February 1979): 132–33 + .

4357. Michels, Therese. "Sins of the Fathers," *Single Parent* 17 (April 1974): 16–17.

4358. Napolitane, Catherine, and Pellegrino, Victoria. *Living and Loving after Divorce*. New York: Atheneum Publishers, 1977.

4359. ———. "You Love him, but He Doesn't Love Back," *New Woman* 9 (March–April 1979): 69–70.

4360. "The New Life of Moshe Dyan's Ex," *New Woman* 4 (January–February 1973): 44.

4361. O'Sullivan, Sonya. "Single Life in a Double Bed," *Cosmopolitan* 180 (April 1976): 140 + .

4362. ———. "When a Woman Makes Marriage her Sole Occupation," *New Woman* 6 (March–April 1976): 61–66.

4363. Pat Loud: Making it as a Divorcée," *New Woman* 4 (July–August 1974): 77 + .

4364. Raphael, Phyllis. "Life after Divorce: Out of the Frying Pan into the Freezer," *Cosmopolitan* 186 (May 1979): 313–16.

4365. Rappold, Judith G. "When a Woman Takes Over Her Life," *Vogue* 169 (November 1979): 265–66.

4366. Salk, Lee. "Guilt and the Single Parent," *Harper's Bazaar* 109 (March 1976): 89 + .

4367. Schenkel, Sue. "PWP Helps Ease the Pain," *Single Parent* 18 (March 1975): 16–18.

4368. Schnall, Maxine. "Learning to Love Again," *Woman's Day* 42 (May 22, 1979): 56 + .

4369. Sealey, Pat. "Divorce Dilemma," *New Woman* 1 (August 1971): 13.

4370. Shephard, Martin. "Would You Be Healthier, Happier without Him?" *New Woman* 6 (September–October 1976): 36 + .

4371. Singleton, Mary A. "What to Do, and What not to Do—about Christmas," *New Woman* 6 (November–December 1976): 62–63.

4372. Smilgis, Martha. "Once Norman's Conquest, the Fourth Mrs. Mailer Fights Her Final Marital Battle," *People* 11 (February 26, 1979): 24–26.

4373. Smith, Shirley. "Deeper Valleys . . . Higher Mountains," *Single Parent*, vol. 22, no. 3 (1979): 5–8 + ; vol. 22, no. 4 (1979): 11–12 + .

4374. Taylor, LaWanda. "Divorcee's Handbook," *Single Parent* 22 (March 1979): 17 + .

4375. Thompson, M. Cordell. "Lola and Butch Want Divorce to Save their Love," *Jet* 49 (September 25, 1975): 28–29.

4376. Tomasson, Verna. "Women as Property," *New Republic* 163 (September 19, 1970): 15–18.

4377. Trotter, Robert J. "Divorce: The First Two Years Are the Worst," *Science News* 110 (October 9, 1976): 237–38.

4378. Tunick, Carl. "Divorce: Women Suffer, Men Survive," *Playboy* 25 (December 1978): 298 + .

4379. Weiss, Robert S. "Someone New for You," *Single Parent* 22 (December 1979): 5–8.

DATING

4380. Africano, Lillian. "Dating and the Single Parent," *Woman's Day* 42 (February 20, 1979): 60 + .

4381. ———. "Dating and the Single Parent," *Single Parent* 22 (July–August 1979): 5–7 + .

4382. Mann, Judy L. "New Woman's Guide to Used Men," *New Woman* 1 (August 1971): 88–92.

4383. Mayer, Nancy. "Back in Circulation Again! (Divorcée's Battle Plan)," *Cosmopolitan* 171 (April 1971): 178.

4384. Rosenthal, Kristine M., and Keshet, Harry F. "Why Would Any Woman Want to Date a Divorced Man with Children?" *New Woman* 8 (September-October 1978): 103 + .

DISPLACED HOMEMAKERS

4385. Abeel, Erica. "School for Ex-Wives," *New York* 11 (October 16, 1978): 95–101.

4386. Bujarski-Greene, Pamela. "Starting Over: A Guide for the Displaced Homemaker," *Family Circle* 91 (July 10, 1978): 14 + .

4387. "Of Women, Knights and Horses," *Time* 113 (January 1, 1979): 64.

EX-SPOUSES

4388. Bennetts, Leslie. "What It's Like to Be Best Friends with Your Ex," *Cosmopolitan* 187 (October 1979): 328–32.

4389. Davidson, Sara. "What Am I Doing Here?" *Ms* 4 (October 1975): 57–59.

4390. Gertz, Kathryn R. "Father's Day: Coping with Your Ex-Husband," *Harper's Bazaar* 112 (February 1979): 135 + .

4391. Marquise, Lois A. "Love Letter to My Ex," *New Woman* 4 (May-June 1974): 59–60.

4392. "My Ex-Husband Is Getting Married, Should I Let Our Children Go to His Wedding?" *Good Housekeeping* 189 (August 1979): 24 + .

4393. Windeler, Robert. "Bob Radnitz and Joanna Crawford Collaborate on G-Rated Films and an X-Rated Private Life," *People* 5 (May 24, 1976): 49–50 + .

FEMALES

4394. Antoniak, Helen; Scott, Nancy L.; and Worcester, Nancy. *Alone: Emotional, Legal, and Financial Help for the Widowed or Divorced Woman.* Millbrae, CA: Les Femmes Publishing, 1979.

4395. Athearn, Louise Montague. *What Every Formerly Married Woman Should Know: Answers to the Most Intimate Questions Formerly Married Women Ask.* New York: David McKay Co., 1973.

4396. ———. *A New Life Plan: A Guide for the Divorced Woman.* Garden City, NY: Dolphin Books, 1978.

4397. Bequaert, Lucia H. *Single Women Alone and Together.* Boston: Beacon Press, 1976.

4398. Bradley, Connie, and Huff, Dan. *Surviving Divorce: A Survival Handbook for Divorced and Divorcing Women.* Boise, ID: Idaho Department of Health and Welfare, Region IV, 1974.

4399. Eisler, Riane T. *Dissolution: No-Fault Divorce, Marriage and the Future of Women.* New York: McGraw-Hill, 1977.

4400. Singleton, Mary A. *Life after Marriage: Divorce as a New Beginning.* New York: Stein and Day, 1974.

4401. Women in Transition, Inc. *Women in Transition: A Feminist Handbook on Separation and Divorce.* New York: Charles Scribner's Sons, 1975.

4402. ———. *Women's Survival Manual: A Feminist Handbook on Separation and Divorce.* New York: Charles Scribner's Sons, 1972.

4403. Women's Legal Center of San Francisco. *Getting Out: A Collective Experience in Self-Help Divorce.* San Francisco, CA: Women's Legal Center of San Francisco, 1974.

4404. Woolley, Persia. *Creative Survival for Single Mothers.* Millbrae, CA: Celestial Arts Publishing Co., 1975.

4405. Yates, Martha. *Coping: A Survival Manual for Women Alone.* Englewood Cliffs, NJ: Prentice-Hall, 1976.

JEWISH

4406. Bissell, Sherry. "My Divorce and My Community," *Sh'ma: A Journal of Jewish Responsibility* 6 (April 16, 1976): 90–92.

4407. Karmen, Marcia. "Wednesday the Rabbi Called about My Divorce," *Ms* 2 (January 1974): 14 + .

MALES

4408. Baber, Asa. "Who Gets Screwed in a Divorce! I Do," *Playboy* 25 (December 1978): 213–16 + .

4409. Collier, James L. "Time to Give Divorced Men a Break," *Reader's Digest* 96 (February 1970): 64–68; (discussion) 96 (May 1970): 39–41.

4410. "Divorcing Father," *Human Behavior* 6 (April 1977): 38 + .

4411. Gilder, George F. *Naked Nomads: Unmarried Men in America.* New York: Quadrangle Books, 1974.

4412. Gordon, Bob. *The Divorced Man's Guide to Girlmanship and the Single Life.* Waltham, MA: American Publishing Corp., 1973.

4413. Gordon, William J., and Price, Steven D. *The Second-Time Single Man's Survival Handbook: With a Coterie of Kibitzers.* New York: Praeger, 1975.

4414. Kahan, Stuart. *For Divorced Fathers Only.* New York: Simon & Schuster, 1978.

4415. Mothner, Ira. "Portrait of the Dumped Male," *Cosmopolitan* 176 (January 1974): 113–15.

4416. Ornstein, J. Alan. *The Lion's Share: A Combat Manual for the Divorcing Male.* New York: Times Books, 1978.

4417. Rubin, Estelle, and Atkin, Edith L. *Part-time Father.* New York: Vanguard Press, 1976.

4418. Skrocki, Merrill R. "What Divorced Fathers Miss Most," *McCalls* 105 (November 1977): 85.

4419. Van Gelder, Lindsy. "Unmarried Man," *Ms* 8 (November 1979): 51–53 + .

MIDDLE-AGED

4420. Broncaccio, Diane. "The Plight of the Middle-Aged Divorcee," *Cleveland* 6 (May 1977): 92–96 + .

4421. Cosneck, Bernard J. "Divorce after Fifteen Years," *Single Parent* 15 (September 1972): 13–15.

4422. Donelson, Ken, and Donelson, Irene. "Twenty Year Fracture: Long-term Marriages," *Harvest Years* 10 (February 1970): 19–21 + .

4423. McGinnis, Tom, and Roesch, Roberta. "Why Middle-Aged Marriages Are Falling Apart," *Kiwanis* 62 (February 1977): 32 + .

4424. "Surge in Divorces: New Crisis in Middle Age," *U.S. News and World Report* 81 (December 20, 1976): 56.

PERSONAL NARRATIVES

4425. Abeel, Erica. *Only When I Laugh.* New York: William Morrow & Co., 1978.

4426. "After the Bitter Break-Up of a Marriage," *Parents Magazine* 48 (June 1973): 36 + .

4427. Baguedor, Eve. *Separation: Journal of a Marriage.* New York: Simon & Schuster, 1972.

4428. Beck, Mimi. "Courage to Stop Being Brave," *Redbook* 145 (August 1975): 51–52.

4429. Braudy, Susan. "After the Marriage Is Over: A Diary of the First 441 Days," *Ms* 2 (April 1974): 48+.

4430. ———. *Between Marriage and Divorce: A Woman's Diary*. New York: William Morrow & Co., 1975.

4431. Brinkley, Ann. "Ex Marks the Spot," *Ladies Home Journal* 95 (February 1978): 147–49.

4432. Coffey, Barbara. "Single Again," *Glamour* 73 (January 1975): 102+.

4433. Coleman, Emily. "The Best Wife Any Man Ever Had," *New Woman* 4 (November–December 1974): 77–87+.

4434. Coleman, Jack D. "In Search of Each Other," *Single Parent* 20 (November 1977): 5–6+.

4435. Cox, Mathilda. "My Children and My Divorce: Was I Right?" *Glamour* 5 (May 1977): 248–49+.

4436. "Divorced After Twenty Years of Marriage," *Good Housekeeping* 171 (October 1970): 56+.

4437. Donaldson, Bryna. "New Doors to Open," *Single Parent* 20 (September 1977): 20–21+.

4438. Dreifus, Claudia. "Changing Life-Styles: Divorced Mom in the Country," *Family Circle* 84, no. 4 (1974): 20+.

4439. Elliott, Anne. "How to Survive Your First Romance after Divorce," *Cosmpolitan* 181 (October 1976): 148+.

4440. "End of a Marriage," *Good Housekeeping* 178 (February 1974): 75+.

4441. Fager, Charles. "Surviving Divorce," *Harper's Weekly* 64 (March 28, 1975): 9.

4442. Francke, Linda. "Johnny Carson's Ex-wife Tells Her Story," *McCalls* 100 (January 1973): 22+.

4443. Fuller, Jan. "The Diary of a Divorce," *Woman's Day*, vol. 37, no. 4 (1974): 74–80.

4444. ———. "Discovering Yourself Afterwards," *New Woman* 5 (May-June 1975): 60–64+.

4445. ———. *Space: The Scrapbook of My Divorce*. New York: A. Fields Books, 1973.

4446. Gold, Don. "Divorce, with Love," *Harper's* 249 (December 1974): 40+.

4447. Hochstein, Rollie. "What Happens When a Homemaker Loses her Job?" *Woman's Day* 41 (August 7, 1978): 10+.

4448. Hormann, Elizabeth. "With a Little Help from My Friends," *Single Parent* 20 (September 1977): 9+.

4449. Johnson, W. J. "Growing Up at 37," *Essence* 9 (May 1978): 76–77.

4450. Jones, Vickie. "Divorce: Two Who Experienced It," *Essence*, vol. 4, no. 12 (1974): 52+.

4451. Klein, Lynn. "Divorce Dilemma," *New Woman* 1 (July 1971): 11+.

4452. Koffend, John B. *Letter to My Wife*. New York: Saturday Review Press, 1972.

4453. Krantzler, Mel. *Learning to Love Again*. New York: Thomas Y. Crowell Co., 1977.

4454. Lee, Sheila. *From Beginning to Beginning: One Woman's Divorce and Life After: A True Story of Courtroom Corruption, 90 Legal Documents, Abuse and Injustice*. Honolulu, HI: Victory Day Co., 1977.

4455. Libman, Joan. "Divorce: Getting through the First Year," *Family Circle* 92 (November 1, 1979): 52+.

4456. "Living through Divorce—A Search for Self," *Sh'ma: A Journal of Jewish Responsibility* 6 (APRIL 16, 1976): 89–90.

4457. Mahan, Bill. *What Is Your Name and Telephone Number?"* Port Washington, NY: Ashley Books, 1975.

4458. Marst, Susan. "Beware the Quickie Divorce," *Harper's Weekly* 64 (March 28, 1975): 1.

4459. Martin, Albert J. *One Man, Hurt*. NY: Macmillan, 1975.

4460. Martin, Michael. "Feathers in His Hair," *Single Parent* 21 (April 1978): 5–6.

4461. Meenan, Monica. "They're Bachelors Again," *Town and Country* 129 (June 1975): 66–67.

4462. "They're Single Again," *New Woman* 7 (September-October 1977): 81–82.

4463. ———. "They're Single Again," *Town and Country* 31 (June 1977): 80–83.

4464. Melton, Emily. "Sharing the Divorce," *Harper's Weekly* 64 (March 28 1975): 9.

4465. Monagan, Charles. "Divorce Bad, Divorce Good," *Playboy* 25 (December 1978): 302.

4466. "My Best Friend's Husband Made a Pass at me," *Good Housekeeping* 188 (January 1979): 28+.

4467. Richtmyer, Shelly. "Big Date for a Divorcée," *Harper's Weekly* 64 (November 10, 1975): 9.

4468. Shary, Jill. "Baby, It's Cold Outside (A Divorcée's Postmortem). *Cosmopolitan* 168 (February 1970): 56+.

4469. Seldin-Schwartz, Ethel. "Diary of a Middle-Aged Divorce," *Ms* 4 (April 1976): 84–87+.

4470. Sims, Carole. "The Risks (and Joys) of Sex with Your Ex," *Cosmopolitan* 179 (November 1975): 208–12.

4471. Slavin, Maeve. "Going It Alone," *Working Woman* 3 (February 1978): 42–44.

4472. Spock, Benjamin. "Letter from a Divorced Mother," *Redbook* 145 (May 1975): 22+.

4473. Taylor, Rita. "Come on Tomorrow . . . ," *Single Parent* 19 (October 1976): 8+.

4474. Towner, Jason. "Time to Let Go," *Saturday Evening Post* 251 (April 1979): 10+.

4475. Van Gelder, Lindsy. "Is Divorce Ever Final? Ten Women Talk about Their Ex-Husbands," *Ms* 7 (January 1979): 61–62+.

4476. Walters, Robert, and Myers, Lisa. "Politics Makes Estranged Bedfellows . . . Also the First Married Couple to Serve in Congress," *Parade* (September 26, 1976): 26–27.

4477. Watts, Carol K. "Scenes from a Divorce," *Redbook* 148 (April 1977): 82+.

4478. Wilkins, Nancy, and Reese, Mary E. *Divorced: A Single Mother's Very Private Life*. New York: Wyden Books, 1977.

4479. Williams, Ned. "Starting Over—Alone," *American Home* 79 (July 1976): 70.

4480. Winslow, Joyce. "Living Alone: The Diary of a Reluctant Single," *Harper's Weekly* 65 (July 26, 1976): 12–15.

4481. Wysor, Betty. "Divorce Dilemma," *New Woman* 1 (October 1971): 10+.

4482. Young, Jane J. "Why These Park Slope Women Dumped Their Husbands," *New Woman* 5 (September–October 1975): 73–75.

4483. ———. "Husband Dumping," *Village Voice* 20 (February 24, 1975): 6–7.

POSTDIVORCE ADJUSTMENT

4484. Helmlinger, Trudy. *After You've Said Goodbye: How to Recover after Ending a Relationship.* Cambridge, MA: Schenkman Publishing Co., 1977.

4485. Lyman, Howard B. *Single Again.* New York: David McKay Co., 1971.

4486. "Oh God, He's Left! How to Meet the Crisis," *New Woman* 7 (November–December 1977): 86–92.

4487. Singleton, Mary A. "Getting Over the First Difficult Weeks/Months," *New Woman* 8 (March–April 1978): 91–92 + .

4488. Tarrant, John J.; Feinberg, Gloria; and Feinberg, Mortimer R. "If Someone Close to You Has Walked Out," *New Woman* 8 (September–October 1978): 93 + .

SEXUAL BEHAVIOR

4489. Adams, Jane. *Sex and the Single Parent.* New York: Coward, McCann and Geoghegan, 1978.

4490. ———. "Sex and the Single Parent," *Harper's Bazaar* 111 (July 1978): 101 + .

4491. Coburn, Judith. "Intelligent Woman's Guide to Sex," *Mademoiselle* 84 (June 1978): 104.

4492. Dullea, Georgia. "Sex and the Single Parent," *Cosmopolitan* 186 (April 1979): 266–69 + .

4493. Eberle, Nancy. "Silent Problem of Single Parenthood: How Do You Handle Your Sex Life?" *Glamour* 76 (November 1978): 266–67 + .

4494. Kaplan, Helen S. "Sexual Freedom or Remarriage or . . .," *Harper's Bazaar* 109 (July 1976): 29 + .

4495. Mayer, Nancy. "The Ingenious Sex Lives of Divorced Mothers," *Cosmopolitan* 180 (January 1976): 92 + .

4496. Muenchow, Susan. "Sex and the Single Parent," *Parents* 54 (June 1979): 55–59.

4497. Napolitane, Catherine, and Pellegrino, Victoria. "Sex and the Formerly Married Woman," *Cosmopolitan* 182 (June 1977): 84 + .

4498. Wright, Barbara. "Mommy, Who's That Man in Your Bed? Problems and Solutions for the Surrogate Father," *Esquire* 91 (June 5, 1979): 85–87.

SUICIDE

4499. Schrut, Albert H. "Suicide Wish among Divorcees," *Intellect* 104 (March 1976): 418–19.

FATHER ABSENCE

4500. Coleman, Jack D. "Defining 'Father,' " *Single Parent* 22 (January–February 1979): 13 + .

4501. Daniel, Glenda. "But What of Girls without Fathers?" *PTA Magazine* 68 (June 1974): 13.

4502. Goldman, Tamara. "Daddy, I Wish I'd Known You," *Seventeen* 33 (August 1974): 122.

4503. Lehr, Claire J. "Fathers in Name Only," *Single Parent* 20 (December 1977): 11–13.

4504. Tavris, Carol. "Boys without Fathers—It's Tougher for White Teens," *Psychology Today* 9 (December 1975): 123.

4505. Wood, Abigail. "Life without Father: Questions and Answers," *Seventeen* 31 (March 1972): 80.

ONE-PARENT FAMILIES

4506. Baruth, Leroy G. *A Single Parent's Survival Guide: How to Raise the Children.* Dubuque, IA: Kendall/Hunt Publishing Co., 1979.

4507. Baum, Patricia. "Private Life of Liv Ullmann: A Mother Alone," *Parents' Magazine* 51 (August 1976): 34–35 + .

4508. Bel Geddes, Joan. *How to Parent Alone: A Guide for Single Parents.* New York: Seabury Press, 1974.

4509. Berman, Eleanor. *The Cooperating Family: How Your Children Can Help Manage the Household—For Their Good as Well as Yours.* Englewood Cliffs, NJ: Prentice-Hall, 1977.

4510. Berman, Susan. "Mother and Daughter: The very Private World of Barbara Walters," *Parents* 54 (July 1979): 57–61.

4511. "Broken Family: Divorce U. S. Style," *Newsweek* 81 (March 12, 1973): 47–57.

4512. Caine, Lynn. "Single Mothers, *Ladies Home Journal* 94 (October 1977): 104 + .

4513. Carro, Geraldine. "Help for Single Parents," *Ladies Home Journal* 92 (December 1975): 18.

4514. ———. "When He Keeps the Kids," *Ladies Home Journal* 96 (April 1979): 24.

4515. Comer, James P., and Poussaint, Alvin F. "You and Your Children: Divorce and Raising a Fatherless Child," *Essence,* vol. 6, no. 6 (1975): 26.

4516. Engel, Laura. "Four Single Mothers: Together on Our Own," *McCalls* 106 (December 1978): 26 + .

4517. Francke, Linda B. "Putting Father Back in the Family," *Newsweek* 86 (September 22, 1975) 54.

4518. Fuld, Charles L. "Scouting and the Single Parent," *Scouting* 67 (October 1979): 44–46.

4519. Gahman, Susan. " 'When I'm at School I Get Mad, I Get Mad,' " *Single Parent* 20 (September 1977): 11–12 + .

4520. Gladston, Richard. "Coping with Behavior Problems: The One-Parent Household," *Parents' Magazine* 52 (October 1977): 97.

1521. Hallett, Kathryn. *A Guide for Single Parents; Transactional Analysis for People in Crisis.* Millbrae, CA: Celestial Arts Publishing Co., 1974.

4522. Harker, Ruth. "A Career . . . A Child . . . A Way of Life," *New Woman* 4 (March–April 1974): 26–29.

4523. Hawke, Sharryl, and Knox, David. "One Parent—One Child," *Single Parent* 21 (March 1978): 8–11 + .

4524. Johnson, Patrice. "In the Family Way," *Encore American and Worldwide News* 6 (May 23, 1977): 8–15.

4525. King, Barbara. "Single Parenthood," *Harper's Bazaar* 110 March 1977): 96 + .

4526. Klein, Carole. *The Single Parent Experience.* New York: Walker, 1973.

4527. *Momma: The Source Book for Single Mothers.* Karol Hope and Nancy Young. New York: New American Library, 1976.

4528. "More Women Head U.S. Homes," *U.S. News and World Report* 77 (December 2, 1974): 85.

4529. Moultrie, Sandra. "Making It as a Divorced Mother," *McCalls* 103 (August 1976): 92 + .

4530. Napolitane, Catherine, and Pellegrino, Victoria. "Left Alone with Kids to Raise? How to Love the Role," *New Woman* 7 (November–December 1977): 58–60.

4531. Ogg, Elizabeth. *One-Parent Families.* Public Affairs Pamphlet No. 543. New York: Public Affairs Committee, 1976.

4532. O'Shea, Ann. "Housing for the Single Parent, Warren Village," *McCalls* 102 (June 1975): 36.

4533. Riley, Harris D., and Woodworth, Karen L. "The Single Parent: Going It Alone," *American Baby* 39 (June 1977): 54–55.

4534. "Rising Problems of Single Parents," *U.S. News and World Report* 75 (July 16, 1975): 32–35.

4535. Rose, Louisa. "Single Parents at Christmas," *American Home* 78 (December 1975): 24 + .

4536. Rosenblum, Arlene. "Help Wanted: Another Pair of Hands," *Single Parent* 19 (October 1976): 5–7.

4537. Russell, Beverly. "Declaration for Independents," *House and Garden* 150 (August 1978): 98–99 + .

4538. Salk, Lee. "Problems and Pleasures of the Single Parent," *Harper's Bazaar* 108 (March 1975): 76 + .

4539. Sharp, Karen. "Mothers Can Too!" *Redbook* 149 (June 1977): 54 + .

4540. Sherberg, Ellen. "Whatever Happened to Motherhood?" *St. Louis* 10 (July 1978): 66 + .

4541. Stencel, Sandra. "Single Parent Families," *Editorial Research Reports* 2 (September 10, 1976): 661–80.

4542. "Women-Headed Households Growing Rapidly," *Dollars and Sense* 37 (May–June 1978): 14–15.

4543. Wood, Sandy. "Without Mother," *Single Parent* 18 (March 1975): 14–15.

FATHERS

4544. Brown, Norman. "Single Fathers: Are They as Good as Mothers? *Pageant* 31 (May 1976): 48–53.

4545. Gatley, Richard H., and Koulack, David. *Single Father's Handbook: A Guide for Separated and Divorced Fathers.* Garden City, NY: Doubleday, 1979.

4546. Gaylin, Jody. "Single Father Is Doing Well," *Psychology Today* 10 (April 1977): 36 + .

4547. Glenn, Claude, Jr. "A Father's Teenager Education," *Single Parent* 18 (March 1975): 12–13 + .

4548. Koubek, Richard F. "A Father's Instincts," *American Home* 80 (June 1977): 18 + .

4549. Levine, James A. *Who Will Raise the Children? New Options for Fathers (and Mothers).* Philadelphia, PA: J. B. Lippincott Co., 1976.

4550. McFadden, Michael. *Bachelor Fatherhood: How to Raise and Enjoy Your Children as a Single Parent.* New York: Walker & Co., 1974.

4551. Stafford, Linley M. *One Man's Family: A Single Father and His Children.* New York: Random House, 1978.

4552. "When Fathers Have to Raise Families Alone," *U.S. News and World Report* 83 (November 21, 1977): 60–61.

PERSONAL NARRATIVES

4553. Griffin, Susan. "Confessions of a Single Mother," *Ramparts* 11 (April 1973): 41–44.

4554. LaFarge, Phyllis. "Third Time, or Why I Sat in the Parking Lot," *Parents* 54 (July 1979): 74–76.

REMARRIAGE

4555. Adler, Bill, and Wagner, Gary. *The Second Time Around Is Better.* Chicago: Playboy Press, 1979.

4556. Baer, Jean. "Facing Life as the Second Wife: Second Wife Etiquette, For Weekend Stepmothers," *New Woman* 5 (July-August 1975): 64+.

4557. ———. *The Second Wife: How to Live Happily with a Man Who Has Been Married Before.* Garden City, NY: Doubleday, 1972.

4558. Birmingham, Nan. "Getting Married Again," *Town and Country* 129 (June 1975): 62–63+.

4559. Block, Joel D. *To Marry Again.* New York: Grosset & Dunlap, 1979.

4560. Blum, Sam. "Making Marriage Work: What Women and Men Learn from Past Mistakes," *Redbook* 138 (February 1972): 84+.

4561. Brothers, Joyce. "Making a Second Marriage Work," *Good Housekeeping* 174 (February 1972): 60+.

4562. Busnitz, Virgie M. "The Perils of Remarrying," *New Woman* 4 (March–April 1974): 63.

4563. Caine, Lynne. "Case against Remarrying Too Soon," *Ladies Home Journal* 95 (February 1978): 151–52.

4564. Cohen, Debra. "Second Time Around, It Seems to Work," *Psychology Today* 10 (March 1977): 34+.

4565. Croake, James W. "Speaking of Remarriage," *Single Parent* 22 (June 1979): 11–12+.

4566. "Don't Rush to Rewed," *Single Parent* 18 (September 1975): 5–7.

4567. Eberle, Nancy. "Do I Want Another Baby?" *McCalls* 106 (November 1978): 45+.

4568. Edmonds, Mim. "The Second Marriage: What Are Its Chances?" *Woman's Day,* vol. 37, no. 11 (1974): 30+.

4569. Fields, Susan. *Getting Married Again.* New York: Dodd, Mead & Co., 1975.

4570. Flach, Frederic F. *A New Marriage, a New Life.* New York: McGraw-Hill, 1978.

4571. Greene, Gail. "Perils of the Second Wife," *Cosmopolitan* 173 (July 1972): 106+.

4572. Gregg, Gary. "Remarriage: Children and Money Are the Big Problems," *Psychology Today* 10 (November 1976): 26+.

4573. Houck, Catherine. "The Availables: Second Time Around Parade," *Cosmopolitan* 182 (February 1977): 191–94.

4574. Hughes, Dee. "My Family, His Family and My Job," *McCalls* 104 (August 1977): 58+.

4575. Hunt, Morton and Hunt, Bernice. "After Divorce: Who Gets Married Again?" *Redbook* 149 (October 1977): 106+.

4576. Hyatt, Ralph. *Before You Marry . . . Again.* New York: Random House, 1977.

4577. Jackson, Elinor. "It's Never Too Late to Grab a Chunk of Life," *Ebony* 33 (November 1977): 123–24+.

4578. Kapit, Hannah, and Kapit, Milton. "Remarriage: Expectation and Reality," (part 1), *Single Parent* 20 (December 1977): 5–7+.

4579. ———. "Remarriage: Expectation and Reality" (part 2), *Single Parent* 20 (January-February 1978): 13–15+.

4580. Kiester, Edwin, Jr. "Marriage the Second Time Around," *Family Circle* 88 (February 1976): 82+.

4581. Kirby, Jonnell H. *Second Marriage.* Muncie, IN: Accelerated Development, 1979.

4582. Klapper, Naomi. "Remarriage: Solution or Illusion?" *Single Parent* 19 (September 1976): 6–9+.

4583. Leonard, John. "Case for Remarriage . . . Among Friends," *Ms* 6 (August 1977): 26–27.

4584. "Let Man Put Asunder?" *Time* 104 (November 18, 1974): 87.

4585. McCord, Jacqueline. "Modern Bride's Guide to Getting Married Again," *Modern Bride* 31 (April-May 1979): 61–68.

4586. Masters, William, and Johnson, Virginia. *The Pleasure Bond: A New Look at Sexuality and Commitment.* Boston: Little, Brown & Co., 1975.

4587. Mayer, Nancy. "Why Marry Again?" *Cosmopolitan* 175 (August 1973): 146+.

4588. Mayleas, Davidyne S. "Remarriage: Survival Manual," *Vogue* 167 (November 1977): 64+.

4589. ———. *Rewedded Bliss: Love, Alimony, Incest, Ex-Spouses, and Other Domestic Blessings.* New York: Basic Books, 1977.

4590. Newman, Mildred, and Berkowitz, Bernard. "Making Second Marriages Work," *Harper's Bazaar* 108 (June 1975): 80+.

4591. Nichols, William C. "Money and Remarriage," *Parents' Magazine* 53 (September 1978): 18.

4592. ———. "Second Time Around," *Parents' Magazine* 53 (July 1978): 10.

4593. Nirenberg, Sue. "Here Comes the Bride: Again," *House Beautiful* 113 (October 1971): 114–15.

4594. O'Malley, Suzanne. "First Marriage, Second Marriage, No Marriage at All: What Are the Odds for Happiness?" *Glamour* 77 (July 1979): 81–83.

4595. Polatin, Phillip, and Philtine, Ellen C. "After Divorce: Another Marriage?" *Single Parent* 18 (July-August 1975): 5–8+.

4596. Poussaint, Ann A. "Are Second Marriages Better?" *Ebony* 30 (March 1975): 55+.

4597. Reingold, Carmel B. *Remarriage.* New York: Harper & Row, 1976.

4598. Rollin, Betty. "The American Way of Marriage: Remarriage," *Look* 35 (September 21, 1971): 62–67.

4599. Ryder, Harriette. *How to Get Married Again!* Tenafly, NJ: Eric Weber Press, 1975.

4600. Rydman, Edward J. "Advice to Second Wives: Interview," *Harper's Bazaar* 106 (April 1973): 104+.

4601. Saline, Carol. "Who's for Seconds?" *Philadelphia* 67 (September 1976): 183–90.

4602. Scofield, Sandra. "How to Live with His Ex-wife," *Cosmopolitan* 183 (October 1977): 244–45+.

4603. Shah, Diane K. "Trade-In Spouses," *Single Parent* 15 (November 1972): 5+.

4604. Stark, Gail U. "Seven on a Honeymoon," *Parents' Magazine* 46 (May 1971): 44+.

4605. Westoff, Leslie A. "The Second Time Around," *Cosmopolitan* 185 (November 1978): 184+.

4606. ———. *The Second Time Around: Remarriage in America.* New York: Viking Press, 1977.

4607. ———. "Two-Time Winners: Remarriage after Divorce," *New York Times Magazine* 88 (August 16, 1976): 72.

4608. Woodward, Kenneth L., and Lisle, Laurie. "Divorced Catholics," *Newsweek* 88 (August 16, 1976): 72.

REMARRIAGE TO FIRST SPOUSE

4609. Cosneck, Bernard J. "Trying It Again," *Single Parent* 15 (November 1972): 4+. R.

4610. Lobsenz, Norman M. "Second Time Around," *Ladies Home Journal* 92 (November 1975): 84+.

SEPARATION

4611. Johnson, Stephen M. "If You Can't Envision Your Future—Without Your First Love," *New Woman* 9 (September-October 1979): 73–78.

4612. "Separation Contracts: Signing Up for Signing Off," *Human Behavior* 7 (August 1978): 34.

4613. Yurasits, Victoria. "Does Separation Have to Mean Divorce?" *Redbook* 148 (January 1977): 93+.

STEPPARENTS AND STEPCHILDREN

STEPCHILDREN

4614. Edmiston, Susan. "Mrs. Greene's Steps to Successful Family Life," *Good Housekeeping* 185 (September 1977): 70+.

4615. Kalter, Suzy. "Instant Parent: How to Deal with Stepchildren," *Harper's Bazaar* 111 (September 1978): 230+.

4616. Roosevelt, Ruth, and Lofas, Jeanette. "These Children Are Not Yours," *Single Parent* 19 (November 1976): 5–7+.

4617. Salk, Lee. "You and Your Stepchildren," *Harper's Bazaar* 10 (June 1975): 81+.

4618. Seligson, Marcia. "The Wicked Stepchild: Your Most Passionate Rival," *Cosmopolitan* 182 (June 1977): 172+.

4619. Spann, Owen, and Spann, Nancy. *Your Child? I Thought It Was My Child.* Pasadina, CA: Ward Ritchie Press, 1977.

4620. " 'You Don't Have to Love Your Stepchildren,' Says an Expert, 'Just Be a Good Parent,' " *People* 9 (April 3, 1978): 56–58.

STEPFATHERS

4621. Bohanna, Paul, and Erickson, Rosemary. "Stepping In Stepfathers," 11 (January 1978): 52–54+.

4622. Hill, Archie. *Closed World of Love.* New York: Simon & Schuster, 1976.

4623. Price, Robert. "Notes of an Instant Father," *Essence* 5 (February 1975): 44–45+.

STEPMOTHERS

4624. Cox, Georgia L. "Confessions of a Wicked Stepmother," *Ladies Home Journal* 88 (March 1971): 104+.

4625. Disney, Dorothy C. "My Husband Put His Son First," *Ladies Home Journal* 96 (January 1979): 12+.

4626. Hidalgo, Marty A. "Wicked Stepmother Doesn't Live Here Anymore," *Redbook* 149 (August 1977): 22+.

4627. Howe, Louise K. "In Praise of Stepchildren," *McCalls* 107 (November 1979): 16+.

4628. Lowe, Patricia T. *The Cruel Stepmother.* Englewood Cliffs, NJ: Prentice-Hall, 1970.

4629. McClenaghan, Judy C., and Most, Bruce W. "How to Make His Child Love You: Stepmothers," *Saturday Evening Post* 250 (April 1978): 34+.

4630. Raphael, Phyllis. "Stepmother Trap," *McCalls* 105 (February 1978): 116–17+.

STEPPARENTS

4631. Auerbach, Stevanne. "From Stepparent to Real Parent," *Parents' Magazine* 51 (June 1976): 34–35 + .

4632. Capaldi, Frederick, and McRae, Barbara. *Stepfamilies: Cooperative Responsibility*. New York: Franklin Watts, 1979.

4633. Crosby, Jan. "What Am I Supposed to Call You?" *Single Parent* 20 (December 1977): 8–10 + .

4634. Dodson, Fitzhugh. "Weaving Together Two Families into One," *Family Health* 9 (September 1977): 44–47 + .

4635. Einstein, Elizabeth. "Stepfamily Lives," *Human Behavior* 8 (April 1979): 62–68.

4636. Hetherington, Kim. "You're Not My Real Mother!" *Washingtonian* 15 (October 1979): 115–32.

4637. Lund, Dorothy. "Stepparent on Trial," *Parents' Magazine* 50 (January 1975): 38 + .

4638. Maddox, Brenda. *The Half-Parent: Living with Other People's Children*. New York: M. Evans & Co., 1975.

4639. ———. "Neither Witch nor Good Fairy," *New York Times Magazine* (August 8, 1976): 16 + .

4640. Marks, Jane. "Adjusting to a Stepparent," *Seventeen* 35 (June 1976): 126–27.

4641. Marks, Judi. "Cinderella Syndrome: Working Out Stepparent Problems," *Teen* 22 (May 1978): 19–20 + .

4642. "One Step at a Time," *Family Health* 9 (April 1977): 54 + .

4643. Roosevelt, Ruth H., and Lofas, Jeanette. *Living in Step*. New York: Stein and Day, 1976.

4644. Rosenbaum, Jean, and Rosenbaum, Veryl. *Stepparenting*. Corte Madera, CA: Chandler & Sharp Publishers, 1977.

4645. Spencer, Sue N. "Stepparenting: Proceed with Caution," *Single Parent* 22 (June 1979): 15–16 + .

V. Nonprint Materials on Divorce

CHILD CUSTODY

AUDIOTAPES

4646. Fulton, Julie. "Divorce, Custody, and the Fragmented Family." Minneapolis, MN: National Council on Family Relations, 1974.

4647. Gardner, Richard A. "Custody Litigation and the Mental Health Professional." Portland, OR: Association of Family Conciliation Courts, 1979.

4648. Solnit, Albert. "Custody Litigation and the Mental Health Professional." Portland, OR: Association of Family Conciliation Courts, 1979.

FILMSTRIPS

4649. "Who Gets Baby Marta?: An Exercise in Law and Family Relations." Pleasantville, NY: Sunburst Communications, 1977.

CHILD SUPPORT

AUDIOTAPES

4650. Chambers, David L. "Enforcement of Support Obligations." Portland, OR: Association of Family Conciliation Courts, 1979.

MOTION PICTURES

4651. "My Husband Stopped Support Payments." Washington, DC: Department of Health, Education and Welfare, Assistance Payments Administration, 1976.

CHILDREN OF DIVORCED PARENTS

AUDIOTAPES

4652. Brown, Daniel G., et al. "The Divorce Experience: How Children Cope." Portland, OR: Association of Family Conciliation Courts, 1979.

4653. "Dr. Gardner Talks to Boys and Girls about Divorce." New York: Psychotherapy and Social Science Tape Library, 1976.

4654. Kelly, Joan B. "Children of Divorce." Psychology Today Library, tape no. 85. New York: Ziff-Davis Publishing Co., 1977.

4655. ———. "Effects of Divorce on Children." Psychology Today Library, no. 38. New York: Ziff-Davis Publishing Co., 1976.

4656. Wallerstein, Judith S. "The Effect of Divorce on Children." San Francisco, CA: California Medical Association, 1975.

4657. ———. "The Effect of Divorce on the Young Child." University of California Tape Library, 1974.

4658. ———. "The Role of the Father in Personality Development." New York: Psychotherapy Tape Library, 1976. 2 tapes.

FILMSTRIPS

4659. "Broken Homes and Families." Chicago: Society for Visual Education, 1970.

4660. "Family Circle." Pasadena, CA: Barr Films, 1977.

MOTION PICTURES

4661. "Breakup." Bloomington, IN: Agency for Instructional Television, 1973.

4662. "Children of Divorce." New York: National Broadcasting Corp., 1976.

4663. Children of Divorce. "Transitional Issues for Elementary School Age" (part 1); "Transitional Issues for Junior High and High School Ages" (part 2). Washington, DC: American Personnel and Guidance Association, 1978.

4664. Crisis Intervention. "Runaway" (part 1). Darien, CT: Fiorelli Films, 1972.

4665. "The Difference Is Friendship." Chicago: Perspective Films, 1975.

4666. "Eugenie," New York: Susan Sussman, 1977.

4667. "Family in the Purple House." Seattle, WA: King Screen Productions, 1970.

4668. "Feeling Left Out." Glendale, CA: AIMS Instructional Media Services, 1975.

4669. "First It Seemed Kinda Strange." Wilmette, IL: Films, Inc., 1974.

4670. "First Year A.D." Los Angeles: Franciscan Communications Center, 1975.

4671. "It Has Nothing to Do with You." Beverly Hills, CA: CRM Productions, 1974.

4672. "Me and Dad's New Wife." New York: Time-Life Films, 1976.

4673. "Mom and Pop Split Up." Pasadena, CA: Barr Films, 1978.

4674. "Papa You're Crazy." Hollywood, CA: Oxford Films, 1972.

4675. "Things Are Different Now." Solana Beach, CA: Media Guild, 1978.

VIDEOTAPES

4676. "Divorce: A Child's Rights." Minneapolis: University of Minnesota, 1975. 2 parts.

4677. Magid, Ken, and Schreibman, Walt. "Children Facing Divorce—A Treatment Program." Evergreen, CO: Human Development and Research Center, 1976.

DESERTION

MOTION PICTURES

4678. "I Love You, Goodbye." New York: Learning Corporation of America, 1974.

4679. "My Husband Left Out on Us." Washington, DC: Department of Health, Education, and Welfare, Assistance Payments Administration, 1975.

DIVORCE

AUDIOTAPES

4680. Brassard, Jane A. "The Ecology of Divorce: A Case Study Analysis of Personal Social Networks and Mother-Child Interaction in Divorced and Married Families," tape no. 1023. Minneapolis, MN: National Council on Family Relations, 1979. R.

4681. "Divorce." Hollywood, CA: Seven Arts Press, 1975.

4682. "Divorce and Disruption: Dilemmas for Policy," tape no. 69 (includes "Policy Ambiguity, and Career Mobility of Ever-Divorced Clergy," by Ira W. Hutchinson and Katherine R. Hutchinson; "Longitudinal Study of the Link between Broken Homes and Criminality," by Joan McCord; "Effects of Divorce on Ego Development and Identity Formation of College Students," by Sharyn M. Crossman, Judy Shea, and Gerald R. Adams). Minneapolis, MN: National Council on Family Relations, 1978. R.

4683. "Divorce," tape no. 72 (includes "Conflict Resolution and Patterns of Male Adjustment to Divorce," by Margaret S. Herrman and Ruth F. Weber; "An Analysis of Mothers' Post-divorce Adjustment," by Jeanne Pais and Priscilla White). Minneapolis, MN: National Council on Family Relations, 1978. R.

4684. Gardner, Richard A. "The Mental Health Professional and Divorce Litigation." New York: Psychotherapy Tape Library, 1974.

4685. ———. "Social, Legal and Therapeutic Changes Necessary to Lessen Psychological Trauma of Divorce." Portland, OR: Association of Family Conciliation Courts, 1979.

4686. Glick, Paul, et al. "Trends and Issues in Marital Dissolution," tape no. 34. Minneapolis, MN: National Council on Family Relations, 1976.

4687. Goldsmith, Jean. "The Everyday Life of the Divorced Family: The Continuing Relationships between Former Spouses," tape no. 1024. Minneapolis, MN: National Council on Family Relations, 1979. R.

4688. Graham, LeRoy, and Hunt, Morton. "Contemporary Values Related to Divorce." Claremont, CA: American Association of Marriage and Family Therapists, 1971.

4689. Sparks, Zoe A. "Socioeconomic Correlates of Divorce and Nondivorce among Rural-Urban Professional Women in Louisiana," tape no. 1067. Minneapolis, MN: National Council on Family Relations, 1979. R.

4690. Steiner, Hinda. "The Postdivorce Family." Portland: OR: Association of Family Conciliation Courts, 1979.

4691. Vahanian, Tilla. "The Divorce Experience and Its Impact on the Family." Portland, OR: Association of Family Conciliation Courts, 1979.

FILMSTRIPS

4692. "The Broken Marriage," Wilton, CT: Current Affairs Films, 1977. 6 filmstrips and cassettes.

4693. "Divorce." New York, Butterick, 1976. 2 filmstrips and cassettes.

4694. "Divorce in the United States." Stanford, CA: Multi-Media Production 6, 1976. 4 filmstrips and cassettes.

4695. "Divorce and Separation." Elmsford, NY: Parents' Magazines Films. 5 filmstrips and cassettes.

4696. "Divorce/Separation: Marriages in Trouble." White Plains, NY: Guidance Associates, 1976. 2 filmstrips.

4697. "Don't You Love Me Anymore?" Wilton, CT: Current Affairs Films, 1977. 4 filmstrips and cassettes.

4698. "Families in Crisis: Divorce." Chicago: Coronet Instructional Media, 1976.

4699. It Takes Two. "Separation" (part 3). Irvine, CA: Doubleday Multimedia, 1975.

4700. "My Parents Are Getting a Divorce." White Plains, NY: Human Relations Media, 1976.

4701. "Other Places, Other Faces." Chicago: Coronet Instructional Media, 1973.

4702. "Separated Parents," Wilton, CN: Current Affairs Films, 1977. 4 filmstrips and cassettes.

4703. "Understanding Changes in the Family." White Plains, NY: Guidance Associates, 1973.

4704. "When Two Divide." Shawnee Mission, KS: Marshfilm, 1977.

MOTION PICTURES

4705. "Divorce." Washington, DC: American Personnel and Guidance Association, 1975. 2 parts.

4706. "Divorce: For Better, for Worse," Beverly Hills, CA: CRM Productions, 1976.

4707. "The Failing Marriage." Glenside, PA: Transactional Dynamics Institute, 1978.

4708. "A Family Album." Bloomington, IN: Indiana University Audio-visual Center, 1973.

4709. "Family Matters," Bloomington, IN: Agency for Instructional Television, 1975.

4710. "Implosion." New York: Time-Life Films, 1972.

4711. "My Dad Lives in a Downtown Hotel." Santa Ana, CA: Doubleday Multimedia, 1975.

4712. "Not Together Now: End of a Marriage." Boston: Polymorph Films, 1975.

4713. "Six American Families: The Greenbergs of California." New York: Carousel Films, 1978.

SLIDES

4714. "Family Crisis—When Parents Divorce." White Plains, NY: Human Relations Media Center, 1978.

4715. "Marriage and Divorce in the United States." San Jose, CA: Lansford Publishing Co., 1972.

VIDEOTAPES

4716. "Divorce." Women and the Law Series. South Orange, NJ: School of Law, Seton Hall University, n.d.

4717. "Divorce: A Legal Perspective." Minneapolis, MN: University of Minnesota, 1975.

4718. "Divorce—Grief or Relief." Minneapolis, MN: University of Minnesota, 1975. 2 parts.

4719. "Social Context of Divorce." Minneapolis, MN: University of Minnesota, 1975.

DIVORCE COUNSELING

AUDIOTAPES

4720. Fisher, Esther O. "Divorce Counseling." New York: Psychotherapy and Social Science Tape Library, 1976. 3 cassettes.

4721. Folley, Francis J, III. "Resources for Marriage and Dissolution Counseling." Portland, OR: Association of Family Conciliation Courts, 1979.

4722. Framo, James. "Divorce Therapy, tape no. 15 Minneapolis, MN: National Council on Family Relations, 1974.

4723. Lawrence, Jean; Juhasz, Ann M.; and Mayo, Judy. "The Use of Theoretical Models in Divorce Counseling," tape no. 1028 Minneapolis, MN: National Council on Family Relations, 1979.

4724. "Sequence on Divorce," tape no. 55. "Cognitive Developmental Considerations for Divorce Counseling with Children," by Nancy Moore; "Child of Divorce—A Community Support Group," by Lucy Jordan and Louise Gurney. Minneapolis, MN: National Council on Family Relations, 1977. R.

4725. Turner, Nathan W. "A Comprehensive Model for Separation and Divorce Therapy," tape no. 1026 Minneapolis, MN: National Council on Family Relations, 1979.

4726. Walters, Jennifer. "The Implications of the Divorce Court Experience for Counseling Divorcing Couples," tape no. 1029. Minneapolis, MN: National Council on Family Relations, 1979.

DIVORCED PERSONS

AUDIOTAPES

4727. Davis, Wallace M., and Goldbern, Martin. "After Divorce: Individual, Marital and Family Adjustments." Claremont, CA: American Association of Marriage and Family Therapists, 1971.

4728. "Dr. Gardner Talks to Divorced Parents." New York: Psychotherapy and Social Science Tape Library, 1975.

4729. Fisher, Bruce F. "Divorce: Make It a Healing Process," tape no. 280 Claremont, CA: American Association of Marriage and Family Therapists, 1977.

4730. "Professional Persons Face Divorce—Their Own." Claremont, CA: American Association of Marriage and Family Therapists, 1972.

4731. Smoke, Jim. "Growing through Divorce." Pittsburgh, PA: Thesis Theological Cassettes, 1979.

4732. Stultz, Fred, et al. "Love, Sex, Marriage, and Divorce in the Middle Years," tape no. 57 Minneapolis, MN: National Council on Family Relations, 1977.

4733. Vahanian, Tilla. "Separation: Coping with the Breakup of a Marriage." Westport, CT: Lessons for Living, 1976. 4 cassettes.

MOTION PICTURES

4734. "And They Lived Happily Ever After." New York: The National Film Board of Canada, 1976.

4735. "Bobby's Ax." Beverly Hills, CA: American Film Institute Center for Advanced Films, 1973.

4736. "Chris and Bernie." New York: FSM/Pandora Films, 1974.

4737. "A Free Woman." New York: New Yorker Films, 1974.

4738. "Let No Man Put Asunder." Washington, DC: WRC–TV, 1973.

4739. "Mothers After Divorce." Boston: Polymorph Films, 1976.

4740. "One Woman." Edmonton, Alberta, Canada: Filmwest Associates, 1972.

4741. "Sunday Father." Wilmette, IL: Films Incorporated, 1974.

VIDEOTAPES

4742. "Standing Alone." Minneapolis, MN: University of Minnesota, 1975.

FATHER ABSENCE

MOTION PICTURES

4743. What Are We Doing to Our Children? "Welfare and the Fatherless Family" (part 2). New York: Carousel Films, 1973.

ONE-PARENT FAMILIES

AUDIOTAPES

4744. Nickols, Sharon Y. "Community Support Services for Single-Parent Families," tape no. 1070 Minneapolis, MN: National Council on Family Relations, 1979.

4745. Wylie, Mary L., and Hardman, Helaine. "Interaction and Role Strain: One-Parent versus Two-Parent Situations," tape no. 1025 Minneapolis, MN: National Council on Family Relations, 1979.

MOTION PICTURES

4746. "A Matter of Life." New York: National Film Board of Canada, 1970.

4747. "Single Parent," Solana Beach, CA: Media Guild, 1975.

RELIGION AND DIVORCE

AUDIOTAPES

4748. Finnegan, John T. "Compassion: Return from Exile." Notre Dame, IN: Ave Maria Press, 1979.

4749. Noonan, John T. "The Family and the Court." Kansas City, MO: National Catholic Reporter Publishing Co., 1974.

4750. Ottenweller, Albert. "The Separated and Divorced in Today's Church." Notre Dame, IN: Ave Maria Press, 1979.

4751. Ripple, Paula. "Christianity—The Inward Journey." Notre Dame, IN: Ave Maria Press, 1979.

4752. ———. "Ministering to the Separated and Divorced." Kansas City, MO: National Catholic Reporter Publishing Co., 1979.

4753. Young, James. "Catholics: Divorce and Remarriage." Kansas City, MO: National Catholic Reporter Publishing Co., 1979. 10 cassettes.

4754. ———. "New Directions for the Divorce Ministry." Notre Dame, IN: Ave Maria Press, 1979.

REMARRIAGE

AUDIOTAPES

4755. Strauss, Dorothy. "Marriage and Remarriage in Later Life: Resetting the Sights," tape no. 315 Claremont, CA: American Association of Marriage and Family Therapists, 1977.

MOTION PICTURES

4756. "Honeymoon." New York: ACI Films, 1974.

SEPARATION

FILMSTRIPS

4757. "For the Sake of the Children."
Costa Mesa, CA: Concept Media, 1977.

4758. "A Marriage Ending: Frank and
Jenny." Costa Mesa, CA: Concept Media,
1977.

STEPPARENTS AND STEPCHILDREN

MOTION PICTURES

4759. "Stepparenting: New Families, Old
Ties." Boston: Polymorph Films, 1976.

4760. "Stepparents: Where Is the Love?"
Glendale, CA: Walt Disney Educational
Media Co., 1975.

VI. Addendum and Appendix

ADDENDUM

4761. Roper Organization. *The 1980 Virginia Slims American Women's Opinion Poll.* New York: Roper Organization, 1980.

4762. Siegel, Seymour. "Divorce." In *The Second Jewish Catalog,* edited by Sharon Strassfeld and Michael Strassfeld, pp. 108–22. Philadelphia, PA: Jewish Publication Society of America, 1976.

APPENDIX

INDEXES AND ABSTRACTS

The following 73 indexes and abstract journals have been systematically checked for books, articles, documents, and non-print materials on divorce and divorce-related subjects that were published during the 1970s:

Abstracts of Popular Culture vol. 1A (1976)–Vol. 1D (1977).
Abstracts on Criminology and Penology vol. 10 (1970)–vol. 19 (1979).
Abstracts on Police Science vol. 1 (1973)–vol. 7 (1979).
Access: The Supplementary Index to Periodicals vol. 1 (1975)–vol. 5 (1979).
Accountants' Index vol. 19 (1970)–vol. 28; no. 3 (1979).
Air University Library Index to Military Periodicals vol. 21 (1970)–vol. 30, (1979).
America, History and Life vol. 7 (1970)–vol. 16 (1979).
American Statistics Index 1970-4–1979.
Bibliographic Index vol. 10 (1970)–vol. 19 (1979).
Books in Print, Subject Guide 1975–1979.
Business Periodicals Index vol. 12 (1970)–vol. 22, no. 8 (1980).
Catholic Periodical and Literature Index vol. 15 (1970)–vol. 19 (1979).
Child Development Abstracts and Bibliography vol. 44 (1970)–vol. 53 (1979).
Christian Periodical Index 1970–1978.
Cumulative Book Index 1970–March 1980.
Cumulative Index to Nursing Literature vol. 15, (1970)–v. 24, (1979).

Current Index to Journals in Education vol. 2, (1970)–vol. 12, no. 5 1980.
Current Opinion 1973–1975, and 1977.
Directory of Published Proceedings vol. 5 (1970)–vol. 14, no. 4 (1979).
Dissertation Abstracts International vol. 30 (1970)–v. 40, no. 12 (1980).
Education Index vol. 20, 1969–70–vol. 30 (March 1980).
Essay and General Literature Index 1970–1979.
Excerpta Medica: Psychiatry vol. 23 (1970)–vol. 40 (1979).
Excerpta Medica: Public Health vol. 16 (1970)–vol. 33 (1979).
Government Reports Announcements and Index vol. 70 (1970)–vol. 80, no. 8 (1980).
Guide to Social Science and Religion in Periodical Literature vol. 6 (1970)–vol 15, no. 3 (1979).
Historical Abstracts vol. 16 (1970)–vol. 25 (1979).
Humanities Index vol. 1 (1974-75)–vol. 6 (March 1979–80).
Index Medicus vol. 11 (1970)–vol. 21, no. 5 (1980).
Index to Dental Literature 1970–1979.
Index to Jewish Periodicals vol. 7 (1969–70)–vol. 16, no. 1 (1979).
Index to Legal Periodicals 1970–May, 1980.
Index to Periodical Articles by and about Blacks 1970–1978.
Index to Periodical Articles Related to Law vol. 12 (1970)–vol. 21 (1979).
Index to Periodicals of the Church of Jesus Christ of Latter-Day Saints 1970–1978.
Index to U.S. Government Periodicals vol. 1 (1972)–vol. 8, no. 3 (1979).

Insurance Periodicals Index 1970–1978.
International Bibliography of Social and Cultural Anthropology vol. 16 (1970)–vol. 22 (1976).
International Bibliography of Sociology vol. 20 (1970)–vol. 27 (1977).
International Nursing Index vol. 5 (1970)–vol. 14 (1979).
Law Books in Print vol. 2 (1970)–vol. 10, no. 1 (1979).
Library of Congress Catalogs: Films and Other Materials for Projection 1968-70–July-September 1979.
Library of Congress Catalogs: Subject Catalog 1970–July-September 1979.
Magazine Index 1976–April 1980.
Master's Abstracts vol. 8 (1970)–vol. 17 (1979).
Master's Theses in Education vol. 19 (1969–70)–vol. 28 (1978–9).
Master's Theses in the Arts and Social Sciences vol. 1 (1976–77)–vol. 3 (1978–79).
Monthly Catalog of United States Government Publications 1970–1979.
Monthly Checklist of State Publications vol. 61 (1970)–vol. 69 1968).
Monthly Periodical Index vol. 1 (1978)–vol. 2 (1979).
New Periodical Index vol. 1 (1977)–vol. 2 (1978).
Popular Periodical Index vol. 1 (1973)–vol. 14 (1979).
Proceedings in Print vol. 7 (1970)–vol. 16 (1979).
Psychological Abstracts vol. 44 (1970)–vol. 64, no. 4 (1980).
Public Affairs Information Service vol. 56 (1969–70)–vol. 65 (December 1979).

Readers' Guide to Periodical Literature vol. 29 (1969–70)–vol. 39, no. 1 (1980).

Religion Index One: Periodicals (formerly *Index to Religious Periodical Literature*) vol. 9 (1970)–vol. 14 (1979).

Religious and Theological Abstracts vol. 13 (1970)–vol. 22 (1979).

Resources in Education (formerly *Research in Education*) vol. 5 (1970)–vol. 15, no. 5 (1980).

Sage Family Abstracts vol. 1 (1979)–vol. 2, no. 1 (1980).

Seventh-Day Adventist Periodical Index vol. 1 (1971)–vol. 2 (1972) and vol. 4 (1975)–vol. 6 (1977).

Social Sciences and Humanities Index vol. 23 (1969–70)–vol. 26 (1973).

Social Sciences Citation Index 1970–January–April 1980.

Social Sciences Index vol. 1 (1973)–vol. 6 (March 1980).

Social Work Research and Abstracts (formerly *Abstracts for Social Workers*) vol. 6 (1970)–vol. 16, no. 1 (1980).

Sociological Abstracts vol. 18 (1970)–vol. 27, no. 5 (1979).

Southern Baptist Periodical Index 1970–1979.

Subject Index to Selected Periodical Literature—Mosher Library, Dallas Theological Seminary vol. 1, (1970)–vol. 11, no. 3 (1980).

United Methodist Periodical Index vol. 10 (1970)–vol. 20, no. 2 (1980).

Vertical File Index vol. 39 (1970)–vol. 48 (1979).

Women Studies Abstracts vol. 1 (1972)–vol. 8 (1979).

Work Related Abstracts 1970–November 1979.

Writings on American History 1962-73–1977-78.

LEGAL PERIODICALS

Case and Comment vol. 75 (1970)–vol. 84 (1979).

Conciliation Courts Review vol. 8 (1970)–vol. 17 (1979).

Family Advocate vol. 1 (1978)–vol. 2 (1979).

Family Law Newsletter 1970–1978

Family Law Reporter vol. 1 (1975)–vol. 5 (1979).

Unauthorized Practiced News vol. 35 (1970)–vol. 40 (1977).

POPULAR PERIODICALS

Family Circle 1970–1974.*

New Woman vol. 1 (1971)–vol. 9 (1979).

Penthouse 1970–1974.*

Playboy 1970–1974.*

Single Parent vol. 13 (1970)–vol. 22 (1979).

Woman's Day 1970–1974.*

* Indexing began in 1975.

VII. Indexes

AUTHOR INDEX

Aardal, Danny C., 3151
Aarnas, Laila E., 1681
Abad Salvador, Federico, 3562
Abarbanel, Alice R., 105–06
Abbin, Byrle M., 2729, 3129
Abeel, Erica, 4012, 4385, 4425
Abraham, Willard, 1293
Abrahams, Sally, 3891
Abrahams, Samuel, 2553
Abrams, Nola, 958
Abt, Lawrence E., 192
Ackerman, Lillian A., 439
Adair, Alvis V., 1363
Adam, John H., 4013
Adam, Nancy W., 4013
Adams, Alice, 4932
Adams, Fred M., 2744, 2745
Adams, Gerald R., 4682
Adams, Jane, 3940, 4489, 4490
Adams, Jay, 3657
Adams, Paul L., 41
Adams, Terry K., 2029
Addeo, Edmond G., 4014
Adkinson, Clayton J. M., 2339
Adler, Bill, 4555
Adler, Jan M., 2823–24
Africano, Lillian, 4380, 4381
Agatstein, Sylvan, 2215, 2859
Ahern, Stephen F., 2092
Ahrons, Constance R., 107
Akers, Monte E., 2644
Albers, Daniel T., 2130
Albrecht, Stan L., 372, 1480
Alcott, Mark H., 3152
Aldous, Joan, 1161
Alexander, Sharon J., 49, 121
Alford, John G., 1942
Aliber, Stephen D., 1712
Allan, Kathryn H., 703
Allen, C. Ermal, 3280
Allen, Charles M., 4214
Allen, Michael L., 1970
Allen, Nany, 958
Allman, T. D., 4015
Alston, Jon P., 409
Ament, Richard J., 3362
Amerine, Janet, 3011
Ames, Loretta, 1919
Ancel, Sorelle J., 2400
Anderson, Carol E., 1997
Anderson, Clifford R., Jr., 2840
Anderson, Elaine A., 1512, 2904, 2905
Anderson, G. Wells, 2217
Anderson, Geraldine P., 3389
Anderson, Hilary, 133
Anderson, John A., 3012
Anderson, Margaret, 884
Anderson, R. Dennis, 2645, 2814

Anderson, Wayne J., 3682
Andress, Elizabeth L., 892
Andrew, Jan, 4016
Andrew, June M., 1413
Anglea, Berneice, 3013
Ansell, Charles, 982
Anspach, Donald F., 480
Anthony, E. James, 242, 244, 281
Antoniak, Helen, 4394
Appelbaum, Alan S., 1307
Archbell, Roy A., 1631
Ard, Ben N., Jr., 893
Areen, Judith, 2133
Arella, Gerard J., 3230, 3249
Aresty, Joel M., 2671
Argue, Douglas W., 3153
Arlen, Michael J., 3942
Armstrong, Ann, 4303
Armstrong, Herbert, 3560
Armstrong, Ron, 4304
Arndt, Joseph M., III, 2100
Arnold, David, 2176
Arnold, Marilyn, 3759
Arnold, William V., 3460
Arvidson, R. Regner, 3014
Ashby, Deborah H., 3858
Asher, Shirley J., 1137, 1138
Ashley, Paul P., 4162
Aslin, Alice L., 885
Athearn, Forden, 4017
Athearn, Louise M., 4395, 4396
Atkin, Edith L., 4417
Atkins, Michael B., 2219
Atkins, Shirley M., 1286
Atkinson, Brian R., 1162
Atwood, Andrew, 3353
Aubry, Jerold E., 2511
Auerbach, Lynn S., 1474
Auerbach, Marshall J., 2209, 2322, 2730
Auerbach, Stevanne, 4631
Auerbach, Sylvia, 4143
Aulik, Elizabeth J., 1963
Auster, Simon L., 754
Austin, Eugene, 4126
Austin, Jack F., 1731
Austin, Roy L., 1236
Avakian, Spurgeon, 3461
Awad, George A., 65
Ayres, George W., 2163

Baber, Asa, 4408
Babigain, Haroutun M., 1152
Bach, George R., 894
Bacon, Lloyd, 486
Badaines, Joel S., 1191–92
Badal, Cathy M., 1941
Baden-Marotz, Ramona, 1294
Baer, Jean, 4556, 4557

Baer, Joseph W., 2323
Bagby, Trudy K., 755
Baginski, Joseph C., 865
Bagley, Christopher, 1147
Baguedor, Eve, 4427
Bahm, Robert M., 1253
Bahr, Stephen J., 676, 698, 2593–94
Baideme, Sally M., 756
Bailey, Fred, Jr., 4018
Bailey, Robert W., 3354
Bain, Jeffrey M., 2646
Bair, Emily S., 2115
Baker, Adrian J., 418
Baker, David A., 2392
Baker, Russell, 4019
Bakos, Susan C., 3892
Balbirer, Arthur E., 1889, 2372–74, 2603
Baldwin, Rignal W., 1654
Ballantine, Constance, 164
Bandel, Betty, 533
Bane, Mary J., 134–36
Bank, Raymond L., 1751
Baptiste, David A., 1248
Barker, Edward L., 1906
Barkin, Robert, 4187
Barnard, Charles P., 2231
Barnard, Everett, 3548, 3697
Barnett, Bernard, 3016
Barnhart, Joe E., 3338
Barnhart, Mary A., 3338
Barnhill, Diane, 895
Barnwell, William, 3462
Baron, Robert E. C., 2359
Baroni, Diane, 4305
Barrett, John D., 2672
Barrett, Leo J., 1734
Barrett, Roger K., 945
Barrier, Joseph L., 4217
Barringer, Kenneth D., 1295, 3514, 3740–41
Barron, Gene, 3281
Barry, Ann, 1296
Barton, Freeman, 3282
Barton, Kaye, 3530
Bartz, Karen W., 87
Baruth, Leroy G., 4506
Bashinsky, Thomas M., 3017
Basi, Bart A., 3154
Baskin, Henry, 4020
Bass, Gill E., 2757
Bass, Howard L., 137, 4166, 4167
Bassett, William W., 3809
Batson, Jean W., 567
Batt, John, 1812
Baum, Charlotte, 3859, 3893
Baum, John, 567
Baum, Patricia, 4507
Baxter, Lynn, 3760

Beal, Edward W., 138
Bean, Frank D., 444
Beatrice, Dory K., 757
Bebensee, Barbara A., 825
Beck, Aaron T., 1154
Beck, Mimi, 4428
Beck, Phyllis W., 1683
Beck, Robert T., 842
Becker, Carmelita D., 3829
Becker, Gary S., 504
Becker, Russell J., 3463
Becker, Stephen, 1249
Beckert, Paul R., Jr., 2096
Bedell, Susan, 4182
Bedell, Susanna E., 946, 4306
Beebe, Mike D., 1604
Begleiter, Michael L., 556
Behles, Daniel J., 2439
Behles, Jennie D., 2439
Beifuss, Joan, 3704
Beigler, Jerome S., 2393
Belén Frías, Ana, 2472
Belfer, Myron L., 557
Bel Geddes, Joan, 4508
Bell, Michael L., 1168
Bellington, Janice E., 1813
Bellison, Leonard E., 1729–30
Belson, Robert J., 1903
Belt, Terry L., 2784
Belz, Joel, 3391
Bendiksen, Robert A., 218, 219
Benedek, Elissa P., 13, 14, 108, 122, 284,
    1752–54
Benedek, Richard S., 13–14, 108, 122,
    284, 1753–54
Benford, Gary A., 2926
Ben-Horin, Giora, 3132
Benians, R. C., 243
Bennetts, Leslie, 4388
Benson, Barbara, 367
Benson, Roger L., 2093
Bentler, Peter M., 321
Bentley, Eloise, 666
Bequaert, Lucia H., 4397
Berdon, Robert I., 1814, 1890
Berg, Berthold, 257, 285
Berg, Elayne C., 2305
Berg, Pearl, 2131
Berger, Michael J., 2798
Berger, Penny, 1667
Berger, Vivian O., 2673
Berk, Richard A., 1416
Berkebile, James M., 3474
Berkowitz, Bernard J., 1977, 4590
Berlin, Gerald A., 1743–44
Berlin, Joyce E., 552
Berman, Diana D., 2408
Berman, Eleanor, 4307, 4509
Berman, John J., 2299, 2343
Berman, Robert S., 1959
Berman, Susan, 4510
Bernard, Janine M., 139
Bernard, Jessie, 410, 1297
Bernard, W. David, 1950
Bernard, Will, 3860

Bernet, Mary F., 1978
Bernhardt, Jeanne R., 1163
Bernstein, Alan, 1715
Bernstein, Barbara E., 1209
Bernstein, Barton E., 88, 758–59
Bernstein, Blanche, 677
Bernstein, Jay S., 4224
Bernstein, Joanne E., 826
Bernstein, Lawson F., 3018
Berry, Newton, 3563
Bersoff, Donald N., 1801
Berson, Barbara, 4308
Bertelsen, Judy, 322
Bessinger, Tina P., 286
Bettelheim, Bruno, 3943, 3988
Beuche, Larry W., 1658
Bevilacqua, Anthony J., 3564
Bianchi, Suzanne M., 505, 1357
Bianco, Thomas C., 2565
Biblin, Allan E., 3019–20
Biederman, Frana, 2716
Bienenfeld, Florence, 123
Bierman, Jacquin D., 2120, 2927, 3021–
    24
Bilbe, Kathleen, 1637
Bilby, John W., 2333
Bild, Brian, 2860
Biller, Henry B., 1164–65, 1210, 1250–
    53, 1532
Billingsley, Nancy, 2746
Bird, Thomas L., 1692
Birdwell, Rawson P., Jr., 1029
Birmingham, Nan, 4558
Birtchnell, John, 425
Bisbee, Margaret K., 2027
Bishop, Thomas A., 1755
Biskind, Elliott L., 2620
Bissell, Sherry, 4406
Bizer, Linda S., 1382
Black, Kathryn N., 667, 3944
Black, Melvin, 760, 761
Black, Paul, 4205
Blackwell, Robert, 4022
Blanchard, Robert W., 1210
Blank, Diane S., 1586
Blanshard, Paul, 323
Blau, Cecile A., 2062
Blechman, Elaine, 1383
Bledsoe, Eugene, 651, 668
Bleyer, Rosemary, 16
Bliss, Elsie, 4309
Block, Jean L., 4023
Block, Joel D., 4559
Block, Winston J., 4251
Blond, Irwin E., 2914
Blood, Margaret C., 324
Blood, Robert O., Jr., 324
Bloom, Bernard L., 1137–38, 1494
Bloskas, John D., 3549
Blum, Sam, 4560
Bodenheimer, Brigitte M., 1756, 1815,
    1848, 1865, 1885, 1971, 2180, 2703
Boerner, Laurel L., 2532
Bohannan, Paul, 325–26, 440, 866, 928,
    1004, 1026, 1542, 2181, 2586, 4621

Bohmer, Carol, 327
Boice, James M., 3283
Boies, Judith, 1698, 2674
Bolas, Donald M., 2306
Bolhouse, Lana G., 896
Bonavich, Peter, 3155
Bond, Catherine, 1298
Bondurant, Stephen B., 867
Bonesio, W. M., 2487
Bonkowski, Sara E., 762
Bontrager, G. Edwin, 3413
Boone, Gregory K., 2647
Boone, Sherle L., 1237, 1266
Booth, Gerald V., 976
Borenzweig, Herman, 897
Borgen, Mack, 2642, 2785
Borghese, Phyllis, 2928–29, 2995, 3025–
    27
Bosco, Antoinette, 3566–67, 3758
Bosley, Wade R., 1979
Bost, John C., 3124
Bost, T. G., 3156
Bostwick, Sylvia H., 833–34, 3959
Boudreaux, Adrienne E., 983
Bouma, Mary L., 3658
Bova, Ben, 4308
Bowen, Henry C., 1612, 2566
Bowman, Gene, 2786
Boyance, Rudolph E., 4197
Boyd, Mary, 3527
Boyer, Sherry, 1450
Boyle, Larry M., 1897
Boyle, William, 1428
Braaten, Carl E., 3662
Brackley, Judith, 1232
Bradbrook, Adrian, 1816
Bradbury, Katharine, 678–79
Bradford, Lawrence J., 898
Bradley, Connie, 4398
Bradley, W. P., 3531
Brady, James B., 328
Brady, Kathleen, 3841–42
Branca, John G., 2675
Brandwein, Ruth A., 899, 1299–1300
Brandzel, Jacob R., 3028
Brassard, Jane A., 4680
Bratt, Carolyn S., 1849
Bratt, David A., 1909, 2071
Braudy, Susan, 4429–30
Braun, Julius, 4252
Braun, Samuel J., 140
Brazelton, T. Berry, 291
Bredehoft, David, 3397
Breen, Joseph, 3568
Breezeel, Gary L., 1659
Breig, James, 3569
Brenton, Myron, 4005–06
Brett, Wesley E., 3509
Brevitz, Ruth A., 2612
Bridgers, Sue E., 3946
Bridges, Marybeth, 763
Brightman, Carol, 1388
Brightman, Lloyd A., 1211
Briles, Ingrid, 3861
Brill, Steven, 4206

Brinkley, Ann, 4431
Briscoe, C. William, 947–50
Brockelbank, William J., 1998
Brockert, John E., 329
Brockhouse, John D., 3028
Brocki, Severine J., 951
Broden, Barry C., 2731
Brodie, D. W., 2132
Brody, Stephen A., 1278, 1287
Brody, Stuart A., 2203
Broncaccio, Diane, 4420
Bronfenbrenner, Urie, 488, 1301
Bronstein, Eli H., 2345
Brookins, Elwood, 1417
Brooks, Charles, 2533
Brosky, John G., 1942
Brothers, Joyce, 4561
Brower, Elizabeth, 3742
Brown, Autry, 3355
Brown, Bertram R., 2717
Brown, Bob W., 3799
Brown, Carol A., 900, 925, 1300
Brown, Daniel G., 4652
Brown, Emily M., 491, 868–69
Brown, Evelyn C., 952
Brown, George H., 634
Brown, Gerald L., 3724
Brown, J. Michael, 2861
Brown, James M., 2908
Brown, Norman, 4544
Brown, Prudence, 330, 879, 901, 980,
    984–85
Brown, Robert T., 2489
Brown, Terry, 1405
Brubaker, Ellen A., 3398, 3830
Bruce, Jackson M., 2534
Bruce, Larry B., 2787
Bruch, Carol S., 1972, 2909, 3194
Brun, Gudrun, 244
Bry, Adelaide, 4025
Bryant, Barbara E., 902
Bubis, Gerald B., 3735
Buchanan, Margaret R., 3862
Buchman, Arnold E., 1745
Buckley, Elizabeth Y., 141
Buesser, Frederick G., Jr., 2232
Buhr, Kenneth S., 1533
Bujarski-Greene, Pamela, 4386
Bulka, Reuven P., 3441
Bullard, Edward T., 1902
Bumpass, Larry, 142–43, 331, 449, 461–
    62
Bundesen, Russell, 2394
Bunton, Peter L., 1424
Burch, Ernest S., Jr., 440
Burchell, R. Clay, 764
Burdge, Walter A., 765
Burger, Robert E., 4014
Burgess, Jane K., 1302
Burgoyne, Shirley J., 50
Burke, George B., 2246
Burke, Sharon O., 1433
Burlage, Dorothy D., 1139, 1351
Burnett, Dennis J., 2535
Burns, Robert A., 1279

Burns, Robert J., 3550
Burnside, Betty, 688
Burnstein, Jules, 332
Burry, V. F., 556
Burstein, Carole, 2536
Burtle, Vasanti, 894
Burton, John D., 3797
Busch, Joseph P., 2040
Busnitz, Virgie M., 4562
Bustanoby, Andre, 3284, 3481
Butler, Annie L., 144
Butler, C.O., 4310
Buttenweiser, Helen R., 3947
Buxton, Martin, 17
Byron, Brian, 3307

Caballero, Romualdo C., 2266
Cadden, Vivian, 4127
Cage, Lowell T., 1951
Caine, Lynne, 4512, 4563
Calbreath, Dean, 4233
Caldwell, Bettye M., 1176
Caldwell, Steven B., 626
Callahan, Betsy N., 766
Callahan, Parnell J. T., 4168–69
Callen, Barry L., 3659
Callner, Bruce W., 1716
Callow, William G., 1757
Calof, Michael P., 2758
Calvert, Sheryl E., 245
Calvert, Stuart, 3356
Camara, Kathleen A., 145, 208
Cameron, Catherine, 1471
Campbell, Alma L., 3532
Campbell, Bruce L., 534
Campbell, Eugene E., 534
Campbell, Regis W., 2676
Campbell, Ross W., 101
Camper, Diane, 3851
Candela, Joseph L., 535
Cannell, John D., 2226
Cannell, Lin, 3928
Cannon, Melissa, 3515
Cantey, Richard E., 1254
Cantor, Donald J., 4170
Cantor, Dorothy W., 146, 827
Cantor, Irwin, 66
Cantwell, Robert E., III, 2311
Canudo, Eugene R., 4253
Capaldi, Frederick, 1547, 3835, 4632
Cappas, A. Thomas, 400
Cardwell, Albert L., 3802
Cardwell, Ronald E., 1949
Carey, J. Matthew, 1600
Cargill, Joan, 3410
Carlson, David K., 2729, 3129
Carlson, Elwood, 635
Carmichael, H. Alan, 2815
Carmody, Mary E., 2816
Carp, Gerald I., 3133–34
Carpenter, Teresa, 4212
Carr, Jo, 3399
Carrico, Bill, 370
Carro, Geraldine, 3863, 4311, 4513–14
Carroll, Anne K., 3414

Carroll, Katherine, 4026
Carsola, Anthony T., 1735
Carswell, Kenneth R., 2383
Carter, Dianne K., 886, 891
Carter, Hugh, 610
Carter, Velma, 3737
Casasanto, Michael D., 1802
Case, Karen A., 2281, 2677
Casey, Rick, 3705–06, 3725
Cashion, Barbara G., 333
Casperson, Paul, 839
Cassetty, Judith H., 1999–2000
Cassidy, Robert, 4027
Cassius, Joseph, 767
Castellano, Vianne M., 1238
Castleberry, James N., Jr., 2886
Casto, Robert F., 1015–16
Catchpole, David R., 3268
Cathey, Maurice, 2356
Catoir, John T., 3207, 3238
Cauthen, William H., 3668
Cavenaugh, Ralph C., 2241
Cease, Lory, 1850
Cerling, C.E., Jr., 3482
Ceravolo, Anthony J., 3157
Chambers, Cheryl A., 221
Chambers, David L., 2028–29, 4650
Chambers, Marjorie B., 472
Chan, Janet, 3843
Chang, Frederic C., 558
Chapman, Benson J., 3029
Chapman, Michael, 1212
Chardavoyne, David G., 2419
Charnas, Jane F., 18
Chase, Gary A., 51, 124
Chase, Mary T., 3687
Chavis, William M., 441–42
Cherlin, Andrew J., 246, 426, 506, 680,
    704, 1454, 1495
Cherney, Walter, 4270
Chess, Stella, 68, 279
Chesser, Barbara, 1335, 1385
Chester, Robert, 334–35
Chester, Stephanie A., 1948
Chiancola, Samuel P., 1496
Chiland, Colette, 244
Chilton, Roland J., 1414
Chiodo, John J., 669
Chiriboga, David A., 903, 1140, 1497,
    1498
Christensen, John C., 3683
Christensen, Larry, 336, 1441
Christie, Lyle E., 3343
Chu, Daniel, 3915
Church, Virginia A., 1717, 2319
Citron, Rebecca, 2134
Claerbaut, David, 3685
Claire, Anne, 3973
Clark, Homer, H., Jr., 2183–84, 2567,
    2572–73
Clark, Mary F., 2320
Clarke, Juanne N., 386
Clayton, Dorothy H., 2135
Clayton, Patricia N., 1420
Clayton, Paula J., 975

Clemente, Virginia, 3812
Cleveland, C. Anthony, 1891
Cleveland, Martha, 473
Clifford, Garry, 3916–17
Clinard, Keith A., 1702
Cline, Brenda J., 1304
Cline, David W., 247, 2174
Cline, Foster W., 148
Cline, Stephen R., 2826
Coane, James, 785
Coates, William H., 3030
Cobb, Anita D., 3031
Cobe, Patricia, 337, 1305
Coburn, Judith, 3844, 4491
Coché, Judith, 887
Cochran, Thomas C., Jr., 557
Cockburn, Christine, 529
Coffey, Barbara, 4432
Coffman, Jennifer B., 2850
Cohan, Michael C., 2073
Cohen, Alan L., 507
Cohen, Debra, 4564
Cohen, Herbert L., 2206
Cohen, Keith D., 2849
Cohen, Neil P., 2479
Cohen, Richard B., 2440
Cohen, Sarah B., 455
Cohen, Stanley N., 67
Cohen, Warren H., 2537
Cohn, Henry S., 536
Colburn, Virginia C., 1933
Cole, C. Donald, 3732
Cole, Charles L., 338
Cole, Tom, 1866
Coleman, Emily, 4433
Coleman, Gerald D., 3571
Coleman, Jack D., 4434, 4500
Coleman, James P., 1660
Coleman, Susan L., 2405
Coleman, William L., 3347
Coleman, William M., 3285
Collada, Henry B., 63, 132
Colletta, Nancy D., 904, 1166, 1368–69
Collier, James L., 4409
Collyer, Keith E., 2136, 2910
Colón Rodríguez, Victor L., 1690
Colton, Jerome G., 1731
Combs, E. Raedene, 508
Combs, Elizabeth R., 2848
Comer, James P., 4515
Comisky, Myra, 4313
Confusione, Michael J., 1425
Conley, John A., 412
Connally, John B., III, 3158
Connery, John R., 3308
Conroy, Donald B., 3572
Constance, Richard, 1661
Constantine, Diane, 3950
Constantine, Joan M., 339
Constantine, Larry L., 339
Conti, Lee A., 2066
Conway, Jim, 3286
Conway, Paul M., 768
Conyers, Mary G., 657
Coogler, O. J., 851–853

Cook, Helen, 1167
Cook, James J., 3153
Cook, Jimmie, 670
Cookson, Bernard, 4129
Coombs, Lolagene C., 456
Coombs, Russell M., 1867
Cooper, Arthur, 4314
Copeland, Terry F., 1557
Corcoran, Mary, 474
Corfman, Eunice, 1017, 1542
Cornish, Edward, 4104
Corrigan, Brian T., 2101, 2817
Cosgrove, Thomas H., 3707
Cosneck, Bernard J., 3998, 4421, 4609
Costa, Simeon, 4028
Cotroneo, Margaret, 1817
Cott, Nancy F., 537–38
Coulter, James A., 3208
Courtney, Dan E., 1213–14, 1222
Covill, Bruce, 4274–76
Covino, John A., 2870
Cowan, Ronnie, 4315
Cowan, Thomas A., 2138
Cowen, Emory L., 229
Cowley, Susan C., 3930
Cox, Georgia L., 4624
Cox, Martha J., 163, 209, 287, 293, 919–
    21, 1141, 1244
Cox, Mary J., 1850
Cox, Mathilda, 4435
Cox, Roger, 163, 209, 287, 293, 919–21,
    1141
Cox, W. O., 3525
Coyne, James C., 1262
Coyne, Thomas A., 19
Crady, Luther, Jr., 3516
Crandall, Louise, 1172
Crandall, Patricia I., 2902
Crawford, Don R., 340
Crawford, Robert L., 923
Creswell, Richard W., 2480
Crickmore, Jack, 769
Cristy, Carl W., 2054
Croake, James W., 4565
Cromley, Brent R., 2636
Cronkhite, John A., 3035, 3159
Crook, Roger H., 3688
Crosby, Jan, 4633
Cross, Harry M., 2704
Crossman, Sharyn M., 4682
Crouch, Garrett R., II, 3036
Crouch, Richard E., 1798, 2122
Crown, Jeffrey L., 3037
Crum, Robert A., 3302
Crystal, Nathan M., 2477
Cuenin, Walter J., 3250
Cuff, E. C., 341
Culbreth, Marcene C., 1434
Cull, John G., 213–14, 237, 240, 356–57,
    767, 770, 789, 967, 982, 986, 1003,
    1025, 1519–20
Cullimore, James A., 3315, 3424
Culpepper, Emily E., 905
Cunningham, Thomas G., 3318
Curran, Charles E., 3573–76

Curran, Jan W., 4316
Curry, Douglas L., 2430
Curtin, William B., 3363, 3813
Curtis, Orlie L., 3038
Cuse, Arthur, 1
Cusick, David M., 2259
Cusick, Kathleen M., 906
Cutler, Loraine, 1140
Cutright, Phillips, 509, 689
Cutshaw, Gina, 3743
Cybulski, Donald, 2649
Cypen, Irving, 1614
Cypen, Stephen H., 1614
Czajka-Narins, Dorice M., 559

Dahl, Barbara B., 740
Dakin, Carol F., 2554
D'Amico, John, Jr., 2732
Damon, Parker, 652
Dancey, Elizabeth, 3895
Daniel, Glenda, 4501
Daniel, Ralph M., 149
Daniels, Deborah, 1851, 1922
Daniels, Eugene O., 3039
Daniels, Jack L., 993
Danilov, Dan P., 2139
Dannenberg, Linda, 4029
Darsa, Stephanie D., 465
Dart, John M., Jr., 2538
Dash, Jerry, 749
Daskal, Robert H., 3129
Datesman, Susan K., 1415
Davenport, Caroline V., 130
Davey, James, 3689
David, Lester, 4031
Davidson, Charles W., 1168
Davidson, Jessica, 3883
Davidson, Sara, 4389
Davies, John H., 2933
Davies, Robert O., 1623
Davies, Rosalie C., 1838
Davis, Charles, 3577
Davis, Douglas, 4032
Davis, Flora, 4033
Davis, Helen G., 2140
Davis, Hermione G., 1421
Davis, Michael E., 2827
Davis, Muller, 2323
Davis, Wallace M., 4727
Dawson, Dickson R., 987
Dawson, Paul, 1215
Day, H. D., 303
Day, Ingeberg, 4317
Day, Randal D., 510
Dean, George W., 4188
Dean, Gillian, 489, 1455, 1488
Dean, Katherine I., 1193
Dean, Paula D., 2917
de Bessonet, Cary, 2911
Deckert, Pamela, 427
Decter, Midge, 4318
de Dubovay, Diana, 3951
DeFazio, V. J., 771
DeFrain, John, 1335, 1385
DeFronzo, James, 1306

Deitz, Susan, 3896
de Kemper, Magaly Bello, 2126
Del Campo, Rogert L., 14
Del Cotto, Louis A., 1699, 2981, 3040
Delevett, J., Allen F., Jr., 3041–42
Dell, Paul F., 1307
Delooz, Pierre, 3578
Demarest, Vicci, 3980
Dembitz, Nanette, 1799
Demeter, Anna, 3918
Denman, Sidney B., 1182
Denton, David, 772
DePalma, Anthony, 4135
Depue, Roger L., 747
De Ranitz, Richard, 3579
Derdeyn, Andre P., 20, 52, 68, 99–100,
    828, 1559
Desimone-Luis, Judith, 205
Desteian, John, 21
Detec, David A., 1592
Deur, Jan L., 1258
Deutsch, Ellen S., 3160
Deutsch, Morton, 798- 3423
Devine, James R., 1930
DeWeese, Allen, 1615
DeWolf, Rose, 4172, 4235
De Zutter, Albert, 3364
Diamond, S.J., 4199
Diaz, Robert E., 2002
Dibrell, Cooper G., 1952
Dick, LaVernae J., 3512
Dickey, Gordon, 3365, 3726
Dickinson, Lloyd J., 2759
Dickinson, Martin B., Jr., 3161
Dickson, Jane J., 1981
Dickson, Robert J., 2395
Dienstag, Eleanor, 342
Dienstag, Gary E., 1747
Dillingham, Charles, 3162
DiMento, Carol A.G., 2514
Dinerman, Miriam, 1308
DiPiazza, Nicholas C., 1992
DiPronio, Blaise, 2507
Disanto, Edmund, 2003
Disney, Dorothy C., 4625
Diss, William T., 2936
Dixon, Beth, 988
Dixon, Ruth B., 1792
Dlugokinski, Eric, 343
Dobson, James C., 3403
Dodson, Fitzhugh, 4634
Doherty, Dennis J., 3209, 3584, 3585
Dohrenwend, Barbara S., 1143
Dohrenwend, Bruce P., 1143
Donahoe, Mike, 773
Donahue, Charles, Jr., 3210
Donaldson, Bryna, 4437
Donelson, Irene, 4422
Donelson, Ken, 4421
Donley, Joseph M., 1685
Donnelly, Francis, 3211
Donohue, William J., 1686
Donovan, Michael L., 3319
Doppler, George F., 4172
Dorfman, John R., 4271

Dostart, Thomas J., 2708
Dougherty, Ruth, 3884, 3885
Downey, Charles E., 4190
Doyle, R. F., 4173
Doyle, Richard H., IV, 2117
Drake, Charles T., 1280
Drake, Ellen A., 653
Drakeford, John W., 3551
Dranov, Paula, 344
Draughon, Margaret, 1543
Drayton, Ethel L., 1228
Dreifus, Claudia, 4034, 4438
Dresen, Sheila, 1309
Dreskin, Wendy, 3954
Dreyfus, Edward A., 774
Dries, Robert M., 907
Drinan, Robert F., 150, 3411
Druckman, Joan M., 69
Drummond, Paul A., 2796
Duberman, Lucile, 1456, 1457, 1548
Dubose, Eugene Z., 1568
Du Canto, Joseph N., 1563, 1718, 2678–
    81, 3044–48, 3164–65
Duchene, Josianne, 636
Duffin, Sharyn R., 1549
Duke, Marshall P., 1169
Dulick, H. L., 2887, 2888
Dullea, Georgia, 4492
Dumon, Denise M., 2822
Duncan, Darlene, 4035
Duncan, Greg J., 1310
Duncan, Jane, 23
Duncan, Lois, 3784
Duncan, T. Roger, 4035
Dunigan, Vincent, 3586
Dunn, George T., 4174
Duquette, Donald N., 70–71
Durbin, Karen, 4036
Durkin, John J., 2747
Durkin, Mary G., 3587
Durner, James A., 748
Dusyn, Kenneth F., 2051
Dutton, Diana, 2760
DuVal, Kathleen, 2539
Dworak, Richard F., 2012
Dykes, William T. F., 3147

Earl, Loveline, 1194
Earle, George R., 3533
Eberle, Nancy, 4493, 4567
Eberstein, Isaac W., 443–44
Eby, Lynn C., 2083
Eckard, Joyce D., 880
Eddy, John P., 228
Eddy, R. Lee, III, 4254
Eden, Philip, 1980, 2033–34
Eder, Vera J. (Vicki), 72, 109
Edmiston, Jane L., 2031
Edmiston, Susan, 4614
Edmonds, Michael E., 2455
Edmonds, Mim R., 4037, 4568
Edmonds, Patty, 3708–09
Edwards, Jerome E., 539
Edwards, Marie, 908
Edwards, O.C., Jr., 3480

Ehrlich, Stanton L., 1565, 2005
Einbinder, Sandra S., 1514
Einstein, Elizabeth, 4635
Eisler, Riane T., 4399
Elder, Glen H., Jr., 393
Eldred, Quentin T., 2055
El Ghatit, Ahmed Z., 561, 562
Elkin, Meyer, 110, 125, 126, 775, 2204,
    2582, 2583
Elkins, James R., 1739
Ellingson, Catherine, 3766
Elliott, Elizabeth, 3865
Elliot, Ralph E., 3384
Elliott, Anne, 4439
Elliott, Carla J., 83
Elliott, Patricia C., 3049
Ellis, Paul N., 3486
Ellisen, Stanley A., 3487
Ellison, Edythe J., 663, 664
Elser, Marsha B., 1892
Eltzroth, Marjorie, 2026
Elvart, Ann C., 989
Emmons, Keith E., 1626
Emrich, Ernestine H., 3767
Emswiler, James P. 3367
Engel, Laura, 4516
England, J. Lynn, 637
Engler, Calvin, 3050
Enochs, Elizabeth, 2574
Ensworth, George, 3287
Ephron, Nora, 4136
Eppinger, Paul, 3346
Epstein, Alan, 3866
Epstein, Edward Z., 4266
Epstein, Joseph, 4038
Epstein, Marsha F., 1311
Erhard, Tom, 3833
Erhardt, Carl L., 552
Erickson, Rosemary, 4621
Erikson, Alden, 4130
Erskine, Rita K., 990
Eshleman, J. Ross, 386
Esman, Aaron H., 248
Espenshade, Thomas J., 511
Epsinoza, Renato, 1528
Ester, John W., 2412
Ethridge, Deborah, 2682
Evans, David S., 3517–18
Evans, Gayle S., 2568
Evans, John F., 3120
Evans, Larry E., 2097
Evans, William H., 1852
Evensen, Martha A., 2828
Everly, Kathleen G., 345, 909
Ewing, Lee, 4277, 4278

Faber, Stuart J., 2600
Fabricatore, Joseph M., 749
Fagan, Stephen H., 60
Fager, Charles, 3897, 4441
Fain, Harry M., 346, 1842, 2555, 2829
Fairbanks, James D., 2141
Fairbanks, Joseph M., 2913
Fakouri, M. Ebrahim, 1170
Falconer, Barbara, 4236

Falk, Mark, 682
Falk, Phyllis, L.C., 1312
Fannin, David C., 2072
Farber, Bernard, 347
Farber, Stephanie S., 1882
Farley, Florence S., 1313
Farley, Leo C., 3589
Farley, Margaret, 3590
Farley, Reynolds, 505, 638, 1357
Farrell, Margaret D., 2326
Farrell, Michael F., 2282,
Farrell, William P., 3728
Farson, Richard, 288
Fast, Anita H., 1393
Faust, James E., 3427
Feder, Chris W., 3880
Federico, Joseph, 348
Fehren, Henry, 3591
Feig, Ellen, 1173
Feigenbaum, Dolly, 3380
Feinberg, Gloria, 4488
Feinberg, Mortimer R., 4488
Feinhandler, Sherwin, 568
Feld, Alan L., 2988
Feldberg, Roslyn, 490, 925
Felder, Raoul L., 4039
Feldman, David M., 2102
Feldman, Stephen R., 2185
Felici, P., 3320
Felner, Robert D., 229, 249, 1882
Fenelon, Bill, 639
Fennel, Justus J., 3269
Fennessey, Robert E., 2056
Fenton, Kennard L., 1759
Fenton, Norman S., 151
Ferguson, Adelaide, 776
Ferguson, Dennis, 1405
Ferguson, Harold L., Jr., 2303
Ferguson, Larry, 4040
Ferguson, Patricia L., 24, 66
Ferraro, Kathleen J., 874
Ferrell, Ruth M., 2317
Ferris, Abbot L., 623
Ferriss, Franklin, 2216
Fethke, Carol, 2719
Fetterly, Patricia C., 2884, 3052
Field, David L., 428
Fields, Sidney, 3442
Fields, Susan, 4569
Filteau, Jerry, 3212
Fine, Amy R., 1981
Fink, Albert J., 2762
Finkel, Esther, 1421
Finnegan, John T., 3336, 4748
Fiol Matta, Liana, 2473
First, Curry, 1778, 1779
Fisch, Edith L., 2142
Fischer, James M., 2656, 3270
Fisher, Bruce F., 777, 870–71, 4729
Fisher, Esther O., 778–80, 4720
Fisher, Jerry, 3443
Fisher, Mitchell S., 2084
Fishman, Gideon, 405, 1160
Fisk, Mary, 1868
FitzMaurice, Gregory, 2844

Fitzmyer, Joseph A., 3309
Flach, Frederic F., 4570
Flamion, Allen, 2733
Flanagan, William, 4041–42, 4137–38,
    4191, 4298
Flanzer, Jerry P., 1370
Flater, Morris E., 2999
Fleck, Charles J., 1869
Fleer, Bryson, 1017
Fleming, Clarence E., Jr., 2840
Fleming, Jennifer B., 4321
Flinn, Richard, 4322
Floyd, Sally, 25
Flynn, Jon R., 2710
Fogarty, Gerald P., 3592
Folberg, H. Jay, 1853
Foley, Daniel M., 2683
Foley, Leander J., 2556
Foley, Leonard, 3593
Folley, Francis J., III, 4721
Fonte, Verona H., 1030
Foote, Caleb, 2575
Ford, Charlotte, 4323
Ford, Jon R., 2718
Fordham, W. W., 3534
Forgeron, Hy Theodore, 2208
Forlines, Fay, 3803
Forrest, Deborah A., 1510
Forrtenot, Gerald J., 1910
Forst, Bradley P., 1714
Fortinberry, Alicia, 152
Foster, Henry H., Jr., 1566, 1587, 1594,
    1761, 1797, 1800, 1830, 1854, 1870–
    71, 1973, 2006–07, 2085, 2143,
    2186–89, 2220, 2271–77, 2283,
    2443, 2512, 2576, 2581, 2585, 2621,
    2657, 2684–86, 2763, 2878
Fournie, Judith A., 1974
Fowler, Patrick C., 1216, 1217
Fowler, Ray, 349, 2862
Fox, Billy R., 1288
Fox, Elizabeth M., 1300
Fox, Hannah, 330
Fox, Roberta, 1894
Fox, William F., 1760, 2118–19, 2199
Framo, James L., 350, 4722
Francis, D. W., 341
Francis, Robert, 3265
Francke, Linda B., 3992, 4043, 4442,
    4517
Frank, Alan H., 2343
Frank, Frederick N., 2470
Frank, Neil, 1965
Franke, Carl W., 3488
Franks, Maurice R., 2527–28, 3845
Franks, Violet, 330, 894
Fraydouni, Nasser, 351
Freed, Doris J., 1566, 1587, 1594, 1761,
    1830, 1854, 1870–71, 1973, 2006–
    07, 2085, 2188–89, 2220, 2253,
    2262, 2269–77, 2283, 2443, 2581,
    2621, 2657, 2685, 2686, 2763, 2878
Freed, Rae, 153
Freedman, Deborah S., 457
Freeland, James J., 3053

Freeman, Harrop A., 1740
Freeman, Haskell C., 2413–14
Freeman, Marvin A., 1567, 2599, 2601
Freeman, Patricia, 2637
Freeman, Stanley J. J., 1473
French-Wixson, Judith, 1289
Freud, Anna, 27
Freund, John, 781
Frideres, James S., 501
Friedman, James T., 2324
Friedman, Lawrence M., 2251
Friedman, Philip, 1363
Friggens, Paul, 3956
Frisbie, W. Parker, 443–44
Frisch, Robert E., 3054–55
Frohlich, Newton, 782, 4175
Froiland, Donald J., 165, 783, 830
Frumkes, Melvin B., 1892–93
Fuld, Charles L., 4518
Fuller, B. Latham, 742
Fuller, Jan, 4443–45
Fullenweider, Donn C., 2102
Fulton, James A., 2254
Fulton, Julie A., 206, 4646
Fulton, Robert, 219
Furby, Tommy E., 2423
Furfine, Allen, 4324
Furner, Joanne F., 2304
Furstenberg, Frank F., Jr., 458–59

Gabler, Ronald G., 2042
Gabor, Zsa Zsa, 4044
Gach, Linda, 2830
Gaddis, Stephen M., 111, 854
Gaffney, James, 3594
Gahman, Suzan, 4519
Gallagher, Charles, 3595–97
Gallagher, John T., 2318
Galligan, Richard J., 698
Gallin, Martin, 4131
Galloway, Dale E., 3661
Galper, Miriam, 3898
Galvin, William R., 2008
Gamlin, Joanne, 2799
Gangel, Kenneth O., 3271
Ganley, Paul M., 2284
Gans, Herbert J., 408
Garai, Josef E., 3957
Gardiner, Anne M., 3368
Gardner, Richard A., 154, 207, 230, 250,
    1523, 3958, 4647, 4653, 4684–85,
    4728
Gardner, Sandra, 3993
Garian, Harry Z., 2938–44, 3000–01
Garland, T. Neal, 978
Garrett, David J., 3148
Garrett, W. Walton, 1588, 2481
Garrity, Robert W., 4255
Gasser, Rita D., 1394
Gates, Samuel K., 4220
Gath, Ann, 563
Gatley, Richard H., 4545
Gatz, Margaret J., 1771
Gault, Duncan, 1953
Gay, Arthur, 3489

Gaylin, Jody, 4546
Gaylord, C. L., 2190, 2508
Geaney, Dennis J., 3793
Gebhard, Paul, 1026
Gebhart, Barton L., 2077
Geldard, Mark, 3272
Geller, Markham J., 3267
George, Carol V. R., 544
George, Vic, 1426
Gerhart, Frederick J., 2982
Gerhartz, Johannes G., 3598
Gerken, Robert T., 1694
German, Judith M., 2327
Gerow, Ann, 4283
Gershansky, Ira S., 1255
Gershenson, Milton G., 2445
Gersick, Kelin E., 89–90
Gertz, Kathryn R., 4325, 4390
Gettleman, Susan, 4045–46
Getto, Charles A., 2658
Getz, Sandra, 910
Giacalone, David A., 1601, 2035
Gibeau, Dawn, 3214, 3251, 3599
Gibble, Kenneth L., 3475
Giboney, Daniel W., 4226
Gibson, Gifford G., 3890
Gibson, Helen E., 2509
Gilbert, Craig C., 1481
Gilbert, Douglass W., 3670
Gilbert, John P., 3744
Gilder, George F., 4411
Gillen, Frances C., 784
Gillen, Rebecca O., 2482
Gilles, Jean, 4160
Gilreath, James R., 2983
Gilstrap, Frank, 4222
Gittelson, Natalie, 3919, 4047
Gladston, Richard, 4520
Glass, Shirley P., 911
Glasser, Claire L., 26
Glautz, Oscar, 1195
Glendon, Mary A., 2557
Glenn, Claude, Jr., 4547
Glenn, Grant M., 2404
Glenn, Norval D., 752, 1482
Glick, Paul C., 155, 352–53, 378–79,
    610, 627, 738, 1458, 4686
Glickfeld, Bruce S., 3167
Glieberman, Herbert A., 2513, 2687
Glosband, Benjamin A., 2514
Glustrom, Simon, 3345
Goddard, John L., 2602
Goddard, Wendell H., 2307
Godeke, Dan A., 3056
Goebel, Julius, Jr., 2578
Goethal, Kurt G., 991
Goetting, Ann, 640, 912, 1459
Goff, Thomas J., 2540
Gokel, Ruth L., 3168
Gold, Don, 4446
Gold, Tracy, M., 4004
Goldberg, B. Abbott, 2788
Goldbern, Martin, 4727
Goldenberg, Ronald, 654
Goldberger, Gustav, 2541

Goldfarb, Robert S., 693
Goldman, Henry T., 1738, 2668
Goldman, Janice, 785, 887
Goldman, Tamara, 4502
Goldscheider, Robert, 3899
Goldsmith, Jean, 4687
Goldsmith, Mary A., 690
Goldstein, Harris S., 156, 1245, 1255
Goldstein, Joseph, 27
Goldstone, Patricia, 4237
Gomberg, Edith, 330
Gongla, Patricia A., 1500
Gonso, Jonni L., 251
Gonzalez, Carmen C., 2851
Gooblar, Howard M., 1171
Goodman, Ellen, 2
Goodman, Emily J., 3900–01, 4192
Goodman, Emmett, L., Jr., 2064
Goodman, Max A., 2043
Goodwin, Donald W., 564
Goot, Mary V., 3339
Gordon, Bob, 4412
Gordon, Bud, 4048
Gordon, Kathie, 4193
Gordon, Michael, 4116
Gordon, Philip B., 28
Gordon, Richard E., 739
Gordon, Victor M., 2371
Gordon, William J., 4413
Gore, Delores, 1168
Goudy, Willis J., 1462
Gough, Aidan R., 4238
Goulden, Joseph, 4183
Gourley, Ruth L., 29, 1256
Gove, Walter R., 913, 953–54, 1148
Gover, Kathryn R., 737
Gozansky, Nathaniel E., 1824, 2321
Grab, Nancy H., 3755
Graber, Richard F., 786
Grach, Brian, 3169
Grafton, Samuel, 1793
Graham, George P., 3600
Graham, LeRoy, 4688
Graham, Marva, 1853
Graham, William T., 1898
Granat, Jay P., 565
Grande, Donald I., 2734
Grant, Isabella H., 2831
Granvold, Donald K., 787–88, 822, 992
Graves, Edward S., 3057–58
Gray, Gloria M., 914–15
Gray, Susan W., 1201
Greeley, Andrew M., 3601
Green, Barbara J., 845
Green, Leslie, 4326
Green, Mark, 4215
Green, Robert W., 1907
Green, Samuel, 2376
Green, Thomas J., 3215–16, 3239, 3369–
    70
Green, Tony, 4184
Greenbaum, Martin, 1796
Greenbaum, Richard, 1796
Greenberg, Blu, 3444
Greenberg, Judith B., 1395

Greenberg, Simon, 3445
Greene, A. C., 4327
Greene, Freda, 4200
Greene, Gail, 4571
Greene, Karen L., 157
Greene, Roberta S., 91, 1396, 4049
Greene, Scott, 2869
Greenfield, Lawrence, 682
Greenstone, James L., 855
Greer, Steven, 1147
Gregg, Gary, 1475, 4572
Greif, Judith B., 92, 916, 1855
Gremillion, Glenn B., 1639
Gremillion, Jed G., 1911
Grenier, Henri, 3321
Grey, Catherine, 158
Griffin, Susan, 4553
Griffis, Charles B., 1640
Griffith, Benjamin E., 2424
Grigg, Linda L., 2688
Grigg, Susan, 1460
Grimsal, A., Gregory, 1912
Grinnell, Richard M., Jr., 221
Groenveld, Lyle P., 701
Grollman, Earl A., 159, 3989–90, 4050
Grollman, Sharon H., 159
Gromek, Carl L., 2542
Grose, Madison, 1703
Gross, Beatrice, 34
Gross, Leonard, 1165
Gross, Paul, 4146
Gross, Ronald, 34
Gross, Steven J., 942
Grossberg, Sidney H., 1172
Grossman, Allyson S., 726–27
Grote, Douglas F., 112
Groves, Linda C., 2890
Groves, Patricia H., 1736
Gruba, Glen H., 917
Gruenberg, Max F., 1883
Grüner, O. P. N., 566
Guadagno, Mary Ann N., 527
Gubrium, Jaber F., 354
Gudebski, John J., 2764
Guentert, Kenneth, 3602
Guidry, Hervin A., 1641
Gullahorn, Jeanne E., 1141
Gunn, Alan, 1700, 3059
Gunter, B. G., 466, 2252
Gunther, Max, 4009
Gurak, Douglas T., 1455, 1488
Gurevitz, Mark S., 1943
Gurney, Louise, 829, 4724
Gutman, Harry L., 3094
Guze, Samuel B., 975

Haberle, Therese M., 2446
Hackney, Gary R., 872
Haddad, William F., 118, 1856, 3902
Haddy, Theresa B., 559
Hagy, James C., 1719
Hails, Judy, 2044
Haine, William R., 2459
Haines, Marjorie W., 2863–64
Hainline, Louise, 1173, 1255

Hajal, Fady, 1384
Haldy, Ronald L., 2460
Halem, Lynne C., 2144
Hall, Clifford, 2638
Hall, Douglas A., 30
Hall, Sarah M., 3867
Hallett, Garth, 3322
Hallett, Kathryn, 4051, 4521
Halliwell, Anne S., 671
Halpern, Gerard, 2689
Halpert, David H., 2945
Halverson, Richard, 3491
Hamilton, George, 1954
Hamilton, Harper, 4203
Hamilton, Marshall, L., 1174
Hamman, Cathryn L., 1906
Hammer, Bernard, 2177
Hammond, Janice M., 160, 231, 289–90
Hampe, Gary D., 979
Hampton, Robert L., 445–46, 512
Haney, Daniel Q., 3745
Hanks, George F., 4272
Hannan, Michael T., 699–701
Hansen, Robert W., 31, 355
Hanson, Richard W., 5617-62
Hanson, Shirley M. H., 93
Harburg, Ernest, 985
Hardie, L. Glenn, 2765–2767
Hardin, David R., 712
Hardisty, James H., 2178
Hardman, Helaine, 4745
Hardy, Richard E., 213–14, 237, 240,
    356–57, 767, 770, 789, 967, 982,
    986, 1003, 1025, 1519–20
Hare-Mustin, Rachel T., 451
Haring, Bernard, 3217
Harker, Ruth, 4522
Harkey, Ira, III, 4256
Harmelink, Herman, III, 3686
Harmelink, Philip J., 3060–61
Harrell, Irene B., 3694
Harris, David J., 556
Harris, Elizabeth C., 3768
Harris, John W., 2946
Harris, Steven M., 3170
Harris, Thelma, 3780
Harshman, Gordon A., 357
Hart, Betty K., 392
Harter, Richard M., 3062
Hartnagle, Timothy F., 1196
Hartstein, Gordon, 2768
Hartstein, Norman B., 818
Harvey, John V., 2416
Haspel, Eleanor C., 4052
Hastings, Donald W., 487
Hatch, Jonathan C., 1940
Hatherly, John E., 1886
Hatten, William M., 2489
Haugh, William E., 2422
Haughey, John, 3603
Haulman, Clyde A., 2061
Hauserman, Nancy R., 2719
Hausheer, Myron, 1634
Haut, Irwin H., 3446
Hauver, Constance L., 2690

Havens, Elizabeth, 513
Hawke, Sharryl, 4523
Hayashi, Janet W., 3350
Hayden, Jan M., 1913
Hayden, Trudy R., 3935
Hayes, James A., 2308
Hayes, Maggie P. 438, 475
Hayghe, Howard, 705–08, 728–29
Haynes, John M., 856–57
Heard, Drew R., 2659
Heedy, Michael A., 2091
Heer, David, 1149
Heffernan, John, 2315
Heffernan, Virginia A., 3604
Heger, Donna T., 1442
Heinrich, Albert, 447
Heiss, Jerold, 448
Helland, Mark D., 2422
Helmlinger, Trudy, 4328, 4484
Henao, Sergio, 217
Henderson, Robert H., 2901
Henderson, Roger C., 2431
Hendricks, Howard, 3392
Hendricks, William L., 3304
Hendrickson, Wendy E., 358
Hendrix, Lewellyn, 382
Hennen, Claudia M., 4267
Hennessy, Michael, 1416
Hennigan, Joelyn L., 413
Henning, James S., 32, 161
Henoch, Monica J., 567
Henry, B.W., 955
Henry, Gaylord L., 2284
Henry, Linda, 2558
Henry, Ronald T., 1595
Hensley, Dennis E., 4272
Hensley, John C., 3690
Henson, John P., 3063
Henszey, Benjamin N., 1975
Henzlik, William C., 3671
Heritage, Jeannette G. (Lena J. G.), 993–
    94
Hermalin, Albert I., 638
Herman, Jeanne, 910
Herman, Sonya J., 956, 1150, 1501
Hernandez, Irma V., 1616
Herrick, Jeannette E., 918
Herring, Clyde L., 3698
Herrman, Margaret S., 858, 1725, 1728,
    4683
Hertel, James R., 3605
Hervey, James E., 2311
Herz, Fredda M., 1371
Herzog, Briant, 558
Herzog, Elizabeth, 1175–78
Hess, Robert D., 208
Hetherington, E. Mavis, 162–63, 209,
    291–93, 919–21, 1141, 1257–58
Hetherington, Kim, 4636
Hettinger, Clarence J., 3218
Hetzel, Alice M., 612
Heyman, Michael G., 2210
Hickman, Hoyt L., 3519
Hidalgo, Marty A., 4626
Higgins, James R., Jr., 1602

Higgins, Malcolm B., 2095
Higgins, Warren, 3195
Hight, Evelyn S., 1515
Hill, Archie, 4622
Hill, Charles T., 360–61
Hill, Hank A., 756
Hill, Thomas H., 2145
Hillabrant, Walter J., 395
Hinchey, John W., 2387
Hinson, Sandra, 4207, 4329
Hire, Richard P., 3323
Hirsch, Barbara B., 4053
Hirsch, Seth L., 1358
Hirschmann, Maria A., 3782
Hitchcock, James, 3587, 3606
Hitchens, Donna J., 102, 1839
Hittner, David, 743
Hjorth, Roland L., 3067–68
Hoban, Christine, 568
Hobart, James F., 873
Hobbet Richard D., 2948
Hoch, Jered L., 2467
Hochstein, Rollie, 4447
Hodge, Harvey G., 1534
Hodges, William F., 164
Hoehn, G.H., 3535
Hoffer, William, 4074
Hofferth, Sandra L., 1329
Hoffman, Arthur S., 2949
Hoffman, Blair W., 1762
Hoffman, Howard A., 293
Hoffman, James W., 4330
Hoffman, Judy, 1668
Hoffman, Martin L., 1246
Hoffman, Mary F., 2082
Hoffman, Richard C., 790
Hoffman, Richard G., 2335
Hoffman, Saul, 514–15
Hofstein, Saul, 3736
Hogoboom, William P., 2309–10
Hogue, Jon, 1632
Holbrook, Betty, 3404
Holdahl, Shirley, 839
Holder, Angela R., 1732
Holland, Ronald E., 3695
Hollis, Robert A., 3064
Hollstein, Richard W., 2543
Holly, Marcia, 3904
Holman, Adele M., 1259
Holman, Nancy A., 2350, 2505
Holmes, John, 515
Holmes, U. T., III, 3480
Holt, Joel H., 1696
Holz, Marvin C., 53, 1960
Holzman, Robert S., 3065
Honig, Alice S., 1190, 1372
Honig, Marjorie, 691–92
Honigman, Jason L., 2336
Hooker, Lizzie B., 1260
Hoopes, Margaret H., 3428
Hoover, John K., 2800
Hope, Karol, 4527
Hopson, Dan, 2401
Horiuchi, Shiro, 641
Hormann, Elizabeth, 4054, 4448

Horn, Jack C., 362, 642, 4331
Horner, Catherine T., 1352
Horowitz, June A., 1281, 1314
Horvitz, Jerome S., 3195
Hosier, Helen K., 3273
Hoskins, Dalmer, 529
Houck, Catherine, 4573
Houck, John H., 363
Houle, Philip P., 1568
Hover, Dorothea, 4304
Howard, Jeffrey C., 2711
Howard, Margaret, 1982
Howe, Louise K., 4627
Howe, Ruth-Arlene W., 364
Howell, John C., 4223
Hoyne, Stephen D., 2079
Hozman, Thomas L., 165, 783, 830
Hudak, Leona M., 1843–44
Hudson, R. Lofton, 3804
Hudson, Robert L., 3464
Hudson, William E., 1763
Huebner, Daniel L., 1720
Huff, Dan, 4398
Huff, Glenn, 1929
Huffaker, John B., 3139–40
Hughes, Dee, 4574
Hull, Addis E., 3172
Hull, Darrell M., 1282
Hull, E. A., 1596
Hullum, Everett, 3357
Hult, James M., 1967
Humphrey, Kyler, 3905
Humphrey, Stephen L., 2211, 2406
Humphreys, Sarah A. L., 2045
Hungerford, Nancy, 1451
Hunt, Bernice, 4056–58, 4108, 4332, 4575
Hunt, Dennis, 205
Hunt, Janet G., 1179, 1197
Hunt, Larry L., 1179, 1197
Hunt, Morton M., 4055–58, 4108, 4332,
    4575, 4688
Hunter, Brenda, 3769
Hunter, Edna J., 740
Hunter, John L., 1927
Hunter, Laura, 3552
Hunter, Nan D., 1840
Hunter, Robert L., 2397
Hunting, Margaret, 1688
Hurley, Suzanne, 1810
Hurley, Virg, 3288
Hurowitz, Neil, 1983
Hurst, Gloria, 3770
Hussain, Syed J., 2191
Huston, Brett A., 1923
Hutchens, Robert M., 683
Hutchison, Ira W., 3679, 4682
Hutchison, Katherine R., 3679, 4682
Hyatt, Ralph, 4576
Hyde, Heather R., 846
Hyman, Jeffrey A., 1706
Hynes, Winifred J., 1315

Imperio, Anne-Marie, 1261
Infausto, Felix, 1984, 1998
Inker, Monroe L., 1572, 1657, 1764,
    1803, 2335, 2857–58

Irving, Howard H., 862
Irwin, Lee J., 4333
Iseman, James M., Jr., 1985
Isenberg, Roy M., 294
Isenhart, Mary-Alice, 73
Israel, Stanley, 420

Jackson, Elinor, 4577
Jackson, Erwin D., 995
Jackson, Julie H., 1765
Jackson, Lorraine D., 3710
Jackson, Magnolia, 1443
Jacobs, Laura J., 1316
Jacobson, Doris S., 252–54, 1550
Jacobson, Gerald F., 1151, 1516
Jacobson, Robert L., 2712
Jaffe, Dennis T., 1502
James, Adrienne, 3886
James, Edward, 3252
James, Frank S., III, 1748
James, H. Wynne, III, 2885
Jameson, Mark, 3836
Jancourtz, Isabella, 4211
Jantz, Richard K., 1224
Jarobe, J. Michael, 1857
Jarrett, John L., 1845
Jarrett, Rose, 3393
Jason, Judy, 4334
Jauch, Carol, 1317
Javaras, Lee S., 1422
Jeffrey, Shirley H., 3400, 3401, 3746–53
Jenkins, Elizabeth A., 1617
Jenkins, Richard L., 33
Jenkins, Shirley, 166
Jennes, Gail, 3995
Jennings, Kathryn A., 2769
Jensen, Herbert L., 2953
Jensen, Marilyn, 4335
Jersin, Nikki K., 2720
Jewett, Paul K., 3278, 3303
Jewett, Richard, 3536
Joffe, Wendy, 760, 761, 1517, 1518
Johannes, Jack, 2490
John Paul II (Pope), 3325
Johnson, Beverly L., 709–10, 729
Johnson, Charles W., 2360, 2770–71
Johnson, David W., 2103
Johnson, Dick, 3385–86
Johnson, Doyle P., 2252
Johnson, Flora, 1721
Johnson, Frank C., 492
Johnson, Gary C., 1950
Johnson, James E., 4204
Johnson, Jill M., 996
Johnson, Joel, 2125
Johnson, Joyce S., 1144
Johnson, Judy, 167
Johnson, Larry, 3387
Johnson, Lynell A., 168
Johnson, Nora, 4059
Johnson, Patrice, 4524
Johnson, Phyllis H., 2202
Johnson, Phyllis J., 711
Johnson, Richard, 1976
Johnson, S. Greg, 2845

Johnson, Sandra R., 2660
Johnson, Stephen M., 4336–37, 4611
Johnson, Thomas J., III, 2075
Johnson, Virginia, 4586
Johnson, W. J., 4449
Johnson, Walter D., 314, 365, 516, 1726,
    1986, 2146, 2285, 2325
Jones, Carroll F., 1929
Jones, Cathy J., 1964
Jones, Christopher, 1662
Jones, David L., 2832
Jones, F. Nolan, 255
Jones, Hugh E., 1283
Jones, Judy, 4338
Jones, Marvin W., 1955
Jones, Mary S., 2297
Jones, Robert B., 2227
Jones, Robert C., 2770–71
Jones, Shirley M., 1461
Jones, Vickie, 4450
Jordahl, Leigh, 3663–64
Jordon, Lucy, 829, 4724
Jovovich, Susan, 2764
Joyner, Robert C., 2954
Juenger, Frederich, 2255
Juhasz, Ann M., 366, 4723

Kagel, Steven A., 1262–63
Kahan, James P., 1537
Kahan, Stuart, 4414
Kahn, Lawrence E., 2147
Kahn, Robert W., 2147
Kalben, John F., 2943–44
Kalcheim, Michael W., 1628, 2846
Kalenik, Sandra, 4224
Kaler, Patrick, 3607
Kalish, Richard A., 4060, 4339
Kallen, David J., 559
Kalman, Benjamin, 2879
Kalter, Neil, 232
Kalter, Suzy, 4615
Kane, Barbara, 791
Kanter, Rosabeth M., 1502
Kapit, Hanna, 4340, 4578–79
Kapit, Milton, 4578–79
Kaplan, Alan S., 2544
Kaplan, Helen S., 388, 823, 4494
Kaplan, Howard B., 1318
Kaplan, Stuart L., 831
Kapner, Leiws, 1893
Karawia, Wafaa T., 429
Karch, Gary C., 2772
Kargman, Marie W., 54, 2192
Karmen, Marcia, 4407
Kaseman, Charlotte M., 1319
Katz, Lucy, 1818
Katz, Sanford N., 34, 1657, 2559
Kaufman, Michael, 2773
Kavanaugh, Karen, 3405
Kavanaugh, Kathryn A., 1551
Kay, Herma H., 2586
Kayani, Ashraf K., 629, 643
Keating, Gerald, 3071
Keeffe, Arthur J., 2148, 2661
Keeton, H. Dale, 3756

Kehoe, Michael E., 1858
Keir, Margaret S., 752
Keith, Judith A., 1552
Keith, Pat M., 1462
Keleher, Thomas D., 1671
Kellam, Sheppard G., 1320
Kelleher, Stephen J., 3219, 3220, 3608–10, 3711, 3817
Keller, Lillian M., 415
Keller, Peter A., 1198
Kellogg, Mary A., 3906
Kelly, Clifton M., 2057
Kelly, Dennis M., 2912
Kelly, F. Donald, 1373
Kelly, Janice M., 922
Kelly, Joan B., 127, 169, 200–02, 256, 278–81, 821, 832, 4654–55
Kelly, Joan M., 295
Kelly, Robert, 257, 285
Kelly, William, 3611
Kelsey, Linda J., 859
Kempton, Beverly, 4341
Kenkel, William F., 367
Kenkelen, Bill, 3241–42
Kennalley, John M., 2330
Kennedy, Fred, 2721
Kennedy, Robert T., 3336
Kenny, Walter F., 3221
Kent, Judith S., 1882
Kerckhoff, Alan C., 517
Kern, Patricia, 3712
Keshet, Harry F., 713, 1397–99, 1545, 4384
Kessler, Sheila, 421, 792–97, 833–34, 860, 3959, 4061
Kessler, Stuart, 2984
Kestenbaum, Clarice J., 1180
Khanlian, John F., 847
Kiefer, Louis, 1766
Kiel–Friedman, Sonya, 4020
Kienzle, Susan L., 1675
Kiester, Edwin, Jr., 4109, 4580
Kilbourne, James C., 1928
Kimball, Spencer W., 3429–31
King, Barbara, 3960, 3981, 4525
King, Donald B., 1880
King, Richard, 222
King, Rory P., 2229
Kirby, Jonnell H., 4581
Kircher, Kathleen, 3337
Kirkland, Karyn K., 258
Kirkpatrick, Elizabeth K., 3
Kirshner, Sheldon G., 1825
Kitabchi, Gloria, 923
Kitson, Gay C., 924
Kittleson, Mark J., 170
Kizer, Elizabeth J., 997
Kizirian, Lucy B., 1483
Klapper, Naomi, 4582
Klarman, Barbara, 2420
Klausner, Samuel Z., 1321
Klebanow, Sheila, 1374
Klein, Carole, 4526
Klein, Lynn, 4451
Klein, Michael F., Jr., 2991, 3072

Kleinbard, Martin, 3073
Kleinman, Judith, 1463
Klemesrud, Judy, 4128
Klenbort, I., 771
Knight, George W., 3554
Knight, Linda W., 1597
Knowles, Laurence W., 2560
Knox, David, 4523
Knox, L. Mason, 3470, 3612
Koch, Harry W., 4257
Koch, Joanne, 3868
Koch, Lew, 4139
Koffend, John B., 4452
Kohen, Janet A., 490, 925
Kohn, Sherwood D., 171, 368
Kohut, Nestor C., 4176
Kolb, Charles E. M., 2286
Kole, Janet, 4177
Kolodji, Joseph N., 369–70
Kolyer, Peter R., 2662
Komora, Edward J., 3222
Koonce, Jay, 767
Koopman, Elizabeth J., 297
Kop, P. P. A. M., 613
Kopf, Kathryn E., 1229
Kornhauser, Lewis, 2151
Kosicki, Evelyn L., 1935
Kosner, Alice, 4163, 4342
Kosnik, Anthony, 3371
Koubek, Richard F., 4548
Koulack, David, 4545
Koupernik, Cyrille, 242, 244, 281
Kraft, David P., 1152
Kram, Shirley W., 1965
Krantzler, Mel, 4062, 4063, 4343–45, 4453
Kraus, Sharon, 371
Krause, Harry D., 2561, 2577
Krauskopf, Joan M., 1573, 1663–64, 1924, 2862, 2865–66
Krauss, Herbert H., 1153
Kray, Dorothy J., 74
Krell, Robert, 55
Krebs, Richard, 3684
Kressel, Kenneth, 798–99, 861, 1727, 3423
Kriegsmann, John K., 712
Kriesberg, Louis, 1181
Krishnan, Parameswara, 628–29, 643
Krol, John, 3643
Kroll, Arthur H., 2774
Krom, Howard A., 2205
Kruse, Janet K., 1322
Kubie, Lawrence S., 35
Kulka, Richard A., 259
Kulzer, Barbara A., 2691
Kuntz, J. M., 3327
Kuntz, Joel D., 3074
Kunz, Phillip R., 372, 637
Kuo, Eddie C. Y., 493
Kupperman, Stephen H., 2809
Kurdek, Lawrence A., 210, 223
Kutun, Barry, 1894
Kysar, Myrna, 3274
Kysar, Robert, 3274

La Barre, Harriet, 4346
Labovitz, Irving D., 1574
Ladbrook, Dennis, 551
Laeger, Karen V., 998
La Farge, Phyllis, 4554
Lager, Eric, 481
Lake, Alice, 4147
Lamb, Jane, 3779
Lamb, Michael E., 296, 1251
Lambert, Clinton E., Jr., 957
Lambert, Vickie A., 957
Lamp, Herschel C., 3537
Lancaster, William, Jr., 1169
Land, Kenneth C., 615, 624
Landes, Aaron, 3447
Landes, Elizabeth M., 504, 1575
Landgraf, John R., 3831
Landrum, Faye, 3773
Landsman, Kim J., 1819
Lane, Gary L., 1635
Lane, Laura, 4161
Laner, Mary R., 494–96
Lang, Judith, 3448
Langelier, Regis, 427
Langum, David J., 2361
Lansky, Shirley B., 569
Lantz, Herman R., 1503
Laosa, Luis M., 1290
LaPoint, Velma D., 1359
Larentzakis, Gregor, 3435
Larkin, Mark D., 2705
LaRoche, Shirley S., 1535
Larson, Alan, 3846
Larson, Bianca G., 1606
Larson, Philip M., 3691
Lasch, Christopher, 540
Laser, Alvin, 2545
Laser, Martin S., 204
Lauerman, Nora, 1767
Lavercombe, Robert R., 2287
Lavin, John J., 1676
Lavoie, Rachel, 4148
Lawrence, Jean, 4723
Lawson, Gary B., 3175
Layne, Abner A., 744
Lazorick, Paul S., 2052
Leader, Arthur L., 800
Leavenworth, J. Lynn, 3737
Leavitt, Shelley, 1385
Lebbos, Betsey W., 120
Lebel, Robert B., 3223
Lebow, Richard N., 327
Leck, Ian, 570
LeClaair, Robert J., 2389
LeCorgne, Lyle L., 1290
Ledbetter, Jack W., 2630
Lee, B.H., 2214
Lee, Harold B., 3432
Lee, James R., 2546
Lee, Joe, 1677
Lee, Sheila, 4454
Lee, Wayne J., 2852
Leezenbaum, Ralph, 373
Lefco, Stanley M., 1895
Leggett, Marshall J., 3492

Lehmann, Karl, 3328
Lehr, Claire J., 4347, 4503
Lemov, Penelope, 4149
Lenihan, Genie O., 999
Leo, Roger J., 2348
Leonard, Elizabeth D., 926
Leonard, John, 4583
Leonard, Martha F., 1768
Leonard, Robert H., 3076
Leonoff, A., 116
Lerner, Samuel, 172
Lessing, Elsie E., 1218
Lester, Andrew D., 3305
Lester, David, 1154
Lester, Eva P., 75
LeVan, Gerald, 2810
Levi, Jeffrey H., 3176
Levin, Marshall A., 1918
Levin, Martin L., 1478
Levin, Noel A., 2776
Levine, Aaron, 2955, 3077
Levine, David I., 4030, 4194
Levine, James A., 4549
Levine, Marcia W., 801
Levinger, George, 62, 90, 263, 361, 377,
    379, 430, 459, 467, 497, 498, 546,
    685, 704, 925, 1138, 1502, 1504,
    1507
Levitin, Teresa E., 173
Levitt, Zola, 3495
Levy, Alan M., 1826
Levy, Robert J., 2517–18, 2520, 2575
Levy, Terry M., 1517–18
Lewis, Doris, 260
Lewis, Jane A., 1872
Lewis, Ken, 1400, 1444, 1831, 1873
Lewis, Larry, 3394
Lewis, Melvin, 56
Lewis, Shawn D., 4348
Lewis, William E., 1642
Libman, Joan, 4455
Lichtenstein, Grace, 3907, 4064
Lightener, John, 1769
Lightman, Ernie S., 862
Limmer, Ruth, 1411
Lind, Stephen A., 3053
Lindahl, Alan, 3358
Lindenthal, Jacob J., 1143
Lindey, Alexander, 2906
Lindsley, Byron F., 57, 1770
Linett, E. S., 2956, 3004, 3141
Liotta, James A., 2112
Lipman, Eugene F., 3449
Lipman-Blumen, Jean, 499
Lipten, Clarie R., 1323
Lipton, Roslyn A., 2149
Lira, Frank T., 579
Lisle, Laurie, 4608
Little, Jeannette, 2386
Little, Suzanne, 3982
Littlefield, Daniel F., 541
Littner, Ner, 76, 261
Lloyd, Ann, 3493
Lloyd, Cynthia B., 714

Lobsenz, Norman N., 4110, 4239, 4349,
    4610
Locke, Carey P., 2891
Locker, Barbara B., 2009
Lofas, Jeanette, 4616, 4643
Loge, Betty J., 1324
Lohmann, Nancy, 1194
Long, Ann, P. H., 1325
Long, John V., 2376
Long, Sandra M., 262
Longabaugh, Richard, 1219
Longfellow, Cynthia, 263
Longman, Douglas C., Jr., 1643
Loper, Amy T., 2754
Loucks, Richard R., 1733
Lowder, Paul D., 3673
Lowe, Patricia T., 4628
Lowenstein, Joyce S., 297, 1401
Lowery, Donald W., 1291
Lozoff, Michael D., 1968
Luboff, Eileen B., 3931
Luepnitz, Deborah A., 264, 265
Luker, William H., 2663
Lumry, Gayle K., 1159
Lund, Dorothy, 4637
Lundbom, Jack R., 3289
Lupo, Mary E., 2058
Lurvey, Ira H., 2833
Lutes, Dennis L., 2645
Lutzke, Jim, 1402
Lyles, Gladys J., 441–42
Lyman, Howard B., 888, 4485
Lynch, Dennis E.A., 1932
Lynch, Nancy N., 2789
Lysaght, Brian C., 1887

McAlister, Cecil M., 3555
McAndrew, David T., 3372
McAnerney, Robert M., 2316
McAninch, William S., 2547
McCall, Robert, 3999, 4350
McCarren, V. Louise, 4225
McCarron, Gerald J., 3613
McCarthy, Abigail, 3713
McCarthy, Colman, 1326
McCarthy, James, 460, 630, 1031, 3417
McClanahan, John H., 3696
McClelland, Muriel, 2083
McClenaghan, Judy C., 3834, 4629
McClure, Cecilia A., 3754
McClure, Jerry, 2692
McConaughey, Dan E., 2387, 4258
McConnell, Judith A., 233
McConnell, Lynda L., 4351
McCord, Jacqueline, 4585
McCord, Joan, 4682
McCormick, Mona, 1529
McCormick, Richard A., 3614–16
McCourtney, Lorena, 4352
McCowan, Richard J., 1265
McCroskey, Doris, 3406
McCubbin, Hamilton I., 740
McCulloch, Sandy, 802
McDaniel, Charles-Gene, 3390

McDermott, John F., Jr., 77, 266
McDevitt, Anthony, 3818
McDonald, Debbie, 1441
McDonald, John, 625
MacDonald, Maurice M., 526, 687, 1476
MacDonald, Scott K., 2784
MacDonald, Steve, 3847
MacDonald, William E., 1804
McDougall, Daniel, 1280
Mace, David R., 3520
McEaddy, Beverly J., 1429
MacEoin, Gary, 3254
McEvoy, Lawrence T., 2340
McFadden, Leo E., 3224
McFadden, Michael, 4550
McGee, Michael H., 4218
McGinness, Susan K., 1000
McGinnis, Tom, 4423
McGough, Lucy S., 1896
McGovern, Sheila E., 2416
McGrady, Patrick, Jr., 3921
McGuigan, Dorothy G., 984
McGuire, Claire V., 1264
McGuire, William J., 1264
McHale, John, 3617
Machtinger, Steven N., 2362
McHugh, James T., 2288–89, 3618, 3619
McIntosh, Phillip, 1644
McIsaac, Hugh, 129
McIvor, Daniel L., 889
MacKay, Ann, 1426
McKay, Richard W., 3787
McKenna, David L. 3494
McKenney, Mary, 422
McKenney, Paul L. B., 3177–78
McKenry, Patrick C., 28, 853, 858, 927,
    1032, 1725, 1728
McKeown, H. Mary, 2664
Mackey, Robert D., 1883
McKinney, Sally, 4353–54
MacKinnon, Dolores, 1001
MacKinnon, Douglas, 1149
McKisson, Michael P. 2834
McKnight, Joseph W., 2491, 2892
McLachlan, C. Ian, 2242, 2603
McLaughlin, Jon M.A., 2595
MacLean, John V., 2596
McMahon, Mary S., 3620
MacMillan, Dalphine, 2790
McMillan, Mae F., 217
McMillian, Theodore, 2556, 2563
McMullen, Richard, 2893
McMurray, Lucille, 1142
McNair, Bruce, 654
McNamara, T. Neal, 2801
McNeal, Robert E., 174
McNeive, Peggy A., 2067
McRae, Barbara, 1547, 3835, 4632
McRae, Ferrill D., 1603
Madden, Myron C., 3556, 3837
Maddi, Dorothy L., 2587
Maddox, Brenda, 4638–39
Madras, Patrik, 689
Magid, Kenneth M., 835, 4677

Magrab, Phyllis R., 267
Mahan, Bill, 4457
Maher, John, 3255
Maher, Thomas E., 2802
Mahoney, Dennis C., 3078
Maida, Adam J., 3243
Main, Frank O., 1373
Main, Margaret H., 672
Maio, Greta, 753
Makaitis, Regina T., 1805
Maller, Allen S., 3450–51
Maloney, George A., 3436–37
Maloney, Joseph E., 2803
Malouf, Roberta E., 1327–28
Maloy, Richard H. W., 4259–61
Manela, Roger, 879, 901
Manfredi, Lynn A., 175
Mann, Judy L., 4382
Mannes, Marya, 4084
Manosevitz, Martin, 1268, 1556
Marcantonio, Clement, 1002
Marcelous, Elinor W., 1239
Margolin, Frances M., 58, 128
Margolis, Randie, 1521
Marino, Cena D., 1265
Markey, Christian E., Jr., 129
Markham, Margaret, 4355
Markle, Gerald E., 1414
Markowitz, Janet, 4045–46
Marks, Jane, 4000, 4640
Marks, Judi, 4641
Marks, Ronald A., 2880
Marquise, Lois A., 4391
Marroni, E., 3714
Marschall, Patricia H., 1771, 2225
Marshall, Patrick C., 2110
Marshner, William H., 3244
Marst, Susan, 4458
Martelet, Gustave, 3621
Martin, Albert J., 4459
Martin, Allan L., 1874
Martin, Del, 102
Martin, Gilbert I., 234
Martin, John R., 3340
Martin, Michael, 4460
Martin, Norma, 3495
Martin, Patricia, 571
Masingale, Eula M., 1199
Maskin, Michael B., 1417
Mass, Earl H., Jr., 2311
Massey, Raymond L., 2407
Masters, William, 4586
Matano, Gary R., 2548
Mathews, Marilyn, 919
Matluck, Hannah, 3983
Matthews, Graham P., 1200
Matthews, Stephen D., 375
Maxwell, Mervyn, 3538–39
Maxwell, Ralph B., 2150
May, Elaine T., 542, 543
May, William E., 3622, 3310
Maye, Patricia A., 1375
Mayer, Michael F., 4178
Mayer, Nancy, 4383, 4495, 4587
Mayfield, Peter N., 1003

Mayleas, Davidyne S., 3869, 4356, 4588–89
Maynard, Fredelle, 4065, 4111–12
Mayo, Judy, 4723
Mazur-Hart, Stanley F., 2298–99, 2343
Mead, Margaret, 1004, 4066, 4156
Meade, Marion, 3850
Medeiros, Gladys, 3794
Medeiros, Julie P., 1553
Medsger, Anne R., 572
Meeker, Larry K., 3081
Meenan, Monica, 4461–63
Meezan, William Jr., 677
Meier, Paul D., 3496–97
Meislin, Bernard J., 3452
Meldman, Robert E., 3082
Melia, Elias, 3438
Melman, Carla, 4067
Melton, Emily, 4464
Melton, Willie, III, 1033
Mendes, Helen A., 94, 1403–04, 1447
Menéndez Menéndez, Emilio, 2474
Menken, Jane, 460
Merder, I. David, 1741
Meredith, Dennis, 1165, 1532
Meredith, Nancy G., 3961
Meroney, Anne A., 863
Merrill, Maurice E., 2519
Messner, Edward, 580
Messinger, Lillian, 1468–69, 1472–73
Metcalfe, Barbara L., 803
Metzger, Emily B., 1908
Meyendorff, Jean, 3316
Meyer, D. Eugene, 3418
Meyers, Judith C., 1511
Meyners, Hazel S., 905
Michael, Robert T., 431, 504, 644–45
Michels, Therese, 4357
Michels, Toni, 1157
Middlebrook, Janet S., 3180
Middleton, Glen S., 1536
Midonick, Millard L., 2085
Miller, Ann M., 4301
Miller, Arthur A., 928
Miller, David J., 1859
Miller, Diane, 905
Miller, Emily, 59
Miller, Michael H., 469
Miller, Milton H., 823
Miller, Ovvie, 1607
Miller, Paul W., 298
Miller, Pauline, 3781
Miller, Robert L., 2267
Miller, Rosalie D., 1554
Miller, Steven R., 2011
Miller, Thomas W., 2212
Miller, John R. (J. R.), 2461, 2627
Mills, Carol S., 2665
Mills, Robert A., 3181
Milmed, Paul K., 1806
Milne, Ann, 78, 112
Milner, John E., 2078
Minarik, Joseph J., 693
Mincer, Jacob, 376
Mindel, Charles H., 977

Minehart, Gordon, 3674
Minow, Martha L., 1819
Mitchell, Marilyn H., 1920
Mitchelson, Marvin M., 4228
Mlott, Sylvester R., 579
Mlyniec, Wallace J., 1807
Mnookin, Robert H., 1772, 1820, 2151–52
Mobley, Richard, 2357
Moen, Phyllis, 1432
Moerk, Ernst L., 1230
Moerlin, Elinor B., 804
Moffett, Robert K., 4068
Mohan, Raj P., 500
Moles, Oliver C., 62, 90, 263, 361, 377, 379, 430, 459, 467, 498, 546, 684, 685, 704, 925, 1138, 1502, 1504, 1507
Molinoff, Daniel D., 3887, 3908
Molloy, Don, 1711
Momjian, Albert, 2628
Monagan, Charles, 4465
Monahan, Thomas P., 470–71, 2193
Montare, Alberto, 1266
Montgomery, Luetilla, 929
Moody, Edward O., 1773
Moore, Kristin A., 930, 1329
Moore, Lynn S., 4195
Moore, Marvin, 3540
Moore, Nancy V., 130, 299, 4724
Moore, Sylvia F., 432–34, 730
Moran, Patricia A., 1240
Morell, Jerry, 2894
Morgan, Marilyn, 3788
Morgan, Mary, 102
Morganthau, Tom, 3851
Morgenstern, Debora, 3909
Morris, Craig, 1774
Morris, J.H.C., 2256
Morris, James D., 805–07, 810, 811
Morris, Jeffrey B., 1155
Morris, Lydia, 1330
Morris, Michael J., 1969
Morris, Roger B., 1360
Morris, William O., 2635
Morrison, James R., 300
Morrissey, Francis J., Jr., 1689, 2194, 2468
Mortland, Jean A., 2693, 2694, 2907
Morse, William C., 178
Moseley, Jim, 2493
Moskowitz, Joel A., 407
Moskowitz, Lawrence A., 1775
Moss, Milton O., 1737
Most, Bruce W., 3834, 4629
Mothner, Ira, 4415
Mott, Frank L., 432–34
Mouledoux, Andre J., 1645
Moultrie, Sandra, 4529
Mowatt, Marian H., 1555
Mudrick, Nancy R., 694
Mueller, Charles W., 435–37
Mueller, E. Jane, 1220
Muenchow, Susan, 4496
Muir, Martha F., 177, 1284
Mull, Richard L., 2111

Mullaney, Tom, 3715–16
Mulligan, Elizabeth, 4070
Mulligan, Michael D., 3142
Mulligan, William G., 1786
Mulliken, John B., 557
Mumbauer, Corinne C., 1201
Mungavan, Mary, 3256
Munger, Richard, 178
Munson, Douglas A., 2722, 2835
Murphy, Michael C., 2842
Murphy, Richard H., 1672
Murray, Daniel E., 2378
Murray, Edward J., 1198
Murray, Robert M., 4240
Murray, Thomas J., 519, 720, 4071
Murrell, Patricia H., 923
Muse, Diane, 2895
Musetto, Andrew P., 79, 131
Mussehl, Robert C., 1742
Myers, Allen, 3656
Myers, Jerome K., 1143
Myers, Lisa, 4476
Myers, Martha M., 1331
Mynko, Lizabeth, 1156
Myricks, Noel, 2153

Nadeau, Judith S., 60
Nadelmann, Kurt H., 2258
Nadler, Janice H., 1544
Nagata, Robert Y., 2046
Nakagawa, Mike K., 2047
Napier, Augusta Y., 931
Napier, Douglas W., 2456
Napolitane, Catherine, 4358–59, 4497, 4530
Narron, James W., 2918
Natale, Samuel M., 3225, 3257
Nathan, Max, Jr., 3083
Naturale, Cynthia, 1777
Nay, William D., 1937
Neeley-Kvarme, Janet, 1756
Neff, David, 3541
Neff, LaVonne, 3541
Nehls, Nadine M., 114
Nelsen, Edward, 1292
Nelson, Dorothy, 1218
Nelson, Geoffrey B., 1005
Nelson, Hal, 1332
Nelson, James E., 2588
Nelson, Kristine, 1361
Nelson, Meredith A., 2363
Nelson, N. Royce, 2549
Nelson, Robert L., 2030
Nelson, Verne E., 632
Nessel, William J., 3375
Nestor, Byron L., 103
Neumark, Victor, 2847
Neustadt, Leslie B., 2872
Nevaldine, Anne, 468
Newbern, David, 2202
Newcomb, Michael D., 321
Newman, Donald J., 1704
Newman, Gustav, 1182
Newman, Mildred, 4590

Newman, Yvonne, 1528
Newsome, Oliver D., 932
Nichols, George D., 2992
Nichols, Robert C., 80
Nichols, Sharon Y., 1389, 4744
Nichols, William C., 646, 808, 4591–92
Nicholson, Deirdre T., 4225
Nici, Janice, 1489
Nielson, Priscilla H., 1860
Nirenberg, Sue, 4593
Nisnewitz, Freda S., 2589
Nix, Christine, 817
Nobile, Philip, 3856
Noble, June, 3870
Noble, William, 3870
Nodgaard, John C., 2695
Noelker, Timothy, 2550
Noland, Jane, 2505
Noller, Patricia, 1376
Noonan, John T., 3245, 4749
Nordstrom, Ervin E., 4180
Norman, Sam R., 3381
Norman, William H., 478
Norris, Allen E., 2228
Norton, Arthur J., 353, 378–79, 627, 1430, 1458
Norton, George N., 2748
Nosenzo, Maryann E., 268
Noshpitz, Joseph D., 202, 1525
Nowak, Clara J., 3376
Nowell, Robert, 3330
Nuttall, Ena V., 1445
Nye, F. Ivan, 501
Nyswonger, J. Stephen, 1836

Oaks, Mary A., 670
Oberman, I. Allan, 2043
O'Brien, David J., 978
O'Brien, John E., Jr., 380, 476
O'Brien, Patricia, 3623
O'Callaghan, Denis, 3624
O'Connell, Frederick P., 2521
O'Connor, Nancy D.V., 381
O'Connor, William A., 1367
Oden, Marilyn B., 3402
Odencrantz, George D., 30
O'Donnell, Cletus S., 3820, 3821
Oelbaum, Harold, 1576–77
O'Farrell, Timothy J., 1505
Offord, David R., 958, 1418
O'Flarity, James P., 2155
Ogg, Elizabeth, 4072, 4531
Oglesby, William B., Jr., 3466
Ogston, Donald G., 1162
O'Hara, Clinton Joseph, 1478, 1479
O'Hare, William S, 2571
Ohle, B. Robert, 2304
Ohlson, E. LaMonte, 1333
Oken, Jean, 453, 454
Okpaku, Sheila R., 1827
Oldham, J. Thomas, 161, 1578
Olds, Sally W., 3996, 4073, 4114
Olen, Stanley, 4262
Oliver, Stephen R., 2836

Olmstead, Gerald T., 750
Olsen, Shirley, 3085
Olsen, V. Norskov, 3311
Olshewsky, Thomas M., 3466
Olson, David H. L., 863
Olson, K. Richard, 2511
Olson, Lester, 2312
O'Mahoney, Katherine, 205
O'Malley, Suzanne, 4594
O'Meara, Frank, 3625
Onaitis, Susan, 3377
O'Neil, Maureen, 115–16
O'Neill, William L., 544
O'Phelan, Lou, 4115
Opland, David V., 2458
Oppenheimer, Randolph C., 2462
O'Reilly, J., 3997
Oremland, Evelyn K., 307
Oremland, Jerome D., 307
Ornstein, J. Alan, 4416
Orlando, Frank A., 2590
O'Rourke, Thomas W., 412
Orsy, Ladislas, 3331, 3332
Orthner, Dennis K., 1405, 1831
Orthwein, Stephen A., 2379
Ortiz Alvarez, Pedro E., 2920
Ortmeyer, Carl E., 552
Osborne, Gwendolyn E., 1362
Osburn, Richard G., 1707
O'Shea, Ann, 4532
Oshman, Harvey P., 1267–68, 1556
Ostien, J. Keith, 809
O'Sullivan, Sonya, 4361–62
Ottenweller, Albert, 4750
Overall, John E., 955, 959, 962
Overton, Philip R., 2749
Owsley, Harriet C., 545
Ozburn, Samuel D., 1625

Paige, Roger, 3341
Pais, Jeanne S., 1006–07, 4683
Palley, Michael R., 4263
Palmer, Helaine B., 1987
Palmer, Paul F., 3333, 3626, 3822
Palsson, Lennart, 2127
Pantell, Steven, 658
Pantoga, Fritzie, 3627
Paoli, Sylvia, 2804
Paolin, Jo, 3717
Paolucci, Beatrice, 1451
Papa, Mary, 3378
Pardes, Herbert, 399
Pared, Howard J., 1516
Pared, Libbie G., 1516
Parish, Thomas S., 301, 1233–34, 1557
Parker, Allan J., 2960
Parker, Denise, 836
Parker, James O., 2483
Parks, Ann, 837
Parley, Louis, 1861
Parmer, David L., 2230
Parnell, Patrick A., 3561
Parrott, Leslie, 3523
Parrow, Alan A., 1221

Parslow, Richard N., 2049
Parsons, Lynne W., 2818
Pascal, Harold J., 1484
Pascal, Robert A., 2409, 2611, 2853
Pascoe, Elizabeth J., 3963
Pascoe, Jean, 4157
Pate, Dove H., 226
Pati, Prasanna K., 452
Patsavos, Lewis J., 3439–40
Patterson, Joya, 1334
Patterson, Sandra K., 1202
Pattiz, Henry A., 2805
Patton, Robert D., 1027
Pauley, Raymond J., 2087
Pauline, G. David, 2666
Paulsen, Monrad, 2578–79
Payne, Anne T., 1841
Payne, Raymond J., 3086
Payton, Patrick H., 1905
Peak, Lynda, 3521
Peak, Paul, 3757
Pearce, William W., 4074
Pearl, William, 2778
Pearlin, Leonard I., 1144
Pearson, Jessica, 1881
Pearson, Willie Jr., 382
Peck, Bruce B., 1386
Peck, Harry F., 1778–79
Pecot, Michael G., 179
Pedersen, Frank A., 1183, 1269–70
Pedler, Leigh M., 992
Peggs, Jack, 2068
Pellegrino, M., 3628
Pellegrino, Victoria, 4358–59, 4497, 4530
Pennell, Stephen R., 1629
Pentacost, Dorothy H., 3692
Peplau, Ltitia A., 360–61
Pepper, Max P., 1143
Peppler, Alice S., 3467
Percival, Robert V., 2251
Percy, Ryland, 1709
Perdue, Bobbie J., 1314
Perkins, Cheryl G., 3087
Perkins, Sandra L., 2510
Perkins, Terry F., 1537, 1558
Perkowski, Stefan G., 224
Perlberger, Norman, 2469, 2628
Perlstein, Robert S., 2265
Perocchi, Paul P., 1572, 2723, 2857–58
Perretta, Charlotte A., 1803
Perrucci, Carolyn C., 454
Perry, Joseph N., 3629
Perry, Lorraine, 985
Perske, Robert, 3798
Peschel, John L., 2965, 3143
Peskin, Tsipora R., 383
Peter, Val J., 3630
Peters, George W., 3290–93, 3800
Peters, Jack W., 2328
Peters, John F., 384–86, 1490
Peters, Paula, 2856
Peterson, Linda C., 960–61
Petosa, Jason, 3258
Petri, Darlene, 3498
Pett, Marjorie G., 1008

Petty, Charles, 3557
Pfnausch, Edward G., 3259, 3367
Phelps, Arthur W., 2500, 2634
Phelps, Joseph D., 2156
Phelps, Nancy C., 2903
Phillips, B. Ellis, 2012
Phillips, Carol A., 890
Phillips, E. Lakin, 180
Phillips, Earl, 2580
Philtine, Ellen C., 4075, 4595
Pick, Grant, 1832
Pickler, Harold T., 2695
Pierce, David E., 2667
Pike, Donald W., 129
Pinder, Robert H., 3699
Pinnell, Robert E., 2713
Pinson, William M., Jr., 3558
Piper, Thomas S., 3294
Pipher, Mary B., 1285
Pitcairn, Robert A., Jr., 2365
Pitcher, Griffith F., 2966–67, 3088–89
Plata, Maximo, 1412
Plattner, Andy, 4287
Platts, Barbara, 3806
Pleck, Elizabeth H., 315
Ploscowe, Morris, 2581
Podell, Ralph J., 181, 1778–79, 1961, 2522–23
Podolski, Lawrence A., 2003
Podurgiel, William C., 2088
Pokorny, Alex D., 962, 1318
Polansky, Norman A., 1184
Polatin, Phillip, 4075, 4595
Polaw, Bertram, 1780
Polikoff, Nancy D., 1840
Polis, Sheri, 4221
Polizoti, Leo F., 933
Polson, Leonard, 3334
Poole, Samuel N., Jr., 1914
Pope, Hallowell, 435–37
Popenoe, Paul, 4076
Porter, Blaine R., 1335
Porter, Everette M., 1888, 2366
Porteus, Barbara D., 2284
Portuges, Stephen H., 934, 1151, 1516
Portuondo y de Castro, José, 2629
Posner, Constance L., 3931
Potts, Nancy, 3700
Poussaint, Alvin F., 4515
Poussaint, Ann A., 4596
Powell, Morgan K., 2881
Power, Dierdre, 1618
Power, Richard W., 2867
Powers, B. Ward, 3295
Powers, Edward A., 338, 1462
Prescott, Mary R., 805–07, 810–11
Preston, Samuel H., 625, 631
Prewitt, Maryon P.W., 1423
Price, Barbara, 1839
Price, James H., 273
Price, Randall K., 2896
Price, Robert, 4623
Price, Steven D., 4413
Price-Bonham, Sharon, 927, 1012
Prince, Raymond H., 1146

Pritchard, James W., 1464
Projector, Murray, 2724–25
Propper, Grant E., 2837
Provence, Sally, 1768
Provost, James H., 3260–61, 3632, 3823
Pullen, Robert L., Jr., 1465
Putney, Richard S., 1522

Quinn, Garnet, 4293
Quoist, Michel, 3795

Raab, Robert A., 4078
Rabbino, Anna A., 1862
Rabinowitz, Stanley, 3453
Rabow, Jerome A., 3167
Rabwin, Marcella, 4120
Rac, Frank, 2569
Radcliff, David H., 1944
Radloff, Lenore, 963
Ragland, Francine L., 1538
Rakeffet-Rothkoff, Aaron, 3202
Rallings, E.M., 1539
Ramey, Martha L., 1863
Ramm, Bernard L., 3499
Ramos, Suzanne, 3871
Ramsey, James L., 3522
Ransom, Jane W., 1559
Raphael, Marc L., 3454
Raphael, Phyllis, 4364, 4630
Raphael, Robert, 2470
Rapp, Don W., 28
Rappold, Judith G., 4365
Raschke, Helen J., 211, 302, 1009–11, 1145
Raschke, Vernon J., 302
Rashke, Richard, 3633
Rasmussen, Dennis D., 1427
Rasmussen, Paul K., 874
Rasor, Reba G., 2631
Ratner, Helen, 3634
Raup, Cal L., 1695
Ravich, Robert A., 388
Ravikoff, Ronald B., 3170
Rawlings, Edna I., 891
Ray, Edward L., 1722
Ray, LaVon, 3542
Ray, Rayburn W., 3701
Rayner, John D., 3455
Reckling, William J., 1678
Records, T. Herbert, 2159
Reed, Gerald, 3524
Reese, Mary E., 4478
Reice, Sylvie, 4079
Reich, Warren T., 3589
Reid, Verna L., 812
Rein, M. L., 4166–67
Reingold, Carmel B., 4597
Reinhard, David W., 269–70
Reinhardt, Hazel, 1431
Reinhardt, Marion J., 3229–30, 3246
Reinhart, Gail E., 1377
Reinhart, John B., 4001
Reisman, Louis A., 2767
Reiss, David, 293
Rembar, James C., 236

Renne, Karen S., 553
Rennick, Charles H., 2819
Reppy, Susan W., 2367
Reppy, William A., Jr., 2806
Resh, Warren H., 2233–34
Resnik, H.L.P., 1516
Reyes, Tito F., 1241
Reynolds, Jason G., 2380
Reynolds, Louis B., 3543
Rheinstein, Max, 2160, 2290, 2698
Rhett, Teel O., 2873
Rhode, Deborah L., 2241
Rhodes, Clifton A., 69
Ricci, Isolina, 389, 1336
Ricciuti, Henry H., 1176
Rice, David G., 390–91
Rice, George P., Jr., 182
Rice, Joy K., 935
Rich, Adrienne C., 36
Richards, Arlene K., 183
Richards, Herbert C., 1217
Richards, Pamela J., 1416
Richardson, J., Michael, 1670
Richmond-Hawkins, James, 2104
Richtmyer, Shelly, 4467
Rico-Velasco, Jesus, 1156
Riddle, Dorothy I., 104
Ried, Dianne E., 1646–47
Riederer, Henry A., 2426
Rieke, Luvern V., 2506
Riga, Peter J., 3635
Riley, Harris D., 4533
Rindfuss, Ronald R., 142–43, 461–62
Rinn, Peter E., 2070
Ripple, Paula, 3718, 3733, 4751, 4752
Ritchie, Agnes M., 237
Ritter, Barbara, 881
Rivera Quintero, Marcia, 1947
Robbins, Norman N., 81, 2161, 2179, 2291, 2591
Robbins, Patricia V., 2032
Roberts, Albert R., 184
Roberts, Beverly J., 184
Roberts, John, 1498
Roberts, Wesley K., 392
Robertson, Bruce A., 2639
Robertson, Edward H., 3090
Robertson, R. J., Jr., 1590
Robinson, George H., Jr., 1648
Robinson, H., 572
Robinson, Louie, 3984
Robinson, Mary J., 574
Robson, Bonnie E., 3985
Rockwell, Richard C., 393
Rodgers, Thomas A., 1781
Roesch, Roberta, 4423
Rogers, Clayton W., 838
Rogers, Harry E., 4201
Rogers, Jim, 4291
Rogers, Joy, 1468
Rogers, Lynn C., 2464
Rogers, Rita R., 185
Rohrlich, John A., 271
Rollin, Betty, 4598
Rollins, Elaine G., 1580

Roman, Melvin (Mel), 117–18, 1856, 3902
Rombauer, Marjorie D., 2162
Rombro, Robert A., 3091
Romero, Ernest J., 2013
Rone, Jemera, 1586
Roop, Eugene E., 3476–77
Roosevelt, Ruth H., 4616, 4643
Rosario, Anny, 889
Rose, Cayton W., Jr., 2347
Rose, K. Daniel, 745–46
Rose, Louisa, 4535
Rose, Vicki L., 1012
Rosel, James, 3185
Rosen, Lawrence, 394
Rosen, Martin A., 1630
Rosen, Rhona, 37, 272
Rosenbaum, Jean, 4644
Rosenbaum, Veryl, 4644
Rosenbaum, Warren B., 2268
Rosenberg, Edward D., 2280
Rosenberg, Elinor B., 1384, 1463
Rosenberg, Herbert F., 2053
Rosenblatt, Paul C., 395
Rosenblatt, S.M., 575
Rosenblum, Arlene, 4536
Rosenfeld, Jona M., 1448
Rosenman, Linda S., 731–32
Rosenstein, Eliezer, 1448
Rosenstock, George K., 1936
Rosenthal, David M., 1378
Rosenthal, Erich, 3419
Rosenthal, Kristine M., 713, 1398–99, 1545, 4384
Rosenthal, Perihan A., 238
Rosow, Irving, 745–46
Ross, David J., 393
Ross, Heather L., 1337
Ross, Michele, 4258
Roth, Allan, 1966
Rothenberg, Charles, 2624–25
Rothschild, Carl J., 38
Rowatt, G. Wade, 3559
Rowse, Ruth A., 2612
Rozsman, John N., 2807
Ruark, Katherine L., 3680
Rubenstein, Carin, 186
Rubenstein, Judith L, 1270
Rubin, Estelle, 3964, 4417
Rubin, Lisa D., 273
Rubin, Roger H., 1203–05
Rubin, Theodore I., 3965, 4080
Rubin, Zick, 360, 361
Rudberg, Morton A., 2105
Rue, James J., 3636–38, 3719–20
Ruhland, Robert G., 1665
Rushing, William A., 964
Russell, Beverly, 4537
Russell, Deborah M., 1956
Russell, James R., 2069
Rutter, J.E.T., 2838
Rutter, Paul S., 3186
Ryan, Karen C., 3082
Ryan, Michael, 4134
Ryan, Robert S., 3359

Ryan, William F., Jr., 2076
Ryburn, Jack T., 2235
Ryder, Harriette, 4599
Rydman, Edward J., 4600
Ryker, Millard J., 659
Ryrie, Charles C., 3296

Sabalis, Robert F., 2163
Sacco, Lynn A., 2164
Sachs, Sidney S., 1723, 1738, 2668
Safier, I. Jay, 2984
Sage, Joseph F., 2820
Sager, Clifford J., 388, 823
Saks, Howard J., 2738
Sales, Bruce D., 1823
Saline, Carol, 4601
Salinger, Robert M., 2669
Salituro, Patricia, 1858
Salk, Lee, 95, 3966, 4081, 4366, 4538, 4617
Salts, Connie, 813, 875
Saltzman, Leon, 3231
Sampson, John J., 2494–95, 2897
Sams, Marjorie L., 4050
Samuel, Cynthia, 2854
Samuels, Dorothy J., 3093
Sandbote, Louis J., 2791
Sander, Frank A.E., 2575, 2969, 3094
Sanders, James L., 3297
Sanders, Judith A., 1875
Sanders, Marie, 3790
Sandor, Paul E., 3197
Sanford, Jill L., 61
Sang, Dorothy M., 140
Sanson, Robert J., 3262
Santella, Chris, 839
Santon, Marshall, 3352
Santos, Fredericka P., 714
Santrock, John W., 96, 187, 673–74, 1185, 1242, 1247, 1271–73
Sardanis-Zimmerman, Irene, 1546
Sasaki, Joanne, 1682
Sass, Stephen L., 2329
Sasser, Donald J., 1619
Sassower, Doris L., 1782, 2221–22
Sattler, Henry V., 3639
Sauber, Mignon, 2089
Saucy, Robert L., 3500
Saul, Edwin S., 2313
Saul, Elward L., 2551
Saul, Suzanne C., 1013
Savage, James E., Jr., 1363
Savage, Judith A., 814
Savitsky, Charles, Jr., 3640
Sawhill, Isabel V., 520, 1337–38, 1364
Saxe, David B., 39, 2084
Scales, Alice M., 675, 3968
Scanzoni, John, 546
Scaramella, Thomas J., 478
Scarano, Thomas P., 1466
Scarpitti, Frank R., 1415
Scarr, Daphne, 815
Schaengold, Marilyn, 1243
Schaper, Donna, 3468
Schary, Jill, 4468

Schecter, Martha J., 3456
Scheffner, David, 212
Schell, Leo M., 1214, 1222
Schellie, Susan G., 992
Schenkel, Sue, 4367
Scherer, Jack F., 4068
Scherman, Avraham, 274
Schick, Roy J., 3131
Schiller, Donald C., 1783, 2398
Schlender, E. Lee, 2279
Schlenger, Jacques T., 3147–48
Schlesinger, Benjamin, 188–89, 1339,
    1354–55, 1407–08, 1467, 1485, 3967
Schlesinger, Stephen, 1559
Schlissel, Stephen W., 2530
Schmehl, John W., 2099
Schmidt, David D., 580
Schmidt, Katherine, 3510
Schmidt, Ted A., 2739
Schnall, Maxine, 4368
Schoen, Robert, 396, 615, 632, 648
Schoenlaub, Fred E., 2292
Schoonmaker, Samuel V., III, 2316,
    2372–74
Schorr, Alvin L., 1432
Schowalter, John E., 1809
Schreibman, Walt, 4677
Schrut, Albert H., 1157–58, 4499
Schuckit, Marc A., 965
Schulhofer, Edith, 840
Schulman, Gerda L., 1560
Schulman, R.E., 2070, 2331–32
Schultz, Phyllis, 1694
Schultz, Thomas M., 1713
Schuntermann, Peter, 60
Schuppert, Ken, 2780
Schutzer, A.I., 521
Schwabe, Clara, 2090
Schwartz, Herbert E., 3167
Schwartz, Lawrence I., 4263
Schwartz, Stanley A., 2455
Schwartz, Victor E., 2165
Schwenkmeyer, Barry, 4345
Sciara, Frank J., 1206–07, 1223–24
Sciolino, Elaine, 3915, 3936
Scofield, Sandra, 4602
Scoliard, Nancy B., 966
Scott, Carol, 453–54
Scott, Charles V., 660
Scott, Donald G., 1666
Scott, John A., 967
Scott, John P., 968
Scott, Karen, 3511
Scott, Nancy L., 4394
Scott, Sandra R., 1620
Scragg, Walter R.L., 3544
Scribner, John, 275
Scudder, Townsend, 397
Seagull, Arthur A., 40
Seagull, Elizabeth A.W., 40
Seal, Karen L., 522, 2839
Sealey, Pat, 4369
Sear, Alan M., 463
Seaton, Lloyd, Jr., 2689
Seegel, V. F., 554

Seegmiller, Bonni R., 1186
Seglem, Betty S., 438
Seidelson, David E., 2166
Seidenberg, Faith, 5
Seixas, Suzanne, 4151
Seldin-Schwartz, Ethel, 4469
Seligson, Marcia, 4618
Sell, Betty H., 424
Sell, Kenneth D., 119, 423–24, 1724,
    2236, 2300
Sellman, John R., 2014
Senay, Edward C., 968
Serrano, Alberto C., 237
Serratelli, Lori K, 1989
Serritella, Daniel A., 756
Shackelford, James N., 1340
Shaffer, Helen B., 3932, 4246
Shah, Diane K., 4603
Shanahan, Louise, 3232, 3637–38, 3719–
    20, 3722–23
Shank, J. Ward, 3501
Shankweiler, Richard T., 2381
Shapiro, Andrew O., 3923, 4152, 4229
Shapiro, Lee S., 2341, 2427
Shapiro, Terry H., 969
Sharenow, Eric, 2231
Sharma, Prakash C., 649
Sharp, Karen, 4539
Shartar, Martin, 4140
Shaw, Jean, 3502
Shaw, John W., 2812
Shaw, Leslie, 4083
Shaw, Lois B., 523–24
Shea, Judy, 4682
Sheehan, Frank X., 3379
Sheehan, John T., Jr., 1784
Sheffner, David J., 816
Shelton, Sharon C., 817
Shepard, Martin, 4370
Shepardson, Anne L., 876
Shepherd, Bobby E., 1785
Shepherd, Herman, 3641
Shepherd, Robert E., Jr., 1828
Shepperd, Sarah Y., 2484
Sherberg, Ellen, 4121, 4540
Sheresky, Norman, 4084
Sheridan, Kathleen, 4085
Sheridan, Thomas I., III, 2670
Sherman, Charles E., 4202
Sherman, David R., 1649
Sherman, Linda K.G., 1014
Sherwood, Hugh C., 716, 3096
Shideler, Mary M., 3382
Shields, Laurie, 477
Shill, Merton A., 1274
Shindell, Lawrence M., 1896
Shinn, Marybeth, 1187
Shipman, Gordon, 2592
Shivanandan, Mary, 3420
Shorter, Edward, 398
Shrum, Wesley, 3421
Shryock, Harold 3545
Shufeit, Lawrence, 576
Shugrue, Noreen A., 2128
Shultz, Susan, 4141

Shurtz, Nancy E., 3060. 3061
Siegel, David M., 1810
Siegel, Symour, 4762
Siesky, Albert E., Jr., 210, 223
Silden, Isabel, 4086
Siller, Sidney, 1581
Silva-Ruiz, Pedro F., 2475
Silverman, Manuel S., 228
Silverman, Paul N., 2438
Silverman, Stephen M., 3872
Silvern, Steven B., 655
Simms, Richard D., 2213
Simon, Barbara, 1343
Simon, Michael J., 2811
Simon, Werner, 1159
Simons, Richard C., 399
Simpkins, Loy M., 2632
Simpson, Jacqueline L., 190
Simpson, Lee K., 2882
Sims, Carole, 4470
Singer, Karla, 1379
Singer, Laura J., 981
Singleton, Mary A., 4087, 4371, 4400,
    4487
Sinks, Robert F., 3275
Skoloff, Gary N., 2618–19, 2699
Skrocki, Merrill, R., 4418
Slavin, Maeve, 4471
Slifkin, Morrie, 1786
Sloane, L., 2970
Small, Dwight, H., 3342, 3801
Smaller, Deborah, 1863
Smart, Laura S., 936
Smedes, Lewis B., 3471, 3503
Smidchens, Uldis, 661, 1341
Smilgis, Martha, 3882, 4268, 4372
Smith, Bruce L., 3504
Smith, Charles M., 2354
Smith, Chuck, 3505
Smith, Craig A., 2868
Smith, Dianne, 2813
Smith, Donald R., 2631
Smith, Elizabeth J., 1821
Smith, Eugene L., 2106
Smith, George A., 1636
Smith, Gerald M., 1925
Smith, Gloria S., 675, 3968
Smith, Harold I., 1028
Smith, Helen, 3506
Smith, James B., 947–50
Smith, Michael J., 1390
Smith, Pamela J., 1598
Smith, Richard M., 1409
Smith, Richard P., 2740–41
Smith, Shirley, 4373
Smith, Stephanie H., 1829
Smith, Sue, 3774
Smith, Sunde, 3992
Smoke, Jim, 3693, 4731
Snow, Barbara W., 848
Snow, Jacquelyn E., 1365
Snow, M. Lawrence, 3675
Snyder, George E., 2338
Snyder, Lillian M., 316–18
Snyder, Peggy D., 841

Sobota, Walter L., 400
Sokolik, J. Brian, 2898
Solnit, Albert J., 27, 3863, 4648
Solomon, Daniel, 1225
Solomon, Howard B., 3098
Solomon, Philip F., 1833–34
Solow, Robert A., 41
Sommer, Leslie, 4213
Sommers, Tish, 477
Sonne, John C., 2598
Sopkin, Charles, 4185
Sorosky, Arthur D., 276, 3457
Southwick, Lawrence, Jr., 686
Spaht, Katherine S., 2854
Spanier, Graham B., 1015–17, 1512
Spann, Nancy, 4619
Spann, Owen, 4619
Sparer, Ellen A., 1380
Sparks, Zoe A. D., 751, 4689
Speca, John M., 1811, 1926
Spector, Barbara, 2808
Spellman, Howard H., 1749
Spencer, Janet M., 1787–88
Spencer, Sue N., 4645
Spicer, Jerry W., 979
Spikol, Art, 4088
Spillane, Dennis, 1876
Spinks, William B., Jr., 970
Spinnanger, Ruthe T., 3395
Spjut, Robert J., 3187
Spock, Benjamin, 3911, 3986–87, 4472
Spooner, A. Boyce, 3507
Spring, Frank L., 2875
Sproger, Charles E., 1899
Spurgeon, Edward D., 3143
Staal, Debra L., 937
Stabile, Thomas P., 1750
Stack, Carol B., 42
Stack, Steve, 2919
Stafford, Linley M., 4551
Stamets, Connie S., 2883
Stanley, Marjorie T., 2781
Stanton, Elizabeth C., 547
Stanton, L. Vance, 2107
Staples, Robert, 1366
Stark, Gail U., 4604
Stechert, Robert B., 3188
Steele, Richard, 3936
Stein, Judith A., 1498
Stein, Robert H., 3298
Stein, Robert L., 1391
Steinbeck, Mark A., 2388
Steinberg, Joseph L., 877, 2293
Steinberg, Marvin A., 1231
Steinbock, Delmar D., Jr., 2294
Steiner, Hinda, 4690
Steinzor, Bernard, 3969
Stencel, Sandra, 4541
Stender, Fay, 1863
Stephen, Beverly, 3937
Stephens, Nancy, 303
Stephens, Richard B., 3053
Stephenson, Don C., 2700
Stern, Norton B., 548
Stern, Phyllis N., 1540–41

Stern, Richard, 1877
Sterner, R. Eugene, 3472
Stetson, Dorothy M., 2195, 2301–02
Stevens, Joseph H., Jr., 919
Stevens, Marie, 3796
Stevenson, Victoria, 2349
Stewart, Oliver, 3263
Stewart, Robert J., 239
Stewart, Suzanne, 3738, 3775
Stickley, William, 3665
Stickman, H. Norman, 3458
Stigamire, James C., 3189
Stiles, Michael R., 2543
Stinnett, Charlotte A., 1486
Stinnett, Nick, 1335, 1385
Stock, Augustine, 3312
Stocking, Holly, 3999, 4350
Stoddard, Maynard G., 4090
Stogel, Elaine T., 2145
Stokes, Kathleen D., 733
Stolberg, Arnold L., 229, 304–06
Stoloff, Carolyn R., 1018
Stone, Judith P., 1342
Stone, Michael H., 1180
Stone, R. Thomas, Jr., 1583, 1621
Stone, Sam V., Jr., 2749
Storer, Janet K., 2402
Stott, John R.W., 3299
Stouder, Judith B., 2015
Strackbein, Howard E., 2792
Strassfeld, Michael, 4762
Strassfeld, Sharon, 4762
Strassler, Philip F., 3029
Stratman, Steven F., 3100
Strausberg, Gary I., 1656
Strauss, Dorothy, 399, 4755
Streshinsky, Shirley, 4002
Streuk, Robert, 2261
Stuart, Irving R., 192
Stubblefield, Jerry, 3360
Stubbs, Robert S., II, 2607
Stulting, Janet S., 2714
Stultz, Fred, 4732
Suarez, John M., 816, 818
Sudia, Cecelia E., 1175–78
Sugar, Harriet S., 2457
Sugar, Max, 193, 194
Sullivan, James J., 2715
Sullivan, Wallace E., 938
Summers, George M., 1232
Summers, William J., 4272
Sumner, David W., 2793
Sundbye, Ronald L., 4091
Susco, Wendy, 3865
Sussman, Marvin B., 924
Sutherland, James E., 2701
Swann, Mary C., 1693
Swann, Tommy J., 2821
Sweet, James A., 331, 449, 455, 939
Swerdlow, Edith L., 82
Swift, David A., 1679
Swink, Jack W., 2167
Swisher, Peter N., 2570
Swords, Betty, 4248

Tabac, William L., 1680
Taggart, John Y., 3101
Taibbi, Robert, 1019
Taittonen, Edith, 2089
Talkington, Larry, 1343
Talley-Morris, Neva B., 2564
Tarantino, Dominic A., 2971
Targ, Dena B., 454
Tarrant, John J., 4488
Tarrant, Marguerite, 4153
Tatsuguchi, Rosalie K., 1020
Tauber, Yale D., 2774
Tavris, Carol, 4504
Taylor, Claribel M., 1394
Taylor, Gail, 3791
Taylor, Geraldine, 4092
Taylor, Henry D., 3433
Taylor, James C., 301
Taylor, Laura, 43
Taylor, LaWanda, 4374
Taylor, Leigh H., 1900
Taylor, Patricia A., 734
Taylor, Rita, 4473
Taylor, Robert B., 4106
Taylor, Vincent S., 4209
Tavris, Carol, 4504
Tcheng Laroche, Francoise C., 940, 1146
Teague, Franklin L., 4217
Teitelbaum, Lee L., 2223
Teitell, Conrad, 2986
TenBrook, Tammany D., 2168
Tener, Elizabeth, 3970
Tengbom, Mildred, 3776
Tennery, Elizabeth, 2334
Tesser, A., 1153
Tessman, Lora H., 195
Tcw, B. J., 577
Thayer, Charlotte P., 2342
Theus, Robert, 277
Thies, Jill M., 1477
Thiessen, Jake D., 1021
Thistle, Frank, 4269
Thomas, Alexander, 68, 279
Thomas, Bruce, 2721
Thomas, Lowell S., Jr., 3106
Thomas, Lucille, 4293
Thomas, M. Donald, 196
Thomas, Rhona C., 1573
Thomas-More, Jane L., 1592
Thompson, Beatrice R., 1275
Thompson, Bettye D., 1022
Thompson, Cheryl L., 1344
Thompson, Dorothy, 3873
Thompson, Dorothy K., 3407
Thompson, Eugene W., 661, 1341
Thompson, James G., 402
Thompson, Kendrick S., 1034–36
Thompson, M. Cordell, 4375
Thompson, M. Karen, 2916
Thornton, Arland, 403–04, 457, 464, 1491
Thornton, J. Edward, 2353
Tierney, Terence E., 3233
Timko, Andrea A., 1878
Tinder, Donald, 3335
Tischler, Saul, 2874

Title, Peter S., 1835
Tittle, Diana, 4264
Todd, Stephen, 2785
Todres, Rubin, 319, 1408
Tolbert, Malcolm, 3306
Toman, Walter, 502
Tomasson, Verna, 4376
Tomeny, Ann E., 1650
Tomlinson, Allen, 2978
Tompkins, Iverna, 3694, 3778
Toney, Felicia G., 2410
Toolan, David S., 3642
Tooley, Kay, 225
Toomin, Marjorie K., 213–14, 240, 1519, 1520
Torrez, Barbara J., 2825
Towey, Damian, 3248
Towner, Jason, 4474
Townsend, Karen, 2429
Trachtman, Richard S., 1276
Tracy, Robert E., 3643
Tracy, Russel L., 673–74
Trager, Oliva, 4094
Trapnell, Emily M., 1957
Trenker, Thomas R., 1789
Trías Grimes, Peter, 2921
Triplett, Timothy W., 2428
Tritico, Lila, 1915
Troester, James D., 80
Trombetta, Diane, 120
Trotter, Marcia, 1938
Trotter, Robert J., 4377
Trudgeon, Jon H., 2782
True, Michael, 3644
Trunnell, Thomas L., 1790
Truxillo, Douglas W., 1916
Trypsiani, Marina, 941
Tu, Edward J., 487
Tubbs, Ace L., 819
Tuchman, Bruce M., 864
Tucker, Carll, 4095
Tucker, Vicki O., 1958
Tuma, Nancy B., 700–01
Tunick, Carl, 4378
Turley, Edward W., Jr., 2496, 3107
Turner, Bruce E., 3162
Turner, Christopher, 725
Turner, Eric D., 1946
Turner, Marcia C., 942
Turner, Nathan W., 478, 4725
Tynan, Susan A., 942

Udinsky, Jerald H., 2726–27
Uhlenberg, Peter, 450
Ulfelder, Linda C., 215
Ullman, Lois, 1673
Underhill, Lonnie E., 541
Ungar, Sanford J., 3938
Urbanski, Wanda, 3971
Uslander, Arlene S., 197–98
Uviller, Rena K., 1791

Vahanian, Tilla, 4693, 4733
Valiulis, Anthony, 2399
van Bergen, Adriane, 1277

Vanderlinde, Susan K., 1994
Van de Veer, Hugh G., 2783
Van Gelder, Lawrence, 4142
Van Gelder, Lindsy, 3924, 4419, 4475
Vangen, Patricia, 1292
Van Pelt, Samuel, 2344
Vanton, Monte, 4096
Van Wade, David, 3832
Van Wade, Sarah, 3832
Van Zile, Philip T., III, 2171
Vargon, Melanie M., 1188–89
Varin-Hommen, Alvora, 1989
Vasser, Albert G., 2358
Vath, William R., 3264
Vaughn, Diane, 943
Vaughn, Jack M., 3110–14, 3190
Vaughn, Thomas J., Jr., 971
Vaughn, Victor C., 291
Vawter, Bruce, 3313–14
Vayhinger, John M., 3469
Vazquez Bote, Eduardo, 1691, 2476
Veith, Nancy A., 1608
Velez Torres, Berenith A., 2641
Velie, Lester, 3972, 4249
Verbrugge, Lois M., 555
Verhey, Allen, 3279
Vernick, Shelia K., 1023
Veron, Enid L., 1995
Veverka, Donald J., 1901
Victor, Edward G., 2762, 3191
Victor, Ira, 3888
Vigderhous, Gideon, 405, 1160
Vigeveno, H. S., 3973
Viorst, Judith, 4097
Visher, Emily B., 1524–25, 1530–31
Visher, John S., 1524–25, 1530–31
Vitousek, Betty M., 820
Voeckler, Pamela R. P., 4265
Vogel-Moline, Mary E., 972
Volk, Michael D., 2497
Vollman, Stanton H., 3115
Volterra, Max, 2335
Vonderweidt, Joyce, 1345
von Mehren, Arthur T., 2258
Votolato, Arthur N., Jr., 1582
Vroegh, Karen S., 1226–27

Wadlington, Walter, 2172, 2504, 2578–79
Wagner, Gary, 4555
Wainwright, Sally, 4196
Wakeford, Herbert W., 3200
Wakin, Edward, 3827
Wald, Michael S., 199
Walder, Eugene, 4098
Waldman, Elizabeth, 717–18, 736–37, 1452–53
Walker, Barth P., 2728
Walker, Charles M., 1990
Walker, Greta, 4099
Walker, Joyce W., 3422
Walker, Kenneth N., 1468–69, 1473
Walker, Libby, 1470
Walker, Mike, 3116
Walker, Sharon G., 849
Walker, Timothy B., 2295, 2314

Wall, John E., 2552
Wallace, Arla S., 503
Wallace, Lee, 336
Wallace, Richard J., Jr., 665
Wallerstein, Judith S., 127, 169, 200–02, 216–17, 256, 278–82, 307, 821, 832, 4656–58
Wallop, Malcolm, 1879, 3925
Walsh, Joseph F., 1888
Walsh, Joseph H., 1572, 2723, 2857–58
Walsh, Lawrence, 3939
Walsh, Michael R., 2060
Walters, Jennifer, 4726
Walters, Robert, 4476
Walther, David L., 1962
Walton, Abbott B., Jr., 2643
Walzer, Stuart B., 724, 2173, 2750–51, 2755, 2841
Wan, Thomas, 649
Wanner-Westly, Brenda, 762
Warburg, Ronald, 1846
Ward, C. M., 3526
Ward, Larry D., 3009, 3192
Warder, Francis L., Jr., 1591
Ware, Ciji, 3912
Warheit, George J., 973
Warkov, Seymour, 1306
Warner, Nancy S., 83
Warren, Thomas B., 3301
Warshak, Richard A., 96–97
Washburn, Robert M., 1996
Washburne, Carolyn K., 4321
Wasser, Dennis M., 1609
Wasserman, Herbert L., 1208
Watson, Andrew S., 203
Watson, Clark, 2780
Watson, Raymond, 1561
Wattenberg, Esther, 1431
Watts, Carol K., 4477
Watts, Virginia, 3739
Waxman, Robert M., 2037
Waybright, Roger J., 2382
Weathers, Diane, 4216
Weaver, Charles N., 1482
Webb, Carla F., 3734
Webb, Garn H., 2565
Webb, James B., 662
Weber, Ruth E., 853, 859, 1725, 1728, 4683
Wechsler, Henry, 578
Wechsler, Ralph C., 164
Wecht, Cyril H., 203
Weed, James A., 406
Wegher, Arnold C., 3117
Weihofen, Henry, 1740
Weiler, Robert K., 2454
Weiner, I. R., 1178
Weiner, Karen C., 1991
Weingarten, Helen, 259
Weinglass, Janet, 3423
Weininger, Otto, 1346
Weinstein, Arlene S., 407
Weinstein, Elliott W., 3154
Weinstein, Jeffrey P., 112
Weinstein, Marc, 719

Weinstein, Meyer H., 2278
Weintruab, Russell J., 2498
Weisbard, George L., 3118
Weisberg, K. Kelly, 549
Weisberger, Bernard A., 550
Weisel, Joye E., 1381
Weisfeld, David, 204
Weiss, Robert S., 48, 62, 408, 1347–49, 1449, 1506–08, 3974, 4379
Weiss, Warren W., 63, 132
Weitzman, Lenore J., 1792
Welch, Gary J., 787–88, 822
Welker, Patricia Z., 1509
Wellborn, Jacquelyn, 3838
Wells, J. Gipson, 2300
Welsh, Jane A., 1350
Wenham, Gordon J., 3459
Wenig, Mary M., 3119
Wenke, Robert A., 2368
Wenke, William F., 2571, 3120
Werner, Emmy, 43
West, Morris L., 3265
West, William K., Jr., 2486
Westbrook, Craig, 2899
Western, Joset F., 3762
Westgate, Bob, 3926
Westman, Jack C., 64, 241, 247, 308–09, 2174
Westoff, Leslie A., 4605–07
Weston, David L., 3121
Weston, Nancy L., 818
Wetton, Marcy B., 4316
Whaling, Michael J., 2296
Wheat, Penny L., 2043
Wheeler, Michael, 4250
Wheeler, Ronald J., 2478
Whelan, Charles M., 3646
Whetstone, James D., 3361
Whitaker, Carl A., 823
White, C. Dale, 3676–77
White, Henry E., Jr., 824
White, Kenneth R., 1583, 1621, 2061
White, Lynn K., 501, 1487
White, Priscilla N., 927, 1007, 4683
White, Raymond M., 1262
White, S. K., 1410
White, Sharon J., 310
White, Stephen W., 1137–38, 1513
White, Thomas C., 2259
Whiteside, Mary F., 1463, 1474
Whitmore, Robert, 718, 1452
Whittenburg, Gerald E., 3124
Widmann, Randall M., 2369
Wiegner, Kathleen K., 525, 4165
Wieser, Francis, 3647
Wight, Jermy B., 697
Wilcox, Maurice K. C., 1808
Wildemann, Ann P., 1526
Wilder, Joanne R., 2470
Wilding, Paul, 1426
Wiley, Thomas W., 2702
Wilkerson, Albert E., 19, 31, 35, 150
Wilkerson, Pinkie C., 2129
Wilkins, Nancy, 4478
Wilkinson, Carl E., 3126
Wilkinson, Charles B., 1367

Wilkinson, Gary S., 842–43
Wilkinson, Joseph C., 1710
Wilkinson, Karen, 1419
Williams, David, 4205
Williams, Dennis A., 3927
Williams, Foster J., 3678
Williams, John W., Jr., 740–41, 4295
Williams, Mona, 4101
Williams, Ned, 4479
Williams, Nelda, 3408
Williams, Roger, 6
Williams, Ronald G., 2900
Williams, Theodore J., Jr., 2094
Willimon, William H., 3470
Willis, Irene, 183
Willoughby, Barry M. 2471
Wilson, Frank H., 656
Wilson, Kenneth L., 1527
Wilson, Leland, 3478
Wilson, Neal C., 3546
Wilson, Wallace R., 3300
Windeler, Robert, 4393
Winiarski, Mark, 3648, 3681
Winkler, Win A., 3888
Winner, Leslie, 1654
Winslow, Gerald, 3547
Winslow, Joyce, 4480
Winston, Marian P., 320
Winter, Edward J., Jr., 1822, 3889
Winter, Walter T., 3975
Winton, Ward, 1264
Wise, Sherry M., 2855
Wiseman, Dennis G., 850
Wiseman, Reva S., 878
Witcher, Wayne C., 87
Withrow, Oral C., 3473
Wohlford, Paul, 1185
Wolf, Abraham, 1387
Wolf, Douglas A., 702
Wolf, Edwin H., 2224
Wolf, Judi, 2531
Wolf, Marshall J., 2531
Wolf, Wendy C., 526, 687, 1476
Wolfe, Linda, 4125
Wolff, Richard J., 3225
Wolfington, Dave, 84
Wolfstone, Gary L., 2980
Wolynski, Mara, 4132
Wood, Abigail, 3976, 4505
Wood, Britton, 3349
Wood, Linda A., 974
Wood, Sandy, 4543
Woodard, Francis M., 2593, 2594
Woodbury, Roger, 226
Woodcock, Eldon, 3276–77, 2594
Woodrow, Karen, 487
Woodruff, Robert A., 975
Woods, Hammond C., 2081
Woodson, Leslie H., 3508
Woodward, Kenneth L., 4608
Woodworth, Karen L., 4533
Woody, Jane D., 227, 844
Woody, Robert H., 44–45, 85–86, 98, 1823, 3876
Woody, Wayne S., 1584
Wooldridge, Barbara, 3409, 3792

Woolley, Persia, 1864, 3877, 3913, 4404
Worcester, Nancy, 4394
Wortman, Ruth, 3977
Wrenn, Lawrence G., 3236, 3266, 3649–50
Wright, Barbara, 4498
Wright, Douglas, 479
Wright, Gerald C., Jr., 2301, 2302
Wright, H. Norman, 4102
Wright, Robert L., 2039
Wright, Thomas L., 911
Wunsch, Guillame, 636
Wuster, Stanley, 576
Wuthnow, Robert, 3417
Wylie, Evan M., 4231
Wylie, Mary L., 4745
Wysong, Robert J., 4208
Wysor, Betty, 4481

Yahraes, Herbert, 1542
Yannacone, Victor J., Jr., 1793
Yarrow, Leon J., 1270
Yates, Martha, 4154, 4405
Yawkey, Thomas, 655
Yearout, Megan, 2023
Yee, Lucy M., 2050
Young, Amy R., 3703
Young, Anne M., 736
Young, Carl D., 1585
Young, D. Michael, 2794–95
Young, David M., 882–83
Young, Don J., 1974
Young, Earl R., 1233–34
Young, Gregory, 3878
Young, James J. 3336, 3373, 3412, 3644, 3651–55, 3731, 3822, 3828, 4753, 4754
Young, Jane J., 4482–83
Young, Nancy, 4527
Young, Rowland L., 2797
Young, Sheila, 1975
Younger, Judith T., 2391, 4103
Yurasits, Victoria, 4613

Zabel, William D., 3128
Zagorin, Susan W., 1218
Zainaldin, Jamil S., 1837
Zammit, Joseph P., 1787–88
Zaritsky, Howard M., 2987
Zeisel, Elliot, 1715
Zeiss, Antonette M., 1024
Zeiss, Robert A., 1024
Zenor, Donna J., 2196
Zett, James, 2455
Zimmer, C. Thomas, 1622
Zimmering, Paul L., 1651
Zimmerman, Beatrice S., 283
Zold, Anthony C., 1235
Zuckerman, Jacob T., 46
Zuckman, Harvey L., 2197–99
Zuckman, Jacob T., 2200
Zumbrun, Ronald A., 2049
Zumeta, Zena, 456
Zunkel, C. Wayne, 3479
Zusne, Helen, 1025
Zwink, William E., 47

GEOGRAPHIC INDEX

Alabama
  alimony, 11, 1592, 1595, 1603, 2170
  annulments, statistics, 622
  child custody, 2170
  child support, 2019, 2036, 2170
  children of divorced parents, 622
  divorce, 2170,2353
    grounds for, 2269–77
    no-fault 2303–04
    statistics, 621–22
  divorced persons, statistics 1045, 1095–96
  property settlements, 1603
  remarriage, statistics 622
Alaska
  alimony, 11, 2170
  annulments, statistics, 622
  attorney fees, 2170
  child custody, 1883–84, 2170
  child support, 2019, 2037, 2170
  children of divorced parents, 622
  divorce, 440, 2170
    do-it-yourself, 2238
    grounds for, 2269–77
    statistics, 621–22
  divorced persons, statistics, 1045, 1095–96
  domicile and residence, 2647, 2664
  property settlements, 2170, 2822
  remarriage, statistics, 622
Arizona
  alimony, 11
  annulments, 1705–06
    statistics, 622
  attorney fees, 2170
  child custody, 29, 2038–39, 2170
  child support, 2019, 2170
  children of divorced parents
    Tucson, 151
  community property, 2739
  divorce, 2170, 2354, 4141
    do-it-yourself, 4195–96
    grounds for, 2269–77
    reform, 2201
    statistics, 621–22
  divorced persons, statistics, 1045, 1095–96
  property settlements, 2823–25
Arkansas
  alimony, 11, 1604, 2170
  child custody, 2170
  child support, 2019, 2170
  divorce, 751, 2170, 2355–58
    grounds for, 2269–77
    reform, 2202
    statistics, 621–22
  divorced persons, statistics, 1045, 1095–96

property settlements, 2170
remarriage, 2355
California
  alimony, 11, 1593, 1605–09, 2170, 2829, 2833, 2839, 3931
  annulments, 1707
    statistics, 622
  attorney's fees, 1748
  child custody, 1762, 1885–88, 2042, 2170, 3931
    Los Angeles, 129
  child support, 1605, 2019, 2024, 2040–49, 2170, 2839, 3931
  children of divorced parents, 200, 622, 3975
  community property, 2024, 2768, 2801–04, 2808, 2826, 2834
  divorce, 542, 648, 750, 1707, 1748, 2170, 2359–69, 2447, 2586, 2764, 2788, 2831, 3450, 3461, 4142, 4257, 4263
    do-it-yourself, 2234, 2239, 4197–202
    grounds for, 2269–2277
    Los Angeles, 129, 543
    no-fault, 396, 2305–14, 4233, 4234, 4236, 4238, 4244
    reform, 2203–05, 2826
    San Diego, 548
    Shasta Co., 369–70
    statistics, 621, 622
  divorced persons, 4403
    statistics, 1045, 1095–96
  domestic relations, 2586, 2599–602
  one-parent families, 1361
  property settlements, 724, 2042, 2744, 2748, 2751, 2766, 2787, 2798–808, 2826–41, 3186–87
  remarriage, statistics, 622
  separation, 2836, 2908–09
  taxes, 3020, 3186–87
Canada
  divorce, 384–85, 424
  remarriage, 1467
Colorado
  alimony, 11, 1610, 2170
  annulments, statistics, 622
  attorney fees, 2170
  child custody 1881, 2170
  child support, 1610, 2019, 2050, 2170
  divorce, 2170, 2370, 3097
    Denver, 701
    do-it-yourself, 2234, 2240, 4203–05
    grounds for, 2269–77
    statistics, 621–22
  divorced persons, statistics, 1045, 1095–96
  property settlements, 2170, 2709, 2714

Connecticut
  alimony, 11, 1611, 2170, 2373–74, 2603
  annulments, statistics, 622
  attorney's fees, 1745
  child custody, 1818, 1889–90, 2170, 2373–74, 2603
  child support, 2019, 2051–53, 2170, 2373, 2603
  children of divorced parents, 622
  divorce, 536, 1745, 2170, 2371–74, 2538
    do-it-yourself, 2234, 2241–42
    no-fault, 2206, 2315–16
    reform, 2206–07
    statistics, 621–22
  divorced persons, 2538
    statistics, 1045, 1095–96
  domestic relations, 2603
  property settlements, 2170, 2373
  remarriage, statistics, 622

Delaware
  alimony, 11, 2170
  annulments, statistics, 622
  child custody, 2170
  child support, 2019, 2170
  divorce, 2170
    grounds for, 2269–77
    no-fault, 2317–18
    statistics, 621–22
  divorced persons, statistics, 1045, 1095–96
  property settlements, 2170
  remarriage, statistics, 622
District of Columbia
  alimony, 11, 2170
  child custody, 2170, 2376
  child support, 2019, 2170
  divorce, 2170, 2375–76
    do-it-yourself, 4224
    grounds for, 2269–77
    statistics, 621–22
  divorced persons, statistics, 1045, 1095–96
    property settlements, 2170
    remarriages, statistics, 622
Dominican Republic, divorce, 2260–61, 2265, 2475, 4123, 4125

Europe, divorce, 3, 334, 367, 2195, 2557

Florida
  alimony, 11, 1612–22, 2170, 2058, 2320, 2378
  annulments, statistics, 622
  attorney's fees, 2170

child custody, 1891–94, 2059, 2170, 2320, 2378
child support, 1621, 2019, 2054–61, 2170
divorce, 2170, 2377–82, 4259, 4261
  do-it-yourself, 2234, 2243, 4206–07
  grounds for, 2269–77
  no-fault, 2319, 2320
  statistics, 621–22
divorced persons, statistics, 1045, 1095–96
domestic relations, 2590, 2604, 4260
property settlements, 1616, 2059, 2170, 2842
remarriage, statistics, 622
separation, 2377, 2910

Georgia
  alimony, 11, 1623–25, 2170, 2387, 4258
  annulments, 1708
    statistics, 622
  child custody, 1895–96, 2170, 2387, 4258
  child support, 2019, 2062–65, 2170
  children of divorced parents, 622
  divorce, 649, 2170, 2383–88, 2843, 4140, 4258, 4265
    grounds for, 2269–77
    no-fault, 2321, 4265
    statistics, 621–22
  divorced persons, statistics, 1045, 1095–96
  domestic relations, 2605–07
  property settlements, 1624, 2843
  remarriage, statistics, 622
Great Britain, 424

Haiti, divorce, 2262–65, 2364, 4123
Hawaii
  alimony, 11, 2170
  annulments, statistics, 622
  child custody, 2170
  child support, 2019, 2170
  children of divorced parents, 622
  divorce, 469, 2170, 2389–90
    grounds for, 2269–77
    statistics, 621–22
  divorced persons, statistics, 1045, 1095–96
  domicile and residence, 2390
  property settlements, 2170
  remarriage, statistics, 622

Idaho
  alimony, 11
  annulments, statistics, 622
  child custody, 1897–98, 2170
  child support, 2019, 2170
  children of divorced parents, 622
  divorce, 2170, 2391
    grounds for, 2269–77
    reform, 2208
    statistics, 621–22

divorced persons, 4398
  statistics, 1045, 1095–96
property settlements, 2170, 2745, 2786, 2844
remarriage, statistics, 622
separation, 2844
Illinois
  alimony, 11, 1626–28, 2170, 2847
  annulments, statistics, 622
  attorney's fees, 1747
  child custody, 1899–901, 2170
  child support, 2019, 2025–26, 2066, 2170
  children of divorced parents, 622
  divorce, 850, 1721, 1747, 2170, 2392–99, 2569, 3046, 4139, 4251
    do-it-yourself, 4208
    grounds for, 2269–77
    no-fault, 2322–25
    reform, 2209–10
    statistics, 621–22
  divorced persons, statistics, 1045, 1095–96
  domestic relations, 2608–10
  nonsupport, 314
  property settlements, 2170, 2845–47, 3155, 3157
  remarriage, statistics, 622
  taxes, 1628, 3157
India, 2191
Indiana
  alimony, 11, 1629–30, 2170
  annulments, statistics, 622
  child custody, 1902, 2170
  child support, 2019, 2170
  divorce, 2170, 2400–02, 2848
    do-it-yourself, 4209
    grounds for, 2269–77
    statistics, 622
  divorced persons, statistics, 1045, 1095–96
  property settlements, 2170, 2848
  remarriage, statistics, 622
Iowa
  alimony, 11, 1631–33, 2170, 2326
  annulments, 1633
    statistics, 622
  child custody, 1903–05, 2170
  child support, 2019, 2170
  children of divorced parents, 622
  divorce, 2170, 2403
    grounds for, 2269–77
    no-fault, 2326–29
    statistics, 621–22
  divorced persons, statistics, 1045, 1095–96
  domicile and residence, 2661
  property settlements, 2170, 2326
  public opinion, 414
  remarriage, statistics, 622

Kansas
  alimony, 11, 1634–35, 2170
  annulments, 2170
    statistics, 622

attorney fees, 2170
child custody, 1836, 1906–08, 2170
child support, 2019, 2067–70, 2170, 2404
children of divorced parents, 622
divorce, 471, 2170, 2404
  grounds for, 2269–77
  no-fault, 2330–32
  statistics, 621–22
divorced persons, 2549
  statistics, 1045, 1095–96
property settlements, 2170, 2849, 3188
remarriage, statistics, 622
separation, 2170
taxes, 3188
Kentucky
  alimony, 11, 1636, 2170
  annulments, statistics, 622
  child custody, 1909
  child support, 2019, 2071–72, 2170
  children of divorced parents, 622
  community property, 2170
  divorce, 2405–07
    grounds for, 2269–77
    no-fault, 1909, 2333
  reform, 2211–13
  statistics, 621–22
  divorced persons, statistics, 1045, 1095–96
  property settlements, 2170, 2753, 2850
  remarriage, statistics, 622

Louisiana
  alimony, 11, 1637–51, 1709–10, 2170
  annulments, 1650, 1709–10, 4254
    statistics, 622
  attorney's fees, 2073
  child custody, 1910–16, 2170
  child support, 1643, 2019, 2073–75, 2170
  community property, 2809, 2852, 4254
  divorce, 413, 1651, 1710, 2170, 2408–10, 2536, 4254, 4256
    grounds for, 2269–77
    statistics, 622
  divorced persons, 2536, 2551, 4689
    statistics, 1045, 1095–96
  domestic relations, 2611, 4254
  property settlements, 2170, 2809–11, 2851–55
  remarriage, statistics, 622
  separation, 1638, 1640, 1710, 2170, 2851, 2911–12, 4254

Maine
  alimony, 11, 1652, 2170
  annulments, statistics, 622
  child custody, 2170
  child support, 2019, 2170
  divorce, 2170
    do-it-yourself, 4210
    grounds for, 2269–77
    statistics, 621–22
  divorced persons, statistics, 1045, 1095–96

property settlements, 2170
remarriage statistics, 622
Maryland
    alimony, 11, 1653–56, 2170
    annulments, statistics, 622
    child custody, 1874, 1917–18, 2170
    child support, 1654, 1656, 2019, 2076,
        2170
    desertion, 1656, 2913
    divorce, 2170, 2411–12, 4136
        do-it-yourself, 4224
        grounds for, 2269–77
        no-fault, 2334
        statistics, 621–22
    divorced persons, statistics, 1045, 1095–
        96
    nonsupport
        Baltimore, 318
    property settlements, 2856, 3176
    remarriage, statistics, 622
    separation, 1653, 1655, 2170, 2412,
        2913
    taxes, 3176
Massachusetts
    alimony, 11, 1657, 2170, 2857–58
    annulments, statistics, 622
    attorney fees, 2170
    child custody, 2170
    child support, 2019, 2026–27, 2170
    children of divorced parents, 3993,
        3995, 3997
    desertion, Boston, 315
    divorce, 537–38, 549, 2170, 2413–18
        do-it-yourself, 4211
        grounds for, 2269–77
        no-fault, 2335, 4232
        statistics, 621–22
    divorced persons, statistics, 622, 1045,
        1095–96
    property settlements, 2170, 2857–58
    remarriage, statistics, 622
    separation, 2170
Mexico
    divorce, 2266–68, 4122, 4124, 4170,
        4286
Michigan
    alimony, 11, 2170
    annulments, statistics, 622
    child custody, 13, 14, 1919–20, 2170
    child support, 2019, 2028–30, 2077,
        2170
    children of divorced parents, 622
    desertion, 2030
    divorce, 2170, 2419–21
        Detroit, 441–42
        do-it-yourself, 2234, 2237
        grounds for, 2269–77
        no-fault, 2336–38
        reform, 2214
        statistics, 621–22
    divorced persons, statistics, 1045, 1095–
        96
    domestic relations, 2612
    one-parent families, 1359

property settlements, 2170
remarriage, statistics, 622
Minnesota
    alimony, 11, 2170
    annulments, statistics, 622
    child custody, 1921, 2170
    child support, 2019, 2170
    divorce, 2170, 2422, 4255
        do-it-yourself, 2234, 2244
        grounds for, 2269–77
        statistics, 621, 622
    divorced persons, 815
        statistics, 1045, 1095–96
    domestic relations, 776, 2613
    property settlements, 2170
    public opinion, 416, 417
    remarriage, statistics, 622
Mississippi
    alimony, 11, 2170
    annulments, statistics, 622
    child custody, 1922, 2170
    child support, 2019, 2078, 2170
    divorce, 2170, 2423, 2424
        grounds for, 2269–77
        no-fault, 2339
        statistics, 621–22
    divorced persons, statistics, 1045, 1095–
        96
    property settlements, 2170
    remarriage, statistics, 622
Missouri
    alimony, 11, 1658–66, 2170
    annulments, 1658
        statistics, 622
    child custody, 1759, 1923–27, 2170,
        3905
    child support, 1661–62, 1665, 2019,
        2079–81, 2170
    children of divorced parents, 622
    community property, 2867
    divorce, 2170, 2425–28, 2914, 3059
        grounds for, 2269–77
        no-fault, 2340–42
        reform, 2215–16
        statistics, 621–22
    divorced persons, statistics, 1045, 1095–
        96
    domestic relations, 2614
    property settlements, 2170, 2812, 2859–
        68
    remarriage, statistics, 622
    separation, 2170, 2914
    taxes, 2864, 3059
Montana
    alimony, 11
    annulments, 1711
        statistics, 622
    child custody, 1928
    child support, 2019, 2170
    children of divorced parents, 622
    divorce, 2170, 2429
        grounds for, 2269–77
        statistics, 621–22
    divorced persons, statistics, 1045, 1095–
        96

property settlements, 2170
remarriage, statistics, 622

Nebraska
    alimony, 11, 1667–68, 2170, 2432
    annulments, statistics, 622
    child custody, 2170
    child support, 2019, 2170
    children of divorced parents, 622
        Omaha, 227
    divorce, 2170, 2430–32, 2535
        grounds for, 2269–77
        no-fault, 1667, 2298–99, 2343–44,
            4241
        statistics, 621–22
    divorced persons, 2535
        statistics, 1045, 1095–96
    property settlements, 1668, 2170, 2869
    remarriage, statistics, 622
    separation, 2170, 2432
    taxes, 2432, 3030
Nevada
    alimony, 11, 2170
    annulments, statistics, 622
    child custody, 2170
    child support, 2019, 2170
    divorce, 539, 2170
        do-it-yourself, 2234, 2245
        grounds for, 2269–77
        statistics, 621–22
    divorced persons, statistics, 1045, 1095–
        96
    property settlements, 2170
New Hampshire
    alimony, 11, 2170
    annulments, statistics, 622
    child custody, 1802, 1929, 2170
    child support, 2019, 2170
    divorce, 2170, 2433
        grounds for, 2269–77
        reform, 2217
        statistics, 621, 622
    divorced persons, statistics, 1045, 1095–
        96
    property settlements, 2170, 2433
    remarriage, statistics, 622
    taxes, 2433
New Jersey
    alimony, 11, 1669–70, 2170
    annulments, 1670, 1712
        statistics, 622
    child custody, 1930, 2170, 4252
    child support, 1669, 2019, 2170
    divorce, 542, 2170, 2263, 2434–38,
        4135, 4252, 4262
        do-it-yourself, 4212–13
        grounds for, 2269–77
        reform, 2218
        statistics, 621–22
    divorced persons, statistics, 1045, 1095–
        96
    domestic relations, 2615–19
    one parent families, Camden, 1365
    property settlements, 2170, 2870–74,
        2916

remarriage, statistics, 622
separation, 2438, 2915–16
New Mexico
  alimony, 11, 2170
  annulments, statistics, 622
  child custody, 2170
  child support, 2019, 2082–83, 2170
  divorce, 2170, 2439
    grounds for, 2269–77
    statistics, 621–22
  divorced persons, statistics, 1045, 1095–96
  property settlements, 2170, 2875
  separation, 2439
  taxes, 3116
New York
  alimony, 11, 1671–73, 2170, 2443, 2446
  annulments, 1713
    statistics, 622
  child custody, 1847, 1856, 1877, 1931–32, 2170, 2443, 2445
  child support, 2019, 2084–90, 2170, 2443
  children of divorced parents, 622
  divorce, 2170, 2257, 2262, 2268, 2440–54, 4064, 4137–38, 4229
    do-it-yourself, 2234, 2246, 4214–16
    grounds for, 2269–77
    no-fault, 2345–46
    reform 2219–24
    statistics, 621–22
  divorced persons, 2440, 2548
    statistics, 1045, 1095–96
  domestic relations, 2584, 2588, 2620–25
  property settlements, 2086, 2170, 2446, 2876–79
  remarriage, statistics, 622
  separation, 2170, 2346, 2443, 2452
North Carolina
  alimony, 11, 2170
  annulments, 2170
    statistics, 622
  child custody, 1878, 2170
  child support, 2019, 2091, 2170
  divorce, 2170, 2456, 2457
    do-it-yourself, 4217–18
    grounds for, 2269–77
    reform, 2225
    statistics, 621–22
  divorced persons, statistics, 1045, 1095–96
  property settlements, 2170
  remarriage, statistics, 622
  separation, 2917–18
North Dakota
  annulments, statistics, 622
  child custody, 2019, 2170
  divorce, 2170, 2458
    grounds for, 2269–77
    statistics, 621–22
  divorced persons, 1045, 1095–96

Ohio
  alimony, 11, 1674–80, 2170
  annulments, statistics, 622
  child custody, 1933–36, 2170
  child support, 1680, 2019–92, 2170
  children of divorced parents, 622
  community property, 2880
  divorce, 1034–36, 2170, 2459–62, 3357, 4264
    grounds for, 2269–77
    no-fault, 2226, 2347
    reform, 2226–28
    statistics, 621–22
  divorced persons, statistics, 1045, 1095–96
  domestic relations, 2626–27, 2880
  property settlements, 2170, 2880
  remarriage, statistics, 622
  separation, 1676–79
Oklahoma
  alimony, 11, 1714, 2170
  annulments, 1714
    statistics, 622
  child custody, 1937–38, 2019, 2093–94, 2170
  child support, 2093–94
  divorce, 541, 2170, 2463–64
    grounds for, 2269–77
    statistics, 621–22
  divorced persons, statistics, 1045, 1095–96
  property settlements, 2170, 2813, 2881–83
  separation, 2919
Oregon
  alimony, 11, 1681–82, 2170, 2349
  annulments, statistics, 622
  child custody, 1939–40, 2170, 2349
  child support, 2019, 2095, 2170
  children of divorced parents, 622
  divorce, 2170
    do-it-yourself, 2234, 2247–49, 4219
    grounds for, 2269–77
    no-fault, 2348–49
    statistics, 621–22
  divorced persons, statistics, 1045, 1095–96
  property settlements, 2170, 2349, 2884, 3012
  remarriage, statistics, 622
  separation, 2170
  taxes, 3012

Pennsylvania
  alimony, 11, 1683–89
  annulments, statistics, 622
  child custody, 1683, 1941–46, 2170
  child support, 1683–84, 2019, 2096–99, 2170
  children of divorced parents, 622
  divorce, 2170, 2465–71, 2543, 4184
    do-it-yourself, 4220–21
    grounds for, 2269–77
    no-fault, 4245

  statistics, 621–22
  divorced persons, 2098, 2543
    statistics, 1045, 1095–96
  domestic relations, 2628
  domicile and residence, 2465, 2469
  property settlements, 1683
  remarriage, statistics, 622
  separation, 2468, 2904–05
Puerto Rico
  alimony, 1690–91
  child custody, 1947
  divorce, 2472–76, 3420
    statistics, 622
  divorced persons, statistics, 1097, 1119
  domestic relations, 2629
  domicile and residence 2641
  one-parent families, 1330, 1445
  remarriage, statistics, 622
  separation, 2920–21
  taxes, 2921

Rhode Island
  alimony, 11
  annulments, statistics, 622
  child support, 2019, 2170
  children of divorced parents, 622
  divorce, 2170
    grounds for, 2269–77
    statistics, 621–22
  divorced persons, statistics, 1045, 1095–96
  property settlements, 2170
  remarriage, statistics, 622

South Carolina
  alimony, 11, 2100, 2170
  annulments, statistics, 622
  child custody, 2170
  child support, 2019, 2100, 2170
  children of divorced parents, 622
  divorce, 2170, 2477
    grounds for, 2269–77
    statistics, 621–22
  divorced persons, statistics, 1045, 1095–96
  property settlements, 2170
  remarriage, statistics, 622
South Dakota
  alimony, 11, 1692, 2170
  annulments, statistics, 622
  child custody, 1948, 2170, 2229
  child support, 2019, 2170
  children of divorced parents, 622
  divorce, 2170, 2478, 2532
    grounds for, 2269–77
    reform, 2229
    statistics, 621–22
  divorced persons, 2532
    statistics, 1045, 1095–96
  domicile and residence, 2652
  remarriage, statistics, 622

Tennessee
  alimony, 11, 1693, 2481
  annulments, statistics, 622
  child custody, 1949, 2481
  child support, 1693, 2019, 2170
  children of divorced parents, 622
  divorce, 487, 2170, 2479–86, 2885
    grounds for, 2269–77
    statistics, 621–22
  divorced persons, statistics, 1045, 1095–96
  domestic relations, 2485
  property settlements, 2885
  remarriage, statistics, 622
  separation, 2885
Texas
  alimony, 11, 1694–95, 2101, 2496, 3107
  annulment, 2490
    statistics, 622
  attorney fees, 1748, 2493, 2497
  child custody, 1950–55, 2170, 2495, 2498
  child support, 1951, 2019, 2031, 2101–07, 2170, 2498, 3107
  community property, 2816, 2818, 2821, 2887–88, 2896
  divorce, 1748, 2170, 2487–98, 2789, 2888
    do-it-yourself, 4222
    grounds for, 2269–77
    statistics, 621–22
  divorced persons, statistics, 1045, 1095–96
  domestic relations, 855, 2630–33
  domicile and residence, 2644, 2648
  property settlements, 2102, 2105, 2170, 2744, 2784, 2792, 2814–21, 2886–900, 3107, 3180
  separation, 2170
  taxes, 3107, 3114

Utah
  alimony, 11
  annulments, statistics, 622
  child support, 2019, 2108, 2170
  children of divorced parents, 622
  divorce, 329, 534, 2170, 2901
    grounds for, 2269–77
    statistics, 621–22
  divorced persons, statistics, 1045, 1095–96
  domestic relations, 2597
  property settlements, 2901
  remarriage, statistics, 622

Vermont
  alimony, 11, 2170
  annulments, statistics, 622
  attorney fees, 2170
  child custody, 2170
  child support, 2019, 2170
  children of divorced parents, 622
  divorce, 533, 2170
    grounds for, 2269–77
    do-it-yourself, 4225
    statistics, 621–22
  divorced persons, statistics, 1045, 1095–96
  property settlements, 2170
  remarriage, statistics, 622
Virgin Islands
  alimony, 2170
  child custody, 2170
  child support, 2170
  children of divorced parents, 622
  divorce, 2170
    statistics, 621–22
  divorced persons, statistics, 1098
  property settlements, 2170
  remarriage, statistics, 622
  separation, 2170
Virginia
  alimony, 11, 1696, 2170, 2500
  annulments, statistics, 622
  child custody, 1956–57, 2170, 2501
  child support, 1696, 2019, 2109, 2170
  children of divorced parents, 622
  divorce, 545, 2170, 2499–504, 2534
    do-it-yourself, 4223–24, 4240
    grounds for, 2269–77
    statistics, 621–22
  divorced persons, 2534
    statistics, 1045, 1095–96
  domestic relations, 2634
  property settlements, 2170
  remarriage, statistics, 622
  separation, 2170, 2501–03

Washington
  alimony, 11, 2170
  annulments, statistics, 622
  child support, 1993, 2019, 2110–11, 2170
  community property, 2704
  divorce, 2170, 2505–06
    do-it-yourself, 4226
    grounds for, 2269–77
    no-fault, 2350
    Seattle, 701
    statistics, 621–22

divorced persons, statistics, 1045, 1095–96
  domicile and residence, 2639
  property settlements, 2170, 2744, 2747, 2902–03
  separation, 2170
West Virginia
  alimony 11, 2170, 2230, 2500
  annulments, statistics, 622
  child custody, 1958, 2170
  child support, 2019, 2112, 2170
  divorce, 2170, 2500
    grounds for, 2269–77
    reform, 2230
    statistics, 621–22
  divorced persons, statistics, 1045, 1095–96
  domestic relations, 2635
  property settlements, 2170
  remarriage, statistics, 622
Wisconsin
  alimony 11, 2170
  annulments, statistics, 622
  child custody, 1858, 1930, 1959–62, 2170
  child support, 2019, 2032, 2113, 2170
  children of divorced parents, 622
  divorce, 2170, 2507–11
    do-it-yourself, 2234, 2250, 4227
    grounds for, 2269–70
    no-fault, 2351–52, 2507
    reform, 2231
    statistics, 621–22
  divorced persons, statistics, 1045, 1095–96
  domicile and residence, 2666
  property settlements, 2170
  remarriage, statistics, 622
  separation, 2509
  taxes, 3078
Wyoming
  alimony 11, 2170
  annulments, statistics, 622
  child custody, 2170
  child support, 2019, 2170
  children of divorced parents, 622
  divorce, 402, 2170
    grounds for, 2269–77
    statistics, 621–22
  divorced persons, statistics, 1045, 1095–96
  property settlements, 2170
  remarriage, statistics, 622

SUBJECT INDEX

Accidents, 551
  auto, 1130, 1142
Accountants, 2755
  fees, 3117
Actors, divorced, 715
ADAM (American Divorce Association for Men), 4320
Addicts, narcotics, 1712. *See also* Drug use.
Adjustment. *See* Children of divorced parents; One-parent families; Postdivorce adjustment; Separated persons; Stepchildren; Stepfathers.
Adolescents, 183, 275, 281, 303, 305, 1179, 1221, 1238, 1257, 1267, 1285, 1288, 1344
Adoptions, 4329
Adultery. *See* Extramarital relations.
Adventists. *See* Seventh Day Adventists.
Advertising, divorce, 1724
AFDC (Aid to Families with Dependent Children), 688–97, 2041
Aggression, children of divorced parents, 168, 1198, 1266
Air Force, 740, 741
Alcoholism, 564, 575, 601, 602, 608. *See also* Drinking habits; Remarriage, wives of alcoholics.
  separated persons, 1505
Alimony and maintenance, 1–6, 346, 359, 522, 902, 1562–700, 1702, 1709, 1714, 1726, 1760, 2058, 2084, 2100–01, 2152, 2188–89, 2230, 2320, 2326, 2345, 2349, 2373–74, 2378, 2387, 2443, 2446, 2481, 2496, 2500, 2675, 2680, 2688, 2697, 2769, 2829, 2833, 2839, 2847, 2857–58, 2922, 3010, 3016, 3021, 3023, 3110, 3138, 3145, 3193, 3839–52, 3931, 4146, 4147, 4258, 4589. *See also* Domestic relations.
  attitudes toward, 4761
  enforcement of, 1586–89, 1662, 1669
  estimating, 1583, 2034
  foreign decrees, 1587, 1590–91, 2253
  laws, 2272, 2277
  life insurance as, 1648
  for males, 1592–99, 1614, 1649, 3849–52
  modification of, 1587, 1600–02, 1604, 1615, 1654, 1673, 1675
  older women and, 5
  paid, 7–12
  received, 7–12
  by states. *See* Geographic Index for individual states.

statistics, 7–12, 2114. *See also* Geographic Index for individual states.
  taxes. *See* Taxes, alimony.
  trusts, alimony. *See* Taxes, alimony trusts.
Alternative life-styles, 1323, 1393, 2171
American Baptist Church, divorce ministry, 3346
American Indians. *See* Native Americans.
Androgyny, 465
Anemia, 559
Annulments, 1633, 1650, 1658, 1670, 1701–14, 2134, 2490, 3127, 3201–66, 3853–57, 4178
  Church of Jesus Christ of Latter-Day Saints, 3201, 3424
  foreign decrees, 1704
  joint tax returns, 1701
  Jewish, 3202
  Roman Catholic, 970, 3203–66, 3367, 3600, 3624, 3856
    canon law, 3237–48, 3853–55
    grounds for, 3223, 3226, 3229, 3230, 3243
    investigations, 3262, 3264
    personal narratives, 3796
    rates, 3609
    tribunals, 3244, 3249–66, 3332, 3857, 4749
  statistics, 622, 1131
  by states. *See* Geographic Index for individual states.
  tapes, audio, 4749
  taxes, 1701
Anomie, 333
Antenuptial agreements, 1562, 1593, 1611–12, 1618, 1622–23, 1626, 1641, 1682, 1692, 2355, 2356, 2462, 2566–71, 2843, 2883, 2903, 2906
  Jewish, 3447
Antiques, evaluation of, 2716
Arbitration, 856, 862–63, 1787–88, 2087, 2505
Art, evaluation of, 2716
Arthritis, 567
  rheumatoid, 572, 573
Art therapy, 157
Aspirin, use of, 1134
Assertiveness training, 802
Attachment theory, 503
Attitudes toward
  child custody, 130, 4761
  divorce, 227, 375, 409–15, 618, 850, 3334, 4067, 4761
    attorneys, 799, 1725–28
    Baptist Churches, 3355, 3557, 3697

children of divorced parents, 146, 162, 1325
  clergy, 375, 799, 1727
  counselors
    child, 415
    family, 415
    marriage, 415
    pastoral, 375
  divorced persons, 929
  Jewish persons, 3443
  judges, 1726
  psychologists, 375
  social workers, 772
  stepparents, 1526
  therapists, 798–99, 1727
  sex, divorced persons, 881, 1027
  sex roles, 985
Attorneys, divorce, 86, 364, 1715–50, 2147, 2564, 4139, 4182–85. *See also* Cooperation, interdisciplinary.
  advertising, 1724
  attitudes of 799, 1725–28
  attorney–client relations, 1729–33
  client interviews, 1734–38
  counseling by, 1739–42
  ethics, 2477
  fees, 1724, 1743–50, 2073, 2493, 2497, 2929, 2945, 3054, 3055, 3117
  representation, simultaneous, 1719
  role of, 1716
Audiotapes
  annulment, 4749
  child custody, 4646–48
  child support, 4650
  children of divorced parents, 4652–58
  divorce, 4680–91
    counseling, 4720–26
    ministry, 4752, 4754
  divorced persons, 4727–33, 4748, 4750–51, 4753
  one-parent families, 4744–45
  separated persons, 4724, 4750
Audiovisuals, 1352, 4646–760
Audits, 2683
Austrian Americans, divorced, 1109

Bankruptcy, 1582, 1585, 1693, 1703, 2176–77, 2400, 2828
Baptists. *See* American Baptist Church; Southern Baptist Churches.
Bars, and divorced persons, 4327
Behavioral scientists, interdisciplinary cooperation, 46, 70
Bereavement, children of divorced parents, 218–19

"Best interests of the child," doctrine of, 15, 81, 1976–97, 1896, 1906, 1917, 1930, 1941, 1952, 1970, 1975
Beyond the "best interests of the child," 17, 27, 1798–800, 3949
Biblical teaching on divorce. See Divorce, biblical teachings.
Bibliography
    child custody, 48
        joint, 119
    children of divorced parents, 666
    children of separated parents, 826
    divorce, 418–24, 491, 3334–37
    father absence, 1190
    one-parent families, 1351–1356
    religious, 3334–37
    remarriage, 1470
    stepfathers, 1529
    stepparents, 1528
Bibliotherapy, 826, 2531
Blacks. See Children of divorced parents, Blacks; Divorce, Blacks; Divorced persons, Blacks; Father absence, Blacks; One-parent families, Black.
Blood alcohol levels, 578
Boy Scouts of America, 4518
Brethern, Church of the
    divorce, 3291, 3474–79, 3767
    remarriage, biblical teachings, 3475
British Americans, divorced, 1109
Burns, 558
Businessmen, 720, 4296, 4298

Camps and camping, 3977
Canadian Americans, 1109
Cancer, 569, 589, 590
    cervical, 570
    children of divorced parents, 569
Canon law, 2629
    annulment, 3237–48, 3853–55
    personal narratives, 3796
Careers, 910, 996
    dual, 725
    planning, 923
Case studies, divorced persons, 105, 876, 918, 981, 999, 1331
Celebrities, divorced, 3882, 4315, 4360, 4372, 4375, 4507, 4510, 4555
Czech Americans, 1109
Chicanos. See Mexican Americans.
Child advocates, 31–32, 53–54, 181, 1801–08, 1819, 1852, 1890, 1918, 1930, 1960–61
Child custody, 13–132, 161, 195, 197, 244, 346, 909, 996, 999, 1034, 1499, 1726, 1751–969, 2042, 2059, 2151– 52, 2188, 2229, 2320, 2349, 2373– 74, 2376, 2378, 2387, 2443, 2445, 2481, 2495, 2498, 2501, 2515, 2640, 3391, 3858–927, 4035, 4252, 4258, 4646–49. See also "Best interests of the child" doctrine; Beyond the "best interests of the child"; Child advo-

cates; Domestic relations; Kidnapping of children; Uniform Child Custody Jurisdiction Act; Visitation.
    assessment, 75
    attitudes toward, 130, 4761
    audiotapes, 4646–48
    bibliography, 48
    child's preferences, 1809–11, 1886
    consultations, 20
    contested, 49–64, 100, 1805, 1812–23, 1829, 1839, 1845, 1893, 1896, 1921, 1960, 3879–82, 3889, 4647
    counseling, 60, 63
    criteria, 86
    and death of custodial parent, 1785
    decisions, 61, 67, 70–71, 73, 77
    determinations, 65–66, 68–69, 74, 76, 78, 81–82, 85, 1825–29, 1905
    enforcement of, 1589
    evaluations, 72, 79–80, 83–84
        psychiatric, 51
    by fathers, 87–98, 1393, 1396, 1401, 1657, 1830–35, 1897, 1909, 1920, 1949, 3880, 3883–89, 3955
    filmstrips, 4649
    foreign decrees, 1836, 2253, 2399
    history of, 99–100, 1837
    and homosexual parents, 101–04, 1838– 41, 3890
    interstate, 1842–45, 1887, 1950
    investigations, 1824
    Jewish, 1846
    joint custody, 62, 92, 105–20, 916, 1755–66, 1847–64, 2184, 2188, 3888, 3891–913, 4527
        bibliography, 119
    judicial preference, 74
    laws, 1752, 2272–73, 2277
    legal issues, 23, 52
    legislation, 1753–54
    maternal preference, 1818, 1937–38
    mediation, 1880–81
    medical aspects of, 23, 76
    modifications, 1815, 1848, 1902–03, 1928, 1939, 1951, 1955, 1967
    personal narratives, 3290, 3881
    policy, 1882
    and prisoners, 1765
    problems, 131
    psychiatric aspects, 39
    psychiatrists and, 38, 64, 1781, 1826
    psychological aspects, 23, 82
    psychological parent, 18, 1768, 1818, 1829
    psychologists and, 1823
    sexual behavior of parent and, 74, 1767
    states. See Geographic Index for individual states.
    stepparent, 1963
    taxes and, 2991–94
    tender years doctrine, 1830, 1923, 1944, 1948, 1956, 1958, 1964–66
    videotapes, 4676

Child psychiatrists. See Psychiatrists, child.
Child rearing by
    divorced persons, 996, 1166, 1248
    one-parent families, 1368–81, 4515
    stepfathers, 1535–36, 1542
    stepparents, 1552
Child snatching. See Kidnapping of children.
Child support, 30, 346, 522, 697, 902, 1564, 1569, 1579, 1605, 1610, 1621, 1643, 1656, 1665, 1680, 1683–84, 1693–94, 1696, 1761, 1792, 1951, 1977–2119, 2152, 2373, 2443, 2498, 2697, 2769, 2839, 2922, 3109, 3193, 3839, 3928–39, 4146, 4650–51. See also Domestic relations; Military, support of dependents; Taxes, child support; Uniform Reciprocal Enforcement of Support Act.
    age of majority and, 1992–96, 2036, 2038, 2092, 2095, 2404
    attitudes, 5093
    college education, 1993–95, 2088, 2096
    enforcement of, 1588, 1661–62, 1669, 1997–2032, 2040, 2050, 2054– 2055, 2057, 2060, 2072, 2083, 2107, 3935–3939
        interstate, 1998, 2001
        military, 2002, 2012, 4278
    estimating, 1583, 2033–34, 2089
    female, 1990, 3934
    foreign decrees, 2064, 2094, 2253
    grandparent, 2074
    and inflation, 1980
    laws, 2273
    legislation, 1984
    modifications, 1601, 1654, 1951, 2035, 2077, 2082
    motion pictures, 4651
    postmajority, 1992, 1996
    by states. See Geographic Index for individual states.
    statistics, 2114. See also Geographic Index for individual states.
    tapes, audio, 4650
    temporary, 2115
Children of divorced parents, 14, 133–313, 717–18, 919, 1180, 1294, 1373, 1452, 1772, 2174, 2561, 3940–4004, 4081, 4114, 4120, 4426, 4652–77, 4735–4736, 4741. See also Adolescents; Counseling; Counseling, group; Delinquency, juvenile; Students, college; Students, high school.
    achievements of, 174, 1360
        academic, 174, 289, 310, 657–62, 1206–08, 1210–11, 1213, 1216– 17, 1221–23, 1225–27, 1275, 1313, 1341, 1378
        motivation, 1259
        reading, 661, 1214, 1224
    adjustment of, 252, 1231, 1232, 1235, 1285, 1481

to divorce, 205–06, 208–10, 212,
     214–17, 655, 836, 1000, 1005,
     1008, 1371, 3398, 3980–87
  psychological, 211, 1230, 1233–34,
     1255
  psychosocial, 207, 663–64
  school, 258, 1229, 1275, 1340
  social, 211, 1228, 1290
as adults, 186, 259
aggression, 168, 1198, 1266
alienation, social, 225
anemia, 559
arthritis, 567, 572, 573
assertiveness, 1274
attitudes, 146, 162, 1325
audiotapes, 4652–58
behavior of, 304, 1236–43
  antisocial, 225, 1238, 1344
  classroom, 251, 663–65
  disordered, 218–19, 227
  school, 290
bereavement, 218–19
bibliotherapy, 666
Blacks, 1191–93, 1195–203, 1205–08,
     1216, 1221, 1224, 1266, 1367
camps and camping, 3977
castration anxiety, 1274
child neglect, 1184
Church of Jesus Christ of Latter-Day
     Saints, 3389
communication, 3401
  about divorce, 159, 3988–90
creativity, 1249, 1254
crises, psychological, 161
dating, parental, 1366
day care, 140
death fantasies, 1268
dependency, 1240, 1291
development of, 655, 1269, 1270, 1433
  cognitive, 226, 291–93, 299, 304,
     1187, 1212, 1273
  ego, 1261, 4682
  emotional, 291, 293, 1376
  intellectual, 1244
  moral, 187, 1201, 1244–47
  oedipal, 1276
  personality, 97, 294, 296, 308–09,
     1250–52, 1257, 4658, 4682
  psychological, 1255
  psychosocial, 307, 1258, 1267, 1556
  sex role, 1240, 1278–85
  social, 96, 163, 291–93, 1258, 1286–
     92, 1351
discipline, 222
divorce counseling, 825–45
divorce education for, 651, 827, 829,
     833–34, 837, 839, 842–43, 845,
     847, 850, 3991–97
and education, 652–56, 1215, 1332,
     1365, 3397, 3410
effects of divorce on, 242–44, 246–56,
     258, 260–68, 271, 273–83, 290,
     296, 308–09, 3998–4002, 4104,
     4655–57

emotional disturbances, 220, 1262
evaluations, clinical, 239
Evangelical churches, 3391–95
family concepts, 145
family interaction, 292
family relations, 1344
family size, future, 190
father-child relations, 93, 149, 168, 298,
     4658
filmstrips, 4659–60, 4700
grief, 238
growth experiences, 288
handicapped, 167, 576, 1412, 1433
hospitalization, 554
household management, 4509
identity, 1179, 1272, 4682
  gender, 1263–64, 1274, 1278, 1380
  sex role, 303, 1193, 1202, 1284
  sexual, 1263
institutionalized, 1193
I.Q., 1218
Jewish, 172
latency, 256, 278, 1232
life-style, 838
living arrangements, 155, 183
loss, 213–14
lower class, 1195–96, 1223–25, 1290,
     1292
Lutheran Church, 3397
male models for, 1213, 1222, 1287,
     1291
maternal behavior of, 1247
mate selection, 1188–89
mathematics skills, 1209
maturity of, 1288
mental health, 1320
mental retardation, 1343
Mexican Americans, 1191–92, 1238,
     1290
Methodist Church, 3398–402
mother-child relations, 251, 1219
motion pictures, 4661–75, 4709, 4735–
     36, 4741
needs of, 154, 284
neglected, 1184
neurotic, 1261
nutrition, 559
occupational aspirations of, 1378
only children, 236
parental attitudes of, 153
parental relationships, 208
parent-child communication, 254
parents, perception of, 1261
peer relationships, 168
personality characteristics of, 305–06
personal narratives, 3396, 3789, 4003–
     04, 4392
play of, 163, 1286
political beliefs of, 1195
preschool, 164, 175, 217, 238, 279–80,
     307, 1172, 1278, 1342, 1380
pregnancy, premarital, 1256
Protestant churches, 3390
psychiatric illness, 300

psychiatric patients, 232
psychopaths, 1261
reactions to divorce, 180, 257, 269–70,
     272, 3979
religious education of, 3412
research, 177, 245
residential treatment for, 1279
role perception, 1163
role playing, 1199
Roman Catholic Church, 3367, 3410–12
  personal narratives, 3795
self-concept, 268, 286, 290, 295, 298,
     301–02, 310, 1196, 1203, 1253,
     1275, 1277, 1379
self-esteem, 258, 285, 289, 297, 303,
     1205, 1264, 1281, 1378, 1381,
     1401
Seventh Day Adventist Church, 3403–04
sex roles, 291, 1290
  perceptions of, 1424
  preferences toward, 1191–92
sex typing, 1272
sexual
  attitudes of, 1277
  behavior, 1292
  identification, 1263
social interaction, 163
socialization, 287
  political, 1289
social relations, 168
Southern Baptist churches, 3405–09
  personal narratives, 3789
statistics, 311–13, 618, 1047, 1060–63,
     1067–68, 1121, 1125, 2114
  age, 1049, 1050, 1053–55, 1071
  living arrangements, 1059, 1069
stereotypes of, 673–74
stress in, 152, 164
teacher influence, 1215
teachers of, 666–75, 1215, 3397, 3410,
     3968
theory, 141
therapy with, 230, 305
values, 1288
verbal skills, 1220
videotapes, 4676–77
Children of separated parents, 192, 215,
     239, 252–54, 261, 828, 3836
  bibliography, 826
  counseling, 3996
  perceptions of, 1509
  reactions to separation, 180, 238
Chinese Americans, divorced, 1105, 1109,
     1123
Children's rights, 34, 49, 122, 150–51,
     3873, 4676
Christian and Missionary Alliance Church,
     divorce, 3413, 3687, 3689
  biblical teachings, 3276, 3277
  remarriage, biblical teachings, 3276
Christian Reformed Church,
  divorce, 3278, 3339, 3471, 3656
  biblical teachings, 3279
  divorced persons, 3685–86

Christmas, 3754, 4351, 4371, 4535
Church of Christ, divorce, biblical
    teaching, 3332
Church of the Brethern. See Brethern,
    Church of.
Church of God, divorce, 3472–73, 3659
Church of Jesus Christ of Latter-Day
    Saints, 534. See also Annulments;
    Children of divorced parents; Divorce;
    Divorced persons, personal narratives;
    Marriage, indissolubility; One-parent
    families; Remarriage.
Church of the Nazarene. See Nazarene,
    Church of.
Cigarettes, smoking of, 1134
Cirrhosis of the liver, 589, 590. See also
    Liver conditions.
Civil divorce. See Divorce, civil.
Clergy, 3423
    attitudes of, 375, 799, 1727
    divorced, 3657–81, 4682
        Evangelical, 3657–61
        Lutheran, 3662–65
        Methodist, 3666–78
        personal narratives, 3276, 3361,
            3670–72
        Presbyterian, 3679–80, 4682
        Roman Catholic, 3681
        wives of, 3767, 3773
Cohabitation, divorced persons, 353, 1069,
    1578, 1671, 1673, 2530, 4315
Coffee drinking, 1134
Colectomy, 566
Colitis, 566, 595
Communes, divorce in, 1502
Communication, 1171
    children of divorced parents, 3277
    about divorce, 159, 3988–90
    divorced persons, 898, 997
    one-parent families, 1375
    parent-child, 254
    remarriage, 1464
    skills training, 1021
Community property, 1694, 2024, 2672,
    2677, 2692, 2695, 2701–06, 2726,
    2739, 2758, 2760, 2768, 2770–71,
    2781, 2787, 2791, 2801–04, 2808–
    09, 2816, 2818, 2821, 2826, 2830,
    2834, 2852, 2867, 2869, 2880, 2887–
    88, 2896, 2976–77, 3067, 3085,
    3111–13, 3124, 3156, 3158, 3181,
    3185–87. See also Taxes, community
    property.
    income from, 2676
    states. See Geographic Index for indi-
        vidual states.
Conciliation courts, 43, 63, 66, 132, 775.
    See also Courts.
Conflict of laws, 1887, 2120–29, 2475
Constipation, 595
Contraceptives, use of, 1127
Co-parenting, See Custody, joint.

Cooperation, interdisciplinary
    attorneys, 22, 46, 70–71, 88, 758–61,
        1715, 1769
    behavioral scientists, 46, 70
    clergy, 759
    clinicians, 22
    counselors, 758, 1715
    child, 88
    judges, 46
    therapists, 760–761
Co-parenting. See Custody, joint.
Counseling. See also Counselors; Divorce
    counseling; Therapy.
    by attorneys, 1739–42
    child custody, 60, 63
        children of divorced parents, 26, 59,
            228–31, 234–38, 240, 305, 418,
            830–32, 838, 840–41
            group, 233, 797, 3991–97, 4663,
                4677, 4724
        of separated parents, 828, 3996
    divorced persons, 893, 3339
    one-parent families, 1384, 1386
    remarriage, 1471
    separated persons, 766, 790, 810, 822,
        1514–20, 3831
    stepparents, 1555
    visitation, 22, 63, 123
    vocational, 923
Counselors, 88, 758, 860, 1715
    family, 415
    marriage, 340, 415
    pastoral, 375, 3340, 3831
Counties, divorces by. See Divorce, statis-
    tics, county.
Courts
    conciliation, 43, 63, 66, 132, 775
    domestic relations, 2582–94
    family, 2087
Crisis theory, 371, 499, 878
Cruelty, 2223, 2278, 2424
    mental, 2394
Cuban Americans, divorced, 1109, 1116
Cystic fibrosis, 556

Danish Americans, divorced, 1109
Dating
    divorced persons, 937, 1366, 4380–84,
        4412, 4492, 4498
    parental, 1366
Day care, 140
Deacons, 3359, 3702
Deafness, 574
Death. See Death of custodial parent; fan-
    tasies among children of divorced par-
    ents, 1268; Rates, among divorced
    persons, 589–90, 620, 913.
Decrees, foreign
    alimony, 1587, 1590–91, 2253
    annulments, 1704
    child support, 2064, 2094, 2253
    divorce, 2064, 2253–68, 2364, 2399,
        2482, 2887–88, 4122–25, 4170,
        4286

Defenses, legal, 2178–79. See also Re-
    crimination.
Delinquency, juvenile, 221, 224, 226,
    439, 958, 1193, 1228, 1236, 1239–
    40, 1261, 1289, 1413–19, 3962,
    4682
    father absence and, 1228, 1236, 1239–
        40
    one-parent families and, 1413–19
    recidivism, 1417
Dental care, among divorced persons, 592
Dentists, 721–24, 2752–53
Depression, among divorced persons, 947–
    48, 963, 968, 972, 1144, 4312
Desertion, 314–19, 638, 1656, 2030,
    2913, 3936, 3937, 4005–11, 4678–79
    historical aspects, 315
    motion pictures, 4678–79
    wives, 319, 4009, 4011, 4678
Detectives, divorce, 4074
Developmental crises, Erickson's, 1271
Diabetes, 560, 582, 589–90
Discipline
    children of divorced parents, 222
    one-parent families, 4520
    by stepfathers, 1540–41
Disengagement-enmeshment, 1304
Displaced homemakers, 472, 477, 3713,
    4385–87
Disability, work, 703
    statistics, 1106, 1118
Divorce, 190, 199, 321–503, 1581, 1651,
    1707, 1710, 2130–526, 2532, 2534–
    36, 2538, 2543, 2569, 2691, 2764,
    2831, 2843, 2848, 2873, 2885, 2901,
    3395, 3413–3655, 4012–302, 4680–
    719. See also Alcoholism; Attitudes,
    divorce; Intermarriage; Stress; Taxes,
    and divorce; Uniform Marriage and
    Divorce Act.
    advertising, 1724
    age at first marriage, 406, 648
    alternatives to, 349, 357, 3523
    benefits of, 371, 877, 925, 3940, 4055,
        4345
    bibliographies, 418–24, 491, 3335–37
    Blacks, 436–37, 441–46, 448–49, 753,
        985
    Black-White differentials in, 638, 1357
    Brethern, Church of the, 3413, 3474–
        79, 3767
    causes of, 425–34, 438, 475, 645, 687,
        3468, 3493, 3548, 3493, 4104–06,
        4364
    chains, 326, 1459
    childlessness and, 395
    Christian and Missionary Alliance
        Church, 3413, 3687, 3689
    Christian Reformed Church, 3278, 3339,
        3471, 3656
    Church of God, 3472, 3437
    Church of Jesus Christ of Latter-Day
        Saints, 3315, 3424–34
        temple divorce, 3424

civil
    Jewish, 3452
    Roman Catholic, 3231
cohort analysis, 623–25, 635
in communes, 1502
comparative studies, 367
coping with, 337, 343
decision making and, 854
decision to, 348, 476
detectives, 4074
do-it-yourself, 2232–50, 4186–227,
    4240, 4403
    manuals, 4195–227
    by states. See Geographic Index for
        individual states.
Dominican Republic. See Geographic
    Index.
dramas, 146, 3515
duration of marriage, to, 648
Eastern Orthodox Church, 3435–40
economic
    consequences of, 474, 477, 687,
        2189, 3620
    determinants of, 426
and education, 651–56
education for, 392, 400, 804, 808, 822,
    850, 871, 991, 3361
    evaluation of, 880, 888
    effects of divorce on children. See
        Children of divorced parents,
        effects of divorce on.
effects on family, 4691
emotional aspects, 2163
Episcopal Church, 3413, 3480
ethical aspects, 3471, 3483, 3577, 3590
etiquette, 4120–21, 4323
Evangelical Church, 3413, 3481–508
fertility and, 455–56, 461–64
filing for, 466, 467, 2251–52, 4181
filmstrips, 4692–704
foreign decrees, 2064, 2253–68, 2364,
    2399, 2482, 2887–88, 4122–25,
    4170, 4286
friendly, 324, 350, 3382, 4126–28
geographic mobility, 402
granted to wife, 1131
grounds for, 410, 1131, 2269–78
Haiti. See Geographic Index.
historical aspects, 533–50, 625, 2297,
    2361, 3558, 4024
humor, 4129–31
ideology, 2144
illegitimacy, 462
immigration, 2139
industrialization and, 338
initiation of, 465, 468, 960–61, 1001–
    02, 1024, 1035
insurance, divorce, 3425, 4156–58
intergenerational transmission of, 435–
    37
interstate, 2122, 2279
invalid, 2280, 3100, 3104–05, 3126
Jewish, 548, 3441–59, 4132, 4762
kin, interaction with, 480–81

laws, 327, 2135, 2269–77, 2297
    development of, 2141, 2144
    legal, popular works, 4166–273
legislation, 521, 4228–31
Lutheran Church, 3413, 3509–11
mail order, 4142
marital happiness and, 372
Mennonite Church, 3340, 3413, 3512–
    13
Methodist Church, 3413, 3514–22
Mexico. See Geographic Index.
middle age, 427, 472–79, 524
migration and, 376, 402, 486
military. See Military, divorce.
mixed marriages and. See Intermarriage.
by month of marriage, 613
motion pictures, 4705–13
multiple, 326, 4060
myths, 342
Nazarene, Church of the, 3413, 3523–
    24, 3766
no-fault, 344, 396, 410, 522, 1580,
    1667, 1729–30, 1760, 1909, 2206,
    2226, 2281–352, 2507, 2592,
    2839, 3378, 3494, 3618–19, 4223,
    4232–50, 4265, 4399
    and increasing divorce rates, 2298–
        302, 2340, 2343
Pentecostal Church, 3525–26
personality and, 362
philosophy of, 2138
physician's role in, 579–80
poetry, 3405, 4454
policy, 489, 976, 978. See also Policy,
    social.
politics, 322
postdivorce family, 4690
pregnancy, premarital, 457–60, 486
prediction of, 388, 467, 4048
Presbyterian Church, 3413, 3679–80,
    4682
among prisoners. See Prisoners, di-
    vorced.
probabilities of, 626–33
problems in, 4086
process, 479, 865–78, 936, 956, 995,
    4114–15, 4723, 4725
Protestant churches, 3460–70
pseudodivorce, 390
racial differences in, 507, 1357
rates, 619–20, 622, 634–50, 1035,
    1126, 1131, 2114, 2297–302,
    4116–19, 4424
    age-specific, 643–44
    changing, 2297. See also Divorce, no-
        fault, and increasing divorce
        rates.
    historical, 625, 644, 647
    states, See Geographic Index.
records, 482–85
Reformed Church in America, 3527–28
reform, divorce law, 491, 2180–231,
    2517, 2826, 4144, 4172. See also
    Uniform Marriage and Divorce Act.

and religion, 372, 3421
and religious affiliation, 3417
research, 345, 365
ritual, 3380–88, 4077
    Methodist, 3383–86
    Roman Catholic, 3388
    satire, 3387
role expectations, 351
Roman Catholic Church, 3336, 3436–
    37, 3562–655, 4133–34
    canon law, 3207, 3370, 3568, 3589,
        3631
rural-urban differences in, 486–87
Seventh Day Adventist Church, 3529–47
sex differences in, 330, 3517
slides, 4714–15
social characteristics, 426, 512
social determinants of, 426
social indicators, 405
social mobility, 335, 4089
Southern Baptist churches, 3409, 3548–
    59
by states. See Geographic Index for indi-
    vidual states.
statistics, 610–50, 2114
    by counties, 622
    by standard metropolitan statistical
        areas, 622
    by states, 621–22, 1095. See also
        Geographic Index for individual
        states.
and suicide, 749, 1147–60, 4499
suits, 203, 4266–69, 4454
tapes, audio, 4680–91
tapes, video, 4716–19
teenage, 3629, 4031
theology of, 3269, 3271, 3275, 3278,
    3303, 3306, 3615–16
    Evangelical, 3271
theory of, 338, 492–503, 508, 873, 875,
    878, 898, 1007
trauma of, 4685
trials, 2512–14, 4262
violence and, 380
Wesleyan Methodist Church, 3486, 3765
Worldwide Church of God, 3560–61,
    3691
Divorce, biblical teachings, 3267–314
    Christian and Missionary Alliance
        Church, 3267–68
    Christian Reformed Church, 3279
    Church of Christ, 3301
    Evangelical churches, 3271, 3280–301
    Evangelical Covenant Church, 3289
    Jewish, 3267, 4762
    Methodist Church, 3302
    Protestant churches, 3268–306
    Roman Catholic Church, 3307–14
    Southern Baptist churches, 3304–06
Divorce, education for. See Children of di-
    vorced parents, education for divorce.
Divorce, medical aspects. See Medical
    aspects, divorce.

Divorce and welfare, 134, 676–702, 730,
    1288, 1308, 1329, 1337, 1392, 4743
  Aid to Families with Dependent Chil-
      dren, 688–97, 2041
  Puerto Rican, 1330
  statistics, 1128
Divorce and work, 506, 682, 704–53, 963,
    1139, 1378, 1453, 4296–302, 4393.
    See also Accountants: Actors;
    Businessmen, Careers; Dentists; Di-
    vorced persons, statistics, occupations;
    Family life educators; Farmers; Inter-
    views, job; Job effectiveness; Labor
    force participation; Military; Musi-
    cians; Physicians; Police; Politicians;
    Sociologists; Unemployment; Wives,
    working; Disability, work.
Divorce Attitude Inventory, 786
Divorce ceremonies. *See* Divorce, rituals.
Divorce counseling, 392, 418, 479, 516,
    754–891, 933, 1501, 1550, 1741,
    3338–42, 3423, 3864, 3959, 4107–
    09, 4111–13, 4720–26
  children of divorced parents, 825–845
  effectiveness of, 881
  evaluation of, 880, 883
  Evangelical, 3342
  families, 821
  fathers, 774, 800
  groups, 755, 762, 765–66, 769, 773,
      777, 784, 787, 793–95, 806–07,
      810–13, 816, 820, 822, 824, 846,
      848–49, 889–90, 972, 1021, 3361
  leadership training, 784
  Roman Catholic, 3343
  satisfaction with, 879, 882
  tapes, audio, 4720–4726
  women, 884–891
Divorce ministry, 3345–79, 3408, 3508,
    4752, 4754
  American Baptist, 3346
  evaluation of, 3358
  Evangelical, 3347–49, 3508
  Jewish, 3345
  Methodist, 3350–52
  Reformed Church in America, 3353
  Roman Catholic, 3328, 3362–79, 4752,
      4754
  Southern Baptist, 3354–61, 3408, 3757
Divorce organizations, 4385. *See also*
    ADAM; Divorced Catholics
    Movement; Parents without Partners;
    WAVE.
Divorce Registration Areas, 1126
Divorced Catholics Movement, 3377,
    3724–31
Divorced in literature, 1352
Divorced persons, 503, 849, 876, 892–
    1160, 1324, 1331, 2527–52, 3656–
    731, 4303–499, 4727–42, 4748,
    4750–51, 4753. *See also* Attitudes;
    Careers; Career planning; Celebrities;
    Child rearing; Communication;
    Dating; Depression; Ex-spouses;
    Fathers; Friends, divorced; Grief;

Growth, personal; Guilt; Health, In-
    digents; Kin; Males; Mental hospital
    admissions; Mental illness; Mothers;
    Postdivorce adjustment; Postdivorce
    attachment; Prisoners; Psychiatric
    admissions; Psychiatric patients;
    Stress; Terman sample; Therapy;
    Veterans; Women
  accidents, 551
    auto, 1130, 1142
  adoptions, 4329
  age at divorce, 622
  age at first marriage, 930
  audiotapes, 4727–33
  Black, 702, 929, 1033, 1366
  case studies, 105, 876, 918, 981, 999,
      1331
  and church, 3502, 3685–86, 3696, 3698
  Church of Jesus Christ of Latter-Day
      Saints, 3682, 3759-62
  cohabitation, 353, 1578, 1671, 1673,
      2530, 4315
  counseling, 893
  crises, 934, 960–61, 976
  crisis intervention, 1516
  deacons, 3742
  death rates, 589–90, 620, 913
  decision making, 4341
  dental care, 592
  disabled, 739
  drinking habits, 568, 578. *See also*
      Alcoholism.
  duration of marriage, 619, 622
  early marriage and, 428, 930
  education, 622, 935
  effects of divorce, 914, 924
  emotional disorders, 945
  Eskimos, 440, 447
  ethnic, 918
  Evangelical, 3687–94, 3763–78
  father-child relationship, 40, 149, 916,
      932, 1397
  fear of failure, 952
  friends. *See also* Friends, divorced.
    attitudes of, 928
    opposite sex, 941
  health, 551–55, 1146, 4355
  home ownership, 1055
  illness, chronic, 588
  incarcerated, 1684. *See also* Prisoners,
      divorced.
  isolation, 1371
  Jewish, 3345, 4406–07, 4762
  leisure, 909
  life-style changes, 896, 922, 943, 1003
  living arrangements, 939
  loneliness, 967, 974
  low income, 1315
  maternal characteristics, 1282
  men's rights, 4320
  mental health of, 951, 969, 973
  Methodist, 3695, 3779
  Mexican Americans, 443–44, 450, 4319
  middle aged, 989, 4420–24, 4436,
      4469, 4732

  motion pictures, 4665, 4734–41
  parent-child relations, 223, 253, 1141
  perceptions of children, 210
  personality characteristics, 393, 938,
      970–71, 1002, 1248, 4331
  personal narratives, 574, 721–22, 922,
      3881, 4031, 4420, 4425–83, 4529
  Church of Jesus Christ of Latter-Day
      Saints, 3759–62
  Evangelicals, 3661, 3672, 3763–78
  Jewish, 4132, 4456
  Methodist, 3779
  military, 4293
  Pentecostal, 3780
  Presbyterian, 3781
  Roman Catholic, 3240, 3366, 3793–
      96
  Seventh Day Adventists, 3782
  Southern Baptist, 3783–92
  powerlessness, 1371
  previous marriages, 622
  Protestant, 3684
  psychological aspects, 957
  religious affiliation, 3683
  religiosity, 915, 1028
  resource choice, 906
  risk taking, 952
  role redefinition, 997
  roles, sex, 1029
    female, 901
  Roman Catholic, 918, 970, 3377, 3704–
      31, 3793–96, 4748, 4750–51, 4753
  school involvement, 656, 4311
  self-acceptance, 933
  self-actualization, 465, 907, 1030
  self-concept, 784, 813, 888
  self-disclosure, 987, 1333
  self-esteem, 809, 907, 966, 972,1381
  sex discrimination, 2527–28
  sexual attitudes, 881, 1027
  sexual behavior, 185, 473, 1026–28,
      1675, 1767, 2172, 3704, 4470,
      4489–98
  social adjustment, 1022
  social characteristics, 987, 1029–36,
      3683
  social participation, 1009, 1022
  Southern Baptist, 3697–703
  Spanish origin, 607
  statistics, 618, 1038–136
    age, 1038, 1048–54, 1059–69, 1072–
        74, 1085–86, 1101, 1107, 1113–
        14, 1120, 1125
    at divorce, 1071, 1126
    at first marriage, 1099
  in agriculture, 1104
  aspirin, use of, 1134
  auto accidents, 1130
  Black, 1093, 1108, 1110, 1121
  by census tracts, 1122
  children, 1103, 1113
  children ever born, 1102
  cigarette smoking, 1134
  coffee drinking, 1134

cohabitation, 1069
contraceptive use, 1127
criminal victimization, 1124
duration of marriage, 1125
education, 1046, 1056, 1058, 1071,
    1075, 1076, 1091–92, 1096,
    1107, 1125
elderly, 1091–92
employment, 1102
ethnic groups, 1105, 1109, 1116–17,
    1119, 1123
head of household, 1103
home ownership, 1055
income, 1056–58, 1072–76, 1107,
    1120
institutionalized persons, 1077, 1095,
    1114
labor force participation, 1037, 1094–
    96, 1102
labor reserve, 1115
living abroad, 1101
marital history, 1071
marriage order, 1126
mental illness, 599–600, 603–04, 607
migration, 1088, 1108, 1112
in nursing homes, 1114
occupation, 1107, 1111
occupational mobility, 1112
poor, 1038–44, 1106
personality characteristics, 1248
prisoners, 1114, 1135, 1230
    death row, 1135–36
race, 1049, 1055, 1060–65, 1067–69,
    1072–74, 1085–86, 1092, 1094,
    1102, 1104, 1107, 1111, 1113–
    14, 1120, 1125–26
redivorce rate, 1438
residence, 1048–1053, 1055, 1060–
    64, 1067–69, 1089–90, 1103,
    1107, 1113, 1126
rural-urban residence, 1095–96
self-disclosure, 1333
sex, 1038, 1049, 1057, 1059–69,
    1092–93, 1102–03, 1107
sleeping pill use, 1134
Spanish origin, 607, 1053, 1055,
    1078, 1103, 1111, 1116, 1117
    age, 1079–84
    female head, 1079
teenagers, 1131
unemployment, 1094, 1115, 1160
veterans, 608–09, 1120
welfare recipients, 1128
work disability, 1106, 1118
stereotypes, 910
suicide, 749, 1147–60, 4499
support systems, 903–04, 966, 1522
videotapes, 4742
vocational counseling, 923
weight gain, 4330
Do-it-yourself divorce. See Divorce, do-it-
    yourself.

Domestic relations, 1776, 2485, 2553–635,
    4254, 4260
    cases, 2572–81
    court counseling, 2595–98
    courts, 2582–94
    enforcement, 2558
    states, 2599–635. See also Geographic
        Index for individual states.
Domicile and residence, 2364, 2465, 2469,
    2636–70
    military, 2642–43
    residency requirements, 2390, 2644–70
    states. See Geographic Index for indi-
        vidual states.
    taxes, 3199
Dramas
    divorce, 146, 3369
    stepchildren, 3833
    stepfathers, 3833
Drinking habits, divorced persons, 568,
    578
Drugs, use of, children of divorced pa-
    rents, 1168
Dual careers, 725
Durkheim, Emil, 333
Dutch Americans, divorced, 1109

Eastern Orthodox Church
    divorce, 3435–40
    marriage, indissolubility of, 3316
Economic aspects, 477, 504–32, 744,
    1166, 4143–55. See also Bankruptcy;
    Child support; Community property;
    Divorce, economic consequences; Di-
    vorced persons, statistics, income; In-
    come maintenance; Industrialization;
    Labor force participation; One-parent
    families, economic characteristics, in-
    come, resource management, working
    mothers; Poverty; Property settle-
    ments; Remarriage, economic aspects,
    financial problems, income; Separa-
    tion, economic determinants; Social
    Security; Taxes; Unemployment;
    Wills.
Educational aspects. See Child support,
    college education; Children of di-
    vorced parents, achievement; Children
    of divorced parents, adjustment,
    school; Children of divorced parents,
    behavior, classroom; Children of di-
    vorced parents, and education; Chil-
    dren of divorced parents, mathematics
    skills; Children of divorced parents,
    I.Q.; Children of divorced parents,
    teacher influence; Children of di-
    vorced parents, teachers of; Children
    of divorced parents, verbal skills; Di-
    vorce, education; Divorced persons,
    education; Divorced persons, school
    involvement; Father absence,
    academic achievement; One-parent
    families, education of children; Prop-
    erty settlements, education as; Step-
    children, classroom behavior;
    Students; Teachers.

Employment, 506, 507, 1102
Encopresis, 1243
Energy consumption, one-parent families,
    1306, 1321
Episcopal Church, 3413, 3480
Equal Rights Amendment, 1672, 1683,
    1685–88, 2042, 2097, 2153, 2407,
    3564, 4325
Erickson's theory, 936, 1271
Erasmus, Desiderius, 3311
ERISA (Employee Retirement Income
    Security Act), 1579, 2756–57, 2761,
    2769, 2772, 2774, 2783, 2803, 2806,
    3155
Eskimos, 440, 447
Estate planning, 3129–31, 4161
Estates, See Taxes, estate.
Ethics. See Attorneys, ethics; Divorce,
    ethical aspects.
Etiquette, divorce, 4120–21, 4323
Evangelical Churches. See Children of
    divorced parents; Clergy, divorced;
    Divorce; Divorce, Biblical teachings;
    Divorce ministry; Divorce counseling;
    Divorced persons; Divorced persons,
    personal narratives; One-parent
    families; Remarriage, biblical
    teachings.
Evangelical Covenant Church, divorce,
    biblical teachings, 3289
Exchange theory, 492, 501, 932
Excommunication, 3220, 3588, 3592,
    3818, 3820–21
Ex-spouses, 912, 4388–93, 4470, 4475,
    4589, 4602, 4687
Extramarital relations, 395, 911, 1521,
    1751, 3342, 4105. See also Separated
    persons, sexual behavior.

Family Courts, 2087. See also Courts.
Famiy life cycle, 1511
Family life educators, divorced, 738
Farmers, divorced, 1104, 4159, 4161
Farms, evaluation of, 2718. See also Prop-
    erty settlements, farms.
Father absence, 168, 187, 209, 301, 303,
    686, 1005, 1161–292, 1313, 1320,
    1346, 1376, 1386, 1556, 1999, 3049,
    4500–05, 4743
    academic achievement and, 1209–27
    bibliography, 1190
    Black, 1191–208
    causes of, 1185
    delinquency, juvenile and, 1228, 1236,
        1239–40
    effects on children, 1231, 1260, 1265
    and imprisonment, 1182
    motion pictures, 4743
Father custody. See Child custody, father.
Fathers, divorced persons, 40, 920–21,
    1532, 4410, 4414, 4417–18
Fees. See Accountants, fees; Attorneys,
    fees.
Feminism, 451–54, 915, 1791, 1795, 4103

Fertility and divorce, 455–56, 461–64, 1439
Fertility and remarriage, 456, 733, 1478–79, 4567
Field theory, 493
Filipino Americans, divorced, 1105, 1123
Films. *See* Motion pictures.
Filmstrips
    children of divorced parents, 4659–60, 4700
    divorce, 4692–704
    separation, 4757–58
Fisher Divorce Adjustment Scale, 871
Foreign decrees. *See* Decrees, foreign.
Foreign Divorces. *See* Divorces, foreign.
French Americans, divorced, 1109
Friends, divorced, 3732–34, 4339, 4466
Friends of the court, 14
Furman, Rosemary, 4207

Gall bladder, 595
Garnishment, 2069, 2091
    of federal employees, 1579, 1660, 1988, 2005, 2010, 2023, 2101
    of military personnel, 1694, 2012–13, 2815, 4277–78, 4280–84
Gay persons. *See* Divorced persons, homosexual; Child custody, homosexual parents; Homosexuality.
German Americans, divorced, 1109
Grandparents, 2074, 4028
    visitation by, 126, 1953, 1970, 1973
Greek Americans, divorced, 1109
Gregory, Pope, 3611
Grief
    children of divorced parents, 238
    divorced persons, 381, 781, 956–57, 1013
Growth, personal,
    children of divorced parents, 288
    divorced persons, 757, 980–81, 3693, 4062, 4731
Guardian ad litem. *See* Child advocates.
Guilt, divorced persons, 960–61, 4307, 4366

Head Start, 1220
Health, divorced persons, 551–55, 1146, 4355
Hernias, 595
Historical aspects
    child custody, 99–100, 1837
    desertion, 315
    divorce, 533–50, 625, 2144, 2297, 2361, 3558, 4024
    remarriage, 1460
    separation, 1503
Homemaker's services, evaluation of, 2719
Home ownership, 1055
Homosexuals. *See* Child custody, homosexual parents; Divorced persons, homosexual; Homosexuality.
Homosexuality, 3215, 3221, 3462
Honeymoons, 4604

Hospital expenses, 584
Hospitalization, 554, 583, 587, 593–94, 605
Humor, divorce, 4129–31
Hungarian Americans, divorced, 1109

Ideal mate, 1188–89. *See also,* Mate selection.
Illegitimacy, 462
Illness, chronic, 588
Immigration, 2139
Imprisonment, *See* prisoners.
Incapacitation, 583, 588
Incest, 4589
Income, 506, 513, 526, 687, 700–01, 4145
    maintenance, 698–702
Indians, American. *See* Native Americans.
Indigents, 1684, 2098, 2440, 2532–52, 2659, 4064. *See also* Legal aid.
Industrialization, 338
In-laws, 481. *See also* Kin; Mothers-in-law.
Insanity, 2178, 2504
Insurance. *See* Alimony and maintenance, life insurance as; Divorce insurance; Insurance, hospital and surgical; Life insurance; Property settlements, life insurance.
Insurance, hospital and surgical, 585–86
Intermarriage
    racial, 469–71, 1891
    religious, 3419, 3450
Interviews, job, 4300
Intimacy, 1376, 1395
Inuit. *See* Eskimos.
Irish Americans, divorced, 1109
Italian Americans, divorced, 1109

Jackson, Mrs. Andrew, 545
Japanese Americans, divorced, 1105, 1109, 1123
Jews. *See also* Annulments; Antenuptial agreements; Attitudes, divorce; Child custody; Children of divorced parents; Divorce; Divorce, biblical teachings; Divorced persons, personal narratives; Jewish divorce law; Jewish-Gentile divorce; One-parent families; Remarriage
    divorce law, 3202, 3444–46, 3453, 4762
Jewish-Gentile divorce, 3450
Job effectiveness, 712
Joint custody. *See* Child custody, joint.
Journal of Divorce, 2148
Judges, 28, 1726

Kidnapping, 1865–79, 3914–27
    personal narratives, 3918, 3920
Kin, interaction with. *See also* In-laws; Mothers-in-law.
    divorced persons, 480–81, 976–79, 1307, 3740, 4317
    separated persons, 1500
    stepparents, 1548

Labor force participation, 727–37, 1037, 1094, 1102
    one-parent families, 1452
Labor supply, 702
Latency, 56, 256, 278, 1232
Latin Americans, divorced, 1109, 1116
Lawyers. *See* Attorneys.
Legal aid, 2540–41. *See also* Divorced persons, indigents.
Leisure, divorced persons, 909
Licenses, professional, 2753
Life insurance, 527, 2729–43. *See also* Alimony and maintenance, life insurance as; Property settlements, life insurance.
    children, 2729
    evaluation of, 2722
Life-styles, alternative. *See* Alternative life-styles.
Life tables, 615
Living together. *See* Cohabitation.
Literature, juvenile, fiction, 1352, 3989
    one-parent families, writing about, 1352
Liver conditions, 595. *See also* Cirrhosis of the liver.
Loneliness, 967, 974
Lithuanian Americans, divorced, 1109
Luther, Martin, 3509
Lutheran Church
    clergy, divorced, 3662–65
    divorce, 3413, 3509–11
    remarriage, 3397
        Biblical teachings, 3509

Males, divorced, 989, 4027, 4408–419
Malpractice, 742
Marital adjustment, 336
Marital happiness, 372
Marital status, 2154
Marriage, indissolubility of, 3315–33, 3621. *See also* Intermarriage.
    Church of Jesus Christ of Latter-Day Saints, 3315
    Eastern Orthodox Church, 3316
    Roman Catholic Church, 3317–33, 3621
Mate selection. *See also* Ideal mate.
    children of divorced parents, 1188–89
    remarriage, 1488–90
Mediation
    child custody, 1880–81
    divorce, 851–64, 4110
    low-income families, 851
    separation, 1515
Medical aspects. *See also* Alcoholism; Mental health; Mental hospitals; mental illness; Psychiatric patients.
    anemia, 559
    arthritis, 567
        rheumatoid, 572–73
    burns, 558
    cancer, 569, 589–90
        cervical, 570
    children
        abnormal, 563
        handicapped, 167, 576, 1412, 1433

cirrhosis of the liver, 589, 590
colectomy, 566
colitis, 566, 595
constipation, 595
child custody, 23, 76
cystic fibrosis, 556
deafness, 574
dental care, 592
dentists, 721–24, 2752–53
diabetes, 560, 582, 589–90
disability, work, 703
encopresis, 1243
gall bladder, 595
health, 551–55, 1146, 4355
hernias, 595
hospital expenses, 584
hospitalization, 554, 583, 587, 593–94, 605
illness, chronic, 588
incapacitation, 583, 588
insurance, hospital and surgical, 585–86
liver conditions, 595
malpractice, 742
mental retardation, 565, 1343
nursing home residents, 581, 588, 591, 1077
nutrition, 559
physicians, 579–80, 742–46, 4297
  visits to, 583
psychosomatic illness, 1510
spina bifida cystica, 571, 577
spinal cord injuries, 561–562
statistics, 581–609
surgery, cosmetic, 557
tuberculosis, 589–90, 596
ulcers, 595
weight gain, 4330
Mennonite Church
  divorce, 3340, 3413, 3512–13
  remarriage, biblical teachings, 3513
Men's rights, 4320
Mental health
  children of divorced persons, 1320
  divorced persons, 95, 969, 973
  workers, 364, 4684
Mental hospital admissions. See Psychiatric hospital admissions.
Mental illness, divorced persons, 599–600, 603–04, 607, 949–50, 953–55, 958–59, 964, 1418
Mental retardation, 565
  children of divorced parents, 1343
Methodist Church. See Children of divorced parents; Clergy, divorced; Divorce; Divorce, biblical teachings; Divorce ministry; Divorced persons; Divorced persons, personal narratives; One-parent families; Wesleyan Methodists.
Mexican Americans, 1109–16. See also Spanish origin.
  children of divorced parents, 1191–92, 1238, 1290
  divorced persons, 443–44, 450, 4319

Migration, 376, 402, 450, 486
Military aspects. See also Veterans.
  child support, enforcement of, 2002, 2012, 4278
  divorce, 739, 4274–95
  domicile and residence, 2642–43
  medical benefits, 4285, 4287
  officers, divorced, 741
  personnel, divorced, 740
  retirement benefits, property settlements, 1694, 2784–95, 4274–76, 4279, 4289–90
  support of dependents, garnishment, 4277–78, 4280–84
Milton, John, 3313
Ministers. See Clergy.
  wives of. See Clergy, wives of.
Ministry, divorce. See Divorce ministry.
MMPI (Minnesota Multiphasic Personality Inventory), 969–70
Mormons. See also Church of Jesus Christ of Latter-Day Saints.
Mother absence, 303. See also Desertion.
Mothers, 897, 899, 906, 925, 939, 1006, 1141, 1423, 4404, 4490, 4492–93, 4495–96, 4498, 4683, 4739
  behavior, 187
  working, 711, 717–18, 1244. See also Wives, working; One-parent families, working mothers.
Mothers-in-law, 4317
Motion pictures
  child support, 4651
  children of divorced parents, 4661, 4675–709, 4735–36, 4741
  desertion, 4678–79
  divorce, 4705–13
  divorced persons, 4734–41
  father absence, 4743
  one-parent families, 4738, 4746–47
  remarriage, 4756
  stepchildren, 4756
  stepparents, 4759–60
Moynihan Report, 753, 1357
Musicians, divorced, 715

Narcotics, addicts. See Addicts, narcotics; see also Drugs, use of.
Narcissism, 391, 3222
National Center for Divorce Studies, 365
Native Americans, 439, 1100, 2125, 2458, 2537
Nazarene, Church of the, 3413, 3523–24, 3766
Neurotics, children of divorced parents, 1261
Nez Perces, divorced, 439
No-fault divorce. See Divorce, no-fault.
Nonsupport, 314, 316–18, 320
Norwegian Americans, divorced, 1109
Nursing home residents, 581, 588, 591, 1077
  visitation, 581
Nutrition, children of divorced parents, 559

Obesity. See Weight gain.
Occupations. See Careers; Divorce and work.
Oil and gas wells, evaluation of, 2728
One-parent families, 147, 167, 176, 302, 574, 677–79, 689, 695–96, 731, 940, 1293–453, 1554, 3735–58, 3973, 4428, 4478, 4501, 4506–54, 4738, 4744–47
  adjustment to divorce, 1008, 1324
  attitudes towards, 1325
  audiotapes, 4744–45
  bibliography, 1351–56
  birth order and, 1313
  Black, 1204–05, 1207, 1357–67, 4524
  child care, 1372
  child rearing, 1368–81, 4515
  Church of Jesus Christ of Latter-Day Saints, 3201
  communication in, 1375
  counseling, 418, 1384, 1386
  decision making in, 1328
  delinquency, juvenile and, 1413–19
  discipline, 4520
  economic aspects, 1388–92, 3751
  economic characteristics, 1351, 1364, 1429
  education of children, 656, 1365
  effectiveness of, 1370
  energy consumption, 1306, 1321
  Evangelical, 3737–39
  family size, 1313
  father head, 297, 713, 1393–410, 1434, 3745, 4544–52
  female head, 966, 1146, 1181, 1345, 1395, 1431
  holidays, 3754, 4351, 4371, 4535
  household management, 4509
  housing, 1411, 3742, 4532
    discrimination in, 1412
  income in, 710, 1369, 1391
  Jewish, 3735–36
  labor force participation, 1452
  maternal role, 1424
  maternal satisfaction, 1368
  Methodist, 3740–54
  motion pictures, 4738, 4746–47
  needs of, 1359, 1392, 1420–23
  personal narratives, 1297, 3781, 4551, 4553–54
  power in, 1327–28
  pregnancy, premarital, 1329
  problems of, 1316
  psychological characteristics, 1428
  Puerto Rican, 1330, 1445
  Reformed Church in America, 3755
  relationship styles, 1377
  resource management, 1389
  role adjustments, 1324
  role strain, 1139, 1324, 4745
  Roman Catholic, 3758
  rural, 1444
  self-esteem in, 1322
  services for, 1421, 4744

sex roles, 1424–27
sibling conflicts, 1373
social characteristics, 1363, 1428–1431
social climate, 1377
socialization, 1376
Southern Baptist, 3795–96
statistics, 618, 1047, 1435–40, 2114
    female head, 1051–52, 1055, 1093,
        1435, 1437–40
        age, 1438–40
        education, 1439
        fertility of, 1439
        race, 1435, 1438–40
        residence, 1436
status, family, 1390
stress in, 1369, 1433–34, 4745
successful, 1296
support systems, 1369, 1441–46
taxes, 4270
theory, 1448–49
training of, 1382–83, 1385, 1387, 1444
trends, 1431
types of, 1447
working mothers, 1186, 1451–53
Orthodox Church. See Eastern Orthodox
    Church.

Parents without Partners, 837, 1295, 4367
Pensions. See Property settlements, retire-
    ment benefits.
Pentecostal Church
    divorce, 3525–26
    divorced persons, personal narratives,
        3780
Perception, 336
Personal narratives. See Annulments; Child
    custody; Children of divorced parents;
    Divorced persons; Kidnapping; One-
    parent families; Remarriage; Separated
    persons; Stepfathers; Stepmothers;
    Teachers.
Phenomenology, 922
Philosophy of divorce, 2138
Physicians. See also Medical aspects,
    physician's role.
    divorced, 742–46, 4297
    visits to, 583
Pickford, Mary, 539
Poetry, divorce, 3405, 4454
Poisson process model, 624
Police, divorced, 747–50
Policy, social, 488–91, 1392, 1428, 1432,
    1882, 2000, 2141
Polish Americans, divorced, 1109
Politicians, divorced, 4302, 4476
Politics and divorce, 322
Postdivorce adjustment, 359, 371, 381,
    392, 777, 787–88, 793, 809, 813,
    817, 820, 853, 866–67, 872, 881,
    907, 925, 934, 980, 982–1025, 1141,
    1145, 1295, 2531, 3714, 3700, 4484–
    88, 4683, 4727, 4729. See also Fisher
    Divorce Adjustment Scale.

men, 982, 989, 4683
prediction, 1006, 1008
women, 984, 985, 992, 997–98, 1006,
    1018, 1020, 1025, 1315, 4683
Postmarital attachment, 1023
Poverty, 320, 681, 1181. See also Divorce
    and welfare; Divorced persons, indi-
    gent.
Power, 1327, 1328
Pregnancy, premarital
    among children of divorced parents,
        1256
    and divorce, 457–60, 486
    one-parent families, 1329
Presbyterian Church
    clergy, divorced, 3679, 3680, 4682
    divorce, 3413
Prisoners
    and child custody, 1765
    conjugal visits, 332
    on death row, 1135–36
    divorced, 332, 1230, 1684, 2362
    statistics, 1114, 1135–36
    of war, 4288
Private ordering, 2152
    probability of divorce, 626–29
    of remarriage, 630, 633
Property settlements, 359, 508, 522, 858,
    1566, 1570, 1603, 1616, 1624, 1668,
    1683, 1760, 2042, 2059, 2086, 2102,
    2105, 2189, 2326, 2345, 2349, 2373,
    2446, 2671–921, 3040, 3085, 3111,
    4162–65, 4229, 4420. See also
    Domestic relations; Taxes, property
    settlements.
    agreements, 2837, 3190
    community property, 2703–06. See also
        Community property.
    determinations, 2679
    education as a, 2707–15, 2721, 2886
    evaluations, 2716–28
    farms, 2718, 4159–60
    and inflation, 2678, 2727
    laws, 2272–73, 2277, 2685
    life insurance, 2071, 2722, 2729–43,
        2835, 2871, 2943, 2945, 2947,
        2955, 2959, 3054–55, 3098, 3119,
        3133–34, 3140–41, 3147, 3170
    professional goodwill, 2721, 2744–51,
        2827, 2833, 2889, 2891
    profession as a, 724, 2752–55
    retirement benefits, 528, 1499, 1579,
        2210, 2724–26, 2756–83, 3155,
        4164
        federal employees, 2775
        military personnel, 1694, 2784–95,
            4274–76, 4279, 4289, 4290
        Railroad Retirement, 2796–97
        states, 2798–903. See Geographic Index
            for individual states.
Protestant churches
    divorce, 3460–70
        biblical teachings, 3268–306
        remarriage, biblical teachings, 3465,
            3797–807

Pseudodivorce, 390
Psychiatric
    hospital admissions, 575, 597–600, 603–
        04, 606–07
    hospital discharges, 605
    patients, 955, 962, 965, 975
    treatment, 954
Psychiatrists, 38, 86, 235, 946
    child, 41, 103, 241
    child custody and, 38, 64, 1781, 1826
    forensic, 203
Psychiatry, 823, 1723, 2180
Psychologists, 86, 986, 1823
Psychopaths, children of divorced parents,
    1261
Psychosomatic illness, 1510
Psychotherapy. See Therapy
Public opinion, 414, 416–417, 535, 4761
    presidents, divorced, 411
    religious leaders, 3415
Puerto Ricans
    one-parent families, 1330, 1445
    statistics, 1116, 1119

Quality-of-life data, 1349

Ravich Interpersonal Game Test, 388
Real property, evaluation of, 2717
Reconstituted families, 156, 1456–57,
    1463, 1485, 4634. See also Stepfami-
    lies.
Recrimination, 2130, 2358, 2395–96,
    2402, 2408, 2410, 2434, 2459, 2478,
    2484
Reformed Church in America
    divorce, 3527–28
    one-parent families, 3755
Religious aspects. See under individual
    churches, Clergy; Children of di-
    vorced parents, religious education of;
    Divorce, and religion; Divorce, ethical
    aspects; Divorce, religious affiliation;
    Divorce, ritual; Divorce, theology of;
    Divorce, biblical teachings; Divorce
    ministries; Divorced persons, and the
    church; Divorced persons, deacons;
    Divorced persons, religious affiliation;
    Divorced persons, religiousity; Mar-
    riage, indissolubility of; Remarriage,
    biblical teachings; Remarriage, cere-
    monies.
Remarriage, 156, 326, 379, 389, 397,
    456, 460, 464, 480, 504, 526, 553,
    630, 676, 683, 840, 959, 1013,
    1454–93, 1547, 1577, 2355, 2693,
    2968, 3037, 3043, 3416, 3419, 3422,
    3976, 4056, 4316, 4453, 4555–610,
    4753, 4755–56. See also Stepfamilies;
    Stepparents.
    biblical teachings, 3800
        Church of the Brethern, 3475
        Church of Jesus Christ of Latter-Day
            Saints, 3201
        Christian and Missionary Alliance
            Church, 3276

Jewish, 3459
Lutheran, 3509
Mennonite, 3513
Protestant, 3274, 3465, 3797–3807
Roman Catholic, 3324, 3328, 3424–
    25, 3428, 3573, 3583–86, 3590,
    3596, 3604–05, 3608, 3610–11,
    3614–16, 3622, 3630, 3632,
    3634, 3636, 3639, 3642–49,
    3715, 3808–28, 4753
Seventh Day Adventists, 3529, 3531,
    3537, 3540, 3544, 3546–47,
    3807
Southern Baptist, 3304, 3550, 3802–
    06
bibliography, 1470
ceremonies, 3798, 4558
    type of, 622
children and, 840, 1475, 4572
communication, 1464
counseling for, 1471
developmental tasks, 1463
economic aspects, 1475–76, 4591
education for, 808, 1472–73
effects on children, 1477
Evangelical, 3290–91, 3300–01, 3481–
    82, 3484, 3487, 3492, 3500, 3506,
    3799–801
failure in, 1483
and fertility, 733, 1478–79, 4567
financial problems of, 1475
to first spouse, 3802, 4609–10
historical aspects, 1460
husband and wife relations, 1480–87
income, 1476
Luther, Martin, 3512
marital adjustment, 1483–85
marital happiness of, 1480, 1482, 1487
mate selection, 1488–90
middle age, 1486, 4755
motion pictures, 4756
personal narratives, 4594
    Southern Baptist, 3792
probabilities of, 633
problems of, 4562, 4571
    financial, 4572
ritual, 3798, 4558
role structure, 1465
satisfaction, 1486
social characteristics, 1455, 1459
social interaction, 1466
statistics, 616–18, 622, 647, 1070–71,
    1085, 1129, 1131, 1491–93
    by age, 622
    children, 1113
    month of marriage, 1493
    previous marriage, 1493
    race, 622
    type of ceremony, 622, 1493
success, 1483, 4568
tapes, audio, 4753, 4755
taxes, 3126, 3193
therapy, 1474
wives of alcoholics, 1489

Residency. See Domicile and residence.
Retirement benefits. See also Property set-
    tlements, retirement benefits.
    evaluation of, 2724, 2725.
Rights of children. See Children's rights.
Role
    of attorney, 1716
    of children of divorced parents, 1163,
        1199
    expectations, 351
    one-parent families
        adjustment, 1324
        strain, one-parent families, 1139,
            1324, 4745
    redefinition, 997
    structure, in remarriage, 1465
Role theory, 501, 1409
Roles, sex, 953, 985, 992
    attitudes toward, 985
    of children of divorced parents, 291,
        1290
        development of, 1240, 1278–85
        preferences, 1191–92
    divorced persons, 901, 1029
    one-parent families, 1424–27
Roman Catholic Church. See Annulments;
    Children of divorced parents; Clergy,
    divorced; Divorce; Divorce, biblical
    teachings; Divorce, civil; Divorce
    counseling; Divorce ministry; Di-
    vorced persons; Divorced persons,
    personal narratives; Marriage, indis-
    solubility of; One-parent families; Re-
    marriage; Separated persons.
Rorschach tests, 926
Russian Americans, divorced, 1109

Sacraments, 3363, 3369, 3598, 3643,
    3647, 3818–19, 3826
School involvement, divorced persons, 656
Semantic differential, 400
Separated persons, 1397–98. See also Chil-
    dren of separated parents.
    adjustment, 987, 989, 1009, 1014–16,
        1145, 1510–13, 1517–18, 2904,
        2905, 3714
        groups, 846, 849
    audiotapes, 4733, 4750
    counseling, 766, 790, 810, 822, 1501,
        1514–20, 3831
    crisis intervention, 1516
    Evangelical, 3832
    fathers, 1397–98, 4545
    health of, 1510
    mothers, 1139
    personal narratives, 3832
    Roman Catholic, 3714, 3718, 3829,
        4750
    self-concept, 1501
    sexual behavior, extramarital, 1521,
        2172
    statistics, 1108–09, 1121
        census, 1095
        census tracts, 1122
        migration, 1088

suicide, 1151
support systems, 1522
Separation, 48, 62, 180, 223, 331, 377,
    381, 387, 391, 399, 430, 448, 726–
    27, 753, 784, 867, 922, 930, 940,
    966, 968, 972, 1494–522, 1638,
    1640, 1653, 1655, 1710, 2346, 2377,
    2412, 2432, 2438, 2439, 2443, 2452,
    2468, 2501–03, 2509, 2836, 2844,
    2851, 2885, 2904–21, 2923, 2928,
    2957, 3060, 3829–32, 4082, 4098,
    4166, 4401–02, 4427, 4757–58. See
    also Taxes, and separation.
    agreements, 863, 1676, 1679, 1994,
        2004, 2914, 2916–18, 3136, 3200,
        4612
    and alcoholism, 1505
    economic determinants of, 426, 1495
    education for, 1514
    emotional aspects, 1507
    filmstrips, 4757–58
    foreign decrees, 2258
    historical aspects, 1503
    kin, interaction with, 1500
    legal aspects, 1512
    mediation, 1515
    no-fault, 2911
    process, 1496
    and religious affiliation, 3417
    social determinants of, 426
    social relations, 1500
    states, 2908–21. See Geographic Index
        for individual states.
    statistics, 620, 622, 1131
    stress and, 1497–98
    theory, 1502
Sermons, 3297, 3670
Seventh Day Adventists. See Children of
    divorced parents; Divorce; Divorced
    persons, personal narratives; Remar-
    riage.
Sex
    attitudes towards, 985
    extramarital, 395, 911, 1521, 1751,
        3342, 4105
    differences, in divorce, 330, 3517
    discrimination, 2527–28
    roles, 953, 985, 922
    typing, children of divorced parents,
        1272
Sexism, 45
Sexual
    attitudes, children of divorced persons,
        1277
    attraction, in stepfamilies, 1523, 4589
    behavior. See also Cohabitation.
        and child custody, 74, 1767
        children of divorced parents, 1292
        divorced persons, 185, 473, 1026–28,
            1675, 1767, 2172, 3704, 4470,
            4489–98
        separated persons, 1521, 2172
    identification, children of divorced par-
        ents, 1263
    stereotypes, 910

Sleeping pills, use of, 1134
Slides, divorce, 4714–15
Smoking, cigarette, 1134
Socialization
    children of divorced parents, 287
    political, 1289
    one-parent families, 1376
Social indicators, 405
Social mobility, 335, 4089
Social Security, 529–31, 2706, 2773, 2806
Social service agencies, 817
Social work, 856
Social workers, 86, 772
Sociologists, divorced, 752
Southern Baptist Churches. *See* Attitudes,
        divorce; Children of divorced parents;
        Divorce; Divorce, biblical teachings;
        Divorced persons; Divorced persons,
        personal narratives; Divorce ministry;
        One-parent families; Remarriage.
Spina bifida cystica, 571, 577
Spinal cord injuries, 561–62
Standard metropolitan statistical areas. *See*
        Divorce, statistics, standard metropoli-
        tan statistical areas.
States, *See* Geographic Index.
Statistics. *See* Alimony and maintenance;
        Annulments; Child support; Children
        of divorced parents; Divorce; Divorce
        and welfare; Divorced persons; One-
        parent families; Remarriage; Separ-
        ation; Separated persons.
Stepchildren, 1461, 1474, 1523–61, 1977,
        4614–20, 4627, 4629, 4633–34,
        4639, 4643, 4756
    adjustment, 4640
    behavior, classroom, 665
    dramas, 3833
    motion pictures, 4756
    sexual attraction, 1523, 4589
Stepfamilies. *See also* Reconstituted fami-
        lies.
    myths, 1560
    process, 1559
Stepfathers, 1212, 1532–42, 2103, 3002–
        03, 4621–23
    adjustment, 1534
    bibliography, 1529
    childrearing, 1535–36, 1542
    discipline by, 1540–41
    dramas, 3833
    personal narratives, 4622
    role, 1535, 1538–39
Stepmothers, 1543–46, 3832–34, 4624–30
    myths, 1546
    personal narratives, 3838, 4626–28
    stress, 1544
Stepparents, 301, 690, 1284, 1320, 1461,
        1472, 1481, 1523–61, 1722, 1963,
        1977, 2529, 3835–38, 4556–57,
        4559, 4619–20, 4631–45, 4759–60
    attitudes, 1526
    bibliography, 1528–29

child custody, 1963
child rearing, 1552
counseling, 1555
marital interaction, 1533
motion pictures, 4759–60
myths, 1550
problems, 1530–31
self concept, 1557
sexual attraction, 1523, 4589
Southern Baptist, 3836–38
successful, 4614
stress, 1533
Stereotypes
    children of divorced parents, 673–74
    sexual, divorced persons, 910
Sterilization, 2134
Stress
    children of divorced parents, 152, 164
    divorced persons, 903, 909, 980, 1010–
        11, 1131, 1137–46, 4356
    one-parent families, 1369, 1433–34,
        4745
    separation, 867, 1497–98
    stepmothers, 1544
    stepparents, 1533
Stress scale, 1145
Students
    children of divorced parents, 1173,
        1212, 1233–34, 1283, 4682
    college, 811, 1173, 1283, 5014
    high school, 174, 222, 656, 662, 1253,
        1340
Suicide
    and divorce, 749, 1147–60, 4499
    and separation, 1151
Support of dependents. *See* Child support.
Support systems
    divorced persons, 903–04, 966, 1522
    one-parent families, 1369, 1441–46
    separated persons, 1522
Surgery, cosmetic, 557
Swedish Americans, divorced, 1109
Systems theory, 138

Tapes, audio. *See* Audiotapes.
Tapes, video. *See* Videotapes.
TAT (Thematic Apperception Test), 1274
Taxes, 1628, 2922–3200
    alimony and maintenance, 1648, 1697,
        1700, 2281, 2432, 2922–80, 2985,
        2987, 3008, 3017–18, 3020–21,
        3053–55, 3103, 3137, 3144–47,
        3156, 3183–84
    alimony trusts, 2981–87
    annulments, 1701
    avoidance of taxes by divorce and re-
        marriage, 2264, 2988–90, 3025
    child custody, 2991–94
    child support, 2281, 2932, 2934–35,
        2945, 2955, 2958, 2969–70, 2995–
        3009, 3017, 3054–55, 3068, 3098,
        3109, 3142

community property, 2677, 3019–20,
        3158
conflict of laws, 3103–05
divorce, 1577, 2128, 2405, 2672, 2702,
        2737, 2742, 2922, 2925–26, 2931,
        2940, 2982, 2984, 2986, 2991,
        3000–01, 3010–28, 3153, 3167,
        4270–73
    domicile, 3199
    estate, 2735, 2736, 2938, 2960, 3042,
        3098, 3128, 3132–48, 3161
    gift, 2960, 3042, 3098, 3128, 3132,
        3143
    legal expenses and, 3149–50
    marital deduction and, 3037, 3043, 3139
    one-parent families, 4270
    property settlements, 2281, 2433, 2677,
        2767, 2864, 2945, 3009, 3011–12,
        3019–20, 3024, 3033, 3084, 3098,
        3151–92
    remarriage, 3126, 3193
    separation, 2912, 2921, 3013, 3029,
        3032, 3041, 3047, 3056–57, 3063–
        64, 3076, 3083–84, 3086, 3088–
        89, 3094, 3098, 3101, 3106, 3194–
        200
Tax returns. *See* Annulment.
Teachers, 3397
    of children of divorced parents, 666–75,
        1215, 3397, 3410, 3968
    personal narratives, 671–72
    resources for, 666
    stereotypes, children of divorced par-
        ents, 673–74
    teaching about divorce, 669
Temple divorces, 3424
Terman sample, divorced persons, 431
Theory
    attachment, 503
    crisis, 371, 499, 878
    divorce, 338, 492–503, 508, 873, 875,
        898, 1007
    exchange, 492, 501, 932
    field, 493
    one-parent family, 1448–49
    role, 501, 1409
    separation, 1502
    systems, 138
Therapists, 760–61, 798–99, 1727
    family, 44, 358
Therapy. *See also* Counseling.
    art, 157
    conjoint, 756
    children of divorced parents, 230, 305
    divorced persons, 204, 894
    family, 785
    remarriage, 1474
Transactional analysis, 805, 4521
Tribunals. *See* Annulments, Roman Catho-
        lic, tribunals.
Trusts, 2674, 2690, 2693, 2926, 3125,
        3148
    alimony, 1697–700, 2981–87
Tuberculosis, 589–90, 596

Ulcers, 595
Unemployment, 507, 729, 753, 1160
  statistics, divorced persons, 1094, 1115
Uniform Child Custody Jurisdiction, 1773,
      1848, 1870, 1877, 1892, 1894,
      1898, 1908, 1919, 1921, 1924,
      1933, 1935, 1940, 1943, 1957,
      1959, 1962, 1967–69, 2550
Uniform Marriage and Divorce Act, 1757,
      2071, 2186–87, 2197, 2202, 2429,
      2515–26, 2697, 3166
Uniform Reciprocal Enforcement of Sup-
      port Act, 2068, 2075, 2080, 2116–
      19

Values, 778, 4688
  children of divorced parents, 1288
  teaching of, 668
Veterans, divorced persons, 608, 739
  hospitalization, 609
  statistics, 1120

Videotapes
  children of divorced parents, 4676–77
  divorce, 4716–19
  divorced persons, 4742
Violence, 380, 1413
Visitation
  counseling, 22, 63, 123
  disputes, 79, 128, 131
  grandparent, 126, 1953, 1970, 1973
  parent, 82, 121–22, 124–25, 127, 129–
      31, 1766, 1786, 1792, 1814, 1819,
      1821, 1851–52, 1922, 1951, 1971–
      72, 1974–76, 3942, 3964, 4514
Vocational counseling, divorced persons,
      923
Voltaire, 323

Warren Village, 3742, 4532
Walters, Barbara, 4510
WAVE, 4200

Weight gain, divorced persons, 4330
Welfare, dependence, 320. See also Di-
      vorce and welfare.
Wesleyan Methodist Church, divorce,
      3486, 3765
West Indian Americans, divorced, 1109
Wills, 532, 2419, 2694, 2901
Wiretapping, 2149
WISC (Wechsler Intelligence Scale for
      Children), 1218
Wives, working, 4301. See also Mothers,
      working.
Women, divorced, 907, 918, 933, 985,
      998, 1020, 4394–405, 4683
  professional, 751, 4299, 4689
Work bonus, 2017
Worldwide Church of God, divorce, 3560–
      61, 3691

Yugoslav Americans, divorced, 1109